STERLING
Test Prep

DAT

GENERAL CHEMISTRY

Practice Questions

with detailed explanations

6th edition

www.Sterling-Prep.com

Copyright © 2016 Sterling Test Prep

6   5   4   3   2   1

ISBN-13: 978-1-5001957-7-9

Sterling Test Prep products are available at special quantity discounts for sales, promotions, premed counseling offices and other educational purposes.

For more information contact our Sales Department at

Sterling Test Prep
6 Liberty Square #11
Boston, MA 02109

info@sterling-tprep.com

© 2016 Sterling Test Prep

Published by Sterling Test Prep

 Printed in the U.S.A.

Dear Future Dentist!

Congratulations on choosing this book as part of your DAT preparation!

Scoring well on the General Chemistry portion of the DAT is important for admission into dental school. To achieve a high score, you need to develop skills to properly apply the knowledge you have and quickly choose the correct answer. You must solve numerous practice questions that represent the style and content of the DAT questions. Understanding key science concepts is more valuable than memorizing terms.

This book provides over 1,800 chemistry practice questions that test your knowledge of all DAT General Chemistry topics. At the back of the book, you will find answer keys (use them to verify your answers) and explanations to questions. These explanations provide step-by-step solutions for quantitative questions and detailed explanations for conceptual questions. They also cover the foundations of general chemistry topics needed to answer related questions on the test. By reading these explanations carefully and understanding how they apply to solving the question, you will learn important chemistry concepts and the relationships between them. This will prepare you for the test and you will significantly increase your score.

All the questions are prepared by our science editors that possess extensive credentials, are educated in top colleges and universities. Our editors are experts on teaching sciences, preparing students for standardized science tests and have coached thousands of undergraduate and graduate school applicants on admission strategies.

We wish you great success in your future academic achievements and look forward to being an important part of your successful preparation for DAT prep!

Sterling Test Prep Team

160122gdx

Share your opinion

Your feedback is important because we strive to provide the highest quality prep materials. If you are satisfied with the content of this book, post your review on Amazon, so others can benefit from your experience.

If you have any questions or comments about the material, email us at info@sterling-prep.com and we will resolve any issues to your satisfaction.

Visit www.Sterling-Prep.com for DAT online practice tests

Our advanced online testing platform allows you to practice these and other DAT questions on the computer and generate Diagnostic Reports for each test.

By using our online DAT tests and Diagnostic Reports, you will be able to:

- Assess your knowledge of different topics tested on the DAT science sections
- Identify your areas of strength and weakness
- Learn important scientific topics and concepts
- Improve your test taking skills by solving numerous practice questions

To access the online tests at a special pricing
go to page 422 for web address

Table of Contents

Our Commitment to the Environment

Sterling Test Prep is committed to protecting our planet's resources by supporting environmental organizations with proven track records of conservation, environmental research and education and preservation of vital natural resources. A portion of our profits is donated to support these organizations so they can continue their important missions. These organizations include:

 Ocean Conservancy For over 40 years, Ocean Conservancy has been advocating for a healthy ocean by supporting sustainable solutions based on science and cleanup efforts. Among many environmental achievements, Ocean Conservancy laid the groundwork for an international moratorium on commercial whaling, played an instrumental role in protecting fur seals from overhunting and banning the international trade of sea turtles. The organization created national marine sanctuaries and served as the lead non-governmental organization in the designation of 10 of the 13 marine sanctuaries. In twenty five years of International Coastal Cleanups, volunteers of Ocean Conservancy have removed over 144 million pounds of trash from beaches. Ocean Conservancy mobilizes citizen advocates to facilitate change and protect the ocean for future generations.

 For 25 years, Rainforest Trust has been saving critical lands for conservation through land purchases and protected area designations. Rainforest Trust has played a central role in the creation of 73 new protected areas in 17 countries, including Falkland Islands, Costa Rica and Peru. Nearly 8 million acres have been saved thanks to Rainforest Trust's support of in-country partners across Latin America, with over 500,000 acres of critical lands purchased outright for reserves. Through partnerships and community engagement, Rainforest Trust empowers indigenous people to steward their own resources offering them education, training, and economic assistance.

 Since 1980, Pacific Whale Foundation has been saving whales from extinction and protecting our oceans through science and advocacy. As an international organization, with ongoing research projects in Hawaii, Australia and Ecuador, PWF is an active participant in global efforts to address threats to whales and other marine life. A pioneer in non-invasive whale research, PWF was an early leader in educating the public, from a scientific perspective, about whales and the need for ocean conservation. In addition to critically important whale education and research, PWF was instrumental in stopping the operation of a high-speed ferry in whale calving areas, prohibiting smoking and tobacco use at all Maui County beaches and parks, banning the display of captive whales and dolphins in Maui County, and supporting Maui County's ban on plastic grocery bags.

Thank you for choosing our products to achieve your educational goals.

With your purchase you support environmental causes around the world.

Periodic Table of the Elements

Legend:
Atomic Number — Valence Charge
Symbol
Name
Atomic Mass

Group																	
1 IA 1A	2 IIA 2A	3 IIIB 3B	4 IVB 4B	5 VB 5B	6 VIB 6B	7 VIIB 7B	8 VIII 8	9 VIII	10	11 IB 1B	12 IIB 2B	13 IIIA 3A	14 IVA 4A	15 VA 5A	16 VIA 6A	17 VIIA 7A	18 VIIIA 8A

Period 1:
1 +1 H Hydrogen 1.008 — 2 0 He Helium 4.003

Period 2:
3 +1 Li Lithium 6.941; 4 +2 Be Beryllium 9.012; 5 +3 B Boron 10.811; 6 +2,+4,−4 C Carbon 12.011; 7 −3,+5,+3 N Nitrogen 14.007; 8 −2 O Oxygen 15.999; 9 −1 F Fluorine 18.998; 10 0 Ne Neon 20.180

Period 3:
11 +1 Na Sodium 22.990; 12 +2 Mg Magnesium 24.305; 13 +3 Al Aluminum 26.982; 14 +4 Si Silicon 28.086; 15 −3,+5,+3 P Phosphorus 30.974; 16 −2,+2,+4,+6 S Sulfur 32.066; 17 −1,+5,+1 Cl Chlorine 35.453; 18 0 Ar Argon 39.948

Period 4:
19 +1 K Potassium 39.098; 20 +2 Ca Calcium 40.078; 21 +3 Sc Scandium 44.956; 22 +4 Ti Titanium 47.867; 23 +5,+4,+3 V Vanadium 50.942; 24 +6,+3,+2 Cr Chromium 51.996; 25 +7,+4,+2 Mn Manganese 54.938; 26 +3,+2 Fe Iron 55.845; 27 +3,+2 Co Cobalt 58.933; 28 +2 Ni Nickel 58.693; 29 +2,+1 Cu Copper 63.546; 30 +2 Zn Zinc 65.38; 31 +3 Ga Gallium 69.723; 32 +2,+4 Ge Germanium 72.631; 33 +3 As Arsenic 74.922; 34 −2,+4 Se Selenium 78.971; 35 −1,+5,+1 Br Bromine 79.904; 36 0 Kr Krypton 84.798

Period 5:
37 +1 Rb Rubidium 85.468; 38 +2 Sr Strontium 87.62; 39 +3 Y Yttrium 88.906; 40 +4 Zr Zirconium 91.224; 41 +5 Nb Niobium 92.906; 42 +6,+4 Mo Molybdenum 95.95; 43 +7,+4 Tc Technetium 98.907; 44 +4,+3 Ru Ruthenium 101.07; 45 +3 Rh Rhodium 102.906; 46 +2,+4 Pd Palladium 106.42; 47 +1 Ag Silver 107.868; 48 +2 Cd Cadmium 112.414; 49 +3 In Indium 114.818; 50 +2,+4 Sn Tin 118.711; 51 −3,+5,+3 Sb Antimony 121.760; 52 −2,+4 Te Tellurium 127.6; 53 −1,+5,+1 I Iodine 126.904; 54 0 Xe Xenon 131.294

Period 6:
55 +1 Cs Cesium 132.905; 56 +2 Ba Barium 137.326; 57–71 La–Lu; 72 +4 Hf Hafnium 178.49; 73 +5 Ta Tantalum 180.948; 74 +6,+4 W Tungsten 183.84; 75 +7,+4,+3 Re Rhenium 186.207; 76 +4 Os Osmium 190.23; 77 +4,+3 Ir Iridium 192.217; 78 +4,+2 Pt Platinum 195.085; 79 +3,+1 Au Gold 196.967; 80 +2,+1 Hg Mercury 200.592; 81 +3,+1 Tl Thallium 204.383; 82 +2 Pb Lead 207.2; 83 +3 Bi Bismuth 208.980; 84 +2 Po Polonium (208.982); 85 At Astatine 209.987; 86 0 Rn Radon 222.018

Period 7:
87 +1 Fr Francium 223.020; 88 +2 Ra Radium 226.025; 89–103 Ac–Lr; 104 Rf Rutherfordium (261); 105 Db Dubnium (262); 106 Sg Seaborgium (266); 107 Bh Bohrium (264); 108 Hs Hassium (269); 109 Mt Meitnerium (268); 110 Ds Darmstadtium (269); 111 Rg Roentgenium (272); 112 Cn Copernicium (277); 113 Uut Ununtrium unknown; 114 Fl Flerovium (289); 115 Uup Ununpentium unknown; 116 Lv Livermorium (298); 117 Uus Ununseptium unknown; 118 Uuo Ununoctium unknown

Lanthanide Series:
57 +3 La Lanthanum 138.905; 58 +3 Ce Cerium 140.116; 59 +3 Pr Praseodymium 140.908; 60 +3 Nd Neodymium 144.908; 61 +3 Pm Promethium 144.913; 62 +3 Sm Samarium 150.36; 63 +3 Eu Europium 151.964; 64 +3 Gd Gadolinium 157.25; 65 +3 Tb Terbium 158.925; 66 +3 Dy Dysprosium 162.500; 67 +3 Ho Holmium 164.930; 68 +3 Er Erbium 167.259; 69 +3 Tm Thulium 168.934; 70 +2 Yb Ytterbium 173.055; 71 +3 Lu Lutetium 174.967

Actinide Series:
89 +3 Ac Actinium 227.028; 90 +4 Th Thorium 232.038; 91 +5 Pa Protactinium 231.036; 92 +6 U Uranium 238.029; 93 +5 Np Neptunium 237.048; 94 +4 Pu Plutonium 244.064; 95 +3 Am Americium 243.061; 96 +3 Cm Curium 247.070; 97 +3 Bk Berkelium 247.070; 98 +3 Cf Californium 251.080; 99 +3 Es Einsteinium (254); 100 +3 Fm Fermium 257.095; 101 +2 Md Mendelevium 258.1; 102 +2 No Nobelium 259.101; 103 +3 Lr Lawrencium (262)

DAT
GENERAL CHEMISTRY
PRACTICE QUESTIONS

Chapter 1. ATOMIC AND MOLECULAR STRUCTURE; PERIODIC PROPERTIES

1. Which choice below represents an element?

   A. glucose   **B.** sodium chloride   **C.** methanol   **D.** hydrogen   **E.** brass

2. Which of the following is a general characteristic of a metal?

   A. conductor of heat   **C.** solid state
   B. high density   **D.** malleable   **E.** all of the above

3. How many electrons can occupy the *f* subshell?

   A. 2   **B.** 6   **C.** 10   **D.** 14   **E.** 18

4. How many valence electrons are in the Lewis dot structure of C_2H_6?

   A. 10   **B.** 14   **C.** 20   **D.** 28   **E.** 32

5. Which fact regarding the periodic table is false?

   A. The elements are classified into groups by electronic structure
   B. The noble gases make up the most stable period
   C. Horizontal rows represent periods
   D. Elements in the same family have similar chemical properties
   E. Vertical rows represent groups

6. Both ^{65}Cu and ^{65}Zn have the same:

   A. mass number   **C.** number of ions
   B. number of neutrons   **D.** number of electrons   **E.** number of protons

7. Which group of elements contains only non-metals?

   A. Br, Ar, Na   **B.** S, As, Se   **C.** Be, Ca, Sr   **D.** Fe, Ru, Mn   **E.** N, Se, Br

8. If one mole of an element weighs 12 grams, the mass number of this element has a value of approximately:

   A. 6.02×10^{23} **B.** 12   **C.** 1   **D.** $12 \times 6.02 \times 10^{23}$ **E.** 24

9. According to John Dalton, atoms of a given element:

   A. are divisible   **C.** are identical
   B. have the same shape   **D.** have different masses   **E.** none of the above

10. In which order must elements on the periodic table be listed for their properties to repeat at regular intervals?

   A. increasing atomic mass   **C.** increasing atomic number
   B. decreasing atomic mass   **D.** decreasing atomic number
                                          E. decreasing density

11. Which of the following is a general characteristic of a metallic element?

   A. high melting point

   B. conductor of electricity

   C. ductile

   D. shiny luster

   E. all of the above

12. Which of the following represents only alkali metals?

   I. Li

   II. Ba

   III. Rb

   IV. Ca

   A. II and IV   **B.** I and III   **C.** III and IV   **D.** I and II   **E.** I and IV

13. Elements that appear in the same column of the periodic table and have similar chemical properties are called:

   A. congeners

   B. epimers

   C. anomers

   D. monomers

   E. diastereomers

14. Which of the following is an alkali metal?

   A. N   **B.** He   **C.** Cl   **D.** Ga   **E.** K

15. An element can be determined by:

   A. A + C   **B.** C only   **C.** A only   **D.** Z only   **E.** none of the above

16. Based on the Law of Mass Conservation, Lavoisier hypothesized that:

   A. an element is a combination of substances

   B. carbon dioxide is a fundamental element

   C. an element is made of a fundamental substance that cannot be broken down further

   D. matter can lose mass as hot, dry, cold or moist qualities change

   E. matter can gain mass as hot, dry, cold or moist qualities change

17. Elements constituting a period in the periodic table:

   A. are always in the same group

   B. have consecutive atomic numbers

   C. are called isotopes

   D. have similar chemical properties

   E. are called ions

18. Which of the following biochemical elements is classified as a trace element?

   A. selenium   **B.** magnesium   **C.** potassium   **D.** chloride   **E.** oxygen

19. Which of the following is a general characteristic of a metallic element?

   A. reacts with nonmetals

   B. reacts with metals

   C. dull, brittle solid

   D. low melting point

   E. none of the above

20. Which of the following gives the ground-state electron configuration of a Ca^{2+} atom?

   A. [Ar] $4s^2\,3d^2$

   B. [Ar] $4s^2\,4p^2$

   C. [Ar]

   D. [Ar] $4s^2$

   E. [Ar] $4s^2\,4p^1$

21. Which of the following represent(s) only halogens?

    I. O   III. I

    II. He   IV. Br

  A. II and III   **B.** I and IV   **C.** I and II   **D.** III and IV   **E.** I and IV

22. Sulfur has three common oxidation states: +2, 0, –2. Which oxidation state has the largest radius?

  A. anion   **C.** neutral atom

  B. cation   **D.** all are about the same size   **E.** cation and anion

23. Which of the following substances does NOT contain cathode ray particles?

  A. H_2O **C.** hydrogen atoms

  B. Na   **D.** all contain cathode ray particles   **E.** He

24. Mg is an example of:

  A. a halogen   **C.** an alkali metal

  B. a noble gas   **D.** a transition metal   **E.** an alkaline earth metal

25. Which has a mass of approximately 1 amu?

  A. 1 atom of ^{12}C **C.** 1 proton

  B. 1 mole of ^{12}C **D.** 1 electron   **E.** 1 mole of electrons

26. Which of these does NOT describe a metal at room temperature?

  A. liquid   **B.** shiny   **C.** bendable   **D.** solid   **E.** gas

27. Which of the following sets of elements consists of members of the *same* group in the periodic table?

  A. ^{14}Si, ^{15}P and ^{16}S **C.** ^{9}F, ^{10}Ne and ^{11}Na

  B. ^{20}Ca, ^{26}Fe and ^{34}Se **D.** ^{31}Ga, ^{49}In and ^{81}Tl **E.** ^{11}Na, ^{20}Ca and ^{39}Y

28. Which of the following is a general characteristic of a nonmetal?

  A. low density   **C.** brittle

  B. nonconductor of heat   **D.** solid or gaseous state   **E.** all of the above

29. Which of the following elements is a metal?

  A. Hydrogen   **B.** Magnesium   **C.** Silicon   **D.** Chlorine   **E.** Carbon

30. Which element has the greatest ionization energy?

  A. Al   **B.** Cl   **C.** P   **D.** S   **E.** Fr

31. What is the number of neutrons in an As isotope?

  A. 34   **B.** 36   **C.** 42   **D.** 40   **E.** 44

32. Which classification of the element is incorrect?

   A. Ce − Transition metal   **C.** Cd − Transition metal

   B. Ne − Noble gas   **D.** Li − Alkali metal   **E.** Br − Halogen

33. Which elements are most common in living organisms?

   A. O, Na, H, Ca   **C.** C, S, K, Mg

   B. H, O, N, C   **D.** Ca, O, S, Cl   **E.** H, Ca, Na, Cl

34. Which of the following is a general characteristic of a nonmetallic element?

   A. nonconductor of electricity   **C.** dull appearance

   B. low melting point   **D.** reactivity with metals   **E.** all of the above

35. Which of the following is the electron configuration of a boron atom?

   A. $1s^2\,2s^1\,2p^2$ **C.** $1s^2\,2s^2\,2p^2$

   B. $1s^2\,2p^3$ **D.** $1s^2\,2s^2\,2p^1$ **E.** $1s^2\,2s^1\,2p^1$

36. Which of the following elements is a nonmetal?

   A. Sodium   **B.** Chlorine   **C.** Aluminum   **D.** Magnesium   **E.** Palladium

37. Which element would most likely be a metal with a low melting point?

   A. K   **B.** B   **C.** N   **D.** C   **E.** Cl

38. Which of the following particles would NOT be deflected by charged plates?

   A. alpha particles   **C.** hydrogen atoms

   B. protons   **D.** cathode rays   **E.** All are deflected by charged plates

39. How many electrons can occupy the $n = 2$ shell?

   A. 2   **B.** 6   **C.** 8   **D.** 18   **E.** 32

40. How much does 4 moles of Na weigh?

   A. 5.75 grams   **B.** 23 amu   **C.** 23 grams   **D.** 92 grams   **E.** 92 amu

41. Which of these is NOT a metal?

   A. rubidium   **C.** aluminum

   B. sodium   **D.** vanadium   **E.** selenium

42. Which of the following elements occupies a position in Period 5 and Group IIIA on the periodic table?

   A. In   **B.** As   **C.** Tl   **D.** P   **E.** Sr

43. Which of the following is a general characteristic of a nonmetallic element?

   A. reacts with nonmetals   **C.** pliable

   B. high melting point   **D.** shiny luster   **E.** none of the above

44. Which of the following elements is a metalloid?

   A. Copper   **B.** Iron   **C.** Silicon   **D.** Bromine   **E.** Palladium

45. Which characteristic is responsible for the changes seen in ionization energy when moving down a column?

   A. Increased shielding of electrons
   B. Increasing nuclear attraction for electrons and larger atomic or ionic radii
   C. Increasing nuclear attraction for electrons
   D. Decreasing nuclear attraction for electrons
   E. Increased shielding of electrons and larger atomic radii

46. How many electrons can occupy the $n = 4$ shell?

   A. 8   **B.** 10   **C.** 18   **D.** 32   **E.** 40

47. Which represents the charge on 1 mole of electrons?

   A. 6.02×10^{23} e$^-$ **C.** 6.02×10^{23} grams
   B. 6.02×10^{23} C   **D.** 1 C   **E.** 1 e

48. Which of these properties describes a metal?

   A. fragile   **C.** good conductor of heat
   B. transparent   **D.** brittle   **E.** poor conductor of electricity

49. The elements in groups IA, VIIA and VIIIA are called, respectively:

   A. alkaline earth metals, transition metals and halogens
   B. alkali metals, halogens and noble gases
   C. alkali metals, alkali earth metals and halogens
   D. alkaline earth metals, halogens and alkali metals
   E. halogens, alkali earth metals and noble gases

50. What does a positive charge on an atom signify?

   A. more protons than neutrons   **C.** more electrons than protons
   B. more neutrons than protons   **D.** more protons than electrons
                         E. more electrons than neutrons

51. From the periodic table, which of the following elements is a semimetal?

   A. Ar   **B.** As   **C.** Al   **D.** Ac   **E.** Am

52. Which of the following is true of an element in an excited state?

   A. It has emitted a photon and its energy has decreased
   B. It has emitted a photon and its energy has increased
   C. It has absorbed a photon and its energy has decreased
   D. It has absorbed a neutron and its energy has increased
   E. It has absorbed a photon and its energy has increased

53. Which of the following represents a compound rather than an element?

I. O_3

II. CCl_4

III. S_8

IV. H_2O

    A. I and III   **B.** II and IV   **C.** I and II   **D.** III and IV   **E.** I and IV

54. Which element has the lowest electronegativity?

    A. Mg   **B.** Al   **C.** Cl   **D.** Br   **E.** I

55. Uranium exists in nature in the form of several isotopes that have different:

    A. numbers of electrons   **C.** atomic numbers

    B. numbers of protons   **D.** charges   **E.** numbers of neutrons

56. How many electrons can occupy the 4*s* subshell?

    A. 1   **B.** 2   **C.** 6   **D.** 8   **E.** 10

57. The most common isotope of hydrogen contains how many neutrons?

    A. 0   **B.** 1   **C.** 2   **D.** 3   **E.** 4

58. Based on experimental evidence, Dalton postulated that:

    A. atoms of different elements have the same mass

    B. not all atoms of a given element are identical

    C. atoms can be created and destroyed in chemical reactions

    D. each element consists of indivisible minute particles called atoms

    E. none of the above

59. What is the maximum number of electrons in the n = 3 shell?

    A. 32   **B.** 18   **C.** 10   **D.** 8   **E.** 12

60. Referring to the periodic table, which of the following is a solid metal under normal conditions?

    A. Ce   **B.** Os   **C.** Ba   **D.** Cr   **E.** all of the above

61. What must be the same if two atoms represent the same element?

    A. number of neutrons   **C.** number of electron shells

    B. atomic mass   **D.** atomic number

    E. number of valence electrons

62. Electron affinity is the:

    A. ability of an atom to attract electrons when it bonds with another atom

    B. energy needed to remove an electron from a neutral atom of the element in the gas phase

    C. energy liberated when an electron is added to a gaseous neutral atom converting it to an anion

    D. A and B

    E. A and C

63. How many electrons can occupy the $4d$ subshell?

   A. 2   **B.** 6   **C.** 8   **D.** 10   **E.** 12

64. Which statement is true regarding the relative abundances of the ^{6}lithium or ^{7}lithium isotopes?

   A. The relative proportions change as neutrons move between the nuclei
   B. The isotopes are in roughly equal proportions
   C. The relative ratio depends on the temperature of the element
   D. ^{6}Lithium is much more abundant
   E. ^{7}Lithium is much more abundant

65. An element in its ground state absorbs photons of 2.3 eV and 4.1 eV, but no intermediate energies. If the element in its ground state absorbs a photon of energy 4.1 eV, it emits a photon of 4.1 eV and a photon of:

   A. 1.8 eV   **B.** 6.4 eV   **C.** 2.3 eV   **D.** 4.1 eV   **E.** 0.8 eV

66. In the ground state of an atom:

   A. the energy of the electrons are at a maximum
   B. the protons and neutrons fill all the available energy states
   C. all the electrons are in their lowest energy levels
   D. the excited states are all filled
   E. none of the above

67. Each atom of an element has the same number of:

   A. electrons   **C.** photons
   B. neutrons   **D.** protons   **E.** protons and electrons

68. Refer to the periodic table and predict which of the following is a solid nonmetal under normal conditions.

   A. Cl   **B.** F   **C.** Se   **D.** As   **E.** Ar

69. Except for helium, the valence shell of electrons in the noble gases has which of the following electron configurations?

   A. ns^2np^2 **B.** ns^2np^4 **C.** ns^8np^2 **D.** ns^2np^8 **E.** ns^2np^6

70. Which particle is in the nucleus?

   A. protons and neutrons   **C.** protons only
   B. protons and electrons   **D.** neutrons only   **E.** neutrons and electrons

71. Which element would most likely be a metalloid?

   A. B   **B.** Mg   **C.** Cl   **D.** H   **E.** C

72. All isotopes of an element possess the same:

A. number of electrons, atomic number and mass, but have nothing else in common

B. atomic number and mass, but have nothing else in common

C. chemical properties and mass, but have nothing else in common

D. number of electrons, atomic number and chemical properties

E. mass only

73. What is the maximum number of electrons that can occupy the 4*f* orbitals?

A. 6 **B.** 8 **C.** 14 **D.** 16 **E.** 18

74. ^{63}Cu is 69% of the naturally occurring isotope of Cu. If only one other isotope is present for natural copper, what is it?

A. ^{59}Cu **B.** ^{65}Cu **C.** ^{61}Cu **D.** ^{62}Cu **E.** ^{60}Cu

75. Which of the following statements best describes an element?

A. has consistent physical properties **C.** consists of only one type of atom

B. consists of more than one type of atom **D.** material that is pure

E. material that has consistent chemical properties

76. Which of the following statements are true?

    I. The *f* subshell contains 7 orbitals

    II. The third energy shell (n=3) has no *f* orbitals

    III. There are ten *d* orbitals in the *d* subshell

    IV. The second energy shell contains only *s* and *p* orbitals

    V. A *p* subshell can accommodate a maximum of 6 electrons

A. II and IV **B.** I, II and IV **C.** I, II, IV and V **D.** II, III and V **E.** II, III and IV

77. What is the term for the value which indicates the number of protons for an atom of a given element?

A. atomic mass **C.** atomic notation

B. mass number **D.** atomic number **E.** none of the above

78. Almost all of the mass of an atom exists in its:

A. electrons **C.** outermost energy level

B. nucleus **D.** first energy level **E.** valence electrons

79. Which phrase describes the alkali metals (group IA)?

A. Form strong ionic bonds with nonmetals **C.** More reactive than group IIA elements

B. Little or no reaction with water **D.** A and C

E. B and C

80. Which group contains only metalloids?

A. Pm, Sm and Nd **C.** Cu, Ag and Au

B. Ar, Xe and Rn **D.** Po, Cs and Ac **E.** Si, B and Sb

81. What is the mass of one mole of glucose which has a molecular formula of $C_6H_{12}O_6$?

   A. 90 g   **B.** 132 g   **C.** 180 g   **D.** 194 g   **E.** 360 g

82. Metalloids are elements:

   A. larger than nonmetals   **C.** smaller than metals

   B. found in asteroids   **D.** that have some properties like metals and some like nonmetals

   E. that have properties different from either the metals or the nonmetals

83. Which of the following subshells is lowest in energy?

   A. 5*f*   **B.** 4*s*   **C.** 3*d*   **D.** 6*s*   **E.** 5*p*

84. Consider an atom with the electron configuration $1s^2 2s^2 2p^6 3s^2 3p^6$. Which of the following is an accurate statement concerning this atom?

   A. This atom would probably be chemically inert   **C.** This atom is in an excited state

   B. This atom has a non-zero angular momentum   **D.** The atomic number $Z = 11$

   E. This atom is most likely to give rise to an ion with charge +2e

85. What is the term for a broad uninterrupted band of radiant energy?

   A. ultraviolet spectrum   **C.** continuous spectrum

   B. visible spectrum   **D.** radiant energy spectrum   **E.** none of the above

86. Compared to the electronegativity of iodine, the electronegativity of chlorine is:

   A. lower, because increased nuclear shielding results in a weaker pull on the valence electrons

   B. greater, because decreased nuclear shielding allows for a stronger pull on the valence electrons

   C. lower, because Cl has a smaller nuclear charge which results in a smaller force exerted on electrons

   D. greater, because Cl has a greater nuclear charge which results in a greater force exerted on electrons

   E. greater, because Cl has a greater electron charge which results in a greater force exerted on the nucleus

87. Cobalt is element 27. ^{60}Cobalt is used in the medical treatment of cancer. How many neutrons and protons are contained in the nucleus of the ^{60}Cobalt isotope?

   A. 27 neutrons and 27 protons   **C.** 27 neutrons and 33 protons

   B. 33 neutrons and 33 protons   **D.** 33 neutrons and 33 electrons

                                                  E. 33 neutrons and 27 protons

88. Metalloids:

     I. have some metallic and some nonmetallic properties

     II. may have low electrical conductivities

     III. contain elements in group IIIB

   A. I and III only   **C.** II and III only

   B. II only   **D.** I and II only   **E.** I, II and III

89. All atoms of a particular element have the same:

   A. atomic number and chemical properties, but not necessarily the same mass

   B. chemical properties and the same mass, but lack other similarities

   C. number of electrons, the same atomic number, the same mass, but lack other similarities

   D. mass and the same chemical properties, but lack other similarities

   E. atomic number and the same mass, but lack other similarities

90. What is the atomic number and the mass number of ^{79}Br, respectively?

   A. 35; 44   **B.** 44; 35   **C.** 35; 79   **D.** 79; 35   **E.** 35; 114

91. With what charge do alkaline earth metals form ions?

   A. –2   **B.** –1   **C.** 0   **D.** +1   **E.** +2

92. Which of the following is a metalloid?

   A. antimony (Sb)   **C.** iodine (I)

   B. uranium (U)   **D.** zinc (Zn)   **E.** selenium (Se)

93. Which types of subshells are present for the n = 2 energy level?

   A. *d*   **B.** *p*   **C.** *s*   **D.** both *d* and *p*   **E.** both *s* and *p*

94. What is the term for the shorthand description of the arrangement of electrons by sublevels according to increasing energy?

   A. continuous spectrum   **C.** atomic notation

   B. electron configuration   **D.** atomic number   **E.** none of the above

95. Adding one proton to the nucleus of an atom:

   A. causes no change in the atomic number and decrease in the atomic mass

   B. increases its atomic number by one unit, but does not change its atomic mass

   C. increases its atomic mass by one unit, but does not change its atomic number

   D. increases the atomic number and the mass number by one unit

   E. causes no change in the atomic mass and decrease in the atomic number

96. Which subshell has a principal quantum number of 4 and an angular momentum quantum number of 2?

   A. 4*d*   **B.** 4*f*   **C.** 2*p*   **D.** 4*s*   **E.** none of the above

97. Which characteristics describe the mass, charge and location of a proton, respectively?

   A. approximate mass 5×10^{-4} amu; charge +1; inside nucleus

   B. approximate mass 1 amu; charge 0; inside nucleus

   C. approximate mass 1 amu; charge +1; inside nucleus

   D. approximate mass 5×10^{-4} amu; charge –1; outside nucleus

   E. approximate mass 1 amu; charge +1; outside nucleus

98. Halogens form ions by:

A. gaining two electrons   C. gaining one neutron

B. gaining one electron   D. losing one electron   E. losing two electrons

99. Which statement about a neutron is FALSE?

A. It is a nucleon

B. It is often associated with protons

C. It is more difficult to detect than a proton or an electron

D. It is much more massive than an electron

E. It has a charge equivalent but opposite to an electron

100. What is the maximum number of electrons that can be placed into the *f* subshell, *d* subshell and *p* subshell respectively?

A. 14, 10 and 6   C. 10, 14 and 6

B. 12, 10 and 6   D. 2, 12 and 20   E. 16, 8 and 2

101. How many neutrons are in a Beryllium atom with an atomic number of 4 and atomic mass of 9?

A. 4   B. 5   C. 9   D. 16   E. 20

102. Classify the following three elements of S, As & Ga as a metal, metalloid, or nonmetal:

A. As, metal; Ga, metalloid; S, nonmetal   C. Ga, metal; As, metalloid; S, nonmetal

B. Ga, metal; S, metalloid; As, nonmetal   D. S, metal; Ga, metalloid; As, nonmetal

    E. S, metal; As, metalloid; Ga, nonmetal

103. Which of the following elements has the greatest ionization energy?

A. scandium   C. potassium

B. titanium   D. calcium   E. magnesium

104. Isotopes have the:

A. same number of neutrons but different number of electrons

B. same number of protons but different number of neutrons

C. same number of protons but different number of electrons

D. none of the above

E. all of the above

105. Which characteristic is NOT a property of the transition elements?

A. Colored ions in solution   C. Multiple oxidation states

B. Complex ions formed   D. Nonmetallic in character

    E. None of the above

106. Which species shown below has 24 neutrons?

A. $_{24}^{52}\text{Cr}$ B. $_{25}^{55}\text{Mn}$ C. $_{12}^{24}\text{Mg}$ D. $_{23}^{51}\text{V}$ E. $_{21}^{45}\text{Sc}$

107. Hydrogen exists as three isotopes which have different numbers of:

A. neutrons   **C.** protons

B. electrons   **D.** charges   **E.** protons and neutrons

108. The elements of silver, iron, mercury and rhodium are:

A. transduction metals   **C.** alkaline earth metals

B. actinoids   **D.** transition metals   **E.** lanthinides

109. Which atom is largest?

A. Li   **B.** Na   **C.** K   **D.** H   **E.** Rb

110. Rank the elements below in order of decreasing atomic radius:

A. Al > P > Cl > Na > Mg   **C.** Mg > Na > P > Al > Cl

B. Cl > Al > P > Na > Mg   **D.** Na > Mg > Al > P > Cl

       E. P > Al > Cl > Mg > Na

111. Which of the following produces the "atomic fingerprint" of an element?

A. excited protons dropping to a lower energy level

B. excited protons jumping to a higher energy level

C. excited electrons dropping to a lower energy level

D. excited electrons jumping to a higher energy level

E. none of the above

112. How many neutrons are in a neutral atom of ^{40}Ar?

A. 18   **B.** 22   **C.** 38   **D.** 40   **E.** 60

113. Paramagnetism, the ability to be pulled into a magnetic field, is demonstrated by:

A. any substance containing unpaired electrons

B. nonmetal elements that have unpaired *p* orbital electrons

C. transition elements that have unpaired *d* orbital electrons

D. nonmetal elements that have paired *p* orbital electrons

E. any substance containing paired electrons

114. The number of neutrons in an atom is equal to:

A. the mass number   **C.** mass number minus atomic number

B. the atomic number   **D.** atomic number minus mass number

       E. mass number plus atomic number

115. The element calcium belongs to which family?

A. representative elements   **C.** alkali metals

B. transition metals   **D.** lanthanides

       E. alkaline earth metals

116. Which of the following elements would be shiny and flexible?

A. bromine (Br)

B. selenium (Se)

C. helium (He)

D. ruthenium (Ru)

E. silicon (Si)

117. Which of the following subshell notations for electron occupancy is an impossibility?

A. $4f^{11}$ **B.** $2p^1$ **C.** $5s^3$ **D.** $4p^5$ **E.** $3p^3$

118. How many protons, neutrons and electrons does a Platinum atom have respectively, if an uncharged atom of Platinum has an atomic number of 78 and an atomic mass of 195?

A. 78, 156, 78

B. 117, 273, 117

C. 117, 78, 117

D. 117, 78, 78

E. 78, 117, 78

119. Lines were observed in the spectrum of uranium ore identical to those of helium in the spectrum of the Sun. Which of the following produced the lines in the helium spectrum?

A. excited protons jumping to a higher energy level

B. excited protons dropping to a lower energy level

C. excited electrons jumping to a higher energy level

D. excited electrons dropping to a lower energy level

E. none of the above

120. Compared to the atomic radius of calcium, the atomic radius of gallium is:

A. smaller because increased nuclear charge causes electrons to be held more tightly

B. larger because its additional electrons increase the atomic volume

C. smaller because gallium gives up more electrons, thereby decreasing its size

D. larger because increased electron charge requires that the same force be distributed over a greater number of electrons

E. larger because decreased electron charge requires that the same force be distributed over a smaller number of electrons

121. What is the average atomic mass of an element that contains three isotopes of 16.0 amu, 17.0 amu, and 18.0 amu with relative abundances of 20%, 50% and 30%, respectively?

A. 16.9 amu

B. 17.1 amu

C. 17.2 amu

D. 17.4 amu

E. 17.5 amu

122. Element X has an atomic number of 7 and an atomic mass of 13. Element X has:

A. 6 neutrons

B. 6 electrons

C. 6 protons

D. 13 electrons

E. 7 neutrons

123. Which species shown below has 24 electrons?

A. $^{52}_{24}Cr$ **B.** $^{55}_{25}Mn$ **C.** $^{24}_{12}Mg$ **D.** $^{45}_{21}Sc$ **E.** $^{51}_{23}V$

124. An atom that contains 47 protons, 47 electrons and 60 neutrons is an isotope of:

A. Nd   **B.** Bh   **C.** Ag   **D.** Al   **E.** cannot be determined

125. Which element listed below has the greatest electronegativity?

    A. I   **B.** Fr   **C.** H   **D.** He   **E.** F

126. Oxygen atoms form H_2O molecules. Do oxygen atoms in O_2 and in H_2O have similar properties?

    A. No, compounds are uniquely different from the elements from which they are made
    B. No, but their similar properties are only a coincidence
    C. Yes, but it is only a coincidence that their properties are similar
    D. Yes, and this explains how fish are able to breathe water
    E. Yes, compounds and the elements they originate from are identical

127. In an atom with many electrons, which of the following orbitals would be highest in energy?

    A. $4f$ **B.** $4p$ **C.** $6d$ **D.** $7s$ **E.** $8g$

128. Which element has the electron configuration of $1s^2 2s^2 2p^6 3s^2$?

    A. Na   **B.** Si   **C.** Ca   **D.** Mg   **E.** none of the above

129. Which of the following represents a pair of isotopes?

    A. $^{32}_{16}S$, $^{32}_{16}S^{2-}$ **C.** $^{14}_{6}C$, $^{14}_{7}N$

    B. O_2, O_3 **D.** $^{1}_{1}H$, $^{2}_{1}H$ **E.** none of the above

130. The atomic mass of sodium is 22.989 g/mole. This atomic mass is not an integer because of:

    A. quanta   **C.** Pauli exclusion principle
    B. uneven density   **D.** spin direction   **E.** isotopes

131. How many protons and neutrons are in ^{35}Cl, respectively?

    A. 35; 18   **B.** 18; 17   **C.** 17; 18   **D.** 17; 17   **E.** 35; 17

132. The element with the least electronegativity is:

    A. Cl   **B.** Fr   **C.** I   **D.** F   **E.** C

133. What is the name of the compound composed of $CaCl_2$?

    A. dichloromethane   **C.** carbon chloride
    B. dichlorocalcium   **D.** calcium chloride   **E.** dicalcium chloride

134. The electron configuration for manganese (Mn) is:

    A. $1s^2 2s^2 2p^6 3s^2 3p^6$ **C.** $1s^2 2s^2 2p^6 3s^2 3p^6 4s^2 3d^6$
    B. $1s^2 2s^2 2p^6 3s^2 3p^6 4s^2 3d^{10} 4p^1$ **D.** $1s^2 2s^2 2p^6 3s^2 3p^6 4s^2 3d^6$
    E. $1s^2 2s^2 2p^6 3s^2 3p^6 4s^2 3d^5$

135. Different isotopes of one element have an equal number of [ ], but different number of [ ].

    A. protons, electrons   **C.** neutrons, protons
    B. neutrons, electrons   **D.** protons, neutrons   **E.** electrons, protons

136. Which of the following is the best description of the Bohr atom?

    A. sphere with a heavy, dense nucleus surrounded by electrons

    B. sphere with a heavy, dense nucleus encircled by electrons in orbits

    C. indivisible, indestructible particle

    D. homogeneous sphere of *plum pudding*

    E. sphere with a heavy, dense nucleus surrounded by electron orbitals

137. All of the following are examples of polar molecules, EXCEPT:

    A. H_2O **B.** CCl_4 **C.** CH_2Cl_2 **D.** HF   **E.** CO

138. The element rhenium (Re) exists as two stable and eighteen unstable isotopes. ^{185}Rhenium has a nucleus that contains:

    A. 110 protons and 130 neutrons   **C.** 75 protons and 130 neutrons

    B. 130 protons and 75 neutrons   **D.** 75 protons and 75 neutrons

                                                 E. 75 protons and 110 neutrons

139. Which is the principal quantum number?

    A. *n*   **B.** *m*   **C.** *l*   **D.** *s*   **E.** +1/2

140. The atomic mass of a naturally occurring isotope of iron is reported as 55.434 amu, which means that the average mass is:

    A. 55.434/1.0079 times greater than a ^{1}H atom

    B. 55.434/12.000 times greater than a ^{12}C atom

    C. 55.434 times greater than a ^{12}C atom

    D. 55.434 times greater than a ^{1}H atom

    E. 55.434/12.011 times greater than a ^{12}C atom

141. An atom containing 29 protons, 29 electrons and 34 neutrons has a mass number of:

    A. 5   **B.** 29   **C.** 34   **D.** 63   **E.** 92

142. Ionization energy is generally defined as the energy:

    A. released when an element forms ions within an aqueous solution

    B. necessary to add an electron to an element in its standard state

    C. necessary to remove an electron from an element in its liquid state

    D. absorbed when an element forms ions within an aqueous solution

    E. necessary to remove an electron from an element in its gaseous state

143. Which of the following physical properties is expected for krypton (Kr)?

    A. brittle   **C.** exists as a gas at room temperature

    B. shiny   **D.** hard   **E.** conducts electricity

144. Which element has the electron configuration $1s^2 2s^2 2p^6 3s^2 3p^6 4s^2 3d^{10} 4p^6 5s^2 4d^{10} 5p^2$?

    A. Sn   **B.** As   **C.** Pb   **D.** Sb   **E.** In

145. In its ground state, how many unpaired electrons does a sulfur atom have?

A. 0   **B.** 1   **C.** 2   **D.** 3   **E.** 4

146. The masses on the periodic table are expressed in what units?

A. picograms   **C.** Grams

B. nanograms   **D.** micrograms   **E.** Amu's

147. The *l* quantum number refers to the electron's:

A. angular momentum   **C.** spin

B. magnetic orientation   **D.** energy level   **E.** shell size

148. Which characteristics describe the mass, charge and location of a neutron, respectively?

A. approximate mass 1 amu; charge 0; inside nucleus

B. approximate mass 5×10^{-4} amu; charge 0; inside nucleus

C. approximate mass 1 amu; charge +1; inside nucleus

D. approximate mass 1 amu; charge –1; inside nucleus

E. approximate mass 5×10^{-4} amu; charge –1; outside nucleus

149. Which of the following elements most easily accepts an extra electron?

A. He   **B.** Ca   **C.** Cl   **D.** Fr   **E.** Na

150. What happens to the properties of elements across any period of the periodic table?

A. Elements tend to become more metallic because of the increase in atomic number

B. The properties of the elements change gradually across any period of the periodic table

C. The elements get much larger in size because of the addition of more protons and electrons

D. All of the above are true

E. None of the above is true

151. How many electrons are there in the outermost shell and subshell, respectively, in an atom with the electron configuration $1s^2 2s^2 2p^6 3s^2 3p^6 4s^2 3d^{10} 4p^1$?

A. 4, 1   **B.** 3, 1   **C.** 10, 1   **D.** 2, 2   **E.** 5,1

152. Compared to nonradioactive isotopes, radioactive isotopes:

A. have a lower number of neutrons   **C.** have a higher number neutrons

B. have a higher number of protons   **D.** are more stable

                                              E. are less stable

153. What terms refer to a vertical column in the periodic table of elements?

A. period or series   **C.** group or series

B. period or family   **D.** group or family   **E.** none of the above

154. A β– particle is emitted by a lithium nucleus. The resulting nucleus is an isotope of:

A. helium   **B.** carbon   **C.** beryllium   **D.** boron   **E.** lithium

155. How many electrons are in the highest energy level of sulfur?

   A. 2   **B.** 4   **C.** 6   **D.** 8   **E.** 10

156. Which statement is NOT true?

   A. The first four subshells that correspond to $l = 0$, 1, 2, and 3 are s, p, d, and f
   B. In the shell n= 2, there is 1 subshell
   C. The values of l range from 0 to (n − 1)
   D. The numbers of possible values for l describes the number of subshells in a shell
   E. The spin can be either + ½ or − ½

157. Which of the following is NOT an alkali metal?

   A. Fr   **B.** Cs   **C.** Ca   **D.** Na   **E.** Rb

158. Which characteristics describe an electron?

   A. approximate mass 5×10^{-4} amu; charge −1; outside nucleus
   B. approximate mass 5×10^{-4} amu; charge 0; inside nucleus
   C. approximate mass 1 amu; charge −1; inside nucleus
   D. approximate mass 1 amu; charge +1; inside nucleus
   E. approximate mass 1 amu; charge 0; inside nucleus

159. In a bond between any two of the following atoms, the bonding electrons would be most strongly attracted to:

   A. I   **B.** He   **C.** Cs   **D.** Cl   **E.** Fr

160. Dmitri Mendeleev's chart of elements:

   A. predicted the behavior of missing elements
   B. developed the basis of our modern periodic table
   C. predicted the existence of elements undiscovered at his time
   D. placed elements with the same number of valence electrons in the same horizontal row
   E. all of the above

161. Which element has the electron configuration $1s^2 2s^2 2p^6 3s^2 3p^6 4s^2 3d^{10} 4p^6 5s^2 4d^1$?

   A. Y   **B.** La   **C.** Si   **D.** Sc   **E.** Zr

162. Which of the following elements contains 6 valence electrons?

   A. S   **B.** Cl   **C.** Si   **D.** P   **E.** Ca^{2+}

163. The magnetic quantum number does NOT:

   A. suggest that there are always odd numbers of orbitals in a subshell
   B. have values which range from $-l$ to $+l$
   C. give the particular orbitals in a subshell
   D. describe the spin of the electron
   E. none of the above

164. Write the formula for the ionic compound formed from magnesium and sulfur:

    A. Mg_2S **B.** Mg_3S_2 **C.** MgS_2 **D.** MgS_3 **E.** MgS

165. Which has the largest radius?

    A. Br^- **B.** K^+ **C.** Ar **D.** Ca^{2+} **E.** Cl^-

166. Which pair of elements have the correct magnetic properties?

    A. Ba: paramagnetic   Xe: diamagnetic
    B. Ba: paramagnetic   Xe: paramagnetic
    C. Ba: diamagnetic   Xe: diamagnetic
    D. Ba: diamagnetic   Xe: paramagnetic
    E. B and D are correct

167. What is the maximum number of electrons to fill the atom's second electron shell?

    A. 18   **B.** 2   **C.** 4   **D.** 12   **E.** 8

168. Approximately what percent of a ^{14}carbon sample remains after 2,000 years if ^{14}carbon has a half-life of 5,700 years?

    A. 20%   **B.** 32%   **C.** 52%   **D.** 78%   **E.** 92%

169. Which of the following is the sulfate ion?

    A. SO_4^{2-} **B.** S^{2-} **C.** CO_3^{2-} **D.** PO_4^{3-} **E.** S^-

170. What is the value of quantum numbers n and l in the highest occupied orbital for the element carbon that has an atomic number of 6?

    A. $n = 1, l = 1$ **C.** $n = 1, l = 2$
    B. $n = 2, l = 1$ **D.** $n = 2, l = 2$ **E.** $n = 3, l = 3$

171. Which element is a halogen?

    A. Os   **B.** I   **C.** O   **D.** Te   **E.** Se

172. Which of the following is the correct sequence of atomic radii from smallest to largest?

    A. $Al \rightarrow S \rightarrow Al^{3+} \rightarrow S^{2-}$ **C.** $Al^{3+} \rightarrow Al \rightarrow S \rightarrow S^{2-}$
    B. $S \rightarrow S^{2-} \rightarrow Al \rightarrow Al^{3+}$ **D.** $Al^{3+} \rightarrow S \rightarrow Al \rightarrow S^{2-}$ **E.** $Al^{3+} \rightarrow Al \rightarrow S^{2-} \rightarrow S$

173. Early investigators proposed that the ray of the cathode ray tube was due to the cathode because the ray:

    A. could be diverted by a magnetic field
    B. was not seen from the positively charged anode
    C. was attracted to the electric plates that were positively charged
    D. would change colors depending on the gas used within the tube
    E. was observed in the presence or absence of a gas

174. Which of the following atoms is paramagnetic?

   A. Zn   **B.** O   **C.** Ca   **D.** Ar   **E.** Xe

175. What is the electron configuration for an atom of silicon?

   A. $1s^2 2s^2 2p^4$ **C.** $1s^2 2s^2 2p^6 3s^2 3p^2$

   B. $1s^2 2s^2 2p^6 3s^2$ **D.** $1s^2 2s^2 2p^6 3s^2 3p^4$ **E.** $1s^2 2s^2 2p^6 3s^2 3p^5$

176. What is the atomic number of an element with an electron configuration: $1s^2$, $2s^2$, $2p^6$, $3s^2$, $3p^4$?

   A. 16   **C.** 12

   B. 14   **D.** 10   **E.** Not enough information is provided

177. The smallest amount of an element that retains that element's characteristics is the:

   A. molecule   **B.** neutron   **C.** atom   **D.** electron   **E.** proton

178. The attraction of the nucleus on the outermost electron in an atom tends to:

   A. decrease from right–left and bottom–top on the periodic table
   B. decrease from left–right and bottom–top on the periodic table
   C. decrease from left–right and top–bottom of the periodic table
   D. increase from right–left and top–bottom on the periodic table
   E. decrease from right–left and top–bottom on the periodic table

179. What is the number of unpaired electrons in the electron configuration of arsenic?

   A. 1   **B.** 3   **C.** 2   **D.** 0   **E.** 4

180. How many electrons are in its outermost electron shell if Oxygen has an atomic number of 8?

   A. 2   **B.** 6   **C.** 8   **D.** 16   **E.** 18

181. What is the mass of the sample of oxygen that contains 2.5 moles of O_2 molecules?

   A. 25 g   **B.** 40 g   **C.** 60 g   **D.** 80 g   **E.** 88 g

182. Which of the following is the carbonate ion?

   A. CO_3^{2-} **B.** CO_3 **C.** CO_2 **D.** CO_3^- **E.** SO_4^{2-}

183. Which of the following is NOT implied by the spin quantum number?

   A. The two spinning electrons generate magnetic fields
   B. The values are $+\frac{1}{2}$ or $-\frac{1}{2}$ **D.** A and B
   C. Orbital electrons have opposite spins   **E.** None of the above

184. Which statement does NOT describe the noble gases?

   A. The heavier noble gases react with other elements
   B. They belong to group VIIIA (or 18)
   C. They contain at least one metalloid
   D. He, Ne, Ar, Kr, Xe, Rn and Uuo are part of the group
   E. They were once known as the inert gases

185. The greatest dipole moment within a bond is when:

   A. both bonding elements have low electronegativity
   B. one bonding element has high electronegativity and the other has low electronegativity
   C. both bonding elements have high electronegativity
   D. one bonding element has high electronegativity and the other has moderate electronegativity
   E. both bonding elements have moderate electronegativity

186. Which of the elements would be in the same group as the element whose electronic configuration is $1s^2 2s^2 2p^6 3s^2 3p^6 4s^1$?

   A. ^{18}Ar **B.** ^{34}Se **C.** ^{12}Mg **D.** ^{15}P **E.** ^3Li

187. Which of the following is the symbol for the chlorite ion?

   A. ClO_2^- **B.** ClO^- **C.** ClO_4^- **D.** ClO_3^- **E.** ClO_2

188. The *f* subshell contains:

   A. 3 orbitals   **B.** 5 orbitals   **C.** 7 orbitals   **D.** 9 orbitals   **E.** 12 orbitals

189. Another name for atomic mass unit (amu) is the:

   A. Dalton   **B.** Kekule   **C.** Kelvin   **D.** Avogadro   **E.** Mendeleev

190. How many quantum numbers are needed to describe a single electron in an atom?

   A. 1   **B.** 2   **C.** 3   **D.** 4   **E.** 5

191. Early investigators proposed that the ray of the cathode tube was actually a negatively charged particle because the ray was:

   A. not seen from the positively charged anode
   B. diverted by a magnetic field
   C. observed in the presence or absence of a gas
   D. able to change colors depending on which gas was within the tube
   E. attracted to positively charged electric plates

192. If an element has an electron configuration ending in $3p^4$, which statements about the element's electron configuration is NOT correct?

   A. There are six electrons in the 3rd shell
   B. Five different subshells contain electrons
   C. There are eight electrons in the 2nd shell
   D. The 3rd shell needs two more electrons to be completely filled
   E. none of the above

193. An atom with an electrical charge is referred to as a(n):

   A. compound   **B.** ion   **C.** radioactive   **D.** isotope   **E.** element

194. What is the total mass of the H atoms contained in 3 moles of glucose ($C_6H_{12}O_6$)?

   A. 3g   **B.** 12g   **C.** 36g   **D.** 48g   **E.** 58g

195. Which orbital is NOT correctly matched with its shape?

A. *d*, spherically symmetrical C. *s*, spherically symmetrical
B. *p*, dumbbell shaped D. B and C E. A and B

196. The transition metals occur in which period(s) on the periodic table?

A. 2 B. 3 C. 4 D. 1 E. All of the above

197. The shell level of an electron is defined by which quantum number?

A. electron spin quantum number C. azimuthal quantum number
B. magnetic quantum number D. principal quantum number
E. principal quantum number and electron spin quantum number

198. Which of the elements is an alkaline earth metal?

A. ^{54}Xe B. ^{34}Se C. ^{21}Sc D. ^{37}Rb E. ^{38}Sr

199. Which one of the following correctly represents the electron configuration of sulfur in an excited state?

A. $1s^2 2s^2 2p^6 3s^2 3p^4 4s^1$ C. $1s^2 2s^2 2p^6 3s^2 3p^5$
B. $1s^2 2s^2 2p^6 3s^2 3p^3 4s^1$ D. $1s^2 2s^2 2p^6 3s^2 3p^4$ E. $1s^2 2s^2 2p^6 3s^1 3p^5$

200. Electrons fill up subshells in order of:

    I. decreasing distance from the nucleus
    II. increasing distance from the nucleus
    III. increasing energy

A. I only B. II only C. I and II only D. II and III only E. I, II and III

201. Which set of quantum numbers describe the highest energy electron?

A. $n = 2; l = 1; m_l = 0; m_s = -1/2$ C. $n = 1; l = 1; m_l = 0; m_s = +1/2$
B. $n = 3; l = 2; m_l = 2; m_s = -1/2$ D. $n = 1; l = 0; m_l = 0; m_s = -1/2$
E. $n = 2; l = 2; m_l = 2; m_s = -1/2$

202. Which of the following elements is NOT correctly classified?

A. Mo – transition element C. K – representative element
B. Sr – alkaline earth metal D. Ar – noble gas
E. Po – halogen

203. Which of the following Dalton's proposals is still valid?

A. Compounds contain atoms in small whole number ratios
B. Atoms of different elements combine to form compounds
C. An element is composed of tiny particles called atoms
D. All of the above
E. None of the above

204. Why does a chlorine atom form anions more easily than cations?

   A. Chlorine has a high electronegativity value

   B. Chlorine has a large positive electron affinity

   C. Chlorine donates one electron to complete its outer shell

   D. Chlorine gains one electron to complete its outer shell

   E. Chlorine has a low electronegativity value

205. Which principle or rule states that only two electrons can occupy an orbital?

   A. Pauli exclusion principle   **C.** Heisenberg's uncertainty principle

   B. Hund's rule   **D.** Newton's principle   **E.** None of the above

206. Arrange the following elements in order of increasing atomic radius: Sr, Rb, Sb, Te, In

   A. Te < Sb < In < Sr < Rb   **C.** Te < Sb < In < Rb < Sr

   B. In < Sb < Te < Sr < Rb   **D.** Rb < Sr < In < Sb < Te   **E.** In < Sb < Te < Rb < Sr

207. Which set of quantum numbers is possible?

   A. $n = 1; l = 2; m_l = 3; m_s = -1/2$ **C.** $n = 2; l = 1; m_l = 2; m_s = -1/2$

   B. $n = 4; l = 2; m_l = 2; m_s = -1/2$ **D.** $n = 3; l = 3; m_l = 2; m_s = -1/2$

                                              E. $n = 2; l = 3; m_l = 2; m_s = -1/2$

208. Which of the following pairs has one metalloid element and one nonmetal element?

   A. ^{82}Pb and ^{83}Bi **C.** ^{51}Sb and ^{20}Ca

   B. ^{19}K and ^{9}F **D.** ^{3}As and ^{14}Si **E.** ^{32}Ge and ^{9}F

209. Which of the following ions has the same charge as the hydroxide ion?

   A. CO_3^{2-} **B.** PO_4^{3-} **C.** NO_3^- **D.** NH_4^+ **E.** H_3O^+

210. When an atom is most stable, how many electrons does it contain in its valence shell?

   A. 4   **B.** 6   **C.** 8   **D.** 10   **E.** 12

211. The shell with a principal quantum number 3 can accommodate how many electrons?

   A. 2   **B.** 3   **C.** 10   **D.** 18   **E.** 8

212. What is the number of known nonmetals relative to the number of metals?

   A. about two times greater   **C.** about four times less

   B. about fifty percent   **D.** very small in comparison   **E.** about three times greater

213. Which type of subshell is filled by the distinguishing electron of an alkaline earth metal?

   A. *s*   **B.** *p*   **C.** *f*   **D.** *d*   **E.** both *s* and *p*

214. An excited state of an atom is represented by which electron configuration?

   A. $1s^2 2s^2 2p^6 3s^1$ **C.** $1s^2 2s^2 2p^1$

   B. $1s^2 2s^2 2p^6$ **D.** $1s^2 2s^2 3s^1$ **E.** $1s^2 2s^2 2p^6 3s^2$

215. An excited hydrogen atom emits a light spectrum of specific, characteristic wavelengths. The light spectrum is a result of:

A. energy released as H atoms form H_2 molecules
B. the light wavelengths which are not absorbed by valence electrons when white light passes through the sample
C. particles being emitted as the hydrogen nuclei decay
D. excited electrons being promoted to higher energy levels
E. excited electrons dropping to lower energy levels

216. Which electron configuration depicts an excited state of potassium that has an atomic number of 19?

A. $1s^2\, 2s^2\, 2p^6\, 3s^2\, 3p^6$
B. $1s^2\, 2s^2\, 2p^6\, 3s^2\, 3p^6\, 4s^2$
C. $1s^2\, 2s^2\, 2p^6\, 3s^2\, 3p^5\, 4s^2$
D. $1s^2\, 2s^2\, 2p^6\, 3s^2\, 3p^7$
E. $1s^2\, 2s^2\, 2p^6\, 3s^2\, 3p^2\, 4s^6$

217. Which statement is true of the energy levels for an electron in a hydrogen atom?

A. The energy levels are identical to the levels in the He^+ ion
B. The energy of each level can be computed from a known formula
C. The distance between energy levels for $n = 1$ and $n = 2$ is the same as the distance between the $n = 3$ and $n = 4$ energy levels
D. Since there is only one electron, the electron must be located in the lowest energy level
E. The distance between the $n = 3$ and $n = 4$ energy levels in the same as the distance between the $n = 4$ and $n = 5$ energy levels

218. Ignoring hydrogen, which area of the periodic table contains both metals and nonmetals?

A. both p and d areas
B. p area only
C. s area only
D. both s and p areas
E. both s and d areas

219. When an excited electron returns to the ground state, it releases:

A. photons
B. protons
C. beta particles
D. alpha particles
E. gamma particles

220. Which of the following molecules does NOT exist?

A. OF_5 **B.** $NaLiCO_3$ **C.** ICl **D.** UF_6 **E.** all of the above exist

221. Which column of the periodic table has 3 nonmetal and 2 metalloid elements?

A. Group IIIA
B. Group IVA
C. Group VA
D. Group IA
E. Group VIA

222. Given that parent and daughter nuclei are isotopes of the same element, the ratio of α to β decay produced by the daughter must be:

A. 1 to 1   **B.** 1 to 2   **C.** 2 to 1   **D.** 2 to 3   **E.** 3 to 2

223. Which is the name of the elements that have properties between true metals and true nonmetals?

A. alkaline earth metals
B. metalloids

C. nonmetals
D. metals

E. halogens

224. An ion is represented by which of the following electron configurations?

I. $1s^2 2s^2 2p^6$ II. $1s^2 2s^2 2p^6 3s^2$ III. $1s^2 2s^2 2p^2 3s^2 3p^6$

A. I only
B. I and II only

C. II and III only
D. I, II, and III

E. II only

225. Which subshell has the correct order of increasing energy?

A. 3s, 3p, 4s, 3d, 4p, 5s, 4d
B. 3s, 3p, 4s, 3d, 4p, 4d, 5s

C. 3s, 3p, 3d, 4s, 4p, 4d, 5s
D. 3s, 3p, 3d, 4s, 4p, 5s, 4d
E. 3s, 3p, 4s, 3d, 4d, 4p, 5s

226. Which of the following electron configurations represents an excited state of an atom?

A. $1s^2 2s^2 2p^6 3s^2 3d^3 3p^6 4s^2$
B. $1s^2 2s^2 2p^6 3s^2 3p^6 3d^{10} 4s^2 4p^6$

C. $1s^2 2s^2 2p^6 3s^2 3d^{10}$
D. $1s^2 2s^2 2p^6 3s^2 3p^6 4s^1$
E. $1s^2 2s^2 2p^6 3s^2 3p^6 3d^{10} 4s^2 4p^3$

Chapter 2. CHEMICAL BONDS

1. Based on the Lewis structure and formal charge considerations, how many resonance structures, if any, can be drawn for the PO_4^{3-} ion?

    A. original structure only   **B.** 2   **C.** 3   **D.** 4   **E.** 5

2. Which of the substances below would have the largest dipole?

    I. CO_2 II. SO_2^- III. H_2O

    A. I   **C.** III

    B. II   **D.** each dipole is the same magnitude   **E.** none of the molecules has a dipole

3. What is the type of bond that forms between oppositely charged ions?

    A. dipole   **B.** covalent   **C.** London   **D.** induced dipole   **E.** ionic

4. How many valence electrons are in a chlorine atom and a chloride ion?

    A. 17 and 18, respectively   **C.** 7 and 8, respectively

    B. 8 and 7, respectively   **D.** 1 and 8, respectively   **E.** none of the above

5. What is the formula of the sulfite ion?

    A. SO_3^{2-} **B.** S^{2-} **C.** HSO_4^{2-} **D.** SO_4^{2-} **E.** none of the above

6. Which of these molecules has trigonal pyramidal molecular geometry?

    A. SO_3 **B.** NF_3 **C.** AlF_3 **D.** BF_3 **E.** CH_4

7. The valence shell is the:

    A. innermost shell that is complete with electrons

    B. last partially filled orbital of an atom

    C. shell of electrons in an atom that is the least reactive

    D. outermost shell of electrons around an atom

    E. same as the orbital configuration

8. The metaphosphate ion, PO_3^-, is the structural analog of the NO_3^- ion with respect to the arrangement of the atoms. From the Lewis structure for the metaphosphate ion, what is the number of resonance structures for the Lewis structure?

    A. original structure only   **B.** 2   **C.** 3   **D.** 4   **E.** 5

9. A characteristic of a cation is that:

    A. the number of neutrons is related to the number of electrons

    B. it has less electrons than protons

    C. it has equal numbers of electrons and protons

    D. it has less protons than electrons

    E. it has equal numbers of electrons and protons but a different number of neutrons

10. Which is sufficient for determining the molecular formula of a compound?

    A. The % by mass and the molecular weight of a compound

    B. The % by mass and the empirical formula of a compound

    C. The % by mass of a compound

    D. The molecular weight of a compound

    E. The empirical formula of a compound

11. An ionic bond forms between two atoms when:

    A. protons are transferred from the nucleus of the nonmetal to the nucleus of the metal

    B. each atom acquires a negative charge

    C. electron pairs are shared

    D. four electrons are shared

    E. electrons are transferred from metallic to nonmetallic atoms

12. Which of the following statements is true?

    A. $-\Delta H_f^{\circ}$ reactions produce stable compounds

    B. An endothermic reaction produces a fairly stable compound

    C. Bond formation tends to increase the potential energy of the atoms

    D. A compound with $-\Delta H_f^{\circ}$ is unstable as it decomposes into its elements

    E. A compound with $+\Delta H_f^{\circ}$ is stable as it decomposes into its elements

13. The property that describes the ease with which an atom loses an electron to form a positive ion is:

    A. electronegativity   **C.** hyperconjugation

    B. ionization energy   **D.** electron affinity   **E.** none of the above

14. For a representative element, valence electrons are electrons:

    A. located in the outermost orbital   **C.** that are located closest to the nucleus

    B. located in the outermost *d* subshell   **D.** occupying the outermost *s* and *p* orbitals

                                         E. located in the outermost *f* subshell

15. What bond forms between: $Na^+ + Cl^- \rightarrow NaCl$?

    A. dipole   **B.** van der Waals   **C.** covalent   **D.** hydrogen   **E.** ionic

16. What is the total number of valence electrons in a sulfite ion, SO_3^{2-}?

    A. 22   **B.** 24   **C.** 26   **D.** 34   **E.** None of the above

17. How many valence electrons are in the electron configuration of $1s^2 2s^2 2p^6 3s^2 3p^5$?

    A. 6   **B.** 7   **C.** 5   **D.** 2   **E.** 1

18. An ion is:

    A. a molecule such as galactose

    B. a substance formed by the combination of two elements

    C. an atom that has an electrical charge

    D. another term for an atom

    E. an element with differences in the number of neutrons

19. Covalent bonds:

      I. involve the sharing of electrons so each atom acquires a noble gas configuration
      II. can be either polar or nonpolar
      III. are stronger than ionic bonds

    A. I only   **B.** II only   **C.** III only   **D.** I and II only   **E.** I, II and III

20. How many valence electrons do the elements in groups IIA and VA of the periodic table have, respectively?

    A. 2 and 5   **B.** 3 and 4   **C.** 2 and 6   **D.** 2 and 2   **E.** 2 and 4

21. Based on the ΔH°_{f} data, which compound is the most stable?

    A. PH_3 (*g*), +5.3 kJ/mol   **C.** H_2S (*g*), –20.5 kJ/mol
    B. N_2H_4 (*g*), +94.4 kJ/mol   **D.** NH_3 (*g*), –46.5 kJ/mol
                                 E. N_2O_4 (*g*), +9.8 kJ/mol

22. What is the valence shell electron configuration of the ion formed from a halogen?

    A. ns^2 **B.** ns^2np^2 **C.** ns^2np^4 **D.** ns^2np^8 **E.** ns^2np^6

23. A single covalent bond is formed by how many electrons?

    A. 1   **B.** 2   **C.** 3   **D.** 4   **E.** 0

24. What is the number of valence electrons in antimony (Sb)?

    A. 1   **B.** 2   **C.** 3   **D.** 4   **E.** 5

25. Which statement is true about the valence shell?

    A. The valence shell determines the electron dot structure
    B. The electron dot structure is made up of each of the valence shells
    C. The valence shell is the innermost shell
    D. The valence shell is usually the most unreactive shell
    E. None of the above

26. Which bond is formed by the equal sharing of electrons?

    A. covalent   **B.** dipole   **C.** ionic   **D.** London   **E.** van der Waals

27. What is the number of valence electrons in tin (Sn)?

    A. 14   **B.** 8   **C.** 2   **D.** 4   **E.** 5

28. Which of the following occurs naturally as nonpolar diatomic molecules?

    A. sulfur   **C.** argon
    B. chlorine   **D.** all of the above   **E.** none of the above

29. Which of the following describes the orbital geometry of an sp^2 hybridized atom?

    A. bent   **C.** trigonal bipyramidal

    B. tetrahedral   **D.** linear   **E.** trigonal planar

30. An ion with an atomic number of 34 and 36 electrons has what charge?

    A. +2   **B.** −36   **C.** +34   **D.** −2   **E.** neutral

31. The "octet rule" relates to the number eight because:

    A. all orbitals can hold 8 electrons

    B. electron arrangements involving 8 valence electrons are extremely stable

    C. all atoms have 8 valence electrons

    D. only atoms with 8 valence electrons undergo a chemical reaction

    E. each element can accommodate a number of electrons as an integer of 8

32. Covalently bonded substances:

    A. have higher melting-point substances than ionic solids

    B. are found only in liquid and gas phases

    C. are good conductors of heat

    D. are good conductors of electricity

    E. are soft

33. Which of the following represents the breaking of a noncovalent interaction?

    A. Ionization of water   **C.** Hydrolysis of an ester

    B. Decomposition of hydrogen peroxide   **D.** Dissolving of salt crystals

                                                E. None of the above

34. Which of the following statements about noble gases is NOT correct?

    A. They have very stable electron arrangements

    B. They are the most reactive of all gases

    C. They exist in nature as individual atoms rather than in molecular form

    D. They have 8 valence electrons

    E. They have a complete octet

35. Which species has eight valence electrons in the Lewis structure?

    A. S^{2-} **B.** Mg^+ **C.** F^+ **D.** Ar^+ **E.** Si

36. The property that describes the energy released by a gas phase atom from adding an electron is:

    A. ionization energy   **C.** electron affinity

    B. electronegativity   **D.** hyperconjugation   **E.** none of the above

37. Which of the following must occur for an atom to obtain the noble gas configuration?

    A. lose, gain or share an electron   **C.** lose an electron

    B. lose or gain an electron   **D.** share an electron   **E.** share or gain an electron

38. As bond length between a pair of atoms increases, the bond strength:

   A. decreases and bond energy increases   **C.** remains constant as does bond energy

   B. increases and bond energy decreases   **D.** increases and bond energy increases

                                                       E. decreases as does bond energy

39. Which of the following elements has two valence electrons?

   A. Ne   **B.** H   **C.** Mg   **D.** K   **E.** Li

40. In the process of forming sodium nitride (Na_3N), what happens to the electrons of each sodium atom and the electrons of each nitride atom, respectively?

   A. lose one; gain three   **C.** lose three; gain one

   B. lose three; gain three   **D.** lose one; gain two   **E.** lose two; gain three

41. How many covalent bonds can a neutral sulfur form?

   A. 0   **B.** 1   **C.** 2   **D.** 3   **E.** 4

42. Which of the following molecules can form hydrogen bonds?

   A. NH_3 **C.** HF

   B. H_2O **D.** all of the above   **E.** none of the above

43. Which of the following pairings of ions shown are NOT consistent with the formula?

   A. Co_2S_3 (Co^{3+} and S^{2-})   **C.** Na_3P (Na^+ and P^{3-})

   B. K_2O (K^+ and O^-)   **D.** BaF_2 (Ba^{2+} and F^-)

                                                       E. KCl (K^+ and Cl^-)

44. The term for a bond where the electrons are shared unequally is:

   A. ionic   **C.** coordinate covalent

   B. nonpolar covalent   **D.** nonpolar ionic

                                                       E. polar covalent

45. Which atom would NOT be bound to hydrogen in a hydrogen bond?

   A. S   **B.** N   **C.** F   **D.** O   **E.** A and B

46. Which is the correct formula for the ionic compound formed between Ca and I?

   A. Ca_3I_2 **B.** Ca_2I_3 **C.** CaI_2 **D.** Ca_2I **E.** Ca_3I_5

47. Which species below has the least number of valence electrons in its Lewis symbol?

   A. S^{2-} **B.** Mg^{2+} **C.** Ar^+ **D.** Ga^+ **E.** F^-

48. Which has the greatest ionization energy?

   A. P   **B.** Al   **C.** Ne   **D.** Br   **E.** Ca

49. Which statement is NOT correct?

    A. Cations and anions combine in the simplest ratio which results in electrical neutrality

    B. The number of electrons lost by the cation equals the number of electrons gained by the anion in an ionic compound

    C. Ionic compounds may contain one metal and one nonmetal

    D. Ionic compounds may contain one metal and one halogen

    E. Formulas of ionic compounds are written with the anion first, followed by the cation

50. When a bond is broken, energy is:

    A. absorbed if the bond strength is negative   **C.** always released

    B. released if the bond strength is negative   **D.** always absorbed

                                                            E. absorbed if the bond strength is positive

51. A dipole is a:

    A. nonpolar entity   **C.** separation of charges

    B. form of electronegativity   **D.** molecule with parallel bonds

                                                            E. form of hyperconjugation

52. Which of the compounds is most likely ionic?

    A. N_2O_5 **B.** $SrBr_2$ **C.** CBr_4 **D.** GaAs   **E.** CH_2Cl_2

53. What bond holds hydrogens and oxygen together within a water molecule?

    A. covalent   **C.** hydrophilic

    B. dipole   **D.** hydrogen   **E.** van der Waals

54. Which molecular geometry CANNOT result in a nonpolar structure?

    A. diatomic covalent   **C.** tetrahedral

    B. square planar   **D.** trigonal planar   **E.** bent

55. Which of the statements is an accurate description of the structure of the ionic compound NaCl?

    A. Alternating rows of Na^+ and Cl^- ions are present

    B. Each ion present is surrounded by six ions of opposite charge

    C. Alternating layers of Na and Cl atoms are present

    D. Alternating layers of Na^+ and Cl^- ions are present

    E. Repeating layers of Na^+ and Cl^- ions are present

56. The term for a bond where the electrons are shared equally:

    A. coordinate covalent   **C.** polar covalent

    B. ionic   **D.** nonpolar covalent   **E.** nonpolar ionic

57. Given that the first ionization energy of cesium is +376 kJ/mol and the electron affinity of bromine is –325 kJ/mol, calculate ΔE for the reaction: Cs (g) + Br (g) → Cs^+ (g) + Br^- (g)

    A. +51 kJ/mol   **C.** +376 kJ/mol

    B. –701 kJ/mol   **D.** +701kJ/mol   **E.** –51 kJ/mol

58. What term best describes the smallest whole number repeating ratio of ions in an ionic compound?

    A. lattice

    B. unit cell

    C. formula unit

    D. covalent unit

    E. ionic unit

59. The property defined as the energy required to remove one electron from an atom in the gaseous state is:

    A. electronegativity

    B. ionization energy

    C. electron affinity

    D. hyperconjugation

    E. none of the above

60. What is the name for the force holding two atoms together in a chemical bond?

    A. gravitational force

    B. strong nuclear force

    C. weak hydrophobic force

    D. weak nuclear force

    E. electrostatic force

61. A polyatomic ion:

    A. develops a charge as a result of the combination of two or more types of atoms

    B. does not bond further with other ions

    C. has a negative charge of less than -1

    D. contains both a metal and a nonmetal

    E. remains neutral from the combination of two or more types of atoms

62. Which of the following is the strongest form of an interatomic attraction?

    A. dipole-induced dipole interaction

    B. dipole-dipole interaction

    C. ion-dipole interaction

    D. covalent bond

    E. induced dipole-induced dipole interaction

63. Water is a polar molecule because oxygen:

    A. is at one end with the hydrogens at the other end of the molecule

    B. has a partial negative charge while the hydrogens have a partial positive charge

    C. has a partial positive charge while the hydrogens have a partial negative charge

    D. is bonded between the two hydrogens

    E. attracts the hydrogen atoms

64. Which formula for an ionic compound is NOT correct as written?

    A. NH_4ClO_4 **B.** MgS **C.** KOH **D.** $Ca(SO_4)_2$ **E.** KF

65. Which of the following describes the attraction between two NH_3 molecules?

    A. nonpolar covalent bond

    B. polar covalent bond

    C. coordinate covalent bond

    D. hydrogen bond

    E. none of the above

66. Which of the following molecules is polar?

    A. SO_3 **B.** SO_2 **C.** CO_2 **D.** CH_4 **E.** CCl_4

67. What is the chemical formula for a compound that contains K^+ and CO_3^{2-} ions?

   A. $K(CO_3)_3$ **B.** $K_3(CO_3)_2$ **C.** $K_3(CO_3)_3$ **D.** KCO_3 **E.** K_2CO_3

68. Why does H_2O have an unusually high boiling point compared to H_2S?

   A. Hydrogen bonding
   B. Van der Waals forces
   C. H_2O molecules pack more closely than H_2S
   D. Covalent bonds are stronger in H_2O
   E. This is a false statement, because H_2O has a similar boiling point to H_2S

69. Which is the most likely noncovalent interaction between an alcohol and a carboxylic acid?

   A. formation of an anhydride bond   **C.** dipole-charge interaction
   B. dipole-dipole interaction   **D.** charge-charge interaction
                                               E. induced dipole-dipole interaction

70. Which formula for an ionic compound is NOT correct?

   A. $Al_2(CO_3)_3$ **B.** Li_2SO_4 **C.** Na_2S **D.** $MgHCO_3$ **E.** K_2O

71. Which of the following solids is likely to have the smallest exothermic lattice energy?

   A. Al_2O_3 **B.** $AlCl_3$ **C.** NaCl   **D.** LiF   **E.** $CaCl_2$

72. A halogen is expected to have [   ] ionization energy and [   ] electron affinity?

   A. small; small   **C.** large; large
   B. small; large   **D.** large; small   **E.** none of the above

73. What is the total number of valence electrons in a molecule of SOF_2?

   A. 18   **B.** 20   **C.** 8   **D.** 19   **E.** 26

74. Two atoms are held together by a chemical bond because:

   A. atomic nuclei are attracted to the bonding electrons
   B. bonding electrons form an electrostatic cloud with the nuclei on the exterior
   C. atomic nuclei attract each other
   D. bonding electrons attract each other
   E. bonding electrons form an electrostatic cloud that contains both nuclei

75. Which of the following is the weakest form of interatomic attraction?

   A. dipole-dipole   **C.** covalent bond
   B. dipole-induced dipole   **D.** ion-dipole   **E.** induced dipole-induced dipole

76. What is the total number of electrons shown in a correctly written Lewis structure for OF_2?

   A. 20   **B.** 26   **C.** 32   **D.** 18   **E.** 22

77. What type of bond joins adjacent water molecules?

   A. dipole   **B.** hydrogen   **C.** hydrophilic   **D.** covalent   **E.** induced dipole

78. From the electronegativities below, which covalent single bond is the most polar?

Element:	H	C	N	O
Electronegativity	2.1	2.5	3.0	3.5

A. O–C   **B.** O–N   **C.** N–C   **D.** C–H   **E.** C–C

79. Which of the molecules contains a covalent triple bond?

A. SO_2 **B.** HCN   **C.** Br_2 **D.** $C_2H_2Cl_2$ **E.** C_2H_6

80. Use the data to calculate the lattice energy of sodium chloride. $\Delta H_{lattice}$ equals:

$$Na\ (s) \rightarrow Na\ (g) \qquad \Delta H_1 = +108\ kJ$$
$$\tfrac{1}{2}Cl_2\ (g) \rightarrow Cl\ (g) \qquad \Delta H_2 = +120\ kJ$$
$$Na\ (g) \rightarrow Na^+\ (g) + e^- \qquad \Delta H_3 = +496\ kJ$$
$$Cl\ (g) + e^- \rightarrow Cl^-\ (g) \qquad \Delta H_4 = -349\ kJ$$
$$Na\ (s) + \tfrac{1}{2}Cl_2\ (g) \rightarrow NaCl\ (s) \qquad \Delta H^{\circ}_f = -411\ kJ$$

A. –429 kJ/mol   **C.** –349 kJ/mol
B. –760 kJ/mol   **D.** 786 kJ/mol   **E.** –786 kJ/mol

81. An alkaline earth element is expected to have [   ] ionization energy and [   ] electron affinity.

A. small; large   **C.** large; small
B. small; small   **D.** large; large   **E.** none of the above

82. Which of the statements concerning covalent double bonds is correct?

A. They always involve the sharing of 2 electron pairs
B. They occur only between atoms containing 4 valence electrons
C. They are found only in molecules containing polyatomic ions
D. They are found only in molecules containing carbon
E. They occur only between atoms containing 8 valence electrons

83. The distance between two atomic nuclei in a chemical bond is determined by the:

A. size of the valence electrons
B. size of the nucleus
C. size of the protons
D. balance between the repulsion of the nuclei and the attraction of the nuclei for the bonding electrons
E. size of the neutrons

84. Two molecules, X and Y, are not miscible and have very different physical properties. Molecule X boils at 70 °C and freezes at –20 °C, while molecule Y boils at 45 °C and freezes at –90 °C. Which molecule is likely to have the largest dipole?

A. molecule X   **C.** not enough information to determine
B. molecule Y   **D.** both have similar dipoles
E. X and Y are the same molecule but with different physical properties

85. Which of the general statements regarding covalent bond characteristics is NOT correct?

A. Double and triple bonds are shorter than single bonds

B. Triple bonds are possible when 3 or more electrons are needed to complete an octet

C. Triple bonds are stronger than double bonds

D. Double bonds are stronger than single bonds

E. Double bonding can occur with Group VIIA elements

86. Why are adjacent water molecules attracted to each other?

A. Ionic bonding between the hydrogens of H_2O

B. Covalent bonding between adjacent oxygen

C. Electrostatic attraction between the H of one H_2O and the O of another

D. Covalent bonding between the H of one H_2O and the O of another

E. Electrostatic attraction between the O of one H_2O molecule and the O of another

87. Which of the following is true of a hydrogen bond?

A. The bond length is longer than a covalent bond

B. The bond energy is less than a covalent bond

C. The bond is between H and O, N, or F

D. The bond is between two polar molecules

E. All of the above

88. When drawing a Lewis dot structure, pairs of electrons that are not between atoms but are used to fill the octet are:

A. excess electrons   **C.** lone pairs

B. filled shells   **D.** bonding pairs   **E.** not shown on the structure

89. Which atom is the most electronegative?

A. P   **B.** Cl   **C.** Li   **D.** Cs   **E.** Fr

90. What is the name for the weak forces of attraction between nonpolar molecules due to temporary dipoles between adjacent nonpolar molecules?

A. van der Waals forces   **C.** hydrogen bonding forces

B. hydrophobic forces   **D.** nonpolar covalent forces

                                     E. hydrophilic forces

91. Which bonding is NOT possible for a carbon atom that has four valence electrons?

A. 1 single bond and 1 triple bond   **C.** 4 single bonds

B. 1 double bond and 1 triple bond   **D.** 2 single bonds and 1 double bond

                                                E. 2 double bonds

92. Which statement is true about the formation of the stable ionic compound NaCl?

    A. NaCl is stable because it is formed from the combination of isolated gaseous ions

    B. The first ionization energy of sodium contributes favorably to the overall formation of NaCl

    C. The net absorption of 147 kJ/mol of energy for the formation of the Na^+ (*g*) and Cl^- (*g*) is responsible for the formation of the stable ionic compound

    D. The release of energy as NaCl (*s*) forms leads to an overall increase in the potential energy

    E. The lattice energy provides the necessary stabilization energy for the formation of NaCl

93. The statement that best describes the formation of an ionic compound is that electrons:

    A. move freely among a network of nuclei in fixed positions

    B. are shared between two atoms and discrete molecules are formed

    C. are transferred from a non-metal to a metal, and the resulting charged particles form a crystalline network

    D. are transferred from a metal to a non-metal, and the resulting charged particles form a crystalline network

    E. do not permit each atom to achieve an octet

94. Nitrogen has five valence electrons; which of the following types of bonding is possible?

    A. three single bonds

    B. one triple bond

    C. one single and one double bond

    D. all of the above

    E. none of the above

95. The bond energy of a carbon-carbon double bond, when compared to the energy of a carbon-carbon single bond, is:

    A. twice the bond energy of a single bond

    B. more than twice the bond energy of a single bond

    C. less than the bond energy of a single bond

    D. equal in bond energy to a single bond

    E. greater in bond energy than a single bond, but less than twice the bond energy

96. Which of the following molecules would contain a dipole?

    A. F–F   **B.** H–H   **C.** Cl–Cl   **D.** H–F   **E.** all of the above

97. Which of the following statements concerning coordinate covalent bonds is correct?

    A. Once formed, they are indistinguishable from any other covalent bond

    B. They are always single bonds

    C. One of the atoms involved must be a metal and the other a nonmetal

    D. Both atoms involved in the bond contribute an equal number of electrons to the bond

    E. The bond is formed between two Lewis bases

98. What is the name for the attraction between H_2O molecules?

    A. adhesion

    B. polarity

    C. cohesion

    D. van der Waals

    E. hydrophilicity

99. The approximate bond angle between atoms of a trigonal planar molecule is:

    A. 109.5°   **B.** 180°   **C.** 120°   **D.** 90°   **E.** 104.5°

100. Which of the following is an example of a molecule that contains a coordinate covalent bond?

    A. CH_4 **B.** NH_3 **C.** NH_4^+ **D.** H_2O **E.** C_2H_4

101. For two ions with charges q_1 and q_2 that are separated by distance r, the potential energy can be calculated from Coulomb's law: $E = q_1q_2/k \cdot r$

Calculate the energy released when 1 mole NaCl is formed, if the constant $k = 1.11 \times 10^{-10}$ $C^2/J \cdot m$, the charge on $Na^+ = +e$, and the charge on $Cl^- = -e$ (Note: $e = 1.602 \times 10^{-19}$ C; r = 282 pm)

    A. −494 kJ/mol   **C.** +91.2 kJ/mol

    B. −288 kJ/mol   **D.** +421 kJ/mol   **E.** −464 kJ/mol

102. Which one of the compounds below is most likely to be ionic?

    A. CBr_4 **B.** H_2O **C.** CH_2Cl_2 **D.** NO_2 **E.** $SrBr_2$

103. Calculate the total number of electrons in the Lewis structure for PH_4^+?

    A. 10   **B.** 12   **C.** 9   **D.** 8   **E.** 6

104. What is the mass percent of nitrogen in NO_2?

    A. 12.0%   **B.** 25.5%   **C.** 30.4%   **D.** 33.3%   **E.** 50.0%

105. How do the electron-dot structures of elements in the same group of the periodic table compare?

    A. The number of electrons in the electron-dot-structure equals the group number for each element of the group

    B. Elements of the same group have the same number of valence electrons

    C. The number of valence shell electrons increases by one for each element from the top to the bottom of the group

    D. The structures differ by exactly two electrons between vertically consecutive elements

    E. Elements of the same period have the same number of valence electrons

106. What is the geometry of a molecule with three pairs of bonded electrons and one pair of nonbonded electrons around a central atom?

    A. octahedral   **C.** linear

    B. trigonal planar   **D.** tetrahedral   **E.** trigonal pyramidal

107. A water spider is able to walk on the surface of water because:

    A. hydrophilic bonds hold H_2O molecules together

    B. H_2O has strong covalent bonds within its molecules

    C. surface tension from the adhesive properties of H_2O

    D. surface tension from the cohesive properties of H_2O

    E. a water spider is less dense than H_2O

108. Under what conditions is graphite converted to diamond?

   A. low temperature, high pressure
   C. high temperature, high pressure
   B. high temperature, low pressure
   D. low temperature, low pressure
   E. none of the above

109. What is the geometry of a molecule in which the central atom has 2 bonding electron pairs and 2 nonbonding electron pairs?

   A. trigonal planar
   C. linear
   B. trigonal pyramidal
   D. bent
   E. tetrahedral

110. The approximate bond angle between atoms of a tetrahedral molecule is:

   A. 104.5°
   B. 109.5°
   C. 90°
   D. 120°
   E. 180°

111. Which force is intermolecular?

   A. polar covalent bond
   C. dipole-dipole interactions
   B. ionic bond
   D. nonpolar covalent bond
   E. all are intermolecular forces

112. What is the molecular geometry of Cl_2CO?

   A. tetrahedral
   C. trigonal pyramidal
   B. trigonal planar
   D. linear
   E. bent

113. Which statement is true?

   A. The buildup of electron density between two atoms repels each nucleus, making it less stable
   B. Bond energy is the minimum energy required to bring about the pairing of electrons in a covalent bond
   C. As the distance between the nuclei decreases for covalent bond formation, there is a corresponding decreased probability of finding both electrons near either nucleus
   D. One mole of hydrogen atoms is more stable than one mole of hydrogen molecules
   E. Two electrons in a single covalent bond are paired according to the Pauli exclusion principle

114. Which element forms an ion with the greatest positive charge?

   A. Mg
   B. Sr
   C. Al
   D. Na
   E. P

115. What is the molecular geometry of NCl_3?

   A. tetrahedral
   C. trigonal bipyramidal
   B. trigonal bipyramidal
   D. trigonal pyramidal
   E. bent

116. Which statement describes the bond lengths in CS_3^{2-}?

   A. All bonds are of different lengths
   B. All bonds are of the same length
   C. Two are the same length while the other is longer
   D. Two are the same length while the other is shorter
   E. Depends if the molecule is a solid or liquid

117. How many more electrons can fit within the valence shell of a hydrogen atom?

    A. 1   **B.** 2   **C.** 7   **D.** 0   **E.** 3

118. Which one of the following molecules has a tetrahedral shape?

    A. NH_3 **B.** BF_3 **C.** C_2H_4 **D.** XeF_4 **E.** CF_4

119. Sweat cools the human body because water has:

    A. low specific heat   **C.** low density

    B. high specific heat   **D.** low molecular mass   **E.** high density

120. What is the molecular geometry of a CH_3^+ molecule?

    A. bent   **C.** tetrahedral

    B. trigonal pyramidal   **D.** linear   **E.** trigonal planar

121. What is the molecular geometry of PH_3?

    A. tetrahedral   **C.** trigonal pyramidal

    B. octahedral   **D.** linear   **E.** bent

122. Which bond is the most polar?

    A. H—O   **B.** H—P   **C.** H—N   **D.** H—C   **E.** H—Se

123. To form an octet, an atom of selenium must:

    A. gain 2 electrons   **C.** gain 6 electrons

    B. lose 2 electrons   **D.** lose 6 electrons   **E.** gain 4 electrons

124. What is the molecular geometry of CO_2?

    A. bent   **C.** trigonal planar

    B. tetrahedral   **D.** linear   **E.** trigonal bipyramidal

125. In which compound does carbon have the greatest percent by mass?

    A. $C_3H_7NH_2$ **B.** C_3H_7OH **C.** CH_3OH **D.** CCl_4 **E.** CH_2Cl_2

126. Which of the following has the greatest number of nonbonding pairs of electrons?

    A. He   **B.** F   **C.** C   **D.** H   **E.** S

127. Which of the following pairs is NOT correctly matched?

    <u>Formula</u>   <u>Molecular Geometry</u>

    A. CH_4 tetrahedral

    B. OF_2 bent

    C. PCl_3 trigonal planar

    D. Cl_2CO trigonal planar

    E. $^{\oplus}CH_3$ trigonal planar

128. What is the molecular geometry of a NH_3 molecule?

  A. bent   **C.** tetrahedral

  B. trigonal pyramidal   **D.** trigonal planar   **E.** linear

129. The strongest intermolecular force between molecules is:

  A. hydrophobic   **C.** polar

  B. Van der Waals   **D.** coordinate covalent bonds   **E.** hydrogen bonding

130. Electronegativity is a concept that is used to:

  A. formulate a statement of the octet rule

  B. evaluate if double bonds are present in a molecule

  C. evaluate how many electrons are involved in bonding

  D. evaluate the polarity of a bond

  E. evaluate if electrons are moved further from the nucleus of the electronegative element

131. Arrange the following in increasing electronegativity:

  A. Ga < Ge < As < P   **C.** P < Ga < Ge < As

  B. Ge < P < As < Ga   **D.** As < P < Ga < Ge   **E.** Ga < P < As < Ge

132. The charge on a sulfide ion is:

  A. +3   **B.** +2   **C.** 0   **D.** −2   **E.** −3

133. The ability of an atom in a molecule to attract electrons to itself is:

  A. ionization energy   **C.** electronegativity

  B. paramagnetism   **D.** electron affinity   **E.** hyperconjugation

134. Which of the following compounds is NOT possible?

  A. H^- because H forms only positive ions

  B. PbO_2 because the charge on a Pb ion is only +2

  C. SF_6 because F does not have an empty d orbital to form an expanded octet

  D. CH_3^- because C lacks d orbitals

  E. OCl_6 because O does not have d orbitals to form an expanded octet

135. What is the molecular geometry of CH_2O?

  A. trigonal planar   **C.** linear

  B. tetrahedral   **D.** trigonal pyramidal   **E.** bent

136. In the nitrogen monoxide molecule, the dipole moment is 0.16 D and the bond length is 115 pm. What is the sign and magnitude of the charge on the oxygen atom?

  A. −0.098 e **B.** −0.71 e **C.** −1.3 e **D.** −0.029 e **E.** +1.3 e

137. Which of the following series of elements are arranged in the order of increasing electronegativity?

  A. Fr, Mg, Si, O   **C.** F, B, O, Li

  B. Br, Cl, S, P   **D.** Cl, S, Se, Te   **E.** Br, Mg, Si, N

138. The name of Cl⁻ is:

    A. chlorite ion   **C.** chloride ion

    B. chlorate ion   **D.** chlorine ion   **E.** diatomic chlorine

139. What is the percent by mass of Cl in carbon tetrachloride?

    A. 25%   **B.** 66%   **C.** 78%   **D.** 92%   **E.** 33%

140. Which statement about electronegativity is NOT correct?

    A. Electronegativity increases from left to right within a row

    B. Electronegativity increases from bottom to top within a group

    C. Fluorine is the most electronegative atom of all the elements

    D. Francium is the least electronegative element

    E. Metals generally have higher electronegativity values than nonmetals

141. The number of unpaired valence electrons for an atom is related to the number of bonds that the atom can form because the number of unpaired valence electrons:

    A. is twice the number of bonds that the atom can form

    B. is the same as the number of bonds that the atom can form

    C. has no defined relationship between the number of unpaired valence electrons and number of bonds that the atom can form

    D. is one-half the number of bonds that the atom can form

    E. is not related to the number of bonds that the atom can form

142. Which compound is covalent?

    A. RbF   **B.** HF   **C.** NaF   **D.** LiF   **E.** NaCl

143. Which atom is the least electronegative?

    A. Rb   **B.** Ca   **C.** F   **D.** Si   **E.** I

144. The stability of an ionic crystal is greatest by forming:

    A. strong intramolecular forces

    B. the most symmetrical arrangement of anions and cations

    C. the closest arrangement of anions and cations while minimizing repulsion forces

    D. the most complex arrangement of anions and cations while minimizing repulsion forces

    E. greater distant between anions and cations

145. Based on the Lewis structure, how many non-bonding electrons are on N in the nitrate ion?

    A. 0   **B.** 2   **C.** 4   **D.** 6   **E.** 8

146. A bond where the electrons are shared unequally is:

    A. ionic   **C.** coordinate covalent

    B. nonpolar covalent   **D.** van der Waals force   **E.** polar covalent

147. The name of S^{2-} is:

A. sulfite ion

B. sulfide ion

C. sulfur

D. sulfate ion

E. sulfurous ion

148. What is the empirical formula of the compound with the mass percent of 71.65% Cl, 24.27% C and 4.07% H?

A. ClC_2H_5 B. Cl_2CH_2 C. $ClCH_3$ D. $ClCH_2$ E. CCl_4

149. In chlorine monoxide, chlorine has a charge of $+0.167$ e. If the bond length is 154.6 pm, the dipole moment of the molecule is?

A. 2.30 D   B. 0.167 D   C. 1.24 D   D. 3.11 D   E. 1.65 D

150. Which of the following diatomic molecules contains the bond of greatest polarity?

A. CH_4 B. BrI   C. Cl–F   D. P_4 E. Te–F

151. Which element likely forms a cation with a +2 charge?

A. K   B. S   C. Si   D. Mg   E. Br

152. The mass percent of a compound is as follows: 71.65% Cl, 24.27% C and 4.07% H. If the molecular weight of the compound is 98.96, what is the molecular formula of the compound?

A. $Cl_2C_3H_6$ B. $Cl_2C_2H_4$ C. $ClCH_3$ D. ClC_2H_2 E. CCl_4

153. Based on the Lewis structure for hydrogen peroxide, H_2O_2, how many polar bonds and nonpolar bonds are present?

A. 3 polar bonds and zero nonpolar bonds

B. 2 polar bonds and 2 nonpolar bonds

C. 1 polar bond and 2 nonpolar bonds

D. zero polar bonds and 3 nonpolar bonds

E. 2 polar bonds and 1 nonpolar bond

154. Which compound contains only covalent bonds?

A. $HC_2H_3O_2$ B. NaCl   C. NH_4OH D. $Ca_3(PO_4)_2$ E. LiF

155. Which pair of elements is most likely to form an ionic compound when reacted together?

A. C and F   B. K and Br   C. Al and Si   D. Fe and Ca   E. H and N

156. What is the empirical formula of acetic acid, CH_3COOH?

A. CH_3COOH B. $C_2H_4O_2$ C. CH_2O D. COH_2 E. CHO

157. Which of the following pairs is NOT correctly matched?

Formula	Molecular polarity
A. SiF_4	nonpolar
B. H_2O	polar
C. HCN	nonpolar
D. H_2CO	polar
E. CH_2Cl_2	polar

158. Based on the Lewis structure for $H_3C—NH_2$, the formal charge on N is:

   A. –2   **B.** 0   **C.** –3   **D.** +2   **E.** +3

159. What is the formula of the ammonium ion?

   A. NH_4^- **B.** N_4H^+ **C.** Am^+ **D.** Am^- **E.** NH_4^+

160. What is the empirical formula of the compound that has a mass percent of 6% H and 94% O?

   A. HO   **B.** H_2O **C.** H_2O_2 **D.** H_3O_3 **E.** H_4O_2

161. Which of the following pairs is NOT correctly matched?

Formula	Molecular polarity
A. PF_3	polar
B. BCl_3	nonpolar
C. H_2O	polar
D. BeF_2	polar
E. CCl_4	nonpolar

162. Based on the Lewis structure, how many polar and nonpolar bonds are present for H_2CO?

   A. 1 polar bond and 2 nonpolar bonds   **C.** 3 polar bonds and zero nonpolar bonds

   B. 2 polar bonds and 1 nonpolar bond   **D.** zero polar bonds and 3 nonpolar bonds

                                         E. 2 polar bonds and 2 nonpolar bonds

163. What is the formula of the carbonate ion?

   A. $C_2O_4^{2-}$ **B.** $C_2O_4^{1-}$ **C.** CO_2^{3-} **D.** CO_3^{2-} **E.** $C_2H_3O_2^{1-}$

164. Which of the following molecules is polar?

   A. CBr_4 **B.** C_2Cl_6 **C.** $BeCl_2$ **D.** CCl_4 **E.** NCl_3

165. How many total resonance structures, if any, can be drawn for a nitrite ion?

   A. original structure only   **B.** 2   **C.** 3   **D.** 4   **E.** 5

166. What is the formula of a nitrate ion?

   A. NO_3^{1-} **B.** NO_2^{1-} **C.** NO^{3-} **D.** NO_3^{2-} **E.** none of the above

Chapter 3. STATES OF MATTER: GASES, LIQUIDS, SOLIDS

1. Which of the following laws states that for a gas at constant temperature, the pressure and volume are inversely proportional?

A. Dalton's law

B. Gay-Lussac's law

C. Boyle's law

D. Charles's law

E. None of the above

2. What is the standard atmospheric pressure of 760 mmHg in inches of mercury (inHg)? (2.54 cm = 1 in)

A. 73.00 inHg

B. 29.92 inHg

C. 1,930 inHg

D. 103 inHg

E. 109 inHg

3. 212 °F is equivalent to how many degrees Kelvin?

A. 473   **B.** 278   **C.** 273   **D.** 493   **E.** 373

4. Which characteristics best describe a gas?

A. volume and shape of container; no intermolecular attractions

B. definite volume; shape of container; weak intermolecular attractions

C. definite shape and volume; strong intermolecular attractions

D. definite volume; shape of container; moderate intermolecular attractions

E. volume and shape of container; strong intermolecular attractions

5. Which of the following statements about gases is correct?

A. Formation of homogeneous mixtures, regardless of the nature of non-reacting gas components

B. Relatively long distances between molecules

C. High compressibility

D. No attractive forces between gas molecules

E. All of the above

6. Which of the following laws states that volume and Kelvin temperature are directly proportional for a gas at constant pressure?

A. Gay-Lussac's law

B. Dalton's law

C. Charles's law

D. Boyle's law

E. None of the above

7. What is the name given to the transition from the gas phase directly to the solid phase?

A. deposition

B. sublimation

C. freezing

D. condensation

E. evaporation

8. At what temperature is degrees Celsius equivalent to degrees Fahrenheit?

A. 0   **B.** –20   **C.** –40   **D.** –60   **E.** 10

9. A closed-end manometer was constructed from a U-shaped glass tube. It was loaded with mercury so that the closed side was filled to the top, which was 800 mm above the neck while the open end was 180 mm above the neck. The manometer was taken into a chamber used for training astronauts. What is the highest pressure that can be read with assurance on this manometer?

    A. 62.0 torr   **B.** 620 torr   **C.** 98.0 torr   **D.** 98.5 torr   **E.** 6.20 torr

10. Which characteristics best describe a liquid?

    A. volume and shape of container; no intermolecular attractions

    B. definite volume; shape of container; no intermolecular attractions

    C. definite shape and volume; strong intermolecular attractions

    D. definite volume; shape of container; moderate intermolecular attractions

    E. volume and shape of container; strong intermolecular attractions

11. For a fixed quantity of gas, gas laws describe in mathematical terms the relationships between pressure and which two variables?

    A. chemical identity; mass   **C.** temperature; volume

    B. volume; chemical identity   **D.** temperature; size

                                  E. volume; size

12. Which of the following laws states that the pressure exerted by a gas is inversely proportional to its volume and directly proportional to its Kelvin temperature?

    A. combined gas law   **C.** Boyle's law

    B. Gay-Lussac's law   **D.** Charles's law

                                    E. none of the above

13. Which of these alkanes has the lowest boiling point?

    A. C_8H_{18} **B.** C_6H_{14} **C.** C_4H_{10} **D.** C_2H_6 **E.** $C_{10}H_{22}$

14. What are the units of the gas constant R?

    A. atm·K/l·mol   **C.** mol·l/atm·K

    B. atm·K/mol·l   **D.** mol·K/l·atm

                                  E. l·atm/mol·K

15. Which is NOT a correct statement of Boyle's Law?

    A. $P_1V_1 = P_2V_2$

    B. pressure × volume = a constant

    C. pressure α 1/volume

    D. for a gas at constant temperature, pressure and volume are inversely proportional

    E. none of the above

16. Which of the following is NOT a unit used in measuring pressure?

    A. kilometer Hg   **C.** atmosphere

    B. millimeters Hg   **D.** inches Hg   **E.** torr

17. Which of the following laws states that the pressure exerted by a mixture of gases is equal to the sum of the individual gas pressures?

A. Gay-Lussac's law   **C.** Charles's law

B. Dalton's law   **D.** Boyle's law   **E.** none of the above

18. Which of the following compounds will have the lowest boiling point?

A. CH_4 **B.** $CHCl_3$ **C.** CH_3CH_2OH **D.** NH_3 **E.** CH_2Cl_2

19. What is the volume percent of Ar in a 6.50 L flask that contains 0.200 mole of Ne, 0.300 mole He and 0.600 mole of Ar at STP?

A. 44.3%   **B.** 21.9%   **C.** 36.4%   **D.** 54.5%   **E.** 16.8 %

20. A U.S. Weather Bureau forecast cited the atmospheric pressure at sea level as 768.2 mmHg. What is this value expressed in kilopascals (kPa)?

(1 atm = 101325 Pa = 760 torr = 760 mmHg = 1.01325 bar = 1013.25mb)

A. 778.4 kPa   **C.** 100.3 kPa

B. 1024 kPa   **D.** 91.62 kPa   **E.** 102.4 kPa

21. What is the proportionality of volume and pressure for a gas?

A. directly   **C.** raised to the 2nd power

B. inversely   **D.** none of the above   **E.** all of the above

22. When volatile solvents X and Y are mixed in equal proportions, heat is released to the surroundings. If pure X has a higher boiling point than pure Y, which is NOT true?

A. The vapor pressure of the mixture is less than pure Y
B. The vapor pressure of the mixture is less than pure X
C. The boiling point of the mixture is less than pure X
D. The boiling point of the mixture is less than pure Y
E. Not enough information is provided

23. How, in terms of size, is mmHg of pressure units related to the torr units?

A. 1000 times larger than   **C.** equal to

B. 760 times larger than   **D.** 100 times larger than   **E.** 760 times smaller than

24. What is the term that refers to the frequency and energy of gas molecules colliding with the walls of the container?

A. partial pressure   **C.** atmospheric pressure

B. vapor pressure   **D.** gas pressure   **E.** none of the above

25. Which of the following compounds has the highest boiling point?

A. $CH_3CH_2CH_3$ **C.** CH_3CH_3

B. $CH_3CH_2CH_2CH_3$ **D.** CH_4 **E.** CCl_4

26. 190 torr is equal to how many atmospheres?

    A. 0.19   **B.** 0.25   **C.** 0.30   **D.** 1.9   **E.** 3.8

27. Which characteristics best describe a solid?

  A. definite volume; shape of container; no intermolecular attractions

  B. volume and shape of container; no intermolecular attractions

  C. definite shape and volume; strong intermolecular attractions

  D. definite volume; shape of container; moderate intermolecular attractions

  E. volume and shape of container; strong intermolecular attractions

28. What is standard atmospheric pressure in inches mercury (inHg) where 2.54 cm = 1 in?

  A. 1930 inHg   **C.** 76.0 inHg

  B. 101 inHg   **D.** 88 inHg   **E.** 29.9 inHg

29. Which of the following laws states that pressure and Kelvin temperature are directly proportional for a gas at constant volume?

  A. Gay-Lussac's law   **C.** Charles's law

  B. Dalton's law   **D.** Boyle's law   **E.** none of the above

30. Which of the following alkanes has the highest boiling point?

  A. $CH_3C(CH_3)_2CH_2CH_3$ **C.** $CH_3CH_2CH_2CH_2CH_2CH_2CH_3$

  B. $CH_3CH(CH_3)CH_2CH_2CH_3$ **D.** $CH_3CH(CH_3)CH(CH_3)CH_3$

                                      E. all have equivalent boiling points

31. Under which conditions does a real gas behave most nearly like an ideal gas?

  A. High temperature and high pressure   **C.** Low temperature and low pressure

  B. High temperature and low pressure   **D.** Low temperature and high pressure

  E. If it remains in the gaseous state regardless of temperature or pressure

32. If an ionic bond is stronger than a dipole-dipole interaction, why does water dissolve an ionic compound?

  A. Ions do not overcome their interatomic attraction and therefore are not soluble

  B. Ion-dipole interaction causes the ions to heat up and vibrate free of the crystal

  C. Ionic bond is weakened by the ion-dipole interactions and ionic repulsion ejects the ions from the crystal

  D. Ion-dipole interactions of several water molecules aggregate with the ionic bond and dissociate it into the solution

  E. None of the above

33. The barometric pressure in the eye of a hurricane dips as low as 27.2 inches of Hg. How many millimeters of Hg is this, given that 1 in = 2.54 cm?

  A. 107 mmHg   **C.** 6.91 mmHg

  B. 691 mmHg   **D.** 1.07 mmHg   **E.** 0.691 mmHg

34. Which of the following increases the pressure of a gas?

    A. Decreasing the volume

    B. Increasing the number of molecules

    C. Increasing temperature

    D. None of the above

    E. All of the above

35. Which of the following is true when comparing two compounds of similar molar mass in which compound A is comprised of nonpolar molecules, while compound B is composed of polar molecules?

    A. B boils at a higher temperature than A

    B. B boils at a lower temperature than A

    C. A does not boil

    D. B does not boil

    E. Both compounds have the same boiling point

36. At the molecular level, ideal gases:

    A. do not occupy space

    B. occupy space

    C. do not exhibit intermolecular forces

    D. exhibit intermolecular forces

    E. A and C

37. A sample of a gas in a cylindrical chamber with a movable piston occupied a volume of 4.626 liters when the pressure was 0.983 atm and the temperature was 27.2 °C. By moving the piston, the pressure was adjusted to 1.388 atm. What is the volume occupied under the new conditions if the temperature remains constant?

    A. 0.303 L   **B.** 3.28 L   **C.** 4.68 L   **D.** 6.35 L   **E.** 6.49 L

38. In comparing gases to liquids, gases have:

    A. smaller compressibility and greater density

    B. smaller compressibility and smaller density

    C. greater compressibility and greater density

    D. greater compressibility and smaller density

    E. none of the above

39. 8 liters of O_2 gas is under a pressure of 280 torr. If the volume of this gas is increased to 14 liters at constant temperature, what is the new pressure?

    A. 390 torr   **B.** 160 torr   **C.** 66 torr   **D.** 490 torr   **E.** 6 torr

40. A sample of krypton gas at 75.0 psi and 100 °C expands from 0.100 L to 0.450 L. What is the final pressure in psi when the temperature remains constant?

    A. 16.7 psi   **B.** 75.0 psi   **C.** 1.67 psi   **D.** 3.38 psi   **E.** 33.8 psi

41. Which compound would have the highest boiling point?

    A. CH_3OH

    B. $CH_3CH_2CH_2CH_2CH_2\text{–}OH$

    C. $CH_3\text{–}O\text{–}CH_2\ CH_2CH_2CH_3$

    D. $CH_3CH_2\text{–}O\text{–}CH_2\ CH_2CH_3$

    E. $CH_3CH_2CH_2C(OH)H\text{–}OH$

42. Which transformation describes evaporation?

    A. solid → liquid   **C.** liquid → solid

    B. solid → gas   **D.** liquid → gas   **E.** gas → solid

43. The kinetic-molecular theory of ideal gases assumes which of the following?

    I. Gas molecules move at the same speed

    II. Gas molecules have negligible volume

    III. Gas molecules exert no attractive forces on each other

    A. I only   **C.** II and III only

    B. I and III only   **D.** I, II and III   **E.** III only

44. What is the relationship between the pressure and volume of a fixed amount of gas at constant temperature?

    A. directly proportional   **C.** inversely proportional

    B. equal   **D.** decreased by a factor of 2   **E.** none of the above

45. Assuming constant pressure, if a volume of nitrogen gas at 420 K decreases from 100 mL to 50 mL, what is the final temperature in Kelvin?

    A. 630 K   **B.** 420 K   **C.** 910 K   **D.** 150 K   **E.** 210 K

46. The major intermolecular force in $(CH_3)_2NH$ is:

    A. hydrogen bonding   **C.** London-dispersion forces

    B. dipole-dipole attractions   **D.** ion-dipole attractions   **E.** van der Waals forces

47. Which is an assumption of the kinetic molecular theory of gases?

    A. Nonelastic collisions   **C.** Nonrandom collisions

    B. Constant interaction of molecules   **D.** Gas particles take up space

                                     E. Elastic collisions

48. A cylinder fitted with a movable piston and filled with a gas has a volume of 16.44 liters at 22.4 °C at an applied pressure of 772.2 torr. The temperature of the surrounding oil bath was increased to 184.4 °C while the load on the piston was changed. The volume was 16.60 liters. What is the final pressure in the system?

    A. 496 torr   **B.** 504.2 torr   **C.** 1,184 torr   **D.** 1,209 torr   **E.** 6,288 torr

49. Which transformation describes condensation?

    A. solid → gas   **C.** liquid → gas

    B. solid → liquid   **D.** gas → liquid   **E.** liquid → solid

50. What property primarily determines the effect of temperature on the solubility of gas molecules?

    A. Ionic strength of the gas   **C.** Polarity of the gas

    B. Molecular weight of the gas   **D.** Kinetic energy of the gas

                                     E. Dipole strength of the solvent

51. A 2.50 L sample of He gas has a pressure of 0.925 atm. What is the pressure of the gas if the volume is reduced to 0.350 L?

    A. 6.61 atm   **B.** 0.661 atm   **C.** 0.130 atm   **D.** 0.946 atm   **E.** 13.0 atm

52. A sample of air at 7.50 atm is heated from 220 K to 440 K, while the volume remains constant. What is the final pressure?

    A. 30.0 atm   **B.** 6.15 atm   **C.** 4.57 atm   **D.** 3.75 atm   **E.** 15.3 atm

53. The attraction due to London dispersion forces between molecules depends on what two factors?

    A. Volatility and shape

    B. Molar mass and volatility

    C. Vapor pressure and size

    D. Molar mass and shape

    E. Molar mass and vapor pressure

54. What is the new internal pressure of a given mass of nitrogen gas in a 400-ml vessel at 22 °C and 1.2 atm, when heated to 60 °C and compressed to 300 ml?

    A. (1.2)(0.300)(333) / (0.400)(295)

    B. (0.400)(333) / (1.2)(0.300)(295)

    C. (1.2)(0.400)(295) / (0.300)(333)

    D. (1.2)(0.400)(0.300) / (333)(278)

    E. (1.2)(0.400)(333) / (0.300)(295)

55. The standard reference conditions for gases are:

    A. temperature: 0.00 K; pressure: 1.000 standard atmosphere

    B. temperature: 0.00 °C; pressure: 1.000 standard atmosphere

    C. temperature: 273.15 K; pressure: 1.000 Pascal

    D. temperature: 298.15 K; pressure: 1.000 standard atmosphere

    E. temperature: 298.15 K; pressure: 1.000 Pascal

56. Which transformation describes freezing?

    A. solid → liquid

    B. solid → gas

    C. liquid → solid

    D. liquid → gas

    E. gas → liquid

57. In the ideal gas law, what does V represent?

    A. Volume of a gas molecule

    B. Volume of the container that encloses the gas

    C. Average speed of a gas molecule

    D. Average velocity of a gas molecule

    E. Average kinetic energy of a gas molecule

58. What happens if the pressure of a gas above a liquid increases, such as by pressing a piston above a liquid?

    A. Pressure goes down and the gas moves out of the solvent

    B. Pressure goes down and the gas goes into the solvent

    C. The gas is forced into solution and the solubility increases

    D. The solution is compressed and the gas is forced out of the solvent

    E. The amount of gas in the solution remains constant

59. The mathematical expression of Charles' law is:

    A. $V_1T_1 = V_2T_2$ **C.** $V_1 + T_2 = V_2 + T_1$

    B. $V_1 + T_1 = V_2 + T_2$ **D.** $V_1 / T_2 = T_1 / V_2$ **E.** $V_1 / T_1 = V_2 / T_2$

60. If the temperature of a liquid increases, what happens to its vapor pressure?

    A. unpredictable   **C.** decreases

    B. remains constant   **D.** increases   **E.** none of the above

61. Which of the following statements about intermolecular forces is true?

    A. Hydrogen bonding occurs between any two molecules that contain hydrogen atoms

    B. Dipole-dipole interactions occurs between two polar molecules

    C. London dispersions forces are the strongest of the three types

    D. Intermolecular forces occur within molecules, rather than between the molecules

    E. Intermolecular forces are of about the same magnitude

62. How many moles of carbon atoms are contained in a 22.4 liter sample of a gas at STP that contains, by volume, 20% C_2H_6, 50% CH_4 and 30% N_2?

    A. 0.40   **B.** 0.50   **C.** 0.90   **D.** 1.20   **E.** 0.75

63. Which transformation describes melting?

    A. solid → liquid   **C.** liquid → solid

    B. solid → gas   **D.** liquid → gas   **E.** gas → liquid

64. Which of the following statements gives the best kinetic molecular theory explanation of the Boyle's law observation of increased pressure due to decreased volume?

    A. Particles strike container walls with more force   **C.** Particles have more kinetic energy

    B. Particles strike container walls more frequently   **D.** Particles increase in size

    E. Particles have less kinetic energy

65. Explain why chlorine, Cl_2, is a gas at room temperature while bromine, Br_2, is a liquid.

    A. Bromine ions are held together by ionic bonds

    B. Chlorine molecules are smaller and, therefore, pack tighter in their physical orientation

    C. Bromine atoms are larger, which causes the formation of a stronger induced dipole-induced dipole attraction

    D. Chlorine atoms are larger, which causes the formation of a stronger induced dipole-induced dipole attraction

    E. Bromine molecules are smaller and, therefore, pack tighter in their physical orientation

66. When NaCl dissolves in water, the force of attraction that exists between Na^+ and H_2O is:

    A. van der Waals   **C.** ion-ion

    B. hydrogen bonding   **D.** dipole-dipole   **E.** ion-dipole

67. A sample of an unknown gas was isolated in a gas containment bulb on a manifold. The volume of the bulb was 1.425 liters, the temperature was 25.40 °C, and the manifold pressure was 583.0 torr. What is the volume of this gas at STP?

    A. 1.000 L   **B.** 1.149 L   **C.** 1.670 L   **D.** 2.026 L   **E.** 11.38 L

68. Charles' law involves which of the following?

    A. indirect proportion   **C.** constant volume

    B. varying mass of gas   **D.** varying temperature   **E.** constant temperature

69. What is the vapor pressure of water at 100 °C?

    A. 760 mmHg   **C.** 76 mmHg

    B. 100 mmHg   **D.** 1 mmHg   **E.** none of the above

70. Which type of attractive forces occur in all molecules regardless of the atoms they possess?

    A. Dipole–ion interactions   **C.** Dipole–dipole attractions

    B. Ion–ion interactions   **D.** Hydrogen bonding

    E. London dispersion forces

71. One liter of an ideal gas is placed in a piston at 27 °C. If the pressure is constant and the temperature is changed to 50 K, the final volume is:

    A. 108 ml   **C.** 136 ml

    B. 131 ml   **D.** 167 ml   **E.** 184 ml

72. A sample of a gas occupying a volume of 122.4 ml at STP was placed in a different vessel with a volume of 164.2 ml, in which the pressure was measured as 0.9915 atm. What was its temperature?

    A. 90.2 °C   **B.** 93.1 °C   **C.** 124.1 °C   **D.** 203.6 °C   **E.** 208.3 °C

73. Which transformation describes sublimation?

    A. solid → liquid   **C.** liquid → solid

    B. solid → gas   **D.** liquid → gas   **E.** gas → liquid

74. What is the relationship between temperature and volume of a fixed amount of gas at constant pressure?

    A. equal   **C.** directly proportional

    B. indirectly proportional   **D.** decreased by a factor of 2

    E. none of the above

75. A beaker of water at 22 °C is placed in a closed container and a vacuum pump is used to evacuate the air in the container. Why does the water begin to boil?

    A. The vapor pressure decreases   **C.** The atmospheric pressure is reduced

    B. Air is released from the water   **D.** The vapor pressure increases

    E. none of the above

76. Which quantity contains the greatest number of moles?

    A. 10g SiO_2 **C.** 10g CBr_4

    B. 10g SO_2 **D.** 10g CO_2 **E.** 10g CH_4

77. How does a real gas deviate from an ideal gas?

    I. Molecules occupy a significant amount of space

    II. Intermolecular forces may exist

    III. Pressure is created from molecular collisions with the walls of the container

    A. I only   **C.** I and II only

    B. II only   **D.** II and III only   **E.** I and III only

78. What would be the new pressure if a 400 mL gas sample at 360 mmHg is expanded to 800 mL with no change in temperature?

    A. 180 mmHg   **C.** 720 mmHg

    B. 360 mmHg   **D.** 760 mmHg   **E.** 800 mmHg

79. 10.0 liters of O_2 gas are at a temperature of 23 °C. If the temperature of the gas is raised to 40 °C at constant pressure, the new volume is:

    A. 10.6 liters   **C.** 4.20 liters

    B. 14.1 liters   **D.** 1.82 liters   **E.** 6.80 liters

80. If hydrogen gas is collected over water at 20 °C and 763 mmHg, what is the partial pressure of the H_2? The vapor pressure of water at 20 °C is 17.5 mmHg.

    A. 763 mmHg   **C.** 743 mmHg

    B. 745.5 mmHg   **D.** 17.5 mmHg   **E.** 780.5 mmHg

81. What is the percent by mass of salt in a mixture that contains 150 g of salt, 1.2 kg of flour and 650 g of sugar?

    A. 0.085%   **B.** 7.5%   **C.** 9.1%   **D.** 15%   **E.** 18%

82. A balloon originally had a volume of 4.39 L at 44 °C and a pressure of 729 torr. At constant pressure, to what temperature (in °C) must the balloon be cooled to reduce its volume to 3.78 L?

    A. 73 °C   **B.** 273 °C   **C.** 38 °C   **D.** 0 °C   **E.** 88 °C

83. If oxygen gas is collected over water at 25 °C and 775 torr, what is the partial pressure of the O_2? The vapor pressure of water at 25 °C is 23.8 torr.

    A. 751 torr   **B.** 725 torr   **C.** 23.8 torr   **D.** 750 torr   **E.** 799 torr

84. Which of the following statements bests describes a liquid?

    A. Definite shape but indefinite volume   **C.** Indefinite shape and volume

    B. Indefinite shape but definite volume   **D.** Definite shape and volume

                                                 E. Definite shape but indefinite mass

85. What is the ratio of the diffusion rate of O_2 molecules to the diffusion rate of H_2 molecules when five moles of O_2 gas and five moles of H_2 gas are placed in a large vessel, such that the gases and vessel are at the same temperature?

   A. 4:1   **B.** 1:4   **C.** 12:1   **D.** 1:1   **E.** 2:1

86. Measured at STP, how many liters of pure oxygen gas are required for the complete combustion of 11.2 L of methane gas?

   A. 12.3 L   **B.** 13.2 L   **C.** 22.4 L   **D.** 31.6 L   **E.** 35.8 L

87. Which statement of Gay–Lussac's Law describes the behavior of a fixed amount of gas?

   A. As temperature increases, pressure decreases at constant volume

   B. As temperature increases, pressure increases at constant volume

   C. As pressure increases, volume increases at constant temperature

   D. As pressure increases, volume decreases at constant temperature

   E. As temperature increases, volume increases at constant pressure

88. Which affects the average force per unit area exerted by a gas on the wall of its container?

     I. Average speed of a gas molecule

     II. Frequency of collision between gas molecules and the wall of the container

     III. Volume of a gas molecule

   A. I only   **B.** I and III only   **C.** I and II only   **D.** I, II and III   **E.** II only

89. What is the difference between a dipole-dipole and an ion–dipole interaction?

   A. One involves dipole attraction between neutral molecules, while the other involves dipole interactions with ions

   B. One involves ionic molecules interacting with other ionic molecules, while the other deals with polar molecules

   C. One involves salts and water, while the other does not involve water

   D. One involves hydrogen bonding, while the other does not

   E. None of the above

90. The Gay–Lussac's law of increased pressure due to increased temperature is explained using kinetic molecular theory, stating that the pressure must increase because the:

   A. molecules increase in size   **C.** molecules decrease in size

   B. molecules move slower   **D.** molecules strike the container walls less often

                                      E. molecules strike the container walls more often

91. Which of the following is true of an ideal gas, according to the kinetic theory?

   A. All molecular collisions have the same energy

   B. All molecules have the same kinetic energy   **D.** None of the above

   C. All molecules have the same velocity   **E.** All of the above

92. Which of the following statements best describes a solid?

- **A.** Indefinite shape, but definite volume
- **B.** Definite shape, but indefinite volume
- **C.** Definite shape and volume
- **D.** Indefinite shape and volume
- **E.** Definite shape, but indefinite mass

93. A vessel contains 32 g of CH_4 gas and 8.5 g of NH_3 gas at a combined pressure of 1.8 atm. What is the partial pressure of the NH_3 gas?

- **A.** 0.30 atm
- **B.** 0.22 atm
- **C.** 0.44 atm
- **D.** 0.38 atm
- **E.** 0.36 atm

94. The mathematical expression of Gay-Lussac's law is:

- **A.** $P_1 + T_2 = P_2 + T_1$
- **C.** $P_1 / T_1 = P_2 / T_2$
- **B.** $P_1T_1 = P_2T_2$
- **D.** $P_1 / T_1 = P_2 / T_1$
- **E.** $P_1 + T_1 = P_2 + T_2$

95. What are the conditions for a real gas to behave most like an ideal gas?

- **A.** low temperature, high pressure
- **B.** low temperature, low pressure
- **C.** high temperature, high pressure
- **D.** high temperature, low pressure
- **E.** none of the above

96. Which of the following statements best describes a gas?

- **A.** Definite shape, but indefinite volume
- **B.** Indefinite shape, but definite volume
- **C.** Indefinite shape and volume
- **D.** Definite shape and volume
- **E.** Definite shape, but indefinite mass

97. A sample of gas has a volume of 130 mL at 0.900 atm. What would be the volume if the pressure is decreased to 0.300 atm while temperature is held constant?

- **A.** 65 mL
- **B.** 190 mL
- **C.** 130 mL
- **D.** 180 mL
- **E.** 390 mL

98. If the pressure of a gas sample is doubled, according to Gay–Lussac's law, the gas sample's:

- **A.** Kelvin is doubled
- **B.** Kelvin decreases by a factor of 2
- **C.** volume is doubled
- **D.** volume decreases by a factor of 2
- **E.** volume decreases by a factor of 4

99. According to Boyle's law, what happens to a gas as the volume increases?

- **A.** The temperature increases
- **B.** The temperature decreases
- **C.** The pressure increases
- **D.** The pressure decreases
- **E.** None of the above

100. Matter is nearly incompressible in which of these states?

- **A.** solid
- **B.** liquid
- **C.** gas
- **D.** liquid and gas
- **E.** solid and liquid

101. How many molecules of neon gas are present in 5 liters at 10°C and 300 mmHg?
R=0.0821

A. $(300/760)(0.821)(5) / (6 \times 10^{23})(283)$

C. $(300)(5)(283)(6 \times 10^{23})$

B. $(300/760)(5)(6 \times 10^{23}) / (0.0821)(283)$

D. $(300/760)(5)(283)(6 \times 10^{23}) / (0.821)$

E. $(300/283)(5) (6 \times 10^{23}) / (0.0821)(760)$

102. A chemical reaction A $(s) \rightarrow$ B (s) + C (g) occurs when substance A is vigorously heated.
The molecular mass of the gaseous product was determined from the following experimental data:

Mass of A before reaction: 4.962 g

Mass of A after reaction: 0 g

Mass of residue B after cooling and weighing when no more gas was evolved: 3.684 g

When all of the gas C evolved, it was collected and stored in a 658.5 mL glass vessel at
30.4 °C, and the gas exerted a pressure of 748.5 torr.

From this data, determine the apparent molecular mass of C, assuming it behaves as an ideal gas:

A. 6.46 g mol^{-1}

C. 49.1 g mol^{-1}

B. 46.3 g mol^{-1}

D. 72.2 g mol^{-1}

E. 142 g mol^{-1}

103. What is the new pressure if a sealed container with gas at 3.00 atm is heated from 30 K to 60 K?

A. 0.500 atm

C. 4.50 atm

B. 1.50 atm

D. 4.00 atm

E. 6.00 atm

104. Which of the following is a true statement if vessel I contains a gas at 200 °C, while
vessel II has the same gas at 100 °C?

A. Each gas molecule in vessel I has more mass than each gas molecule in vessel II

B. All of the gas molecules in vessel I move slower than all of the gas molecules in vessel II

C. All of the gas molecules in vessel I move faster than all of the gas molecules in vessel II

D. None of the above statements are true

E. Both A and C are correct

105. The combined gas law can NOT be written as:

A. $V_2 = V_1 \times P_1 / P_2 \times T_2 / T_1$

C. $T_2 = T_1 \times P_1 / P_2 \times V_2 / V_1$

B. $P_1 = P_2 \times V_2 / V_1 \times T_1 / T_2$

D. $V1 = V_2 \times P_2 / P_1 \times T_1 / T_2$

E. none of the above

106. According to Charles's law, what happens to a gas as temperature increases?

A. The volume decreases

C. The pressure decreases

B. The volume increases

D. The pressure increases

E. none of the above

107. Which of the following compounds does NOT exhibit hydrogen bonding?

A. CH_4

B. HF

C. NH_3

D. H_2O

E. CH_3OH

108. The Van der Waals equation $[(P + n^2a / v^2)(V − nb) = nRT]$ is used to describe nonideal gases. The terms n^2a / v^2 and nb stand for, respectively:

    A. volume of gas molecules and intermolecular forces

    B. nonrandom movement and intermolecular forces between gas molecules

    C. nonelastic collisions and volume of gas molecules

    D. intermolecular forces and volume of gas molecules

    E. nonrandom movement and volume of gas molecules

109. How does the volume of a fixed sample of gas change if both the pressure and Kelvin are doubled?

    A. Decreases by a factor of 2   **C.** Doubles

    B. Increases by a factor of 4   **D.** Does not change

    E. Change cannot be determined without more information

110. A hydrogen bond is a special type of:

    A. dipole–dipole attraction involving hydrogen bonded to another hydrogen atom

    B. attraction involving any molecules that contain hydrogens

    C. dipole-dipole attraction involving hydrogen bonded to a highly electronegative atom

    D. dipole–dipole attraction involving hydrogen bonded to any other atom

    E. none of the above

111. If both the pressure and the temperature of a gas are halved, the volume is:

    A. halved   **C.** doubled

    B. the same   **D.** quadrupled   **E.** decreased by a factor of 4

112. According to Gay–Lussac's law, what happens to a gas as temperature increases?

    A. The pressure increases   **C.** The volume increases

    B. The volume decreases   **D.** The pressure decreases

    E. none of the above

113. Which one of these molecules can act as a hydrogen bond acceptor but not a donor?

    A. CH_3NH_2 **B.** CH_3CO_2H **C.** H_2O **D.** C_2H_5OH **E.** $CH_3–O–CH_3$

114. A mixture of gases containing 16 g of O_2, 14 g of N_2 and 88 g of CO_2 is collected above water at a temperature of 25 °C. The total pressure is 1 atm, and the vapor pressure water at 25 °C is 40 torr. What is the partial pressure exerted by CO_2?

    A. 280 torr   **B.** 360 torr   **C.** 480 torr   **D.** 540 torr   **E.** 560 torr

115. What is the mole fraction of H in a gaseous mixture that consists of 8.00 g of H_2 and 12.00 g of Ne in a 3.50 liter container maintained at 35.20 °C?

    A. 0.130   **B.** 0.430   **C.** 0.670   **D.** 0.870   **E.** 0.910

116. A gas initially filled a 3.0 L container. Heat was then added to the gas, which raised its temperature from 100 K to 150 K, while increasing its pressure from 3.0 atm to 4.5 atm. What is the new volume of the gas?

    A. 1.4 L   **B.** 3.0 L   **C.** 2.0 L   **D.** 4.5 L   **E.** 6.0 L

117. How will the pressure of a fixed sample of gas change if its volume is halved and Kelvin is quadrupled, while the moles of gas remain constant?

    A. decrease by a factor of 8   **C.** decrease by a factor of 4
    B. quadruple   **D.** decrease by a factor of 2
                               E. increase by a factor of 8

118. If a piston compresses a gas in a steel cylinder, what happens to the volume in the cylinder?

    A. Increases and the pressure decreases   **C.** Decreases and the pressure decreases
    B. Increases and the pressure increases   **D.** Decreases and the pressure increases
                               E. None of the above

119. What is the predominant intermolecular force that is between two molecules of CH_3CH_2OH?

    A. ion–dipole   **C.** dipole–dipole
    B. ion–ion   **D.** London dispersion forces   **E.** hydrogen bonding

120. As the pressure is increased on solid CO_2, the melting point is:

    A. decreased   **C.** increased
    B. unchanged   **D.** inversely proportional to the square root of the change
                           E. unable to be determined without further information

121. The average speed at which a methane molecule effuses at 28.5 °C is 631 m/s. The average speed at which a krypton molecule effuses at this same temperature is:

    A. 123 m/s   **C.** 312 m/s
    B. 276 m/s   **D.** 421 m/s   **E.** 633 m/s

122. A sample of SO_3 gas is decomposed to SO_2 and O_2.

    $2SO_3\,(g) \rightarrow 2SO_2\,(g) + O_2\,(g)$

If the total pressure of SO_2 and O_2 is 1340 torr, what is the partial pressure of O_2 in torr?

    A. 447 torr   **B.** 1160 torr   **C.** 1340 torr   **D.** 893 torr   **E.** 11.60 torr

123. Which of the following is the definition of standard temperature and pressure?

    A. 0 K and 1 atm   **C.** 298 K and 1 atm
    B. 298 K and 760 mm Hg   **D.** 273 °C and 760 torr   **E.** 273 K and 760 mm Hg

124. A latex balloon has a volume of 500 mL when filled with gas at a pressure of 820 torr and a temperature of 300 K. The balloon contains how many moles of gas? (R = 0.08206 L atm mol^{-1} K^{-1})

    A. 0.022   **B.** 0.22   **C.** 2.2   **D.** 22   **E.** 222

125. Avogadro's law, in its alternate form, is very similar in form to:

A. Charles' law and Gay-Lussac's law   C. Boyle's law

B. Boyle's law and Charles' law   D. Boyle's law and Gay-Lussac's law

E. Charles' law

126. If a helium balloon is placed in a cold freezer, what happens to the temperature in the balloon?

A. Increases and the volume increases   C. Decreases and the volume increases

B. Increases and the volume decreases   D. Decreases and the volume decreases

E. None of the above

127. Which of the following compounds exhibits primarily dipole-dipole intermolecular forces?

A. CO_2 B. F_2 C. $CH_3–O–CH_3$ D. CH_3CH_3 E. H_2O

128. Boiling occurs when the:

A. internal pressure of a liquid is less than the sum of all external pressures

B. vapor pressure of a liquid is greater than the external pressure

C. internal pressure of a liquid is greater than the atmospheric pressure

D. internal pressure of a liquid is greater than the external pressure

E. vapor pressure of a liquid is less than the external pressure

129. Which of the following two variables are present in mathematical statements of Avogadro's law?

A. P and V   B. n and P   C. n and T   D. V and T   E. n and V

130. As an automobile travels the highway, what happens to the temperature of the air inside the tires?

A. Increases and the pressure decreases   C. Decreases and the pressure decreases

B. Increases and the pressure increases   D. Decreases and the pressure increases

E. None of the above

131. How many hydrogen bonds does $CH_3–O–CH_2OH$ form with water?

A. 5   B. 3   C. 4   D. 2   E. 6

132. Which statement is NOT true regarding vapor pressure?

A. Solids have a vapor pressure

B. The vapor pressure of a pure liquid does not depend on the amount of vapor present

C. The vapor pressure of a pure liquid does not depend on the amount of liquid present

D. None of the above

E. A and B

133. According to the kinetic theory of gases, the average kinetic energy of the gas particles is directly proportional to:

A. temperature   C. volume

B. molar mass   D. pressure   E. number of moles of gas

134. How many moles of gas are present in a 10.0 liter sample at STP?

    A. 224 moles   **C.** 10.0 moles

    B. 0.446 moles   **D.** 2.24 moles   **E.** 22.4 moles

135. A balloon contains 40 grams of He with a pressure of 1000 torr. When He is released from the balloon, the new pressure is 900 torr and the volume is half of the original. If the temperature remains the same, how many grams of He remains in the balloon?

    A. 18 grams   **C.** 10 grams

    B. 20 grams   **D.** 40 grams   **E.** 25 grams

136. Which is the strongest form of intermolecular attraction in a water molecule?

    A. ion-dipole   **C.** induced dipole-induced dipole

    B. covalent bonding   **D.** hydrogen bonding

                              E. polar-induced polar

137. An ideal gas differs from a real gas because the molecules of an ideal gas have:

    A. no attraction to each other   **C.** molecular weight equal to zero

    B. no kinetic energy   **D.** appreciable volumes

                              E. none of the above

138. Which of the following describes a substance in the solid physical state?

    A. The substance compresses negligibly   **C.** The substance has a fixed shape

    B. The substance has a fixed volume   **D.** None of the above

                                       E. All of the above

139. For small molecules of comparable molecular weight, which lists the intermolecular forces in increasing order?

    A. dipole-dipole forces < hydrogen bonds < London forces

    B. London forces < hydrogen bonds < dipole-dipole forces

    C. London forces < dipole-dipole forces < hydrogen bonds

    D. hydrogen bonds < dipole-dipole forces < London forces

    E. London forces < dipole-dipole forces = hydrogen bonds

140. Consider the phase diagram for H_2O. The termination of the gas-liquid transition at which distinct or liquid phases do not exist is called the:

    A. critical point   **C.** triple point

    B. end point   **D.** condensation point   **E.** inflection point

141. According to Avogadro's Law, the volume of a gas [ ] as the [ ] increases while [ ] are held constant.

    A. increases… temperature… pressure and number of moles

    B. decreases… pressure… temperature and number of moles

    C. increases… pressure… temperature and number of moles

    D. decreases… number of moles… pressure and temperature

    E. increases… number of moles… pressure and temperature

142. The ideal gas equation CANNOT be written as:

A. PV = nRT
C. R = PV / nT
B. P = nRT / V
D. R = nT / PV
E. none of the above

143. Which of the following describes a substance in the liquid physical state?

A. The substance has a variable shape
C. The substance has a fixed volume
B. The substance compresses negligibly
D. None of the above
E. All of the above

144. Which of the following has only London dispersion forces as the primary attraction between molecules?

A. CH_3OH
C. CH_3CH_3
B. CH_3CH_2OH
D. H_2S
E. H_2O

145. Which of the following does NOT demonstrate colligative properties?

A. Freezing point
C. Vapor pressure
B. Boiling point
D. All of the above demonstrates colligative properties
E. None of the above

146. If container X is occupied by 1.00 mole of O_2 gas, while container Y is occupied by 20.0 grams of N_2 gas and both containers are maintained at 0.00 °C and 650 torr, then:

A. container X must have a volume of 22.4 L
B. the average kinetic energy of the molecules in X is equal to the average kinetic energy of the molecules in Y
C. container Y must be larger than container X
D. the average speed of the molecules in container X is greater than that of the molecules in container Y
E. the number of atoms in container Y is greater than the number of atoms in container X

147. Consider a sample of helium and a sample of neon, both at 30 °C and 1.5 atm. Both samples have a volume of 5.0 liters. Which statement regarding these samples is NOT true?

A. The density of the neon sample is greater than the density of the helium sample
B. Each sample contains the same number of moles of gas
C. Each sample weighs the same amount
D. Each sample contains the same number of atoms of gas
E. None of the above

148. 10 grams of O_2 are placed in an empty 10 liter container at 28 °C. Compared to an equal mass of H that is placed in an identical container at 28 °C, the pressure of the O_2 is:

A. less than the pressure of the H
C. greater than the pressure of the H
B. double the pressure of the H
D. equal to the pressure of the H
E. equal to the square root of the pressure of the H

149. Which singular molecule is most likely to show a dipole-dipole interaction?

A. CH_4
B. H–C≡C–H
C. SO_2
D. CO_2
E. none of the above

150. The value of the ideal gas constant, expressed in units (torr × mL) / mole × K is:

   A. 62.4   **B.** 62,400   **C.** 0.0821   **D.** 1 / 0.0821   **E.** 8.21

151. What is the term for a change of state from a liquid to a gas?

   A. vaporizing   **C.** freezing

   B. melting   **D.** condensing   **E.** none of the above

152. Which of the following pairs of compounds contain the same intermolecular forces?

   A. H_2S and CH_4 **C.** CH_3CH_3 and H_2O

   B. NH_3 and CH_4 **D.** CH_3CH_2OH and H_2O **E.** CCl_4 and CH_3OH

153. When nonvolatile solute molecules are added to a solution, the vapor pressure of the solution:

   A. stays the same   **C.** decreases

   B. increases   **D.** is unable to be determined without further information

                     E. is directly proportional to the square root of the amount added

154. For the following reaction, if 11.2 L of nitrogen are reacted to form NH_3 at STP, how many liters of hydrogen are required to completely consume all of the nitrogen?

       $N_2 + 3H_2 \rightarrow 2NH_2$

   A. 7.4 L   **B.** 6.1 L   **C.** 16.8 L   **D.** 11.2 L   **E.** 33.6 L

155. Using the following chemical reaction, what volume of H_2 gas at 780 mmHg and 23 °C is required to produce 10.6 L of NH_3 gas at the same temperature and pressure?

       $N_2\,(g) + 3H_2\,(g) \rightarrow 2NH_3\,(g)$

   A. 20.0 L   **B.** 15.0 L   **C.** 15.9 L   **D.** 13.0 L   **E.** 10.6 L

156. What is the term for a direct change of state from a solid to a gas?

   A. sublimation   **C.** condensation

   B. vaporization   **D.** deposition   **E.** none of the above

157. What is the molarity of a solution that contains 36 mEq Ca^{2+} per liter?

   A. 0.018 M   **B.** 0.036 M   **C.** 1.8 M   **D.** 3.6 M   **E.** 0.36 M

158. What effect does adding solute to a pure solvent have on the boiling and freezing points, respectively?

   A. decreases, decreases   **C.** increases, decreases

   B. decreases, increases   **D.** increases, increases   **E.** no relationship

159. The van der Waals equation of state for a real gas is

$$\left[P + \frac{n^2a}{V^2}\right](V - nb) = nRT$$

The van der Waals constant, *a*, represents a correction for a:

A. negative deviation in the measured value of P from that of an ideal gas due to the attractive forces between the molecules of a real gas
B. positive deviation in the measured value of P from that of an ideal gas due to the attractive forces between the molecules of a real gas
C. negative deviation in the measured value of P from that of an ideal gas due to the finite volume of space occupied by molecules of a real gas
D. positive deviation in the measured value of P from that of an ideal gas due to the finite volume of space occupied by molecules of a real gas
E. positive deviation in the measured value of P from that of an ideal gas due to the finite mass of the molecules of a real gas

160. Vessels X and Y each contain 1.00 L of a gas at STP, but vessel X contains oxygen while container Y contains nitrogen. Assuming the gases behave ideally, the gases has the same:

    I. number of molecules   II. density   III. kinetic energy

A. II only
C. I and III only
B. III only
D. I, II and III
E. I only

161. Which molecule(s) is/are most likely to show a dipole-dipole interaction?

    I. H–C≡C–H   III. CH_3SH

    II. CH_4 IV. $CH_3\,CH_2OH$

A. I only   B. II only   C. III only   D. III and IV only   E. I and IV only

162. Propane burners are used for cooking by campers. What volume of H_2O gas is produced by the complete combustion of 1.8 L of propane (C_3H_8) gas? Gas volumes are measured at the same temperature and pressure.

$$C_3H_8\,(g) + 5O_2\,(g) \rightarrow 3CO_2\,(g) + 4H_2O\,(g)$$

A. 0.52 L   B. 7.2 L   C. 14 L   D. 1.8 L   E. 5.2 L

163. What is the term for a change of state from a gas to a liquid?

A. vaporizing
C. freezing
B. melting
D. condensing
E. none of the above

164. What is the molarity of the solution obtained by diluting 125 mL of 2.50 M NaOH to 575 mL?

A. 0.272 M   B. 0.543 M   C. 1.84 M   D. 1.15 M   E. 0.115 M

165. What is the boiling point when 90 g of glucose ($C_6H_{12}O_6$) are added to 500 g of H_2O?

    K = 0.52

A. 267.80 K   B. 273.54 K   C. 278.20 K   D. 373.52 K   E. 393.28 K

166. Currently the CO_2 content of the Earth's atmosphere is approximately:

    A. 40.5 %   **B.** 11 %   **C.** 4.21 %   **D.** 0.038 %   **E.** 0.011 %

167. A container is labeled "Ar, 5.0 moles," but has no pressure gauge. By measuring the temperature and determining the volume of the container, a chemist uses the ideal gas law to estimate the pressure inside the container. Unfortunately, the handwriting on the container is illegible, and the container actually contains 5.0 moles of He, not Ar. How does this affect the pressure inside of the container?

    A. The estimate is correct, but only because both gases are monatomic
    B. The estimate is too high
    C. The estimate is slightly too low
    D. The estimate is significantly too low because of the large difference in molecular mass
    E. The estimate is correct because the identity of the gas is irrelevant

168. Which is most likely to have the weakest induced dipole-induced dipole interaction?

    A. I_2 **B.** F_2 **C.** Br_2 **D.** Cl_2 **E.** All have the same interactions

169. How much water must be added when 125 mL of a 2.00 M solution of HCl is diluted to a final concentration of 0.400 M?

    A. 150 mL   **B.** 850 mL   **C.** 625 mL   **D.** 750 mL   **E.** 500 mL

170. The freezing point changes by 10 K when an unknown amount of toluene is added to 100 g of benzene. Find the number of moles of toluene added from the given data.

    $K_{benzene} = 5.0$
    $K_{toluene} = 8.4$

    A. 0.14   **B.** 0.20   **C.** 0.23   **D.** 0.27   **E.** 0.31

171. A laser contains 0.40 mole Ar and 0.60 mole F_2, whereby the total pressure inside the laser cavity is 1.10 atm. What is the partial pressure of Ar inside the laser?

    A. 0.40 atm   **C.** 0.60 atm
    B. 10.0 atm   **D.** 1.0 atm   **E.** 0.44 atm

172. Which of the following atoms could interact through a hydrogen bond?

    A. The hydrogen of an amine and the oxygen of an alcohol
    B. The hydrogen on an aromatic ring and the oxygen of carbon dioxide
    C. The oxygen of a ketone and the hydrogen of an aldehyde
    D. The oxygen of methanol and a hydrogen on the methyl carbon of methanol
    E. None of the above

173. The ozone layer is located in which region of the atmosphere?

    A. troposhere   **C.** mesosphere
    B. stratosphere   **D.** thermosphere   **E.** ecosphere

174. Which of the following statements is true, if three 2.0 L flasks are filled with H_2, O_2 and He, respectively, at STP?

   A. There are twice as many He atoms as H_2 or O_2 molecules

   B. There are four times as many H_2 or O_2 molecules as He atoms

   C. Each flask contains the same number of atoms

   D. There are twice as many H_2 or O_2 molecules as He atoms

   E. The number of H_2 or O_2 molecules is the same as the number of He atoms

175. What is the molarity of a solution formed by dissolving 45 g NaOH in water to give a final volume of 250 mL?

   A. 0.0045 M   **B.** 0.18 M   **C.** 4.5 M   **D.** 9.0 M   **E.** 0.45 M

176. When 25 g of compound X is dissolved in 1 kg of camphor, the freezing point of the camphor falls 2.0 K. What is the approximate molecular weight of compound X?

   $K_{camphor} = 40$

   A. 50 g/mol   **C.** 5,000 g/mol

   B. 500 g/mol   **D.** 5,500 g/mol   **E.** 5,750 g/mol

177. Which of the following best explains the hydrogen bonding that occurs in water?

   A. The structure of liquid water is best described as flickering clusters of H-bonds due to the relative short duration of individual H-bonds

   B. Each water molecule is capable of forming 8 H-bonds

   C. The average number of H-bonds formed by one water molecule is the same in liquid and solid water, the only difference is the duration of the H-bond

   D. The number of H-bonds formed by one water molecule is greater in liquid water than in solid water

   E. None of the above

178. What volume is occupied by 6.21×10^{24} molecules of CO at STP?

   A. 231 L   **B.** 44.3 L   **C.** 22.4 L   **D.** 106 L   **E.** 2.24 L

179. According to the kinetic theory, what happens to the kinetic energy of gaseous molecules when the temperature of a gas decreases?

   A. Increase as does velocity   **C.** Increases and velocity decreases

   B. Remains constant as does velocity   **D.** Decreases and velocity increases

                                                    E. Decreases as does velocity

180. Calculate the volume (in ml) of a 2.75 M solution that must be used to make 1.25 L of a 0.150 M solution.

   A. 0.0682 mL   **B.** 33.0 mL   **C.** 0.0330 mL   **D.** 68.2 mL   **E.** 0.682 mL

181. Calculate the number of O_2 molecules if a 15.0 L cylinder was filled with O_2 gas at STP.

   A. 443 molecules   **C.** 4.03×10^{23} molecules

   B. 6.59×10^{24} molecules   **D.** 2.77×10^{22} molecules   **E.** 4,430 molecules

182. Given the structure of glucose, which statement explains the hydrogen bonding between glucose and water?

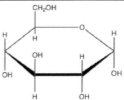

A. Due to the cyclic structure of glucose, H-bonding with water does not occur
B. Each glucose molecule could H-bond with as many as 17 water molecules
C. H-bonds will form with water always being the H-bond donor
D. H-bonds will form with glucose always being the H-bond donor
E. None of the above

183. The conditions known as STP are:

A. 1 mmHg and 273 K   C. 760 mmHg and 273 °C
B. 1 atm and 273 °C   D. 760 atm and 273 K   E. 1 atm and 273 K

184. For a gas to be classified as a *greenhouse gas*, it must:

A. transmit infrared light and absorb visible light
B. be combustible   D. be radioactive
C. transmit visible light and absorb infrared radiation   E. be a product of combustion

185. Which of the following would have the highest boiling point?

A. F_2 B. Br_2 C. Cl_2 D. I_2
E. not enough information given

186. A sample of N_2 gas occupies a volume of 180 mL at STP. What volume will it occupy at 640 mmHg and 295 K?

A. 1.07 L   B. 0.690 L   C. 0.231 L   D. 1.45 L   E. 6.90 L

187. What volume of 8.25 M NaOH solution must be diluted to prepare 2.40 L of 0.500 M NaOH solution?

A. 438 mL   B. 145 mL   C. 39.6 L   D. 0.356 L   E. 35.4 L

188. A properly designed Torricelli mercury barometer should be at least how tall?

A. 100 in   B. 250 mm   C. 76 mm   D. 500 mm   E. 800 mm

189. Which gas has the greatest density at STP:

A. CO_2 B. O_2 C. N_2 D. NO   E. more than one

190. A container contains only N_2, CO_2, O_2 and water vapor. If, at STP, the partial pressure of O_2 is 300 torr, CO_2 is 20 torr, and water vapor is 8 torr, what is the partial pressure of N_2?

A. 165 torr   B. 432 torr   C. 760 torr   D. 330 torr   E. 864 torr

191. What is the mass of one mole of a gas that has a density of 1.34 g/L at STP?

A. 44.0 g   B. 43.9 g   C. 28.0 g   D. 30.0 g   E. 4.39 g

Chapter 4. SOLUTIONS

1. Which of the following solid compounds is insoluble in water?

   A. $BaSO_4$ **C.** $PbCl_2$

   B. Hg_2I_2 **D.** all of the above   **E.** none of the above

2. The sucrose that dissolves in H_2O is the [ ], the H_2O is the [ ], and the sweetened H_2O is the [ ], respectively.

   A. solution, solute, solvent   **C.** solute, solvent, solution

   B. solute, solution, solvent   **D.** solvent, solution, solute

                                 E. solution, solvent, solute

3. The equation for the reaction $Pb(NO_3)_2$ (*aq*) + NaCl (*aq*) → $PbCl_2$ (*s*) + $NaNO_3$ (*aq*) can be written as an ionic equation. In the ionic equation, the spectator ions are:

   A. Pb^{2+} and NO_3^- **C.** Na^+ and Cl^-

   B. Pb^{2+} and Cl^- **D.** Na^+ and Pb^{2+} **E.** Na^+ and NO_3^-

4. All of the following statements describing solutions are true, EXCEPT:

   A. solutions are colorless

   B. the particles in a solution are atomic or molecular

   C. making a solution involves a physical change in size

   D. solutions are homogeneous

   E. solutions are transparent

5. Which of the following is possible?

      I. A gaseous solution consisting of a gaseous solute and a gaseous solvent

      II. A solid solution consisting of a solid solute and a solid solvent

      III. A liquid solution resulting from a gaseous solute and a liquid solvent

   A. I only   **B.** II only   **C.** I and II only   **D.** II and III only   **E.** I, II and III

6. A crystal of solid NaCl is placed into an aqueous NaCl solution. No precipitate forms in the bottom of the container and the final solution is:

   A. saturated   **C.** supersaturated

   B. unsaturated   **D.** polysaturated   **E.** polyunsaturated

7. Which of the following solid compounds is insoluble in water?

   A. Li_2CO_3 **C.** $AgC_2H_3O_2$

   B. $Cu(NO_3)_2$ **D.** all of the above   **E.** none of the above

8. What is the molar concentration of a solution containing 0.5 mol of solute in a 50 cm^3 of solution?

   A. 0.1 M   **B.** 1.5 M   **C.** 3 M   **D.** 10 M   **E.** 1 M

9. Which of the following is/are solutions?

      I. NaCl in water
      II. An alloy of 2% carbon and 98% water
      III. Water vapor in nitrogen gas

A. I only   **C.** II and III only
B. II only   **D.** I, II and III   **E.** I and II only

10. In a solution made from one teaspoon of sugar and one liter of water, which is the solute?

A. the teaspoon   **C.** sugar
B. water   **D.** both sugar and water   **E.** none of the above

11. Which of the following solid compounds is insoluble in water?

A. $BaSO_4$ **C.** $(NH_4)_2CO_3$
B. Na_2S **D.** K_2CrO_4 **E.** $Sr(OH)_2$

12. A saturated solution:

A. contains dissolved solute in equilibrium with undissolved solid
B. will rapidly precipitate if a seed crystal is added
C. contains as much solvent as it can hold
D. contains only electrolytes
E. contains only ions

13. The equation for the reaction $AgNO_3\,(aq) + K_2CrO_4\,(aq) \rightarrow Ag_2CrO_4\,(s) + KNO_3\,(aq)$ can be written as an ionic equation, whereby the spectator ions are:

A. K^+ and CrO_4^{2-} **C.** Ag^+ and K^+
B. CrO_4^{2-} and NO_3^- **D.** Ag^+ and CrO_4^{2-} **E.** K^+ and NO_3^-

14. Which heterogeneous mixture is opaque and has particles large enough to be filtered?

A. colloid   **C.** solution
B. suspension   **D.** both colloids and suspensions
                               E. none of the above

15. Which are characteristics of an ideally dilute solution?

      I. Solute molecules do not interact with each other
      II. Solvent molecules do not interact with each other
      III. The mole fraction of the solvent approaches 1

A. I only   **C.** I and III only
B. II only   **D.** I, II and III   **E.** I and II only

16. A solution in which the rate of crystallization is equal to the rate of dissolution is:

A. saturated   **C.** dilute
B. supersaturated   **D.** unsaturated   **E.** cannot be determined

17. Which of the following symbolizes a precipitate in a chemical equation?

A. *(g)*   **B.** *(aq)*   **C.** *(s)*   **D.** *(l)*   **E.** none of the above

18. What is the molality of a solution that contains 2 moles of glycerin, $C_3H_5(OH)_3$, dissolved in 1000g of water?

    A. 0.2 m   **B.** 0.5 m   **C.** 1 m   **D.** 2 m   **E.** 4 m

19. When 1 ml of a 4 M solution of HCl is diluted to 15 ml, the new concentration of the HCl is:

    A. 0.140 M   **B.** 0.440 M   **C.** 0.325 M   **D.** 0.415 M   **E.** 0.270 M

20. Which is/are characteristic(s) of an ideal solution?

    I. Solute molecules do not interact
    II. Solvent molecules do not interact
    III. Solvent-solute interactions are similar to solute-solute and solvent-solvent interactions

    A. I only   **B.** III only   **C.** II only   **D.** I, II and III   **E.** I and II only

21. In a solution of 77 percent nitrogen and 23 percent oxygen, which is the solvent?

    A. nitrogen   **C.** both
    B. oxygen   **D.** neither   **E.** gases cannot form solutions

22. A supersaturated solution:

    A. contains dissolved solute in equilibrium with undissolved solid
    B. will rapidly precipitate if a seed crystal is added   **D.** contains no double bonds
    C. contains as much solvent as it can hold   **E.** contains only electrolytes

23. Which statement is correct for pure H_2O?

    A. Pure H_2O contains no ions
    B. Pure H_2O is an electrolyte
    C. Pure H_2O contains equal $[^-OH]$ and $[H_3O^+]$
    D. Pure H_2O contains greater $[^-OH^-]$ than $[H_3O^+]$
    E. Pure H_2O contains greater $[H_3O^+]$ than $[OH^-]$

24. Which compound produces three ions per formula unit by dissociation when dissolved in water?

    A. aluminum sulfate   **C.** nickel sulfate
    B. ammonium bromate   **D.** sodium nitrate   **E.** calcium perchlorate

25. Which compound is most likely to be more soluble in benzene (a nonpolar solvent) than in water?

    A. SO_2 **B.** CO_2 **C.** silver chloride   **D.** H_2S **E.** CH_2Cl_2

26. Which of the following statements describes a saturated solution?

    A. Solution where the solvent cannot dissolve any more solute
    B. Carbonated beverage with bubbles
    C. Solution of salt water with salt at the bottom
    D. All of the above
    E. None of the above

27. What is the molarity of a solution formed by dissolving 25.0 g of NaCl in water to make 625 mL of solution?

    A. 0.495 M   **B.** 0.684 M   **C.** 0.328 M   **D.** 0.535 M   **E.** 0.125 M

28. Which statement comparing solutions with pure solvents is NOT correct?

    A. A solution containing a non-volatile solute has a lower boiling point than a pure solvent

    B. A solution will have a greater mass than an equal volume of a pure solvent if the solute has a molar mass greater than the solvent

    C. A solution containing a non-volatile solute has a lower vapor pressure than a pure solvent

    D. A solution containing a non-volatile solute has a lower freezing point than a pure solvent

    E. None of the above

29. Which of the following is the most soluble in benzene (C_6H_6)?

    A. glucose ($C_6H_{12}O_6$)   **C.** octane (C_8H_{18})

    B. sodium benzoate   **D.** hydrobromic acid   **E.** CH_2Cl_2

30. The term miscible describes which type of solution?

    A. solid/solid   **B.** liquid/gas   **C.** liquid/solid   **D.** liquid/liquid   **E.** solid/gas

31. What is the predicted product from the burning of carbon in charcoal?

    A. CO_3 **C.** C_2O

    B. CO_2 **D.** CO   **E.** The product depends on experimental conditions

32. Approximate the freezing point of an aqueous solution containing 25 g of a compound with a molecular weight of 100 g/mol dissolved in 50 g of water. (Note: assume the compound does not dissociate in solution. Molal freezing point constant of water = –1.86 °C/m).

    A. –4.5 °C   **B.** –14 °C   **C.** –9 °C   **D.** –18 °C   **E.** –21 °C

33. Which of the following can serve as the solvent in a solution?

    A. liquid   **C.** solid

    B. gas   **D.** liquid and gas   **E.** All of the above

34. Which is most likely soluble in NH_3?

    A. CO_2 **B.** SO_2 **C.** CCl_4 **D.** N_2 **E.** H_2

35. Water and methanol are two liquids that dissolve in each other. When the two are mixed they form one layer because the liquids are:

    A. unsaturated   **C.** miscible

    B. saturated   **D.** immiscible   **E.** supersaturated

36. What is the predicted product from the burning of sulfur in low-grade coal?

    A. SO_2 **C.** SO

    B. SO_3 **D.** S_2O **E.** The product depends on experimental conditions

37. What volume of 10 M H_2SO_4 is needed to prepare 600 ml of 0.5 M H_2SO_4?

   A. 5 ml   **B.** 10 ml   **C.** 30 ml   **D.** 15 ml   **E.** 60 ml

38. A solute is a:

   A. substance that dissolves into a solvent
   B. substance containing a solid, liquid or gas
   C. solid substance that does not dissolve into water
   D. solid substance that does not dissolve at a given temperature
   E. liquid that does not dissolve into another liquid

39. Salts are more soluble in H_2O than in benzene because:

   A. benzene is aromatic and therefore very stable
   B. the dipole moment of H_2O compensates for the loss of ionic bonding when salt dissolves
   C. the strong intermolecular attractions in benzene must be disrupted to dissolve a salt in benzene
   D. the molecular mass of H_2O is similar to the atomic mass of most ions
   E. the dipole moment of H_2O compensates for the increased ionic bonding when salt dissolves

40. Which of the following interparticle attractions play a part in the formation of a solution?

      I. solute-solute   II. solvent-solute   III. solvent-solvent

   A. I only   **C.** I and II only
   B. III only   **D.** I, II and III   **E.** II and III only

41. What is the product from the reaction of N_2 and O_2 gases in a combustion engine?

   A. N_2O_3 **B.** NO_2 **C.** N_2O **D.** NO   **E.** all of the above

42. Which has the highest boiling point?

   A. 0.1 M $Al(NO_3)_3$ **C.** 0.1 M glucose ($C_6H_{12}O_6$)
   B. 0.1 M $MgCl_2$ **D.** 0.1 M Na_2SO_4 **E.** pure H_2O

43. Octane is less soluble in H_2O than in benzene because:

   A. bonds between benzene and octane are much stronger than the bonds between H_2O and octane
   B. octane cannot dissociate in the presence of H_2O
   C. bonds between H_2O and octane are weaker than the bonds between H_2O molecules
   D. octane and benzene have similar molecular weights
   E. H_2O dissociates in the presence of octane

44. Which of the following is true of a colloid?

   A. Dispersed particles separate in a centrifuge
   B. Dispersed particles pass through filter paper   **D.** All of the above
   C. Dispersed particles are about 1-100 nm in diameter   **E.** None of the above

45. What is the volume of a solution that contains 3.12 moles of NaCl if the concentration is 6.67 M NaCl?

   A. 0.936 L   **B.** 0.468 L   **C.** 20.8 L   **D.** 2.14 L   **E.** 0.234 L

46. Which of the following describes the term concentration?

    A. It is the amount of solute in a given amount of solution

    B. The given amount of solution in a given container

    C. The given amount of solvent per amount of solute

    D. The amount of solvent in a given amount of solution

    E. None of the above

47. Methane (CH_4) can be used as automobile fuel to reduce pollution. What is the coefficient of oxygen in the balanced equation for the reaction?

$$\text{Spark}$$
$$\_\_CH_4\,(g) + \_\_O_2\,(g) \rightarrow \_\_CO_2\,(g) + \_\_H_2O\,(g)$$

    A. 1   **B.** 2   **C.** 3   **D.** 4   **E.** none of the above

48. Determine the boiling point of a 2 molal aqueous solution of NaCl.

Note: boiling point constant of water = 0.51 °C/m

    A. 98.5 °C   **B.** 99.8 °C   **C.** 101 °C   **D.** 102 °C   **E.** 105 °C

49. Of the following, which can serve as the solute in a solution?

    A. gas   **C.** liquid

    B. solid   **D.** gas and liquid only   **E.** all of the above

50. Hexane is significantly soluble in octane because:

    A. entropy increases for the two substances as the dominant factor in the ΔG when mixed

    B. hexane hydrogen bonds with octane

    C. intermolecular bonds between hexane-octane are much stronger than either hexane-hexane or octane-octane molecular bonds

    D. ΔH for hexane-octane is greater than hexane-H_2O

    E. hexane and octane have similar molecular weights

51. The principle *like dissolve like* is not applicable for predicting solubility when the solute is a/an:

    A. nonpolar liquid   **C.** nonpolar gas

    B. polar gas   **D.** ionic compound   **E.** covalent compound

52. Ethane (C_2H_6) gives off carbon dioxide and water when burning. What is the coefficient of oxygen in the balanced equation for the reaction?

$$\text{Spark}$$
$$\_\_C_2H_6\,(g) + \_\_O_2\,(g) \rightarrow \_\_CO_2\,(g) + \_\_H_2O\,(g)$$

    A. 5   **B.** 7   **C.** 10   **D.** 14   **E.** none of the above

53. A 4 M solution of H_3A is completely dissociated in water. How many equivalents of H^+ are found in 1/3 liter?

    A. ¼   **B.** 1   **C.** 1.5   **D.** 3   **E.** 4

54. Which of the following describes a saturated solution?

    A. When the ratio of solute to solvent is small
    B. When it contains less solute than it can hold at 25 °C
    C. When it contains as much solute as it can hold at a given temperature
    D. When it contains 1 g of solute in 100 mL of water
    E. When it is equivalent to a supersaturated solution

55. 15 grams of an unknown substance is dissolved in 60 grams of water. When the solution is transferred to another container, it weighs 78 grams. Which of the following is a possible explanation?

    A. The solution reacted with the second container that formed a precipitate
    B. Some of the solution remained in the first container
    C. The reaction was endothermic, which increased the average molecular speed
    D. The solution reacted with the first container, causing some byproducts to be transferred with the solution
    E. The reaction was exothermic, which increased the average molecular speed

56. Which of the following solutions is the most dilute?

    A. One liter of H_2O with 1 gram of sugar
    B. One liter of H_2O with 2 grams of sugar
    C. One liter of H_2O with 5 grams of sugar
    D. one liter of H_2O with 10 grams of sugar
    E. All have the same volume

57. Which type of compound is likely to dissolve in H_2O?

    I. One with hydrogen bonds
    II. Highly polar compound
    III. Salt

    A. I only   **B.** II only   **C.** III only   **D.** I and III only   **E.** I, II and III

58. Propane (C_3H_8) is flammable and used in rural areas where natural gas is not available. What is the coefficient of oxygen in the balanced equation for the combustion of propane?

$$\underline{}C_3H_8\,(g) + \underline{}O_2\,(g) \xrightarrow{\text{Spark}} \underline{}CO_2\,(g) + \underline{}H_2O\,(g)$$

    A. 1   **B.** 7   **C.** 5   **D.** 10   **E.** none of the above

59. In a mixture of 5 mL water, 10 mL alcohol, and 50 mL acetone, the solvent(s) is/are:

    A. acetone   **C.** alcohol
    B. water   **D.** acetone and alcohol   **E.** alcohol and water

60. Which of the following describes a colloid?

    A. A supersaturated solution of potassium chloride
    B. Carbon dioxide molecules dissolved in a soft drink
    C. Hemoglobin molecules in cytosol
    D. Tiny sand particles dispersed in water which then settle as a precipitate
    E. Food coloring dispersed in water that change the color of the liquid

61. Which response includes all of the following compounds that are soluble in water, and no others?

I. LiF   II. $PbCl_2$ III. NH_4CH_3COO IV. FeS

V. $Mn(OH)_2$ VI. $Cr(NO_3)_3$ VII. $CuCO_3$ VIII. $Ni_3(PO_4)_2$

A. III, IV, V and VIII   **C.** I, III and VI

B. I, II, V and VIII   **D.** II, IV, V and VII   **E.** I, III and VII

62. Butane (C_4H_{10}) is flammable and used in butane lighters. What is the coefficient of oxygen in the balanced equation for the combustion of butane?

$$\text{Spark}$$
$$\_C_4H_{10}\,(g) + \_O_2\,(g) \rightarrow \_CO_2\,(g) + \_H_2O\,(g)$$

A. 9   **B.** 13   **C.** 18   **D.** 26   **E.** none of the above

63. Water boils at a lower temperature at high altitudes because:

A. vapor pressure of water is increased at high altitudes
B. temperature is higher than at low altitudes
C. more energy is available to break liquid bonds at high altitudes
D. atmospheric pressure is lower at high altitudes
E. atmospheric pressure is lower at low altitudes

64. Which of the following aqueous solutions is a poor conductor of electricity?

I. sucrose, $C_{12}H_{22}O_{11}$

II. barium nitrate, $Ba(NO_3)_2$

III. ethylene glycol, $HOCH_2CH_2OH$

IV. calcium bromide, $CaBr_2$

V. ammonium chloride, NH_4Cl

A. I and III only   **C.** I and V only

B. I, IV and V only   **D.** III, IV and V only

                              E. II, IV and V only

65. Which of the following methods does NOT extract colloidal particles?

A. distillation   **C.** evaporation

B. extraction   **D.** dialysis   **E.** simple filtration

66. Which of the following solutions is the most concentrated?

A. one liter of water with 1 gram of sugar   **C.** one liter of water with 5 grams of sugar

B. one liter of water with 2 grams of sugar   **D.** one liter of water with 10 grams of sugar

                                        E. They all have the same volume

67. Octane (C_8H_{18}) is a major component in gasoline. What is the coefficient of oxygen in the balanced equation for the combustion of octane?

$$\text{Spark}$$
$$\_C_8H_{18}\,(g) + \_O_2\,(g) \rightarrow \_CO_2\,(g) + \_H_2O\,(g)$$

A. 17   **B.** 25   **C.** 34   **D.** 50   **E.** none of the above

68. Which of the following is the solvent for a homogenous mixture consisting of 12% ethanol, 28% methanol and 60% water?

   A. Ethanol   **C.** Methanol

   B. Water   **D.** Ethanol and methanol   **E.** Octane

69. Which solution has the greatest osmolarity?

   A. 0.14 M KF   **C.** 0.6 M NaCl

   B. 0.2 M $CaBr_2$ **D.** 0.35 M $AlCl_3$ **E.** 0.10 M KNO_3

70. Which one of the following compounds is NOT soluble in water?

   A. NH_4F **B.** $FeCl_3$ **C.** NaOH   **D.** CH_3OH **E.** CuS

71. Ethanol (C_2H_5OH) is made from fermenting grain and is blended with gasoline as a fuel additive. If combustion of ethanol produces carbon dioxide and water, what is the coefficient of oxygen in the balanced equation?

Spark

$$\_\_C_2H_5OH\ (g) + \_\_O_2\ (g) \rightarrow \_\_CO_2\ (g) + \_\_H_2O\ (g)$$

   A. 1   **B.** 2   **C.** 3   **D.** 6   **E.** none of the above

72. How much NaCl (*s*) (MW = 58) is required to prepare 100 ml of a 4 M solution?

   A. 23.2 g   **B.** 14.5 g   **C.** 232 g   **D.** 145 g   **E.** 15.4 g

73. Which is true when a beam of light shines through a colloid solution?

   A. The path of the light beam is *invisible* in the colloid, but *visible* in the solution

   B. The path of the light beam is *visible* in the colloid, but *invisible* in the solution

   C. The path of the light beam is *invisible* in both the colloid and the solution

   D. The path of the light beam is *visible* in both the colloid and the solution

   E. Depends on the temperature of the experiment

74. Which of the following solutions is the most dilute?

   A. 0.1 liter of H_2O with 1 gram of sugar   **C.** 0.5 liter of H_2O with 5 grams of sugar

   B. 0.2 liter of H_2O with 2 grams of sugar   **D.** 1 liter of H_2O with 10 grams of sugar

                                                    E. They all have the same concentration

75. Which of the following is NOT soluble in H_2O?

   A. iron (III) hydroxide   **C.** potassium sulfide

   B. iron (III) nitrate   **D.** ammonium sulfate   **E.** sodium chloride

76. Methanol (CH_3OH) is derived from natural gas and is blended with gasoline. If the combustion of methanol produces carbon dioxide and water, what is the coefficient of oxygen in the balanced equation?

Spark

$$\_\_CH_3OH\ (g) + \_\_O_2\ (g) \rightarrow \_\_CO_2\ (g) + \_\_H_2O\ (g)$$

   A. 1   **B.** 2   **C.** 3   **D.** 6   **E.** none of the above

77. Calculate the solubility product of AgCl if the solubility of AgCl in H_2O is 1.3×10^{-4} mol/L?

A. 1.3×10^{-4} **C.** 2.6×10^{-4}

B. 1.3×10^{-2} **D.** 3.9×10^{-5} **E.** 1.7×10^{-8}

78. Which statement best explains the meaning of the phrase "like dissolves like"?

   A. Only true solutions are formed when water dissolves a nonpolar solute

   B. Only true solutions are formed when water dissolves a polar solute

   C. A solvent will easily dissolve a solute of similar mass

   D. A solvent and solute with similar intermolecular forces will readily form a solution

   E. None of these statements is correct

79. What is the term for a homogeneous mixture in which the dispersed particles range from 1 to 100 nm in diameter?

   A. colloid   **C.** supersaturated solution

   B. true solution   **D.** saturated solution   **E.** none of the above

80. What causes colloid particles to settle out during coagulation?

   A. Particles bind to the solution and settle out

   B. Particles dissociate and settle out

   C. Particles bind together and settle due to gravity

   D. Particles dissolve and settle due to gravity

   E. Particles break apart and settle due to gravity

81. What statement best describes a mole?

   A. The amount of molecules or atoms in 1 gram of something

   B. A very large number that chemists use to count atoms or molecules

   C. A little furry mammal that lives in the ground

   D. A very small number that chemists use to count atoms or molecules

   E. None of the above

82. Which percentage concentration units are used by chemists?

     I. % (v/v)   II. % (m/v)   III. % (m/m)

   A. I only   **B.** II only   **C.** III only   **D.** I, II and III   **E.** II and III only

83. What is the term for a region in a molecule that has partial negative and partial positive charge resulting from a polar bond?

   A. net dipole   **C.** delta minus

   B. dipole   **D.** delta plus   **E.** none of the above

84. Which is true if the ion concentration product of a solution of AgCl is less than the K_{sp}?

   A. Precipitation occurs   **C.** Precipitation does not occur

   B. The ions are insoluble in water   **D.** A and B only

                                                      E. B and C only

85. Which compound produces four ions per formula unit by dissociation when dissolved in water?

    A. Li_3PO_4 **B.** $Ca(NO_3)_2$ **C.** $MgSO_4$ **D.** $(NH_4)_2SO_4$ **E.** $(NH_4)_4Fe(CN)_6$

86. What principle states that the solubility of a gas in a liquid is proportional to the partial pressure of the gas above the liquid?

    A. solubility principle   **C.** colloid principle

    B. Tyndall effect   **D.** Henry's law   **E.** none of the above

87. Which of the following represents the chlorite ion?

    A. ClO_4^- **B.** ClO_3^- **C.** ClO^- **D.** Cl_2O^- **E.** ClO_2^-

88. If the concentration of a KCl solution is 16.0% (m/v), the mass of KCl in 26.0 mL of solution is:

    A. 4.16 grams   **C.** 2.08 grams

    B. 8.32 grams   **D.** 16.0 grams   **E.** 8.0 grams

89. What is molarity?

    A. number of liters of solute per mole of solution

    B. number of moles of solute per liter of solvent

    C. number of grams of solute per liter of solution

    D. number of moles of solute per liter of solution

    E. number of grams of solute per mole of solution

90. What is the term that refers to liquids that do not dissolve in one another and separate into two layers?

    A. soluble   **C.** insoluble

    B. miscible   **D.** immiscible   **E.** none of the above

91. The $[Pb^{2+}]$ of a solution is 1.25×10^{-3} M. Calculate the $[SO_4^{2-}]$ that must be exceeded before $PbSO_4$ can precipitate. (The solubility product of $PbSO_4$ at 25 °C is 1.6×10^{-8})

    A. 1.3×10^{-4} M   **C.** 2.6×10^{-4} M

    B. 5.2×10^{-6} M   **D.** 1.6×10^{-8} M   **E.** 1.3×10^{-5} M

92. Which of the following statements best describes the phrase "like dissolves like"?

    A. A solvent dissolves a solute that has a similar mass

    B. Only homogenous solutions are formed when water dissolves a nonpolar solute

    C. A solvent and a solute with similar intermolecular forces make a solution

    D. Only true solutions are formed when hydrophobic solvents dissolve polar solutes

    E. A solvent and a solute with different intermolecular forces make a solution

93. Calculate the molarity of a solution prepared by dissolving 15.0 g of NH_3 in 250 g of water with a final density of 0.974 g/mL.

    A. 60.0 M   **B.** 3.42 M   **C.** 0.00353 M   **D.** 0.882 M   **E.** 6.80 M

94. What is the term for the general principle that solubility is greatest when the polarity of the solute and solvent are similar?

    A. solute rule   **C.** like dissolves like rule

    B. solvent rule   **D.** polarity rule   **E.** none of the above

95. How many ions are produced in solution by dissociation of one formula unit of $Co(NO_3)_2 \cdot 6H_2O$?

    A. 2   **B.** 3   **C.** 4   **D.** 6   **E.** 9

96. When a solid dissolves, each molecule is removed from the crystal by interaction with the solvent. This process of surrounding each ion with solvent molecules is called:

    A. hemolysis   **C.** crenation

    B. electrolysis   **D.** dilution   **E.** solvation

97. Which of the following represents the bicarbonate ion?

    A. HCO_3^- **B.** $H_2CO_3^{2-}$ **C.** CO_3^- **D.** CO_3^{2-} **E.** HCO_3^{2-}

98. Coca-Cola is carbonated by injection with carbon dioxide gas. Under what conditions is carbon dioxide gas most soluble?

    A. high temperature, high pressure   **C.** low temperature, low pressure

    B. high temperature, low pressure   **D.** low temperature, high pressure

                                        E. none of the above

99. What is the concentration of ^-OH if the concentration of H_3O^+ is 1×10^{-5}M?

$$[H_3O^+] \times [^-OH] = K_w = 1 \times 10^{-14}$$

    A. 1×10^5 **B.** 1×10^9 **C.** 1×10^{-5} **D.** 1×10^{-14} **E.** 1×10^{-9}

100. What is the concentration in mass-volume percent for 13.9 g CaF_2 in 255 mL of solution?

    A. 5.45%   **B.** 0.950%   **C.** 0.180%   **D.** 2.73%   **E.** 0.360%

101. Soft drinks are carbonated by injection with carbon dioxide gas. Under what conditions is carbon dioxide gas least soluble?

    A. high temperature, low pressure   **C.** low temperature, high pressure

    B. high temperature, high pressure   **D.** low temperature, low pressure

                                        E. none of the above

102. Which of the following can be classified as a colloid?

    A. Grape juice   **C.** Pepsi-Cola

    B. Homogenized milk   **D.** Kool-Aid   **E.** Decaf coffee

103. Which ions are the spectator ions in the reaction below?

$$K_2SO_4\,(aq) + Ba(NO_3)_2\,(aq) \rightarrow BaSO_4\,(s) + 2KNO_3\,(aq)?$$

    A. K^+ and SO_4^{2-} **C.** Ba^{2+} and K^+

    B. Ba^{2+} and NO_3^- **D.** Ba^{2+} and SO_4^{2-} **E.** K^+ and NO_3^-

104. A substance represented by a formula written as $M_xLO_y \cdot zH_2O$ is called a:

  A. solvent   **C.** solid hydrate

  B. solute   **D.** colloid   **E.** suspension

105. Which is the correct order for nitrate, nitrite, sulfate and sulfite?

  A. NO_2^-, NO_3^-, SO_4^-, SO_3^- **C.** NO_3^-, NO_2^-, SO_3^-, SO_4^-

  B. NO_3^-, NO_2^-, SO_4^-, SO_3^- **D.** NO_2^-, NO_3^-, SO_3^-, SO_4^-

                                          E. NO_2^-, SO_3^-, NO_3^-, SO_4^-

106. If the solubility of nitrogen in blood is 1.90 cc/100 cc at 1.00 atm, what is the solubility of nitrogen in a scuba diver's blood at a depth of 150 feet where the pressure is 5.55 atm?

  A. 1.90 cc/100 cc   **C.** 0.190 cc/100 cc

  B. 3.80 cc/100 cc   **D.** 0.380 cc/100 cc   **E.** 10.55 cc/100 cc

107. What is the concentration of ^-OH, if the concentration of H_3O^+ is 1×10^{-8} M?

  $[H_3O^+] \times [^-OH] = K_w = 1 \times 10^{-14}$

  A. 1×10^8 **B.** 1×10^6 **C.** 1×10^{-14} **D.** 1×10^{-6} **E.** 1×10^{-8}

108. What volume of 8.50% (m/v) solution contains 50.0 grams of glucose?

  A. 17.0 mL   **B.** 48.0 mL   **C.** 588 mL   **D.** 344 mL   **E.** 96.0 mL

109. What is the solubility of CaF_2 when it is added to a 0.02 M solution of NaF?

  A. Low because $[F^-]$ present in solution inhibits dissociation of CaF_2

  B. High because of the common ion effect

  C. Unaffected by the presence of NaF

  D. Low because less water is available for solvation due to the presence of NaF

  E. High because $[F^-]$ present in solution facilitates dissociation of CaF_2

110. Which of the following illustrates the *like dissolves like* rule for two liquids?

  A. A polar solute is miscible with a polar solvent

  B. A polar solute is immiscible with a nonpolar solvent

  C. A nonpolar solute is miscible with a nonpolar solvent

  D. All of the above

  E. None of the above

111. If X moles of $PbCl_2$ fully dissociate in 1 liter of H_2O, the K_{sp} product is equivalent to:

  A. X^2 **B.** $2X^4$ **C.** $3X^2$ **D.** $2X^3$ **E.** $4X^3$

112. Which of the following concentrations is dependent on temperature?

  A. mole fraction   **C.** mass percent

  B. molarity   **D.** molality

                                E. more than one of the above

113. An ionic compound that strongly attracts atmospheric water is said to be:

  A. immiscible   **C.** diluted

  B. miscible   **D.** hygroscopic   **E.** soluble

114. Hydration involves the:

  A. formation of bonds between the solute and water molecules

  B. breaking of water–water bonds

  C. breaking of water–solute bonds

  D. breaking of solute–solute bonds

  E. both the breaking of water-water bonds and formation of solute-solute bonds

115. Which of the following illustrates the *like dissolves like* rule for two liquids?

  A. A nonpolar solute is miscible with a nonpolar solvent

  B. A nonpolar solvent is miscible with a polar solvent

  C. A polar solute is miscible with a nonpolar solvent

  D. A polar solute is immiscible with a polar solvent

  E. A polar solvent is immiscible with a polar solute

116. With increasing temperature, many solvents expand to occupy greater volumes. What happens to the concentration of a solution made with such a solvent as temperature increases?

  A. Concentration decreases because the solution has a greater ability to dissolve more solute at a higher temperature

  B. Concentration increases because the solution has a greater ability to dissolve more solute at a higher temperature

  C. Concentration of a solution decreases as the volume increases because concentration depends on how much mass is dissolved in a given volume

  D. Concentration of a solution increases as the solute fits into the new spaces between the molecules

  E. Concentration of a solution increases as the volume increases because concentration depends on how much mass is dissolved in a given volume

117. What mass of H_2O is needed to prepare 148 grams of 12.0% (m/m) $KHCO_3$ solution?

  A. 120 g   **B.** 130 g   **C.** 11.3 g   **D.** 17.8 g   **E.** 12.0 g

118. Which of the following is an example of a true solution?

  A. Apple juice   **C.** Homogenized milk

  B. Mayonnaise   **D.** Blood   **E.** Glass of water with ice

119. The *like dissolves like* rule for two liquids is illustrated by which of the following?

  A. A nonpolar solute is immiscible with a nonpolar solvent

  B. A nonpolar solute is miscible with a polar solvent

  C. A polar solute is immiscible with a polar solvent

  D. A polar solute is miscible with a nonpolar solvent

  E. None of the above

120. What is the concentration of Ag in moles/liter if the K_{sp} for AgCl is A, and the concentration Cl^- in a container is B molar?

    A. A moles/liter   **C.** A/B moles/liter

    B. B moles/liter   **D.** B or C   **E.** none of the above

121. In the reaction KHS (*aq*) + HCl (*aq*) → KCl (*aq*) + H_2S (*g*), which ions are the spectator ions?

    A. H^+ and HS^- **B.** K^+ and HS^- **C.** K^+ and Cl^- **D.** K^+ and H^+ **E.** HS^- and Cl^-

122. A supersaturated solution:

    A. contains a dissolved solute in equilibrium with an undissolved solid

    B. will rapidly precipitate if a seed crystal is added

    C. contains as much solvent as it can hold

    D. contains no double bonds

    E. none of the above

123. Apply the *like dissolves like* rule to predict which of the following liquids is miscible with water.

    A. methyl ethyl ketone, C_4H_8O **C.** formic acid, $HCHO_2$

    B. glycerin, $C_3H_5(OH)_3$ **D.** all of the above

                                       E. none of the above

124. The hydration number of an ion is the number of:

    A. water molecules bonded to an ion in an aqueous solution

    B. water molecules required to dissolve one mole of ions

    C. ions bonded to one mole of water molecules

    D. ions dissolved in one liter of an aqueous solution

    E. water molecules required to dissolve the compound

125. How many grams of sucrose are in 5.0 liters of sugar water that has a concentration of 0.50 grams per liter of solution?

    A. 0.5 g   **B.** 5.0 g   **C.** 2.5 g   **D.** 1.0 g   **E.** 1.5 g

126. What mass of NaOH is contained in 75.0 mL of a 5.0% (m/v) NaOH solution?

    A. 6.50 g   **B.** 15.0 g   **C.** 7.50 g   **D.** 0.65 g   **E.** 3.75 g

127. Apply the like dissolves like rule to predict which of the following liquids is miscible with water.

    A. carbon tetrachloride, CCl_4 **C.** ethanol, C_2H_5OH

    B. toluene, C_7H_8 **D.** all of the above   **E.** none of the above

128. A water solution of sodium chloride is a good conductor of electricity. Therefore, table salt is classified as a(n):

    A. non–electrolyte   **C.** weak electrolyte

    B. semi–electrolyte   **D.** strong electrolyte   **E.** strong ionic compound

129. Which substance does not produce ions when dissolved in water?

A. manganese (II) nitrate   C. CH_2O

B. CsCN   D. KClO   E. NaHS

130. Apply the *like dissolves like* rule to predict which of the liquids is immiscible in water.

A. ethanol, CH_3CH_2OH C. acetic acid, CH_3COOH

B. acetone, C_3H_6O D. all of the above

     E. none of the above

131. Which of the following is/are a strong electrolytes?

     I. salts   II. strong bases   III. weak acids

A. I only   C. III only

B. I and II only   D. I, II and III   E. I and III only

132. How are intermolecular forces and solubility related?

A. Solubility is a measure of how weak the intermolecular forces in the solute are

B. Solubility is a measure of how strong a solvent's intermolecular forces are

C. Solubility depends on the solute's ability to overcome the intermolecular forces in the solvent

D. Solubility depends on the solvent's ability to overcome the intermolecular forces in a solid

E. None of the above

133. Calculate the mass percent of a solution prepared by dissolving 17.2 g of NaCl in 149 g of water:

A. 10.3%   B. 0.103%   C. 12.4%   D. 6.45%   E. 16.9%

134. Apply the *like dissolves like* rule to predict which of the following liquids is miscible with liquid bromine (Br_2)

A. benzene (C_6H_6)   C. carbon tetrachloride (CCl_4)

B. hexane (C_6H_{14})   D. none of the above

     E. all of the above

135. What is the concentration of I^- ions in a 0.40 M solution of magnesium iodide?

A. 0.05 M   B. 0.80 M   C. 0.60 M   D. 0.20 M   E. 0.40 M

136. Calculate the $[N_2]$ gas in water, if N_2 gas at a partial pressure above the water is 0.826 atm and Henry's Law constant for N_2 in water $= 6.8 \times 10^{-4}$ mol/L-atm.

A. 5.6×10^{-4} M   C. 3.2×10^3 M

B. 7.2×10^{-3} M   D. 0.61 M   E. 7.2×10^{-5} M

137. What was the molarity of the original solution if a 20.0 mL sample of a $CuSO_4$ solution was dried and 0.967 g of copper (II) sulfate remained?

A. 0.606 M   B. 0.570 M   C. 0.253 M   D. 0.303 M   E. 0.909 M

Use the following data to answer questions **138** through **141**.

$$K_{sp} \quad PbCl_2 = 1.0 \times 10^{-5}$$
$$K_{sp} \quad AgCl = 1.0 \times 10^{-10}$$
$$K_{sp} \quad PbCO_3 = 1.0 \times 10^{-15}$$

138. Comparing equal volumes of saturated solutions for $PbCl_2$ and $AgCl$, which solution contains a greater concentration of Cl^-?

    I. $PbCl_2$ II. $AgCl$ III. Both have the same concentration of Cl^-

A. I only   **B.** II only   **C.** III only   **D.** I, II and III   **E.** I and II only

139. If the K_{sp} of $MgSO_4$ is 4×10^{-5}, would a precipitate form if 1 liter of 0.03 M $Mg(NO_3)_2$ were mixed with 2 liters of 0.06 M K_2SO_4? (Assume complete dissociation of solutions.)

    A. Yes
    B. No, because the K_{sp} value for $MgSO_4$ is not exceeded
    C. No, because the solution does not contain $MgSO_4$
    D. Not enough data is given
    E. No, because the K_{sp} value for $MgSO_4$ is exceeded

140. Consider a saturated solution of $PbCl_2$. The addition of NaCl would:

    A. decrease $[Pb^{2+}]$ **C.** increase the precipitation of $PbCl_2$
    B. have no affect on the precipitation of $PbCl_2$ **D.** A and B
                                                    E. A and C

141. What occurs when $AgNO_3$ is added to a saturated solution of $PbCl_2$?

    I. AgCl precipitates
    II. $Pb(NO_3)_2$ forms a white precipitate
    III. More $PbCl_2$ forms

A. I only   **B.** II only   **C.** III only   **D.** I, II and III   **E.** I and II only

142. If the solubility of carbon dioxide in a bottle of champagne is 1.45 g per liter at 1.00 atmosphere, what is the solubility of carbon dioxide at 10.0 atmospheres?

    A. 3.40 g/L   **B.** 1.25 g/L   **C.** 0.720 g/L   **D.** 0.145 g/L   **E.** 14.5 g/L

143. Which of the following illustrates the *like dissolves like* rule for a solid solute in a liquid solvent?

    I. A nonpolar compound is soluble in a nonpolar solvent
    II. A polar compound is soluble in a polar solvent
    III. An ionic compound is soluble in a polar solvent

A. I only   **B.** II only   **C.** I and II only   **D.** I, II and III   **E.** None of the above

144. Potassium oxide contains:

    A. ionic bonds and is a weak electrolyte   **C.** covalent bonds and is a non-electrolyte
    B. ionic bonds and is a strong electrolyte   **D.** covalent bonds and is a strong electrolyte
                                                        E. hydrogen bonds and is a non-electrolyte

145. It is determined that 9.86×10^{-3} g of a contaminant is present in 4865 g of a particular solution. What is the concentration of the contaminant in ppm (m/m)?

    A. 3.40 ppm   **B.** 1.50 ppm   **C.** 4.06 ppm   **D.** 2.03 ppm   **E.** 1.70 ppm

146. Which of the following illustrates the *like dissolves like* rule for a solid solute in a liquid solvent?

    A. An ionic compound is soluble in a nonpolar solvent

    B. A nonpolar compound is soluble in a polar solvent   **D.** All of the above

    C. A polar compound is soluble in a nonpolar solvent   **E.** None of the above

147. What happens when the molecule-to-molecule attractions in the solute are comparable to those in the solvent?

    A. The material has only limited solubility in the solvent

    B. The solution will become saturated

    C. The solute can have infinite solubility in the solvent

    D. The solute does not dissolve in the solvent

    E. None of the above

148. A water solution of the table sugar sucrose does not conduct electricity. Due to this property, sucrose is classified as:

    A. semi-electrolyte   **C.** strong electrolyte

    B. non-electrolyte   **D.** weak electrolyte

                          E. neither a strong nor weak electrolyte

149. Calculate the molarity of a 9.55 molal solution of methanol (CH_3OH) with a density of 0.937 g/mL:

    A. 0.155 M   **B.** 23.5 M   **C.** 6.86 M   **D.** 68.6 M   **E.** 2.35 M

150. From the *like dissolves like* rule, predict which of the following vitamins is soluble in water.

    A. α-tocopherol ($C_{29}H_{50}O_2$)   **C.** ascorbic acid ($C_6H_8O_6$)

    B. calciferol ($C_{27}H_{44}O$)   **D.** retinol ($C_{20}H_{30}O$)   **E.** none of the above

151. The equation for the reaction $BaCl_2\,(aq) + K_2CrO_4\,(aq) \rightarrow BaCrO_4\,(s) + KCl\,(aq)$ can be written as an ionic equation. In the ionic equation, the spectator ions are:

    A. K^+ and Cl^- **C.** Ba^{2+} and K^+

    B. B^{2+} and CrO_4^{2-} **D.** K^+ and CrO_4^{2-} **E.** Cl^- and CrO_4^{2-}

152. Which solution is the least concentrated? Each choice refers to the same solute and solvent.

    A. 2.4 g solute in 2 mL solution   **C.** 20 g solute in 50 mL solution

    B. 2.4 g solute in 5 mL solution   **D.** 30 g solute in 150 mL solution

                                E. 50 g solute in 175 mL solution

153. Which of the following is true of a colloid?

    A. Dispersed particles are less than 1 nm in diameter

    B. Dispersed particles demonstrate the Tyndall effect

    C. Dispersed particles pass through biological membranes

    D. All of the above

    E. None of the above

154. Hydrochloric acid contains:

    A. ionic bonds and is a strong electrolyte   **C.** covalent bonds and is a strong electrolyte

    B. hydrogen bonds and is a weak electrolyte   **D.** ionic bonds and is a non-electrolyte

    E. covalent bonds and is a non-electrolyte

155. Apply the *like dissolves like* rule to predict which of the following vitamins is insoluble in water.

    A. niacinamide ($C_6H_6N_2O$)   **C.** retinol ($C_{20}H_{30}O$)

    B. pyridoxine ($C_8H_{11}NO_3$)   **D.** thiamine ($C_{12}H_{17}N_4OS$)

    E. cyanocobalamin ($C_{63}H_{88}CoN_{14}O_{14}P$)

156. Molarity could be used as a conversion factor between:

    A. grams of solute and volume of solution   **C.** grams of solute and moles of solvent

    B. moles of solute and kilograms of solution   **D.** moles of solute and volume of solution

    E. grams of solute and kilograms of solution

157. Which of the following might have the best solubility in water?

    A. CH_3CH_3 **B.** CH_3OH **C.** Cl_2 **D.** O_2 **E.** none of the above

158. If 10.0 mL of blood plasma has a mass of 10.279 g and contains 0.870 g of protein, what is the mass/mass percent concentration of protein in the blood plasma?

    A. 8.70%   **B.** 32.1%   **C.** 0.870%   **D.** 97.3%   **E.** 8.46%

159. At 20 °C, a one-liter sample of pure water has a vapor pressure of 17.5 torr. If 5 g of NaCl is added to the sample, the vapor pressure of the water:

    A. equals the vapor pressure of the added NaCl

    B. remain unchanged at 17.5 torr   **D.** decreases

    C. increases   **E.** increases to the square root of solute added

160. Which of the following is an example of a weak electrolyte?

    A. H_2SO_4 **B.** HNO_3 **C.** $HC_2H_3O_2$ **D.** $MgCl_2$ **E.** Na_2CO_3

161. If 25.0 mL of urine has a mass of 25.725 g and contains 1.929 g of solute, what is the mass/mass percent concentration of solute in the urine sample?

    A. 13.34%   **B.** 7.72%   **C.** 7.499%   **D.** 3.887%   **E.** 97.2%

162. Which information is necessary to determine the molarity of a solution if the chemical formula of the solute is known?

    A. Mass of the solute dissolved and the volume of the solvent added

    B. Molar mass of both the solute and the solvent used

    C. Only the volume of the solvent used

    D. Only the mass of the solute dissolved

    E. Mass of the solute dissolved and the final volume of the solution

163. In the reaction between aqueous silver nitrate and aqueous potassium chromate, what is the identity of the soluble substance that is formed?

    A. potassium nitrate

    B. potassium chromate

    C. silver nitrate

    D. silver chromate

    E. no soluble substance is formed

164. If 25.0 mL of seawater has a mass of 25.895 g and contains 1.295 g of solute, what is the mass/mass percent concentration of solute in the seawater sample?

    A. 5.18%   **B.** 20.00%   **C.** 3.862%   **D.** 5.001%   **E.** 96.5%

165. When salt A is dissolved into water to form a 1 molar unsaturated solution, the temperature of the solution decreases. Under these conditions, which statement is accurate when salt A is dissolved in water?

    A. $\Delta H°$ and $\Delta G°$ are positive

    B. $\Delta H°$ is positive and $\Delta G°$ is negative

    C. $\Delta H°$ is negative and $\Delta G°$ is positive

    D. $\Delta H°$ and $\Delta G°$ are negative

    E. $\Delta H°$, $\Delta S°$ and $\Delta G°$ are positive

166. Under which conditions is the expected solubility of oxygen gas in water the highest?

    A. High temperature and high O_2 pressure above the solution

    B. Low temperature and low O_2 pressure above the solution

    C. Low temperature and high O_2 pressure above the solution

    D. High temperature and low O_2 pressure above the solution

    E. The O_2 solubility is independent of temperature and pressure

167. How many grams of H_3PO_4 are needed to make 175 mL of a 0.175 M H_3PO_4 solution?

    A. 3.00 g   **B.** 5.08 g   **C.** 0.346 g   **D.** 0.764 g   **E.** 2.54 g

168. Which of the following is NOT a unit factor related to a 15.0% aqueous solution of potassium iodide (KI)?

    A. 100 g solution / 85.0 g water

    B. 85.0 g water / 15.0 g KI

    C. 85.0 g water / 100 g solution

    D. 15.0 g KI / 85.0 g water

    E. 15.0 g KI / 100 g water

169. At room temperature, barium hydroxide ($Ba(OH)_2$) is dissolved in pure water. From the equilibrium concentrations of Ba^+ and OH^- ions, which expressions could be used to find the solubility product for barium hydroxide?

A. $K_{sp} = [Ba^{2+}][OH^-]^2$ **C.** $K_{sp} = [Ba^{2+}][OH^-]$

B. $K_{sp} = 2[Ba^{2+}][OH^-]^2$ **D.** $K_{sp} = [Ba^{2+}]2[OH^-]$ **E.** $K_{sp} = 2[Ba^{2+}][OH^-]$

170. Which of the following is an example of a nonelectrolyte?

A. Na_2SO_4 **B.** $NaCl$ **C.** $MgCl_2$ **D.** $HC_2H_3O_2$ **E.** $C_{12}H_{22}O_{11}$

171. What is the mass of a 10.0% blood plasma sample that contains 2.50g of dissolved solute?

A. 21.5 g   **B.** 25.0 g   **C.** 0.215 g   **D.** 0.430 g   **E.** 12.5 g

172. Which of the following would likely form micelles in an aqueous solution?

A. dodecanoic acid   **C.** glucose

B. glutamic acid   **D.** hexane   **E.** none of the above

173. The heat of a solution measures the energy absorbed from:

    I. formation of solvent-solute bonds
    II. breaking of solute-solute bonds
    III. breaking of solvent-solvent bonds

A. I only   **C.** III only

B. II only   **D.** I, II and III   **E.** I and II only

174. What is the mass of a 7.50% urine sample that contains 122 g of dissolved solute?

A. 1550 g   **C.** 9.35 g

B. 935 g   **D.** 15.5 g   **E.** 1630 g

175. Which statement below is true?

A. All bases are strong electrolytes and ionize completely when dissolved in water
B. All salts are strong electrolytes and dissociate completely when dissolved in water
C. All acids are strong electrolytes and ionize completely when dissolved in water
D. All bases are weak electrolytes and ionize completely when dissolved in water
E. All salts are weak electrolytes and ionize partially when dissolved in water

176. What is the molarity of KCl in seawater, if KCl is 12.5% (m/m) and the density of seawater is 1.06 g/mL?

A. 1.78 M   **C.** 2.78 M

B. 17.8 M   **D.** 0.845 M   **E.** 27.8 M

177. What is the molarity of a glucose solution that contains 10.0 g of $C_6H_{12}O_6$ (180.18 g/mol) dissolved in 100.0 mL of solution?

A. 1.80 M   **C.** 0.0555 M

B. 0.555 M   **D.** 0.00555 M   **E.** 18.0 M

178. Why does the reaction proceed if, when solid potassium chloride is dissolved in H_2O, the energy of the bonds formed is less than the energy of the bonds broken?

    A. The electronegativity of the H_2O increases from interaction with potassium and chloride ions
    B. The reaction does not take place under standard conditions
    C. The decreased disorder due to mixing decreases entropy within the system
    D. Remaining potassium chloride which does not dissolve offsets the portion that dissolves
    E. The increased disorder due to mixing increases entropy within the system

179. Which statement supports the fact that calcium fluoride is much less soluble in water than sodium fluoride?

    I. calcium fluoride is not used in toothpaste
    II. calcium fluoride is not used to fluoridate city water supplies
    III. sodium fluoride is not used to fluoridate city water supplies

    A. I only   **C.** III only
    B. II only   **D.** I and II only   **E.** I, II and III

180. What is the molarity of a sucrose solution that contains 10.0 g of $C_{12}H_{22}O_{11}$ (342.34 g/mol) dissolved in 100.0 mL of solution?

    A. 0.292 M   **B.** 3.33 M   **C.** 0.00292 M   **D.** 0.0292 M   **E.** 33.3 M

181. What is the molar concentration of Ca^{2+} (*aq*) in a solution that is prepared by mixing 15 mL of a 0.02 M $CaCl_2$ (*aq*) solution with a 10 mL of a 0.04 M $CaSO_4$ (*aq*) solution?

    A. 0.014 M   **B.** 0.020 M   **C.** 0.028 M   **D.** 0.042 M   **E.** 0.046 M

182. Which is a correctly balanced hydration equation for the hydration of Na_2SO_4?

    A. $Na_2SO_4 (s) \xrightarrow{H_2O} Na^+ (aq) + 2SO_4^{2-} (aq)$

    B. $Na_2SO_4 (s) \xrightarrow{H_2O} 2Na^{2+} (aq) + S^{2-} (aq) + O_4^{2-} (aq)$

    C. $Na_2SO_4 (s) \xrightarrow{H_2O} Na_2^{2+} (aq) + SO_4^{2-} (aq)$

    D. $Na_2SO_4 (s) \xrightarrow{H_2O} 2Na^+ (aq) + SO_4^{2-} (aq)$

    E. $Na_2SO_4 (s) \xrightarrow{H_2O} 2Na^{2+} (aq) + S^{2-} (aq) + SO_4^{2-} (aq) + O_4^{2-} (aq)$

183. What is the molarity of a hydrochloric acid solution prepared by diluting 250.0 mL of 6.00 M HCl to a total volume of 2.50 L?

    A. 2.50 M   **B.** 0.600 M   **C.** 0.250 M   **D.** 0.0600 M   **E.** 6.00 M

184. What happens to DNA when placed into an aqueous solution at physiological pH?

    A. Individual DNA molecules repel each other due to presence of positive charges
    B. DNA molecules bind to negatively charged proteins
    C. Individual DNA molecules attract each other due to presence of positive and negative charges
    D. Individual DNA molecules repel each other due to presence of negative charges
    E. None of the above

185. What is the molarity of a solution prepared by dissolving 3.50 mol NaCl in enough water to make 1.50 L of solution?

A. 0.429 M   **B.** 2.33 M   **C.** 5.25 M   **D.** 87.8 M   **E.** 137 M

186. What is the molarity of a hydrochloric acid solution prepared by diluting 200.0 mL of 0.500 M HCl to a total volume of 1.00 L?

A. 0.250 M   **B.** 1.00 M   **C.** 0.100 M   **D.** 0.200 M   **E.** 2.50 M

187. What does negative heat of solution indicate about solute-solvent bonds as compared to solute-solute bonds and solvent-solvent bonds?

  A. Solute-solute and solute-solvent bond strengths are greater than solvent-solvent bond strength
  B. Heat of solution does not support conclusion about bond strength
  C. Solute-solute and solvent-solvent bonds are stronger than solute-solvent bonds
  D. Solute-solute and solvent-solvent bond strengths are equal to solute-solvent bond strength
  E. Solute-solute and solvent-solvent bonds are weaker than solute-solvent bonds

188. What is the formula of the solid formed when aqueous barium chloride is mixed with aqueous potassium chromate?

  A. K_2CrO_4 **B.** K_2Ba **C.** KCl   **D.** $BaCrO_4$ **E.** $BaCl_2$

189. What is the molarity of a hydrochloric acid solution prepared by diluting 500.0 mL of 1.00 M HCl to a total volume of 2.50 L?

  A. 2.00 M   **B.** 1.00 M   **C.** 2.50 M   **D.** 0.100 M   **E.** 0.200 M

190. Why might sodium carbonate (washing soda, Na_2CO_3) be added to hard water for cleaning?

  A. The soap gets softer due to the added ions
  B. The ions solubilize the soap due to ion-ion intermolecular attraction, which improves the cleaning ability
  C. The hard ions in the water are more attracted to the carbonate ions -2 charge
  D. The hard ions are dissolved by the added sodium ions
  E. None of the above

191. What mass of KOH is needed to produce 22.0 mL of 0.576 M solution?

  A. 2.20 g   **B.** 0.711 g   **C.** 1.48 g   **D.** 0.443 g   **E.** 4.43 g

192. What volume of 12 M acid must be diluted with distilled water to prepare 5.0 L of 0.10 M acid?

  A. 42 mL   **B.** 60 mL   **C.** 0.042 mL   **D.** 6 mL   **E.** 420 mL

193. What is the %v/v concentration of red wine that contains 15 mL of ethyl alcohol in 200 mL?

  A. 0.60 %v/v   **C.** 0.075 %v/v
  B. 0.060 %v/v   **D.** 6.0 %v/v   **E.** 7.5 %v/v

194. If 29.4 g of LiOH is dissolved in water to make 985 mL of solution, what is the molarity of the LiOH solution?

    A. 1.25 M   **B.** 2.29 M   **C.** 0.986 M   **D.** 0.478 M   **E.** 0.229 M

195. What volume of 0.255 M hydrochloric acid reacts completely with 0.400 g of sodium hydrogen carbonate, $NaHCO_3$ (84.01 g/mol) ?

$$NaHCO_3\,(s) + HCl\,(aq) \rightarrow NaCl\,(aq) + H_2O\,(l) + CO_2\,(g)$$

    A. 121 mL   **B.** 53.6 mL   **C.** 18.7 mL   **D.** 4.76 mL   **E.** 132 mL

196. All of the statements about molarity are correct EXCEPT:

    A. volume = moles/molarity

    B. moles = molarity × volume

    C. molarity of a diluted solution is less than the molarity of the original solution

    D. abbreviation is M

    E. interpretation of the symbol is "moles of solute per mole of solvent"

197. What is the v/v% concentration of a solution made by adding 25 mL of acetone to 75 mL of water?

    A. 33 % v/v   **B.** 0.33 % v/v   **C.** 25 % v/v   **D.** 0.25 % v/v   **E.** 3.3 % v/v

198. What volume of 0.115 M hydrochloric acid reacts completely with 0.125 g of sodium carbonate, Na_2CO_3 (105.99 g/mol)?

$$Na_2CO_3\,(s) + 2\,HCl\,(aq) \rightarrow CO_2\,(g) + H_2O\,(l) + 2\,NaCl\,(aq)$$

    A. 20.5 mL   **B.** 41.0 mL   **C.** 9.75 mL   **D.** 10.3 mL   **E.** 97.5 mL

199. What mass of $CaCl_2$ is required to prepare 3.20 L of 0.850 M $CaCl_2$ solution?

    A. 75.5 g   **B.** 160 g   **C.** 320 g   **D.** 302 g   **E.** 151 g

200. What is the net ionic equation for the reaction between HNO_3 and Na_2SO_3?

    A. $H_2O + SO_2\,(g) \rightarrow H^+\,(aq) + HSO_3^-\,(aq)$

    B. $2H^+\,(aq) + SO_3^{2-}\,(aq) \rightarrow H_2O + SO_2\,(g)$

    C. $HNO_3\,(aq) + Na_2SO_3\,(aq) \rightarrow H_2O + SO_2\,(g) + NO_3^-\,(aq)$

    D. $H_2SO_3\,(aq) \rightarrow H_2O + SO_2\,(g)$

    E. $2H^+\,(aq) + Na_2SO_3\,(aq) \rightarrow 2Na^+\,(aq) + H_2O + SO_2\,(g)$

201. What solution conditions are required for a protein to be a positively charged macroion?

    A. pH of solution is less than the protein's pI and ionic strength is low

    B. pH of solution is greater than the protein's pI and ionic strength is low

    C. pH of solution is less than the protein's pI

    D. pH of solution is greater than the protein's pI

    E. None of the above

202. Which of the following symbolizes a liquid in a chemical equation?

    A. (*aq*)   **B.** (*g*)   **C.** (*l*)   **D.** (*s*)   **E.** none of the above

203. How many grams of $FeSO_4$ are present in a 20.0 mL sample of a 0.500 M solution?

    A. 1.52 g   **B.** 0.760 g   **C.** 60.4 g   **D.** 6.04 g   **E.** 7.60 g

204. Which is the net ionic equation for the reaction that takes place when $HC_2H_3O_2$ (*aq*) is added to NH_3 (*aq*)?

    A. $HC_2H_3O_2$ (*aq*) + OH^- (*aq*) → $C_2H_3O_2^-$ (*aq*) + H_2O (*l*)
    B. H^+ (*aq*) + NH_4OH (*aq*) → NH_4^+ (*aq*) + H_2O (*l*)
    C. $HC_2H_3O_2$ (*aq*) + NH_4OH (*aq*) → H_2O (*l*) + NH_4ClO_4 (*aq*)
    D. H^+ (*aq*) + OH^- (*aq*) → H_2O (*l*)
    E. $HC_2H_3O_2$ (*aq*) + NH_3 (*aq*) → NH_4^+ (*aq*) + $C_2H_3O_2^-$ (*aq*)

205. Which of the following statements best describes what is happening in a water softening unit?

    A. The sodium is removed from the water, making the water interact less with the soap molecules
    B. The ions in the water softener are softened by chemically bonding with sodium
    C. The hard ions are all trapped in the softener, which filters out all the ions
    D. The hard ions in water are exchanged for ions that do not interact as strongly with soaps
    E. None of the above

206. Which of the following explains why bubbles form on the inside of a pan of water when the pan of water is heated?

    A. As temperature increases, the vapor pressure increases
    B. As temperature increases, the atmospheric pressure decreases
    C. As temperature increases, the solubility of air decreases
    D. As temperature increases, the kinetic energy decreases
    E. None of the above

207. The density of a $NaNO_3$ solution is 1.24 g/mL. What is the molarity of a 25.0% (m/m) $NaNO_3$ solution?

    A. 15.3 M   **B.** 8.41 M   **C.** 0.760 M   **D.** 3.65 M   **E.** 7.60 M

208. Which is the net ionic equation for the reaction when HNO_3 (*aq*) is added to Fe_2O_3 (*s*)?

    A. $6H^+$ (*aq*) + Fe_2O_3 (*s*) → $2Fe^{3+}$ (*aq*) + $3H_2O$ (*l*)
    B. HNO_3 (*aq*) + OH^- (*s*) → NO_3^- (*aq*) + H_2O (*l*)
    C. H^+ (*aq*) + OH^- (*aq*) → H_2O (*l*)
    D. HNO_3 (*aq*) + Fe_2O_3 (*s*) → $Fe(NO_3)_3$ (*aq*) + H_2O (*l*)
    E. HNO_3 (*aq*) + Fe^{3+} (*aq*) → $Fe(NO_3)_3$ (*aq*) + H^+ (*aq*)

209. How many grams of NaOH are needed to make 750 mL of a 2.5% (w/v) solution?

    A. 2.4 g   **B.** 7.5 g   **C.** 19 g   **D.** 15 g   **E.** 1.5 g

Chapter 5.   ACIDS AND BASES

1. Which of the following is a strong acid?

   A. H_3PO_4 (aq) (~1% ionized)

   B. H_2SO_3 (aq) (~1% ionized)

   C. HNO_2 (aq) (~1% ionized)

   D. all of the above

   E. none of the above

2. Which of the following properties is NOT characteristic of an acid?

   A. Is neutralized by a base

   B. Has a slippery feel

   C. Produces H^+ in water

   D. Has a sour taste

   E. Has a pH reading less than 7

3. When NH_3 is diluted in H_2O, the reaction below occurs. What is the concentration of the ammonium ion, if the concentration of ammonia in a solution is 0.4 M and the pH = 10?

   $$NH_3 + H_2O \rightleftharpoons NH_4^+ + OH^- \qquad K_b = 2 \times 10^{-5}$$

   A. 0.01 M   B. 0.02 M   C. 0.08 M   D. 0.04 M   E. 0.10 M

4. Which of the following is an example of an Arrhenius base?

   A. $NaOH$ (aq)

   B. $Al(OH)_3$ (s)

   C. $Ca(OH)_2$ (aq)

   D. all of the above

   E. None of the above

5. Which of the following substances is produced during an acid/base (i.e. neutralization) reaction?

   A. NaOH   B. CO_2 C. H_2O D. H_2 E. NaCl

6. What atom in the ammonium ion (NH_4^+) bears the positive charge?

   A. Hydrogen atom

   B. Nitrogen atom

   C. Neither atom bears a positive charge

   D. Nitrogen and hydrogen equally share the positive charge

   E. The spectator ion holds the positive charge

7. When dissolved in water, the Arrhenius acid-bases KOH, H_2SO_4 and HNO_3 are, respectively:

   A. base, acid and base

   B. base, base and acid

   C. base, acid and acid

   D. acid, base and base

   E. acid, acid and base

8. What are the predicted products from the following neutralization reaction?

   $$HCl\ (aq) + NH_4OH\ (aq) \rightarrow$$

   A. NH_4Cl and H_2O

   B. NH_4Cl and O_2

   C. NH_3Cl and H_2O

   D. NH_3Cl and O_2

   E. No reaction

9. Which of the following is a weak acid?

   A. OH^- B. NH_3 C. HNO_3 D. HF   E. HI

---

10. A Brønsted-Lowry base is a(n):

A. electron acceptor

B. proton acceptor

C. electron donor

D. proton donor

E. both proton donor and electron acceptor

11. Which of the following pairs of 0.1 M solutions react to form a precipitate?

A. KOH and $Ba(NO_3)_2$

B. NaI and KBr

C. K_2SO_4 and CsI

D. $NiBr_2$ and $AgNO_3$

E. all of the above

12. What are products from the neutralization reaction $HC_2H_3O_2$ *(aq)* + $Ca(OH)_2$ *(aq)* → ?

A. $Ca(C_2H_3O_2)_2$ and H_2

B. $Ca(HCO_3)_2$ and H_2O

C. $Ca(HCO_3)_2$ and H_2

D. $CaCO_3$ and H_2O

E. $Ca(C_2H_3O_2)_2$ and H_2O

13. What is the conjugate base of water?

A. OH^- *(aq)*   B. H^+ *(aq)*   C. H_2O *(l)*   D. H_3O^+ *(aq)*   E. O^{2-} *(aq)*

14. Identify the acid or base for each substance in the reaction: $HSO_4^- + H_2O \rightleftharpoons OH^- + H_2SO_4$

A. HSO_4^- acts as a base, H_2O acts as a base, OH^- acts as a base, H_2SO_4 acts as an acid

B. HSO_4^- acts as an acid, H_2O acts as a base, OH^- acts as a base, H_2SO_4 acts as an acid

C. HSO_4^- acts as a base, H_2O acts as an acid, OH^- acts as an acid, H_2SO_4 acts as a base

D. HSO_4^- acts as an acid, H_2O acts as a base, OH^- acts as an acid, H_2SO_4 acts as a base

E. HSO_4^- acts as a base, H_2O acts as an acid, OH^- acts as a base, H_2SO_4 acts as an acid

15. Which of the following could NOT be a Brønsted-Lowry acid?

A. CN^- B. HS^- C. HF   D. $HC_2H_3O_2$ E. H_2SO_4

16. Which of the following indicators is yellow in an acidic solution and blue in a basic solution?

A. methyl red

B. phenolphthalein

C. bromthymol blue

D. all of the above

E. none of the above

17. Which of the following does NOT act as a Brønsted-Lowry acid?

A. CO_3^{2-} B. HS^- C. HSO_4^- D. H_2O E. H_2SO_4

Questions **18-22** are based on the following titration graph.

Assume that the unknown acid is completely titrated with NaOH.

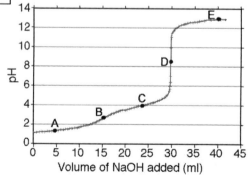

18. The unknown acid shown in the graph must be:

A. monoprotic acid

B. diprotic acid

C. triprotic acid

D. weak acid

E. none of the above

19. The pK_{a2} for this acid is located at point:

   A. A   **B.** B   **C.** C   **D.** D   **E.** E

20. At which point does the acid exist at 50% fully protonated and 50% singly deprotonated?

   A. A   **B.** B   **C.** C   **D.** D   **E.** E

21. At which point is the acid 100% singly deprotonated?

   A. A   **B.** B   **C.** C   **D.** D   **E.** E

22. Which points are the best buffer regions?

   A. A and B   **C.** B and D

   B. A and C   **D.** C and B   **E.** C and D

23. What is the term for a solution that is a good conductor of electricity?

   A. strong electrolyte   **C.** non-electrolyte

   B. weak electrolyte   **D.** aqueous electrolyte   **E.** none of the above

24. Which statement concerning the Arrhenius acid-base theory is NOT correct?

   A. Neutralization reactions produce H_2O plus a salt

   B. Acid-base reactions must take place in aqueous solution

   C. Arrhenius acids produce H^+ in H_2O solution

   D. Arrhenius bases produce OH^- in H_2O solution

   E. All are correct

25. Sodium hydroxide is a very strong base. If a concentrated solution of NaOH spills on a latex glove, it feels like water. Why is it that if the solution were to splash directly on a person's skin, it feels very slippery?

   A. As a liquid, NaOH is slippery, but this cannot be detected through a latex glove because of the friction between the latex surfaces

   B. NaOH destroys skin cells on contact and the remnants of skin cells feel slippery because the cells still contain natural oils

   C. NaOH lifts oil directly out of the skin cells and the extruded oil causes the slippery sensation

   D. NaOH reacts with skin oils, transforming them into soap

   E. NaOH, as a liquid, causes the skin to feel slippery from low viscosity

26. Which of the following pairs of substances could NOT function as a buffer system in aqueous solution?

   A. $NaHCO_3$ and Na_2CO_3 **C.** $HClO_4$ and $KClO_4$

   B. HF and LiF   **D.** HNO_2 and $NaNO_2$

                                            E. none could function as a buffer

27. Which of the following is an example of an Arrhenius acid?

   A. HCl *(aq)*   **C.** HNO_3 *(aq)*

   B. H_2SO_4 *(aq)*   **D.** None of the above   **E.** All of the above

28. Which of the following properties is NOT characteristic of a base?

A. Has a slippery feel

B. Is neutralized by an acid

C. Has a bitter taste

D. Produces H^+ in water

E. All of the above

29. In the expression HCl (*aq*) $\rightleftharpoons H^+ + Cl^-$, Cl is a:

A. weak conjugate base

B. strong conjugate base

C. weak conjugate acid

D. strong conjugate acid

E. strong conjugate base and weak conjugate acid

30. What is the pH of an aqueous solution if the $[H^+] = 0.1$ M?

A. 0   B. 1   C. 2   D. 10   E. 13

31. Which of the following is the strongest weak acid?

A. H_2CO_3 (Ka = 4.3×10^{-7})

B. HNO_2 (Ka = 4.0×10^{-4})

C. HCN   (Ka = 6.2×10^{-10})

D. HClO   (Ka = 3.0×10^{-8})

E. HF   (Ka = 6.8×10^{-4})

32. Which of the following statements describes a neutral solution?

A. $[H_3O^+] / [OH^-] = 1 \times 10^{-14}$

B. $[H_3O^+] / [OH^-] = 1$

C. $[H_3O^+] < [OH^-]$

D. $[H_3O^+] > [OH^-]$

E. $[H_3O^+] \times [OH^-] \neq 1 \times 10^{-14}$

33. Each of the following can act like a Brønsted-Lowry acid and base, EXCEPT:

A. H_2O B. HCO_3^- C. $H_2PO_4^-$ D. NH_4^+ E. HS^-

34. If a light bulb in a conductivity apparatus glows brightly when testing a solution, which of the following must be true about the solution?

A. It is highly reactive

B. It is slightly reactive

C. It is highly ionized

D. It is slightly ionized

E. It is not an electrolyte

35. What is the pH of a solution that has a $[H_3O^+] = 1.2 \times 10^{-3}$?

A. 1.40   B. 2.92   C. 6.20   D. 8.80   E. 11.34

36. Which compound is both a Lewis base and a Brønsted-Lowry base?

A. NH_3 B. NO_3 C. $Ca(OH)_2$ D. BH_3 E. NH_4^+

37. Which of the following explains why distilled H_2O is neutral?

A. $[H^+] = [OH^-]$

B. Distilled H_2O has no OH^-

C. Distilled H_2O has no H^+

D. Distilled H_2O has no ions

E. None of the above

38. If the concentration of H_3O^+ is 3.5×10^{-3} M, what is the molar concentration of OH^-?

   A. 3.5×10^{-10} **C.** 1.0×10^{-3}

   B. 1.0×10^{-7} **D.** 10.5×10^{-4} **E.** 2.9×10^{-12}

39. A strong acid tends to:

   A. form positively charged ions when dissolved in H_2O **C.** be strongly polar

   B. form negatively charged ions when dissolved in H_2O **D.** all of the above

                                                       E. none of the above

40. Which of the following is NOT a strong base?

   A. $Ca(OH)_2$ **B.** $Fe(OH)_3$ **C.** KOH   **D.** NaOH   **E.** NH_2^-

41. What is the term for a substance that donates a proton in an acid-base reaction?

   A. Brønsted-Lowry acid   **C.** Arrhenius acid

   B. Brønsted-Lowry base   **D.** Arrhenius base   **E.** None of the above

42. In an acidic solution, the pH is:

   A. > 9 **B.** < 7 **C.** > 7 **D.** $= 7$ **E.** cannot be determined

43. Which is a strong acid and completely dissociates in H_2O?

   A. H_3PO_4 **B.** CH_3CH_2COOH **C.** HF   **D.** HNO_3 **E.** H_2O

44. If a vinegar sample has a pH of 5, the solution is:

   A. weakly basic   **C.** weakly acidic

   B. neutral   **D.** strongly acidic   **E.** strongly basic

45. Which compound has a very large value of K_a in aqueous solution?

   A. KOH   **B.** H_3PO_4 **C.** HNO_3 **D.** NaCl   **E.** NH_3

46. What is the best explanation for why a person might wash their hands with ashes?

   A. The oils on the skin act as a base and react with the ashes to produce soap

   B. After being burnt in the fire, the acids and bases of the log are neutralized, making it a gentle material to use on the hands

   C. The ashes act as a base and react with skin oils to produce solutions of soap

   D. The ashes act as an acid and react with the skin oils to produce soap

   E. The amino acids on the skin act as a base and react with the ashes to produce soap

47. Which is incorrectly classified as an acid, a base or an amphoteric species?

   A. LiOH / base   **C.** H_2S / acid

   B. HS^- / amphoteric   **D.** NH_4^+ / base   **E.** none of the above

48. Which of the following is a general property of an acidic solution?

   A. pH < 7   **C.** Tastes sour

   B. Neutralizes bases   **D.** Turns litmus paper red   **E.** All of the above

49. What is the conjugate base of ^-OH?

   A. O_2 **B.** O^{2-} **C.** H_2O **D.** O^- **E.** H_3O^+

50. Which is the strongest acid?

Monoprotic Acids	Ka
Acid I	1×10^{-8}
Acid II	1×10^{-9}
Acid III	3.5×10^{-10}
Acid IV	2.5×10^{-8}

   A. I   **B.** II   **C.** III   **D.** IV   **E.** Not enough data to determine

51. The $[^-OH]$ and the pH of 0.035 M KOH at 25 °C are, respectively:

   A. 0.035 M and +12.5   **C.** 0.035 M and −1.46

   B. 2.9×10^{-13} M and −12.5   **D.** 0.035 M and +1.46

                                        E. 2.9×10^{-13} and +12.5

52. What is the conjugate acid of HS^-?

   A. S^- **B.** HS^- **C.** H_2S **D.** S^{2-} **E.** S

53. Which of the following is a weak acid?

   A. HCl (aq) (~100% ionized)   **C.** HNO_3 (aq) (~100% ionized)

   B. $HC_2H_3O_2$ (aq) (~1% ionized)   **D.** All of the above

                                        E. None of the above

54. What is the conjugate acid of water?

   A. H^+ (aq) **B.** OH^- (aq) **C.** O_2^- (aq) **D.** H_2O (l) **E.** H_3O^+ (aq)

55. In the reaction below, what does the symbol $\rightleftharpoons$ indicate?

     $^-OH + NH_4^+ \rightleftharpoons H_2O + NH_3$

   A. The rate of the backward reaction is the same as the forward reaction; H^+ is not transferred

   B. The forward reaction does not progress

   C. The reaction cannot decide which direction produces equilibrium

   D. The forward and backward reactions are occurring simultaneously

   E. None of the above

56. Which of these salts is basic in an aqueous solution?

   A. NaF   **B.** $CrCl_3$ **C.** KBr   **D.** NH_4ClO_4 **E.** None are basic

57. What are the products from the neutralization reaction $HNO_3\,(aq) + Ba(OH)_2\,(aq) \rightarrow$?

   A. $Ba(NO_2)_2$ and H_2O **C.** Ba_3N_2 and H_2O

   B. $Ba(NO_3)_2$ and H_2O **D.** $Ba(NO_2)_2$ and H_2 **E.** $Ba(NO_3)_2$ and H_2

58. At which pH will the net charge on an amino acid be zero, if the pI for it is 7.5?

   A. 2.5   **B.** 5.0   **C.** 7.0   **D.** 7.5   **E.** 10.0

59. Which molecule is a Lewis acid?

   A. NO_3^- **B.** NH_3 **C.** NH_4^+ **D.** CH_3COOH **E.** BH_3

60. A 36.0 mL sample of aqueous sulfuric acid was titrated with 0.250 M NaOH *(aq)* until neutralized. The residue was dried and then weighed with a mass of 861 mg. What is the molarity of the sulfuric acid solution?

   A. 0.0732 M   **B.** 0.168 M   **C.** 0.262 M   **D.** 0.445 M   **E.** 0.894 M

61. What is the pH of an aqueous solution if $[H^+] = 0.000001$ M?

   A. 1   **B.** 4   **C.** 6   **D.** 7   **E.** 9

62. The classification as weak or strong for an acid or base is determined by:

   A. the concentration of the acid or base

   B. the extent of dissociation of the dissolved acid or base

   C. the solubility of the acid or base

   D. the ability to be neutralized by buffering solution

   E. more than one choice is correct

63. Which of the following statements about strong or weak acids is true?

   A. A weak acid reacts with a strong base

   B. A strong acid does not react with a strong base

   C. A weak acid readily forms ions when dissolved in water

   D. A weak acid and a strong acid at the same concentration are equally corrosive

   E. All of the above

64. Which is NOT correctly classified as a base, salt or an amphoteric species?

   A. KF / salt   **C.** HCO_3^- / amphoteric

   B. S^{2-} / amphoteric   **D.** NH_3 / base   **E.** all are correctly classified

65. What is the term for a substance that releases H^+ in H_2O?

   A. Brønsted-Lowry acid   **C.** Arrhenius acid

   B. Brønsted-Lowry base   **D.** Arrhenius base   **E.** none of the above

66. Which compound forms CO_2 and H_2O when reacted with an acid?

   A. $NaC_2H_3O_2$ **B.** NH_3 **C.** $CaCO_3$ **D.** $Mg(OH)_2$ **E.** none of the above

67. The conjugate bases of HSO_4^-, CH_3OH and H_3O^+ are, respectively:

A. SO_4^{2-}, CH_2OH^- and ^-OH

B. CH_3O^-, SO_4^{2-} and H_2O

C. SO_4^-, CH_3O^- and ^-OH

D. SO_4^-, CH_2OH^- and H_2O

E. SO_4^{2-}, CH_3O^- and H_2O

68. What is the term used for an H^+ acceptor?

A. proton acceptor

B. Brønsted-Lowry acid

C. Arrhenius acid

D. amphiprotic

E. none of the above

69. An acid is represented by which of the following?

A. HBr   **B.** C_2H_6 **C.** KOH   **D.** NaF   **E.** $NaNH_2$

70. Which of the following statements describes an acidic solution?

A. $[H_3O^+] / [^-OH] = 1 \times 10^{-14}$

B. $[H_3O^+] \times [^-OH] \neq 1 \times 10^{-14}$

C. $[H_3O^+] < [^-OH]$

D. $[H_3O^+] > [^-OH]$

E. $[H_3O^+] / [^-OH] = 1$

71. Which acid has the strongest conjugate base?

Monoprotic Acids	Ka
Acid I	1×10^{-8}
Acid II	1×10^{-9}
Acid III	3.5×10^{-10}
Acid IV	2.5×10^{-8}

A. I   **B.** II   **C.** III   **D.** IV   **E.** Not enough data to determine

72. In the following reaction, which reactant is a Brønsted-Lowry base?

$$H_2CO_3\,(aq) + Na_2HPO_4\,(aq) \rightarrow NaHCO_3\,(aq) + NaH_2PO_4\,(aq)$$

A. $NaHCO_3$

B. NaH_2PO_4

C. Na_2HPO_4

D. H_2CO_3

E. none of the above

73. Complete neutralization of phosphoric acid with barium hydroxide yields $Ba_3(PO_4)_2$ as one of the products when separated and dried. This indicates that phosphoric acid is a:

A. monoprotic acid

B. diprotic acid

C. hexaprotic acid

D. tetraprotic acid

E. triprotic acid

74. The isoelectric point of an amino acid is defined as the:

A. pH equals the pKa

B. pH at which the amino acid exists in the acidic form

C. pH at which the amino acid exists in the basic form

D. pH at which the amino acid exists in the zwitterion form

E. pH at which the amino acid exists in the protonated form

75. When 37 g of $Ca(OH)_2$ is added to 1000 ml of 0.55 M H_2SO_4, the resulting pOH is:

A. 3   **B.** 8   **C.** 11   **D.** 13   **E.** 14

76. Which reactant is a Brønsted-Lowry acid in HCl (*aq*) + KHS (*aq*) → KCl (*aq*) + H$_2$S (*aq*)?

  A. KCl   **B.** H$_2$S   **C.** HCl   **D.** KHS   **E.** None of the above

77. Citric acid is a triprotic acid with three carboxylic acid groups having pK_a values of 3.1, 4.8 and 6.4. At a pH of 5.5, what is the predominant protonation state of citric acid?

  A. All 3 carboxylic acid groups are deprotonated

  B. All 3 carboxylic acid groups are protonated

  C. 1 carboxylic acid group is deprotonated while 2 are protonated

  D. 2 carboxylic acid groups are deprotonated while 1 is protonated

  E. The protonation state cannot be determined

78. Which of the following is the strongest base?

  A. ClO$_3^-$ **B.** NH$_3$ **C.** ClO$^-$ **D.** ClO$_2^-$ **E.** ClO$_4^-$

79. Which of the following compound-classification pair is incorrectly matched?

  A. HF–weak acid   **C.** NH$_3$–weak base

  B. LiC$_2$H$_3$O$_2$–salt   **D.** HI–strong acid   **E.** Ca(OH)$_2$–weak base

80. Which of the following indicators is orange at pH 5?

  A. phenolphthalein   **C.** bromthymol blue

  B. methyl red   **D.** all of the above   **E.** none of the above

81. Which of the following is a strong base?

  A. Ba(OH)$_2$ **B.** CH$_3$COOH   **C.** NH$_3$ **D.** CH$_3$OH   **E.** NaCl

82. Which one is a Brønsted-Lowry acid?

  A. NH$_3$ **B.** NO$_3^-$ **C.** CH$_3$COOH   **D.** BH$_3$ **E.** CH$_2$Cl$_2$

83. The chemical species present in all acidic solutions is:

  A. H$_2$O$^+$ (*aq*)   **B.** H$_3$O$^+$ (*l*)   **C.** H$_2$O (*aq*)   **D.** $^-$OH (*aq*)   **E.** H$_3$O$^+$ (*aq*)

84. Which of the following is a general property of an acidic solution?

  A. pH greater than 7   **C.** Feels slippery

  B. Turns litmus paper blue   **D.** Tastes sour   **E.** None of the above

85. The H$_3$O$^+$ ion is called the:

  A. protium ion   **C.** hydronium ion

  B. hydrogen ion   **D.** hydroxide ion   **E.** water ion

86. Which molecule is acting as a base in the following reaction $^-$OH + NH$_4^+$ → H$_2$O + NH$_3$?

  A. $^-$OH   **B.** NH$_4^+$ **C.** H$_2$O   **D.** NH$_3$ **E.** H$_3$O$^+$

87. Which of the following is NOT a conjugate acid/base pair?

A. S^{2-} / H_2S

C. H_2O / ^-OH

B. HSO_4^- / SO_4^{2-}

D. PH_4^+ / PH_3

E. all are conjugate acid/base pairs

88. In aqueous solution, what is the term for ions that do not participate in a reaction, and do not appear in the net ionic equation?

A. zwitterions

C. nonelectrolyte ions

B. spectator ions

D. electrolyte ions

E. none of the above

89. An Arrhenius acid is defined as a substance that:

A. decreases $[H^+]$ when placed in aqueous solutions

B. increases $[H^+]$ when placed in aqueous solutions

C. acts as a proton acceptor in any system

D. acts as a proton donor in any system

E. acts as a proton acceptor in aqueous solutions

90. If $[HF]$ (*aq*), $[H^+]$ and $[F^-]$ at equilibrium are 2.5×10^{-1} M, 5.0×10^{-2} M, and 5.0×10^{-5} M respectively, what is the dissociation constant for HF(*aq*) in the reaction HF (*aq*) $\rightleftharpoons H^+ + F^-$?

A. 1×10^{-5}

C. 3.0×10^{-3}

B. 2.5×10^{-4}

D. 5.0×10^{-5}

E. 3.0×10^{-2}

91. Given the pK_a values for phosphoric acid of 2.14, 6.86 and 12.4, what is the ratio of HPO_4^{2-} / $H_2PO_4^-$ in a typical muscle cell when the pH is 7.2?

A. 6.3×10^{-6} **B.** 1.1×10^5 **C.** 0.46   **D.** 2.2   **E.** 3.1×10^3

92. What is the sum of the coefficients for the balanced molecular equation?

$$BaCO_3 \,(aq) + HNO_3 \,(aq) \rightarrow ?$$

A. 9   **B.** 10   **C.** 8   **D.** 3   **E.** 6

93. What is the term for a substance that changes color according to the pH of the solution?

A. Arrhenius acid

C. Acid-base indicator

B. Brønsted-Lowry acid

D. Acid-base signal

E. None of the above

94. Which set below contains *only* weak electrolytes?

A. NH_4Cl (*aq*), $HClO_2$ (*aq*), HCN (*aq*)

B. NH_3 (*aq*), $HC_2H_3O_2$ (*aq*), HCN (*aq*)

C. KOH (*aq*), H_3PO_4 (*aq*), $NaClO_4$ (*aq*)

D. HNO_3 (*aq*), H_2SO_4 (*aq*), HCN (*aq*)

E. NaOH (*aq*), H_2SO_4 (*aq*), $HC_2H_3O_2$ (*aq*)

95. Compared to a solution with a higher pH, a solution with a lower pH has a(n):

A. decreased Ka

C. increased pK_a

B. increased $[^-OH]$

D. increased $[H^+]$

E. decreased $[H^+]$

96. Which is the correct net ionic equation for the hydrolysis reaction of Na_2S?

  A. $Na^+ (aq) + H_2O (l) \rightarrow NaOH (aq) + H_2 (g)$

  B. $Na^+ (aq) + 2H_2O (l) \rightarrow NaOH (aq) + H_2O^+ (aq)$

  C. $S^{2-} (aq) + H_2O (l) \rightarrow 2HS^- (aq) + {}^-OH (aq)$

  D. $S^{2-} (aq) + 2H_2O (l) \rightarrow HS^- (aq) + H_3O^+ (aq)$

  E. $S^{2-} (aq) + H_2O (l) \rightarrow HS^- (aq) + {}^-OH (aq)$

97. What is the molarity of a hydrochloric acid solution if 20.00 mL of HCl is required to neutralize 0.424 g of sodium carbonate (105.99 g/mol)?

$$2HCl (aq) + Na_2CO_3 (aq) \rightarrow 2NaCl (aq) + H_2O (l) + CO_2 (g)$$

  A. 0.150 M   **C.** 0.300 M

  B. 0.250 M   **D.** 0.400 M   **E.** 0.500 M

98. What is the $[H_3O^+]$ of a solution that has a pH = 2.34?

  A. 1.3×10^1 M   **C.** 4.6×10^{-3} M

  B. 2.3×10^{-10} M   **D.** 2.4×10^{-3} M   **E.** $3.6 \ 10^{-8}$ M

99. Which compound is amphoteric?

  A. NO_3 **B.** HBr   **C.** $CH_3CH_2COO^-$ **D.** BH_3 **E.** HSO_4^-

100. If 10.0 mL of 0.100 M HCl is titrated with 0.200 M NaOH, what volume of sodium hydroxide solution is required to neutralize the acid?

$$HCl (aq) + NaOH (aq) \rightarrow NaCl (aq) + H_2O (l)$$

  A. 5.00 mL   **B.** 10.0 mL   **C.** 20.0 mL   **D.** 40.0 mL   **E.** 80.0 mL

101. A requirement for a Brønsted-Lowry base is the:

  A. production of H_3O^+ upon reaction with H_2O

  B. lone pair of electrons in its Lewis dot structure

  C. presence of ^-OH in its formula

  D. presence of H_2O as a reaction medium

  E. presence of a metal ion in its formula

102. Can an acid and a base react to form an acid?

  A. The reaction can only occur if the reactants are organic/carboxylic acids and organic bases

  B. An acid and a base react to form an acid if the acid is a weak acid and the base is a strong base

  C. No, acids always form salts when reacted with bases

  D. The reaction can only occur if the substances reacting are true acids and bases

  E. An acid and a base react to form an acid if the acid is a strong acid and the base is a weak base

103. The Brønsted-Lowry acid and base in $NH_4^+ + CN^- \rightarrow NH_3 + HCN$ are, respectively:

  A. NH_4^+ and CN^- **C.** NH_4^+ and HCN

  B. CN^- and HCN   **D.** NH_3 and CN^-

                              E. NH_3 and NH_4^+

104. In the following reaction, which reactant is a Brønsted-Lowry acid?

$$H_2CO_3\,(aq) + Na_2HPO_4\,(aq) \rightarrow NaHCO_3\,(aq) + NaH_2PO_4\,(aq)$$

A. NaH_2PO_4

B. $NaHCO_3$

C. H_2CO_3

D. Na_2HPO_4

E. None of the above

105. Which one of the following is the weakest acid?

A. HF   ($K_a = 6.5 \times 10^{-4}$)

B. HNO_2 ($K_a = 4.5 \times 10^{-4}$)

C. HClO   ($K_a = 3.0 \times 10^{-8}$)

D. HCN   ($K_a = 6.3 \times 10^{-10}$)

E. HI   ($K_a = 7.1 \times 10^{2}$)

106. Acids and bases react to form:

A. Brønsted-Lowry acids

B. Arrhenius acids

C. Lewis acids

D. Lewis bases

E. salts

107. Which of the following is a general property of a basic solution?

A. Turns litmus paper red

B. pH less than 7

C. Tastes sour

D. Feels slippery

E. None of the above

108. A weak acid is titrated with a strong base. When the concentration of the conjugate base is equal to the concentration of the acid, the titration is at the:

A. end point

B. buffering region

C. equivalence point

D. diprotic point

E. indicator zone

109. Which of the following statements is/are always true for a neutralization reaction?

    I. Water is formed

    II. It is the reaction of an $^-$OH with an H^+

    III. One molecule of acid neutralizes one molecule of base

A. I only   B. II only   C. III. only   D. I and II only   E. I and III only

110. Which of the following is NOT a strong acid?

A. HBr *(aq)*   B. HNO_3 C. H_2CO_3 D. H_2SO_4 E. HCl *(aq)*

111. What is the color of phenolphthalein indicator at pH 7?

A. pink   B. colorless   C. red   D. blue   E. none of the above

112. A Brønsted-Lowry acid is defined as a substance that:

A. acts as a H^+ acceptor in any system

B. acts as a proton donor in any system

C. increases $[H^+]$ when placed in H_2O

D. decreases $[H^+]$ when placed in H_2O

E. acts as lone pair acceptor in any system

113. Which acts as the best buffer solution:

A. Strong acids or bases

B. Strong acids and their salts

C. Salts

D. Weak acids or bases and their salts

E. Strong bases and their salts

114. When fully neutralized by treatment with barium hydroxide, a phosphoric acid yields $Ba_2P_2O_7$ as one of its products. The parent acid for the anion in this compound is:

A. monoprotic acid

B. diprotic acid

C. triprotic acid

D. hexaprotic acid

E. tetraprotic acid

115. What is the term used as a synonym for hydrogen ion donor?

A. Brønsted-Lowry base

B. proton donor

C. amphiprotic

D. Arrhenius base

E. none of the above

116. Which compound has a value of K_a that is close to 10^{-5}?

A. $CH_3CH_2CO_2H$ B. KOH   C. NaCl   D. HNO_3 E. NH_3

117. A base is a substance that:

A. can be used to clean drains

B. accepts electrons

C. accepts an ^-OH

D. accepts an H^+

E. has a bitter taste

118. In which of the following pairs of acids are both chemical species in the pair weak acids?

A. $HC_2H_3O_2$ and HI

B. H_2CO_3 and HBr

C. HCN and H_2S

D. H_3PO_4 and H_2SO_4

E. HCl and HBr

119. Which of the following indicators is colorless in an acidic solution and pink in a basic solution?

A. phenolphthalein

B. bromthymol blue

C. methyl red

D. all of the above

E. none of the above

120. Which of the following is NOT a strong acid?

A. HI (*aq*)   B. $HClO_4$ C. HCl (*aq*)   D. HNO_3 E. $HC_2H_3O_2$

121. What is the name given to a solution that resists changes in pH?

A. neutral   B. basic   C. buffer   D. protic   E. acidic

122. Which would NOT be used to make a buffer solution?

A. H_2SO_4 B. H_2CO_3 C. NH_4OH D. CH_3COOH E. Tricene

123. In the following reaction, which reactant is a Brønsted-Lowry base?

HCl (*aq*) + KHS (*aq*) → KCl (*aq*) + H_2S (*aq*)

A. H_2S B. KCl   C. KHS   D. HCl   E. none of the above

124. The ions, Ca^{2+}, Mg^{2+}, Fe^{2+}/Fe^{3+}, which are present in all ground water, can be removed by pretreating the water with:

A. $PbSO_4$

B. $Na_2CO_3 \cdot 10H_2O$

C. KNO_3

D. $CaCl_2$

E. 0.05 M HCl

125. What is the pI for glutamic acid that contains two carboxylic acid groups (pK$_a$ 2.2 and 4.2) and an amino group (pK$_a$ 9.7)?

    A. 3.2   **B.** 1.0   **C.** 6.4   **D.** 5.4   **E.** 5.95

126. Which of the following is a diprotic acid?

    A. HCl   **B.** H_3PO_4 **C.** HNO_3 **D.** H_2SO_3 **E.** H_2O

127. What are the products from the complete neutralization of carbonic acid with aqueous potassium hydroxide?

    A. $KHCO_4$ (*aq*) and H_2O (*l*)   **C.** K_2CO_3 (*aq*) and H_2O (*l*)
    B. $KC_2H_3O_2$ (*aq*) and H_2O (*l*)   **D.** $KHCO_3$ (*aq*) and H_2O (*l*)
                                            E. $K_2C_2H_3O_2$ (*aq*) and H_2O (*l*)

128. Calculate the pH of 0.00756 M HNO_3.

    A. 2.1   **B.** 12.9   **C.** 11.7   **D.** 7. 93   **E.** 5.67

129. Salts of strong acids and strong bases are:

    A. neutral   **B.** basic   **C.** acidic   **D.** salts   **E.** none of the above

130. Which of the following is a general property of a basic solution?

    A. Neutralizes acids   **C.** Feels slippery
    B. Turns litmus paper blue   **D.** Tastes bitter   **E.** All of the above

131. At 25 °C, the value of K$_w$ is:

    A. 1.0   **B.** 1.0×10^{-7} **C.** 1.0×10^{-14} **D.** 1.0×10^7 **E.** 1.0×10^{14}

132. The main component of bleach is sodium hypochlorite (NaOCl) which consists of sodium ions, Na$^+$ and hypochlorite ions ($^-$OCl). What products are formed when this compound is reacted with the hydrochloric acid (HCl) present in toilet bowl cleaner?

    A. NaOH, O_2 and Cl_2 **C.** NaOH, H_2O and Cl_2
    B. NaCl and HOCl   **D.** NaCl, O_2 and $HClO_2$ **E.** NaCl and NaOH

133. Which of the following pairs of chemical species contains two polyprotic acids?

    A. HNO_3 and $H_2C_4H_4O_6$ **C.** H_3PO_4 and HCN
    B. $HC_2H_3O_2$ and $H_3C_6H_5O_7$ **D.** H_2S and H_2CO_3 **E.** HCN and HNO_3

134. Which of the following is a general property of an acidic solution?

    A. Turns litmus paper blue   **C.** Tastes bitter
    B. Neutralizes acids   **D.** Feels slippery   **E.** None of the above

135. Which one of the following is the strongest weak acid?

    A. CH_3COOH (K$_a$ = 1.8×10^{-5})   **C.** HCN   (K$_a$ = 6.3×10^{-10})
    B. HF   (K$_a$ = 6.5×10^{-4})   **D.** HClO   (K$_a$ = 3.0×10^{-8})
                                               E. HNO_2 (K$_a$ = 4.5×10^{-4})

136. Which acts as a buffer system?

A. $NH_3 + H_2O \rightleftharpoons OH^- + NH_4^+$

B. $H_2PO_4 \rightleftharpoons H^+ + HPO_4^{2-}$

C. $HC_2H_3O_2 \rightleftharpoons H^+ + C_2H_3O_2^-$

D. $CO_2 + H_2O \rightleftharpoons H_2CO_3 \rightleftharpoons HCO_3^- + H^+$

E. All of the above

137. What is the term for a solution for which concentration has been established accurately, usually to three or four significant digits?

A. standard solution

B. stock solution

C. normal solution

D. reference solution

E. none of the above

138. The reaction most likely to lead to the formation of calcium bicarbonate in limestone regions is the reaction between:

A. sodium hydroxide and acetic acid

B. calcium carbonate and carbonic acid

C. calcium chloride and sodium carbonate

D. sodium nitrate and carbonic acid

E. sodium carbonate and calcium carbonate

139. Which of the following statements is correct?

A. In a basic solution, $[H_3O^+] > 10^{-7}$ and $[OH^-] < 10^{-7}$

B. In a basic solution, $[H_3O^+] > 10^{-7}$ and $[OH^-] > 10^{-7}$

C. In a basic solution, $[H_3O^+] < 10^{-7}$ and $[OH^-] < 10^{-7}$

D. In a basic solution, $[H_3O^+] < 10^{-7}$ and $[OH^-] > 10^{-7}$

E. In a basic solution, $[H_3O^+] > 10^{-7}$ and $[OH^-] = 10^{-7}$

140. The hydrogen sulfate ion HSO_4^- is amphoteric. In which of the following equations does it act as an acid?

A. $HSO_4^- + {}^-OH \rightarrow H_2SO_4 + O^{2-}$

B. $HSO_4^- + H_2O \rightarrow SO_4^{2-} + H_3O^+$

C. $HSO_4^- + H_3O^+ \rightarrow SO_3 + 2H_2O$

D. $HSO_4^- + H_2O \rightarrow H_2SO_4 + {}^-OH$

E. None of the above

141. Which of the following is a general property of a basic solution?

A. Neutralizes bases

B. pH less than 7

C. Turns litmus paper red

D. Tastes sour

E. None of the above

142. In the following equation, which is the proton donor and which is the proton acceptor?

$CO_3^{2-} (aq) + H_2O (l) \rightarrow HCO_3^- (aq) + OH^- (aq)$

A. OH^- is the donor and HCO_3^- is the acceptor

B. HCO_3^- is the donor and OH^- is the acceptor

C. H_2O is the donor and CO_3^{2-} is the acceptor

D. CO_3^{2-} is the donor and H_2O is the acceptor

E. CO_3^{2-} is the donor and OH^- is the acceptor

143. What is the pH of 0.001 M HCl?

A. 2   **B.** 1   **C.** 4   **D.** 3   **E.** 5

144. What are the products from the complete neutralization of sulfuric acid with aqueous sodium hydroxide?

A. Na_2SO_3 (*aq*) and H_2O (*l*)

B. $NaHSO_4$ (*aq*) and H_2O (*l*)

C. $NaHSO_3$ (*aq*) and H_2O (*l*)

D. Na_2S (*aq*) and H_2O (*l*)

E. Na_2SO_4 (*aq*) and H_2O (*l*)

145. What is the conjugate acid-base pair in the reaction $CH_3NH_2 + HCl \leftrightarrow CH_3NH_3^+ + Cl^-$?

A. HCl and Cl^-

B. $CH_3NH_3^+$ and Cl^-

C. CH_3NH_2 and Cl^-

D. CH_3NH_2 and HCl

E. HCl and H_3O^+

146. Does a solution become more or less acidic when a weak acid is added to a concentrated solution of HCl?

A. Less acidic, because the concentration of OH^- increases

B. No change in acidity, because [HCl] is too high to be changed by the weak solution

C. Less acidic, because the solution becomes more dilute with a less concentrated solution of H_3O^+ being added to the solution

D. More acidic, because more H_3O^+ are being added to the solution

E. More acidic, because the solution becomes more dilute with a less concentrated solution of H_3O^+ being added to the solution

147. The neutralization of $Cr(OH)_3$ with H_2SO_4 produces which product?

A. $Cr_2(SO_4)_3$ B. SO_2 C. ^-OH D. H_3O^+ E. H_2SO_4

148. In the following reaction, which reactant is a Brønsted-Lowry acid?

$$NaHS \ (aq) + HCN \ (aq) \rightarrow NaCN \ (aq) + H_2S \ (aq)$$

A. NaCN

B. H_2S

C. NaHS

D. HCN

E. none of the above

149. Relative to a pH of 7, a solution with a pH of 4 has:

A. 30 times less $[H^+]$

B. 300 times less $[H^+]$

C. 1000 times greater $[H^+]$

D. 300 times greater $[H^+]$

E. 30 times greater $[H^+$

150. If a salt to acid ratio is 1:10 for an acid with $K_a = 1 \times 10^{-4}$, what is the pH of the solution?

A. 2   B. 3   C. 4   D. 5   E. 6

151. What is the term for a substance that releases hydroxide ions in water?

A. Brønsted-Lowry base

B. Brønsted-Lowry acid

C. Arrhenius base

D. Arrhenius acid   E. None of the above

152. Calculate the hydrogen ion concentration in a solution with a pH = 6.35.

A. 4.5×10^{-7} M

B. 7.55×10^{-8} M

C. 7.65 M

D. 6.35 M

E. 6.35×10^{-8} M

153. Which of the following would be predominantly deprotonated in the stomach if gastric juice has a pH of about 2?

    A. phosphoric acid ($pK_a = 2.2$)   **C.** acetic acid ($pK_a = 4.7$)

    B. lactic acid, ($pK_a = 3.9$)   **D.** phenol ($pK_a = 9.8$)   **E.** hydrochloric acid ($pK_a = -6$)

154. A metal and a salt solution react only if the metal introduced into the solution is:

    A. below the replaced metal in the activity series

    B. above the replaced metal in the activity series

    C. below hydrogen in the activity series

    D. above hydrogen in the activity series

    E. equal to the replaced metal in the activity series

155. What volume of barium hydroxide is required to neutralize the acid when 25.0 mL of 0.100 M HCl is titrated with 0.150 M $Ba(OH)_2$?

$$2HCl\,(aq) + Ba(OH)_2\,(aq) \rightarrow BaCl_2\,(aq) + 2H_2O\,(l)$$

    A. 32.4 mL   **B.** 25.0 mL   **C.** 16.7 mL   **D.** 8.33 mL   **E.** 37.5 mL

156. Identify the Brønsted-Lowry acid and base, respectively: $NH_3 + HCN \rightarrow NH_4^+ + CN^-$

    A. NH_3 and NH_4^+ **C.** HCN and NH_3

    B. NH_4^+ and CN^- **D.** NH_3 and HCN   **E.** NH_3 and NH_4^+

157. Which of the following is NOT an example of an acidic salt?

    A. sodium hydrogen sulfate   **C.** barium dihydrogen phosphate

    B. nickel (II) bichromate   **D.** aluminum bicarbonate

                                     E. potassium hydrogen chloride

158. Calculate $[F^-]$ in a 2 M solution of hydrogen fluoride if the K_a of HF is 6.5×10^{-4}.

    A. $3.6 \times 10^{-2}\,M$ **C.** $1.9 \times 10^{-2}\,M$

    B. $1.7 \times 10^{-2}\,M$ **D.** $1.3 \times 10^{-3}\,M$ **E.** $6.5 \times 10^{-2}\,M$

159. Which of the following must be true if an unknown solution is a poor conductor of electricity?

    A. Solution is slightly reactive   **C.** Solution is highly ionized

    B. Solution is highly corrosive   **D.** Solution is slightly ionized

                                     E. Solution is highly reactive

160. What is the pH of a buffer solution, where acetic acid (with a K_a of 1.8×10^{-5}) and its conjugate base are in a 10:1 ratio?

    A. 1.9   **B.** 3.7   **C.** 5.7   **D.** 7.0   **E.** 7.4

161. Which characteristic of a molecule describes an acid?

    A. Donates hydrogen atoms   **C.** Donates hydrogen ions

    B. Dissolves metal   **D.** Accepts hydrogen atoms

                                      E. Donates hydronium ions

162. Which of the following pairs of acids and conjugate bases is NOT correctly labeled?

Acid	Conjugate Base
A. NH_4^+	NH_3
B. HSO_3^-	SO_3^{2-}
C. H_2SO_4	HSO_4^-
D. HSO_4^-	SO_4^{2-}
E. HFO_2	HFO_3

163. What is the pH of an aqueous solution if the $[H^+] = 0.001$ M?

   A. 1   **B.** 2   **C.** 3   **D.** 10   **E.** 11

164. Which of the following is NOT a strong base?

   A. $Ca(OH)_2$ **B.** KOH   **C.** NaOH   **D.** $Al(OH)_3$ **E.** ^-OH

165. What volume of 0.15 M H_2SO_4 is needed to neutralize 40 ml of 0.2 M NaOH?

   A. 27 ml   **B.** 40 ml   **C.** 65 ml   **D.** 80 ml   **E.** 105 ml

166. In the following titration curve, what does the inflection point represent?

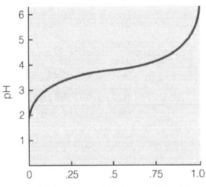

Moles base added per mole acid

   A. The weak acid is 50% protonated and 50% deprotonated

   B. The pH where the solution functions most effectively as a buffer

   C. Equal concentration of weak acid and conjugate base

   D. pH of solution equals pK_a of weak acid

   E. All of the above

167. What is the term for a substance that accepts a proton in an acid-base reaction?

   A. Brønsted-Lowry base   **C.** Arrhenius base

   B. Brønsted-Lowry acid   **D.** Arrhenius acid   **E.** None of the above

168. If $[H_3O^+]$ in an aqueous solution is 7.5×10^{-9} M, the $[OH^-]$ is:

   A. 6.4×10^{-5} M   **C.** 7.5×10^{-23} M

   B. $3.8 \times 10^{+8}$ M   **D.** 1.5×10^{-6} M   **E.** 9.0×10^{-9} M

169. Identify the acid/base behavior of each substance for $H_3O^+ + Cl^- \rightleftharpoons H_2O + HCl$

  A. H_3O^+ acts as an acid, Cl^- acts as a base, H_2O acts a base, HCl acts as an acid

  B. H_3O^+ acts as a base, Cl^- acts as an acid, H_2O acts a base, HCl acts as an acid

  C. H_3O^+ acts as an acid, Cl^- acts as a base, H_2O acts an acid, HCl acts as a base

  D. H_3O^+ acts as a base, Cl^- acts as an acid, H_2O acts an acid, HCl acts as a base

  E. H_3O^+ acts as an acid, Cl^- acts as a base, H_2O acts a base, HCl acts as a base

170. Which of the following is a triprotic acid?

  A. HNO_3 **B.** H_3PO_4 **C.** H_2SO_3 **D.** $HC_2H_3O_2$ **E.** CH_2COOH

171. Which of the following is a strong acid?

  A. HNO_3 (*aq*) (~100% ionized)   **C.** HCl (*aq*) (~100% ionized)

  B. H_2SO_4 (*aq*) (~100% ionized)   **D.** All of the above   **E.** None of the above

172. The K_a of a buffer is 4.5×10^{-4}. If the concentration of an undissociated weak acid is equal to the concentration of the conjugate base, the pH of this buffer system is between:

  A. 1 and 2   **B.** 3 and 4   **C.** 5 and 6   **D.** 7 and 8   **E.** 9 and 10

173. Which is the balanced equation for the neutralization reaction between $Al(OH)_3$ and HCl (*aq*)?

  A. $Al(OH)_3 + 3HCl$ (*aq*) $\rightarrow AlCl_3 + H^+ + OH^-$ **C.** $Al(OH)_3 + 3HCl$ (*aq*) $\rightarrow AlCl_3 + 3H_2O$

  B. $Al^{3+} + OH^- + H^+ + Cl^- \rightarrow AlCl_3 + H_2O$ **D.** $Al(OH)_3 + HCl$ (*aq*) $\rightarrow AlCl_3 + H_2O$

  E. $Al(OH)_3 + HCl$ (*aq*) $\rightarrow AlCl_3 + 3H_2O$

174. Which of the following is an example of an Arrhenius acid?

  A. $KC_2H_3O_2$ (*aq*)   **C.** $NH_4C_2H_3O_2$ (*aq*)

  B. $HC_2H_3O_2$ (*aq*)   **D.** All of the above   **E.** None of the above

175. When acids and bases react, the product other than water is a:

  A. hydronium ion   **B.** metal   **C.** hydrogen ion   **D.** hydroxide ion   **E.** salt

176. What happens to the corrosive properties of an acid and a base after they neutralize each other?

  A. The corrosive properties are doubled because the acid and base are combined in the salt

  B. The corrosive properties remain the same when the salt is mixed into water

  C. The corrosive properties are neutralized because the acid and base no longer exist

  D. The corrosive properties are unaffected because salt is a corrosive agent

  E. The corrosive properties are increased because salt is a corrosive agent

177. Which of the following statements about the reaction of acids with metals is NOT correct?

  A. Metal atoms, which dissolved in acid, become positive metal ions

  B. Hydrogen gas is produced when a metal dissolves in an acid

  C. Any metal above hydrogen in the activity series dissolves in a non-oxidizing acid

  D. Acids react with many, but not all, metals

  E. Any metal below hydrogen in the activity series dissolves in a non-oxidizing acid

178. If an unknown solution is a good conductor of electricity, which of the following must be true?

    A. The solution is highly reactive

    B. The solution is slightly reactive

    C. The solution is highly ionized

    D. The solution is slightly ionized

    E. None of the above

179. Which of the following is the weakest acid?

    A. HCO_3^- $pK_a = 10.32$ **C.** NH_4^+ $pK_a = 9.20$

    B. $HC_2H_3O_2$ $pK_a = 4.76$ **D.** $H_2PO_4^-$ $pK_a = 7.18$

                                          E. CCl_3COOH $pK_a = 2.86$

180. What volume of 0.03 M NaOH is needed to titrate 40 ml of 0.1 N H_3PO_4?

    A. 44ml   **B.** 88 ml   **C.** 133 ml   **D.** 266 ml   **E.** 399 ml

181. If stomach digestive juice has a pH of 2, the solution is:

    A. strongly acidic   **C.** neutral

    B. weakly basic   **D.** weakly acidic   **E.** buffered

182. What is the $[H_3O^+]$ in a solution with pH = 11.61?

    A. 1.05×10^{-14} M   **C.** 2.40×10^1 M

    B. 4.35×10^{-4} M   **D.** 1.65×10^1 M   **E.** 2.45×10^{-12} M

183. Which of the following statements describes a basic solution?

    A. $[H_3O^+] \times [OH^-] \neq 1 \times 10^{-14}$ **C.** $[H_3O^+] > [OH^-]$

    B. $[H_3O^+] / [OH^-] = 1 \times 10^{-14}$ **D.** $[H_3O^+] < [OH^-]$

                                            E. $[H_3O^+] / [OH^-] = 1$

184. What is the sum of the coefficients for the balanced molecular equation for the following acid-base reaction LiOH (*aq*) + H_2SO_4 (*aq*) → ?

    A. 6   **B.** 7   **C.** 8   **D.** 10   **E.** 12

185. Which of the following indicators is pink at a pH of 9?

    A. methyl red   **C.** bromthymol blue

    B. phenolphthalein   **D.** all of the above

                                            E. none of the above

186. In an acidic solution, $[H_3O^+]$ is:

    A. $< 1 \times 10^{-7}$ M   **C.** $< 1 \times 10^{-7}$ M

    B. $> 1 \times 10^{-7}$ M   **D.** 1×10^{-7} M

                                            E. cannot be determined

187. Since $pK_a = -\log K_a$, which of the following is a correct statement?

A. Since the pK_a for conversion of the ammonium ion to ammonia is 9.25, ammonia is a weaker base then the acetate ion

B. For carbonic acid with pK_a values of 6.3 and 10.3, the bicarbonate ion is a stronger base than the carbonate ion

C. Acetic acid ($pK_a = 4.7$) is stronger than lactic acid ($pK_a = 3.9$)

D. Lactic acid ($pK_a = 3.9$) is weaker than all forms of phosphoric acid ($pK_a = 2.1$, 6.9 and 12.4)

E. None of the above

188. What is the molarity of a sulfuric acid solution if 30.00 mL of H_2SO_4 is required to neutralize 0.840 g of sodium hydrogen carbonate (84.01 g/mol)?

$$H_2SO_4\,(aq) + 2\,NaHCO_3\,(aq) \rightarrow Na_2SO_4\,(aq) + 2\,H_2O\,(l) + 2\,CO_2\,(g)$$

A. 0.333 M   **B.** 0.500 M   **C.** 0.167 M   **D.** 0.300 M   **E.** 0.667 M

189. Acetic acid is a weak acid in water because it is:

A. only slightly dissociated into ions

B. unable to hold onto its hydrogen ion

C. only slightly soluble

D. dilute

E. completely dissociated into hydronium ions and acetate ions

190. Why is sulfuric acid a much stronger acid than carbonic acid?

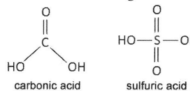

carbonic acid   sulfuric acid

A. The acid strength of two comparative molecules is directly proportional to the number of oxygens bonded to the central atom

B. Since carbonic acid has resonance stabilization and sulfuric acid does not, sulfuric acid is less stable and more acidic

C. The two double bonded oxygens in H_2SO_4 tend to destabilize the single bonded oxygen once the hydrogen ions form, thus making sulfuric acid more acidic

D. In sulfuric acid, the negative charges can move between 4 oxygen atoms, compared to 3 oxygen atoms in carbonic acid

E. In carbonic acid, the positive charge is able to move between two additional oxygens, rather than only one for sulfuric acid

191. What is the pH of a solution that has a hydronium ion concentration of 3.98×10^{-9} M?

A. 8.000   **B.** 3.900   **C.** 5.750   **D.** 2,460   **E.** 8.400

192. What is the term for the product of an acid-base reaction in addition to water?

A. nonelectrolyte   **C.** buffer

B. salt   **D.** electrolyte   **E.** none of the above

193. Which is the correct combination of Brønsted-Lowry bases in the following equilibrium?

$H_2PO_4^- + H_2O \leftrightarrow H_3PO_4 + OH^-$

A. $H_2O + OH^-$

B. $H_2O + H_3PO_4$

C. $H_2PO_4^- + H_3PO_4$

D. $H_2PO_4^- + OH^-$

E. $H_2PO_4^- + H_2O$

194. A buffer solution with pH = 4.0 and an acid with a pK_a of 3.0 should be prepared with a salt to acid ratio of:

A. 1:1　　**B.** 1:1000　　**C.** 1:100　　**D.** 1:5　　**E.** 10:1

195. When a base is added to a buffered solution, the buffer:

A. accepts H^+

B. releases protons

C. releases H_2O

D. releases OH^-

E. accepts H_3O^+

196. What is the term for a substance capable of either donating or accepting a proton in an acid-base reaction?

A. semiprotic

B. nonprotic

C. aprotic

D. amphiprotic

E. none of the above

197. For the reaction $C_5H_5N + H_2CO_3 \leftrightarrow C_5H_6N^+ + HCO_3^-$ the conjugate acid of C_5H_5N is:

A. $C_5H_6N^+$　　**B.** HCO_3^-　　**C.** C_5H_5N　　**D.** H_2CO_3　　**E.** H_3O^+

198. Which species has a K_a of 6.6×10^{-10} if NH_3 has a K_b of 1.8×10^{-5}?

A. H^+　　**B.** NH_2^-　　**C.** NH_4^+　　**D.** H_2O　　**E.** NH_3

199. The two members of the pair do NOT react for which of the following pairs of substances?

A. Na_3PO_4 and HCl

B. KCl and NaI

C. HF and LiOH

D. $PbCl_2$ and H_2SO_4

E. all react

200. If 20.0 mL of 0.500 M KOH is titrated with 0.250 M HNO_3, what volume of nitric acid is required to neutralize the base?

$HNO_3\ (aq) + KOH\ (aq) \rightarrow KNO_3\ (aq) + H_2O\ (l)$

A. 10.0 mL　　**B.** 20.0 mL　　**C.** 25.0 mL　　**D.** 40.0 mL　　**E.** 50.0 mL

201. In a basic solution, the pH is […] and $[H_3O^+]$ is […]:

A. < 7 and $> 1 \times 10^{-7}$ M

B. < 7 and $< 1 \times 10^{-7}$ M

C. $= 7$ and 1×10^{-7} M

D. < 7 and 1×10^{-7} M

E. > 7 and $< 1 \times 10^{-7}$ M

202. What is the ratio of base/acid in the blood stream at pH 7.4 for formic acid ($pK_a = 3.9$), which is the active agent in an ant bite?

A. 3.5　　**B.** 0.54　　**C.** 3.16×10^{-4}　　**D.** 3.16×10^3　　**E.** 1.90

203. Which of the following is the ionization constant expression for water?

A. $K_w = [H_2O] / [H^+] [OH^-]$

B. $K_w = [H^+] [OH^-] / [H_2O]$

C. $K_w = [H^+] [OH^-]$

D. $K_w = [H_2O] [H_2O]$

E. None of the above

204. Which reaction produces $NiCr_2O_7$ as a product?

A. nickel (II) hydroxide and dichromic acid

B. nickel (II) hydroxide and chromic acid

C. nickelic acid and chromium (II) hydroxide

D. nickel (II) hydroxide and chromate acid

E. nickel (II) hydroxide and bichromic acid

205. Which of the following compounds cannot act as an acid?

A. NH_3 **B.** H_2SO_4 **C.** HSO_4^{1-} **D.** SO_4^{2-} **E.** CH_3CO_2H

206. The pH of a solution for which $[H_3O^+] = 8.3 \times 10^{-9}$ is:

A. 5.03   **B.** 11.54   **C.** 9.51   **D.** 5.88   **E.** 8.08

207. If a drain cleaner solution is a strong electrolyte, the drain cleaner is:

A. slightly ionized

B. highly ionized

C. slightly reactive

D. highly reactive

E. None of the above

208. Calculate the $[H_3O^+]$ and the pH of a 0.021 M HNO_3 solution.

A. 0.021 M and 1.68

B. 0.021 M and –1.68

C. 4.8×10^{-13} M and 12.32

D. 4.8×10^{-13} M and –12.32

E. 0.042 and 3.36

209. A sample of $Mg(OH)_2$ salt is dissolved in water and reaches equilibrium with its dissociated ions. Addition of the strong base NaOH increases the concentration of:

A. H_2O^+

B. Mg^{2+}

C. undissociated sodium hydroxide

D. undissociated magnesium hydroxide

E. H_2O^+ and undissociated sodium hydroxide

210. What is the molarity of a nitric acid solution, if 25.00 mL of HNO_3 is required to neutralize 0.500 g of calcium carbonate (100.09 g/mol)?

$$2 \; HNO_3 \, (aq) + CaCO_3 \, (s) \rightarrow Ca(NO_3)_2 \, (aq) + H_2O \, (l) + CO_2 \, (g)$$

A. 0.200 M   **B.** 0.250 M   **C.** 0.400 M   **D.** 0.550 M   **E.** 0.700 M

211. Which of the following compounds is a salt?

A. NaOH   **B.** H_2SO_4 **C.** $C_6H_{12}O_6$ **D.** HBr   **E.** KNO_3

212. Boiler scale forms on the walls of hot water pipes from ground water due to:

  A. transformation of $H_2PO_4^-$ ions to PO_4^{3-} ions, which precipitate with the "hardness ions", Ca^{2+}, Mg^{2+}, Fe^{2+}/Fe^{3+}

  B. transformation of HSO_4^- ions to SO_4^{2-} ions, which precipitate with the "hardness ions", Ca^{2+}, Mg^{2+}, Fe^{2+}/Fe^{3+}

  C. transformation of HSO_3^- ions to SO_3^{2-} ions, which precipitate with the "hardness ions", Ca^{2+}, Mg^{2+}, Fe^{2+}/Fe^{3+}

  D. transformation of HCO_3^- ions to CO_3^{2-} ions, which precipitate with the "hardness ions", Ca^{2+}, Mg^{2+}, Fe^{2+}/Fe^{3+}

  E. The reaction of the CO_3^{2-} ions present in all ground water with the "hardness ions", Ca^{2+}, Mg^{2+}, Fe^{2+}/Fe^{3+}

213. Which of the following statements about weak acids is correct?

  A. Weak acids can only be prepared as dilute solutions

  B. Weak acids have a strong affinity for acidic hydrogens

  C. Weak acids always contain carbon atoms

  D. The percentage dissociation for weak acids is usually in the range of 40-60%

  E. Weak acid have a weak affinity for acidic hydrogens

214. Which of the following is an example of an Arrhenius acid?

  A. H_2O (*l*)　　　　　　**C.** $Ba(OH)_2$ (*aq*)

  B. RbOH (*aq*)　　　　　　**D.** $Al(OH)_3$ (*s*)　　　　　　**E.** None of the above

215. By the Arrhenius definition of acids and bases, a base:

  A. produces OH^-　　　　　**C.** decreases pH

  B. decreases OH^-　　　　　**D.** decreases H_2O　　　　　**E.** increases H_3O^+

216. Which of the following is the strongest weak acid?

  A. HF　　　　　$pK_a = 3.17$　　　　　**C.** $H_2PO_4^-$　　　　　$pK_a = 7.18$

  B. HCO_3^-　　　　$pK_a = 10.32$　　　　　**D.** NH_4^+　　　　　$pK_a = 9.20$

  　　　　　　　　　　　　　　　　　　　　E. $HC_2H_3O_2$　　　　$pK_a = 4.76$

217. If a light bulb in a conductivity apparatus glows dimly when testing a solution, which of the following must be true about the solution?

  A. It is slightly reactive　　　　　**C.** It is slightly ionized

  B. It is highly reactive　　　　　　**D.** It is highly ionized

  　　　　　　　　　　　　　　　　　E. None of the above

218. A Brønsted-Lowry base is a substance which:

  A. donates protons to other substances

  B. accepts protons from other substances

  C. produces hydrogen ions in aqueous solution

  D. produces hydroxide ions in aqueous solution

  E. accepts hydronium ions from other substances

219. Which is a basic anhydride?

   A. BaO   **B.** O_2 **C.** CO_2 **D.** SO_2 **E.** N_2O_5

220. A solution with a pH of 2.1 is:

   A. weakly basic   **C.** strongly acidic

   B. strongly basic   **D.** weakly acidic   **E.** a strong buffer

221. Which of the following indicators is green at pH 7?

   A. phenolphthalein   **C.** methyl red

   B. bromthymol blue   **D.** all of the above   **E.** none of the above

222. A Brønsted-Lowry base is defined as a substance that:

   A. increases $[H^+]$ when placed in water   **C.** acts as proton donor in any system

   B. decreases $[H^+]$ when placed in water   **D.** acts as proton acceptor in any system

                                                     E. acts as a buffer

223. The K_a of formic acid (HCOOH) is 1.8×10^{-4}. What is the pK_b of the formate ion?

   A. $14 - \log(1.8 \times 10^{-4})$ **C.** $-14 - \log(1.8 \times 10^{-4})$

   B. $14 + \log(1.8 \times 10^{-10})$ **D.** $-14 + \log(1.8 \times 10^{-4})$ **E.** $14 + \log(1.8 \times 10^{-4})$

224. Which of the following indicators is yellow in a basic solution and red in an acidic solution?

   A. phenolphthalein   **C.** methyl red

   B. bromthymol blue   **D.** all of the above   **E.** none of the above

225. A typical amino acid has a carboxylic acid and an amine with pK_a values of 2.3 and 9.6, respectively. In a solution of pH 4.5, which describes its protonation and charge state?

   A. Carboxylic acid is deprotonated and negative; amine is protonated and neutral

   B. Carboxylic acid is deprotonated and negative; amine is protonated and positive

   C. Carboxylic acid is protonated and neutral; amine is deprotonated and negative

   D. Carboxylic acid is protonated and neutral; amine is protonated and neutral

   E. Carboxylic acid is deprotonated and negative; amine is deprotonated and neutral

226. Which substance will ionize when completely dissolved in water to form an aqueous solution?

   A. $C_6H_{12}O_6$ (*s*)   **C.** $NaClO_4$ (*s*)

   B. $(NH_4)_2SO_4$ (*s*)   **D.** HNO_3 (*aq*)   **E.** $Ba(OH)_2$ (*s*)

227. Identify a conjugate acid-base pair, whereby the acid is listed first in the pair.

$$H_2PO_4^- + S^{2-} \rightarrow HS^- + HPO_4^{2-}$$

Acid	Conjugate Base		Acid	Conjugate Base
A. $H_2PO_4^-$	HPO_4^{2-}		**C.** S^{2-}	HS^-
B. HS^-	$H_2PO_4^-$		**D.** $H_2PO_4^-$	S^{2-}
			E. HPO_4^{2-}	$H_2PO_4^-$

228. What is the $[H^+]$ in stomach acid that registers a pH of 2 on a strip of pH paper?

    A. 0.2 M   **B.** 0.1 M   **C.** 0.02 M   **D.** 0.01 M   **E.** 2 M

229. Addition of sodium acetate to a solution of acetic acid causes the pH to:

    A. decrease due to the common ion effect
    B. increase due to the common ion effect
    C. remain constant because sodium acetate is a buffer
    D. remain constant because sodium acetate is neither acidic nor basic
    E. remain constant due to the common ion effect

230. Which of the following substances, when added to a solution of nitrous acid (HNO_2), could be used to prepare a buffer solution?

    A. H_2O **B.** $HC_2H_3O_2$ **C.** NaCl   **D.** HCl   **E.** $NaNO_2$

231. If 25.0 mL of 0.100 M $Ca(OH)_2$ is titrated with 0.200 M HNO_3, what volume of nitric acid is required to neutralize the base?

$$2HNO_3 \, (aq) + Ca(OH)_2 \, (aq) \rightarrow 2Ca(NO_3)_2 \, (aq) + 2H_2O \, (l)$$

    A. 25.0 mL   **B.** 40.0 mL   **C.** 12.5 mL   **D.** 20.0 mL   **E.** 50.0 mL

232. What is the pK_a of an unknown acid if, in a solution at pH 7.0, 24% of the acid is in its deprotonated form?

    A. 6.0   **B.** 6.5   **C.** 7.5   **D.** 8.0   **E.** 10.0

233. Which statement is true to distinguish between dissociation and ionization?

    A. Some acids are weak electrolytes and ionize completely when dissolved in H_2O
    B. Some acids are strong electrolytes and dissociate completely when dissolved in H_2O
    C. Some acids are strong electrolytes and ionize completely when dissolved in H_2O
    D. All acids are strong electrolytes and dissociate completely when dissolved in H_2O
    E. Some acids are weak electrolytes and dissociate partially when dissolved in H_2O

234. Which species is formed in the second step of the dissociation of H_3PO_4?

    A. PO_4^{3-} **B.** $H_2PO_4^{2-}$ **C.** $H_2PO_4^-$ **D.** HPO_4^{2-} **E.** H_3PO_3

235. What are the products from the complete neutralization of phosphoric acid with aqueous lithium hydroxide?

    A. $LiHPO_4 \, (aq)$ and $H_2O \, (l)$ **C.** $Li_2HPO_4 \, (aq)$ and $H_2O \, (l)$
    B. $Li_3PO_4 \, (aq)$ and $H_2O \, (l)$ **D.** $LiH_2PO_4 \, (aq)$ and $H_2O \, (l)$ **E.** $Li_2PO_4 \, (aq)$ and $H_2O \, (l)$

236. Which acid has the lowest boiling point elevation?

Monoprotic Acids	Ka
Acid I	1×10^{-8}
Acid II	1×10^{-9}
Acid III	3.5×10^{-10}
Acid IV	2.5×10^{-8}

    A. I   **B.** II   **C.** III   **D.** IV   **E.** Not enough data to determine

237. Based upon the reduction potential: $Zn^{2+} + 2e^- \rightarrow Zn\,(s)$ $E^\circ = -0.76\,V$. Does a reaction take place when Zinc (s) is added to aqueous HCl, under standard conditions?

  A. Yes, because the reduction potential for H^+ is negative
  B. Yes, because the reduction potential for H^+ is zero
  C. No, because the oxidation potential for Cl^- is positive
  D. No, because the reduction potential for Cl^- is negative
  E. Yes, because the reduction potential for H^+ is positive

238. If a battery acid solution is a strong electrolyte, which of the following must be true of the battery acid?

  A. It is highly ionized
  B. It is slightly ionized

  C. It is highly reactive
  D. It is slightly reactive
  E. It is slightly ionized and weakly reactive

239. Which acid or base is least likely to be present in a biochemical reaction?

  A. ammonia   **B.** citric acid   **C.** nitric acid   **D.** acetic acid   **E.** phosphoric acid

240. Which is the acid anhydride for $HClO_4$?

  A. ClO **B.** ClO_2 **C.** ClO_3 **D.** ClO_4 **E.** Cl_2O_7

241. Which of the following does NOT represent a conjugate acid/base pair?

  A. HCl / Cl^-
  B. $HC_2H_3O_2 / {}^-OH$

  C. H_3O^+ / H_2O
  D. HCN / CN^- **E.** All represent a conjugate acid/base pair

242. Which of the following reactions represents the ionization of H_2O?

  A. $H_2O + H_2O \rightarrow 2H_2 + O_2$
  B. $H_2O + H_2O \rightarrow H_3O^+ + OH^-$

  C. $H_2O + H_3O^+ \rightarrow H_3O^+ + H_2O$
  D. $H_3O^+ + OH^- \rightarrow H_2O + H_2O$
  E. None of the above

243. What pH range is generally considered to be within the physiological pH range?

  A. 1.5–3.5   **B.** 4.5–7.3   **C.** 5.5–8.5   **D.** 6.5–8.0   **E.** 7.5–10.0

244. An acid-base neutralization is the reaction of:

  A. $H^+\,(aq)$ with $O_2\,(g)$ to form $H_2O\,(l)$
  B. $Na^+\,(aq)$ with $OH^-\,(aq)$ to form $NaOH\,(aq)$ **D.** $H_2\,(aq)$ with $OH^-\,(aq)$ to form $H_2O\,(l)$
  C. $H_2\,(g)$ with $O_2\,(g)$ to form $H_2O\,(l)$ **E.** $H^+\,(aq)$ with $OH^-\,(aq)$ to form $H_2O\,(l)$

245. In which of the following pairs of substances are both species salts?

  A. NH_4F and KCl
  B. $CaCl_2$ and HCN

  C. $LiOH$ and K_2CO_3
  D. $NaOH$ and HNO_3 **E.** HCN and K_2CO_3

246. If a buffer is made with the pH below the pK_a of the weak acid, the [base] / [acid] ratio is:

  A. equal to 0
  B. equal to 1

  C. greater than 1
  D. less than 1   **E.** cannot be determined

---

247. Which is NOT a strong acid?

A. $HClO_3$ **B.** HF **C.** HBr **D.** HCl **E.** HI

248. A Brønsted-Lowry acid is defined as a substance that:

A. acts as a proton donor in any system

B. acts as a proton acceptor in any system

C. increases $[H^+]$ when placed in water

D. decreases $[H^+]$ when placed in water

E. increases $[H^+]$ in any system

249. Which of the following is the conjugate acid of hydrogen phosphate, HPO_4^{2-}?

A. $H_2PO_4^{2-}$ **B.** H_3PO_4 **C.** $H_2PO_4^-$ **D.** $H_2PO_3^-$ **E.** none of the above

250. Which statement is NOT correct?

A. Acidic salts are formed by partial neutralization of a diprotic acid by a diprotic base

B. Acidic salts are formed by partial neutralization of a triprotic acid by a diprotic base

C. Acidic salts are formed by partial neutralization of a monoprotic acid by a monoprotic base

D. Acidic salts are formed by partial neutralization of a diprotic acid by a monoprotic base

E. Acidic salts are formed by partial neutralization of a polyprotic acid by a monoprotic base

251. The pH of a solution for which $[^-OH] = 1.0 \times 10^{-9}$ is:

A. 8.00 **B.** 1.00×10^{-5} **C.** 1.50 **D.** 5.00 **E.** 9

252. Lysine contains two amine groups (pK$_a$ 9.0 and 10.0) and a carboxylic acid group (pK$_a$ 2.2). In a solution of pH 9.5, which describes the protonation and charge state of lysine?

A. Carboxylic acid is deprotonated and negative; amine (pK$_a$ 9.0) is deprotonated and neutral whereby the amine (pK$_a$ 10.0) is protonated and positive

B. Carboxylic acid is deprotonated and negative; amine (pK$_a$ 9.0) is protonated and positive whereby the amine (pK$_a$ 10.0) is deprotonated and neutral

C. Carboxylic acid is deprotonated and neutral; both amines are protonated and positive

D. Carboxylic acid is deprotonated and negative; both amines are deprotonated and neutral

E. Carboxylic acid is deprotonated and neutral; amine (pK$_a$ 9.0) is deprotonated and neutral whereby the amine (pK$_a$ 10.0) is protonated and positive

253. The acidic anhydride of phosphoric acid (H_3PO_4) is:

A. P_2O **B.** P_2O_3 **C.** PO_3 **D.** PO_2 **E.** P_4O_{10}

Chapter 6.   STOICHIOMETRY AND GENERAL CONCEPTS

1. Which substance listed below is the strongest oxidizing agent given the following spontaneous redox reaction?

$$Mg\ (s) + Sn^{2+}\ (aq) \rightarrow Mg^{2+}\ (aq) + Sn\ (s)$$

A. Mg^{2+} **B.** Sn   **C.** Mg   **D.** Sn^{2+} **E.** none of the above

2. Which of the following is the correct conversion factor to convert mL to L?

A. 1 L = 1000 mL   **C.** 1000 L = 1 mL

B. 1 L = 100 mL   **D.** 10 L = 1 mL   **E.** 10 L = 1000 mL

3. How many grams are in 0.4 mole of $CaCO_3$?

A. 25 g   **B.** 33 g   **C.** 40 g   **D.** 58 g   **E.** 67 g

4. How many moles of C are in a 3.50 g sample of C if the atomic mass of C is 12.011 amu?

A. 3.61 moles   **B.** 0.367 moles   **C.** 1.00 moles   **D.** 3.34 moles   **E.** 0.291 moles

5. Which reaction is NOT correctly classified?

A. $PbO\ (s) + C\ (s) \rightarrow Pb\ (s) + CO\ (g)$ (double-replacement)

B. $CaO\ (s) + H_2O\ (l) \rightarrow Ca(OH)_2\ (aq)$ (synthesis)

C. $Pb(NO_3)_2\ (aq) + 2LiCl\ (aq) \rightarrow 2LiNO_3\ (aq) + PbCl_2\ (s)$ (double-replacement)

D. $Mg\ (s) + 2HCl\ (aq) \rightarrow MgCl_2\ (aq) + H_2\ (g)$ (single-replacement)

E. All are classified correctly

6. What is the molecular formula for lactic acid if the percent composition is 40.00% C, 6.71% H and 53.29% O, with an approximate molar mass of 90 g/mol?

A. CHO_2 **B.** $C_3H_6O_3$ **C.** CHO   **D.** CH_2O **E.** C_6HO_8

7. Consider the balanced equation shown and identify the statement that is NOT true.

$$Na_2SO_4\ (aq) + BaCl_2\ (aq) \rightarrow 2NaCl\ (aq) + BaSO_4\ (s)$$

A. The products are barium sulfate and sodium chloride

B. Barium chloride is dissolved in water

C. Barium sulfate is produced in solid form

D. $2NaCl\ (aq)$ could also be written as $Na_2Cl_2\ (aq)$

E. The coefficient of sodium sulfate is one

8. Which must be true concerning a solution at equilibrium when chemicals are mixed in a redox reaction and allowed to come to equilibrium?

A. $\Delta G° = \Delta G$ **B.** $E = 0$ **C.** $\Delta G° = 0$ **D.** $K = 1$ **E.** $K < 1$

9. Balance the following chemical equation: ___N_2 + ___$H_2 \rightarrow$ ___NH_3

A. 2, 6, 4   **B.** 3, 2, 1   **C.** 1, 2, 3   **D.** 1/2, 3/2, 1   **E.** 1, 3, 2

10. Which reaction is NOT correctly classified?

   A. $BaCl_2 + H_2SO_4 \rightarrow BaSO_4 + 2HCl$ (single-replacement)

   B. $F_2 + 2NaCl \rightarrow Cl_2 + 2NaF$ (single-replacement)

   C. $Fe + CuSO_4 \rightarrow Cu + FeSO_4$ (single-replacement)

   D. $2NO_2 + H_2O_2 \rightarrow 2HNO_3$ (synthesis)

   E. All are classified correctly

11. Which of the following nonmetals in the free state has an oxidation number of zero?

   A. S_8 **B.** P_4 **C.** F_2 **D.** Ar   **E.** all of the above

12. The number of moles of H_2O in a flask of water that contains 4.0×10^{21} molecules is:

   A. 2.4×10^{23} **B.** 6.6×10^{-23} **C.** 6.6×10^{-3} **D.** 2.4×10^{42} **E.** 2.4×10^{23}

13. Avogadro's number is:

   A. number of atoms in 1 mole of any element   **C.** approximately 6.02×10^{23}

   B. number of molecules in a compound   **D.** choices A and C

                                              E. all of the above

14. What is the oxidation number of Cl in $HClO_4$?

   A. -1   **B.** +5   **C.** +4   **D.** +8   **E.** +7

15. Which conversion factor is NOT consistent with the equation below?

       $4NH_3 + 5O_2 \rightarrow 4NO + 6H_2O$?

   A. 5 moles O_2 / 6 moles H_2O **C.** 4 moles NH_3 / 5 moles H_2O

   B. 4 moles NO / 4 moles NH_3 **D.** 4 moles NO / 5 moles O_2

                                              E. all are classified correctly

16. What is the term for a list of the mass percent of each element in a compound?

   A. mass composition   **C.** compound composition

   B. percent composition   **D.** elemental composition

                                              E. none of the above

17. In the following reaction which species is being oxidized and which is being reduced?

       $2Cr\ (s) + 3Cl_2\ (g) \rightarrow 2CrCl_3\ (s)$

   A. Cr is oxidized, while Cl_2 is reduced   **C.** Cr is oxidized, while $CrCl_3$ is reduced

   B. Cl_2 is oxidized, while Cr is reduced   **D.** $CrCl_3$ is oxidized, while Cr is reduced

                                              E. Cr is reduced, while $CrCl_3$ is reduced

18. If two different isotopes of an element are isolated as neutral atoms, the atoms must have the same number of:

    I. protons   II. neutrons   III. electrons

   A. I only   **B.** II only   **C.** I and III only   **D.** I, II and III   **E.** III only

19. What coefficient is needed for the O_2 molecule to balance the following equation?

$2C_4H_{10}\,(g) + \_\_O_2\,(g) \rightarrow 8CO_2\,(g) + 10H_2O\,(l)$

A. 5   **B.** 1   **C.** 8   **D.** 15   **E.** 13

20. Choose the spectator ions: $Pb(NO_3)_2\,(aq) + H_2SO_4\,(aq) \rightarrow PbSO_4\,(s) + 2HNO_3\,(aq)$

A. NO_3^- and H^+ **C.** Pb^{2+} and H^+

B. H^+ and SO_4^{2-} **D.** Pb^{2+} and NO_3^- **E.** Pb^{2+} and SO_4^{2-}

21. What is the oxidation number of Br in $NaBrO_3$?

A. −1   **B.** +1   **C.** +3   **D.** +5   **E.** none of the above

22. How many significant figures are there in the following number: 46,000 pounds?

A. 1   **B.** 2   **C.** 3   **D.** 4   **E.** 5

23. Approximately what percent of $AgNO_3$ is oxygen by weight?

A. 22%   **B.** 24%   **C.** 28%   **D.** 32%   **E.** 34%

24. How many moles of Mg are in a 3.50 g sample of Mg if the atomic mass of Mg is 24.305 amu?

A. 0.0175 moles   **C.** 0.224 moles

B. 0.144 moles   **D.** 0.232 moles   **E.** 1.23×10^{23} moles

25. Which reaction below is a *decomposition* reaction?

A. $2Cr\,(s) + 3Cl_2\,(g) \rightarrow 2CrCl_3\,(s)$ **C.** $C_7H_8O_2\,(l) + 8O_2\,(g) \rightarrow 7CO_2\,(g) + 4H_2O\,(l)$

B. $6Li\,(s) + N_2\,(g) \rightarrow 2Li_3N\,(s)$ **D.** $2KClO_3\,(s) \rightarrow 2KCl\,(s) + 3O_2\,(g)$

                                                   E. None of the above

26. After balancing the following redox reaction, what is the coefficient of O_2?

$Al_2O_3\,(s) + Cl_2\,(g) \rightarrow AlCl_3\,(aq) + O_2\,(g)$

A. 1   **B.** 2   **C.** 3   **D.** 5   **E.** none of the above

27. In a chemical reaction:

A. there is always the same number of products as there are reactants

B. there are equal numbers of atoms on each side of the reaction arrow

C. the number of atoms present in a reaction can vary when the conditions change during the reaction

D. there are equal numbers of molecules on each side of the reaction arrow

E. none of the above

28. A gas sample had $P = 2.0$ atm, $V = 10.5$ L and $T = 298$ K. Based on these measurements, an investigator calculated the number of moles from $PV = nRT$. Which value has the correct number of significant figures? (Note: $R = 0.08206$ L atm K^{-1} mol^{-1})

A. 0.12 mol   **B.** 0.123 mol   **C.** 0.1227 mol   **D.** 0.12270 mol   **E.** 0.1mol

29. For the balanced equation, which term has the highest coefficient: $4H_2 + 2C \rightarrow 2CH_4$?

A. CH_4 **B.** H_4 **C.** H_2 **D.** C   **E.** none of the above

30. Which reaction below is a *synthesis* reaction?

A. $3CuSO_4 + Al \rightarrow Al_2(SO_4)_3 + 3Cu$

B. $SO_3 + H_2O \rightarrow H_2SO_4$

C. $2NaHCO_3 \rightarrow Na_2CO_3 + CO_2 + H_2O$

D. $C_3H_8 + 5O_2 \rightarrow 3CO_2 + 4H_2O$

E. None of the above

31. What is the oxidation number of metallic iron in the elemental state?

A. 0   **B.** +1   **C.** +2   **D.** +3   **E.** none of the above

32. The reactants for this chemical reaction are:

$$C_6H_{12}O_6 + 6H_2O + 6O_2 \rightarrow 6CO_2 + 12H_2O$$

A. $C_6H_{12}O_6$, H_2O, O_2 and CO_2

B. $C_6H_{12}O_6$ and H_2O

C. $C_6H_{12}O_6$

D. $C_6H_{12}O_6$ and CO_2

E. $C_6H_{12}O_6$, H_2O and O_2

33. What is the empirical formula of the compound with the following percent composition?

$C = 15.8\%$ $S = 42.1\%$ $N = 36.8\%$ $H = 5.3\%$

A. N_2H_4CS

B. NH_2C_3S

C. $N_2H_2C_3S$

D. N_3H_2CS

E. $NH_2C_3S_4$

34. The formula mass of $Co(NH_3)_6(ClO_4)_3$ is:

A. 317.76 amu

B. 384.63 amu

C. 403.68 amu

D. 459.47 amu

E. 751.74 amu

35. Which reaction is NOT correctly classified?

A. $AgNO_3 + KCl \rightarrow KNO_3 + AgCl$ (double-replacement)

B. $CH_4 + 2O_2 \rightarrow CO_2 + 2H_2O$ (single-replacement)

C. $Zn + H_2SO_4 \rightarrow ZnSO_4 + H_2$ (single-replacement)

D. $2KClO_3 \rightarrow 2KCl + 3O_2$ (decomposition)

E. All are classified correctly

36. What is the oxidation number of liquid bromine in the elemental state?

A. 0   **B.** –1   **C.** –2   **D.** –3   **E.** None of the above

37. Which of the following is the percent mass composition of acetic acid (CH_3COOH)?

A. 48% carbon, 8% hydrogen and 44% oxygen

B. 52% carbon, 12% hydrogen and 36% oxygen

C. 32% carbon, 6% hydrogen and 62% oxygen

D. 40% carbon, 7% hydrogen and 53% oxygen

E. 34% carbon, 4% hydrogen and 62% oxygen

38. Which of the following has the greatest mass?

A. 34 protons, 34 neutrons and 39 electrons

B. 34 protons, 35 neutrons and 37 electrons

C. 35 protons, 34 neutrons and 37 electrons

D. 34 protons, 35 neutrons and 34 electrons

E. 35 protons, 35 neutrons and 33 electrons

39. Which equation(s) is/are balanced?

    I. $Mg\ (s) + 2HCl\ (aq) \rightarrow MgCl_2\ (aq) + H_2\ (g)$

    II. $3Al\ (s) + 3Br_2\ (l) \rightarrow Al_2Br_3\ (s)$

    III. $2HgO\ (s) \rightarrow 2\ Hg\ (l) + O_2\ (g)$

  A. Only equation III is balanced   **C.** Equations I and III are balanced

  B. Equations II and III are balanced   **D.** All equations are balanced

                                             E. None of the equations are balanced

40. Which of the following is a *double-replacement* reaction?

  A. $2HI \rightarrow H_2 + I_2$ **C.** $HBr + KOH \rightarrow H_2O + KBr$

  B. $SO_2 + H_2O \rightarrow H_2SO_3$ **D.** $CuO + H_2 \rightarrow Cu + H_2O$ **E.** none of the above

41. Which metal in the free state has an oxidation number of zero?

  A. Mg   **B.** Na   **C.** Al   **D.** Ag   **E.** all of the above

42. Which contains the fewest moles?

  A. 10g CH_4 **B.** 10g Si   **C.** 10g CO   **D.** 10g N_2 **E.** 10g AlH_3

43. How many moles are in 40.1g of $MgSO_4$?

  A. 0.25 mole   **B.** 0.33 mole   **C.** 0.45 mole   **D.** 0.55 mole   **E.** 0.67 mole

44. What is the oxidation number of sulfur in the $S_2O_8{}^{2-}$ ion?

  A. −1   **B.** +7   **C.** +2   **D.** +6   **E.** +1

45. By definition, a strong electrolyte must:

  A. be highly soluble in water

  B. contain both metal and nonmetal atoms

  C. be an ionic compound

  D. dissociate almost completely into its ions in solution

  E. none of the above

46. What is the oxidation number of Cl in $LiClO_2$?

  A. −1   **B.** +1   **C.** +3   **D.** +5   **E.** None of the above

47. The oxidation number of sulfur in calcium sulfate, $CaSO_4$, is:

  A. +6   **B.** +4   **C.** +2   **D.** 0   **E.** −2

48. If A of element Y equals 13, then 26 grams of element Y represents approximately:

  A. 26 moles of atoms   **C.** 2 atoms

  B. ½ mole of atoms   **D.** ½ of an atom   **E.** 2 moles of atoms

49. For the balanced reaction $2Na + Cl_2 \rightarrow 2NaCl$, which of the following is a solid?

A. Cl_2 **B.** Cl **C.** Na **D.** $NaCl$ **E.** none are solids

50. Which of the following would be a weak electrolyte in a solution?

A. HBr *(aq)*   **B.** KCl **C.** KOH **D.** $HC_2H_3O_2$ **E.** HI

51. What substance is the oxidizing agent in the following redox reaction?

$$Co\ (s)\ + 2\ HCl\ (aq) \rightarrow CoCl_2\ (aq)\ + H_2\ (g)$$

A. H_2 **B.** $CoCl_2$ **C.** HCl **D.** Co **E.** none of the above

52. Which of the following conversion factors is correct for converting from grams to kilograms?

A. $1000\ g = 1\ kg$ **C.** $1\ g = 100\ kg$

B. $100\ g = 1\ kg$ **D.** $1\ g = 1000\ kg$ **E.** $10\ g = 1\ kg$

53. If the molecular weight of a compound is 219 g/mol, what is the molecular formula of the compound with the following percent composition?

$C = 49.3\%$ $O = 43.8\%$ $H = 6.9\%$

A. $C_3O_2H_5$ **B.** $C_2O_2H_5$ **C.** $C_3O_2H_3$ **D.** $C_3O_2H_4$ **E.** None of the above

54. The formula mass of $C_{14}H_{28}(COOH)_2$ is:

A. 237.30 amu   **C.** 271.24 amu

B. 252.32 amu   **D.** 286.41 amu   **E.** 271.50 amu

55. The net ionic equation for the reaction $CaCO_3 + 2HNO_3 \rightarrow Ca(NO_3)_2 + CO_2 + H_2O$ is:

A. $CO_3^{2-} + H^+ \rightarrow CO_2$ **C.** $Ca^{2+} + 2\ NO_3^- \rightarrow Ca(NO_3)_2$

B. $CaCO_3 + 2\ H^+ \rightarrow Ca^{2+} + CO_2 + H_2O$ **D.** $CaCO_3 + 2\ NO_3^- \rightarrow Ca(NO_3)_2 + CO_3^{2-}$

E. none of the above

56. What substance is reduced in the following redox reaction?

$$F_2\ (g) + 2\ Br^-\ (aq) \rightarrow 2\ F^-\ (aq) + Br_2\ (l)$$

A. F^- **B.** Br_2 **C.** F_2 **D.** Br^- **E.** None of the above

57. Which is the correct equation for the reaction of magnesium with hydrochloric acid to yield hydrogen and magnesium chloride?

A. $2Mg + 6HCl \rightarrow 3H_2 + 2MgCl_2$ **C.** $Mg + 3HCl \rightarrow 3H + MgCl_2$

B. $Mg + 2HCl \rightarrow 2H + MgCl_2$ **D.** $Mg + HCl \rightarrow H + MgCl$

E. $Mg + 2HCl \rightarrow H_2 + MgCl_2$

58. Which represents the balanced double displacement reaction between copper (II) chloride and iron (II) carbonate?

A. $Cu_2Cl + FeCO_3 \rightarrow Cu_2CO_3 + FeC$ **C.** $Cu_2Cl + Fe_2CO_3 \rightarrow Cu_2CO_3 + Fe_2Cl$

B. $CuCl_2 + FeCO_3 \rightarrow CuCO_3 + FeCl_2$ **D.** $CuCl_2 + Fe_2(CO_3)_2 \rightarrow Cu(CO_3)_2 + FeCl_2$

E. $CuCl_2 + 2FeCO_3 \rightarrow 2CuCO_3 + FeCl_2$

59. In a chemical equation, the coefficients:

  A. appear before the chemical formulas

  B. appear as subscripts

  C. reactants always sum up to those of the products

  D. two of the above statements are correct

  E. none of the above statements is correct

60. In which of the following pairs of substances would both species in the pair be written in molecular form in a net ionic equation?

  A. NH_4Cl and $NaCl$ **C.** $LiOH$ and H_2

  B. CO_2 and H_2SO_4 **D.** HF and CO_2 **E.** None of the above

61. What substance is the reducing agent in the following redox reaction?

    $Co\ (s) + 2HCl\ (aq) \rightarrow CoCl_2\ (aq) + H_2\ (g)$

  A. $CoCl_2$ **B.** H_2 **C.** Co **D.** HCl **E.** None of the above

62. Which is a true statement about H_2O as it begins to freeze?

  A. Hydrogen bonds break   **C.** Covalent bond strength increases

  B. Number of hydrogen bonds decreases   **D.** Molecules move closer together

                                   E. Number of hydrogen bonds increases

63. What is the sum of the coefficients in the balanced reaction (no fractional coefficients)?

    $RuS\ (s) + O_2 + H_2O \rightarrow Ru_2O_3\ (s) + H_2SO_4$

  A. 23   **B.** 18   **C.** 13   **D.** 25   **E.** 29

64. How many formula units of $NaCl$ are in 146 grams of sodium chloride?

  A. 3.82×10^{-22} **C.** 1.50×10^{24}

  B. 2.34×10^{24} **D.** 7.45×10^{25} **E.** 4.04×10^{23}

65. In which of the following pairs of substances would both species in the pair be written in ionic form in a net ionic equation?

  A. $AgCl$ and CO_2 **C.** CH_3COOH and HNO_3

  B. KBr and NH_3 **D.** Na_2CO_3 and $Ba(NO_3)_2$ **E.** None of the above

66. What is the oxidation number of I in KIO_4?

  A. −1   **B.** +1   **C.** +3   **D.** +5   **E.** None of the above

67. What is the percent mass composition of H_2SO_4?

  A. 48% oxygen, 50% sulfur and 2% hydrogen

  B. 65% oxygen, 33% sulfur and 2% hydrogen

  C. 75% oxygen, 24% sulfur and 1% hydrogen

  D. 85% oxygen, 14% sulfur and 1% hydrogen

  E. 48% oxygen, 40% sulfur and 12% hydrogen

68. How many atoms of Mg are in a solid 48 g sample of magnesium?

A. $2 \times 6.02 \times 10^{23}$ **C.** 2,400,000

B. 4,800   **D.** $4 \times 6.02 \times 10^{23}$ **E.** 6.02×10^{23}

69. For the balanced reaction $2Na + Cl_2 \rightarrow 2NaCl$, which of the following is a gas?

A. Cl   **B.** NaCl   **C.** Na   **D.** Cl_2 **E.** none are a gas

70. Which of the following is NOT an electrolyte?

A. NaBr   **B.** Ne   **C.** KOH   **D.** HCl   **E.** HI

71. What substance is oxidized in the following redox reaction?

$$F_2(g) + 2\,Br^-(aq) \rightarrow 2\,F^-(aq) + Br_2(l)$$

A. Br_2 **B.** F^- **C.** Br^- **D.** F_2 **E.** None of the above

72. How many mL of solution are there in 0.0500 L?

A. 0.0000500 mL   **B.** 500 mL   **C.** 0.50 mL   **D.** 50.0 mL   **E.** 5.0 mL

73. Assuming STP, if 49 g of H_2SO_4 are produced in the following reaction, what volume of O_2 must be used in the reaction?

$$RuS(s) + O_2 + H_2O \rightarrow Ru_2O_3(s) + H_2SO_4$$

A. 20.6 liters   **C.** 28.3 liters

B. 31.2 liters   **D.** 29.1 liters   **E.** 25.2 liters

74. What is the total number of moles of gas in a sample that contains 16.0 g of CH_4, 16.0 g of O_2, 16.0 g of SO_2 and 33.0 g of CO_2?

A. 2.31 moles   **C.** 2.63 moles

B. 2.50 moles   **D.** 3.10 moles   **E.** 4.20 moles

75. The net ionic equation for the reaction $Ca(OH)_2 + 2HCl \rightarrow 2H_2O + CaCl_2$ is:

A. $OH^- + H^+ \rightarrow H_2O$ **C.** $Ca^{2+} + 2Cl^- \rightarrow CaCl_2$

B. $2OH^- + 2HCl \rightarrow 2H_2O$ **D.** $Ca(OH)_2 + 2H^+ \rightarrow Ca^{2+} + H_2O$

E. none of the above

76. What is the term that expresses the ratio of mass per unit volume for a gas?

A. molar volume   **C.** gas ratio

B. molar mass   **D.** gas density   **E.** none of the above

77. In the reaction shown, what is the oxidizing agent and why?

$$Ni(s) + CuCl_2(aq) \rightarrow Cu(s) + NiCl_2(aq)$$

A. $CuCl_2$ – causes reduction   **C.** Ni – causes reduction

B. $CuCl_2$ – is reduced   **D.** Ni – is reduced   **E.** $NiCl_2$ – is reduced

78. What is the mass of N in a 11.2 liter container when the partial pressure of nitrogen gas is 0.5 atmospheres at 25°C?

    A. 4.5g   **B.** 24g   **C.** 11g   **D.** 22g   **E.** 7g

79. Balance the following equation: ___NO → ___N_2O + ___NO_2

    A. 4, 4, 8   **B.** 1, 2, 4   **C.** 3, 1, 1   **D.** 3, 0, 0   **E.** 6, 2, 1

80. What is the oxidation number of the pure element zinc and a compound like $ZnSO_4$, respectively?

    A. +1 and 0   **B.** 0 and +2   **C.** 0 and 0   **D.** 0 and +1   **E.** +1 and +2

81. The formula for the illegal drug cocaine is $C_{17}H_{21}NO_4$ (303.39 g/mol). What is the percentage of oxygen in cocaine?

    A. 21.09%   **B.** 6.35%   **C.** 4.57%   **D.** 4.74%   **E.** 62.83%

82. How long is 1cm?

    A. 0.01 mm   **B.** 1 mm   **C.** 0.1 mm   **D.** 100 mm   **E.** 10 mm

83. If the following reaction is run at STP with excess H_2O, and 22.4 liters of O_2 react with 67 g of RuS, how many grams of H_2SO_4 are produced?

    $RuS\ (s) + O_2 + H_2O \rightarrow Ru_2O_3\ (s) + H_2SO_4$

    A. 28 g   **B.** 32 g   **C.** 44 g   **D.** 54 g   **E.** 58 g

84. How many oxygen atoms are in 3.62 g of fructose ($C_6H_{12}O_6$)?

    A. 1.34×10^{-21} **C.** 3.28×10^{24}

    B. 7.22×10^{22} **D.** 1.16×10^{23} **E.** 6.85×10^{20}

85. Which species is NOT written as its constituent ions when the equation is expanded into the ionic equation?

    $Mg(OH)_2\ (s) + 2HCl\ (aq) \rightarrow MgCl_2\ (aq) + 2H_2O\ (l)$

    A. $Mg(OH)_2$ only   **C.** HCl

    B. H_2O and $Mg(OH)_2$ **D.** $MgCl_2$ **E.** HCl and $MgCl_2$

86. What substance is oxidized in the following redox reaction?

    $HgCl_2\ (aq) + Sn^{2+}\ (aq) \rightarrow Sn^{4+}\ (aq) + Hg_2Cl_2\ (s) + Cl^-\ (aq)$

    A. Hg_2Cl_2 **B.** Sn^{4+} **C.** Sn^{2+} **D.** $HgCl_2$ **E.** none of the above

87. Which of the following equations is NOT balanced?

    A. $SO_2 + O_2 \rightarrow SO_3$ **C.** $C_3H_8 + 5O_2 \rightarrow 3CO_2 + 4H_2O$

    B. $2H_2 + O_2 \rightarrow 2H_2O$ **D.** $2Na + 2H_2O \rightarrow 2NaOH + H_2$

                                            E. $2Al + 6HCl \rightarrow 2AlCl_3 + 3H_2$

88. What is the total charge of all the electrons in 2 grams of He, whereby the charge on one mole of electrons is given by Faraday's constant ($F = 96,500$ C/mol)?

A. 48,250 C

B. 96,500 C

C. 193,000 C

D. 386,000 C

E. Cannot be determined with the information provided

89. What is the approximate formula mass of sulfur dioxide (SO_2)?

A. 28 amu   B. 36 amu   C. 62 amu   D. 64 amu   E. 68 amu

90. In the following reaction, H_2SO_4 is the:

$$H_2SO_4 + HI \rightarrow I_2 + SO_2 + H_2O$$

A. reducing agent and is reduced

B. reducing agent and is oxidized

C. oxidizing agent and is reduced

D. oxidizing agent and is oxidized

E. oxidizing agent, but is neither oxidized nor reduced

91. How many formula units of lithium iodide (LiI) have a mass equal to 4.24 g?

A. 2.55×10^{24} formula units

B. 5.24×10^{23} formula units

C. 1.90×10^{25} formula units

D. 5.24×10^{26} formula units

E. 1.91×10^{22} formula units

92. During exercise, perspiration on a person's skin can form droplets because of the:

A. ability of H_2O to dissipate heat

B. high specific heat of H_2O

C. adhesive properties of H_2O

D. cohesive properties of H_2O

E. high NaCl content of perspiration

93. If 7 moles of RuS are used in the following reaction, what is the maximum number of moles of Ru_2O_3 that can be produced?

$$RuS\ (s) + O_2 + H_2O \rightarrow Ru_2O_3\ (s) + H_2SO_4$$

A. 3.5 moles   B. 2.8 moles   C. 3.2 moles   D. 2.24 moles   E. 3.8 moles

94. The mass of 5.20 moles of glucose ($C_6H_{12}O_6$) is:

A. 1.54×10^{-21} g   B. 313 g   C. 344 g   D. 937 g   E. 6.34×10^{20} g

95. In which sequence of sulfur-containing species are the species arranged in *decreasing* oxidation numbers for S?

A. SO_4^{2-}, S^{2-}, $S_2O_3^{2-}$

B. $S_2O_3^{2-}$, SO_3^{2-}, S^{2-}

C. SO_4^{2-}, $S_2O_3^{2-}$, S^{2-}

D. SO_3^{2-}, SO_4^{2-}, S^{2-}

E. S^{2-}, SO_4^{2-}, $S_2O_3^{2-}$

96. What law is illustrated if ethyl alcohol always contains 52% carbon, 13% hydrogen, and 35% oxygen by mass?

A. law of constant composition

B. law of constant percentages

C. law of multiple proportions

D. law of conservation of mass

E. none of the above

---

97. If one mole of Ag is produced, how many grams of O_2 gas are produced: $2Ag_2O \rightarrow 4Ag + O_2$?

  A. 6g   **B.** 5g   **C.** 2g   **D.** 12g   **E.** 8g

98. Silicon exists as three isotopes: ^{28}Si, ^{29}Si, and ^{30}Si with atomic masses of 27.98 amu, 28.98 amu and 29.97 amu, respectively. Which isotope is the most abundant in nature?

  A. ^{28}Si **C.** ^{30}Si

  B. ^{29}Si **D.** ^{28}Si and ^{30}Si are equally abundant   **E.** All are equally abundant

99. Is it possible to have a macroscopic sample of oxygen that has a mass of 14 atomic mass units?

  A. No, because oxygen is a gas at room temperature
  B. Yes, because it would have the same density as nitrogen
  C. No, because this is less than a macroscopic quantity
  D. Yes, but it would need to be made of isotopes of oxygen atoms
  E. No, because this is less than the mass of a single oxygen atom

100. The oxidation numbers for the elements in Na_2CrO_4 would be:

  A. +2 for Na, +5 for Cr and −6 for O   **C.** +1 for Na, +4 for Cr and −6 for O

  B. +2 for Na, +3 for Cr and −2 for O   **D.** +1 for Na, +6 for Cr and −2 for O

                                                           E. +1 for Na, +5 for Cr and −2 for O

101. After balancing the following redox reaction, what is the coefficient of NaCl?

    $Cl_2 (g) + NaI (aq) \rightarrow I_2 (s) + NaCl (aq)$

  A. 1   **B.** 2   **C.** 3   **D.** 5   **E.** none of the above

102. What is the mass of 3.61 moles of Ca?

  A. 43 g   **B.** 125 g   **C.** 80 g   **D.** 145 g   **E.** 160 g

103. When aluminum metal reacts with ferric oxide (Fe_2O_3), a displacement reaction yields two products with one of the products being metallic iron. What is the sum of the coefficients of the products of the balanced reaction?

  A. 4   **B.** 6   **C.** 2   **D.** 5   **E.** 3

104. How many molecules of CO_2 are in 154.0 grams of CO_2?

  A. 3.499   **C.** 4.214×10^{24}

  B. 2.107×10^{24} **D.** 9.274×10^{25} **E.** 4.081×10^{27}

105. The oxidation number +7 is for the element:

  A. Mn in $KMnO_4$ **C.** C in MgC_2O_4

  B. Br in $NaBrO_3$ **D.** S in H_2SO_4 **E.** K in $KMnO_4$

106. Which substance listed below is the strongest reducing agent, given the following *spontaneous* redox reaction?

    $FeCl_3 (aq) + NaI (aq) \rightarrow I_2 (s) + FeCl_2 (aq) + NaCl (aq)$

  A. $FeCl_2$ **B.** I_2 **C.** NaI   **D.** $FeCl_3$ **E.** NaCl

107. Which statement regarding balanced chemical equations is NOT true?

  A. When no coefficient is written in front of a formula, the number "one" is assumed

  B. Subscripts may be changed to make an equation simpler to balance

  C. Coefficients are used in front of formulas to balance the equation

  D. The number of each kind of atoms must be the same on each side

  E. Reactants are written to the left of the arrow

108. In the following reaction, which is performed at 600 K, 9.0 moles of N_2 gas are mixed with 22 moles of H_2 gas. What is the percent yield of NH_3 if the reaction produces 12 moles of NH_3?

$$N_2\,(g) + 3H_2\,(g) \rightarrow 2NH_3\,(g)$$

  A. 66%   **B.** 30%   **C.** 20%   **D.** 100%   **E.** 82%

109. Seven grams of nitrogen contain:

  A. 0.5 moles of nitrogen atoms   **C.** 0.25 moles of nitrogen atoms

  B. 1 mole of nitrogen atoms   **D.** 0.75 moles of nitrogen atoms

                              E. Not enough information is given

110. Which substance is functioning as the oxidizing agent in this reaction?

$$14\,H^+ + Cr_2O_7^{2-} + 3\,Ni \rightarrow 3\,Ni^{2+} + 2\,Cr^{3+} + 7\,H_2O$$

  A. H_2O **B.** $Cr_2O_7^{2-}$ **C.** H^+ **D.** Ni   **E.** Ni^{2+}

111. What is the term for the value corresponding to the number of atoms in 12.01g of carbon?

  A. mass number   **C.** Avogadro's number

  B. mole number   **D.** atomic number   **E.** none of the above

112. How many atoms of oxygen does this reaction yield?

$$C_6H_{12}O_6 + 6H_2O + 6O_2 \rightarrow 6CO_2 + 12H_2O$$

  A. 3   **B.** 12   **C.** 14   **D.** 24   **E.** 36

113. From the following reaction, if 0.1 mole of Al is allowed to react with 0.2 mole of Fe_2O_3, how many moles of iron are produced: $2Al + Fe_2O_3 \rightarrow 2Fe + Al_2O_3$

  A. 0.05 mole   **C.** 0.10 mole

  B. 0.075 mole   **D.** 0.15 mole   **E.** 0.25 mole

114. What is the balanced reaction for the combustion of methane?

  A. $CH_4 + OH^- \rightarrow CH_3OH$ **C.** $NH_3 + OH^- \rightarrow NH_4OH$

  B. $CH_4 + \frac{1}{2}O_2 \rightarrow CO_2 + 2H_2O$ **D.** $CH_3OH + 2O_2 \rightarrow CO_2 + 2H_2O$

                              E. $CH_4 + 2O_2 \rightarrow CO_2 + 2H_2O$

115. Which of the following represents 1 mol of phosphine gas (PH_3)?

  A. 22.4 L phosphine gas at STP   **C.** 6.02×10^{23} phosphine molecules

  B. 34.00 g phosphine gas   **D.** all of the above

                              E. none of the above

116. Select the balanced chemical equation:

A. $2C_2H_5OH + 2Na_2Cr_2O_7 + 8H_2SO_4 \rightarrow 2HC_2H_3O_2 + 2Cr_2(SO_4)_3 + 4Na_2SO_4 + 11H_2O$

B. $2C_2H_5OH + Na_2Cr_2O_7 + 8H_2SO_4 \rightarrow 3HC_2H_3O_2 + 2Cr_2(SO_4)_3 + 2Na_2SO_4 + 11H_2O$

C. $C_2H_5OH + 2Na_2Cr_2O_7 + 8H_2SO_4 \rightarrow HC_2H_3O_2 + 2Cr_2(SO_4)_3 + 2Na_2SO_4 + 11H_2O$

D. $C_2H_5OH + Na_2Cr_2O_7 + 2H_2SO_4 \rightarrow HC_2H_3O_2 + Cr_2(SO_4)_3 + 2Na_2SO_4 + 11H_2O$

E. $3C_2H_5OH + 2Na_2Cr_2O_7 + 8H_2SO_4 \rightarrow 3HC_2H_3O_2 + 2Cr_2(SO_4)_3 + 2Na_2SO_4 + 11H_2O$

117. The oxidation number of Cr in $K_2Cr_2O_7$ is:

A. +6   B. +5   C. +4   D. +2   E. +1

118. What is the volume occupied by 10.0 g of NO gas, at STP?

A. 13.4 L   B. 67.2 L   C. 0.333 L   D. 7.46 L   E. 224 L

119. What is the empirical formula of a compound that, by mass, contains 64% silver, 8% nitrogen and 28% oxygen?

A. Ag_3NO B. Ag_3NO_3 C. $AgNO_2$ D. Ag_3NO_2 E. $AgNO_3$

120. Which reaction represents the balanced reaction for the combustion of ethanol?

A. $4C_2H_5OH + 13O_2 \rightarrow 8CO_2 + 10H_2$

B. $C_2H_5OH + 3O_2 \rightarrow 2CO_2 + 3H_2O$

C. $C_2H_5OH + 2O_2 \rightarrow 2CO_2 + 2H_2O$

D. $C_2H_5OH + O_2 \rightarrow CO_2 + H_2O$

E. $C_2H_5OH + ½ O_2 \rightarrow 2CO_2 + 3H_2O$

121. What is the formula mass of a molecule of CO_2?

A. 44 amu   C. 56.5 amu

B. 52 amu   D. 112 amu   E. none of the above

122. What is the oxidizing agent in the redox reaction: $Al + MnO_2 \rightarrow Al_2O_3 + Mn$?

A. O in Al_2O_3 B. O in MnO_2 C. Mn in MnO_2 D. Al   E. Al in Al_2O_3

123. What substance is reduced in the following redox reaction?

$$HgCl_2\ (aq) + Sn^{2+}\ (aq) \rightarrow Sn^{4+}\ (aq) + Hg_2Cl_2\ (s) + Cl^-\ (aq)$$

A. Sn^{4+} B. Hg_2Cl_2 C. $HgCl_2$ D. Sn^{2+} E. None of the above

124. Convert 152 miles into kilometers, using significant figures, given that 1 mile = 1.609 km:

A. 245 km   B. 244.57 km   C. 94 km   D. 94.4 km   E. 244.6 km

125. In acidic conditions, what is the sum of the coefficients in the products of the balanced reaction?

$$MnO_4^- + C_3H_7OH \rightarrow Mn^{2+} + C_2H_5COOH$$

A. 12   B. 16   C. 18   D. 20   E. 24

126. What is the percent by mass of chromium in K_2CrO_4?

A. 26.776 %   B. 31.663 %   C. 41.348 %   D. 43.765 %   E. 52.446 %

127. The oxidation number of C in BaC_2O_4 is:

   A. −3   **B.** −2   **C.** +2   **D.** +3   **E.** +4

128. How many molecules of CH_4 gas have a mass equal to 3.20 g?

   A. 3.01×10^{23} molecules   **C.** 1.20×10^{24} molecules

   B. 1.93×10^{24} molecules   **D.** 3.01×10^{24} molecules   **E.** 1.20×10^{23} molecules

129. When a substance loses electrons it is [   ], while the substance itself is acting as [   ] agent.

   A. reduced… a reducing   **C.** reduced… an oxidizing

   B. oxidized… a reducing   **D.** oxidized… an oxidizing   **E.** dissolved… a neutralizing

130. At constant volume, as the temperature of a sample of gas is decreased, the gas deviates from ideal behavior. Compared to the pressure predicted by the ideal gas law, actual pressure would be:

   A. higher, because of the volume of the gas molecules

   B. higher, because of intermolecular attractions between gas molecules

   C. lower, because of the volume of the gas molecules

   D. lower, because of intermolecular attractions among gas molecules

   E. higher, because of intramolecular attractions between gas molecules

131. How many O_2 molecules are needed to yield $10CO_2$ molecules according to balanced chemical equation: $2CO + O_2 \rightarrow 2CO_2$

   A. 4   **B.** 10   **C.** 5   **D.** 1   **E.** 2

132. In which of the following compounds does Cl have an oxidation number of +7?

   A. $NaClO_2$ **C.** $Ca(ClO_3)_2$

   B. $Al(ClO_4)_3$ **D.** $LiClO_3$ **E.** none of the above

133. Which of the following is a guideline for balancing redox equations by the oxidation number method?

   A. Verify that the total number of atoms and the total ionic charge are the same for reactants and products

   B. In front of the substance reduced, place a coefficient that corresponds to the number of electrons lost by the substance oxidized

   C. In front of the substance oxidized, place a coefficient that corresponds to the number of electrons gained by the substance reduced

   D. Diagram the electrons lost by the substance oxidized and gained by the substance reduced

   E. All of the above

134. What is the coefficient for O_2 when the following equation is balanced with the lowest whole number coefficients?

      $C_3H_7OH + O_2 \rightarrow CO_2 + H_2O$

   A. 4   **B.** 5   **C.** 9   **D.** 10   **E.** 12

135. From the following reaction, if 0.1 mole Al is allowed to react with 0.2 mole Fe_2O_3, what is the limiting reactant in this reaction: $2Al + Fe_2O_3 \rightarrow 2Fe + Al_2O_3$

  A. Fe_2O_3 **B.** Al_2O_3 **C.** Fe_2O_3 and Al_2O_3 **D.** Fe   **E.** Al

136. How many moles of Al are in a 4.56 g sample of Al if the atomic mass of Al is 26.982 amu?

  A. 0.169 moles   **C.** 1.43 moles

  B. 0.230 moles   **D.** 4.34 moles   **E.** 5.87 moles

137. Identify the missing terms in the following definition: "An oxidation number is the [   ] that an atom [   ] when the electrons in each bond are assigned to the [   ] electronegative of the two atoms involved in the bond.

  A. charge… definitely has… more   **C.** number of electrons… definitely has… more

  B. charge… definitely has… less   **D.** number of electrons… appears to have… less

                                         E. charge… appears to have… more

138. Which substance listed below is the weakest oxidizing agent given the following spontaneous redox reaction?

$$Mg\ (s) + Sn^{2+}\ (aq) \rightarrow Mg^{2+}\ (aq) + Sn\ (s)$$

  A. Mg^{2+} **B.** Sn   **C.** Mg   **D.** Sn^{2+} **E.** none of the above

139. The scientific principle that is the basis for balancing chemical equations is:

  A. Law of Conservation of Mass and Energy   **C.** Law of Conservation of Energy

  B. Law of Definite Proportions   **D.** Law of Conservation of Mass

                                         E. Avogadro's Law

140. How many moles of O_2 gas are required for combustion with one mole of $C_6H_{12}O_6$ in the unbalanced reaction: $C_6H_{12}O_6\ (s) + O_2\ (g) \rightarrow CO_2\ (g) + H_2O\ (g)$

  A. 1   **B.** 2.5   **C.** 6   **D.** 10   **E.** 12

141. What are the formula masses of water (H_2O), propene (C_3H_6) and 2-propanol (C_3H_8O)?

  A. water: 18 amu; propene: 44 amu; 2-propanol: 64 amu

  B. water: 18 amu; propene: 42 amu; 2-propanol: 60 amu

  C. water: 18 amu; propene: 42 amu; 2-propanol: 62 amu

  D. water: 18 amu; propene: 40 amu; 2-propanol: 58 amu

  E. water: 18 amu; propene: 42 amu; 2-propanol: 58 amu

142. Which of the following net ionic equations represents a disproportionation reaction?

  A. $ClO^- + Cl^- + 2H^+ \rightarrow Cl_2 + H_2O$ **C.** $Fe + 3Ag^+ \rightarrow Fe^{3+} + 3Ag$

  B. $CH_4 + 2O_2 \rightarrow CO_2 + H_2O$ **D.** $2HNO_3 + SO_2 \rightarrow H_2SO_4 + 2NO_2$

                                             E. None of the above

143. After balancing the following redox reaction, what is the coefficient of CO_2?

$$Co_2O_3\ (s) + CO\ (g) \rightarrow Co\ (s) + CO_2\ (g)$$

  A. 1   **B.** 2   **C.** 3   **D.** 5   **E.** none of the above

144. Round the following number to 3 significant figures: 565.85 grams:

    A. 565.9   **B.** 560   **C.** 565   **D.** 566   **E.** 565.90

145. Oxidation is defined as the:

    A. gaining of protons   **C.** gaining of electrons

    B. losing of neutrons   **D.** gaining of neutrons   **E.** losing of electrons

146. How many potassium atoms are in a sample of $K_3Fe(CN)_6$ that contains 1.084×10^{24} carbon atoms?

    A. 1.124×10^{24} atoms   **C.** 2.238×10^{24} atoms

    B. 5.420×10^{23} atoms   **D.** 3.865×10^{23} atoms   **E.** 3.362×10^{24} atoms

147. In which of the following compounds is the oxidation number of hydrogen NOT +1?

    A. NH_3 **B.** $HClO_2$ **C.** H_2SO_4 **D.** NaH   **E.** none of the above

148. What is the term for the volume occupied by 1 mol of any gas at STP?

    A. STP volume   **C.** standard volume

    B. molar volume   **D.** Avogadro's volume   **E.** none of the above

149. $2AgNO_3\,(aq) + K_2SO_4\,(aq) \rightarrow 2KNO_3\,(aq) + Ag_2SO_4\,(s)$.

The net ionic reaction for the balanced equation shown above is:

    A. $2Ag^+ + SO_4^{2-} \rightarrow Ag_2SO_4$ **C.** $2\,K^+ + SO_4^{2-} \rightarrow K_2SO_4$

    B. $K^+ + NO_3^- \rightarrow KNO_3$ **D.** $Ag^+ + NO_3^- \rightarrow AgNO_3$

                                          E. $H^+ + OH^- \rightarrow H_2O$

150. If the partial pressure of CO_2 is 60 torr at STP, and the gas is 20% CO_2 by mass, with only one other species of gas, which of the following could be the other species of gas?

    A. ethanol   **B.** sulfur   **C.** methane   **D.** hydrogen   **E.** bromine

151. How many grams of H_2O can be formed from a reaction between 10 grams of oxygen and 1 gram of hydrogen?

    A. 11 grams of H_2O are formed since mass must be conserved

    B. 10 grams of H_2O are formed since the mass of water produced cannot be greater than the amount of oxygen reacting

    C. 9 grams of H_2O are formed because oxygen and hydrogen react in an 8:1 mass ratio

    D. No H_2O is formed because there is insufficient hydrogen to react with the oxygen

    E. Not enough information is provided

152. The oxidation number of iron in the compound $FeBr_3$ is:

    A. –2   **B.** +1   **C.** +2   **D.** +3   **E.** –1

153. Which of the following is a method for balancing a redox equation in acidic solution by the half-reaction method?

   A. Multiply each half-reaction by a whole number, so that the number of electrons lost by the substance oxidized is equal to the electrons gained by the substance reduced

   B. Add the two half-reactions together and cancel identical species from each side of the equation

   C. Write a half-reaction for the substance oxidized and the substance reduced

   D. Balance the atoms in each half-reaction; balance oxygen with water and hydrogen with H^+

   E. All of the above

154. Which of the following substances has the lowest density?

   A. A mass of 750 g and a volume of 70 dL   **C.** A mass of 1.5 kg and a volume of 1.2 L

   B. A mass of 5 mg and a volume of 25 μL   **D.** A mass of 25 g and a volume of 20 mL

   E. A mass of 15 mg and a volume of 50 μL

155. How many moles of Sn^{4+} are produced from one mole of Sn^{2+} and excess O_2 and H^+ in the following reaction: $Sn^{2+} + O_2 \rightarrow Sn^{4+}$

   A. 2 moles   **B.** 2.5 moles   **C.** 1 ½ moles   **D.** ½ mole   **E.** 1 mole

156. How many grams of carbon are required to combine with 1.99 g of oxygen in C_2H_5OH?

   A. 1.93 g   **B.** 2.99 g   **C.** 5.26 g   **D.** 4.99 g   **E.** 3.99 g

157. In a redox reaction, the substance that is reduced:

   A. always gains electrons   **C.** contains an element that increases in oxidation number

   B. always loses electrons   **D.** is also the reducing agent

   E. either gains or loses electrons

158. In order for a redox reaction to be balanced, which of the following is true?

   I. Total ionic charge of reactants must equal total ionic charge of products

   II. Atoms of each reactant must equal atoms of product

   III. Electron gain must equal electron loss

   A. I and II only   **C.** II and III only

   B. I and III only   **D.** I, II and III   **E.** None of the above

159. When balanced, the coefficient for CO_2 is:

   ___C_5H_{12} + ___O_2 → ___CO_2 + ___H_2O

   A. 5   **B.** 6   **C.** 8   **D.** 10   **E.** 12

160. How many moles of O_2 gas are required for combustion with 2 moles of hexane in the unbalanced reaction: $C_6H_{14}(g) + O_2(g) \rightarrow CO_2(g) + H_2O(g)$

   A. 11   **B.** 14   **C.** 12   **D.** 20   **E.** 19

161. How many grams of H_2O can be produced from the reaction of 25.0 grams of H_2 and 225 grams of O_2?

    A. 250 grams   **C.** 200 grams

    B. 223 grams   **D.** 25 grams   **E.** 2.50 grams

162. Which of the following represents the oxidation of Co^{2+}?

    A. $Co \rightarrow Co^{2+} + 2\ e^-$ **C.** $Co^{2+} + 2\ e^- \rightarrow Co$

    B. $Co^{3+} + e^- \rightarrow Co^{2+}$ **D.** $Co^{2+} \rightarrow Co^{3+} + e^-$ **E.** $Co^{3+} + 2e^- \rightarrow Co^{1+}$

163. What is the term for the chemical formula of a compound that expresses the actual number of atoms of each element in a molecule?

    A. molecular formula   **C.** elemental formula

    B. empirical formula   **D.** atomic formula   **E.** none of the above

164. What is the coefficient of $HClO_4$ when balanced with smallest whole numbers?

        $Cl_2O_7 + H_2O \rightarrow HClO_4$

    A. 1   **B.** 2   **C.** 3   **D.** 4   **E.** 7

165. A reducing agent:

    A. is oxidized and gains electrons   **C.** is reduced

    B. gains electrons   **D.** loses protons   **E.** is oxidized

166. What is the molecular formula of a compound that has an empirical formula of CHCl with a molar mass of 194g?

    A. $C_4H_4Cl_4$ **B.** $C_2H_2Cl_2$ **C.** $C_3H_3Cl_3$ **D.** CHCl   **E.** $C_4H_3Cl_4$

167. Determine the oxidation number of C in $NaHCO_3$:

    A. +5   **B.** +4   **C.** +12   **D.** +6   **E.** +5

168. After balancing the following redox reaction in acidic solution, what is the coefficient of H^+?

        $Ag\ (s) + NO_3^-\ (aq) \rightarrow Ag^+\ (aq) + NO\ (aq)$

    A. 1   **B.** 2   **C.** 4   **D.** 6   **E.** None of the above

169. When the reaction shown is correctly balanced, the coefficients are:

        $C_6H_{14}\ (l) + O_2\ (g) \rightarrow CO_2\ (g) + H_2O\ (g)$

    A. 1, 3.5, 6, 7   **C.** 1, 6, 6, 7

    B. 1, 9.5, 6, 7   **D.** 2, 19, 12, 14   **E.** 2, 16.5, 12, 7

170. Ten moles of $N_2O_4\ (l)$ are added to an unknown amount of $N_2H_3(CH_3)\ (l)$. When the reaction runs to completion, what is the limiting reagent if 23 moles of H_2O are produced?

        $5N_2O_4\ (l) + 4N_2H_3(CH_3)\ (l) \rightarrow 12H_2O\ (g) + N_2\ (g) + CO_2\ (g)$

    A. $N_2O_4\ (l)$ **C.** $4N_2H_3(CH_3)\ (l)$

    B. $H_2O\ (g)$ **D.** $N_2O_4\ (l)$ **E.** There was no limiting reagent

171. How is Avogadro's number related to the numbers on the periodic table?

  A. The atomic mass listed is the mass of Avogadro's number's worth of atoms

  B. The periodic table provides the mass of one atom, while Avogadro's number provides the number of moles

  C. The masses are all divisible by Avogadro's number, which provides the weight of one mole

  D. The periodic table only provides atomic numbers, not atomic mass

  E. The mass listed is in the units of Avogadro's number

172. What volume of a 0.400 M $Fe(NO_3)_3$ solution is needed to supply 0.850 moles of nitrate ions?

  A. 345 mL   **B.** 0.708 mL   **C.** 222 mL   **D.** 708 mL   **E.** 984 mL

173. As the volume of a sealed container is decreased at constant temperature, the gas begins to deviate from ideal behavior. Compared to the pressure predicted by the ideal gas law, the actual pressure is:

  A. higher because of intermolecular attractions between gas molecules

  B. higher because of the volume of the gas molecules

  C. lower because of intermolecular attractions among gas molecules

  D. lower because of the volume of the gas molecules

  E. higher because of intramolecular attractions between gas molecules

174. How many significant figures are there in the following number: 0.00368 grams?

  A. 1   **B.** 4   **C.** 5   **D.** 2   **E.** 3

175. From the following reaction, if 0.1 mole of Al is allowed to react with 0.2 mole of Fe_2O_3, how many grams of aluminum oxide are produced: $2Al + Fe_2O_3 \rightarrow 2Fe + Al_2O_3$

  A. 3.8 g   **B.** 4.7 g   **C.** 5.1 g   **D.** 8.2 g   **E.** 12.2 g

176. How many atoms are in a sample of phosphorus trifluoride, PF_3, that contains 1.400 moles?

  A. 3.372×10^{24} **C.** 3.4

  B. 5.3   **D.** 2.218×10^{24} **E.** 8.976×10^{23}

177. What is the oxidation number of Br in $NaBrO_4$?

  A. –6   **B.** –4   **C.** +7   **D.** +4   **E.** +5

178. In basic solution, which is a guideline for balancing a redox equation by the half–reaction method?

  I. Verify that the total number of atoms, and that the total ionic charge, are equal for reactants and products

  II. Add the two half–reactions together and cancel identical species on each side of the equation

  III. Multiply each half–reaction by a whole number so that the number of electrons lost by the substance oxidized is equal to the electrons gained by the substance reduced

  IV. Write a balanced half-reaction for the substance oxidized and the substance reduced

  A. I and II only   **C.** II, III and IV only

  B. II and IV only   **D.** I, II and IV only   **E.** I, II, III and IV

179. What is the spectator ion: $2AgNO_3\ (aq) + K_2SO_4\ (aq) \rightarrow 2KNO_3\ (aq) + Ag_2SO_4\ (s)$?

A. silver ion and sulfate ion

B. potassium ion and nitrate ion

C. potassium ion and sulfate ion

D. silver ion and nitrate ion

E. hydrogen ion and hydroxide ion

180. How many moles of O_2 gas are required for combustion with one mole of $C_{12}H_{22}O_{11}$ in the unbalanced reaction: $C_{12}H_{22}O_{11}\ (l) + O_2\ (g) \rightarrow CO_2\ (g) + H_2O\ (g)$

A. 4   B. 8   C. 12   D. 14   E. 20

181. What is the formula mass of a molecule of $C_6H_{12}O_6$?

A. 148 amu   B. 27 amu   C. 21 amu   D. 180 amu   E. none of the above

182. For which of the following compounds is the oxidation number of oxygen NOT -2?

A. $NaClO_2$

B. Li_2O_2

C. $Ba(OH)_2$

D. Na_2SO_4

E. none of the above

183. Which substance listed below the strongest reducing agent given the following spontaneous redox reaction?

$$Mg\ (s) + Sn^{2+}\ (aq) \rightarrow Mg^{2+}\ (aq) + Sn\ (s)$$

A. Sn   B. Mg^{2+} C. Sn^{2+} D. Mg   E. none of the above

184. How many H atoms are in the molecule $C_6H_3(C_3H_7)_2(C_2H_5)$?

A. 27   B. 15   C. 29   D. 10   E. 22

185. In the following reaction: $Cu^{2+} + 2e^- \rightarrow Cu\ (s)$

A. Cu^{2+} is neutralized

B. Cu^{2+} is reduced and neutralized

C. Cu^{2+} is oxidized

D. Cu^{2+} is reduced

E. Cu^{2+} is a reducing agent

186. Upon combustion analysis, a 6.987 g sample of a hydrocarbon yielded 8.398 grams of carbon dioxide. The percent, by mass, of carbon in the hydrocarbon is:

A. 18.26 %   B. 23.27 %   C. 32.80 %   D. 31.37 %   E. 52.28 %

187. Which equation is NOT correctly classified by the type of chemical reaction?

Equation	Reaction Type
A. $AgNO_3 + NaCl \rightarrow AgCl + NaNO_3$	double-replacement/non-redox
B. $Cl_2 + F_2 \rightarrow 2\ ClF$	synthesis/redox
C. $H_2O + SO_2 \rightarrow H_2SO_3$	synthesis/non-redox
D. $CaCO_3 \rightarrow CaO + CO_2$	decomposition/redox
E. all are correctly classified	

188. Which substance is the weakest reducing agent given the spontaneous redox reaction?

$$Mg\ (s) + Sn^{2+}\ (aq) \rightarrow Mg^{2+}\ (aq) + Sn\ (s)$$

A. Sn   B. Mg^{2+} C. Sn^{2+} D. Mg   E. None of the above

189. The balanced equation for the reaction occurring when iron (III) oxide, a solid, is reduced with pure carbon to produce carbon dioxide and molten iron is:

A. $2Fe_2O_3 + 3C\ (s) \rightarrow 4Fe\ (l) + 3CO_2\ (g)$

B. $4Fe_2O_3 + 6C\ (s) \rightarrow 8Fe\ (l) + 6CO_2\ (g)$

C. $2FeO_3 + 3C\ (s) \rightarrow 2Fe\ (l) + 3CO_2\ (g)$

D. $2Fe_3O + C\ (s) \rightarrow 6Fe\ (l) + CO_2\ (g)$

E. $2FeO + C\ (s) \rightarrow 2Fe\ (l) + CO_2\ (g)$

190. 13.5 moles of N_2 gas are mixed with 33 moles of H_2 gas in the following reaction:

$$N_2\ (g) + 3H_2\ (g) \rightarrow 2NH_3\ (g)$$

How many moles of N_2 gas remain if the reaction produces 18 moles of NH_3 gas when performed at 600 K?

A. 0 moles   **B.** 2.25 moles   **C.** 4.5 moles   **D.** 9.0 moles   **E.** 18.0 moles

191. Which is a correctly balanced equation?

A. $2P_4 + 12H_2 \rightarrow 8PH_3$ **C.** $P_4 + 6H_2 \rightarrow 4PH_3$

B. $P_4 + 6H_2 \rightarrow 4PH_3$ **D.** $P_4 + 6H_2 \rightarrow 4PH_3$ **E.** $P_4 + 3H_2 \rightarrow PH_3$

192. Which element is reduced in the redox reaction: $BaSO_4 + 4C \rightarrow BaS + 4CO$?

A. O in CO   **B.** Ba in BaS   **C.** C   **D.** C in CO   **E.** S in $BaSO_4$

193. What is the term for the amount of substance that contains 6.02×10^{23} particles?

A. molar mass   **C.** Avogadro's number

B. mole   **D.** formula mass   **E.** none of the above

194. What is the coefficient for O_2 when balanced with the lowest whole number coefficients?

$$C_2H_6 + O_2 \rightarrow CO_2 + H_2O$$

A. 3   **B.** 4   **C.** 6   **D.** 7   **E.** 9

195. What is the oxidation number of Cr in the compound HCr_2O_4Cl?

A. +3   **B.** +2   **C.** +6   **D.** +5   **E.** +4

196. Select the balanced chemical equation for the reaction: $C_6H_{14} + O_2 \rightarrow CO_2 + H_2O$

A. $3C_6H_{14} + O_2 \rightarrow 18CO_2 + 22H_2O$ **C.** $2C_6H_{14} + 19O_2 \rightarrow 12CO_2 + 14H_2O$

B. $2C_6H_{14} + 12O_2 \rightarrow 12CO_2 + 14H_2O$ **D.** $2C_6H_{14} + 9O_2 \rightarrow 12CO_2 + 7H_2O$

     E. $C_6H_{14} + O_2 \rightarrow CO_2 + H_2O$

197. Which of the following reactions is NOT correctly classified?

A. $AgNO_3\ (aq) + KOH\ (aq) \rightarrow KNO_3\ (aq) + AgOH\ (s)$ non-redox / precipitation

B. $2H_2O_2\ (s) \rightarrow 2H_2O\ (l) + O_2\ (g)$ non-redox / decomposition

C. $Pb(NO_3)_2\ (aq) + 2Na\ (s) \rightarrow Pb\ (s) + 2NaNO_3\ (aq)$ redox / single-replacement

D. $HNO_3\ (aq) + LiOH\ (aq) \rightarrow LiNO_3\ (aq) + H_2O\ (l)$ non-redox / double-replacement

E. All are correctly classified

198. Which substance listed below is the weakest oxidizing agent given the following *spontaneous* redox reaction?

$$FeCl_3\ (aq) + NaI\ (aq) \rightarrow I_2\ (s) + FeCl_2\ (aq) + NaCl\ (aq)$$

A. I_2 **B.** $FeCl_2$ **C.** $FeCl_3$ **D.** NaI   **E.** NaCl

199. The oxidation number of iron in the compound $FeBr_3$ is:

A. -2 **B.** -1 **C.** $+1$ **D.** $+2$ **E.** $+3$

200. Which could NOT be true for the following reaction: $N_2\ (g) + 3H_2\ (g) \rightarrow 2NH_3\ (g)$?

A. 25 grams of N_2 gas reacts with 75 grams of H_2 gas to form 50 grams of NH_3 gas
B. 28 grams of N_2 gas reacts with 6 grams of H_2 gas to form 34 grams of NH_3 gas
C. 15 moles of N_2 gas reacts with 45 moles of H_2 gas to form 30 moles of NH_3 gas
D. 5 molecules of N_2 gas reacts with 15 molecules of H_2 gas to form 10 molecules of NH_3 gas
E. None of the above

201. Which coefficients balance the following equation:___$P_4\ (s) + $___$H_2\ (g) \rightarrow$ ___$PH_3\ (g)$?

A. 2, 10, 8   **B.** 1, 4, 4   **C.** 1, 6, 4   **D.** 4, 2, 3   **E.** 1, 3, 4

202. Which response represents the balanced half reaction for *oxidation* for the reaction:

$$HCl\ (aq) + Fe\ (s) \rightarrow FeCl_3\ (aq) + H_2\ (g)$$

A. $2Fe \rightarrow 2Fe^{3+} + 6e^-$ **C.** $Fe + 3e^- \rightarrow Fe^{3+}$
B. $3Fe \rightarrow Fe^{3+} + 3e^-$ **D.** $6e^- + 6H^+ \rightarrow 3H_2$ **E.** None of the above

203. From the periodic table, how many atoms of cobalt equal a mass of 58.93 g?

A. 58.93   **B.** 59   **C.** 1   **D.** 6.02×10^{23} **E.** 29.5

204. What is the total of all the coefficients when balanced with the lowest whole number coefficients?

$$N_2H_4 + H_2O_2 \rightarrow N_2 + H_2O$$

A. 4   **B.** 8   **C.** 10   **D.** 12   **E.** 14

205. Under acidic conditions, what is the sum of the coefficients in the balanced reaction below?

$$Fe^{2+} + Cr_2O_7^{2-} \rightarrow Fe^{3+} + Cr^{3+}$$

A. 8   **B.** 14   **C.** 17   **D.** 36   **E.** None of the above

206. The oxidation states of sulfur in H_2SO_4 and H_2SO_3, respectively, are:

A. $+2$ and $+6$ **C.** $+2$ and $+4$
B. $+6$ and $+4$ **D.** $+4$ and $+2$ **E.** $+4$ and $+4$

207. Which substance is functioning as the reducing agent:

$$14H^+ + Cr_2O_7^{2-} + 3\ Ni \rightarrow 3Ni^{2+} + 2Cr^{3+} + 7H_2O$$

A. $Cr_2O_7^{2-}$ **B.** H_2O **C.** Ni   **D.** H^+ **E.** Ni^{2+}

208. What is the term for a chemical formula that expresses the simplest whole number ratio of atoms of each element in a molecule?

   A. empirical formula   **C.** atomic formula

   B. molecular formula   **D.** elemental formula   **E.** none of the above

209. The balanced equation for the reaction occurring when calcium nitrate solution is mixed with sodium phosphate solution is:

   A. $3CaNO_3 (aq) + Na_3PO_4 (aq) \rightarrow Ca_3PO_4 (aq) + 3NaNO_3 (s)$

   B. $Ca(NO_3)_2 (aq) + 2NaPO_4 (aq) \rightarrow Ca(PO_4)_2 (s) + 2NaNO_3 (aq)$

   C. $3Ca(NO_3)_2 (aq) + 2Na_3PO_4 (aq) \rightarrow Ca_3(PO_4)_2 (aq) + 6NaNO_3 (aq)$

   D. $2Ca(NO_3)_2 (aq) + 3Na_3PO_4 (aq) \rightarrow 2\ Ca_3(PO_4)_2 (s) + 6NaNO_3 (aq)$

   E. $3Ca(NO_3)_2 (aq) + 2Na_3PO_4 (aq) \rightarrow Ca_3(PO_4)_2 (s) + 6NaNO_3 (aq)$

210. How much phosphorous is required to produce 275 g of phosphorous trichloride when the following reaction is run to completion: $P_4 (s) + 6Cl_2 (g) \rightarrow PCl_3 (l)$

   A. 62 g   **B.** 124 g   **C.** 166 g   **D.** 238 g   **E.** 265 g

211. Balance the equation: ___$H_2 (g)$ + ___$N_2 (g) \rightarrow$ ___$NH_3 (g)$

   A. 3, 2, 2   **B.** 3, 1, 2   **C.** 2, 2, 3   **D.** 2, 2, 5   **E.** 3, 1, 2

212. Which equation is NOT correctly classified by the type of chemical reaction?

Equation	Reaction Type
A. $PbO + C \rightarrow Pb + CO$	single-replacement/non-redox
B. $2Na + 2HCl \rightarrow 2NaCl + H_2$	single-replacement/redox
C. $NaHCO_3 + HCl \rightarrow NaCl + H_2O + CO_2$	double-replacement/non-redox
D. $2Na + H_2 \rightarrow 2NaH$	synthesis/redox
E. All are correctly classified	

213. Which substance is the weakest reducing agent given the spontaneous redox reaction?

     $FeCl_3 (aq) + NaI (aq) \rightarrow I_2 (s) + FeCl_2 (aq) + NaCl (aq)$

   A. NaCl   **B.** I_2 **C.** NaI   **D.** $FeCl_3$ **E.** $FeCl_2$

214. How many O atoms are in the formula unit $GaO(NO_3)_2$?

   A. 3   **B.** 4   **C.** 5   **D.** 7   **E.** 8

215. What is the oxidation state of S in sulfuric acid?

   A. +8   **B.** +6   **C.** −2   **D.** −6   **E.** +4

216. How many electrons are lost or gained by each formula unit of $CuBr_2$ in this reaction?

     $Zn + CuBr_2 \rightarrow ZnBr_2 + Cu$

   A. loses 1 electron   **C.** gains 2 electrons

   B. gains 6 electrons   **D.** loses 2 electrons   **E.** gains 4 electrons

217. What general term refers to the mass of 1 mol of any substance?

   A. gram-formula mass   **C.** gram-atomic mass

   B. molar mass   **D.** gram-molecular mass   **E.** none of the above

218. The net ionic equation for the reaction between zinc and hydrochloric acid solution is:

   A. $Zn^{2+} (aq) + H_2 (g) \rightarrow ZnS (s) + 2H^+ (aq)$

   B. $ZnCl_2 (aq) + H_2 (g) \rightarrow ZnS (s) + 2HCl (aq)$

   C. $Zn (s) + 2H^+ (aq) \rightarrow Zn^{2+} (aq) + H_2 (g)$

   D. $Zn (s) + 2HCl (aq) \rightarrow ZnCl_2 (aq) + H_2 (g)$

   E. None of these

219. If the partial pressure of CO_2 is 60 torr at STP, and nitrogen is the only other gas present, what is the percent by mass of CO_2?

   A. 1%   **B.** 25%   **C.** 40.5%   **D.** 3%   **E.** 12%

220. For a basic solution, which is the correct balanced half reaction?

$$Cr(OH)_4^- \rightarrow CrO_4^{2-}$$

   A. $Cr(OH)_4^- \rightarrow CrO_4^{2-} + 4H_2O + 2e^-$ **C.** $4OH^- + Cr(OH)_4^- \rightarrow CrO_4^{2-} + 3e^- + 4H_2O$

   B. $2OH^- + Cr(OH)_4^- \rightarrow CrO_4^{2-} + 6e^- + 3H_2O$ **D.** $3e^- + Cr(OH)_4^- + 2OH^- \rightarrow CrO_4^{2-} + 2H_2O$

                                                   E. None of the above

221. What principle states that equal volumes of gases, at the same temperature and pressure, contain equal numbers of molecules?

   A. Dalton's theory   **C.** Boyle's theory

   B. Charles' theory   **D.** Avogadro's theory   **E.** None of the above

222. If 64 g of O_2 gas are reacted in the following reaction, how many moles of water are produced?

$$Sn^{2+} + O_2 \rightarrow Sn^{4+}$$

   A. 3 moles   **B.** 2 moles   **C.** 6 moles   **D.** 5 moles   **E.** 4 moles

223. How many moles of phosphorous trichloride are required to produce 365 grams of HCl when the reaction yields 75%: $PCl_3 (g) + 3NH_3 (g) \rightarrow P(NH_2)_3 + 3HCl (g)$.

   A. 1 mol   **B.** 2.5 mol   **C.** 3.5 mol   **D.** 4.5 mol   **E.** 5 mol

224. Which response represents the balanced half reaction for *reduction* for the reaction given below?

$$Fe (s) + CuSO_4 (aq) \rightarrow Fe_2(SO_4)_3(aq) + Cu (s)$$

   A. $3Cu^{2+} + 6e^- \rightarrow 3Cu$ **C.** $2Cu^{3+} + 3e^- \rightarrow 2Cu$

   B. $2Fe \rightarrow 2Fe^{3+} + 6e^-$ **D.** $Fe + 3e^- \rightarrow Fe^{3+}$ **E.** none of the above

225. What is the term for a temperature of 0 °C and a pressure of 1 atm?

   A. standard temperature and pressure   **C.** experimental temperature and pressure

   B. ideal gas temperature and pressure   **D.** atmospheric temperature and pressure

                                                 E. none of the above

226. What are the spectator ions in the reaction between KOH and HNO_3?

   A. K^+ and NO_3^- **C.** K^+ and H^+

   B. H^+ and NO_3^- **D.** H^+ and OH^- **E.** K^+ and OH^-

227. What is the molecular formula of galactose if the empirical formula is CH_2O, and the approximate molar mass is 180 g/mol?

   A. $C_6H_{12}O_6$ **B.** CH_2O_6 **C.** CH_2O **D.** CHO **E.** $C_{12}H_{22}O_{11}$

228. If the relative mass of a ping pong ball is 1/20 that of a golf ball, how many ping pong balls are needed to equal the mass of two golf balls?

   A. 100   **B.** 10   **C.** 20   **D.** 40   **E.** 6.022×10^{23}

229. In the disproportion equation below, what species is undergoing disproportionation?

$$3Br_2 + 6OH^- \rightarrow BrO_3^- + 5Br^- + 3H_2O$$

   A. Br_2 **B.** H_2O **C.** Br^- **D.** OH^- **E.** none of the above

230. What is the volume occupied by 0.750 g of N_2 gas, at STP?

   A. 37.3 L   **B.** 16.8 L   **C.** 0.600 L   **D.** 0.938 L   **E.** 836 L

231. For *n* moles of gas, which term expresses the kinetic energy?

   A. nPA, where n = number of moles of gas, P = total pressure and A = surface area of the container walls

   B. $1/2 \ nPA$, where n = number of moles of gas, P = total pressure and A = surface area of the container walls

   C. $1/2 \ MV^2$, where M = molar mass of the gas and V = volume of the container

   D. MV^2, where M = molar mass of the gas and V = volume of the container

   E. $3/2 \ nRT$, where n = number of moles of gas, R = ideal gas constant and T = absolute temperature

232. How many grams of Ba^{2+} ions are in an aqueous solution of $BaCl_2$ that contains 6.8×10^{22} Cl ions?

   A. 3.2×10^{48} g   **B.** 12g   **C.** 14.5g   **D.** 7.8g   **E.** 9.8g

233. The formula for mustard gas used in chemical warfare is $C_4H_8SCl_2$ (159.09 g/mol). What is the percentage of chlorine in mustard gas?

   A. 20.16%   **B.** 44.57%   **C.** 5.08%   **D.** 30.20%   **E.** 22.28%

234. Which is a good experimental method to distinguish between ordinary hydrogen and deuterium, the rare isotope of hydrogen?

> I. Measure the density of the gas at STP
> II. Measure the rate at which the gas effuses
> III. Determine the number of grams of gas that react with one mole of O_2 to form H_2O

A. I only   **B.** II only   **C.** III only   **D.** I, II, and III   **E.** None of the above

235. Which reaction is the correctly balanced half reaction (in acid solution) for the process below?

$$Cr_2O_7^{2-} \, (aq) \rightarrow Cr^{3+} \, (aq)$$

A. $8H^+ + Cr_2O_7 \rightarrow 2Cr^{3+} + 4H_2O + 3e^-$

B. $12H^+ + Cr_2O_7^{2-} + 3e^- \rightarrow 2Cr^{3+} + 6H_2O$

C. $14H^+ + Cr_2O_7^{2-} + 6e^- \rightarrow 2Cr^{3+} + 7H_2O$

D. $8H^+ + Cr_2O_7 + 3e^- \rightarrow 2Cr^{3+} + 4H_2O$

E. None of the above

236. In the early 1980s, benzene that had been used as a solvent for waxes and oils was listed as a carcinogen by the EPA. What is the molecular formula of benzene if the empirical formula is C_1H_1, and the approximate molar mass is 78 g/mol?

A. CH_{12} **B.** $C_{12}H_{12}$ **C.** CH **D.** CH_6 **E.** C_6H_6

237. Under ideal conditions, which of the following gases is least likely to be ideal?

A. CCl_4 **B.** CH_3OH **C.** O_2 **D.** O_3 **E.** CO_2

238. The reason why ice floats in a glass of water is because, when frozen, H_2O is less dense due to:

A. strengthening of cohesive forces

B. high specific heat

C. decreased number of hydrogen bonds

D. weakening of cohesive forces

E. increased number of hydrogen bonds

Chapter 7.   CHEMICAL EQUILIBRIA AND CHEMICAL KINETICS

1. What is the term for the energy necessary for reactants to achieve the transition state and form products?

A. heat of reaction

B. energy barrier

C. rate barrier

D. collision energy

E. activation energy

2. Which of the following stresses would shift the equilibrium to the left for the following chemical system at equilibrium *heat* + $6H_2O$ (g) + $2N_2$ (g) ↔ $4NH_3$ (g) + $3O_2$ (g)?

A. Increasing the concentration of H_2O

B. Decreasing the concentration of NH_3

C. Increasing the concentration of O_2

D. Increasing the reaction temperature

E. Decreasing the concentration of O_2

3. Which component of the reaction mechanism results in the net production of free radicals?

   I. initiation   II. propagation   III. termination

A. I only   **B.** II only   **C.** III only   **D.** II and III only   **E.** I and III only

4. Nitrogen monoxide reacts with bromine at elevated temperatures according to the equation

$$2NO\ (g) + Br_2\ (g) \rightarrow 2NOBr\ (g)$$

What is the rate of consumption of Br_2 (g) if, in a certain reaction mixture, the rate of formation of NOBr (g) was 4.50×10^{-4} mol L^{-1} s^{-1}?

A. 3.12×10^{-4} mol L^{-1} s^{-1}

B. 8.00×10^{-4} mol L^{-1} s^{-1}

C. 2.25×10^{-4} mol L^{-1} s^{-1}

D. 4.50×10^{-4} mol L^{-1} s^{-1}

E. 4.00×10^{-3} mol L^{-1} s^{-1}

5. For a collision between molecules to result in a reaction, the molecules must possess both a favorable orientation relative to each other and:

A. be in the gaseous state

B. have a certain minimum energy

C. adhere for at least 2 nanoseconds

D. exchange electrons

E. be in the liquid state

6. What is the term for a substance that allows a reaction to proceed faster by lowering the energy of activation?

A. rate barrier

B. energy barrier

C. collision energy

D. activation energy

E. catalyst

7. Reaction rates are determined by all of the following factors, EXCEPT:

A. orientation of collisions between molecules

B. spontaneity of the reaction

C. force of collisions between molecules

D. number of collisions between molecules

E. the activation energy of the reaction

8. For the combustion of ethanol (C_2H_6O) to form carbon dioxide and water, what is the rate at which carbon dioxide is produced if the ethanol is consumed at a rate of 3.0 M s^{-1}?

    A. 1.5 M s^{-1} **C.** 6.0 M s^{-1}

    B. 12.0 M s^{-1} **D.** 9.0 M s^{-1} **E.** 10.0 M s^{-1}

9. If the heat of reaction is endothermic, which of the following is always true?

    A. The energy of the reactants is less than the products   **C.** The reaction rate is slow

    B. The energy of the reactants is greater than the products   **D.** The reaction rate is fast

                                                     E. None of the above

10. Most reactions are carried out in liquid solution or in the gaseous phase, because in such situations:

    A. kinetic energies of reactants are lower

    B. reactant collisions occur more frequently

    C. activation energies are higher

    D. reactant activation energies are lower

    E. reactant collisions occur less frequently

11. Why might increasing the concentration of a set of reactants increase the rate of reaction?

    A. The rate of reaction depends only on the mass of the atoms and therefore increases as you increase the mass of the reactants

    B. The concentration of reactants is unrelated to the rate of reaction

    C. There is an increased ratio of reactants to products

    D. There is an increased probability that any two reactant molecules collide and react

    E. None of the above

12. What is the term for a dynamic state of a reversible reaction in which the rates of the forward and reverse reactions are equal?

    A. dynamic equilibrium   **C.** reversible equilibrium

    B. rate equilibrium   **D.** concentration equilibrium

                                        E. chemical equilibrium

13. Which conditions would favor the reaction to completion?

    $2N_2 (g) + 6H_2O (g) + heat \leftrightarrow 4NH_3 (g) + 3O_2 (g)$

    A. Increase reaction temperature

    B. Continual addition of NH_3 gas to the reaction mixture

    C. Decrease the pressure on the reaction vessel

    D. Continual removal of N_2 gas

    E. Decreases reaction temperature

14. The reaction $\cdot OH + H_2 \rightarrow H_2O + H\cdot$ is an example of a free radical:

    I. initiation   II. propagation   III. termination

    A. I only   **B.** II only   **C.** III only   **D.** II and III only   **E.** I and II only

15. In a particular study of the reaction described by the equation, what is the rate of consumption of CH_4O (g) if the rate of consumption of $O_2(g)$ is 0.400 mol $L^{-1} s^{-1}$?

$$2CH_4O\ (g) + 3O_2\ (g) \rightarrow 2CO_2\ (g) + 4H_2O\ (g)$$

A. 0.150 mol $L^{-1} s^{-1}$
B. 0.267 mol $L^{-1} s^1$

C. 0.333 mol $L^{-1} s^{-1}$
D. 0.550 mol $L^{-1} s^{-1}$
E. 0.500 mol $L^{-1} s^{-1}$

16. Which of the following statements about "activation energy" is correct?

A. Activation energy is the energy given off when reactants collide
B. Activation energy is high for reactions that occur rapidly
C. Activation energy is low for reactions that occur rapidly
D. Activation energy is the maximum energy a reacting molecule may possess
E. Activation energy is low for reactions that occur slowly

17. What is the term for the principle that the rate of reaction is regulated by the frequency, energy and orientation of molecules striking each other?

A. orientation theory
B. frequency theory

C. energy theory
D. collision theory
E. rate theory

18. Which of the following statements can be assumed to be true about how reactions occur?

A. Reactant particles must collide with each other
B. Energy must be released as the reaction proceeds
C. Catalysts must be present in the reaction
D. Energy must be absorbed as the reaction proceeds
E. The energy of activation must have a negative value

19. Given the rate = $k[A]^2[B]^4$, what is the order of the reaction?

A. 1   **B.** 2   **C.** 4   **D.** 6   **E.** 8

20. What is the equilibrium constant expression (K_{sp}) for slightly soluble silver sulfate in an aqueous solution $Ag_2SO_4\ (s) \rightleftarrows 2Ag^+\ (aq) + SO_4^{2-}\ (aq)$?

A. $K_{sp} = [Ag^+]\ [SO_4^{2-}]^2$
B. $K_{sp} = [Ag^+]^2\ [SO_4^{2-}]\ /\ [Ag_2SO_4]$

C. $K_{sp} = [Ag^+]\ [SO_4^{2-}]$
D. $K_{sp} = [Ag^+]\ [SO_4^{2-}]^2\ /\ [Ag_2SO_4]$
E. $K_{sp} = [Ag^+]^2\ [SO_4^{2-}]$

21. The minimum combined kinetic energy reactants must possess for collisions to result in a reaction is:

A. orientation energy
B. activation energy

C. collision energy
D. dissociation energy
E. bond energy

22. Why does a glowing splint of wood burn only slowly in air, but rapidly in a burst of flames when placed in pure oxygen?

    A. A glowing wood splint is actually extinguished within pure oxygen because oxygen inhibits the smoke

    B. Pure oxygen is able to absorb carbon dioxide at a faster rate

    C. Oxygen is a flammable gas

    D. There is an increased number of collisions between the wood and oxygen molecules

    E. There is a decreased number of collisions between the wood and oxygen

23. What is the term for a reaction that proceeds by absorbing heat energy?

    A. isothermal reaction   **C.** endothermic reaction

    B. exothermic reaction   **D.** all of the above   **E.** none of the above

24. All of the following factors may shift the position of equilibrium, EXCEPT:

    A. decreasing reaction temperature   **C.** increasing reaction temperature

    B. doubling the pressure   **D.** reducing reaction volume

                                  E. addition of a catalyst

25. Which factor does NOT describe activated complexes?

    A. May be chemically isolated   **C.** Have specific geometry

    B. Decompose rapidly   **D.** Are extremely reactive

                                    E. At the high point of the reaction profile

26. A 10-mm cube of copper metal is placed in 250 mL of 12 M nitric acid at 25 °C and the reaction below occurs:

$$Cu(s) + 4H^+ (aq) + 2NO_3^- (aq) \rightarrow Cu^{2+} (aq) + 2NO_2 (g) + 2H_2O (l)$$

At a particular instant in time, nitrogen dioxide is being produced at the rate of 2.6×10^{-4} M/min. At this same instant, what is the rate at which hydrogen ions are being consumed?

    A. 2.6×10^{-4} M/min   **C.** 1.3×10^{-4} M/min

    B. 1.0×10^{-3} M/min   **D.** 5.2×10^{-4} M/min   **E.** 6.5×10^{-5} M/min

27. If, at equilibrium, reactant concentrations are slightly smaller than product concentrations, the equilibrium constant would be:

    A. slightly greater than 1   **C.** $\ll 1$

    B. slightly lower than 1   **D.** $\gg 1$ **E.** equal to zero

28. Which of the following influences the rate of a chemical reaction?

    A. Collision orientation   **C.** Collision frequency

    B. Collision energy   **D.** None of the above   **E.** All of the above

29. Which of the following affects all reaction rates?

    A. Temperature of the reactants   **C.** Concentrations of the reactants

    B. Presence of a catalyst   **D.** All are correct

                                    E. None affect the rates

30. If the rate law = $k[A]^{1/2}[B]$, which of the following can be concluded about the reaction?

    A. Reaction mechanism does not occur in a single step

    B. The rate of A is half the rate of B

    C. For every molecule of B, two molecules of A react

    D. For every molecule of A, two molecules of B react

    E. None are true

31. Which of the changes has no effect on the equilibrium for the reversible reaction:

$$SO_3\,(g) + NO\,(g) + heat \leftrightarrow SO_2\,(g) + NO_2\,(g)$$

    A. add a catalyst   **C.** increase volume

    B. add helium gas   **D.** decrease volume   **E.** all of the above

32. The expression for the equilibrium constant, K_{eq}, for the reaction below is:

$$4NH_3\,(g) + 5O_2\,(g) \leftrightarrow 4NO\,(g) + 6H_2O\,(g)$$

    A. $K_{eq} = [NO]^4[H_2O]^6 / [NH_3]^4[O_2]^5$ **C.** $K_{eq} = [NO][H_2O] / [NH_3][O_2]$

    B. $K_{eq} = [NH_3]^4[O_2]^5 / [NO]^4[H_2O]^6$ **D.** $K_{eq} = [NH_3][O_2] / [NO][H_2O]$

                                                E. $K_{eq} = [NH_3]^2[O_2]^5 / [NO]^2[H_2O]^3$

33. Why might increasing temperature alter the rate of a chemical reaction?

    A. The molecules combine with other atoms at high temperature to save space

    B. The density decreases as a function of temperature that increases volume and decreases the reaction rate

    C. The molecules have a higher kinetic energy and have more force when colliding

    D. The molecules are less reactive at higher temperatures

    E. None of the above

34. If the E_{act} is lowered, which of the following is always true?

    A. The reaction is endothermic   **C.** The reaction proceeds slower

    B. The reaction is exothermic   **D.** The reaction proceeds faster

                                               E. None of the above

35. If a reaction proceeds in several steps, the process with the highest activation energy is the:

    A. product formation step   **C.** transition step

    B. activated complex step   **D.** favorable step   **E.** rate-determining step

36. What is the overall order of the reaction if the units of the rate constant for a particular reaction are min^{-1}?

    A. Zero   **B.** First   **C.** Second   **D.** Third   **E.** Fourth

37. Which statement is NOT a correct characterization for a catalyst?

    A. Catalysts are not consumed in a reaction

    B. Catalysts do not actively participate in a reaction

    C. Catalysts lower the activation energy for a reaction

    D. Catalysts can be either solids, liquids or gases

    E. Catalysts do not alter the equilibrium of the reaction

38. What is the term for a reaction that proceeds by releasing heat energy?

  A. Endothermic reaction   **C.** Exothermic reaction

  B. Isothermal reaction   **D.** All of the above   **E.** None of the above

39. For a chemical reaction to occur, all of the following must happen, EXCEPT:

  A. reactant particles must collide with the correct orientation

  B. a large enough number of collisions must occur

  C. chemical bonds in the reactants must break

  D. reactant particles must collide with enough energy for change to occur

  E. chemical bonds in the products must form

40. By convention, what is the equilibrium constant for step 1 in a reaction?

  A. $k_1 k_{+2}$ **B.** $k_1 + k_{+2}$ **C.** k_{-1} **D.** k_1 **E.** k_1 / k_{-1}

41. What is the K_{sp} for calcium fluoride (CaF_2) if the calcium ion concentration in a saturated solution is 0.00021 *M*?

  A. $K_{sp} = 3.7 \times 10^{-11}$ **C.** $K_{sp} = 4.4 \times 10^{-8}$

  B. $K_{sp} = 2.3 \times 10^{-12}$ **D.** $K_{sp} = 8.8 \times 10^{-8}$ **E.** $K_{sp} = 9.3 \times 10^{-12}$

42. Which statement is correct concerning Reaction A, if it releases 24 kJ/mole and has an activation energy of 98 kJ/mole?

  A. The overall reaction is exothermic with a high activation energy

  B. The overall reaction is endothermic with a high activation energy

  C. The overall reaction is exothermic with a low activation energy

  D. The overall reaction is endothermic with a low activation energy

  E. None of the above

43. Why does dough rise faster in a warmer area when yeast in bread dough feed on sugar to produce carbon dioxide?

  A. The yeast tends to become activated with warmer temperatures, which is why baker's yeast is best stored in the refrigerator

  B. The rate of evaporation increases with increasing temperature

  C. There is a greater number of effective collisions among reacting molecules

  D. Atmospheric pressure decreases with increasing temperature

  E. Atmospheric pressure increases with increasing temperature

44. Which is true before a reaction reaches chemical equilibrium?

  A. The amount of reactants and products are equal

  B. The amount of reactants and products are constant

  C. The amount of products is decreasing

  D. The amount of reactants is increasing

  E. The amount of products is increasing

45. Which of the changes shift the equilibrium to the right for the following system at equilibrium:

$$N_2 (g) + 3H_2 (g) \leftrightarrow 2NH_3 (g) + 92.94 \text{ kJ}$$

I. Removing NH_3 III. Removing N_2
II. Adding NH_3 IV. Adding N_2

A. I and III   **B.** II and III   **C.** II and IV   **D.** I and IV   **E.** None of the above

46. Which is NOT an important condition for a chemical reaction?

  A. The molecules must make contact
  B. The molecules have enough energy to react once they collide
  C. The reacting molecules are in the correct orientation to one another
  D. None of the above
  E. The molecules are in the solid, liquid or gaseous state

47. The rate of a chemical reaction in solution can be measured in the units:

  A. mol s L^{-1} **C.** $\text{mol L}^{-1} \text{s}^{-1}$

  B. s^{-2} **D.** $\text{L}^2 \text{mol}^{-1} \text{s}^{-1}$ **E.** $\text{sec L}^{-1} \text{mol}^{-1}$

48. Whether a reaction is exothermic or endothermic is determined by:

  A. an energy balance between bond breaking and bond forming resulting in a net loss or gain of energy
  B. whether a catalyst is present
  C. the activation energy
  D. the physical state of the reaction system
  E. none of the above

49. Which of the changes shifts the equilibrium to the right for the following reversible reaction?

$$SO_3 (g) + NO (g) + heat \leftrightarrow SO_2 (g) + NO_2 (g)$$

  A. decreasing temperature   **C.** increasing $[SO_3]$
  B. increasing volume   **D.** increasing $[SO_2]$ **E.** adding a catalyst

50. In the reaction energy diagrams shown below, reaction A is [   ] and occurs [   ] reaction B.

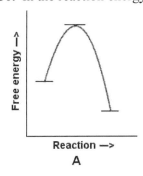
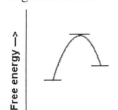

  A. endergonic… slower than
  B. exergonic… slower than
  C. endergonic… faster than
  D. exergonic… faster than
  E. exergonic… at the same rate as

51. In the reaction energy diagrams shown in question 50, reaction B is [ ] and occurs [ ] reaction A.

A. exergonic… slower than

B. endergonic… slower than

C. exergonic… faster than

D. exergonic… at the same rate as

E. endergonic… faster than

52. What is the order of the reaction when the rate law = $k[A][B]^3$?

A. 2   B. 3   C. 4   D. 5   E. 6

53. What is the equilibrium constant expression, K_i, for the following weak acid?

$$H_3PO_4 \, (aq) \leftrightarrow H^+ \, (aq) + H_2PO_4^- \, (aq)$$

A. $K_i = [H_3PO_4] / [H^+] [H_2PO_4^-]$

B. $K_i = [H^+]^3 [PO_4^{3-}] / [H_3PO_4]$

C. $K_i = [H^+]^3 [H_2PO_4^-] / [H_3PO_4]$

D. $K_i = [H^+] [H_2PO_4^-] / [H_3PO_4]$

E. $K_i = [H_3PO_4] / [H^+]^3 [PO_4^{3-}]$

54. Which reaction below is endothermic?

A. $PCl_3 + Cl_2 \rightarrow PCl_5 + heat$

B. $2NO_2 \rightarrow N_2 + 2O_2 + heat$

C. $CH_4 + NH_3 + heat \rightarrow HCN + 3H_2$

D. $NH_3 + HBr \rightarrow NH_4Br + heat$

E. $PCl_3 + Cl_2 \rightarrow PCl_5 + heat$

55. Which of the reactions proceeds the fastest?

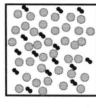 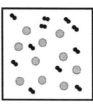 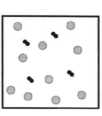

a   b   c

$X + Y \rightarrow Z$

A. a

B. b

C. c

D. all proceed at same rate

E. not enough information given

56. Which of the reactions proceeds the slowest?

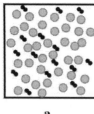 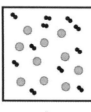 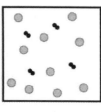

a   b   c

$X + Y \rightarrow Z$

A. a

B. b

C. c

D. all proceed at same rate

E. not enough information given

57. What equilibrium constant applies to a reversible reaction involving a gaseous mixture at equilibrium?

A. Ionization equilibrium constant, K_w

B. General equilibrium constant, K_{eq}

C. Solubility product equilibrium constant, K_{sp}

D. Ionization equilibrium constant, K_i

E. None of the above

58. Coal burning plants release the toxic gas, sulfur dioxide, into the atmosphere while nitrogen monoxide is released into the atmosphere via industrial processes and from combustion engines. Sulfur dioxide can also be produced in the atmosphere by the following equilibrium reaction:

$$SO_3 \ (g) + NO \ (g) + Heat \leftrightarrow SO_2 \ (g) + NO_2 \ (g)$$

Which of the following does NOT shift the equilibrium to the right?

A. [NO$_2$] decrease
B. [NO] increase
C. Decrease the reaction chamber volume
D. Temperature increase
E. All of the above would shift the equilibrium to the right

Questions **59-62** are based on this graph and net reaction.

The reaction proceeds in two consecutive steps.
$$XY + Z \rightleftarrows XYZ \rightleftarrows X + YZ$$

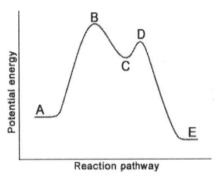

59. Where is the activated complex for this reaction?

A. A
B. A and C
C. C
D. E
E. B and D

60. The activation energy for the reverse reaction is given by:

A. A
B. B
C. C
D. D
E. D and C

61. The activation energy for the forward reaction is given by:

A. A
B. B
C. C
D. D
E. B and D

62. The change in energy (ΔE) of the overall reaction is given by the difference between:

A. A and B
B. A and E
C. A and C
D. B and D
E. B and C

63. Which statement is NOT correct for $aA + bB \rightarrow dD + eE$ whereby rate $= k[A]^q[B]^r$?

A. The overall order of the reaction is q + r
B. The exponents q and r are equal to the coefficients a and b, respectively
C. The exponents q and r must be determined experimentally
D. The exponents q and r are often integers
E. The symbol k represents the rate constant

64. If, at equilibrium, most of the reactants remain unreacted, the equilibrium constant has a numerical value that is:

A. slightly greater than 1.0
B. slightly less than 1.0
C. very large
D. equal to 0
E. very small

---

65. If the heat of reaction is exothermic, which of the following is always true?

A. Energy of the reactants is greater than the products

B. Energy of the reactants is less than the products

C. Reaction rate is fast

D. Reaction rate is slow

E. Energy of the reactants is equal to that of the products

66. Which factors decrease the rate of a reaction?

    I.   Lowering the temperature

    II. Increasing the concentration of reactants

    III. Adding a catalyst

A. I only   **B.** II only   **C.** III only   **D.** II and III only   **E.** I and III only

67. The rate constant for the conversion of methyl propanoate is 1×10^{-4} s^{-1}. A container of methyl propanoate gas has a partial pressure of 100 torr. After 6.4 hours (approx. 23,000 seconds), what is the partial pressure of methyl propanoate gas?

A. 1 torr   **B.** 10 torr   **C.** 5 torr   **D.** 30 torr   **E.** 12.5 torr

68. Which of the changes has no effect on the equilibrium for the reversible reaction?

$$PbI_2\,(s) \leftrightarrow Pb^{2+}\,(aq) + 2I^-\,(aq)$$

A. Decreasing $[Pb^{2+}]$ **C.** Decreasing $[I^-]$

B. Adding solid PbI_2 **D.** Increasing $[Pb^{2+}]$ **E.** Increasing $[I^-]$

69. What does it mean when the position of an equilibrium is described as being "far to the left"?

A. The rate of the reverse reaction is greater than that of the forward reaction

B. Significant amounts of both products and reactants are present in the equilibrium mixture

C. Very few product molecules are present in the equilibrium mixture

D. Very few reactant molecules are present in the equilibrium mixture

E. Many product molecules are present in the equilibrium mixture

70. What is the activation energy?

A. Amount of energy required to separate reactants from the products

B. Energy difference between the reactants and the products

C. Amount of energy required to activate a phase change

D. Amount of energy released from the phase change

E. Minimum amount of energy to break the bonds in the reactants

71. Which of the following increases the collision energy of gaseous molecules?

A. Increasing the temperature   **C.** Increasing the concentration

B. Adding a catalyst   **D.** All of the above   **E.** None of the above

72. For a reaction that has an equilibrium constant of 4.3×10^{-17} at 25 °C, the position at equilibrium is described as:

    A. equal amounts of reactants and products
    B. significant amounts of both reactants and products
    C. mostly products
    D. mostly reactants
    E. amount of product is slightly greater than reactants

73. If the temperature of the system is raised for the reaction $CO\,(g) + 2H_2O\,(g) \rightleftarrows CH_3OH\,(g)$ with $\Delta H < 0$, the equilibrium is:

    A. variable
    B. unaffected
    C. shifted to the left
    D. shifted to the right
    E. shifted to the right by the square root of ΔH

74. Which of the changes shifts the equilibrium to the right for the following reversible reaction?

    $PbI_2\,(s) \leftrightarrow Pb^{2+}\,(aq) + 2\,I^-\,(aq)$

    A. add solid $Pb(NO_3)_2$
    B. add solid PbI_2
    C. decrease $[I^-]$
    D. increase $[Pb^{2+}]$
    E. add solid $NaNO_3$

75. Which of the following is true regarding the K_{eq} expression?

    A. The value of K_{eq} is temperature dependent
    B. The K_{eq} expression contains only substances in the same physical state
    C. The K_{eq} expression was originally determined experimentally
    D. None of the above
    E. All of the above

76. Cyclobutane decomposes as $C_4H_8\,(g) \rightarrow 2C_2H_4\,(g)$. What is the rate of $C_2H_4\,(g)$ formation if, during the course this reaction, the rate of consumption of C_4H_8 was 4.25×10^{-4} mol L^{-1} s^{-1}?

    A. 1.06×10^{-4} mol L^{-1} s^{-1}
    B. 8.50×10^{-4} mol L^{-1} s^{-1}
    C. 2.13×10^{-4} mol L^{-1} s^{-1}
    D. 4.25×10^{-4} mol L^{-1} s^{-1}
    E. 1.81×10^{-3} mol L^{-1} s^{-1}

77. Which of the following changes most likely decreases the rate of a reaction?

    A. Increasing the reaction temperature
    B. Increasing the concentration of a reactant
    C. Increasing the activation energy for the reaction
    D. Decreasing the activation energy for the reaction
    E. Increasing the reaction pressure

78. What is the term for a type of equilibrium in which all of the participating species are not in the same physical state?

    A. Homogeneous equilibrium
    B. Physical equilibrium
    C. Concentration equilibrium
    D. Heterogeneous equilibrium
    E. None of the above

79. A rapid reaction is distinguished by:

    A. having a large activation energy

    B. having a small heat of reaction

    C. having a large heat of reaction

    D. being unaffected by catalysts

    E. having a small activation energy

80. What is the order of B in a reactant with the rate law of $k[A]^2$?

    A. 0   **C.** 2

    B. 1   **D.** ½   **E.** Cannot be determined from the information given

81. For the reaction, $CO\ (g) + 2H_2O\ (g) \rightleftarrows CH_3OH\ (g)$ with $\Delta H < 0$, which factor increases the equilibrium yield for methanol?

    A. Decreasing the volume

    B. Decreasing the pressure

    C. Lowering the temperature of the system

    D. Decreasing the volume or lowering the temperature of the system

    E. None of the above

82. A catalyst functions by:

    A. increasing the rate of a reaction by increasing the heat of reaction

    B. increasing the rate of a reaction by increasing the activation energy of the reverse reaction only

    C. increasing the rate of a reaction by lowering the activation energy of the forward reaction only

    D. increasing the rate of a reaction by decreasing the heat of reaction

    E. increasing the rate of a reaction by providing an alternative pathway with a lower activation energy

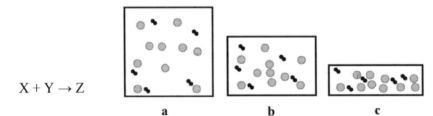

$X + Y \rightarrow Z$

    a   b   c

83. Which of the above reactions proceeds the slowest?

    A. a   **C.** c

    B. b   **D.** All proceed at same rate   **E.** Not enough information given

84. Which of the above reactions in the figures for question 83 proceeds the fastest?

    A. a   **C.** c

    B. b   **D.** All proceed at same rate   **E.** Not enough information given

85. Which of the following increases the collision frequency of molecules?

    A. Adding a catalyst

    B. Increasing the temperature

    C. Decreasing the concentration

    D. All of the above

    E. None of the above

86. For a chemical reaction at equilibrium, which always decreases the concentrations of the products?

A. Decreasing the pressure

B. Increasing the temperature and decreasing the temperature

C. Increasing the temperature

D. Decreasing the temperature

E. Decreasing the concentration of a gaseous or aqueous reactant

87. Which statement is true?

A. The equilibrium constant for a reaction can be determined in part from the activation energy

B. The equilibrium concentrations of reactants can be determined in part from the activation energy

C. The rate constant of a reaction can be determined in part from the activation energy

D. The order of a reaction can be determined in part from the activation energy

E. None of the above is true

88. From the data below, what is the order of the reaction with respect to reactant A?

Determining A Rate Law From Experimental Data

$A + B \rightarrow$ Products

Exp.	Initial [A]	Initial [B]	Initial Rate M/s
1	0.015	0.022	0.125
2	0.030	0.044	0.500
3	0.060	0.044	0.500
4	0.060	0.066	1.125
5	0.085	0.088	?

A. Zero   B. First   C. Second   D. Third   E. Fourth

89. A chemical system is considered to have reached dynamic equilibrium when the:

A. activation energy of the forward reaction equals the activation energy of the reverse reaction

B. rate of production of each of the products equals the rate of their consumption by the reverse reaction

C. frequency of collisions between the reactant molecules equals the frequency of collisions between the product molecules

D. sum of the concentrations of each of the reactant species equals the sum of the concentrations of each of the product species

E. rate of production of each of the product species equals the rate of consumption of each of the reactant species

90. $K_{eq} = 2$ with the initial concentrations of [A] = 4, [B] = 8 and [AB] = 16 at 25 °C.

$$AB + Heat \rightarrow A\ (g) + B\ (g)$$

After a stress has been absorbed by the reaction, the new equilibrium concentrations are: [A] = 2, [B] = 1, and [AB] = 64. The stress absorbed by the equilibrium system was:

A. an increase in [AB]

B. a decrease in [B]   D. a change in the reaction temperature resulting in the change for K_{eq}

C. a decrease in [A]   E. a decrease in [A] and [B]

91. What is the equilibrium constant expression for the reaction CO (*g*) + 2H$_2$ (*g*) ↔ CH$_3$OH (*l*)?

A. K_{eq} = 1 / [CO] [H$_2$]^2

B. K_{eq} = [CO] [H$_2$]^2

C. K_{eq} = [CH$_3$OH] / [CO] [H$_2$]^2

D. K_{eq} = [CH$_3$OH] / [CO] [H$_2$]

E. None of the above

92. If a catalyst is added to the reaction, CO + H$_2$O + *heat* ↔ CO$_2$ + H$_2$, which direction does the equilibrium shift?

A. To the left

B. To the right

C. No effect

D. Not enough information

E. Initially to the right but settles at ½ current equilibrium

93. With respect to A, what is the order of the reaction if the rate law = k[A]^3[B]^6?

A. 2   **B.** 3   **C.** 4   **D.** 5   **E.** 6

94. If a reaction does not occur extensively and gives a low concentration of products at equilibrium, which of the following is true?

A. The rate of the forward reaction is greater than the reverse reaction

B. The rate of the reverse reaction is greater than the forward reaction

C. The equilibrium constant is greater than one; that is, K_{eq} >> 1

D. The equilibrium constant is less than one; that is, K_{eq} << 1

E. None of the above

95. Which of the following conditions characterizes a system in a state of chemical equilibrium?

A. Rate of reverse reaction drops to zero

B. Reactant molecules no longer react with each other

C. Concentrations of reactants and products are equal

D. Rate of forward reaction drops to zero

E. Reactants are being consumed at the same rate they are being produced

---

Questions **96** through **98** are based on the following Figure:

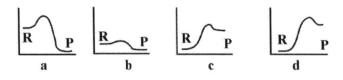

R = reactants   P = products

96. For the above energy profiles, which reaction has the highest activation energy?

  A. a   **B.** b   **C.** c   **D.** d   **E.** c and d

97. For the above energy profiles, which reaction has the lowest activation energy?

  A. a   **B.** b   **C.** c   **D.** d   **E.** a and b

98. For the above energy profiles, which reaction proceeds the slowest?

  A. a   **B.** b   **C.** c   **D.** d   **E.** c and d

99. What is the term for the difference in heat energy between the reactants and the products for a chemical reaction?

    A. Heat of reaction   **C.** Endothermic

    B. Exothermic   **D.** Activation energy   **E.** None of the above

100. If $K_{eq} = 6.1 \times 10^{-11}$, which statement is true?

    A. Both reactants and products are present   **C.** Mostly products are present

    B. The amount of reactants equals products   **D.** Cannot be determined

                                                  E. Mostly reactants are present

---

Questions **101** and **102** are based on the following Equation:

$$H_2 + F_2 \leftrightharpoons 2HF$$

101. What happens when the concentration of H_2 is increased?

        I. equilibrium shifts to the left

        II. consumption of fluorine increases

        III. equilibrium shifts to the right

    A. I only   **B.** II only   **C.** III only   **D.** II and III only   **E.** I and III only

102. If a catalyst is added, which statement is true?

    A. The forward and backward reaction rates are increased by the same proportion

    B. The equilibrium is shifted to the more energetically favorable product

    C. The forward reaction is favored

    D. The equilibrium concentrations shift

    E. The reverse reaction is favored

103. Which change causes the greatest increase in the reaction rate if rate law $= k[A][B]^2$?

    A. Quadrupling [A]   **D.** Doubling [B]

    B. Tripling [B]   **E.** Doubling [A]

    C. Keeping the concentrations constant while decreasing the temperature

104. Increasing the temperature at which a chemical reaction occurs:

    A. increases the reaction rate by lowering the activation energy

    B. causes fewer reactant collisions to take place

    C. lowers the activation energy, thus increasing the reaction rate

    D. raises the activation energy, thus decreasing the reaction rate

    E. increases the reaction rate by increasing reactant collisions per unit time

105. What is the equilibrium constant expression, K_i, for the following weak acid?

$$H_2S \, (aq) \leftrightarrow H^+ \, (aq) + HS^- \, (aq)$$

    A. $K_i = [H^+]^2 \, [S^{2-}] / [H_2S]$ **C.** $K_i = [H^+] \, [HS^-] / [H_2S]$

    B. $K_i = [H_2S] / [H^+] \, [HS^-]$ **D.** $K_i = [H^+]^2 \, [HS^-] / [H_2S]$

                                               E. $K_i = [H_2S] / [H^+]^2 \, [HS^-]$

106. For $2SO_2$ (g) + O_2 (g) ↔ $2SO_3$ (g) + *heat*, increasing pressure causes the equilibrium to:

A. remain unchanged, but the reaction mixture gets warmer

B. remain unchanged, but the reaction mixture gets cooler

C. shift to the right towards products

D. shift to the left towards reactants

E. pressure has no effect on equilibrium

107. Which method could be used to determine the rate law for a reaction?

      I. Measure the initial rate of the reaction at several reactant concentrations
      II. Graph the concentration of the reactants as a function of time
      III. Deduce the reaction mechanism

A. I only   **B.** III only   **C.** II only   **D.** I, II and III   **E.** II and III only

108. What is the equilibrium constant expression for $CaCO_3$ (s) ↔ CaO (s) + CO_2 (g)?

A. $K_{eq} = [CO_2]$ **C.** $K_{eq} = [CaO] [CO_2] / [CaCO_3]$

B. $K_{eq} = 1 / [CO_2]$ **D.** $K_{eq} = [CaO] [CO_2]$ **E.** None of the above

109. Predict which reaction occurs at a faster rate for a hypothetical reaction X + Y → W + Z.

Reaction	Activation energy	Temperature
1	low	low
2	low	high
3	high	high
4	high	low

A. 1   **B.** 2   **C.** 3   **D.** 4   **E.** 1 and 4

110. If the graphs are for the same reaction, which most likely has a catalyst?

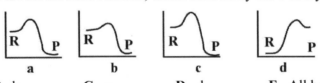

        a   **b**   **c**   **d**

A. a   **B.** b   **C.** c   **D.** d   **E.** All have a catalyst

111. What is the general equilibrium constant expression, K_{eq}, for the reversible reaction:

      A + 3B ↔ 2C?

A. $K_{eq} = [C]^2 / [A] [B]^3$ **C.** $K_{eq} = [A] [B]^3 / [C]^2$

B. $K_{eq} = [C] / [A] [B]$ **D.** $K_{eq} = [A] [B] / [C]$ **E.** None of the above

112. The following reaction is endothermic: $CaCO_3$ (s) ↔ CaO (s) + CO_2 (g).

Which of the following causes the reaction to shift towards yielding more carbon dioxide gas?

A. Increasing the pressure and decreasing the temperature of the system

B. Increasing the pressure of the system

C. Decreasing the temperature of the reaction

D. Increasing the pressure and increasing the temperature of the system

E. Increasing the temperature of the reaction

113. In chemical reactions, catalysts:

A. shift the equilibrium
B. become irreversibly consumed in the reaction
C. lower the activation energy of the original reaction
D. are depleted during the reaction
E. increase the activation energy of the original reaction

114. What is the equilibrium constant expression, K_i, for the following weak acid?

$$H_2CO_3\,(aq) \leftrightarrow H^+\,(aq) + HCO_3^-\,(aq)$$

A. $K_i = [H^+]^2\,[CO_3^{2-}] / [H_2CO_3]$

B. $K_i = [H_2CO_3] / [H^+]\,[HCO_3^-]$

C. $K_i = [H^+]\,[HCO_3^-] / [H_2CO_3]$

D. $K_i = [H^+]^2\,[HCO_3^-] / [H_2CO_3]$

E. $K_i = [H_2CO_3] / [H^+]^2\,[CO_3^{2-}]$

115. Identify the reaction described by the following equilibrium expression:

$$K = [H_2]^2\,[O_2] / [H_2O]^2$$

A. $2H_2O\,(g) \leftrightarrow 2H_2(g) + O_2\,(g)$

B. $H_2O\,(g) \leftrightarrow 2H\,(g) + O\,(g)$

C. $H_2O\,(g) \leftrightarrow H_2\,(g) + \frac{1}{2}O_2\,(g)$

D. $2H_2\,(g) + O_2\,(g) \leftrightarrow 2H_2O\,(g)$

E. $2H_2O\,(g) \leftrightarrow H_2(g) + O_2\,(g)$

116. If the concentration of reactants decreases, which of the following is true?

A. The amount of products increases
B. The heat of reaction decreases
C. The rate of reaction decreases
D. All of the above
E. None of the above

117. Which statement describes how a catalyst works?

A. increases ΔG

B. increases E_{act}

C. decreases ΔH

D. increases ΔH

E. decreases E_{act}

118. What is the equilibrium law for $CaO\,(s) + CO_2\,(g) \leftrightarrows CaCO_3\,(s)$?

A. $K_c = [CaCO_3] / [CaO]$

B. $K_c = 1 / [CO_2]$

C. $K_c = [CaCO_3] / [CaO]\,[CO_2]$

D. $K_c = [CO_2]$

E. $K_c = [CaO]\,[CO_2] / [CaCO_3]$

119. The grams of products present after a chemical reaction reaches equilibrium:

A. must equal the grams of reactants present
B. may be less than, equal to, or greater than the grams of reactants present, depending upon the chemical reaction
C. must be greater than the grams of reactants present
D. must be less than the grams of reactants present
E. none of the above

120. Which of the following statements about catalysts is NOT true?

A. A catalyst does not change the energy of the reactants or the products
B. A catalyst can be used to speed up slow reactions
C. A catalyst can be consumed in a reaction
D. A catalyst alters the rate of a chemical reaction
E. All of the above are true

121. Which of the following changes shifts the equilibrium to the left for the given reversible reaction?

$$SO_3 (g) + NO (g) + heat \leftrightarrow SO_2 (g) + NO_2 (g)$$

A. Decrease temperature

B. Decrease volume

C. Increase [NO]

D. Decrease [SO_2]

E. Add a catalyst

122. What is the expression for the equilibrium constant (K_{eq}) for the reaction is:

$$2NaIO_3 (s) \leftrightarrow 2NaI (s) + 3O_2 (g)$$

A. $K_{eq} = [NaIO_3]^2 / [NaI]^2[O_2]^3$

B. $K_{eq} = [NaI]^2[O_2]^3 / [NaIO_3]^2$

C. $K_{eq} = [O_2]^3 / [NaIO_3]^2$

D. $K_{eq} = [O_2]^3$

E. None of the above

123. If there is too much chlorine in the water, swimmers complain that their eyes burn. Consider the equilibrium found in swimming pools. Predict which increases the chlorine concentration.

$$Cl_2 (g) + H_2O (l) \leftrightarrow HClO (aq) \leftrightarrow H^+ (aq) + ClO^- (aq)$$

A. Decreasing the pH

B. Adding hydrochloric acid, HCl (*aq*)

C. Adding hypochlorous acid, HClO (*aq*)

D. Adding sodium hypochlorite, NaClO

E. All of the above

124. The reaction, $2NO (g) + O_2 (g) \rightarrow 2NO_2 (g)$, was found to be first order in each of the two reactants and second order overall. The rate law is:

A. rate = $k[NO]^2[O_2]^2$

B. rate = $k[NO_2]^2[NO]^{-2}[O_2]^{-\frac{1}{2}}$

C. rate = $k[NO][O_2]$

D. rate = $k[NO]^2$

E. rate = $k([NO][O_2])^2$

125. In writing an equilibrium constant expression, which of the following is NOT correct?

A. Reactant concentrations are always placed in the denominator of the expression

B. Concentrations of pure solids and pure liquids, when placed in the equilibrium expression, are never raised to any power

C. Concentrations are always expressed as molarities

D. Product concentrations are always placed in the numerator of the expression

E. none of the above

126. Which of the following increases the amount of product formed from a reaction?

A. Using a UV light catalyst

B. Adding an acid catalyst

C. Adding a metal catalyst

D. None of the above

E. All of the above

127. In the reaction A + B → AB, which of the following does NOT increase the rate?

A. increasing the temperature

B. decreasing the temperature

C. adding A

D. adding B

E. adding a catalyst

128. What is the equilibrium constant value if, at equilibrium, the concentrations are: $[NH_3]$ = 0.40 M, $[H_2]$ = 0.12 M and $[N_2]$ = 0.040 M [at a certain temperature]?

$$2NH_3\ (g) \leftrightarrow N_2\ (g) + 3H_2\ (g)$$

A. 6.3×10^{12} **C.** 4.3×10^{-4}

B. 7.1×10^{-7} **D.** 3.9×10^{-3} **E.** 8.5×10^{-9}

129. Which of the changes listed below shifts the equilibrium to the left for the following reversible reaction: $PbI_2\ (s) \leftrightarrow Pb^{2+}\ (aq) + 2I^-\ (aq)$?

A. Add $Pb(NO_3)_2\ (s)$ **C.** Decrease $[Pb^{2+}]$

B. Add NaCl (s) **D.** Decrease $[I^-]$

        E. Add nitric acid

130. Given the following reaction, the equilibrium expression will be:

$$4CuO\ (s) + CH_4\ (g) \leftrightarrow CO_2\ (g) + 4Cu\ (s) + 2H_2O\ (g)$$

A. $[Cu]^4 / [CuO]^4$ **C.** $[CH_4] / [CO_2][H_2O]^2$

B. $[CH_4]^2 / [CO_2][H_2O]$ **D.** $[CuO]^4 / [Cu]^4$

        E. $[CO_2][H_2O]^2 / [CH_4]$

131. Find the reaction rate for $A + B \rightarrow C$:

Trial	$[A]_{t=0}$	$[B]_{t=0}$	Initial rate (M/s)
1	0.05 M	1.0 M	1×10^{-3}
2	0.05 M	4.0 M	16×10^{-3}
3	0.15 M	1.0 M	3×10^{-3}

A. rate = $k[A]^2[B]^2$ **C.** rate = $k[A]^2[B]$

B. rate = $k[A][B]^2$ **D.** rate = $k[A][B]$

        E. rate = $k[A]^2[B]^3$

132. What is the general equilibrium constant expression, K_{eq}, for the reversible reaction?

$$2A + 3B \leftrightarrow C$$

A. $K_{eq} = [C] / [A]^2\ [B]^3$ **C.** $K_{eq} = [A]\ [B] / [C]$

B. $K_{eq} = [C] / [A]\ [B]$ **D.** $K_{eq} = [A]^2\ [B]^3 / [C]$

        E. none of the above

133. What is the effect on the equilibrium after adding H_2O to the equilibrium mixture if CO_2 and H_2 react until equilibrium is established: $CO_2\ (g) + H_2\ (g) \leftrightarrow H_2O\ (g) + CO\ (g)$?

A. $[H_2]$ decreases and $[H_2O]$ increases   **C.** $[H_2]$ decreases and $[CO_2]$ increases

B. $[CO]$ and $[CO_2]$ increase   **D.** Equilibrium shifts to the left

        E. Equilibrium shifts to the right

Questions **134** through **136** refer to the rate data
for the conversion of reactants W, X, and Y to product Z.

Trial Number	Concentration (moles/L)			Rate of Formation of Z (moles/l·s)
	W	X	Y	
1	0.01	0.05	0.04	0.04
2	0.015	0.07	0.06	0.08
3	0.01	0.15	0.04	0.36
4	0.03	0.07	0.06	0.08
5	0.01	0.05	0.16	0.18

134. From the above data, what is the overall order of the reaction?

A. 3½   **B.** 4   **C.** 3   **D.** 2   **E.** 2½

135. From the above data, the order with respect to W suggests that the rate of formation of Z is:

A. dependent on [W]   **C.** semidependent on [W]
B. independent of [W]   **D.** unable to be determined   **E.** inversely proportional to [W]

136. From the above data, the magnitude of k for trial l is:

A. 20   **B.** 40   **C.** 60   **D.** 80   **E.** 90

137. For the reaction, $2XO + O_2 \rightarrow 2XO_2$, data obtained from measurement of the initial rate of reaction at varying concentrations are:

Experiment	[XO]	[O$_2$]	Rate (mmol L^{-1} s^{-1})
1	0.010	0.010	2.5
2	0.010	0.020	5.0
3	0.030	0.020	45.0

The rate law is therefore:

A. rate = $k[XO][O_2]$ **C.** rate = $k[XO]^2[O_2]$
B. rate = $k[XO]^2[O_2]^2$ **D.** rate = $k[XO][O_2]^2$ **E.** rate = $k[XO]^2/[O_2]^2$

138. 0.56 mol of NO and 0.38 mol of Br_2 are placed in a container and allowed to react until equilibrium, whereby 0.47 mol of NOBr are present.

$$2NO\,(g) + Br_2\,(g) \rightarrow 2NOBr\,(g)$$

What is the composition of the equilibrium mixture in terms of moles of each substance present?

A. 0.56 mol NO and 0.38 mol Br_2 **C.** 0.56 mol NO and 0.47 mol Br_2
B. 0.47 mol NO and 0.47 mol Br_2 **D.** 0.33 mol NO and 0.09 mol Br_2
     E. 0.09 mol NO and 0.15 mol Br_2

139. What is the equilibrium constant expression, K_i, for the following weak acid?

$$H_2SO_3\,(aq) \leftrightarrow H^+\,(aq) + HSO_3^-\,(aq)$$

A. $K_i = [H_2SO_3] / [H^+][HSO_3^-]$ **C.** $K_i = [H^+]^2[HSO_3^-] / [H_2SO_3]$
B. $K_i = [H^+]^2[SO_3^{2-}] / [H_2SO_3]$ **D.** $K_i = [H^+][HSO_3^-] / [H_2SO_3]$
     E. $K_i = [H_2SO_3] / [H^+]^2[SO_3^{2-}]$

140. When a reaction system is at equilibrium:

    A. rate in the forward and reverse directions are equal

    B. rate in the forward direction is at a maximum

    C. amounts of reactants and products are equal

    D. rate in the reverse direction is at a minimum

    E. reaction is complete and static

141. Which of the following drives the exothermic reaction to the right?

$$CH_4 \, (g) + 2O_2 \, (g) \leftrightarrow CO_2 \, (g) + 2H_2O \, (g)$$

    A. Addition of CO_2 **C.** Increase in temperature

    B. Removal of CH_4 **D.** Decrease in temperature

                                    E. Addition of H_2O

142. Which of the following is the equilibrium expression?

$$CS_2 \, (g) + 4H_2 \, (g) \leftrightarrow CH_4 \, (g) + 2H_2S \, (g)$$

    A. $K_{eq} = [CS_2][H_2]^4 / [CH_4][H_2S]^2$ **C.** $K_{eq} = [CH_4][H_2S]^2 / [CS_2][H_2]^4$

    B. $K_{eq} = [CH_4][H_2S]^2 / [CS_2][H_2]$ **D.** $K_{eq} = [CS_2][H_2]^4 / [CH_4][H_2S]^2$

                                      E. $K_{eq} = [CS_2][H_2]^2 / [CH_4][H_2S]^4$

143. Which of the following is the equilibrium expression?

$$C \, (s) + 2H_2 \, (g) \leftrightarrow CH_4 \, (g)$$

    A. $K_{eq} = [H_2]^2 [C] / [CH_4]$ **C.** $K_{eq} = [C] [H_2]$

    B. $K_{eq} = [CH_4] / [H_2]^2$ **D.** $K_{eq} = [CH_4] / [C] [H_2]^2$

                                      E. $K_{eq} = [CH_4] / [H_2]$

144. Which of the following increases the collision frequency of molecules?

    A. Increasing the concentration   **C.** Decreasing the temperature

    B. Adding a catalyst   **D.** All of the above

                                      E. None of the above

145. What effect does a catalyst have on an equilibrium?

    A. It increases the rate of the forward reaction

    B. It shifts the reaction to the right

    C. It increases the rate at which equilibrium is reached without changing ΔG

    D. It increases the rate at which equilibrium is reached and lowers ΔG

    E. It slows the reverse reaction

146. If k is 4×10^{-4} for $Cl_2 \, (g) \rightleftharpoons 2Cl \, (g)$ at 1000 K, and 1 M $Cl_2 \, (g)$ is placed in a container, what is the concentration of $Cl \, (g)$ at equilibrium?

    A. 0.01 M   **B.** 0.02 M   **C.** 0.04 M   **D.** 0.05 M   **E.** 0.06 M

147. What is the rate law for the reaction, $3B + C \rightarrow E + 2F$, whereby the data for three trials are?

Experiment	[B]	[C]	Rate (mol L^{-1} s^{-1})
1	0.100	0.250	0.000250
2	0.200	0.250	0.000500
3	0.100	0.500	0.00100

A. rate = $k[B]^2[C]^2$
B. rate = $k[B]^2[C]$

C. rate = $k[B]^3[C]$
D. rate = $k[B][C]^2$

E. rate = $k[B][C]$

148. A mixture of 1.40 moles of A and 2.30 moles of B reacted. At equilibrium, 0.90 moles of A are present. How many moles of C are present at equilibrium?

$$3A\ (g) + 2B\ (g) \rightarrow 4C\ (g)$$

A. 2.7 moles   **B.** 1.3 moles   **C.** 0.09 moles   **D.** 1.8 moles   **E.** 0.67 moles

149. What is the equilibrium constant expression (K_{eq}) for the reversible reaction below?

$$2A \leftrightarrow B + 3C$$

A. $K_{eq} = [B]\,[C]^3 / [A]^2$
B. $K_{eq} = [B]\,[C] / [A]$

C. $K_{eq} = [A]^2 / [B]\,[C]^3$
D. $K_{eq} = [A] / [B]\,[C]$

E. none of the above

150. What is the equilibrium expression for the reaction $2CO\ (g) + O_2\ (g) \leftrightarrow 2CO_2\ (g)$?

A. $K_{eq} = 2[CO_2] / 2[CO][O_2]$
B. $K_{eq} = [CO][O_2] / [CO_2]$

C. $K_{eq} = [CO_2]^2 / [CO]^2[O_2]$
D. $K_{eq} = [CO_2] / [CO] + [O_2]$
E. $K_{eq} = [CO]^2[O_2] / [CO_2]^2$

151. What is the rate law when rates were measured at different concentrations for the dissociation of hydrogen gas: $H_2\ (g) \rightarrow 2H\ (g)$?

[H_2]	Rate M/s s^{-1}
1.0	1.4×10^5
1.5	2.8×10^5
2.0	5.6×10^5

A. The rate law cannot be determined from the information given
B. rate = $k[H]^2 / [H_2]$
C. rate = $k[H_2]^2$

D. rate = $k[H_2] / [H]^2$
E. rate = $k2[H] / [H_2]$

152. Which of the changes shifts the equilibrium to the left for the reversible reaction in an aqueous solution: $HNO_2\ (aq) \leftrightarrow H^+\ (aq) + NO_2^-\ (aq)$?

A. Adding solid KNO_2
B. Adding solid KCl

C. Increasing [HNO_2]
D. Increasing pH
E. Adding solid KOH

153. What does a chemical equilibrium expression of a reaction depend on?

A. mechanism
B. stoichiometry and mechanism

C. stoichiometry
D. rate
E. rate and mechanism

154. What is the K_{sp} for slightly soluble copper (II) phosphate in an aqueous solution?

$$Cu_3(PO_4)_2 (s) \rightleftarrows 3Cu^{2+} (aq) + 2PO_4^{3-} (aq)$$

A. $K_{sp} = [Cu^{2+}]^3 [PO_4^{3-}]^2$ **C.** $K_{sp} = [Cu^{2+}]^3 [PO_4^{3-}]$

B. $K_{sp} = [Cu^{2+}] [PO_4^{3-}]^2$ **D.** $K_{sp} = [Cu^{2+}] [PO_4^{3-}]$ **E.** $K_{sp} = [Cu^{2+}]^2 [PO_4^{3-}]^3$

155. Which of the following is true if the concentration of reactants increases?

A. Amount of product decreases   **C.** Heat of reaction increases

B. Rate of reaction increases   **D.** All of the above

     E. Rate of reaction decreases

156. A reaction vessel contains NH_3, N_2, and H_2 at equilibrium with $[NH_3] = 0.1$ M, $[N_2] = 0.2$ M, and $[H_2] = 0.3$ M. For decomposition, what is K for NH_3 to N_2 and H_2?

A. $K = (0.2)(0.3)^3 / (0.1)^2$ **C.** $K = (0.1)^2 / (0.2)(0.3)^3$

B. $K = (0.1) / (0.2)^2(1.5)^3$ **D.** $K = (0.2)(0.3)^2 / (0.1)$ **E.** $K = (0.2)(0.3)^3 / (0.1)$

157. The data provides the rate of a reaction as affected by the concentration of the reactants.

Experiment	[A]	[B]	[C]	Rate (mol L^{-1} hr^{-1})
1	0.200	0.100	0.600	5.0
2	0.200	0.400	0.400	80.0
3	0.600	0.100	0.200	15.0
4	0.200	0.100	0.200	5.0
5	0.200	0.200	0.400	20.0

A. zero order with respect to A

B. order for A is minus one (rate proportional to 1 / [A])

C. first order with respect to A

D. second order with respect to A

E. order for A cannot be determined from data

158. Chemical equilibrium is reached in a system when:

A. complete conversion of reactants to products has occurred

B. product molecules begin reacting with each other

C. reactant concentrations steadily decrease

D. reactant concentrations steadily increase

E. product and reactant concentrations remain constant

159. Dinitrogen tetraoxide decomposes to produce nitrogen dioxide. Calculate the equilibrium constant given the equilibrium concentrations at 100 °C: $[N_2O_4] = 0.800$ and $[NO_2] = 0.400$.

$$N_2O_4 (g) \leftrightarrow 2NO_2 (g)$$

A. $K_{eq} = 0.725$ **C.** $K_{eq} = 0.200$

B. $K_{eq} = 2.50$ **D.** $K_{eq} = 0.500$ **E.** $K_{eq} = 0.750$

160. Which change to this reaction system causes the equilibrium to shift to the right?

$$N_2 (g) + 3H_2 (g) \leftrightarrow 2NH_3 (g) + heat$$

A. Heating the system   **C.** Addition of NH_3 (g)

B. Removal of H_2 (g)   **D.** Lowering the temperature

     E. Addition of a catalyst

161. Which is NOT a difference between a first order and second order elementary reactions?

A. When concentrations of reactants are doubled, the rate of a first order reaction doubles, while the rate of a second order elementary reaction quadruples

B. The rate of a first order reaction is greater than the rate of a second order reaction because collisions are not required

C. A first order reaction is unimolecular, while a second order reaction is bimolecular

D. The half life of a first order reaction is independent of the starting concentration of the reactant, while the half life of a second order reaction depends on the starting concentration of the reactant

E. The rate of a first order reaction is less than the rate of a second order reaction because collisions are required

162. Which is the correct equilibrium expression for the reaction $2Ag\ (s) + Cl_2\ (g) \leftrightarrow 2AgCl\ (s)$?

A. $K_{eq} = [AgCl] / [Ag]^2[Cl_2]$

B. $K_{eq} = [2AgCl] / [2Ag][Cl_2]$

C. $K_{eq} = [AgCl]^2 / [Ag]^2[Cl_2]$

D. $K_{eq} = 1 / [Cl_2]$

E. $K_{eq} = [2AgCl]^2 / [2Ag]^2[Cl_2]$

163. How does a catalyst increase the rate of a reaction?

A. It increases the energy difference between the reactants and products

B. It has no affect on the rate of the reaction

C. It is neither created nor consumed in a reaction

D. It raises the activation energy of the reactants, which makes the reaction proceed faster

E. It lowers the activation energy

164. If the temperature of a reaction increases, which of the following is true?

A. Amount of product decreases

B. Rate of reaction increases

C. Heat of reaction increases

D. All of the above

E. None of the above

165. Given the equation $xA + yB \rightarrow z$, the rate expression reaction in terms of the rate of change of the concentration of c with respect to time is:

A. $k[A]^x[B]^{yz}$

B. $k[A]^y[B]^x$

C. $k[A]^x[B]^y$

D. unable to determine

E. $k[A]^x[B]^y / [z]$

166. Which one of the following changes the value of the equilibrium constant?

A. Varying the initial concentrations of reactants

B. Varying the initial concentrations of products

C. Changing temperature

D. Adding a catalyst at the onset of the reaction

E. Adding other substances that do not react with any of the species involved in the equilibrium

167. Which conditions increase the rate of a chemical reaction?

    I. Lowering the temperature of the chemical reaction

    II. Significantly increasing the concentration of one of the reactants

    III. Adding a catalyst to a reaction

    IV. Increasing the pressure on a gaseous reaction system

A. II and IV only

B. II and III only

C. I and IV only

D. II, III and IV only

E. III and IV only

168. Which change shifts the equilibrium to the right for the reversible reaction in an aqueous solution?

$$HNO_2\,(aq) \leftrightarrow H^+\,(aq) + NO_2^-\,(aq)$$

   A. Add solid NaOH   **C.** Decrease $[H^+]$

   B. Decrease $[NO_2^-]$ **D.** Increase $[HNO_2]$ **E.** All of the above

169. The position of the equilibrium for a system where $K = 4.6 \times 10^{-15}$ can be described as being favored for [ ]; the concentration of products is relatively:

   A. the left; large   **C.** the right; large

   B. the left; small   **D.** the right; small   **E.** neither direction; large

170. In addition to molecular collision, what conditions are required for a reaction?

   A. Sufficient energy of collision and proper spatial orientation of the molecules

   B. Sufficient energy of collision only

   C. Proper spatial orientation of the molecules only

   D. Sufficient temperature and sufficient duration of molecular contact

   E. Sufficient energy of collision and sufficient duration of molecular content

171. Which of the changes shifts the equilibrium to the right for the following reversible reaction?

$$CO\,(g) + H_2O\,(g) \leftrightarrow CO_2\,(g) + H_2\,(g) + heat$$

   A. increasing volume   **C.** increasing $[CO_2]$

   B. increasing temperature   **D.** adding a catalyst   **E.** increasing $[CO]$

172. Increasing the temperature of a chemical reaction increases the rate of reaction because:

   A. both the collision frequency and collision energies of reactant molecules increase

   B. the collision frequency of reactant molecules increases

   C. the activation energy increases

   D. the activation energy decreases

   E. the stability of the products increases

173. Heat is often added to chemical reactions performed in the laboratory to:

   A. compensate for the natural tendency of energy to disperse

   B. increase the rate at which reactants collide

   C. allow a greater number of reactants to overcome the barrier of the activation energy

   D. increase the energy of the reactant molecules

   E. all of the above

174. Which shifts the equilibrium to the left for the reversible reaction in an aqueous solution?

$$HC_2H_3O_2\,(aq) \rightleftarrows H^+\,(aq) + C_2H_3O_2^-\,(aq)$$

   A. add solid KOH   **C.** increase pH

   B. add solid KNO$_3$ **D.** increase $[HC_2H_3O_2]$ **E.** add solid $KC_2H_3O_2$

175. As the temperature of a reaction increases, the reaction rate:

  A. increases, but the rate constant remains constant
  B. increases, along with the rate constant
  C. remains constant, but the rate constant increases
  D. remains constant, as does the rate constant
  E. is not affected

176. Write the mass action expression for the reaction: $4Cr\,(s) + 3CCl_4\,(g) \leftrightarrows 4CrCl_3\,(g) + 4C\,(s)$

  A. $K_c = [C][CrCl_3] / [Cr][CCl_4]$
  B. $K_c = [C]^4[CrCl_3]^4 / [Cr]^4\,[CCl_4]^3$
  C. $K_c = [CrCl_3]^4 / [CCl_4]^3$
  D. $K_c = [CrCl_3] / [CCl_4]$
  E. $K_c = [CrCl_3] + [CCl_4]$

177. Calculate the equilibrium constant for the reaction if, at equilibrium, a 3.25 L tank contains 0.343 mol O_2, 0.0212 mol SO_3 and 0.00419 mol SO_2: $2SO_3\,(g) \leftrightarrow 2SO_2\,(g) + O_2\,(g)$

  A. 4.14×10^{-3} **B.** 4.44×10^{-2} **C.** 5.32×10^{-2} **D.** 1.28×10^{-2} **E.** 4.62×10^{-4}

178. Which of the following is true if a reaction occurs extensively and yields a high concentration of products at equilibrium?

  A. The rate of the reverse reaction is greater than the forward reaction
  B. The rate of the forward reaction is greater than the reverse reaction
  C. The equilibrium constant is less than one; $K_{eq} \ll 1$
  D. The equilibrium constant is greater than one; $K_{eq} \gg 1$
  E. None of the above

179. Which of the following conditions characterizes a system in a state of chemical equilibrium?

  A. Product concentrations are greater than reactant concentrations
  B. Reactant molecules no longer react with each other
  C. Concentrations of reactants and products are equal
  D. Rate of forward reaction has dropped to zero
  E. Reactants are being consumed at the same rate they are being produced

180. For the reaction $CO\,(g) + Cl_2\,(g) \rightarrow COCl_2\,(g)$, the equilibrium constant is 125.

What is the equilibrium constant of the reaction $2CO\,(g) + 2Cl_2\,(g) \rightarrow 2COCl_2\,(g)$?

  A. 2.50×10^3 **B.** 250   **C.** 1.56×10^3 **D.** 1.56×10^4 **E.** 2.50×10^4

181. Given the following decomposition reaction: $PCl_5\,(g) \leftrightarrow PCl_3\,(g) + Cl_2\,(g)$. What is the equilibrium constant for this reaction if 0.84 moles of PCl_5 are placed in a 1.0 L container and, at equilibrium, 0.72 moles of PCl_5 remains?

  A. 0.14   **B.** 0.020   **C.** 0.67   **D.** 0.72   **E.** 1.14

182. Which changes shift the equilibrium to the product side for the following reaction at equilibrium?

$$SO_2Cl_2\,(g) \leftrightarrow SO_2\,(g) + Cl_2\,(g)$$

  I. Addition of SO_2Cl_2 III. Removal of SO_2Cl_2
  II. Addition of SO_2 IV. Removal of Cl_2
  A. I, II and III   **B.** II and III   **C.** I and II   **D.** III and IV   **E.** I and IV

183. Which influences the rate of a chemical reaction?

A. catalyst   C. concentration

B. temperature   D. all of the above   E. none of the above

184. The rate-determining step of a chemical reaction involves:

A. the fastest step   C. the molecules with the smallest molecular mass

B. the slowest step   D. the molecules with the greatest molecular mass

     E. charged molecules transformed into neutral molecules

185. The system, $H_2(g) + X_2(g) \leftrightarrows 2HX(g)$ has a value of 24.4 for K_C. A catalyst was introduced into a reaction within a 3.00 liter reactor containing 0.150 moles of H_2, 0.150 moles of X_2, and 0.600 moles of HX. The reaction proceeds in which direction?

A. to the right, $Q > K$ C. to the right, $Q < K$

B. to the left, $Q > K$ D. to the left, $Q < K$ E. not possible to predict in direction

186. For a hypothetical reaction, $A + B \rightarrow C$, predict which reaction occurs at the slowest rate from the reaction conditions from the data .

Reaction	Activation energy	Temperature
1	103 kJ/mol	15 °C
2	46 kJ/mol	22 °C
3	103 kJ/mol	24 °C
4	46 kJ/mol	30 °C

A. 1   B. 2   C. 3   D. 4   E. not enough information is given

187. What is the equilibrium reaction, given the solubility product expression for slightly soluble iron (III) chromate is $K_{sp} = [Fe^{3+}]^2 [CrO_4^{2-}]^3$?

A. $Fe_2(CrO_4)_3(s) \leftrightarrow 3Fe^{3+}(aq) + 2CrO_4^{2-}(aq)$ C. $Fe_2(CrO_4)_3(s) \leftrightarrow Fe^{3+}(aq) + CrO_4^{2-}(aq)$

B. $Fe_3(CrO_4)_2(s) \leftrightarrow 2Fe^{3+}(aq) + 3CrO_4^{2-}(aq)$ D. $Fe_2(CrO_4)_3(s) \leftrightarrow 2Fe^{3+}(aq) + 3CrO_4^{2-}(aq)$

     E. $Fe_3(CrO_4)_2(s) \leftrightarrow 3Fe^{3+}(aq) + 2CrO_4^{2-}(aq)$

188. The function of a catalyst in a reaction system is to:

A. decrease the amount of reactants consumed

B. decrease the amount of energy consumed by the reaction

C. decrease the amount of heat produced   D. increase the yield of product

     E. increase the rate of the reaction

189. What is an explanation for the observation that the reaction stops before all reactants are converted to products in the following reaction?

$$NH_3(aq) + HC_2H_3O_2(aq) \rightarrow NH_4^+(aq) + C_2H_3O_2^-(aq)$$

A. The catalyst is depleted

B. The reverse rate increases, while the forward rate decreases until they are equal

C. As [products] increases, the acetic acid begins to dissociate, stoping the reaction

D. As [reactants] decreases, NH_3 and $HC_2H_3O_2$ molecules stop colliding

E. As [products] increases, NH_3 and $HC_2H_3O_2$ molecules stop colliding

190. Which statement is NOT true regarding an equilibrium constant for a particular reaction?

A. Does not change as product is removed
B. Does not change as additional quantity of a reactant is added
C. Changes when a catalyst is added
D. Changes as the temperature increases
E. All are true statements

191. Consider the reaction: $2H_2 + 2NO \rightarrow N_2 + 2H_2O$
What rate law is most consistent, given the rates were measured at different concentrations?

$[H_2]$	$[NO]$	Rate/M s^{-1}
0.1	0.3	225
0.2	0.3	450
0.3	0.1	80
0.2	0.1	50

A. rate = $k[H_2]^2[NO]$
B. rate = $k[H_2]^2[NO]^3$
C. rate = $k[H_2]^3[NO]$
D. rate = $k[H_2]^3[NO]^2$
E. rate = $k[H_2][NO]^2$

192. Which changes shift(s) the equilibrium to the right for the reversible reaction in an aqueous solution: $HC_2H_3O_2\,(aq) \leftrightarrow H^+\,(aq) + C_2H_3O_2^-\,(aq)$?

I. Decreasing $[C_2H_3O_2^-]$
II. Decreasing $[H^+]$
III. Increasing $[HC_2H_3O_2]$
IV. Decreasing $[HC_2H_3O_2]$

A. I and II only
B. I and III only
C. II and III only
D. I, II and IV only
E. I, II and III only

193. Which is the rate law when the following experimental data was observed for $A + B \rightarrow C$?

Trial	$[A]_{t=0}$	$[B]_{t=0}$	Initial rate (M/s)
1	1.0 M	1.0 M	6.0×10^{-5}
2	2.0	1.0	1.2×10^{-4}
3	2.0	2.0	2.4×10^{-4}
4	2.0	4.0	4.8×10^{-4}

A. rate = $k[B]^2$
B. rate = $k[A][B]$
C. rate = $k[A]$
D. rate = $k[B]$
E. rate = $k[A]^2$

194. Which statement about chemical equilibrium is NOT true?

A. At equilibrium, the forward reaction rate equals the reverse reaction rate
B. The same equilibrium state can be attained starting either from the reactant or product side of the equation
C. Chemical equilibrium can only be attained by starting with reagents from the reactant side of the equation
D. At equilibrium, [reactant] and [product] are constant over time
E. At equilibrium, [reactant] and [product] may be different

195. At a given temperature, K = 46.0 for the reaction $4HCl\ (g) + O_2\ (g) \leftrightarrow 2H_2O\ (g) + 2Cl_2\ (g)$. At equilibrium, [HCl] = 0.150, [O_2] = 0.395 and [H_2O] = 0.625. What is the concentration of Cl_2 at equilibrium?

    A. 0.153 M   **B.** 0.444 M   **C.** 1.14 M   **D.** 0.00547 M   **E.** None of the above

196. Carbonic acid in blood: $CO_2\ (g) + H_2O\ (l) \leftrightarrow H_2CO_3\ (aq) \rightleftarrows H^+\ (aq) + HCO_3^-\ (aq)$ at equilibrium . If a person hyperventilates, the rapid breathing expels carbon dioxide gas. Predict which decreases when a person hyperventilates?

    A. [HCO_3^-]   **C.** [H_2CO_3]

    B. [H^+]   **D.** None of the above   **E.** All of the above

197. The equilibrium expression for the reaction $A + 2B \leftrightarrow 2C + D$ is:

    A. $[C]^2[D] / [A][B]^2$ **C.** $[A]2[B] / 2[C][D]$

    B. $[A]2[B]^2 / 2[C]^2[D]$ **D.** $2[C][D] / [A]2[B]$ **E.** $[A][B]^2 / [C]^2[D]$

198. Consider the following reaction: $H_2\ (g) + I_2\ (g) \rightarrow 2HI\ (g)$

At 160 K, this reaction has an equilibrium constant of 35. If, at 160 K, the concentration of hydrogen gas is 0.4 M, iodine gas is 0.6 M, and hydrogen iodide gas is 3 M:

    A. system is at equilibrium   **C.** [hydrogen iodide] increases

    B. [iodine] decreases   **D.** [hydrogen iodide] decreases

                                E. [hydrogen] decreases

199. Which statement is true if $K_{eq} = 2.2 \times 10^{12}$?

    A. Mostly products are present   **C.** Mostly reactants are present

    B. There is an equal amount of reactants and products   **D.** None of the above

                                                    E. Need more information

200. When a system is at equilibrium, the:

    A. reaction rate of the forward reaction is small compared to the reverse

    B. amount of products and reactants is exactly equal

    C. reaction rate of the forward reaction is equal to the rate of the reverse

    D. reaction rate of the reverse reaction is small compared to the forward

    E. reaction rate of the reverse reaction is large compared to the forward

201. Which of the following is true before a reaction reaches chemical equilibrium?

    A. The rate of the forward reaction is increasing, and the rate of the reverse reaction is decreasing

    B. The rate of the forward reaction is decreasing, and the rate of the reverse reaction is increasing

    C. The rates of the forward and reverse reactions are increasing

    D. The rates of the forward and reverse reactions are decreasing

    E. None of the above

202. The following data were collected for the reaction A + B + C → D + E:

Trial	$[A]_{t=0}$	$[B]_{t=0}$	$[C]_{t=0}$	Initial rate (M/s)
1	0.1 M	0.1 M	0.1 M	2×10^{-2}
2	0.1	0.1	0.2	4×10^{-2}
3	0.1	0.2	0.1	8×10^{-2}
4	0.2	0.1	0.1	8×10^{-2}

What is the rate law for this reaction?

A. rate = $k[A][B][C] / [D][E]$
B. rate = $k[A]^2[B][C]^2$
C. rate = $k[A][B]^2[C]^2$
D. rate = $k[A][B][C]$
E. rate = $k[A]^2[B]^2[C]$

203. Calculate a value for K_c for the reaction NOCl (g) + ½O$_2$ (g) ⇆ NO$_2$ (g) + ½Cl$_2$ (g), using the data:

$$2NO\ (g) +\ Cl_2\ (g) \leftrightarrows 2NOCl\ (g) \qquad\qquad K_c = 3.20 \times 10^{-3}$$
$$2NO_2\ (g) \leftrightarrows 2NO\ (g) + O_2\ (g) \qquad\qquad K_c = 15.5$$

A. 4.49   **B.** 0.343   **C.** 4.32×10^{-4} **D.** 1.33×10^{-5} **E.** 18.4

204. According to Le Chatelier's principle, which changes shift to the left the equilibrium for:

$$N_2\ (g) + 3H_2\ (g) \leftrightarrow 2NH_3\ (g) + \textit{heat}$$

A. Decreasing the temperature
B. Increasing [H$_2$]
C. Increasing [N$_2$]
D. Decreasing the pressure on the system
E. Increasing [N$_2$] and [H$_2$]

205. Which of the following is true after a reaction reaches chemical equilibrium?

A. The amount of reactants and products are constant
B. The amount of reactants and products are equal
C. The amount of reactants is increasing
D. The amount of products is increasing
E. None of the above

206. Which factors would increase the rate of a chemical reaction?

    I. Increasing the temperature
    II. Removing products as they form
    III. Adding a catalyst

A. I and II   **B.** II and III   **C.** I, II and III   **D.** I only   **E.** II only

207. Which of the following concentrations of CH$_2$Cl$_2$ should be used in the rate law for Step 2 if CH$_2$Cl$_2$ is a product of the fast (first) step and a reactant of the slow (second) step?

A. [CH$_2$Cl$_2$] at equilibrium
B. [CH$_2$Cl$_2$] in Step 2 cannot be predicted because Step 1 is the fast step
C. Zero moles per liter
D. [CH$_2$Cl$_2$] after Step 1 is completed
E. None of the above

208. Which of the changes has no effect on the equilibrium for the following reversible reaction?

$$SrCO_3 (s) \leftrightarrow Sr^{2+} (aq) + CO_3^{2-} (aq)$$

A. Adding solid Na_2CO_3

B. Adding solid $NaNO_3$

C. Increasing $[CO_3^{2-}]$

D. Increasing $[Sr^{2+}]$

E. Adding solid $Sr(NO_3)_2$

209. In which of the following equilibrium systems will the equilibrium shift to the left when the pressure of the system is increased?

A. $H_2 (g) + Cl_2 (g) \leftrightarrow 2HCl (g)$

B. $2SO_2 (g) + O_2 (g) \leftrightarrow 2SO_3 (g)$

C. $4NH_3 (g) + 5O_2 (g) \leftrightarrow 4NO (g) + 6H_2O (g)$

D. $N_2 (g) + 3H_2 (g) \leftrightarrow 2NH_3 (g)$

E. Increased pressure causes all to shift to the left

210. For the reaction, $CO (g) + 2H_2O (g) \rightleftarrows CH_3OH (g)$ with $\Delta H < 0$, which factor decreases the magnitude of the equilibrium constant K?

A. Decreasing the temperature of this system

B. Decreasing volume

C. Decreasing the pressure of this system

D. All of the above

E. None of the above

211. What is the equilibrium constant for $PCl_5 (g) + 2NO (g) \leftrightarrows PCl_3 (g) + 2NOCl (g)$, given the two reactions shown with their equilibrium constants?

$$PCl_3 (g) + Cl_2 (g) \leftrightarrows PCl_5 (g) \qquad\qquad K_1$$
$$2NO (g) + Cl_2 (g) \leftrightarrows 2NOCl (g) \qquad\qquad K_2$$

A. K_1/K_2 **B.** $(K_1K_2)^{-1}$ **C.** K_1K_2 **D.** K_2/K_1 **E.** $K_2 - K_1$

212. Which of the following statements is true concerning the equilibrium system, whereby S combines with H_2 to form hydrogen sulfide, a toxic gas from the decay of organic material?

$$S (g) + H_2 (g) \leftrightarrow H_2S (g) \qquad K_{eq} = 2.8 \times 10^{-21}$$

A. Almost all the starting molecules are converted to product

B. Decreasing $[H_2S]$ shifts the equilibrium to the left

C. Decreasing $[H_2]$ shifts the equilibrium to the right

D. Increasing the volume of the sealed reaction container shifts the equilibrium to the right

E. Very little hydrogen sulfide gas is present in the equilibrium

213. What is the K_{sp} for slightly soluble gold (III) chloride in an aqueous solution for the reaction shown?

$$AuCl_3 (s) \leftrightarrow Au^{3+} (aq) + 3Cl^- (aq)$$

A. $K_{sp} = [Au^{3+}]^3 [Cl^-] / [AuCl_3]$

B. $K_{sp} = [Au^{3+}] [Cl^-]^3$

C. $K_{sp} = [Au^{3+}]^3 [Cl^-]$

D. $K_{sp} = [Au^{3+}] [Cl^-]$

E. $K_{sp} = [Au^{3+}] [Cl^-]^3 / [AuCl_3]$

214. What is the equilibrium expression for $4NH_3 (g) + 5O_2 (g) \rightarrow 4NO (g) + 6H_2O (g)$?

A. $K_{eq} = [H_2O]^6[NO]^4 / [NH_3]^4[O_2]^5$
B. $K_{eq} = [H_2O]^6[NO]^4 / [NH_3]^4$
C. $K_{eq} = [NO]^4 / [NH_3]^4[O_2]^5$
D. $K_{eq} = [6H_2O][4NO] / [4NH_3] [5O_2]$
E. Cannot be determined from the information given

215. Hydrogen gas reacts with iron (III) oxide to form iron metal (which produces steel), as shown in the reaction below. Which statement is NOT correct concerning the equilibrium system?

$$Fe_2O_3 (s) + 3H_2 (g) + heat \leftrightarrow 2Fe (s) + 3H_2O (g)$$

A. Continually removing water from the reaction chamber increases the yield of iron
B. Decreasing the volume of hydrogen gas reduces the yield of iron
C. Lowering the reaction temperature increases the concentration of hydrogen gas
D. Increasing the pressure on the reaction chamber increases the formation of products
E. Decreasing the pressure on the reaction chamber favors the formation of products

216. Which of the following factors increases the rate of a chemical reaction?

A. Decreasing the concentration   **C.** Decreasing the temperature

B. Adding a catalyst   **D.** All of the above   **E.** None of the above

217. A chemical system is considered to have reached equilibrium when the:

A. rate of production of each of the product species is equal to the rate of consumption of each of the reactant species by the reverse reaction
B. rate of consumption of each of the product species by the reverse reaction is equal to the rate of production of each of the reactant species by the reverse reaction
C. sum of the concentrations of each of the reactant species is equal to the sum of the concentrations of each of the product species
D. rate of production of each of the product species is equal to the rate of consumption of each of the product species by the reverse reaction
E. rate of production of each of the product species by the forward reaction is equal to the rate of production of each of the reactant species by the reverse reaction

218. Which of the reactions at equilibrium shift to the left when the pressure is decreased?

A. $N_2 (g) + 3H_2 (g) \leftrightarrow 2NH_3 (g)$ **C.** $2HCl (g) \leftrightarrow H_2 (g) + Cl_2 (g)$
B. $N_2O_4 (g) \leftrightarrow 2NO_2 (g)$ **D.** $2SO_3 (g) \leftrightarrow 2SO_2 (g) + O_2 (g)$
E. All respond to the same degree under a change of pressure

Chapter 8.   THERMODYNAMICS AND THERMOCHEMISTRY

1. What happens to the kinetic energy of a gas molecule when the gas is heated?

A. Depends on the gas

B. Kinetic energy increases

C. Kinetic energy decreases

D. Kinetic energy remains constant

E. None of the above

2. For an isolated system, what can be exchanged between the system and its surroundings?

A. Neither matter nor energy

B. Temperature only

C. Matter only

D. Energy only

E. Both matter and energy

3. When liquids and gases are compared, liquids have [ ] compressibility compared to gases and a [ ] density.

A. smaller… smaller

B. greater… greater

C. greater… smaller

D. smaller… greater

E. same…same

4. Which of the following is a form of energy?

A. chemical

B. mechanical

C. electrical

D. heat

E. all of the above

5. Determine ΔH for the reaction $CH_4(g) + 2O_2(g) \rightarrow CO_2(g) + 2H_2O(l)$ given the following:

$$CH_4(g) + 2O_2(g) \rightarrow CO_2(g) + 2H_2O(g) \quad \Delta H = -802 \text{ kJ/mol}$$

$$2H_2O(g) \rightarrow 2H_2O(l) \quad\quad\quad\quad \Delta H = -88 \text{ kJ/mol}$$

A. –890 kJ/mol

B. –714 kJ/mol

C. 714 kJ/mol

D. 890 kJ/mol

E. –914 kJ/mol

6. For a closed system, what can be exchanged between the system and its surroundings?

A. Both matter and energy

B. Neither matter nor energy

C. Energy only

D. Matter only

E. Temperature only

7. Snow forms in the clouds when water vapor freezes without ever passing through the liquid phase in a process known as:

A. deposition

B. freezing

C. condensation

D. sublimation

E. melting

8. Which of the following is a form of energy?

A. nuclear   B. light   C. heat   D. mechanical   E. all of the above

9. A process or reaction that takes in heat from the surroundings is said to be:

A. exothermic

B. isothermal

C. conservative

D. endothermic

E. endergonic

10. What kind of system is represented when an investigator compresses gas within a leak-proof system by pushing down on the inside of a piston?

    A. isolated   **C.** open

    B. closed   **D.** endergonic   **E.** endothermic

11. Which of the following terms does NOT involve the solid state?

    A. freezing   **C.** evaporation

    B. sublimation   **D.** melting   **E.** none of the above

12. A fuel cell contains hydrogen and oxygen gas that react explosively and the energy converts water to steam which drives a turbine to turn a generator that produces electricity. The fuel cell and the turbine represent which forms of energy?

    A. Electrical and mechanical energy   **C.** Chemical and mechanical energy

    B. Electrical and heat energy   **D.** Chemical and heat energy

                                       E. Nuclear and mechanical energy

13. Which conditions result in a negative ΔG for a reaction?

    A. ΔH is negative and ΔS is positive   **C.** ΔS is positive

    B. ΔH is negative and ΔS is negative   **D.** ΔH is negative

                                       E. ΔH is negative and ΔS is zero

14. A process or reaction that releases heat to the surroundings is:

    A. isothermal   **C.** endothermic

    B. exothermic   **D.** conservative   **E.** exergonic

15. A 500 ml beaker of distilled water is placed under a bell jar, which is then covered by a layer of opaque insulation. After several days, some of the water evaporated. The contents of the bell jar are what kind of system?

    A. endothermic   **B.** exergonic   **C.** closed   **D.** open   **E.** isolated

16. Heat is a measure of:

    A. temperature   **C.** average kinetic energy

    B. internal thermal energy   **D.** potential energy   **E.** none of the above

17. Which of the following is NOT an endothermic process?

    A. Condensation of water vapor   **C.** Water evaporating

    B. Boiling soup   **D.** Ice melting   **E.** All are endothermic

18. A fuel cell contains hydrogen and oxygen gas that react explosively and the energy converts water to steam which drives a turbine to turn a generator that produces electricity. The fuel cell and the steam represent which forms of energy?

    A. electrical and heat energy   **C.** chemical and heat energy

    B. electrical and chemical energy   **D.** chemical and mechanical energy

                                       E. nuclear and mechanical energy

19. Which is a state function?

   A. ΔG **B.** ΔH **C.** ΔS **D.** all of the above   **E.** none of the above

20. A small bomb has exploded inside a sealed concrete bunker. What kind of system are the contents of the bunker, if the shielding of the bunker results in no heat or vibrations being detected by anyone leaning against the exterior wall?

   A. exergonic   **B.** entropic   **C.** open   **D.** closed   **E.** isolated

21. In which of the following pairs of physical changes are both changes exothermic?

   A. Melting and condensation
   B. Freezing and condensation
   C. Sublimation and evaporation
   D. Freezing and sublimation
   E. None of the above

22. A fuel cell contains hydrogen and oxygen gas that react explosively and the energy converts water to steam which drives a turbine to turn a generator that produces electricity. What are the initial and final forms of energy?

   A. Chemical and electrical energy
   B. Nuclear and electrical energy
   C. Chemical and mechanical energy
   D. Chemical and heat energy
   E. Nuclear and mechanical energy

23. Calculate the standard enthalpy change for the reaction: $CaCO_3\,(s) \rightarrow CaO\,(s) + CO_2\,(g)$ using the standard heats of formation shown below:

Compound	ΔH_f°
$CaCO_3\,(s)$	-1206.5 kJ/mol
$CaO\,(s)$	-635.5 kJ/mol
$CO_2\,(g)$	-393.5 kJ/mol

   A. -571 kJ/mol
   B. -242 kJ/mol
   C. 177.5 kJ/mol
   D. 570 kJ/mol
   E. $-1,028.5$ kJ/mol

24. Which scientific principle explains the observation that the amount of heat transfer accompanying a change in one direction is numerically equal but opposite in sign to the amount of heat transfer in the opposite direction?

   A. Law of Conservation of Mass and Energy
   B. Law of Definite Proportions
   C. Avogadro's Law
   D. Law of Conservation of Mass
   E. Law of Conservation of Energy

25. Once an object enters a black hole, astronomers consider it to have left the universe which means the universe is:

   A. entropic   **B.** isolated   **C.** closed   **D.** open   **E.** exergonic

26. Which temperature is the hottest?

     I. $100\,°C$ II. $100\,°F$ III. $100\,K$

   A. I only
   B. II only
   C. III only
   D. I and II are equal
   E. II and III equal

27. Which of the following quantities is needed to calculate the amount of heat energy released as water turns to ice at 0 °C?

    A. Heat of condensation for water and the mass
    B. Heat of vaporization for water and the mass
    C. Heat of fusion for water and the mass
    D. Heat of solidification for water and the mass
    E. Heat of fusion for water only

28. A fuel cell contains hydrogen and oxygen gas that react explosively and the energy converts water to steam which drives a turbine to turn a generator that produces electricity. What energy changes are involved in the process?

    A. Mechanical → electrical energy
    B. Chemical → heat energy
    C. Heat → mechanical energy
    D. None of the above
    E. All of the above

29. A person immersed into 8 °C H_2O would experience hypothermia much more rapidly than if exposed to air of 8 °C because:

    A. immersion in water prevents perspiration from warming the body
    B. H_2O exhibits hydrogen bonding, while air does not
    C. H_2O conducts heat more effectively than air
    D. H_2O conducts heat less effectively than air
    E. air exhibits hydrogen bonding while H_2O does not

30. How many joules of heat must be removed to lower the temperature of a 36.5 g Al bar from 84.1 °C to 56.8 °C? (specific heat of Al = 0.908 J/g °C).

    A. 905 J   **B.** 225 J   **C.** 572 J   **D.** 1063 J   **E.** 888 J

31. A nuclear power plant uses radioactive uranium to convert water to steam, which drives a turbine that turns a generator to produce electricity. The uranium and the steam represent which forms of energy?

    A. Electrical and heat energy
    B. Nuclear and heat energy
    C. Chemical and mechanical energy
    D. Chemical and heat energy
    E. Nuclear and mechanical energy

32. The mathematical equation that expresses the first law of thermodynamics is:

    A. $\Delta H = q + w$
    B. $\Delta H = q + \Delta E$
    C. $\Delta H = \Delta E + p\Delta V$
    D. $\Delta H = \Delta E - p\Delta V$
    E. $\Delta E = q + w$

33. What is the purpose of the hollow walls within a closed hollow walled container that is effective at maintaining the temperature inside?

    A. Traps air trying to escape from the box, which minimizes convection
    B. Acts as an effective insulator, which minimizes convection
    C. Acts as an effective insulator, which minimizes conduction
    D. Provides an additional source of heat for the container
    E. Reactions occur within the walls that maintain the temperature within the container

34. The specific heat of substance A is one fourth that of substance B. The temperature of both a 28.0 g sample of substance A and a 14.0 g sample of substance B were raised 15 °C. Compared to the heat absorbed by substance B, the heat absorbed by substance A was:

A. equal to   **C.** twice

B. one-half   **D.** four times   **E.** square root

35. The ΔG of formation for N_2 (g) at 25 °C is:

A. more information is needed   **C.** negative

B. positive   **D.** 1 kJ/mol   **E.** 0 kJ/mol

36. Which of the following is true for a reaction where products have more stable bonds and more orderly arrangement than the reactants?

A. ΔH is negative and ΔS is positive   **C.** ΔH is negative and ΔS is zero

B. ΔH is positive and ΔS is negative   **D.** ΔH and ΔS are positive

     E. ΔH and ΔS are negative

37. The energy change occurring in a chemical reaction at constant pressure is:

A. ΔE **B.** ΔG **C.** ΔS **D.** ΔH **E.** ΔP

38. Which component of an insulated vessel design minimizes heat conduction?

A. Reflective interior coating   **C.** Double-walled construction

B. Heavy-duty plastic casing   **D.** Tight-fitting, screw-on lid

     E. Heavy-duty aluminum construction

39. Which of the following temperatures is NOT possible?

A. –200 °C   **B.** 0 °C   **C.** 25 K   **D.** –200 K   **E.** 0 °F

40. How much heat energy in Joules is required to heat 16.0 g of copper from 23.0 °C to 66.1 °C? Specific heat of Cu = 0.382 J/g °C.

A. 450 J   **B.** 109 J   **C.** 322 J   **D.** 812 J   **E.** 263 J

41. A nuclear power plant uses ^{235}U to convert water to steam that drives a turbine which turns a generator to produce electricity. What are the initial and final forms of energy?

A. Heat energy and electrical energy   **C.** Chemical energy and mechanical energy

B. Nuclear energy and electrical energy   **D.** Chemical energy and heat energy

     E. Nuclear energy and mechanical energy

42. All of the statements regarding the symbol ΔH are correct, EXCEPT:

A. referred to as a change in entropy

B. referred to as a change in enthalpy

C. referred to as heat of reaction

D. represents the difference between the energy used in breaking bonds and the energy released in forming bonds during the chemical reaction

E. has a negative value for an exothermic reaction

43. Which component of an insulated vessel design minimizes convection?

   A. Heavy–duty aluminum construction   **C.** Tight–fitting, screw–on lid

   B. Reflective interior coating   **D.** Double–walled construction

                                        E. Heavy–duty plastic casing

44. A sample of aluminum absorbed 9.86 J of heat and the temperature increased from 23.2 °C to 30.5 °C. What is the mass of the aluminum? The specific heat of aluminum is 0.90 J/g °C.

   A. 8.1 g   **B.** 5.6 g   **C.** 6.8 g   **D.** 1.5 g   **E.** 11.8 g

45. Which is true of an atomic fission bomb according to the conservation of mass and energy law?

   A. The mass of the bomb and the fission products are identical

   B. A small amount of mass is converted into energy

   C. The energy of the bomb and the fission products are identical

   D. The mass of the fission bomb is greater than the mass of the products

   E. None of the above

46. What is the effect on the energy of the activated complex and on the rate of the reaction when a catalyst is added to a chemical reaction?

   A. Energy of the activated complex increases and the reaction rate decreases

   B. Energy of the activated complex decreases and the reaction rate increases

   C. Energy of the activated complex and the reaction rate increase

   D. Energy of the activated complex and the reaction rate decrease

   E. Energy of the activated complex remains the same, while the reaction rate decreases

47. Which component of an insulated vessel design minimizes heat radiation?

   A. Tight–fitting, screw–on lid   **C.** Double–walled construction

   B. Heavy–duty aluminum construction   **D.** Reflective interior coating

                                        E. Heavy–duty plastic casing

48. Which of the following best describes temperature?

   A. Temperature is the measure of the average amount of kinetic energy in a substance

   B. Temperature is the measure of the heat of an object

   C. Temperature is the measure of the total amount of energy in a substance

   D. All of the above

   E. None of the above

49. What is the final temperature after 336 J of heat energy is removed from 25.0 g of H_2O at 19.6 °C? Specific heat of H_2O = 4.184 J/g °C.

   A. 30.4 °C   **B.** 23.2 °C   **C.** 26.4 °C   **D.** 28.7 °C   **E.** 16.4 °C

50. What term refers to a chemical reaction that absorbs heat energy?

   A. endothermic   **C.** exothermic

   B. isothermal   **D.** exergonic   **E.** all of the above

51. To simplify comparisons, the energy value of fuels is expressed in units of:

   A. kcal/g   **B.** kcal/L   **C.** kcal   **D.** kcal/mol   **E.** some other unit

52. When considering how to keep a cup of coffee warm an office worker, places a lid on the cup. This action reduces heat loss from:

   A. radiation   **C.** conduction

   B. sublimation   **D.** convection   **E.** all of the above

53. What is the heat capacity of 84.0 g of H_2O? Specific heat of H_2O = 4.184 J/g °C.

   A. 485 J/°C   **B.** 513 J/°C   **C.** 92.3 J/°C   **D.** 355 J/°C   **E.** 351 J/°C

54. What term refers to a chemical reaction that releases heat energy?

   A. isothermal   **C.** endothermic

   B. exothermic   **D.** exergonic   **E.** all of the above

55. According to the kinetic theory, which is NOT true of ideal gases?

   A. For a sample of gas molecules, average kinetic energy is directly proportional to temperature

   B. There are no attractive or repulsive forces between gas molecules

   C. All collisions among gas molecules are perfectly elastic

   D. There is no transfer of kinetic energy during collisions between gas molecules

   E. None of the above

56. Which statement below is always true for a spontaneous chemical reaction?

   A. $\Delta S_{sys} - \Delta S_{surr} = 0$ **C.** $\Delta S_{sys} + \Delta S_{surr} < 0$

   B. $\Delta S_{sys} + \Delta S_{surr} > 0$ **D.** $\Delta S_{sys} + \Delta S_{surr} = 0$ **E.** $\Delta S_{sys} - \Delta S_{surr} < 0$

57. Which compound is NOT correctly matched with the predominant intermolecular force associated with that compound in the liquid state?

Compound	Intermolecular force
A. CH_3OH	hydrogen bonding
B. HF	hydrogen bonding
C. Cl_2O	dipole-dipole interactions
D. HBr	van der Waals interactions
E. CH_4	van der Waals interactions

58. Which of the following best describes heat?

   A. Heat can be measured with a thermometer

   B. Objects at the same temperature contain the same quantity of heat

   C. Heat is energy that moves from high to low temperature objects

   D. Heat is a measure of the temperature of an object

   E. Heat is a measure of the average amount of energy in an object

59. How many grams of Ag can be heated from 23 °C to 36 °C when 22 g of Au cools from 95.5 °C to 26.4 °C? Specific heat of Ag = 0.240 J/g °C; Specific heat of Au = 0.130 J/g °C.

   A. 63 g   **B.** 1.5×10^3 g   **C.** 44 g   **D.** 22 g   **E.** 66 g

60. Which statement best describes the reaction: $HCl\ (aq) + KOH\ (aq) \rightarrow KCl\ (aq) + H_2O\ (l)$

A. HCl and potassium hydroxide solutions produce potassium chloride and H_2O
B. HCl and potassium hydroxide solutions produce potassium chloride solution and H_2O
C. Aqueous HCl and potassium hydroxide produce aqueous potassium chloride and H_2O
D. HCl and potassium hydroxide produce potassium chloride and H_2O
E. An acid plus a base produce H_2O and a salt

61. Which reaction tends to be the most stable?

A. Isothermic reaction
B. Exothermic reaction
C. Endothermic reaction
D. All three are equally stable
E. All three are unstable

62. Which of the following properties of a gas is/are a state functions?

      I. temperature   II. heat   III. work

A. I only   **B.** I and II only   **C.** II and III only   **D.** I, II and III   **E.** II only

63. Calculate the mass of gold that requires 468 J to heat the sample from 21.6 °C to 33.2 °C? Specific heat of gold = 0.130 J/g °C

A. 6.72 g   **B.** 483 g   **C.** 262 g   **D.** 63.4 g   **E.** 310 g

64. Which of the statements below best describes the following reaction?

$$HNO_3\ (aq) + LiOH\ (aq) \rightarrow LiNO_3\ (aq) + H_2O\ (l)$$

A. Nitric acid and lithium hydroxide solutions produce lithium nitrate solution and water
B. Nitric acid and lithium hydroxide solutions produce lithium nitrate and water
C. Nitric acid and lithium hydroxide produce lithium nitrate and water
D. Aqueous solutions of nitric acid and lithium hydroxide produce aqueous lithium nitrate and water
E. An acid plus a base produce H_2O and a salt

65. Based on the reaction shown, which statement is true?

$$N_2 + O_2 \rightarrow 2NO \qquad \Delta H = 43.2\ kcal$$

A. 43.2 kcal are consumed when 1.00 mole of O_2 reacts
B. 43.2 kcal are produced when 1.00 mole of NO is produced
C. 43.2 kcal are consumed when 1.00 g of N_2 reacts
D. 43.2 kcal are consumed when 1.00 g of O_2 reacts
E. 43.2 kcal are consumed when 1.00 g of NO is produced

66. Which statement must be true for all objects that radiate heat?

A. Any object that gets warmer must be experiencing conduction or convection
B. First Law of Thermodynamics does not apply to radiation
C. First Law of Thermodynamics applies to convection
D. All objects are gradually getting colder
E. No object can reach the temperature of absolute zero

67. A chicken cutlet provides 6.90×10^2 food Calories (Cal). A food Calorie is equivalent to 4180 J of heat energy. The heat energy provided by the chicken cutlet would be sufficient to heat 59.1 kg of water by how many °C? Specific heat of water = 4.18 J/g °C.

A. 5.32 °C   **B.** 21.8 °C   **C.** 5.91 °C   **D.** 11.7 °C   **E.** 4.18 °C

68. Which of the statements best describes the following reaction?

$$HC_2H_3O_2 \ (aq) + NaOH \ (aq) \rightarrow NaC_2H_3O_2 \ (aq) + H_2O \ (l)$$

A. Acetic acid and sodium hydroxide solutions produce sodium acetate and water
B. Aqueous solutions of acetic acid and sodium hydroxide produce aqueous sodium acetate and water
C. Acetic acid and sodium hydroxide solutions produce sodium acetate solution and water
D. Acetic acid and sodium hydroxide produce sodium acetate and water
E. An acid plus a base produce H_2O and a salt

69. What is the volume of three moles of O_2 at STP?

A. 11.2 L   **B.** 22.4 L   **C.** 67.2 L   **D.** 32.0 L   **E.** 5.51. L

70. Which violates the first law of thermodynamics?

    I. An isolated pendulum that swings indefinitely
    II. A battery that indefinitely maintains its charge
    III. A refrigerator converts all of the interior heat removed to provide electricity to the room in which it is located

A. I only   **B.** II only   **C.** III only   **D.** I, II and III   **E.** II and III only

71. Which of the following elements occurs naturally as diatomic molecules?

A. chlorine gas   **C.** fluorine gas
B. iodine vapor   **D.** all of the above   **E.** none of the above

72. Determine the value of $\Delta E°_{rxn}$ for this reaction, whereby the standard enthalpy of reaction $(\Delta H°_{rxn})$ for $C_2H_2 \ (g) + 2H_2 \ (g) \rightarrow C_2H_6 \ (g)$ is -311.5 kJ mol^{-1}.

A. -306.5 kJ mol^{-1} **C.** -316.0 kJ mol^{-1}
B. -318.0 kJ mol^{-1} **D.** -364.6 kJ mol^{-1} **E.** $+466$ kJ mol^{-1}

73. A process that is unfavorable for enthalpy, but favorable with respect to entropy, could:

A. occur at any temperature
B. not occur regardless of temperature
C. occur at high temperatures, but not at lower temperatures
D. occur at low temperatures, but not at higher temperatures
E. none of the above

74. The combustion of one mole of a gas produces 212 calories of energy. Express the energy released in this reaction in kilojoules:

A. 0.393 kJ   **B.** 0.887 kJ   **C.** 789 kJ   **D.** 348 kJ   **E.** 3.88 kJ

75. Which is a general guideline for balancing an equation?

  A. Check each reactant and product to verify the coefficients
  B. Balance polyatomic ions as a single unit
  C. Begin balancing with the most complex formula
  D. Write correct formulas for reactants and products
  E. All of the above

76. What is the ratio of the diffusion rates of H_2 gas to O_2 gas?

  A. 4:1 **B.** 2:1 **C.** 1:3 **D.** 1:4 **E.** 1:2

77. Which of the following is an intensive property?

  I. volume   II. density   III. specific heat

  A. III only **C.** II and III only
  B. I and II only **D.** I, II and III **E.** II only

78. In a chemical reaction, the bonds being formed are:

  A. more energetic than the ones broken   **C.** the same as the bonds broken
  B. less energetic than the ones broken   **D.** different from the ones broken
  E. none of the above

79. Which statement concerning temperature change as a substance is heated is NOT correct?

  A. As a liquid is heated, its temperature rises until its boiling point is reached
  B. During the time a liquid is changing to the gaseous state, the temperature gradually increases until all the liquid is changed
  C. As a solid is heated, its temperature rises until its melting point is reached
  D. During the time a solid melts to a liquid the temperature remains constant
  E. The temperature remains the same during the phase change

80. Which is NOT a general guideline for balancing an equation?

  A. Balance polyatomic ions as a single unit
  B. Check each reactant and product to verify the coefficients
  C. Write correct formulas for reactants and products
  D. Begin balancing with the most complex formula
  E. Change a subscript in a formula if the equation is not balanced

81. Consider the reaction: $N_2 + O_2 \rightarrow 2NO$. $\Delta H = 43.2$ kcal

When 50.0 g of N_2 reacts, [ ] kcal will be [ ].

  A. 43.2… produced **C.** 77.1… produced
  B. 77.1… consumed **D.** 86.4… consumed **E.** 86.4… produced

82. As an extensive property, if the change in a value for the decomposition of 110 grams of a substance is –45 kJ, what is the change in this value when 330 grams decompose?

  A. –15 kJ **B.** –45 kJ **C.** –135 kJ **D.** –560 kJ **E.** Cannot be determined

83. Which would be the correct units for a heat of condensation value?

  A. Cal / g **B.** g / °C **C.** Cal / °C **D.** J / °C **E.** K / °C

84. Which is NOT a general guideline for balancing an equation?

  A. Balance ionic compounds as a single unit
  B. Balance polyatomic ions as a single unit
  C. Begin balancing with the most complex formula
  D. Write correct formulas for reactants and products
  E. Check each reactant and product to verify the coefficients

85. The thermodynamic systems that have high stability tend to demonstrate:

  A. maximum ΔH and maximum ΔS
  B. maximum ΔH and minimum ΔS
  C. minimum ΔH and maximum ΔS
  D. minimum ΔH and minimum ΔS
  E. none of the above

86. As an intensive property, if the change in μ for the decomposition of 140 grams of a substance is –60 kJ/mol, what is the change in μ from the decomposition of 420 grams?

  A. –20 kJ   **B.** –70 kJ   **C.** –140 kJ   **D.** –80 kJ   **E.** –60 kJ

87. What is an endothermic reaction?

  A. It is a reaction that requires heat as a reactant
  B. It is a reaction where there is a net absorption of energy from a reaction
  C. It is a reaction where the products have more energy than the reactants
  D. All of the above
  E. None of the above

88. What is the coefficient (n) of O_2 gas for the balanced equation?

  $$n\text{P}\,(s) + n\text{O}_2\,(g) \rightarrow n\text{P}_2\text{O}_3\,(s)$$

  A. 1   **B.** 2   **C.** 3   **D.** 5   **E.** none of the above

89. What is the partial pressure due to CO_2 of a mixture of gases at 700 torr that contains 40% CO_2, 40% O_2 and 20% H_2 by pressure?

  A. 760 torr   **B.** 280 torr   **C.** 420 torr   **D.** 560 torr   **E.** 700 torr

90. The standard enthalpy (ΔH°) at 25 °C for $NH_3\,(g) + HCl\,(g) \rightarrow NH_4Cl\,(s)$ is –175.9 kJ mol^{-1}. Determine ΔE°_{rxn}:

  A. –164.8 kJ mol^{-1}
  B. +5134 kJ mol^{-1}
  C. –173.4 kJ mol^{-1}
  D. –180.9 kJ mol^{-1}
  E. –170.9 kJ mol^{-1}

91. Which of the following represent forms of internal energy?

  I. bond energy   II. thermal energy   III. gravitational energy
  A. II only   **C.** II and III only
  B. I and II only   **D.** III only   **E.** I, II and III

92. Which of the following would have the same numerical magnitude?

  A. Heats of sublimation and deposition
  B. Heats of solidification and condensation
  C. Heats of fusion and deposition
  D. Heats of sublimation and condensation
  E. None of the above

---

93. What is the coefficient (n) of O_2 gas for the balanced equation: $nP\ (s) + nO_2\ (g) \rightarrow nP_2O_5\ (s)$?

   A. 1   **B.** 2   **C.** 4   **D.** 5   **E.** none of the above

94. A flask contains a mixture of O_2, N_2 and CO_2. The pressure exerted by N_2 is 320 torr, and exerted by CO_2 is 240 torr. If the total pressure of the gases is 740 torr, what is the percent pressure of O_2?

   A. 20%   **B.** 66%   **C.** 33%   **D.** 24%   **E.** 75%

95. What does internal energy for an ideal gas depend upon?

       I. pressure   II. temperature   III. volume

   A. I only   **C.** I and III only

   B. II only   **D.** I, II and III   **E.** III only

96. What is an exothermic reaction?

      I. It is a reaction where there is a net absorption of energy from a reaction
      II. It is a reaction where the products have more energy than the reactants
      III. It is a reaction that requires heat as a reactant

   A. I and II only   **C.** II and III only

   B. I and III only   **D.** I, II and III   **E.** none of the above

97. What is the coefficient (n) of P for the balanced equation: $nP\ (s) + nO_2\ (g) \rightarrow nP_2O_5\ (s)$?

   A. 1   **B.** 2   **C.** 4   **D.** 5   **E.** none of the above

98. Calculate the enthalpy for the reaction $N_2 + O_2 \rightarrow 2NO$, given the bond dissociation energies of $N_2 = 226$ kcal/mol, $O_2 = 199$ kcal/mol and $NO = 145$ kcal/mol.

   A. 135 kcal/mol   **C.** 280 kcal/mol

   B. –135 kcal/mol   **D.** –280 kcal/mol   **E.** 199 kcal/mol

99. The internal energy of the system increases for which of the following situations?

      I. A clay ball is dropped and sticks to the ground
      II. Hydrogen and oxygen undergo an exothermic reaction to form H_2O
      III. A race car is driven at a constant speed while considering the effect of air resistance

   A. II only   **C.** I and III only

   B. II and III only   **D.** I, II and III   **E.** III only

100. Which of the following quantities are necessary in calculating the amount of heat energy required to change liquid H_2O at 75 °C to steam at 110 °C?

   A. Specific heat of ice and specific heat of H_2O
   B. Heat of fusion for H_2O and heat of condensation for H_2O
   C. Specific heat of steam and heat of fusion for H_2O
   D. Specific heat of H_2O, specific heat of steam, and heat of vaporization for H_2O
   E. Specific heat of H_2O and specific heat of steam

101. What is the coefficient (n) of N_2 gas for the balanced equation: $nN_2\ (g) + nH_2\ (g) \rightarrow nNH_3\ (g)$?

   A. 1   **B.** 2   **C.** 3   **D.** 4   **E.** None of the above

102. Which statement is true for a chemical reaction, whereby ΔH is < 0 and ΔS is < 0?

  A. Reaction may or may not be spontaneous, but spontaneity is favored by low temperatures

  B. Reaction may or may not be spontaneous, but spontaneity is favored by high temperatures

  C. Reaction must be spontaneous, regardless of temperature and becomes even more so at higher temperatures

  D. Reaction must be spontaneous, regardless of temperature and becomes even more so at lower temperatures

  E. No conclusion can be made from the limited information presented

103. Where does the energy released during an exothermic reaction originate from?

  A. Surroundings

  B. Kinetic energy of the reacting molecules   **D.** Thermal energy of the reactants

  C. Potential energy of the reacting molecules   **E.** Kinetic energy of the surrounding

104. If it takes energy to break bonds and you gain energy in the formation of bonds, how can some reactions be exothermic, while others are endothermic?

  A. Some products have more energy than others and they always require energy to be formed

  B. Some reactants have more energetic bonds than others and they will always release energy

  C. It is the total number of bonds that matters. Sometimes you create more bonds than you break and, since all bonds have same amount of energy, you gain or lose energy depending on the number of bonds

  D. It is the total amount of energy that matters. Sometimes some bonds are stronger than others and so you gain or lose energy when you form them

  E. None of the above

105. What is the coefficient (n) of H_2 gas for the balanced equation: $nN_2\,(g) + nH_2\,(g) \rightarrow nNH_3\,(g)$?

  A. 1   **B.** 2   **C.** 3   **D.** 4   **E.** None of the above

106. What is $\Delta H°$ for the decomposition of methane to C and diatomic gases?

    $CH_4\,(g) + 2O_2\,(g) \rightarrow CO_2\,(g) + 2H_2O\,(g)\ \Delta H = -191.8$ kJ/mole

  A. –361.4 kJ   **B.** 17.8 kJ   **C.** –13.6 kJ   **D.** 361.4 kJ   **E.** 33.4 kJ

107. Which expression yields the same value for T_1 and T_2 when both temperatures are in Celsius or Kelvin?

  A. T_1/T_2 **B.** $T_1 T_2$ **C.** $T_1 - T_2$ **D.** $T_1 + T_2$ **E.** $T_1 T_2/2$

108. How much energy is required to change 12.9 g of solid Cu to molten Cu at 1083 °C (melting point)? Heat of fusion for Cu = 205 J/g.

  A. 1320 J   **B.** 1870 J   **C.** 1430 J   **D.** 3540 J   **E.** 2640 J

109. What is the coefficient (n) of NH_3 for the balanced equation $nN_2\,(g) + nH_2\,(g) \rightarrow nNH_3\,(g)$?

  A. 1   **B.** 2   **C.** 3   **D.** 4   **E.** None of the above

110. A quantity of an ideal gas occupies 300 cm^3 at 27 °C. Find its volume at –173 °C at constant pressure.

  A. 50 cm^3 **B.** 150 cm^3 **C.** 100 cm^3 **D.** 900 cm^3 **E.** 200 cm^3

111. How much heat is required to raise 5 grams of a material by 10 K if it requires 40 calories to raise 5 grams of this material by 10 °C?

   A. 0.0040 cal   **B.** 40 cal   **C.** 5 cal   **D.** 50 cal   **E.** 4.0 cal

112. From the energy profile graphs, which reaction is endothermic?

   R= reactants   P= products

   A. a   **B.** b   **C.** c   **D.** d   **E.** None of the above

113. What is the product for the combination reaction Li (s) + O_2 (g) → ?

   A. LiO_2 **B.** Li_2O_3 **C.** LiO   **D.** Li_3O_2 **E.** Li_2O

114. What is the term for a reaction when the bonds formed during the reaction are stronger than the bonds broken?

   A. endergonic   **C.** endothermic
   B. exergonic   **D.** exothermic   **E.** spontaneous

115. If the stationary gas has a kinetic energy of 500 J at 25 °C, what is its kinetic energy at 50 °C?

   A. 125 J   **B.** 450 J   **C.** 540 J   **D.** 1080 J   **E.** 270 J

116. How much heat must be absorbed to evaporate 14 g of NH_3 at −33 °C (condensation point)? Heat of condensation for NH_3 = 1380 J/g.

   A. 62,000 J   **B.** 46,000 J   **C.** 91,000 J   **D.** 19,000 J   **E.** 1,380 J

117. What is the product for the combination reaction Ca (s) + O_2 (g) → ?

   A. Ca_2O_3 **B.** CaO_2 **C.** Ca_2O **D.** CaO   **E.** Ca_3O_2

118. An ideal gas fills a closed rigid container. As the number of moles of gas in the chamber is increased at a constant temperature:

   A. volume increases   **C.** pressure decreases
   B. pressure remains constant   **D.** the effect on pressure cannot be determined
                                          E. pressure increases

119. When the temperature of a suspension bridge changes from −10 °C on a winter night to 0 °C during the daylight, an iron bolt expands in diameter from 1.0000 cm to 1.0022 cm. What is the coefficient of linear expansion for iron? (Note: ΔL/L = aΔT.)

   A. $(2.2 \times 10^{-4})(10)$ °C   **C.** $10 / (2.2 \times 10^{-4})$ °C
   B. $(2.2 \times 10^{-4})/10$ °C   **D.** $1 / (10 \times 2.2 \times 10^{-4})$ °C
                                                 E. $(2.2 \times 10^{-4})(10) / (2.2 \times 10^{-4})$ °C

120. Given that the following energy profiles have the same scale, which of the reactions is the most exothermic?

   R = reactants   P = products

   A. a   **B.** b   **C.** c   **D.** d   **E.** Cannot be determined

121. What is the product from heating magnesium metal and nitrogen gas?

  A. Mg_2N **B.** Mg_2N_3 **C.** MgN **D.** MgN_2 **E.** Mg_3N_2

122. Consider the reaction: $C_3H_8 + 5O_2 \rightarrow 3CO_2 + 4H_2O + 488$ kcal

The reaction is [   ] and the sign of ΔH is [   ].

  A. exothermic … negative   **C.** exothermic … positive
  B. endothermic … negative   **D.** endothermic … positive
                                       E. exothermic … neither positive nor negative

123. Which of the following expressions defines enthalpy? (q is heat; U is internal energy; P is pressure, V is volume)

  A. $q - \Delta U$ **B.** $U + q$ **C.** q **D.** ΔU **E.** $U + PV$

124. What is the product from heating potassium metal and powdered phosphorus?

  A. K_2P_3 **B.** K_3P **C.** KP_3 **D.** KP **E.** K_3P_2

125. Given the following data, what is the heat of formation for ethanol?

    $C_2H_5OH + 3O_2 \rightarrow 2CO_2 + 3H_2O$
    $\Delta H = 327.0$ kcal/mole
    $H_2O \rightarrow H_2 + \frac{1}{2}O_2$
    $\Delta H = +68.3$ kcal/mole
    $C + O_2 \rightarrow CO_2$
    $\Delta H = -94.1$ kcal/mole

  A. –720.1 kcal   **C.** +720.1 kcal
  B. –327.0 kcal   **D.** +76.2 kcal   **E.** +327.0 kcal

126. For an ideal gas, ΔH depends upon:

    I. density   II. temperature   III. volume

  A. I only   **B.** II only   **C.** III only   **D.** I and II only   **E.** I and III only

127. What is the heat of vaporization in J/g of an unknown liquid, if 6,823 J of heat is required to vaporize 58.0 g of it at its boiling point?

  A. 981 J/g   **B.** 28,100 J/g   **C.** 516 J/g   **D.** 118 J/g   **E.** 6,823 J/g

128. What is the product from heating cadmium metal and powdered sulfur?

  A. CdS_2 **B.** Cd_2S_3 **C.** CdS **D.** Cd_2S **E.** Cd_3S_2

129. Which of the following is true about Liquid A, if the vapor pressure of Liquid A is greater than that of Liquid B?

  A. Liquid A has a higher heat of fusion than B
  B. Liquid A has a higher heat of vaporization than B
  C. Liquid A forms stronger bonds than B
  D. Liquid A boils at a higher temperature than B
  E. Liquid A boils at a lower temperature than B

130. Under standard conditions, which reaction has the largest difference between the energy of reaction and enthalpy,?

A. C (*graphite*) → C (*diamond*)

B. C (*graphite*) + O_2 (*g*) → C (*diamond*)

C. 2C (*graphite*) + O_2 (*g*) → 2CO (*g*)

D. C (*graphite*) + O_2 (*g*) → CO_2 (*g*)

E. CO (*g*) + NO_2 (*g*) → CO_2 (*g*) + NO (*g*)

131. Given the energy profiles with the same scale, which of the reactions requires the most energy?

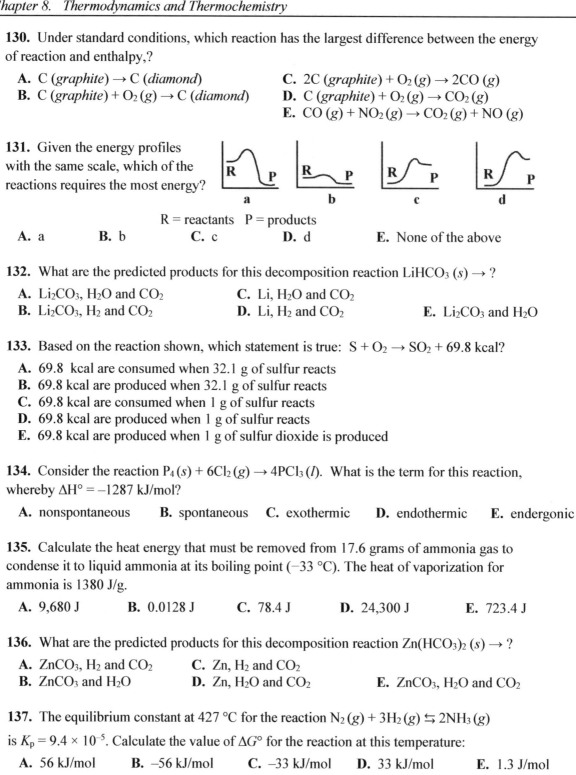

R = reactants   P = products

A. a   **B.** b   **C.** c   **D.** d   **E.** None of the above

132. What are the predicted products for this decomposition reaction $LiHCO_3$ (*s*) → ?

A. Li_2CO_3, H_2O and CO_2

B. Li_2CO_3, H_2 and CO_2

C. Li, H_2O and CO_2

D. Li, H_2 and CO_2

E. Li_2CO_3 and H_2O

133. Based on the reaction shown, which statement is true: S + O_2 → SO_2 + 69.8 kcal?

A. 69.8 kcal are consumed when 32.1 g of sulfur reacts

B. 69.8 kcal are produced when 32.1 g of sulfur reacts

C. 69.8 kcal are consumed when 1 g of sulfur reacts

D. 69.8 kcal are produced when 1 g of sulfur reacts

E. 69.8 kcal are produced when 1 g of sulfur dioxide is produced

134. Consider the reaction P_4 (*s*) + $6Cl_2$ (*g*) → $4PCl_3$ (*l*). What is the term for this reaction, whereby $\Delta H° = -1287$ kJ/mol?

A. nonspontaneous   **B.** spontaneous   **C.** exothermic   **D.** endothermic   **E.** endergonic

135. Calculate the heat energy that must be removed from 17.6 grams of ammonia gas to condense it to liquid ammonia at its boiling point (−33 °C). The heat of vaporization for ammonia is 1380 J/g.

A. 9,680 J   **B.** 0.0128 J   **C.** 78.4 J   **D.** 24,300 J   **E.** 723.4 J

136. What are the predicted products for this decomposition reaction $Zn(HCO_3)_2$ (*s*) → ?

A. $ZnCO_3$, H_2 and CO_2

B. $ZnCO_3$ and H_2O

C. Zn, H_2 and CO_2

D. Zn, H_2O and CO_2

E. $ZnCO_3$, H_2O and CO_2

137. The equilibrium constant at 427 °C for the reaction N_2 (*g*) + $3H_2$ (*g*) ⇆ $2NH_3$ (*g*) is $K_p = 9.4 \times 10^{-5}$. Calculate the value of $\Delta G°$ for the reaction at this temperature:

A. 56 kJ/mol   **B.** −56 kJ/mol   **C.** −33 kJ/mol   **D.** 33 kJ/mol   **E.** 1.3 J/mol

138. What is the standard enthalpy change for the reaction?

$$3P_4 (s) + 18Cl_2 (g) → 12PCl_3 (l)$$

$$P_4 (s) + 6Cl_2 (g) → 4PCl_3 (l) \qquad \Delta H° = -1289 \text{ kJ/mol}$$

A. 426 kJ/mol   **B.** −1345 kJ/mol   **C.** −366 kJ/mol   **D.** 1289 kJ/mol   **E.** −3837 kJ/mol

139. Which of the following reaction energies is the most endothermic?

A. 540 kJ/mole

C. 125 kJ/mole

B. −540 kJ/mole

D. −125 kJ/mole

E. Not enough information given

140. What are the predicted products for this decomposition reaction $Al(HCO_3)_3$ (*s*) → ?

A. Al, H_2O and CO_2

C. $Al_2(CO_3)_3$, H_2O and CO_2

B. $Al_2(CO_3)_3$, H_2 and CO_2

D. Al, H_2 and CO_2

E. $Al_2(CO_3)_3$ and H_2O

141. If a substance is in the gas phase at STP, what occurs as the pressure of the surroundings is decreased at constant temperature?

A. no phase change

C. evaporation

B. sublimation

D. condensation

E. freezing

142. Given the data, what is the standard enthalpy change for $4PCl_3$ (*l*) → P_4 (*s*) + $6Cl_2$ (*g*)?

$$P_4\,(s) + 6Cl_2\,(g) \rightarrow 4PCl_3\,(l) \qquad \Delta H^\circ = -1274 \text{ kJ/mol}$$

A. 318.5 kJ/mol

C. −1917 kJ/mol

B. −637 kJ/mol

D. 1274 kJ/mol

E. −2548 kJ/mol

143. How much heat is needed to convert 10.0 g of ice at −10 °C to H_2O (*l*) at 10 °C? Specific heat of ice = 2.09 J/(g °C); heat of fusion of ice = 334 J/g; specific heat of water = 4.18 J/g °C.

A. 6,210 J

B. 3970 J

C. 2760 J

D. 1,070 J

E. 5230 J

144. What are the products for the single-replacement reaction Zn (*s*) + $CuSO_4$ (*aq*) → ?

A. CuO and $ZnSO_4$

C. Cu and $ZnSO_4$

B. CuO and $ZnSO_3$

D. Cu and $ZnSO_3$

E. no reaction

145. A reaction that is spontaneous can be described as:

A. releasing heat to the surroundings

B. proceeding without external influence once it has begun

C. proceeding in both the forward and reverse directions

D. having the same rate in both the forward and reverse directions

E. increasing in disorder

146. Given that the ΔH° is 92.4 kJ/mol, what is the heat of formation of NH_3 (*g*) of the following reaction: $2NH_3$ (*g*) → N_2 (*g*) + $3H_2$ (*g*)?

A. −92.4 kJ/mol

C. 46.2 kJ/mol

B. −184.4 kJ/mol

D. 92.4 kJ/mol

E. −46.2 kJ/mol

147. Which of the following reaction energies is the least exothermic?

A. 562 kJ/mole

C. 126 kJ/mole

B. −562 kJ/mole

D. −126 kJ/mole

E. Not enough information given

148. Which solid compound is soluble in water?

A. Na_2CO_3

C. $CuC_2H_3O_2$

B. $AgNO_3$

D. None of the above

E. All of the above

149. If ΔG is negative, then the reaction is described as:

A. spontaneous and endothermic   C. spontaneous with an increase in entropy

B. spontaneous and exothermic   D. nonspontaneous because of the decrease in entropy

    E. spontaneous because of the decrease in entropy

150. The heat of formation of water vapor is:

A. positive, but greater than the heat of formation for H_2O (*l*)

B. positive and greater than the heat of formation for H_2O (*l*)

C. negative, but greater than the heat of formation for H_2O (*l*)

D. negative and less than the heat of formation for H_2O (*l*)

E. positive and equal to the heat of formation for H_2O (*l*)

151. Which constant does *C* represent in the calculation used to determine how much heat is needed to convert 50 g of ice at −20 °C to steam at 300 °C?

(A)(50 g)(20 °C) + (heat of fusion)(50 g) + (B)(50 g)(100 °C) + (heat of vap.)(50 g) +

+ (C)(50 g)(200 °C) = total heat.

A. Heat capacity of water   C. Specific heat of water

B. Specific heat of steam   D. Specific heat of ice   E. Heat capacity of steam

152. Which solid compound is soluble in water?

A. $AlPO_4$ B. $PbSO_4$ C. $CaCO_3$ D. All of the above   E. None of the above

153. Which reaction is accompanied by an *increase* in entropy?

A. Na_2CO_3 (*s*) + CO_2 (*g*) + H_2O (*g*) → $2NaHCO_3$ (*s*)

B. BaO (*s*) + CO_2 (*g*) → $BaCO_3$ (*s*)   D. ZnS (*s*) + $3/2O_2$ (*g*) → ZnO (*s*) + SO_2 (*g*)

C. CH_4 (*g*) + H_2O (*g*) → CO (*g*) + $3H_2$ (*g*)   E. N_2 (*g*) + $3H_2$ (*g*) → $2NH_3$ (*g*)

154. The greatest entropy is observed for which 10 g sample of CO_2?

A. CO_2 (*g*)   B. CO_2 (*aq*)   C. CO_2 (*s*)   D. CO_2 (*l*)   E. All are equivalent

155. A chemical reaction is when:

A. two solids mix to form a heterogeneous mixture

B. two liquids mix to form a homogeneous mixture

C. one or more new compounds are formed by rearranging atoms

D. a new element is formed by rearranging nucleons

E. a liquid undergoes a phase change and produces a solid

156. Which solid compound is soluble in water?

A. CuS B. Ag_3PO_4 C. $PbCrO_4$ D. $NiCO_3$ E. $Ba(OH)_2$

157. At equilibrium, increasing the temperature of an exothermic reaction likely:

A. increases the heat of reaction

B. decreases the heat of reaction

C. increases the forward reaction

D. decreases the forward reaction

E. increases the heat of reaction and increases the forward reaction

158. Entropy can be defined as the amount of:

  A. equilibrium in a system
  B. chemical bonds that are changed during a reaction
  C. energy required to initiate a reaction
  D. energy required to rearrange chemical bonds
  E. disorder in a system

159. Which is ranked from lowest to highest entropy per gram of NaCl?

  A. NaCl(s), NaCl (l), NaCl (aq), NaCl (g)
  B. NaCl (s), NaCl (l), NaCl (g), NaCl (aq)
  C. NaCl (g), NaCl (aq), NaCl (l), NaCl (s)
  D. NaCl (s), NaCl (aq), NaCl (l), NaCl (g)
  E. NaCl (l), NaCl (s), NaCl (g), NaCl (aq)

160. A chemical equation is a:

  A. representation of the atoms undergoing a chemical equalization
  B. chemical combination of equal numbers of reactants and products
  C. sum of the masses of the products and reactants
  D. shorthand notation for illustrating a chemical reaction
  E. type of reaction that occurs only when energy is consumed by the reaction

161. Which constant does A represent in the calculation used to determine how much heat is needed to convert 50 g of ice at −20 °C to steam at 300 °C?

(A)(50 g)(20 °C) + (heat of fusion)(50 g) + (4.18 J/g °C)(50 g)(100 °C) + (B)(50 g) +

+ (C)(50 g)(200 °C) = total heat.

  A. Specific heat of water   **C.** Heat of condensation
  B. Heat of vaporization of water   **D.** Heat capacity of steam
                                  E. Specific heat of ice

162. What phase change is observed by a researcher working with a sample of neon at 278 K and a pressure of 60 atm when the pressure is reduced to 38 atm?

  A. liquid → solid   **C.** solid → gas
  B. solid → liquid   **D.** liquid → gas   **E.** gas → liquid

163. At constant temperature and pressure, a negative ΔG indicates that the:

  A. reaction is exothermic   **C.** reaction is spontaneous
  B. reaction is fast   **D.** $\Delta S > 0$ **E.** reaction is endothermic

164. Which statement is true regarding entropy?

    I. It is a state function
    II. It is an extensive property
    III. It has an absolute zero value
  A. I only   **C.** I and III only
  B. III only   **D.** I, II and III   **E.** I and II only

165. Is the potential energy of the reactants or the potential energy of the products higher in an endothermic reaction?

    A. The potential energy of the reactants equals the potential energy of the products
    B. Initially, the potential energy of the reactants is higher, but the potential energy of the products is higher in the later stages
    C. The potential energy of the products is higher than the potential energy of the reactants
    D. The potential energy of the reactants is higher than the potential energy of the products
    E. Not enough information is provided to make any conclusions

166. Which of the following is a true statement regarding evaporation?

    A. Increasing the surface area of the liquid decreases the rate of evaporation
    B. The temperature of the liquid changes during evaporation
    C. Decreasing the surface area of the liquid increases the rate of evaporation
    D. Molecules with greater energy escape from the liquid
    E. Not enough information is provided to make any conclusions

167. What are the products for this double-replacement reaction $AgNO_3$ (*aq*) + NaCl (*aq*) → ?

    A. $AgClO_3$ and $NaNO_2$ **C.** AgCl and $NaNO_2$
    B. AgCl and $NaNO_3$ **D.** Ag_3N and $NaClO_3$ **E.** $AgClO_3$ and $NaNO_3$

168. The noble gas Xe can exist in the liquid phase at 180 K, which is a temperature significantly greater than its normal boiling point, if:

    A. external pressure > vapor pressure of xenon
    B. external pressure < vapor pressure of xenon   **D.** temperature is increased quickly
    C. external pressure = partial pressure of water   **E.** temperature is increased slowly

169. What is the heat of reaction in the combustion of 60 grams of ethane from the data and balanced reaction below?

$$2C_2H_6 + 7O_2 \rightarrow 4CO_2 + 6H_2O \ (g)$$

$$\Delta H_f^o(C_2H_6) = -20.2 \ \text{kcal/mol}$$
$$\Delta H_f^o(CO_2) = -94.1 \ \text{kcal/mol} \qquad \Delta H_f^o(H_2O \ (g)) = -57.8 \ \text{kcal/mol}$$

    A. –682.8 kcal   **B.** –515.3 kcal   **C.** –332.7 kcal   **D.** –243.2 kcal   **E.** –60.0 kcal

170. For the second law of thermodynamics, which statement(s) is/are true?

    I. Heat never flows from a cooler to a warmer object
    II. Heat cannot be converted completely to work in a cyclic process
    III. The entropy of the universe never decreases

    A. III only   **B.** I and II only   **C.** II and III only   **D.** I, II and III   **E.** I and III only

171. Use the bond energies to determine if the reaction is exothermic: $H_2 + Cl_2 \rightarrow 2HCl$

H–H (436 kJ/mol); Cl–Cl (243 kJ/mol); H–Cl (431 kJ/mol)

    A. Exothermic with less than 50 kJ of energy released
    B. Endothermic with less than 50 kJ of energy absorbed
    C. Exothermic with more than 50 kJ of energy released
    D. Endothermic with more than 50 kJ of energy absorbed
    E. Endothermic equal to 50 kJ of energy absorbed

172. A nonvolatile liquid would have:

A. a highly explosive propensity
B. strong attractive forces between molecules
C. weak attractive forces between molecules
D. a high vapor pressure at room temperature
E. weak attractive forces within molecules

173. What are gases A and B likely to be if, at STP, a mixture of gas A and B has the average velocity of gas A twice that of B?

A. Ar and Kr **B.** C and Ti **C.** He and H **D.** Mg and K **E.** B and Ne

174. In the reaction, $2H_2 (g) + O_2 (g) \rightarrow 2H_2O (g)$, entropy is:

A. increasing **C.** inversely proportional
B. the same **D.** unable to be determined **E.** decreasing

175. Which statement for the reaction $2NO (g) + O_2 (g) \rightarrow 2NO_2 (g)$ is true when $\Delta H° = -113.1$ kJ/mol and $\Delta S° = -145.3$ J/K mol?

A. Reaction is at equilibrium at 25 °C under standard conditions
B. Reaction is spontaneous at only high temperatures
C. Reaction is spontaneous at only low temperatures
D. Reaction is spontaneous at all temperatures
E. $\Delta G°$ becomes more favorable as temperature increases

176. When the system undergoes a spontaneous reaction, is it possible for entropy of a system to decrease?

A. No, because this violates the second law of thermodynamics
B. No, because this violates the first law of thermodynamics
C. Yes, but only if the reaction is endothermic
D. Yes, but only if the entropy gain of the environment is greater in magnitude than the magnitude of the entropy loss in the system
E. Yes, but only if the entropy gain of the environment is smaller in magnitude than the magnitude of the entropy loss in the system

177. From the given bond energies, how many kJ of energy are released or absorbed from the reaction of one mole of N_2 with three moles of H_2 to form two moles of NH_3?

$N\equiv N + H-H + H-H + H-H \rightarrow NH_3 + NH_3$

$H-N$ (389 kJ/mol); $H-H$ (436 kJ/mol); $N\equiv N$ (946 kJ/mol);

A. −80 kJ/mol released **C.** −946 kJ/mol released
B. +89.5 kJ/mol absorbed **D.** +895 kJ/mol absorbed **E.** +946 kJ/mol absorbed

178. The vapor pressure of $SnCl_4$ reaches 400 mmHg at 92 °C, the vapor pressure of SnI_4 reaches 400 mmHg at 315 °C, the vapor pressure of PBr_3 reaches 400 mmHg at 150 °C, and the vapor pressure of PCl_3 reaches 400 mmHg at 57 °C. At 175 °C, which substance would have the lowest vapor pressure?

A. PCl_3 **B.** $SnCl_4$ **C.** SnI_4 **D.** PBr_3 **E.** Hg

179. If a chemical reaction is spontaneous, which must be negative?

    A. C_p **B.** ΔS **C.** ΔG **D.** ΔH **E.** K_{eq}

180. Consider the reaction $2CO\ (g) + O_2\ (g) \rightarrow CO_2\ (g) + 135.2$ kcal. This reaction is [   ] because the sign of ΔH is [   ].

    A. endothermic; negative   **C.** endothermic; positive
    B. exothermic; negative   **D.** exothermic; positive
                                          E. exothermic; neither positive nor negative

181. When which quantity increases, does entropy increase?

    I. volume   II. moles   III. temperature

    A. II only   **C.** II and III only
    B. III only   **D.** I, II and III   **E.** I and III only

182. Decreasing the temperature of a liquid by 20 °C, at constant pressure, has what effect on the magnitude of its vapor pressure?

    A. no change   **C.** increase
    B. insufficient information given   **D.** inversely proportional   **E.** decrease

183. Which of the following conditions favors the formation of NO (g) in a closed container for the equilibrium: $N_2\ (g) + O_2\ (g) \leftrightarrow 2\ NO\ (g)$ $\Delta H = +181$ kJ/mol

    A. Increasing the temperature
    B. Decreasing the temperature
    C. Increasing the pressure
    D. Decreasing the pressure
    E. Decreasing the temperature and increasing the pressure

184. Which statement(s) is/are correct for the entropy?

    I. Higher for a sample of gas than for the same sample as liquid
    II. A measure of the *randomness* in a system
    III. Available energy for conversion into mechanical work

    A. I only   **B.** II only   **C.** III only   **D.** I and II only   **E.** I, II and III

185. Determine the equilibrium constant (K_c) at 25 °C for the reaction:

$$2NO\ (g) + O_2\ (g) \leftrightarrows 2NO_2\ (g)$$

$$(\Delta G°_{rxn} = -69.7 \text{ kJ/mol})$$

    A. 1.63×10^{12} **B.** 8.28×10^{-2} **C.** 2.60   **D.** 13.4   **E.** 6.07×10^{-13}

186. Which is NOT true for entropy in a closed system according to the equation $\Delta S = Q / T$?

    A. Entropy decreases as temperature decreases
    B. The equation is only valid for a reversible process
    C. Entropy changes due to heat transfer are greater at low temperatures
    D. Entropy of the system decreases as heat is transferred out of the system
    E. Entropy increases as temperature decreases

187. What role does entropy play in chemical reactions?

  A. The entropy change determines whether the reaction occurs spontaneously
  B. The entropy change determines whether the chemical reaction is favorable
  C. The entropy determines how much product is actually produced
  D. The entropy change determines whether the reaction is exothermic or endothermic
  E. The entropy determines how much reactant remains

188. The boiling point of a liquid is:

  A. the temperature where sublimation occurs
  B. the temperature where the vapor pressure of the liquid is less than the pressure over the liquid
  C. always 100 °C or greater
  D. the temperature where the rate of sublimation equals evaporation
  E. the temperature where the vapor pressure of the liquid equals the pressure over the liquid

189. What are the products for this double-replacement reaction $BaCl_2$ (*aq*) + K_2SO_4 (*aq*) → ?

  A. $BaSO_3$ and $KClO_4$ **C.** BaS and $KClO_4$
  B. $BaSO_4$ and KCl **D.** $BaSO_3$ and KCl **E.** $BaSO_4$ and $KClO_4$

190. Increased pressure results in:

  A. an increase in the forward reaction due to decreased volume
  B. an increase in the reverse reaction due to increased volume
  C. an increase in the forward reaction due to increased volume
  D. an increase in the reverse reaction due to decreased volume
  E. no effect since the reaction is at equilibrium

191. The process of H_2O (*g*) → H_2O (*l*) is nonspontaneous under pressure of 760 torr and temperatures of 378 K because:

  A. $\Delta H = T\Delta S$ **C.** $\Delta H > 0$
  B. $\Delta G < 0$ **D.** $\Delta H < T\Delta S$ **E.** $\Delta H > T\Delta S$

192. Using these bond energies, $\Delta H°$:

     C—C: 348 kJ   C=C: 612 kJ   C≡C: 960 kJ   C—H: 412 kJ
     C—O: 360 kJ   C=O: 743 kJ   H—H: 436 kJ   H—O: 463 kJ

Calculate the value of $\Delta H°$ of reaction for:

$$O=C=O \ (g) + 3 \ H_2 \ (g) \rightarrow CH_3—O—H \ (g) + H—O—H \ (g)$$

  A. –272 kJ   **B.** +272 kJ   **C.** –191 kJ   **D.** –5779 kJ   **E.** +5779 kJ

193. All of the statements regarding the symbol ΔG are true, EXCEPT it:

  A. identifies an endergonic reaction
  B. identifies an exothermic reaction
  C. predicts the spontaneity of a reaction
  D. refers to the free energy of the reaction
  E. describes the effect of both enthalpy and entropy on a reaction

194. A negative ΔG signifies a spontaneous reaction when which conditions are constant?

    I. pressure   II. temperature   III. volume

  A. I only   **B.** II only   **C.** I and II only   **D.** I, II and III   **E.** III only

195. What happens to the entropy of a system as the components of the system are introduced to a larger number of possible arrangements, such as when liquid water transforms into water vapor?

  A. Entropy of a system is solely dependent upon the amount of material undergoing reaction
  B. Entropy of a system is independent of introducing the components of the system to a larger number of possible arrangements
  C. Entropy increases because there are more ways for the energy to disperse
  D. Entropy decreases because there are less ways in which the energy can disperse
  E. Entropy increases because there are less ways for the energy to disperse

196. Which statement about the boiling point of water is NOT correct?

  A. At sea level and at a pressure of 760 mmHg, the boiling point is 100 °C
  B. In a pressure cooker, shorter cooking times are required due to the change in boiling point
  C. The boiling point is greater than 100 °C in a pressure cooker
  D. The boiling point is less than 100 °C for locations at low elevations
  E. The boiling point is greater than 100 °C for locations at low elevations

197. If a chemical reaction has a positive ΔH and a negative ΔS, the reaction tends to be:

  A. at equilibrium   **C.** spontaneous
  B. nonspontaneous   **D.** unable to be determined   **E.** irreversible

198. The species in the reaction $KClO_3\,(s) \rightarrow KCl\,(s) + 3/2\,O_2\,(g)$ have the values for standard enthalpies of formation at 25 °C:

$$KClO_3\,(s),\ \Delta H^\circ_f = -391.2\ \text{kJ mol}^{-1}$$

$$KCl\,(s),\ \Delta H^\circ_f = -436.8\ \text{kJ mol}^{-1}$$

Make the assumption that, since the physical states do not change, the values of ΔH° and ΔS° are constant throughout a broad temperature range, and use this information to determine which of the following conditions may apply:

  A. The reaction is nonspontaneous at low temperatures, but spontaneous at high temperatures
  B. The reaction is spontaneous at low temperatures, but nonspontaneous at high temperatures
  C. The reaction is nonspontaneous at all temperatures over a broad temperature range
  D. The reaction is spontaneous at all temperatures over a broad temperature range
  E. It is not possible to make conclusion about spontaneity because of insufficient information

199. Which statement is NOT true for spontaneous reactions?

  A. Reaction rate is determined by the value of ΔG
  B. If the enthalpy change is unfavorable, the reaction occurs at a high temperature
  C. $\Delta G < 0$
  D. A catalyst does not affect ΔG
  E. Reaction is exergonic

200. Which condition(s) must be constant for $\Delta G = \Delta H - T\Delta S$ to be valid?

          I. pressure   II. temperature   III. volume

  A. I only   **B.** II only   **C.** III only   **D.** I, II and III   **E.** I and II only

201. The reaction rate is:

  A. the ratio of the masses of products and reactants
  B. the ratio of the molecular masses of the elements in a given compound
  C. the speed at which reactants are consumed or product is formed
  D. the balanced chemical formula that relates the number of product molecules to reactant molecules
  E. none of the above

202. Which substance would be expected to have the highest boiling point?

  A. Nonvolatile liquid
  B. Nonpolar liquid with van der Waal interactions
  C. Polar liquid with hydrogen bonding
  D. Nonpolar liquid
  E. Nonpolar liquid with dipole–induced dipole interactions

203. What are the products for this double-replacement reaction $AgNO_3\,(aq) + Li_3PO_4\,(aq) \rightarrow$?

  A. Ag_3PO_4 and $LiNO_2$ **C.** Ag_3PO_3 and $LiNO_2$
  B. Ag_3PO_3 and $LiNO_3$ **D.** Ag_3P and $LiNO_3$
                                       E. Ag_3PO_4 and $LiNO_3$

204. The ΔG of a reaction is the maximum energy that the reaction releases to do:

  A. P–V work only   **C.** any type of work
  B. work and release heat   **D.** non P–V work only
                                       E. work and generate heat

205. If a chemical reaction has $\Delta H = X$, $\Delta S = Y$, $\Delta G = X - RY$ and occurs at R °K, the reaction is:

  A. spontaneous   **C.** nonspontaneous
  B. at equilibrium   **D.** irreversible   **E.** unable to be determined

206. Calculate the standard free energy change ($\Delta G°$) for $NO_2\,(g) + SO_2\,(g) \rightarrow NO\,(g) + SO_3\,(g)$ using the standard free energies of formation:

    $NO_2\,(g)$, $\Delta G_f^o = +51.84$ kJ mol^{-1} $SO_2\,(g)$, $\Delta G_f^o = -300.0$ kJ mol^{-1}

    $NO\,(g)$, $\Delta G_f^o = +86.69$ kJ mol^{-1} $SO_3\,(g)$, $\Delta G_f^o = -370.0$ kJ mol^{-1}

  A. –35.15 kJ   **B.** –104.9 kJ   **C.** –429.2 kJ   **D.** –619.6 kJ   **E.** –808.5 kJ

207. Consider the contribution of entropy to the spontaneity of the reaction

$$2Al_2O_3\,(s) \rightarrow 4Al\,(s) + 3O_2\,(g), \Delta G = +138 \text{ kcal}$$

As written, the reaction is [   ] and the entropy of the system [   ].

  A. non-spontaneous… decreases   **C.** spontaneous… decreases
  B. non-spontaneous… increases   **D.** spontaneous… increases
                                       E. non-spontaneous… does not change

208. Which statement(s) is/are true for ΔG?

    I. ΔG of the universe is conserved
    II. ΔG of a system is conserved
    III. ΔG of the universe decreases with each reaction

  A. I only   **B.** II only   **C.** III only   **D.** I and II only   **E.** I and III only

209. An Alka-Seltzer antacid tablet bubbles vigorously when placed in water, but only slowly when placed in an alcoholic beverage of the same temperature containing a 50:50 mix of alcohol and H_2O. Propose a probable explanation involving the relationship between the speed of a reaction and molecular collisions.

  A. In a 50:50 mix there are fewer H_2O molecules for the antacid molecules to collide with
  B. The tablet reacts chemically with H_2O, but not the alcohol
  C. Alcohol molecules are more massive than H_2O molecules, hence they move slower and their collisions are not as forceful
  D. The alcohol absorbs the carbon dioxide bubbles before they escape the liquid phase
  E. In a 50:50 mix there are more H_2O molecules for the antacid molecules to collide with

210. Calculate the value of $\Delta H°$ of reaction for:

$$H_2C{=}CH_2\,(g) + H_2\,(g) \rightarrow CH_3{-}CH_3\,(g)$$

The bond energies are:

    C—C: 348 kJ   C=C: 612 kJ   C≡C: 960 kJ
    C—H: 412 kJ   H—H: 436 kJ

  A. –388 kJ   **B.** +224 kJ   **C.** –560 kJ   **D.** –124 kJ   **E.** –212 kJ

211. Which decreases as the strength of the attractive intermolecular force increases?

  A. melting point
  B. vapor pressure of a liquid
  C. viscosity
  D. normal boiling temperature
  E. density

212. The bond dissociation energy is:

  A. useful in estimating the enthalpy change in a reaction
  B. the energy required to break a bond between two gaseous atoms
  C. the energy released when a bond between two gaseous atoms is broken
  D. A and B
  E. all of the above

213. A spontaneous reaction:

  A. is endothermic and releases heat
  B. cannot be endothermic
  C. occurs quickly
  D. occurs slowly
  E. can do work on the surroundings

214. A catalyst changes which of the following?

  A. ΔS **B.** ΔG **C.** ΔH **D.** $E_{activation}$ **E.** $\Sigma(\Delta H_{products})$

215. When NaCl dissolves in water, what is the force of attraction between Na^+ and H_2O?

    A. ion–dipole   **C.** ion–ion

    B. hydrogen bonding   **D.** dipole–dipole   **E.** van der Waals

216. Identify the decreased ordering of attractions among particles in the three states of matter.

    A. solid < gas < liquid   **C.** solid > liquid > gas

    B. gas < solid < liquid   **D.** solid < liquid < gas   **E.** solid > gas > liquid

217. Which is true for the thermodynamic functions G, H and S in $\Delta G = \Delta H - T\Delta S$?

    A. G refers to the universe, H to the surroundings and S to the system

    B. G refers to the system, H to the system and S to the system

    C. G refers to the surroundings, H to the surroundings and S to the system

    D. G refers to the system, H to the system and S to the surroundings

    E. G refers to the system, H to the surroundings and S to the system

218. Which statement is the best explanation for the fact that the reaction rates of many thermodynamically spontaneous reactions are actually very slow?

    A. ΔS is negative   **C.** $\Delta G°$ for the reaction is positive

    B. K_P for the reaction < 1   **D.** Such reactions are endothermic

                                 E. The activation energy of the reaction is large

219. A solid sample at room temperature spontaneously sublimes forming a gas. This change in state is accompanied by which of the changes in the sample?

    A. Entropy decreases and energy increases   **C.** Entropy and energy decrease

    B. Entropy increases and energy decreases   **D.** Entropy and energy increase

                                            E. Entropy and energy are equal

220. What is true of a reaction if an endothermic reaction causes a decrease in ΔS of the system?

    A. Only occurs at low temperatures when ΔS is insignificant

    B. Occurs if coupled to an endergonic reaction

    C. Never occurs because it decreases ΔS of the system

    D. Never occurs because ΔG is positive

    E. None of the above

221. What can be deduced about the activation energy of a reaction that takes billions of years to go to completion and reaction that takes only a fraction of a second.

    A. The slow reaction has high activation energy, while the fast reaction has low activation energy

    B. The slow reaction must have slow activation energy, while the fast reaction must have high activation energy

    C. The activation energy of both reactions is very low

    D. The activation energy of both reactions is very high

    E. The activation energy of both reactions is equal

222. Use the following bond dissociation energies to determine what the energy change is for:
$2O_2 + CH_4 \rightarrow CO_2 + 2H_2O$?

        C—C   350 kJ/mole
        C—H   410 kJ/mole
        O=O   495 kJ/mole
        O—H   460 kJ/mole
        C=O   720 kJ/mole

A. 880 kJ/mole   **C.** –650 kJ/mole

B. –700 kJ/mole   **D.** –1158 kJ/mole   **E.** None of the above

223. Given the data, calculate $\Delta G°$, for the reaction $H_2(g) + I_2(s) \rightarrow 2HI(g)$?

$$H_2(g), \Delta H_f^o = 0 \text{ kJ mol}^{-1}, S° = +130.6 \text{ J mol}^{-1}\text{K}^{-1}$$

$$I_2(s), \Delta H_f^o = 0 \text{ kJ mol}^{-1}, S° = +116.12 \text{ J mol}^{-1}\text{K}^{-1}$$

$$HI(g), \Delta H_f^o = +26 \text{ kJ mol}^{-1}, S° = +206 \text{ J mol}^{-1-1}\text{K}^{-1}$$

A. +128.2 kJ   **B.** +2.7 kJ   **C.** –46.5 kJ   **D.** +64.1 kJ   **E.** –165.3 kJ

224. Since the physical states do not change, assume the values of ΔH and ΔS do not change as temperature is increased in the reaction below. Using the following values at 25 °C, calculate a value for the free energy change, ΔG_T^0.

$$CaCO_3(s) \rightarrow CaO(s) + CO_2(g) \text{ at } 815 \text{ °C}$$

$$CaO(s), \Delta H_f^o = -635.5 \text{ kJ mol}^{-1}, S° = +40.0 \text{ J mol}^{-1}\text{K}^{-1}$$

$$CaCO_3(s), \Delta H_f^o = -1207 \text{ kJ mol}^{-1}, S° = +92.9 \text{ J mol}^{-1}\text{K}^{-1}$$

$$CO_2(g), \Delta H_f^o = -394 \text{ kJ mol}^{-1}, S° = +213.6 \text{ J mol}^{-1}\text{K}^{-1}$$

A. +2.6 kJ   **B.** +42.5 kJ   **C.** +147.1 kJ   **D.** +312.2 kJ   **E.** +5.94 kJ

Chapter 9.   ELECTROCHEMISTRY

1. What is the term for the electrode in an electrochemical cell where oxidation occurs?

- **A.** oxidation electrode
- **B.** reduction electrode
- **C.** anode
- **D.** cathode
- **E.** none of the above

2. Based on the following data, which of the following is a true statement?

$$Li^+ (aq) + e^- \qquad E° = -3.05 \text{ V}$$

$$Na^+ (aq) + e^- \qquad E° = -2.71 \text{ V}$$

- **A.** Li^+ is more easily oxidized than Na^+
- **B.** Li^+ is more easily reduced than Na^+
- **C.** Na^+ and Li^+ are both spontaneously reduced
- **D.** Na^+ is more easily oxidized than Li^+
- **E.** Na^+ and Li^+ are both spontaneously oxidized

3. If in a battery, the following two oxidation-reduction reactions occur, which reaction takes place at the cathode?

$$rxn \text{ A: } Zn \rightarrow Zn^{2+} + 2e^-$$

$$rxn \text{ B: } 2NH_4^+ + 2e^- \rightarrow 2NH_3 + H_2$$

- **A.** rxn A
- **B.** rxn B
- **C.** Both reactions occur at both the anode and cathode
- **D.** Both reactions occur at the electrode
- **E.** The reaction occurs at the electrode

4. Which is NOT true for the following redox reaction occurring in a spontaneous electrochemical cell?

$$Sn (s) + Cu^{2+} (aq) \rightarrow Cu (s) + Sn^{2+} (aq)$$

- **A.** Electrons flow from the Sn electrode to the Cu electrode
- **B.** Anions in the salt bridge flow from the Cu half-cell to the Sn half-cell
- **C.** Sn is oxidized at the anode
- **D.** Cu^{2+} is reduced at the anode
- **E.** Cu^{2+} is reduced at the cathode

5. How many Faradays are consumed to completely electrolyze 5 moles of H_2O_2 when in the reaction $H_2O_2 + 2H^+ + 2e^- \rightleftarrows 2H_2O$?

- **A.** 5.0
- **B.** 2.5
- **C.** 7.5
- **D.** 12.5
- **E.** 10.0

6. How much charge is required to liberate 10 moles of H_2O when hydrogen peroxide is electrolyzed in the reaction $H_2O_2 + 2H^+ + 2e^- \rightleftarrows 2H_2O$?

- **A.** 96,500 coulombs
- **B.** 9,650 coulombs
- **C.** 48,250 coulombs
- **D.** 965,000 coulombs
- **E.** 4,825 coulombs

7. How long must a current of 2 amps run to liberate 2 moles of H_2O when is electrolyzed in the reaction $H_2O_2 + 2H^+ + 2e^- \rightleftarrows 2H_2O$?

- **A.** 4.83×10^4 sec
- **B.** 4.83×10^5 sec
- **C.** 9.65×10^4 sec
- **D.** 2.41×10^5 sec
- **E.** 9.65×10^3 sec

8. In an acidic media, how many electrons are needed to balance the half-reaction for

$$NO_3^- \rightarrow NH_4^+.$$

A. 8 e⁻ on the left side

B. 4 e⁻ on the left side

C. 3 e⁻ on the right side

D. 2 e⁻ on the left side

E. 8 e⁻ on the right side

9. What happens at the anode when rust forms if Fe is in contact with H_2O?

$$4Fe + 3O_2 \rightarrow 2Fe_2O_3$$

A. Fe is reduced

B. Oxygen is reduced

C. Oxygen is oxidized

D. Fe is oxidized

E. None of the above

10. Which is NOT true for the following redox reaction occurring in a nonspontaneous electrochemical cell?

$$Cd\,(s) + Zn(NO_3)_2\,(aq) \xrightarrow{\text{Electricity}} Zn\,(s) + Cd(NO_3)_2\,(aq)$$

A. Cd^{2+} is produced at the anode

B. Zn metal is produced at the anode

C. Oxidation half-reaction: $Cd \rightarrow Cd^{2+} + 2e^-$

D. Reduction half-reaction: $Zn^{2+} + 2e^- \rightarrow Zn$

E. Zn metal is produced at the cathode

11. Which of the following species is the oxidizing agent in the following redox reaction?

$$Zn + Cu^{2+} \rightarrow Zn^{2+} + Cu$$

A. Cu^{2+} **B.** Cu   **C.** Zn^{2+} **D.** Zn   **E.** both

12. Why is the anode of a battery indicated with a negative (–) sign?

A. Electrons move to the anode to react with NH_4Cl in the battery

B. It indicates the electrode where the chemicals are reduced

C. Electrons are attracted to the negative electrode

D. The cathode is the source of negatively charged electrons

E. The electrode is the source of negatively charged electrons

13. What is the term for a substance that causes the reduction of another substance in a redox reaction?

A. oxidizing agent

B. reducing agent

C. anode

D. cathode

E. none of the above

14. In galvanic cells, reduction occurs at the:

A. salt bridge

B. cathode

C. anode

D. both cathode and anode

E. both salt bridge and anode

15. How many grams of chromium would be electroplated by passing a constant current of 5.2 amps through a solution containing chromium (III) sulfate for 45.0 minutes? (Cr: 52.00 g/mol)

A. 2.3×10^{10} g

B. 24 g

C. 0.042 g

D. 9.3×10^{-4} g

E. 2.5 g

16. Which of the following species is the oxidizing agent?

$$2CuBr \rightarrow 2Cu + Br_2$$

A. Cu^+ **B.** Br^- **C.** Cu   **D.** CuBr   **E.** Br_2

17. What is the term for a process characterized by the gain of electrons?

A. reduction   **B.** redox   **C.** oxidation   **D.** electrochemistry   **E.** reduction agent

18. In an electrolytic cell containing molten $MgCl_2$ (*l*):

A. Mg^{2+} is oxidized at the cathode and Cl^- is reduced at the anode
B. Mg^{2+} is reduced at the anode and Cl^- is oxidized at the cathode
C. Mg^{2+} is oxidized at the anode and Cl^- is reduced at the cathode
D. Mg^{2+} is reduced at the cathode and Cl^- is oxidized at the anode
E. Mg^{2+} and Cl^- are reduced at the cathode

19. What is the relationship between an element's ionization energy and its ability to function as an oxidizing agent?

A. As ionization energy increases, the ability of an element to function as an oxidizing agent remains the same

B. As ionization energy increases, the ability of an element to function as an oxidizing agent decreases

C. As ionization energy increases, the ability of an element to function as an oxidizing agent increases

D. As ionization energy increases, the ability of an element to function as a reducing agent remains the same

E. As ionization energy increases, the ability of an element to function as a reducing agent increases

20. Which is true regarding the following redox reaction occurring in a spontaneous electrochemical cell?

$$Sn \ (s) + Cu^{2+} \ (aq) \rightarrow Cu \ (s) + Sn^{2+} \ (aq)$$

A. Anions in the salt bridge flow from the Cu half-cell to the Sn half-cell
B. Electrons flow from the Cu electrode to the Sn electrode
C. Cu^{2+} is oxidized at the cathode
D. Sn is reduced at the anode
E. None of the above

21. In electrolysis, E° tends to be:

A. zero   **B.** neutral   **C.** positive   **D.** greater than 1   **E.** negative

22. In basic media, how many electrons are needed to balance the half-reaction:

$$C_8H_{10} \rightarrow C_8H_4O_4{}^{2-}?$$

A. 8 electrons to the left side   **C.** 4 electrons to the left side
B. 12 electrons to the left side   **D.** 12 electrons to the right side
                                           E. 8 electrons to the right side

23. How are photovoltaic cells different from many other forms of solar energy?

  A. Light is reflected and the coolness of the shade is used to provide a temperature differential
  B. Light is passively converted into heat
  C. Light is converted into heat and then into steam
  D. Light is converted into heat and then into electricity
  E. Light is converted directly to electricity

24. What is the term for an electrochemical cell in which the anode and cathode reactions do not take place in aqueous solutions?

  A. voltaic cell
  B. electrolytic cell

  C. dry cell
  D. battery

  E. galvanic cell

25. The following two half-reactions occur in a voltaic cell:

  Reaction I: $Cr_2O_7^{2-}(aq) + 14H^+(aq) + 6e^- \rightarrow 2Cr^{3+}(aq) + 7H_2O\ (l)$

  Reaction II: $6I^-(aq) \rightarrow 3I_2(s) + 6e^-$

  Which one of the following statements is true?

  A. Reaction II is oxidation and occurs at the cathode
  B. Reaction II is oxidation and occurs at the anode
  C. Reaction I is reduction and occurs at the anode
  D. Reaction I is oxidation and occurs at the anode
  E. Reaction I is reduction and occurs at both the anode and cathode

26. Which of the following is most likely to undergo reduction?

  A. Cl_2 **B.** Cl^- **C.** Na   **D.** Na^+ **E.** both Cl^- and Na^+

27. What is the general term for an apparatus that contains two solutions with electrodes in separate compartments that are connected by a wire and salt bridge?

  A. electrolytic cell
  B. voltaic cell

  C. battery
  D. electrochemical cell

  E. dry cell

28. A galvanic cell is constructed with the following two elements and their ions. What is the E° for the net reaction of the oxidation of Mg (s) and the reduction of Pb (s)?

$$Mg\ (s) \rightarrow Mg^{2+} + 2e^- \qquad E° = 2.37\ V$$
$$Pb\ (s) \rightarrow Pb^{2+} + 2e^- \qquad E° = 0.126\ V$$

  A. −2.496 V   **B.** 2.496 V   **C.** −2.244 V   **D.** 740 V   **E.** 2.244 V

29. Which is capable of oxidizing Cu (s) to $Cu^{2+}(aq)$ when added to Cu (s) in solution?

  A. $Al^{3+}(aq)$ **B.** $Ag^+(aq)$ **C.** Ni (s)   **D.** $I^-(aq)$ **E.** $Au^{3+}(aq)$

30. Electrolysis is an example of a(n):

  A. acid-base reaction
  B. exothermic reaction

  C. physical change
  D. chemical change

  E. state function

31. Which is NOT true regarding the following redox reaction occurring in a nonspontaneous electrochemical cell?

$$3C + 2Co_2O_3 \xrightarrow{\text{Electricity}} 4Co + 3CO_2$$

- **A.** CO_2 (g) is produced at the anode
- **B.** Co metal is produced at the anode
- **C.** Oxidation half-reaction: $C + 2O^{2-} \rightarrow CO_2 + 4e^-$
- **D.** Reduction half-reaction: $Co^{3+} + 3e^- \rightarrow Co$
- **E.** Co metal is produced at the cathode

32. What happens to an element when it is oxidized?

- **A.** Loses electrons and its oxidation state decreases
- **B.** Gains electrons and its oxidation remains the same
- **C.** Gains electrons and its oxidation decreases
- **D.** Gains electrons and its oxidation state increases
- **E.** Loses electrons and its oxidation state increases

33. For a battery, what is undergoing reduction for the following oxidation-reduction reaction?

$$Mn_2O_3 + ZnO \rightarrow 2MnO_2 + Zn$$

- **A.** Mn_2O_3 **B.** MnO_2 **C.** ZnO **D.** Zn **E.** Mn_2O_3 and Zn

34. What is the term for the electrode in an electrochemical cell at which reduction occurs?

- **A.** oxidation electrode
- **B.** reduction electrode
- **C.** anode
- **D.** cathode
- **E.** anode and cathode

35. The anode in a galvanic cell attracts:

- **A.** cations
- **B.** neutral particles
- **C.** anions
- **D.** both anions and neutral particles
- **E.** both cations and neutral particles

36. How many e^- are needed to balance the half reaction $Cl_2O_7 \rightarrow HClO$ in an acidic solution?

- **A.** 12 e^- to the left side
- **B.** 6 e^- to the right side
- **C.** 2 e^- to the left side
- **D.** 3 e^- to the right side
- **E.** 8 e^- to the left side

37. How many e^- are gained or lost in the following half-reaction: $2Na \rightarrow 2Na^+$?

- **A.** ½ e^- is lost
- **B.** 2 e^- are gained
- **C.** 2 e^- are lost
- **D.** ½ e^- is gained
- **E.** 4 e^- are gained

38. Given the reaction for recharging a NiCad battery, what substance is being reduced?

$$Cd(OH)_2 (s) + Ni(OH)_2 (s) \rightarrow Cd (s) + NiO_2 (s) + 2H_2O (l)$$

- **A.** $Ni(OH)_2$ **B.** H_2O **C.** NiO_2 **D.** Cd **E.** $Cd(OH)_2$

39. In an electrolytic cell, the electrochemical reaction is:

    A. nonspontaneous with oxidation at the cathode
    B. nonspontaneous with the oxidation at the anode
    C. spontaneous with oxidation at the cathode
    D. spontaneous with oxidation at the anode
    E. spontaneous with oxidation at both the anode and cathode

40. Which of the following statements about electrochemistry is NOT true?

    A. The study of how protons are transferred from one chemical compound to another
    B. The use of electrical current to produce an oxidation-reduction reaction
    C. The use of a set of oxidation-reduction reactions to produce electrical current
    D. The study of how electrical energy and chemical reactions are related
    E. The study of how electrons are transferred from one chemical compound to another

41. What is the term for an electrochemical cell in which a nonspontaneous redox reaction occurs by forcing electricity through the cell?

    A. wet cell
    B. voltaic cell
    C. electrolytic cell
    D. dry cell
    E. none of the above

42. What is E° for the electrochemical cell of $CuSO_4$ and LiCl?

$$Cu^{2+} + 2e^- \rightarrow Cu\ (s) \qquad E° = 0.337$$
$$Li^+ + e^- \rightarrow Li\ (s) \qquad E° = -3.03$$

    The net reaction is: $Cu\ (s) + Li^+ \rightarrow Cu^{2+} + Li\ (s)$

    A. 3.367 V
    B. −3.367 V
    C. 2.693 V
    D. −2.693 V
    E. −6.397 V

43. The reaction for the data given for the electrochemical cell consisting of $CuSO_4$ and LiCl?

$$Cu^{2+} + 2e^- \rightarrow Cu\ (s) \qquad E° = 0.337$$
$$Li^+ + e^- \rightarrow Li\ (s) \qquad E° = -3.03$$

    The net reaction is: $Cu\ (s) + Li^+ \rightarrow Cu^{2+} + Li\ (s)$

    A. Proceeds spontaneously as written
    B. Is at equilibrium
    C. Proceeds in the opposite direction
    D. Moves in both directions
    E. None of the above

44. The electrode with the standard reduction potential of 0 V is assigned, as the standard reference electrode and uses the half-reaction:

    A. $2NH_4^+\ (aq) + 2e^- \leftrightarrows H_2\ (g) + 2NH_3\ (g)$
    B. $Ag^+\ (aq) + e^- \leftrightarrows Ag\ (s)$
    C. $Cu^{2+}\ (aq) + 2e^- \leftrightarrows Cu\ (s)$
    D. $Zn^{2+}\ (aq) + 2e^- \leftrightarrows Zn\ (s)$
    E. $2H^+\ (aq) + 2e^- \leftrightarrows H_2\ (g)$

45. How many e^- are gained or lost in the following half-reaction: $Na \rightarrow Na^+$?

    A. 1 e^- is gained
    B. ½ e^- is lost
    C. ½ e^- is gained
    D. 1 e^- is lost
    E. 2 e^- are gained

46. Which is true regarding the redox reaction occurring in a spontaneous electrochemical cell?

$$Sn\ (s) + Cu^{2+}\ (aq) \rightarrow Cu\ (s) + Sn^{2+}\ (aq)$$

A. Electrons flow from the Sn electrode to the Cu electrode

B. Anions in the salt bridge flow from the Sn half-cell to the Cu half-cell

C. Sn is oxidized at the cathode

D. Cu^{2+} is reduced at the anode

E. None of the above

47. Which substance is NOT an electrolyte?

A. NaOH   **B.** NH_4NO_3 **C.** HBr   **D.** KCl   **E.** CH_4

48. Which of the materials is most likely to act as an oxidizing agent?

A. Cl^- **B.** Cl_2 **C.** Na^+ **D.** Na   **E.** both Cl^- and Na

49. Which is NOT true regarding the redox reaction occurring in a spontaneous electrochemical cell
$Cl_2\ (g) + 2Br^-\ (aq) \rightarrow Br_2\ (l) + 2Cl^-\ (aq)$

  A. Cations in the salt bridge flow from the Br_2 half-cell to the Cl_2 half-cell

B. Electrons flow from the anode to the cathode   **D.** Br^- is oxidized at the cathode

C. Cl_2 is reduced at the cathode   **E.** Br^- is oxidized at the anode

50. In electrolytic cells, oxidation occurs at:

A. the anode   **C.** both the anode and cathode

B. the cathode   **D.** neither the anode or cathode   **E.** depends on the voltage

51. Which statement is correct about reduction if a galvanic cell has two electrodes?

A. Reduction occurs at the uncharged dynode

B. Reduction occurs at the negatively charged cathode

C. Reduction occurs at the positively charged anode

D. Reduction occurs at the negatively charged anode

E. Reduction occurs at the positively charged cathode

52. How many e^- are gained or lost in the following half-reaction: $Cl_2 \rightarrow 2Cl^-$?

A. 2 e^- are gained   **C.** ½ e^- is gained

B. ½ e^- is lost   **D.** 2 e^- are lost   **E.** 4 e^- are gained

53. Which of the statements listed below is true regarding the following redox reaction
occurring in a nonspontaneous electrochemical cell?

$$\overset{Electricity}{3C\ (s) + 4AlCl_3\ (l)\ \ \longrightarrow\ \ 4Al\ (l) + 3CCl_4\ (g)}$$

A. Cl^- is produced at the anode

B. Al metal is produced at the cathode

C. Oxidation half-reaction is $Al^{3+} + 3e^- \rightarrow Al$

D. Reduction half-reaction is $C + 4Cl^- \rightarrow CCl_4 + 4e^-$

E. None of the above

54. Which is the strongest reducing agent for the following half-reaction potentials?

$Sn^{4+}(aq) + 2e^- \rightarrow Sn^{2+}(aq)$ $E° = -0.14$ V

$Ag^+(aq) + e^- \rightarrow Ag(s)$ $E° = +0.80$ V

$Cr^{3+}(aq) + 3e^- \rightarrow Cr(s)$ $E° = -0.74$ V

$Fe^{2+}(aq) + 2e^- \rightarrow Fe(s)$ $E° = -0.44$ V

A. Cr (*s*)   **B.** $Fe^{2+}(aq)$ **C.** $Sn^{2+}(aq)$ **D.** Ag (*s*)   **E.** $Sn^{2+}(aq)$ and Ag (*s*)

55. Which of the following species undergoes oxidation in $2CuBr \rightarrow 2Cu + Br_2$?

A. Cu^+ **B.** Br^- **C.** Cu   **D.** CuBr   **E.** Br_2

56. What is the term for a substance that causes oxidation in a redox reaction?

A. oxidized   **C.** anode

B. reducing agent   **D.** cathode   **E.** oxidizing agent

57. If $\Delta G°$ for a cell is positive, the $E°$ is:

A. neutral   **C.** positive

B. negative   **D.** unable to be determined   **E.** greater than 1

58. A galvanic cell consists of a Cu (*s*) | $Cu^{2+}(aq)$ half-cell and a Zn (*s*) | $Zn^{2+}(aq)$ half-cell connected by a salt bridge. Oxidation occurs in the zinc half-cell. The cell can be represented in standard notation as:

A. Cu (*s*) | $Cu^{2+}(aq)$ | Zn (*s*) | $Zn^{2+}(aq)$ **C.** Zn (*s*) | $Zn^{2+}(aq)$ || Cu (*s*) | $Cu^{2+}(aq)$

B. $Cu^{2+}(aq)$ | Cu (*s*) || Zn (*s*) | $Zn^{2+}(aq)$ **D.** Zn (*s*) | $Zn^{2+}(aq)$ || $Cu^{2+}(aq)$ | Cu (*s*)

     E. $Zn^{2+}(aq)$ | Zn (*s*) || Cu (*s*) | $Cu^{2+}(aq)$

59. What is undergoing reduction for a battery if the following two oxidation-reduction reactions take place?

Reaction I: $Zn + 2OH^- \rightarrow ZnO + H_2O + 2e^-$

Reaction II: $2MnO_2 + H_2O + 2e^- \rightarrow Mn_2O_3 + 2OH^-$

A. OH^- **B.** H_2O **C.** Zn   **D.** ZnO   **E.** MnO_2

60. What is the term for a porous device that allows ions to travel between two half-cells to maintain an ionic charge balance in each compartment?

A. salt bridge   **C.** oxidation half-cell

B. reduction half-cell   **D.** electrochemical cell   **E.** none of the above

61. Using the following half-reaction potentials, determine the cell potential and whether the following reaction as written is spontaneous under standard conditions.

$$F_2(g) + 2Br^-(aq) \rightarrow Br_2(l) + 2F^-(aq)$$

$Br_2(l) + 2e^- \rightarrow 2Br^-(aq)$ $E° = 1.07$ V

$F_2(g) + 2e^- \rightarrow 2F^-(aq)$ $E° = 2.87$ V

A. $E° = 1.80$ V and nonspontaneous   **C.** $E° = 3.94$ V and spontaneous

B. $E° = 1.80$ V and spontaneous   **D.** $E° = -1.80$ V and nonspontaneous

     E. $E° = -1.80$ V and spontaneous

62. What is the relationship between an element's ionization energy and its ability to function as an oxidizing and reducing agent?

  A. Elements with high ionization energy behave as strong oxidizing and weak reducing agents

  B. Elements with high ionization energy behave as weak oxidizing and weak reducing agents

  C. Elements with high ionization energy behave as strong oxidizing and strong reducing agents

  D. Elements with high ionization energy behave as weak oxidizing and strong reducing agents

  E. Elements with high ionization energy behave as weak oxidizing and neutral reducing agents

63. Which is true regarding the redox reaction occurring in the spontaneous electrochemical cell for $Cl_2 (g) + 2Br^- (aq) \rightarrow Br_2 (l) + 2Cl^- (aq)$?

  A. Electrons flow from the cathode to the anode

  B. Cl_2 is oxidized at the cathode

  C. Br^- is reduced at the anode

  D. Cations in the salt bridge flow from the Br_2 half-cell to the Cl_2 half-cell

  E. Br^- is reduced at the anode and Cl_2 is oxidized at the cathode

64. In which type of cell does the following reaction occur when electrons are forced into a system by applying an external voltage?

$$Fe^{2+} + 2e^- \rightarrow Fe (s) \qquad E° = -0.44 \text{ V}$$

  A. concentration cell   **C.** electrochemical cell

  B. battery   **D.** galvanic cell   **E.** electrolytic cell

65. If a galvanic cell has two electrodes, which statement is correct?

  A. Oxidation occurs at the negatively charged cathode

  B. Oxidation occurs at the positively charged cathode

  C. Oxidation occurs at the negatively charged anode

  D. Oxidation occurs at the positively charged anode

  E. Oxidation occurs at the uncharged dynode

66. The purpose of the salt bridge in a voltaic cell is to:

  A. allow for a balance of charge between the two chambers

  B. allow the Fe^{2+} and the Cu^{2+} to flow freely between the two chambers

  C. allow for the buildup of positively charged ions in one container and negatively charged ions in the other container

  D. prevent any further migration of electrons through the wire

  E. allow for a separation of charge between the two chambers

67. Which of the statements is NOT true regarding the following redox reaction occurring in a nonspontaneous electrochemical cell?

$$3C (s) + 4AlCl_3 (l) \xrightarrow{\text{Electricity}} 4Al (l) + 3CCl_4 (g)$$

  A. Al metal is produced at the cathode   **D.** $CCl_4 (g)$ is produced at the cathode

  B. oxidation half-reaction: $C + 4Cl^- \rightarrow CCl_4 + 4e^-$ **E.** $CCl_4 (g)$ is produced at the anode

  C. reduction half-reaction: $Al^{3+} + 3 e^- \rightarrow Al$

68. Which is a strong electrolyte in an aqueous solution?

   A. CCl_4 **B.** NH_3 **C.** KNO_3 **D.** CH_3OH **E.** CH_2Cl_2

69. For a battery, what is undergoing oxidation in the oxidation-reduction reaction?

$$Mn_2O_3 + ZnO \rightarrow 2MnO_2 + Zn$$

   A. MnO_2 **B.** ZnO **C.** Zn **D.** Mn_2O_3 **E.** Zn and MnO_2

70. What is the term for a chemical reaction that involves electron transfer between two reacting substances?

   A. reduction reaction   **C.** oxidation reaction

   B. electrochemical reaction   **D.** half-reaction

                                              E. redox reaction

71. If 8 amps run for 2 minutes at the cathode where reaction, $Ag^+ + e^- \rightarrow Ag\ (s)$, how many grams of $Ag\ (s)$ plate at the cathode? ($Ag = 108$ g/mole)

   A. 10.8 g   **C.** 1.07 g

   B. 1.20 g   **D.** 1.12 g   **E.** 1.50 g

72. How many coulombs are required to electroplate 35.0 grams of chromium by passing an electrical current through a solution containing aqueous $CrCl_3$?

       ($Cr = 52.00$ g/mol, $Cl = 35.453$ g/mol)

   A. 1.60×10^3 coulomb   **C.** 6.50×10^4 coulomb

   B. 6.40×10^4 coulomb   **D.** 1.95×10^5 coulomb

                                                 E. 1.01×10^7 coulomb

73. In an operating photovoltaic cell, electrons move through the external circuit to the negatively charged p-type silicon wafer. How can the electrons move to the negatively charged silicon wafer if electrons are negatively charged?

   A. The p-type silicon wafer is positively charged

   B. The energy of the sunlight moves electrons in the nonspontaneous direction

   C. Advancements in photovoltaic technology has solved this technological impediment

   D. An electric current occurs because the energy from the sun reverses the charge of the electrons

   E. The p-type silicon wafer is negatively charged

74. Which of the statements is NOT true regarding the redox reaction occurring in a spontaneous electrochemical cell $Zn\ (s) + Cd^{2+}\ (aq) \rightarrow Cd\ (s) + Zn^{2+}\ (aq)$?

   A. Anions in the salt bridge flow from the Zn half-cell to the Cd half-cell

   B. Electrons flow from the Zn electrode to the Cd electrode

   C. Cd^{2+} is reduced at the cathode

   D. Zn is oxidized at the anode

   E. Anions in the salt bridge flow from the Cd half-cell to the Zn half-cell

75. The half-reaction at the anode during electrolysis of aqueous potassium bromide solution is:

A. $2H^+(aq) + e^- \rightarrow H_2(g)$

B. $2H_2O \rightarrow O_2(g) + 4H^+(aq) + 4e^-$

C. $2Br^-(aq) \rightarrow Br_2(l) + 2e^-$

D. $Br_2(g) + 2e^- \rightarrow 2Br^-(aq)$

E. $Na^+(aq) + e^- \rightarrow Na(s)$

76. Which of the following statements about oxidation and reduction reactions is true?

A. Only neutral atoms are formed in oxidation and reduction reactions

B. A half-reaction is only used for reduction reactions

C. More than one electron can be transferred in an oxidation and reduction reaction

D. In a half-reaction, only half of an electron is transferred

E. None of the above

77. What is the term for the providing of electricity to a nonspontaneous redox process to cause a reaction?

A. hydrolysis

B. protolysis

C. electrochemistry

D. electrolysis

E. none of the above

78. If 1 amp of current passes a cathode for 10 minutes, how much Zn (s) forms in the following reaction $Zn^{2+} + 2e^- \rightarrow Zn(s)$?   Zn = 65 g/mole

A. 0.10 g

B. 10.0 g

C. 0.65 g

D. 2.20 g

E. 0.20 g

79. Which is true for the redox reaction occurring in a spontaneous electrochemical cell?

$$Zn(s) + Cd^{2+}(aq) \rightarrow Cd(s) + Zn^{2+}(aq)$$

A. Electrons flow from the Cd electrode to the Zn electrode

B. Anions in the salt bridge flow from the Cd half-cell to the Zn half-cell

C. Zn is reduced at the anode

D. Cd^{2+} is oxidized at the cathode

E. None of the above

80. How many electrons are needed to balance the charge for the half-reaction in acidic media?

$$C_2H_6O \rightarrow HC_2H_3O_2$$

A. 6 electrons to the right side

B. 4 electrons to the right side

C. 3 electrons to the left side

D. 2 electrons to the left side

E. 8 electrons to the right side

81 Which of the half-reactions would be complementary and balance the half-reaction:

$$Zn^{2+} \rightarrow Zn?$$

A. $2K^+ \rightarrow 2K$

B. $2Cu \rightarrow 2Cu^{2+}$

C. $K^+ \rightarrow K$

D. $Cu \rightarrow Cu^{2+}$

E. $Cl_2 \rightarrow 2Cl^-$

82. Which statement is true regarding the following redox reaction occurring in a nonspontaneous electrochemical cell?

$$\text{Electricity}$$
$$3C\,(s) + 2Co_2O_3\,(l) \quad \rightarrow \quad 4Co\,(l) + 3CO_2\,(g)$$

A. CO_2 gas is produced at the anode

B. Co^{3+} is produced at the cathode

C. Oxidation half-reaction: $Co^{3+} + 3e^- \rightarrow Co$

D. Reduction half-reaction: $C + 2O^{2-} \rightarrow CO_2 + e^-$

E. None of the above

83. The half-reaction that occurs at the cathode during electrolysis of aqueous $CuCl_2$ solution is:

A. $2H_2O + 2e^- \rightarrow H_2\,(g) + 2OH^-\,(aq)$ **C.** $Cl_2\,(g) + 2e^- \rightarrow 2Cl^-\,(aq)$

B. $Cu^+\,(aq) + e^- \rightarrow Cu\,(s)$ **D.** $2Cl^-\,(aq) \rightarrow Cl_2\,(g) + 2e^-$

                                                         E. $Cu^{2+}\,(aq) + 2e^- \rightarrow Cu\,(s)$

84. Which of the following species is the reducing agent in $2CuBr \rightarrow 2Cu + Br_2$?

A. Br^- **B.** Cu^+ **C.** CuBr   **D.** Cu   **E.** Br_2

85. What is the term for the conversion of chemical energy to electrical energy from redox reactions?

A. redox chemistry   **C.** cell chemistry

B. electrochemistry   **D.** battery chemistry   **E.** none of the above

86. Using the following metal ion/metal reaction potentials:

$$Cu^{2+}\,(aq)|Cu\,(s) \quad Ag^+\,(aq)|Ag\,(s) \quad Co^{2+}\,(aq)|Co\,(s) \quad Zn^{2+}\,(aq)|Zn\,(s)$$
$$+0.34\text{ V} \qquad\quad +0.80\text{ V} \qquad\quad -0.28\text{ V} \quad -0.76\text{ V}$$

Calculate the standard cell potential for the cell whose reaction is:

$$Co\,(s) + Cu^{2+}\,(aq) \rightarrow Co^{2+}\,(aq) + Cu\,(s)$$

A. +0.62 volt   **C.** +0.48 volt

B. –0.62 volt   **D.** –0.48 volt   **E.** +0.68 volt

87. The following set of redox reactions takes place as shown:

           Vessel I   Vessel II

      $Fe \rightarrow Fe^{2+} + 2e^-$ $Cu^{2+} + 2e^- \rightarrow Cu$

If you had two vessels filled with the ion solution described above with a wire connecting a piece of iron (in vessel I) and a piece of copper (in vessel II) and a salt-bridge connecting the two vessels, which way do the electrons flow?

A. From vessel II to vessel I

B. The electrons flow back and forth between the two vessels

C. There is no continuous flow of electrons between the two vessels

D. The electrons only move within their original vessel

E. From vessel I to vessel II

88. What is the term for a process characterized by the loss of electrons?

A. redox
C. electrochemistry

B. reduction
D. oxidation
E. none of the above

89. A galvanic cell consists of an Ag (s)|Ag$^+$ (aq) half-cell and a Zn (s)|Zn^{2+} (aq) half-cell connected by a salt bridge. If oxidation occurs in the zinc half-cell, the cell can be represented in standard notation as:

A. Ag$^+$ (aq)|Ag (s)||Zn (s)|Zn^{2+} (aq)
C. Zn (s)|Zn^{2+} (aq)||Ag$^+$ (aq)|Ag (s)

B. Zn^{2+} (aq)|Zn (s)||Ag (s)|Ag$^+$ (aq)
D. Zn (s)|Zn^{2+} (aq)||Ag (s)|Ag$^+$ (aq)

E. Ag (s)|Ag$^+$ (aq)|Zn (s)|Zn^{2+} (aq)

90. A battery operates by:

A. oxidation
C. both oxidation and reduction

B. reduction
D. neither oxidation nor reduction
E. none of the above

91. Which of the statements is true regarding the following redox reaction occurring in a spontaneous electrochemical cell?

$$Cl_2 (g) + 2 Br^- (aq) \rightarrow Br_2 (l) + 2 Cl^- (aq)$$

A. Cations in the salt bridge flow from the Cl$_2$ half-cell to the Br$_2$ half-cell

B. Electrons flow from the anode to the cathode

C. Cl$_2$ is reduced at the anode

D. Br$^-$ is oxidized at the cathode

E. None of the above

92. How many electrons are needed to balance the half reaction H$_2$S $\rightarrow$ S$_8$, in acidic media?

A. 14 electrons to the left side
C. 12 electrons to the left side

B. 6 electrons to the right side
D. 8 electrons to the right side

E. 16 electrons to the right side

93. In the oxidation–reduction reaction Mg (s) + Cu^{2+} (aq) $\rightarrow$ Mg^{2+} (aq) + Cu (s), which atom/ion is reduced and which atom/ion is oxidized?

A. The Cu^{2+} ion is reduced (gains electrons) to form Cu metal, while Mg metal is oxidized (loses electrons) to form Mg^{2+}

B. Since Mg goes from a solid to an aqueous solution and Cu goes from an aqueous solution to a solid, no oxidation–reduction reaction occurs

C. The Cu^{2+} ion is oxidized (gains electrons) from Cu metal, while Mg metal is reduced (loses electrons) to form Mg^{2+}

D. The Mg^{2+} ion is reduced (gains electrons) from Cu metal, while Cu^{2+} is oxidized (loses electrons) to the Mg^{2+}

E. None of the above

94. Which of the statements is true regarding the following redox reaction occurring in a nonspontaneous electrochemical cell?

Electricity

$$3C\ (s) + 4AlCl_3\ (l)\ \rightarrow\ 4Al\ (l) + 3CCl_4\ (g)$$

A. Al^{3+} is produced at the cathode

B. CCl_4 gas is produced at the anode

C. Reduction half-reaction: $C + 4Cl^- \rightarrow CCl_4 + 4e^-$

D. Oxidation half-reaction: $Al^{3+} + 3e^- \rightarrow Al$

E. None of the above

95. For the electrochemical cell Ni (s) | Ni^{2+}(1 M) ‖ H^+(1 M) | H_2(1 atm) | Pt (s), which of the following changes causes a *decrease* in the cell voltage?

A. Decreasing the concentration of Ni^{2+} ion

B. Lowering the pH of the cell electrolyte

C. Decreasing the mass of the nickel electrode

D. Increasing the pressure of H_2 to 2.0 atm

E. None of the above

96. Which relationship explains an element's electronegativity and its ability to act as an oxidizing and reducing agent?

A. Atoms with great electronegativity tend to act as strong oxidizing and strong reducing agents

B. Atoms with great electronegativity tend to act as weak oxidizing and strong reducing agents

C. Atoms with great electronegativity tend to act as strong oxidizing and weak reducing agents

D. Atoms with great electronegativity tend to act as weak oxidizing and weak reducing agents

E. None of the above

97. What is the term for a reaction that represents separate oxidation or reduction processes?

A. reduction reaction

B. redox reaction

C. oxidation reaction

D. half-reaction

E. none of the above

98. In a battery, the following two oxidation-reduction reactions occur:

Reaction I: $Zn \rightarrow Zn^{2+} + 2e^-$

Reaction II: $2NH_4^+ + 2e^- \rightarrow 2NH_3 + H_2$

Which reaction is taking place at the anode?

A. Reaction I

B. Reaction II

C. Both reactions occur at the anode and cathode

D. Both reactions occur at the electrode

E. The reactions occur at the electrode, but not the anode

99. Nickel-cadmium batteries are used in rechargeable electronic calculators. In the reaction for recharging a NiCad battery, what substance is being oxidized?

$$Cd(OH)_2\ (s) + Ni(OH)_2\ (s) \rightarrow Cd\ (s) + NiO_2\ (s) + 2H_2O\ (l)$$

A. H_2O **B.** $Cd(OH)_2$ **C.** Cd   **D.** NiO_2 **E.** $Ni(OH)_2$

100. Which of the following materials is most likely to undergo oxidation?

A. Cl_2 **B.** Cl^- **C.** Na   **D.** Na^+ **E.** both Cl_2 and Cl^-

101. What is the term for any electrochemical cell that spontaneously produces electrical energy?

A. half-cell   **C.** dry cell

B. electrolytic cell   **D.** battery   **E.** none of the above

102. Which of the following species undergoes reduction in $2CuBr \rightarrow 2Cu + Br_2$?

A. Br^- **B.** Cu^+ **C.** CuBr   **D.** Cu   **E.** Br_2

103. What is the term for an electrochemical cell that has a single electrode where oxidation or reduction can occur?

A. half-cell   **C.** dry cell

B. voltaic cell   **D.** electrolytic cell   **E.** none of the above

104. Why might disposing of a lead–acid, nickel–cadmium or mercury battery in a landfill be undesirable?

A. Mercury, cadmium and lead are radioactive and release radiation

B. Mercury, cadmium and lead are very reactive

C. Mercury, cadmium and lead are toxic metals

D. Mercury, cadmium and lead generate highly unstable compounds

E. All of the above

105. Which of the statements is true regarding the following redox reaction occurring in a nonspontaneous electrochemical cell?

$$3C\ (s) + 2Co_2O_3\ (l) \xrightarrow{\text{Electricity}} 4Co\ (l) + 3CO_2\ (g)$$

A. Co metal is produced at the cathode   **C.** Reduction half-reaction: $C + 2O^{2-} \rightarrow CO_2 + 4e^-$

B. O^{2-} is produced at the anode   **D.** Oxidation half-reaction: $Co^{3+} + 3e^- \rightarrow Co$

    E. None of the above

106. How is electrolysis different from the chemical process inside a battery?

A. Pure compounds cannot be generated *via* electrolysis

B. Electrolysis only uses electrons from a cathode

C. Electrolysis does not use electrons

D. They are the same process in reverse

E. Chemical changes do not occur in electrolysis

107. What is the term for the value assigned to an atom in a substance that indicates whether the atom is electron-poor or electron-rich compared to a free atom?

A. reduction number   **C.** cathode number

B. oxidation number   **D.** anode number   **E.** none of the above

108. Why is recycling aluminum better for the environment than electrolysis of the aluminum ore bauxite?

 A. Bauxite is extremely rare

 B. Electricity is extremely cheap and it is better to use inexpensive electricity

 C. It takes less energy to recycle aluminum

 D. Electrolysis releases harmful gases into the atmosphere

 E. There is a large supply of aluminum

109. Which of the statements is true regarding the following redox reaction occurring in a nonspontaneous electrochemical cell?

$$\text{Br}_2\,(l) + 2\text{NaCl}\,(aq) \xrightarrow{\text{Electricity}} \text{Cl}_2\,(g) + 2\text{NaBr}\,(aq)$$

 A. Br_2 liquid is produced at the cathode

 B. Cl_2 gas is produced at the cathode

 C. Reduction half–reaction: $2\text{Cl}^- \rightarrow \text{Cl}_2 + 2\text{e}^-$

 D. Oxidation half–reaction: $\text{Br}_2 + 2\text{e}^- \rightarrow 2\text{Br}^-$

 E. Cl_2 gas is produced at the anode

110. The anode of a battery is indicated with negative (–) sign because the anode is:

 A. where electrons are adsorbed

 B. positive

 C. negative

 D. where electrons are generated

 E. determined by convention

111. What is the term for the relative ability of a substance to undergo reduction?

 A. oxidation potential

 B. reduction potential

 C. anode potential

 D. cathode potential

 E. none of the above

112. In a battery, which of the following species in the two oxidation-reduction reactions is undergoing oxidation?

 Reaction I: $\text{Zn} + 2\text{OH}^- \rightarrow \text{ZnO} + \text{H}_2\text{O} + 2\text{e}^-$

 Reaction II: $2\text{MnO}_2 + \text{H}_2\text{O} + 2\text{e}^- \rightarrow \text{Mn}_2\text{O}_3 + 2\text{OH}^-$

 A. H_2O **B.** MnO_2 **C.** ZnO **D.** Zn **E.** OH^-

113. In the reaction for a discharging nickel–cadmium battery, which substance is being oxidized?

 $\text{Cd}\,(s) + \text{NiO}_2\,(s) + 2\text{H}_2\text{O}\,(l) \rightarrow \text{Cd(OH)}_2\,(s) + \text{Ni(OH)}_2\,(s)$

 A. H_2O **B.** Cd(OH)_2 **C.** Cd **D.** NiO_2 **E.** Ni(OH)_2

114. Which of the following is the balanced chemical reaction for the electrolysis of brine (i.e. concentrated salt water) as a major source of chlorine gas?

 A. $2\text{NaCl}\,(aq) + \text{H}_2\text{O} \rightarrow 2\text{NaH}\,(aq) + \text{Cl}_2\text{O}^-\,(aq)$

 B. $2\text{NaCl}\,(aq) + 2\text{H}_2\text{O} \rightarrow 2\text{Na}\,(s) + \text{O}_2\,(g) + 2\text{H}_2\,(g) + \text{Cl}_2\,(g)$

 C. $2\text{NaCl}\,(aq) + \text{H}_2\text{O} \rightarrow \text{Na}_2\text{O}\,(aq) + 2\text{HCl}\,(aq)$

 D. $2\text{NaOH}\,(aq) + \text{Cl}_2\,(g) + 2\text{H}_2\,(g) \rightarrow 2\text{NaCl}\,(aq) + 2\text{H}_2\text{O}$

 E. $2\text{NaCl}\,(aq) + 2\text{H}_2\text{O} \rightarrow 2\text{NaOH}\,(aq) + \text{Cl}_2\,(g) + 2\text{H}_2\,(g)$

115. What is the term for an electrochemical cell in which electrical energy is generated from a spontaneous redox reaction?

    A. voltaic cell   **C.** dry cell

    B. photoelectric cell   **D.** electrolytic cell   **E.** wet cell

116. By which method could electrolysis be used to raise the hull of a sunken ship?

    A. Electrolysis could only be used to raise the hull if the ship was made of iron. If so, the electrolysis of the iron metal might produce sufficient gas to lift the ship

    B. The gaseous products of the electrolysis of H_2O are collected with bags attached to the hull of the ship, and the inflated bags raise the ship

    C. The electrolysis of the H_2O beneath the hull of the ship boils H_2O and creates upward pressure to raise the ship

    D. An electric current passed through the hull of the ship produces electrolysis, and the gases trapped in the compartments of the vessel would push it upwards

    E. Electrolysis of the ship's hull decreases its mass and the reduced weight causes the ship to rise

117. Which of the statements is true regarding the following redox reaction occurring in a nonspontaneous electrochemical cell?

$$\overset{\text{Electricity}}{Br_2 (l) + 2NaCl (aq) \rightarrow Cl_2 (g) + 2NaBr (aq)}$$

    A. Cl^- is produced at the anode

    B. Br^- is produced at the anode

    C. Oxidation half-reaction: $Br_2 + 2e^- \rightarrow 2Br^-$

    D. Reduction half-reaction: $2Cl^- \rightarrow Cl_2 + 2e^-$

    E. Br^- is produced at the cathode

118. A major source of chlorine gas is from the electrolysis of concentrated salt water, NaCl (*aq*). What is the sign of the electrode where the chlorine gas is formed?

    A. Neither since chlorine gas is a neutral molecule and there is no electrode attraction

    B. Negative, since the chlorine gas needs to deposit electrons to form chloride ions

    C. Positive, since the chloride ions lose electrons to form chlorine molecules

    D. Both, since the chloride ions from NaCl (*aq*) are attracted to the positive electrode to form chlorine molecules, while the produced chlorine gas molecules move to deposit electrons at the negative electrode

    E. Positive, since the chloride ions gain electrons to form chlorine molecules

119. Given that the following redox reactions go essentially to completion, which of the metals listed below has the greatest tendency to undergo oxidation?

$$Co (s) + Cu^{2+} (aq) \rightarrow Cu (s) + Co^{2+} (aq)$$

$$Mg (s) + Mn^{2+} (aq) \rightarrow Mn (s) + Mg^{2+} (aq)$$

$$Cu (s) + Ag^+ (aq) \rightarrow Ag (s) + Cu^{2+} (aq)$$

$$Mn (s) + Co^{2+} (aq) \rightarrow Co (s) + Mn^{2+} (aq)$$

    A. Cu   **B.** Mg   **C.** Ag   **D.** Co   **E.** Mn

120. Rust has a tendency to form when iron comes in contact with water. According to the following reaction $4Fe + 3O_2 \rightarrow 2Fe_2O_3$, what is happening at the cathode region?

- **A.** Oxygen is being reduced
- **B.** Iron is being reduced
- **C.** Iron is being oxidized
- **D.** Oxygen is being oxidized
- **E.** None of the above

121. Given that the following redox reactions go essentially to completion, which of the metals listed below has the greatest tendency to undergo oxidation?

$$Ni \ (s) + Ag^+ \ (aq) \rightarrow Ag \ (s) + Ni^{2+} \ (aq)$$
$$Al \ (s) + Cd^{2+} \ (aq) \rightarrow Cd \ (s) + Al^{3+} \ (aq)$$
$$Cd \ (s) + Ni^{2+} \ (aq) \rightarrow Ni \ (s) + Cd^{2+} \ (aq)$$
$$Ag \ (s) + H^+ \ (aq) \rightarrow \text{no reaction}$$

- **A.** (H)
- **B.** Cd
- **C.** Ni
- **D.** Ag
- **E.** Al

122. What is the primary difference between a fuel cell and a battery?

- **A.** Fuel cells oxidize to supply electricity, while batteries reduce to supply electricity
- **B.** Batteries supply electricity, while fuel cells supply heat
- **C.** Batteries can be recharged, while fuel cells cannot
- **D.** Fuel cells do not run down because they can be refueled, while batteries run down and need to be recharged
- **E.** Fuel cells do not use metals as oxidants and reductants, while batteries have a static reservoir of oxidants and reductants

123. Nickel-cadmium batteries are used in rechargeable electronic calculators. Given the reaction for a discharging NiCad battery, what substance is being reduced?

$$Cd \ (s) + NiO_2 \ (s) + 2H_2O \ (l) \rightarrow Cd(OH)_2 \ (s) + Ni(OH)_2 \ (s)$$

- **A.** $Cd(OH)_2$
- **B.** H_2O
- **C.** NiO_2
- **D.** Cd
- **E.** $Ni(OH)_2$

124. After balancing the following redox reaction in acidic solution, what is the coefficient of H^+?

$$Mg \ (s) \ + NO_3^- \ (aq) \rightarrow Mg^{2+} \ (aq) + NO_2 \ (aq)$$

- **A.** 1
- **B.** 2
- **C.** 4
- **D.** 6
- **E.** none of the above

ANSWER KEYS

235

Chapter 1: Atomic and Molecular Structure; Periodic Properties

1: D	26: E	51: B	76: C	101: B	126: A	151: B	176: A	201: B
2: E	27: D	52: E	77: D	102: C	127: C	152: E	177: C	202: E
3: D	28: E	53: B	78: B	103: B	128: D	153: D	178: E	203: D
4: B	29: B	54: A	79: D	104: B	129: D	154: C	179: B	204: D
5: B	30: B	55: E	80: E	105: D	130: E	155: C	180: B	205: A
6: A	31: C	56: B	81: C	106: E	131: C	156: B	181: D	206: A
7: E	32: A	57: A	82: D	107: A	132: B	157: C	182: A	207: B
8: B	33: B	58: D	83: B	108: D	133: D	158: A	183: E	208: E
9: C	34: E	59: B	84: A	109: E	134: E	159: D	184: C	209: C
10: C	35: D	60: E	85: C	110: D	135: D	160: E	185: B	210: C
11: E	36: B	61: D	86: B	111: C	136: B	161: A	186: E	211: D
12: B	37: A	62: C	87: E	112: B	137: B	162: A	187: A	212: C
13: A	38: C	63: D	88: D	113: A	138: E	163: D	188: C	213: A
14: E	39: C	64: E	89: A	114: C	139: A	164: E	189: A	214: D
15: D	40: D	65: A	90: C	115: E	140: B	165: A	190: D	215: E
16: C	41: E	66: C	91: E	116: D	141: D	166: C	191: E	216: C
17: B	42: A	67: D	92: A	117: C	142: E	167: E	192: D	217: B
18: A	43: A	68: C	93: E	118: E	143: C	168: D	193: B	218: B
19: A	44: C	69: E	94: B	119: D	144: A	169: A	194: C	219: A
20: C	45: E	70: A	95: D	120: A	145: C	170: B	195: A	220: A
21: D	46: D	71: A	96: A	121: B	146: E	171: B	196: C	221: E
22: A	47: A	72: D	97: C	122: A	147: A	172: D	197: D	222: B
23: D	48: C	73: C	98: B	123: A	148: A	173: E	198: E	223: B
24: E	49: B	74: B	99: E	124: C	149: C	174: B	199: B	224: D
25: C	50: D	75: C	100: A	125: E	150: B	175: C	200: D	225: A
								226: C

Chapter 2: Chemical Bonding

1: D	26: A	51: C	76: A	101: A	126: B	151: D
2: C	27: D	52: B	77: B	102: E	127: C	152: B
3: E	28: B	53: A	78: A	103: D	128: B	153: E
4: C	29: E	54: E	79: B	104: C	129: E	154: A
5: A	30: D	55: B	80: E	105: B	130: D	155: B
6: B	31: B	56: D	81: B	106: E	131: A	156: C
7: D	32: E	57: A	82: A	107: D	132: D	157: C
8: C	33: D	58: C	83: D	108: C	133: C	158: B
9: B	34: B	59: B	84: A	109: D	134: E	159: E
10: A	35: A	60: E	85: E	110: B	135: A	160: A
11: E	36: C	61: A	86: C	111: C	136: D	161: D
12: A	37: A	62: D	87: E	112: B	137: A	162: C
13: B	38: E	63: B	88: C	113: E	138: C	163: D
14: D	39: C	64: D	89: B	114: C	139: D	164: E
15: E	40: A	65: D	90: A	115: D	140: E	165: B
16: C	41: C	66: B	91: B	116: B	141: B	166: A
17: B	42: D	67: E	92: E	117: A	142: B	
18: C	43: B	68: A	93: D	118: E	143: A	
19: D	44: E	69: C	94: D	119: B	144: C	
20: A	45: A	70: D	95: E	120: E	145: A	
21: D	46: C	71: C	96: D	121: C	146: E	
22: E	47: D	72: C	97: A	122: A	147: B	
23: B	48: C	73: E	98: C	123: A	148: D	
24: E	49: E	74: A	99: C	124: D	149: C	
25: A	50: D	75: E	100: C	125: A	150: E	

Chapter 3: States of Matter: Gases, Liquids, Solids

1: C	26: B	51: A	76: E	101: B	126: D	151: A	176: B
2: B	27: C	52: E	77: C	102: C	127: C	152: D	177: A
3: E	28: E	53: D	78: A	103: E	128: B	153: C	178: A
4: A	29: A	54: E	79: A	104: D	129: E	154: E	179: E
5: E	30: C	55: B	80: B	105: C	130: B	155: C	180: D
6: C	31: B	56: C	81: B	106: B	131: A	156: A	181: C
7: A	32: D	57: B	82: D	107: A	132: D	157: A	182: B
8: C	33: B	58: C	83: A	108: D	133: A	158: C	183: E
9: B	34: E	59: E	84: B	109: D	134: B	159: A	184: C
10: D	35: A	60: D	85: B	110: C	135: A	160: C	185: D
11: C	36: E	61: B	86: C	111: B	136: D	161: D	186: C
12: A	37: B	62: C	87: B	112: A	137: A	162: B	187: B
13: D	38: D	63: A	88: C	113: E	138: E	163: D	188: E
14: E	39: B	64: B	89: A	114: C	139: C	164: B	189: A
15: E	40: A	65: C	90: E	115: D	140: A	165: D	190: B
16: A	41: E	66: E	91: D	116: B	141: E	166: D	191: D
17: B	42: D	67: A	92: C	117: E	142: D	167: E	
18: A	43: C	68: D	93: E	118: D	143: E	168: B	
19: D	44: C	69: A	94: C	119: E	144: C	169: E	
20: E	45: E	70: E	95: D	120: C	145: D	170: B	
21: B	46: A	71: D	96: C	121: B	146: B	171: E	
22: D	47: E	72: A	97: E	122: A	147: C	172: A	
23: C	48: C	73: B	98: A	123: E	148: A	173: B	
24: D	49: D	74: C	99: D	124: A	149: C	174: E	
25: B	50: D	75: C	100: E	125: A	150: B	175: C	

Chapter 4: Solutions

1: D	26: D	51: D	76: C	101: A	126: E	151: A	176: A	201: C
2: C	27: B	52: B	77: E	102: B	127: C	152: D	177: B	202: C
3: E	28: A	53: E	78: D	103: E	128: D	153: B	178: E	203: A
4: A	29: C	54: C	79: A	104: C	129: C	154: C	179: D	204: E
5: E	30: D	55: D	80: C	105: B	130: E	155: C	180: A	205: D
6: B	31: E	56: A	81: B	106: E	131: B	156: D	181: C	206: C
7: E	32: C	57: E	82: D	107: D	132: D	157: B	182: D	207: D
8: D	33: E	58: C	83: B	108: C	133: A	158: E	183: B	208: A
9: D	34: B	59: A	84: C	109: A	134: E	159: D	184: D	209: C
10: C	35: C	60: C	85: A	110: D	135: B	160: C	185: B	
11: A	36: E	61: C	86: D	111: E	136: A	161: C	186: C	
12: A	37: C	62: B	87: E	112: B	137: D	162: E	187: E	
13: E	38: A	63: D	88: A	113: D	138: A	163: A	188: D	
14: B	39: B	64: A	89: D	114: E	139: A	164: D	189: E	
15: C	40: D	65: E	90: D	115: A	140: E	165: B	190: C	
16: A	41: E	66: D	91: E	116: C	141: A	166: C	191: B	
17: C	42: A	67: B	92: C	117: B	142: E	167: A	192: A	
18: D	43: C	68: B	93: B	118: A	143: D	168: E	193: E	
19: E	44: D	69: D	94: C	119: E	144: B	169: A	194: A	
20: B	45: B	70: E	95: B	120: D	145: D	170: E	195: C	
21: A	46: A	71: C	96: E	121: C	146: E	171: B	196: E	
22: B	47: B	72: A	97: A	122: B	147: C	172: A	197: C	
23: C	48: D	73: B	98: D	123: D	148: B	173: D	198: A	
24: E	49: E	74: E	99: E	124: A	149: C	174: E	199: D	
25: B	50: A	75: A	100: A	125: C	150: C	175: B	200: B	

Chapter 5: Acids & Bases

1: E	26: C	51: A	76: C	101: B	126: D	151: C	176: C	201: E	226: D
2: B	27: E	52: C	77: D	102: E	127: C	152: A	177: E	202: D	227: A
3: C	28: D	53: B	78: C	103: A	128: A	153: E	178: C	203: C	228: D
4: D	29: A	54: E	79: E	104: C	129: A	154: B	179: A	204: A	229: B
5: C	30: B	55: D	80: B	105: D	130: E	155: D	180: C	205: D	230: E
6: B	31: E	56: A	81: A	106: E	131: C	156: C	181: A	206: E	231: A
7: C	32: B	57: B	82: C	107: D	132: B	157: E	182: E	207: B	232: C
8: A	33: D	58: D	83: E	108: C	133: D	158: A	183: D	208: A	233: C
9: D	34: C	59: E	84: D	109: E	134: E	159: D	184: A	209: D	234: D
10: B	35: B	60: B	85: C	110: C	135: B	160: B	185: B	210: C	235: B
11: D	36: A	61: C	86: A	111: B	136: E	161: C	186: B	211: E	236: E
12: E	37: A	62: B	87: A	112: B	137: A	162: E	187: E	212: D	237: B
13: A	38: E	63: A	88: B	113: D	138: B	163: C	188: C	213: B	238: A
14: E	39: D	64: B	89: B	114: E	139: D	164: D	189: A	214: E	239: C
15: A	40: B	65: C	90: A	115: B	140: B	165: A	190: D	215: A	240: E
16: C	41: A	66: C	91: D	116: A	141: E	166: E	191: E	216: A	241: B
17: A	42: B	67: E	92: E	117: D	142: C	167: A	192: B	217: C	242: B
18: B	43: D	68: A	93: C	118: C	143: D	168: D	193: D	218: B	243: D
19: C	44: C	69: A	94: B	119: A	144: E	169: A	194: E	219: A	244: E
20: A	45: C	70: D	95: D	120: E	145: A	170: B	195: B	220: C	245: A
21: B	46: C	71: C	96: E	121: C	146: C	171: D	196: D	221: B	246: D
22: B	47: D	72: C	97: D	122: A	147: A	172: B	197: A	222: D	247: B
23: A	48: E	73: E	98: C	123: C	148: D	173: C	198: C	223: E	248: A
24: E	49: B	74: D	99: E	124: B	149: C	174: B	199: B	224: C	249: C
25: D	50: D	75: D	100: A	125: A	150: B	175: E	200: D	225: B	250: C
									251: D
									252: A
									253: E

Chapter 6: Stoichiometry and General Concepts

1: D	26: C	51: C	76: D	101: B	126: A	151: C	176: A	201: C	226: A
2: A	27: B	52: A	77: B	102: D	127: D	152: D	177: C	202: A	227: A
3: C	28: A	53: E	78: E	103: E	128: E	153: E	178: E	203: D	228: D
4: E	29: C	54: D	79: C	104: B	129: B	154: B	179: B	204: B	229: A
5: A	30: B	55: B	80: B	105: A	130: D	155: E	180: C	205: D	230: C
6: B	31: A	56: C	81: A	106: C	131: C	156: B	181: D	206: B	231: E
7: D	32: E	57: E	82: E	107: B	132: B	157: A	182: B	207: C	232: D
8: B	33: A	58: B	83: C	108: E	133: E	158: D	183: D	208: A	233: B
9: E	34: D	59: A	84: B	109: A	134: C	159: A	184: E	209: E	234: D
10: A	35: B	60: D	85: B	110: B	135: E	160: E	185: B	210: A	235: C
11: E	36: A	61: C	86: C	111: C	136: A	161: B	186: C	211: B	236: E
12: C	37: D	62: E	87: A	112: D	137: E	162: D	187: D	212: A	237: B
13: D	38: E	63: A	88: B	113: C	138: A	163: A	188: A	213: E	238: E
14: E	39: C	64: C	89: D	114: E	139: D	164: B	189: A	214: D	
15: C	40: C	65: D	90: C	115: D	140: C	165: E	190: C	215: B	
16: B	41: E	66: E	91: E	116: E	141: B	166: A	191: D	216: C	
17: A	42: E	67: B	92: D	117: A	142: A	167: B	192: E	217: B	
18: C	43: B	68: A	93: A	118: D	143: C	168: C	193: B	218: C	
19: E	44: B	69: D	94: D	119: E	144: D	169: D	194: D	219: E	
20: A	45: D	70: B	95: C	120: B	145: E	170: C	195: E	220: C	
21: D	46: C	71: C	96: A	121: A	146: B	171: A	196: C	221: D	
22: B	47: A	72: D	97: E	122: C	147: D	172: D	197: B	222: E	
23: C	48: E	73: E	98: A	123: C	148: B	173: C	198: A	223: D	
24: B	49: D	74: B	99: E	124: A	149: A	174: E	199: E	224: A	
25: D	50: D	75: A	100: D	125: D	150: C	175: C	200: A	225: A	

Chapter 7: Chemical Equilibria and Chemical Kinetics

1: E	26: D	51: E	76: B	101: D	126: D	151: C	176: C	201: B
2: C	27: A	52: C	77: C	102: A	127: B	152: A	177: A	202: E
3: A	28: E	53: D	78: D	103: B	128: C	153: C	178: D	203: A
4: C	29: D	54: C	79: E	104: E	129: A	154: A	179: E	204: D
5: B	30: A	55: A	80: A	105: C	130: E	155: B	180: D	205: A
6: E	31: E	56: C	81: D	106: C	131: B	156: A	181: B	206: C
7: B	32: A	57: B	82: E	107: D	132: A	157: C	182: E	207: A
8: C	33: C	58: C	83: A	108: A	133: D	158: E	183: D	208: B
9: A	34: D	59: E	84: C	109: B	134: E	159: C	184: B	209: C
10: B	35: E	60: B	85: B	110: B	135: B	160: D	185: C	210: E
11: D	36: B	61: B	86: E	111: A	136: D	161: B	186: A	211: D
12: E	37: B	62: B	87: C	112: E	137: C	162: D	187: D	212: E
13: A	38: C	63: B	88: A	113: C	138: E	163: E	188: E	213: B
14: B	39: B	64: E	89: B	114: C	139: D	164: B	189: B	214: A
15: B	40: E	65: A	90: D	115: A	140: A	165: D	190: C	215: D
16: C	41: A	66: A	91: A	116: C	141: D	166: C	191: E	216: B
17: D	42: A	67: B	92: C	117: E	142: C	167: D	192: E	217: D
18: A	43: C	68: B	93: B	118: B	143: B	168: E	193: B	218: A
19: D	44: E	69: C	94: D	119: B	144: A	169: B	194: C	
20: E	45: D	70: E	95: E	120: C	145: C	170: A	195: A	
21: B	46: D	71: A	96: D	121: A	146: B	171: E	196: E	
22: D	47: C	72: D	97: B	122: D	147: D	172: A	197: A	
23: C	48: A	73: C	98: D	123: E	148: E	173: D	198: D	
24: E	49: C	74: C	99: A	124: C	149: A	174: E	199: A	
25: A	50: B	75: E	100: E	125: B	150: C	175: B	200: C	

Chapter 8: Thermodynamics and Thermochemistry

1: B	26: A	51: A	76: A	101: A	126: B	151: B	176: D	201: C
2: A	27: D	52: D	77: C	102: A	127: D	152: E	177: A	202: C
3: D	28: E	53: E	78: D	103: C	128: C	153: C	178: C	203: E
4: E	29: C	54: B	79: B	104: D	129: E	154: A	179: C	204: D
5: A	30: A	55: D	80: E	105: C	130: C	155: C	180: B	205: E
6: C	31: B	56: B	81: B	106: B	131: D	156: E	181: D	206: A
7: A	32: E	57: D	82: C	107: C	132: A	157: D	182: E	207: B
8: E	33: C	58: C	83: A	108: E	133: B	158: E	183: A	208: C
9: D	34: B	59: A	84: A	109: B	134: C	159: A	184: D	209: A
10: B	35: E	60: C	85: C	110: C	135: D	160: D	185: A	210: D
11: C	36: E	61: B	86: E	111: B	136: E	161: E	186: E	211: B
12: C	37: D	62: A	87: D	112: D	137: B	162: D	187: B	212: D
13: A	38: C	63: E	88: C	113: E	138: E	163: C	188: E	213: E
14: B	39: D	64: D	89: B	114: D	139: A	164: E	189: B	214: D
15: E	40: E	65: A	90: E	115: C	140: C	165: C	190: A	215: A
16: B	41: B	66: E	91: B	116: D	141: A	166: D	191: E	216: C
17: A	42: A	67: D	92: A	117: D	142: D	167: B	192: C	217: B
18: C	43: C	68: B	93: D	118: E	143: B	168: A	193: B	218: E
19: D	44: D	69: C	94: D	119: B	144: C	169: A	194: C	219: D
20: E	45: B	70: B	95: B	120: A	145: B	170: D	195: C	220: B
21: B	46: B	71: D	96: E	121: E	146: E	171: C	196: D	221: A
22: A	47: D	72: A	97: C	122: A	147: D	172: B	197: B	222: C
23: C	48: A	73: C	98: A	123: E	148: E	173: B	198: D	223: B
24: E	49: E	74: B	99: C	124: B	149: B	174: E	199: A	224: A
25: D	50: A	75: E	100: D	125: A	150: C	175: C	200: B	

Chapter 9: Electrochemistry

1: C	26: A	51: E	76: C	101: D
2: A	27: D	52: A	77: D	102: B
3: B	28: E	53: B	78: E	103: A
4: E	29: B	54: A	79: B	104: C
5: E	30: D	55: B	80: B	105: A
6: D	31: B	56: E	81: D	106: D
7: C	32: E	57: B	82: A	107: B
8: A	33: C	58: D	83: E	108: C
9: D	34: D	59: E	84: A	109: E
10: B	35: C	60: A	85: B	110: D
11: A	36: A	61: B	86: A	111: B
12: E	37: C	62: A	87: E	112: D
13: B	38: E	63: D	88: D	113: C
14: B	39: B	64: E	89: C	114: E
15: E	40: A	65: C	90: C	115: A
16: C	41: C	66: A	91: B	116: B
17: A	42: B	67: D	92: E	117: E
18: D	43: C	68: C	93: A	118: C
19: C	44: E	69: D	94: B	119: B
20: A	45: D	70: E	95: D	120: A
21: E	46: A	71: C	96: C	121: E
22: D	47: E	72: D	97: D	122: D
23: E	48: B	73: B	98: A	123: C
24: C	49: D	74: A	99: E	124: C
25: B	50: A	75: C	100: C	

Share your opinion

Your feedback is important because we strive to provide the highest quality prep materials. If you are satisfied with the content of this book, post your review on Amazon, so others can benefit from your experience.

If you have any questions or comments about the material, email us at info@sterling-prep.com and we will resolve any issues to your satisfaction.

DAT
GENERAL CHEMISTRY
PRACTICE QUESTIONS

Chapter 1. ATOMIC AND MOLECULAR STRUCTURE; PERIODIC PROPERTIES

1. D is correct. An element is a pure chemical substance that consists of a single type of atom. Every element has an atomic number based on the number of protons that it contains. Hydrogen has the atomic number 1, and it is the first element on the periodic table of elements.

The other answer choices contain more than one type of atom, so they are referred to as chemical compounds. Glucose and methanol contain carbon, oxygen and hydrogen atoms. Sodium chloride, as its name suggests, contains sodium and chlorine. Brass contains copper and zinc.

2. E is correct. Metals are excellent conductors of both heat and electricity because the molecules in metal are very closely packed together, i.e. they have a high density. Metals are generally in a solid state at room temperature, and are also known to be very malleable, meaning that they can be pressed or hammered into different shapes without breaking.

3. D is correct. There is one *s* orbital, three *p* orbitals, five *d* orbitals, and seven *f* orbitals. The number of orbitals in a subshell is different than the maximum number of electrons in the subshell. Each orbital can hold two electrons, so the capacity of an *f* subshell is $7 \times 2 = 14$ electrons.

4. B is correct.

$$\begin{array}{c} \text{H}\ \ \text{H} \\ \text{H} : \overset{..}{\underset{..}{\text{C}}} : \overset{..}{\underset{..}{\text{C}}} : \text{H} \\ \text{H}\ \ \text{H} \end{array}$$

5. B is correct. The noble gases are the most stable *group* (not period).

6. A is correct.

7. E is correct.

8. B is correct. The mass number is an approximation of the atomic weight of the element as amu (or grams per mole).

9. C is correct. Dalton's Atomic Theory, developed in the early 1800s, states that atoms of a given element are identical in mass and properties. Today, we know that the masses of atoms of a particular element may be not identical, although all atoms of an element must have the same number of protons; they can have different numbers of neutrons (and are called isotopes).

10. C is correct. The properties of the elements on the periodic table repeat at regular intervals, creating "groups" or "families" of elements. Each column on the periodic table is considered to be a group, and elements within groups have similar physical and chemical characteristics (due to the orbital location of their outermost electron). These column groups would only exist if the elements of the periodic table were listed by increasing atomic number.

11. E is correct.

12. B is correct.

13. A is correct. Congeners are chemical substances related by origin, structure, or function. In regards of the periodic table, congeners are the elements of the same group which share similar properties (e.g. copper, silver and gold are congeners of Group 11). Anomers and epimers are discussed in organic chemistry.

14. E is correct.

15. D is correct. The atomic number (Z) defines the element.

16. C is correct. French chemist Antoine Lavoisier performed a series of experiments that established the Law of Mass Conservation, which states that *whenever matter undergoes a change, the total mass of the products of the change is the same as the total mass of the reactants*. From this idea, he further proposed that an element is any material made of a fundamental substance that cannot be broken down into anything else.

17. B is correct.

18. A is correct.

19. A is correct.

20. C is correct. A calcium atom contains 20 electrons. As a +2 charge, it lost 2 electrons and has 18 electrons.

21. D is correct.

22. A is correct. The anion has the largest radius because it has the greatest number of electrons occupying the valence orbitals around the nucleus.

23. D is correct.

24. E is correct.

25. C is correct. 1 amu is 1/12 the mass of ^{12}C atoms which is approximately the mass of one proton.

26. E is correct.

27. D is correct.

28. E is correct.

29. B is correct.

30. B is correct. Ionization energy is smallest on the left and bottom of the table.

31. C is correct. The mass of As (arsenic) is 74.9 and the atomic number (i.e. # of protons) is 33. Since the mass of both protons and neutrons is approximately 1 amu, the number of neutrons is 75 – 33 = 42 which is valid because (in this example) there is only one naturally occurring isotope. Otherwise there is a mixture of isotopes with 41 and 43 neutrons.

32. A is correct.

33. B is correct.

34. E is correct.

35. D is correct. Boron's atomic number is 5, therefore it contains 5 electrons.

Use Aufbau's principle to determine order of orbital filing. Remember that each electron shell starts with a new *s* orbital. Answer: $1s^2 2s^2 2p^1$

36. B is correct.

37. A is correct. The alkali metals have very low melting points for metals.

38. C is correct. Charged plates are a pair of plates with positive charge on one plate and negative on the other. Particles will be shot at a high speed in between those plates. If a particle is deflected, it will be travelling in a curve towards one of the plates. A particle will be deflected if it has positive or negative charge and it will travel towards the plate with opposite charges.

Hydrogen atom has an equal number of protons and electrons, which means that the overall charge on the molecule is zero. Therefore, it won't be affected by the positive or negative charges on the charged plates. The other options (alpha particles, protons, and cathode rays) are charged particles and they will be deflected by charged plates.

39. C is correct.

40. D is correct. The atomic mass of Na is 23.0 and the mass of 1 mole of Na is 23.0 grams; 4 moles has a mass of $4 \times 23 = 92.0$ grams.

41. E is correct.

42. A is correct.

43. A is correct.

44. C is correct.

45. E is correct. The elements listed at the bottom of the periodic table have low ionization energies. This is due to the shielding from the positive charge of the nucleus, and therefore these elements have large atomic radii. The greater the distance between the electrons and the nucleus, the easier it is to remove the outer valence electrons.

46. D is correct. $n = 4$ shell has 4 orbitals: *s, p, d, f*

Maximum number of electrons in each shell:

$$s = 2$$

$$p = 6$$

$$d = 10$$

$$f = 14$$

Total $= 2 + 6 + 10 + 14 = 32$ electrons

47. A is correct. The charge on 1 electron is negative; one mole is Avogadro's number $\times$ e⁻.

48. C is correct. Metals are good conductors of both heat and electricity, because the molecules in metals are closely packed together. Metals are not brittle or fragile (i.e. they do not break easily); to the contrary, they are malleable and can be pressed or hammered without breaking. Metals are opaque and not transparent because all of the atoms in metal are surrounded by free moving electrons, therefore any light that strikes the metal will hit these electrons, which will absorb and re-emit it, and the light is not able to pass through.

49. B is correct.

50. D is correct. Protons have a +1 charge, electrons have a –1 charge and neutrons have no charge (0). If there are more protons than electrons, the positive charges must outweigh the negative charges, creating a net positive charge.

51. B is correct.

52. E is correct. Electrons become excited when gaining energy from absorbing a photon.

53. B is correct.

54. A is correct. Electronegativity is the relative attraction of the nucleus for bonding electrons. It increases from left to right and from bottom to top (similar to the trend for ionization energy).

55. E is correct.

56. B is correct. Electron shells represent the orbit that electrons follow around an atom's nucleus. Each shell is composed of one or more subshells, which are named using lowercase letters (*s*, *p*, *d*, *f*).

Shell name	Subshell name	Subshell max electrons	Shell max electrons
K	1s	2	**2**
L	2s	2	**2 + 6 = 8**
	2p	6	
M	3s	2	**2 + 6 + 10 = 18**
	3p	6	
	3d	10	
N	4s	2	**2 + 6 + + 10 + 14 = 32**
	4p	6	
	4d	10	
	4f	14	

The first shell has one subshell (1*s*), the second shell has two subshells (2*s*, 2*p*), the third subshell has three subshells (3*s*, 3*p*, 3*d*), etc.

An *s* subshell hold 2 electrons, and each subsequent subshell in the series can hold 4 more (*p* holds 6, *d* holds 10, *f* holds 14). The number before the *s* (i.e. 4 in this example) does not affect how many electrons can occupy the subshell.

57. A is correct. The atomic mass of H is 1.0 amu and a single proton has a mass of 1 amu, the most common isotope contains no neutrons. Alternatively, from acid-base chemistry, hydrogen ions are referred to as *protons* (H^+) with zero neutrons in the nucleus.

58. D is correct. English chemist John Dalton is known for his Atomic Theory, which states that *elements are made of small particles called atoms, which cannot be created or destroyed*.

59. B is correct. The n = 3 shell contains subshells 3*s*, 3*p* and 3*d*. An *s* shell can contain 2 electrons, a *p* shell can contain up to 6 electrons, and a *d* shell can contain up to 10 electrons. 2 + 6 + 10 = 18, so the maximum number of electrons in the n = 3 shell is 18. Also, see explanation to question **56**.

60. E is correct.

61. D is correct. An element is a pure chemical substance that consists of a single type of atom, distinguished by its atomic number (i.e. the number of protons that it contains).

62. C is correct. This is the definition of electron affinity.

A: definition of electronegativity.

B: definition for ionization energy.

63. D is correct.

64. E is correct. Since naturally occurring lithium has a mass of 6.9 g/mol and both protons and neutrons have a mass of approximately 1 g/mol, ^{7}lithium is the predominant isotope.

65. A is correct. The electron could fall to the intermediate level, giving off an energy of 4.1 – 2.3 = 1.8 eV.

66. C is correct. Energy levels for electrons in an atom include the ground state and various excited states. In the ground state, all the electrons are in their lowest energy levels. After an electron absorbs energy, it may jump to a higher energy excited state.

67. D is correct. All atoms of a given element must have the same number of protons (this is their atomic number). They may have different numbers of neutrons, forming isotopes of the same elements. They may also have different numbers of electrons, forming charged particles called ions.

68. C is correct.

69. E is correct. Noble gas electronic configurations are characterized by filled valence *s* and *p* subshells.

70. A is correct. The nucleus is the dense central core of the atom that contains positively-charged protons and neutral neutrons (joined by the nuclear force). Therefore, the nucleus is positively-charged. It has most of the mass of an atom, but only a small fraction of the volume. The nucleus is surrounded by an electron cloud.

71. A is correct. Metalloids are semimetallic elements (i.e. between metals and nonmetals). The following elements are metalloids: B, Si, Ge, As, Sb, Te, Po and At.

72. D is correct.

73. C is correct.

74. B is correct. Cu has an atomic weight of 63.5 grams. Therefore, the other isotope of Cu must be heavier than the more common ^{63}Cu and the atomic weight is closer to 65.

75. C is correct.

76. C is correct.

77. D is correct. The atomic number, sometimes represented by the symbol *Z*, is the number of protons for an atom of a given element. In the periodic table, the elements are listed by order of increasing atomic number.

78. B is correct. The nucleus, the dense central core of an atom, contains most of the atom's mass. It consists of protons and neutrons, which each have a mass of approximately 1 amu. A cloud of orbiting electrons surrounds the nucleus, and each electron has a mass of approximately 1/1837 amu. Clearly, the electrons contribute to only a tiny fraction of the mass of an atom.

79. D is correct. The alkali metals have low electronegativity and react violently with water. An example is the violent reaction of sodium with water.

80. E is correct.

81. C is correct. From the periodic table:

C (6 × 12 grams) + H (12 × 1 gram) + O (6 × 16 grams) = 180 g.

82. D is correct. See explanation for question **71**.

83. B is correct. Electron shells represent the orbit that electrons follow around an atom's nucleus. Each shell is composed of one or more subshells, which are named using lowercase letters (*s*, *p*, *d*, *f*). The *s* subshell is the lowest energy subshell and the *f* subshell is the highest energy subshell. The number before the lowercase letter represents the number of the shell. There is no 6*s* subshell because the largest shell is the n=5 shell, therefore the answer is 4*s*.

84. A is correct.

85. C is correct. A continuous spectrum refers to a broad uninterrupted spectrum of radiant energy. The visible spectrum refers to the light that we can see and includes the colors of the rainbow. The ultraviolet spectrum refers to electromagnetic radiation with wavelength shorter than visible light but longer than X-rays. The radiant energy spectrum refers to electromagnetic (EM) waves of all wavelengths, but the bands of frequency in an EM signal may be sharply defined with interruptions, or they may be broad.

86. B is correct. The periodic trend for electronegativity predicts that Cl is more electronegative than I. Since I (Z = 53) has more protons than Cl (Z=17) it has a greater nuclear charge.

87. E is correct. Cobalt's atomic number is 27

Atomic weight = 60
Number or protons = number of electrons = atomic number = 27
Atomic weight = atomic number + number of neutrons
Number of neutrons = atomic weight – atomic number
Number of neutrons = 60 – 27 = 33

88. D is correct. The metalloids have some properties of metals and some properties of nonmetals. However, the elements in the IIIB group are transition metals, not metalloids.

89. A is correct. All atoms of a particular element have the same chemical properties and the same number of protons. This number of protons is the atomic number of the element. Atoms of a particular element do not necessarily have the same mass, because they may have different numbers of neutrons (i.e. they are isotopes of the element). Atoms of an element may also have different numbers of electrons, forming charged ions.

90. C is correct. The mass number is already provided by the problem: ^{79}Br means the mass number is 79.

The atomic number of ^{79}Br can be obtained from the periodic table. Br is in group VIIA/17 and its atomic number is 35.

91. E is correct. Ions typically form with the same electron configuration of the noble gases (i.e. complete octet).

92. A is correct. See explanation for question **71**.

93. E is correct. Electron shells represent the orbit that electrons follow around an atom's nucleus. Each shell is composed of one or more subshells, which are named using lowercase letters (*s, p, d, f*). The first shell, n = 1, has one subshell (1*s*), the second shell, n = 2, has two subshells (2*s*, 2*p*), the third shell, n = 3, has three subshells (3*s*, 3*p*, 3*d)*, etc.

94. B is correct. The electron configuration is the arrangement of electrons by sublevels (known as shells) according to increasing energy. An electron shell represents the orbit of the electrons in that energy level. Each shell can hold a maximum number of electrons, and the outermost shell contains electrons of the highest energy.

A continuous spectrum refers to an uninterrupted spectrum of waves or frequencies. Atomic number is the number of protons in an atom of a particular element, and atomic notation refers to the way that a chemical symbol is written, with the mass number as a superscript and the atomic number as a subscript.

95. D is correct.

96. A is correct. If $n = 4$, the subshell must be either a 4*s*, 4*p*, 4*d*, or 4*f*. If $l = 2$, the *l* values range from 0 to 2 (0, 1, 2); and the $l = 2$ value must correspond to the third subshell on the 4th shell, the 4*d* subshell. If $l = 1$, the subshell would have been 4*p*, and if $l = 0$, the subshell would have been 4*s*.

97. C is correct. Protons are the positively-charged particles located inside the nucleus of an atom. Like neutrons (which are also in the nucleus), protons have a mass of approximately 1 amu. However, the difference between protons and neutrons is that protons have a +1 charge while neutrons have a charge of 0 (i.e. they are neutral). Electrons, on the other hand, are negatively-charged particles that are much smaller than protons and neutrons, having a mass of about 5×10^{-4} amu.

98. B is correct. Ions typically form with the same electron configuration as the noble gases (i.e. complete octet).

99. E is correct. Neutrons, like protons, are nucleons, meaning that they are one of the particles that make up the nucleus of an atom. Neutrons are closely associated with protons, held together by the nuclear force. Both neutrons and protons have a mass of about 1 amu, and are therefore much more massive than electrons. Neutrons are neutral and thus have a charge of 0. This makes them more difficult to detect than protons (which have a +1 charge) and electrons (which have a –1 charge).

100. A is correct.

101. B is correct.

102. C is correct.

103. B is correct. Ionization energy generally increases to the right across a row in the periodic table.

104. B is correct. Isotopes are variants of the same element that have a different number of neutrons. Since they are the same element, they must have the same number of protons, so choice A can be eliminated. Atoms that have the same number of protons but a different number of electrons are called ions, so choice C is also incorrect.

105. D is correct. The transition elements are metals.

106. E is correct.

107. A is correct.

108. D is correct.

109. E is correct. All of the atoms in the options (Li, Na, K, H, Rb) are Group IA / 1 elements. Within a group, the radius of an atom increases from top to bottom. The atom with the largest radius (size) will be the lowest atom in the group, which is Rb.

110. D is correct.

111. C is correct. In Bohr's model of the atom, electrons can jump to higher energy levels, gaining energy, or drop to lower energy levels, releasing energy. When electric current flows through an element in the gas phase, a glowing light is produced. By directing this light through a prism, a pattern of lines known as the atomic spectra can be seen. These lines are produced by excited electrons dropping to lower energy levels. Since the energy levels in each element are different, each element has a unique set of lines, which is why the spectrum is called the "atomic fingerprint" of the element.

112. B is correct. First, determine the atomic number of Ar using the periodic table. Ar is located in Group VIII/18 and its atomic number is 18.

The atomic mass of $^{40}Ar = 40$.

To get the number of neutrons, subtract the atomic number from the atomic mass:

$40 - 18 = 22$ neutrons

113. A is correct. Paramagnetic elements are substances that tend to move into a magnetic field and tend to have one or more unpaired electrons. Most transition metals and their compounds in oxidation states involving incomplete inner electron subshells are paramagnetic.

114. C is correct. The mass number is the total number of nucleons (i.e. protons and neutrons) in an atom. The atomic number is the number of protons in an atom. The number of neutrons in an atom can be calculated by subtracting the atomic number from the mass number.

115. E is correct.

116. D is correct.

117. C is correct.

118. E is correct.

  Platinum. Atomic number = 78

  Atomic weight = 195

  number or protons = number of electrons = atomic number = 78

  Atomic weight = atomic number + number of neutrons

  number of neutrons = atomic weight – atomic number

  number of neutrons = 195 – 78

  number of neutrons = 117

119. D is correct.

120. A is correct. Atomic radius generally decreases to the right across a row in the periodic table. Therefore, comparing the 4th period elements of calcium and gallium, gallium has the smaller radius.

121. B is correct.

  Average atomic mass = sum of (relative abundance × atomic mass)

  Average atomic mass = (20% × 16.0 amu + 50% × 17.0 amu + 30% × 18.0)

  Average atomic mass = 17.1 amu

122. A is correct. The atomic number depends on the number of protons or electrons in the neutral atom. The atomic mass is the sum of the number of protons and neutrons. This element has 7 protons, 7 electrons, and (13 – 7) or 6 neutrons.

123. A is correct.

124. C is correct. The atom has 47 protons, 47 electrons, and 60 neutrons.

Because the periodic table is arranged by atomic number, the fastest way to identify an element is to determine its atomic number. The atomic number is equal to the number of protons or electrons, which means that this atom's atomic number is 47. Use this information to locate element #47 in the table, which is Ag (silver).

To confirm the identity, check the atomic mass, which is equal to atomic number + number of neutrons. For this atom, the mass is 60 + 47 = 107. The mass of Ag on the periodic table is listed as 107.87, which is the average mass of all Ag isotopes. But it is pretty close – usually all isotopes of an element has similar masses (within 1-3 amu to each other).

125. E is correct.

126. A is correct.

127. C is correct.

128. D is correct. Electron configuration: $1s^2 2s^2 2p^6 3s^2$

The fastest way to identify an element using the periodic table is by using its atomic number. The atomic number is equal to the number of protons or electrons. In this problem, the total number of electrons can be determined by adding up all the electrons in the provided electron configuration: 2 + 2 + 6 + 2 = 12. Locate element #12 in the periodic table. Answer: Mg

129. D is correct.

130. E is correct. Atomic masses are not often integers because many elements have isotopes. Isotopes are atoms with the same number of protons but different numbers of neutrons. For example the three forms of hydrogen are protium (1 proton, 1 electron), deuterium (1 proton, 1 neutron, 1 electron), and tritium (1 proton, 2 neutrons, and 1 electron). When the relative numbers of these forms of hydrogen are multiplied by their atomic weights, the average value for the atomic weight for hydrogen is greater than 1.

131. C is correct. The problem only specifies the atomic mass of Cl: 35 amu. The atomic number was not given but the information is available in the periodic table (atomic number = 17).

number of neutrons = atomic weight – atomic number

number of neutrons = 35 – 17

number of neutrons = 18

132. B is correct.

133. D is correct.

134. E is correct. Start by obtaining the atomic number of Mn from the periodic table. Mn is a transition metal and it is located in Group VIIB/7; its atomic number is 25.

Use Aufbau's principle to fill up the orbitals of Mn:

$1s^2 2s^2 2p^6 3s^2 3p^6 4s^2 3d^5$

135. D is correct.

136. B is correct. The Rutherford-Bohr model of the hydrogen atom, often referred to as simply the Bohr atom, depicts a sphere with a heavy, dense nucleus encircled by electrons in orbits, held together by the electrostatic forces between the positively-charged nucleus and the negatively-charged electrons.

137. B is correct. Although each C–Cl bond is very polar, the dipole moments of each of the four bonds in CCl_4 (carbon tetrachloride) cancel because the molecule is a symmetric tetrahedron.

138. E is correct.

139. A is correct.

n is the principal quantum number

l stands for the angular momentum quantum number.

s stands for the spin quantum number.

m stands for the magnetic quantum number.

140. B is correct. The atomic mass unit (amu) was designed using carbon-12 isotope as the reference. 1 amu = 1/12 mass of a C-12 atom. Masses of other elements are measured against this standard.

If the mass of an atom 55.434 amu, it means that the atom's mass is 55.434 × (1/12 mass of carbon-12)

Option E offers a similar answer, except the ratio is 55.434/12.011 (versus 55.434/12.000 in option B). 12.011 is the average molecular mass for carbon, which takes into account other isotopes of carbon. The amu standard was only based on carbon-12 isotope.

141. D is correct.

142. E is correct. Ionization energy is the energy necessary to remove an electron from an element in its gaseous state and form a positively-charged gaseous ion. The ionization energy can be specified in units of electronvolts (eV) or as a molar quantity (e.g. kJ/mol or kcal/mol). The ionization energies for bigger atoms are larger than the ionization energies for smaller atoms.

The *first* ionization energy is the energy needed to remove the outermost electron from a neutral gas phase atom. Similarly, the ionization energies to remove subsequent electrons are named the *n*th ionization energy.

143. C is correct.

144. A is correct. The fastest way to identify an element using the periodic table is by using its atomic number. The atomic number is equal to the number of protons or electrons. In this problem, the total number of electrons can be determined by adding up all the electrons in the provided electron configuration: $2 + 2 + 6 + 2 + 6 + 2 + 10 + 6 + 2 + 10 + 2 = 50$. Look up element #50 in the periodic table to identify it. Answer: Sn

145. C is correct. The ground state configuration of sulfur is $[Ne]3s^23p^4$. According to Hund's rule, the *p* orbitals separately fill and then start to pair the electrons. The first three *p* electrons fill separate orbitals and then the fourth electron doubles up with two unpaired electrons remaining.

146. E is correct. The masses on the periodic table are the atomic masses of the elements. The atomic mass is a weighted average of the various isotopes of the element (the mass of each isotope multiplied by its abundance). Atomic mass is sometimes called atomic weight, but the term atomic mass is more accurate. This mass is expressed in atomic mass units (amu), also called Daltons (D). 1 amu is equal to 1 g/mol. An amu is defined as one-twelfth the mass of a neutral carbon-12 atom.

147. A is correct. The quantum number *l* refers to the angular momentum of the electron.

See explanation for question **139**.

148. A is correct. Neutrons are the neutral particles located inside the nucleus of an atom. See explanation to question **97** for further discussion.

149. C is correct. Accepting electrons is a characteristic of non-metals to form the same electron configuration of the noble gases (i.e. complete octet).

150. B is correct. Periods are the rows on the periodic table (while groups are the columns on the table). From left to right across a period, the atomic number does increase, but this does not mean that the elements tend to get more metallic. The elements across a period get only incrementally larger in size, since it is just one proton being added to each subsequent element across a period.

The properties of the elements are similar within columns (groups), indicating that they must change across any period of the periodic table.

151. B is correct. Outermost shell: the shell with the largest number. In this problem, that would be 4.

The sum of electrons within the fourth shell: $2 + 1 = 3$

Outermost subshell: the subshell within the shell that has the outermost electron/last added electron. Usually it's the very last orbital in the electron configuration. In this problem, that would be $4p$, which only has 1 electron. Answer: 3, 1

152. E is correct. Radioactive isotopes of atoms lose energy by emitting ionizing radiation. This occurs due to nuclear instability. The instability of nuclei results from the intense conflict between two extremely strong forces, the attractive nuclear force and the repulsive electromagnetic force. If this balance is broken, due to very few or too many neutrons, the isotope is unstable and radioactive decay occurs.

153. D is correct. A period is a horizontal row in the periodic table of elements. A group or family is a vertical column, and elements within groups share similar properties. However, there are regions of the periodic table where horizontal trends are more significant than vertical trends; for example, the actinides and lanthanides form two important series of elements.

154. C is correct. The result of β decay is the transformation of a neutron to a proton and an expelled β electron particle. Therefore, the atomic number increases by one. The original atom lithium ($Z = 3$) is converted to the daughter atom beryllium ($Z = 4$).

155. C is correct.

156. B is correct. In the second shell, there are two subshells (i.e. s and p subshells).

157. C is correct.

158. A is correct. Electrons are the negatively-charged particles (charge -1) located in the electron cloud, orbiting around the nucleus of the atom. Electrons are extremely tiny particles, much smaller than protons and neutrons, and they have a mass of about 5×10^{-4} amu.

159. D is correct. Chlorine has the highest electronegativity which is a characteristic of non-metals.

160. E is correct. Russian chemist Dmitri Mendeleev created the original prototype version of the periodic table of elements, in which he placed elements with the same number of valence electrons in the same horizontal row.

Mendeleev's table was the basis of the modern day periodic table, although our modern day table has an opposite system where elements with the same number of valence electrons are in the same vertical column (i.e. the same group or family) rather than horizontal row. Mendeleev predicted the existence of undiscovered elements, along with their behavior.

161. A is correct. The fastest way to identify an element using the periodic table is by using its atomic number. The atomic number is equal to the number of protons or electrons. In this problem, the total number of electrons can be determined by adding up all the electrons in the provided electron configuration: $2 + 2 + 6 + 2 + 6 + 2 + 10 + 6 + 2 + 1 = 39$. Element #39 in the periodic table is Y.

162. A is correct.

163. D is correct. The magnetic quantum number m_l gives the particular orbitals in a subshell and the orientation of these subshells. The value of m_l depends on the orbital angular momentum quantum number l; it can range from $-l$ to $+l$, and therefore can be a negative integer, zero, or a positive integer. Restrictions on the possible values for m_l and the other quantum numbers gives rise to the pattern of each subshell divided into orbitals that increase by odd numbers. However, the magnetic quantum number does not describe the spin of the electrons; instead, this is done by the spin quantum number s.

164. E is correct.

165. A is correct. Negative ions (anions) are *much larger* than their neutral counterparts while positive ions (cations) are *much smaller*. All examples are isoelectronic because of the same number of electrons.

Options: Br^-, K^+, Ar, Ca^{2+}, Cl^-
Atomic numbers:
$$Cl = 17$$
$$Br = 35$$
$$K = 19$$
$$Ca = 20$$
$$Ar = 18$$

The general trend for atomic radius is to decrease from left to right and increase from top to bottom in the periodic table. When the ion gains or loses an electron to create a new charged ion, its radius would change slightly but the general trend of radius still applies. Cl^-, K^+, Ca^{2+}, and Ar all have identical numbers of electrons. On the other hand, Br is located below Cl and its atomic number is almost twice as high as the others. It means Br has more electrons and its radius must be significantly larger than the other atoms.

166. C is correct.

167. E is correct.

168. D is correct. It takes 5,700 years for 50% (i.e. definition of half-life) of a ^{14}C sample to decay. After only 2,000 years, much less than 50% decays, leaving much more than 50% remaining.

169. A is correct.

170. B is correct. Carbon has an atomic number of 6 and an electron configuration of $1s^2$, $2s^2$, $2p^2$. Therefore, electrons are in the second shell ($n = 2$) and two subshells are in the outermost shell ($l = 1$); only the greatest value of l is given. Therefore, the values of l are 0 and 1 whereby only the largest value of l, ($l = 1$) is reported.

171. B is correct.

172. D is correct. Positive ions (cations) are *much smaller* than their neutral counterparts while negative ions (anions) are *much larger*. Since the size of neutral atoms decreases from left to right across the periodic table, neutral aluminum is larger than neutral sulfur.

173. E is correct.

174. B is correct.

175. C is correct. Silicon atomic number = 14, therefore there are 14 electrons in a neutral silicon atom.

Use Aufbau's Principle to determine the order of orbital filling. Answer: $1s^22s^22p^63s^23p^2$

176. A is correct. The # of electrons = # of protons, and the sum of electrons (2 + 2 + 6 + 2 + 4 = 16) is equivalent to the atomic number.

177. C is correct. Atoms of a given element retain the element's characteristics. Protons, neutrons and electrons are much smaller particles within the atom, and they do not retain an element's characteristics. Molecules are formed by the combination of multiple atoms, and if all the atoms in the molecule are the same (e.g. O_2), they will retain the element's characteristic, but this is not the correct answer because molecules are larger than atoms.

178. E is correct. The attraction of the nucleus on the outermost electrons determines the ionization energy, which increases towards the right and increases up on the periodic table.

179. B is correct.

180. B is correct. Oxygen has 8 electrons. The first shell can hold 2 electrons and the remaining 6 electrons will be located within the orbitals of the next shell.

181. D is correct. One mole of O_2 has a mass of 2 ×16 g = 32 g.

   2.5 moles has a mass of 2.5 × 32 g = 80 g.

182. A is correct.

183. E is correct. The choices correctly describe the spin quantum number.

184. C is correct.

185. B is correct. Electronegativity is a measure of how strongly an element attracts electrons within a bond. Dipole moment depends on the overall shape of the molecule, the length of the bond, and whether the electrons are pulled to one side of the bond (or the molecule overall). For a large dipole moment, one element must pull electrons more strongly (i.e. differences in electronegativity).

186. E is correct. Electron configuration: $1s^22s^22p^63s^23p^64s^1$

There are two ways to obtain the proper answer to this problem:

1. Using atomic number: calculate the atomic number by adding up all the electrons.

   2 + 2 + 6 + 2 + 6 + 1 = 19

Find element number 19 in the periodic table. Once the element is identified, check the group where it is located to see other elements that belong to the same group.

Element number 19 is potassium (K), so the element that belong to the same group (IA) is Lithium (Li).

2. Using subshell: identify the outermost subshell and use it to identify its group in the periodic table. In this problem, the outermost subshell is 4s1.

Relationship between outermost subshell and group:

s1 = Group IA
s2 = Group IIA
p1 = Group IIIA
p2 = Group IVA
…
p6 = Group VIII A
d = transition element
f = lanthanide/actinide element

187. A is correct.

188. C is correct. The *s* subshell contains 1 orbital, the *p* has 3 orbitals, the *d* has 5 orbitals, and the *f* has 7 orbitals.

189. A is correct.

190. D is correct. n, l, m_l and m_s.

191. E is correct.

192. D is correct.

193. B is correct. Atoms with electrical charge are referred to as ions. If an atom gains electrons, it becomes negatively charged and is called an anion. If an atom loses electrons, it becomes positively charged and is called a cation.

An element is a pure chemical substance that consists of a single type of atom. A compound is a chemical substance that consists of two or more elements. Isotopes of a particular element have different numbers of neutrons, although they have the same number of protons. Some isotopes may be radioactive, meaning that the nucleus of the atom is unstable, causing it to emit ionizing radiation.

194. C is correct. The mass of one mole of H atoms is 1 g. Glucose contains 12 H atoms; one mole of glucose contains 12 g of hydrogen. Three moles of glucose contain 3×12 g = 36 g of hydrogen.

195. A is correct. Electrons cannot be precisely located in space at any point in time and orbitals describe probability regions for finding the electrons. In terms of shape, *s* subshells are spherically symmetrical, *p* orbitals have a dumbbell shape, and *d* orbitals have four lobes.

196. C is correct. The transition metals occur in groups 3-12 (vertical columns) of the period table. They occur in periods 4-7 (horizontal rows). Transition metals are defined as elements that have a partially-filled *d* or *f* subshell in a common oxidative state. This group of elements includes silver, iron and copper.

197. D is correct.

198. E is correct.

199. B is correct. A sulfur atom contains 16 electrons. $1s^2 2s^2 2p^6 3s^2 3p^4$ is the electronic configuration of a ground-state sulfur atom.

200. D is correct.

201. B is correct. Energy depends primarily on *n*.

202. E is correct.

203. D is correct.

204. D is correct. Chlorine completes its octet when it gains an electron so chlorine atoms form anions (i.e. gain electrons) much more easily than form cations (i.e. lose electrons).

205. A is correct.

B: Hunds' rule describes that the electrons enter each orbital of a given type singly and with identical spins before any pairing of electrons of opposite spin occurs within those orbitals.

C: Heisenberg's uncertainty principle states that it is impossible to accurately determine both the momentum and the position of an electron simultaneously.

206. A is correct.

207. B is correct. *l* must be less than *n* while m_l must be less than or equal to *l*.

208. E is correct.

209. C is correct.

210. C is correct.

211. D is correct. For *n*=3, *s*, *p*, and *d* orbitals exist. Two electrons can occupy the *s* orbitals, six electrons can occupy the *p* orbitals, and ten electrons can occupy the *d* orbitals. Note, the *n* = 4 shell starts filling before the *n* = 3 shell is complete (however, not relevant for this question).

212. C is correct. The vast majority of elements on the periodic table (over 100 elements) are metals. There are about four times more metals than nonmetals.

213. A is correct.

214. D is correct. In the ground state, the 2*s* subshell should be filled and then followed by the 2*p* subshell for the configuration of a neutral atom. $1s^2 2s^2 3s^1$ represents the excited state for boron.

215. E is correct. The specific, characteristic line spectra for atoms result from photons being emitted when excited electrons drop to lower energy levels.

216. C is correct. Atoms in excited states have electrons in lower energy orbitals promoted to higher energy orbitals.

The electron configuration of potassium in ground state is $1s^2\ 2s^2\ 2p^6\ 3s^2\ 3p^6\ 4s^1$

A: has only 18 electrons, not the 19 electrons of potassium.

B: has 20 electrons, not the 19 electrons of potassium.

217. B is correct. According to the Bohr Model and quantum theory, the energy levels of the electron occur at quantified and calculable energies. For hydrogen the energy of each level is found by:

$$E = -13.6 \text{ eV}/n^2$$

The negative is by convention to indicate that this would be the amount of energy needed to ionize the electron completely. D is not correct because the electron can be at higher energy levels although there is just one.

218. B is correct.

219. A is correct. Only photons are released as electrons move from higher to lower energy orbitals.

Alpha particles are helium nuclei and beta particles are electrons.

220. A is correct. Second period elements lack *d* orbitals and cannot have more than four bonds to the central atom.

221. E is correct.

222. B is correct. Alpha decay results in the loss of two protons while ordinary beta decay results in the gain of one proton. Since isotopes of the same element have the same number of protons, the number of protons lost by α decay must equal the number gained by β decay. Therefore, twice as many β decays as α decays occurs for a ratio of 1:2 for α to β decay.

223. B is correct. Metalloids, which include the elements boron, silicon and arsenic, are found along the stair-step line of the period table which divides metals and nonmetals. They have properties between metals and nonmetals. They typically have a metallic appearance but are only fair conductors of electricity (as opposed to metals which are excellent conductors). Metalloids tend to be brittle, and chemically they behave more like nonmetals.

224. D is correct. Ions often have the same electronic configuration as neutral atoms of a different element (e.g. F$^-$ is isoelectronic with Ne), but this is not always true for exited states. An ion can have any electron configuration that is consistent with the rules of quantum numbers.

225. A is correct. The order for filling subshells by electrons is 1*s*, 2*s*, 3*p*, 3*s*, 3*p*, 4*p*, 5*s*, 4*d*, 5*p*, and so forth.

226. C is correct. In the ground state, the 3*p* orbitals fill before the 3*d* orbitals.

Chapter 2.   CHEMICAL BONDS

1. D is correct. In PO_4^{3-}, the central atom is P and it has 5 electrons. To reach stability, it will need 3 more electrons. 3 oxygen atoms will each donate one electron to create a single covalent bond with phosphate. After creating those bonds, phosphate has 8 total electrons and has reached stability. It still has a free electron pair, which is used to form a coordinate covalent bond with the fourth oxygen atom. The other 3 oxygen atoms will each gain an electron to reach stability, which will result in a negatively-charged phosphate ion.

Calculate the formal charges. Remember that electrons in covalent coordinate bonds are treated as free electrons.

Phosphate:

   5 valence electrons – 3 bonding pairs – 2 electrons in covalent coordinate bond = 0

For each of the 3 oxygens that gained an electron:

   6 valence electrons – 5 free electron – 1 bonding pair – 1 gained electron = –1

Oxygen with coordinate covalent bond:

   6 valence electrons – 6 free electrons = 0

(This oxygen didn't contribute any electrons to the coordinate bond.)

Total charge of ion: –3

Because there are 4 oxygen atoms, there are 4 possible combinations in which one of the oxygen atoms has covalent coordinate bond with phosphate and the remaining 3 atoms are attached to phosphate. Therefore PO_4^{3-} has 4 resonance structures.

2. C is correct.

3. E is correct. In atoms or molecules that are ions, the number of electrons is not equal to the number of protons, which gives the molecule a charge (either positive or negative). Oppositely charged ions are attracted to each other and this attraction result in ionic bonds. In an ionic bond, electron(s) are transferred from a metal to a nonmetal, giving both molecules a full valence shell and causing the molecules to closely associate with each other.

4. C is correct. Chlorine belongs to group VIIA/17 in the periodic table, which means that it has 7 valence electrons. To reach stability, it has to have 8 electrons. To do so, a chloride ion will gain an electron and end up with 8 electrons.

5. A is correct.

6. B is correct.

7. D is correct. The valence shell is the outermost shell of electrons around an atom. Atoms with a complete valence shell (i.e. containing the maximum number of electrons), such as the noble gases, are the most non-reactive elements. Atoms with only one electron in their valence shells (alkali metals) or those just missing one electron from a complete valence shell (halogens) are the most reactive elements.

8. C is correct. In a metaphosphate ion, the phosphorus atom is bonded to 3 oxygen atoms. Two of those bonds are single covalent bonds and the oxygen atoms have an extra electron each. The remaining oxygen has a double bond with phosphate.

Because there are three different oxygen atoms with different bond types, there are 3 possible resonance structures.

9. B is correct. Cations have fewer electrons than protons, which gives them an overall positive charge. Anions have more electrons than protons, which gives them an overall negative charge.

10. A is correct. The molecular weight alone is not sufficient because two different compounds might have similar molecular weights. Additionally, the % by mass alone is not sufficient because it yields only the empirical formula.

If both molecular mass and % by mass are known, the empirical formula can be multiplied by a factor to determine the molecular weight. Use that constant to multiply the coefficients in the empirical formula to determine the molecular formula.

11. E is correct. Ionic bonds involve electrostatic interactions between oppositely charged atoms. Electrons from the metallic atom are transferred to the nonmetallic atom, giving both atoms a full valence shell.

12. A is correct.

13. B is correct. Ionization energy is the minimum amount of energy required to remove an electron from an atom or molecule in its gaseous state. When this electron (usually the outermost or highest-energy electron) is removed, the atom constitutes a positive ion because it now has more protons than electrons.

14. D is correct.

15. E is correct.

16. C is correct. To find the total number of valence electrons in a sulfite ion, SO_3^{2-}, start by adding the valence electrons of each atom:

Sulfur = 6

Oxygen = $6 \times 3 = 18$

Total = 24

This ion has a net charge of –2, which indicates that it has 2 extra electrons. Therefore the total number of valence electrons would be $24 + 2 = 26$ electrons.

17. B is correct. In the electron configuration $1s^2 2s^2 2p^6 3s^2 3p^5$, valence electrons are located in the outermost shell, which in this case is n = 3. All electrons in level 3 orbitals are included in the calculation. Total number of electrons = $2 + 5 = 7$.

18. C is correct. Ions do not have the same number of electrons and protons, giving them either a positive or negative electrical charge. If they have more electrons than protons, they are negatively charged and are called anions. If they have more protons than electrons, they are positively charged and are called cations.

19. D is correct. Covalently bonded compounds that involve unequal sharing of electrons due to large electronegativity differences between the atoms are polar covalent. However, with little or no difference in electronegativity between the atoms, it is a nonpolar covalent bond. But in either case, the electrons are shared so that each atom acquires a noble gas configuration. Therefore, I and II are true.

III is false because ionic bonds (in dry conditions) are considered stronger than covalent bonds. In aqueous conditions, ionic bonds are weak and the compound spontaneously dissociates into ions (e.g. table salt in a glass of water).

20. A is correct.

21. D is correct.

22. E is correct. Halogen atoms are located in group VII/17, which means that they have 7 valence electrons. If n is the outermost shell of the halogen, the 7 electrons will occupy s and p orbitals in ns^2np^5 configuration.

When this halogen atom becomes an ion, it gains one electron. This extra electron will occupy the remaining free space in the outermost p orbital, and the new electron configuration is ns^2np^6.

23. B is correct. Two electrons form a covalent bond.

24. E is correct.

25. A is correct. The valence shell is the outermost shell of an atom. Electron dot structure (also known Lewis dot structure) is a visual representation of the valence electron configuration around an atom. It is drawn by placing dots that represent valence electrons around a chemical symbol.

1A								0
H·	2A		3A	4A	5A	6A	7A	He:
Li·	Be·		·B·	·C·	·N·	:O·	:F:	:Ne:

26. A is correct. Covalent bonds are chemical bonds that involve the sharing of electron pairs between atoms. These electrons can be shared equally (if the atoms have the same electronegativity) or unequally (if the electrons have different electronegativity).

However, the answer must be "covalent" because the other choices do not involve the sharing of electrons at all. Ionic bonds involve the transfer of electrons, while dipole, London and van der Waals are weak intermolecular forces.

27. D is correct.

28. B is correct.

29. E is correct. Hybridization of the central atom and the corresponding molecular geometry: sp – linear, sp^2 – trigonal planar, sp^3 – tetrahedral, sp^3d – trigonal bipyramid.

30. D is correct.

31. B is correct. The octet rule states that atoms of main-group elements tend to combine in a way that each atom has eight electrons in its valence shell. This occurs because electron arrangements involving eight valence electrons are extremely stable, as is the case with the noble gasses.

32. E is correct. Covalently bounded substances are poor conductors, have lower melting points and exist in solid, liquid and gaseous forms.

33. D is correct. Salt crystals are held together by ionic bonds. Salts are composed of cations and anions and are electrically neutral. When salts are dissolved, and they split into their constituent ions by breaking of noncovalent interactions.

The hydrogen atoms in water molecule are covalently bonded to the oxygen atom.

Hydrogen peroxide molecule has one more oxygen atom than water molecule does, and is also held together by covalent bonds.

Hydrolysis of an ester breaks covalent bonds to split it into its constituent carboxylic acid and alcohol.

34. B is correct.

35. A is correct.

36. C is correct.

37. A is correct. The noble gas configuration simply refers to eight electrons in the atom's outermost valence shell. Depending on how many electrons it starts with, an atom may have to lose, gain or share an electron to obtain the noble gas configuration.

38. E is correct. Bond energy is related to bond dissociation energy (i.e. energy required to break a bond). Bond length is inversely related to bond strength. Therefore, longer bonds have less strength and lower bond energy.

39. C is correct.

40. A is correct. $Na_3N \rightarrow 3Na^+ + N^{3-}$

Each sodium ion loses one electron to form Na^+ ions.

Nitrogen gains 3 electrons to form N^{3-} ion.

41. C is correct.

42. D is correct.

43. B is correct.

44. E is correct. In covalent bonds, the electrons can be shared either equally or unequally. If the covalent bond is between atoms of different electronegativities, the electrons will be shared unequally, resulting in what is known as a polar covalent bond. An example of this is water, where there is a polar covalent bond between oxygen and hydrogen. This is why water is considered to be a polar molecule.

45. A is correct. N, F and O, bonded directly to hydrogen, participate in hydrogen bonds.

46. C is correct.

47. D is correct.

48. C is correct.

49. E is correct. The choice that states that formulas of ionic compounds are written with the anion first, followed by the cation is incorrect. Formulas of ionic compounds are written with the cation first, followed by the anion. A common example is Na^+Cl^-, which is the formula for sodium chloride. Na^+ is the symbol for the positively-charged sodium cation, while Cl^- is the symbol for the negatively-charged chloride anion.

All the other statements are true of ionic compounds.

50. D is correct. Bond formation decreases entropy and is always exothermic. Bond breaking is always endothermic and requires energy.

51. C is correct. Polar molecules have dipole moments due to non-uniform distributions of charge. A partial positive charge may be on one side of the atom, while a partial negative charge is on the other side.

52. B is correct.

53. A is correct. The oxygen and two hydrogens of a water molecule are held together by covalent bonds, which involve the sharing of electron pairs. It is a polar covalent bond because the electrons are closer to the oxygen than the hydrogen. Although water molecule can engage in hydrogen bonding with other water molecules due to this polar nature, this is not the bond that is holding its atoms together.

54. E is correct. Complete symmetry around the central atom is necessary for the molecule to be nonpolar. For example, H_2O is a bent molecule that lacks symmetry because both pairs of lone pair electrons are on the same side of the central atom.

55. B is correct.

56. D is correct. Covalent bonds involve the sharing of electrons. When the atoms involved in a covalent bond are of the same electronegativity, the electrons are shared equally resulting in a nonpolar covalent bond. When the atoms are of different electronegativity, the electrons are shared unequally resulting in a polar covalent bond.

57. A is correct.

$$Cs\ (g) + Br\ (g) \rightarrow Cs^+\ (g) + Br^-\ (g)$$

Separate the reaction into half-reactions of each element.

$$Br\ (g) \rightarrow Br^-\ (g)\ :\ \text{electron affinity}$$

Electron affinity is the amount of energy released by a mole of gaseous atom to capture one electron.

$$Cs\ (g) \rightarrow Cs^+\ (g)\ :\ \text{ionization energy}$$

Ionization energy is the amount of energy required to remove one electron from each atom in a mole of gaseous element.

To obtain the overall reaction enthalpy, add the two provided values:

$$376\ kJ/mol + (-325\ kJ/mol) = 51\ kJ/mol$$

58. C is correct.

59. B is correct.

60. E is correct. Both positively charged nuclei pull on the bonding electrons.

61. A is correct.

62. D is correct.

63. B is correct. The hydrogens and oxygen in water molecule are held together by covalent bonds. However, the electrons are closer to the oxygen nucleus than the hydrogen nucleus, due to the geometry of the molecule and the electronegativity difference between oxygen and hydrogen. This gives oxygen a partial negative charge and the hydrogens a partial positive charge.

64. D is correct.

65. D is correct.

66. B is correct.

67. E is correct. In a compound, the sum of ionic charges must equal to zero. For the charges of K^+ and CO_3^{2-} to even out, there has to be 2 K^+ ions for every CO_3^{2-} ion. The formula of this balanced molecule is K_2CO_3.

68. A is correct. Polar molecules have high boiling points because of polar interaction. H-bonding is a polar interaction involving hydrogen forming bonds to the electronegative atoms such of F, O or N that accounts for the high boiling points of water.

69. C is correct.

70. D is correct.

71. C is correct.

72. C is correct.

73. E is correct. The total number of valence electrons in a molecule is equal to the sum of valence electrons in each atom.

Check the periodic table to determine valence electrons of each element.

For SOF_2:

$S = 6$

$O = 6$

$F = 2 \times 7 = 14$

Total electrons: $6 + 6 + 14 = 26$

74. A is correct. Atomic nuclei are positively charged, while electrons are negatively charged. A chemical bond is an attraction between two atoms, and it is caused by the electrostatic force of attraction between the oppositely charged nuclei and electrons.

75. E is correct.

76. A is correct.

77. B is correct.

78. A is correct.

79. B is correct.

80. E is correct. Lattice energy is the energy released when one mole of solid compound is created from its gaseous ions.

For NaCl, the lattice energy is represented by this reaction: $Na^+ (g) + Cl^- (g) \rightarrow NaCl (s)$

Arrange the provided reactions so when they are all added up, all other terms will cancel and the remaining reaction is the lattice reaction described above. When reversing a reaction, change the positive/negative sign of ΔH.

$$Na (s) + \tfrac{1}{2}Cl_2 (g) \rightarrow NaCl (s) \quad \Delta H = -411 \text{ kJ}$$

$$Na (g) \rightarrow Na (s) \quad \Delta H = -108 \text{ kJ}$$

$$Cl (g) \rightarrow \tfrac{1}{2}Cl_2 (g) \quad \Delta H = -120 \text{ kJ}$$

$$Cl^- (g) \rightarrow Cl (g) + e^- \quad \Delta H = +349 \text{ kJ}$$

$$Na^+ (g) + e^- \rightarrow Na (g) \quad \Delta H = -496 \text{ kJ}$$

$$\overline{Na^+ (g) + Cl^- (g) \rightarrow NaCl (s) \quad \Delta H = -786 \text{ kJ}} \quad (+)$$

81. B is correct.

82. A is correct. Covalent bonds involve the sharing of electron pairs between atoms. Covalent single bonds involve the sharing of one electron pair, while covalent double bonds involve the sharing of two electron pairs. Double bonds are stronger and shorter than single bonds.

83. D is correct. Positively charged nuclei repel each other while each attracts the bonding electrons. These opposing forces reach equilibrium at the bond length.

84. A is correct. Start by analyzing the boiling points. A higher boiling point indicates stronger intermolecular forces. Molecules with higher dipole moment have stronger intermolecular bonds compared to non-polar molecules. X has a higher boiling point than Y, which means X is most likely more polar than Y.

Next, consider the fact that X and Y are not miscible. This most likely means that one of them is polar and the other one is nonpolar. This fact supports the hypothesis that X is more polar than Y: if X has strong polar characteristics, it'll be the more polar component and it won't be miscible with the nonpolar Y.

85. E is correct. Not all elements can form double or triple covalent bonds because there must be at least two vacancies in an atom's valence electron shell for the double bond formation, and at least three vacancies for triple bond formation. The elements of Group VIIA have seven valence electrons with one vacancy. Therefore, all covalent bonds formed by these elements are single covalent bonds.

86. C is correct.

87. E is correct.

88. C is correct.

89. B is correct.

90. A is correct. Van der Waals forces involve nonpolar (hydrophobic) molecules such as hydrocarbons. The van der Waals force is the sum total of attractive or repulsive forces between molecules, and therefore can be either attractive or repulsive. It can include the force between two permanent dipoles, the force between a permanent dipole and a temporary dipole, or the force between two temporary dipoles. The question provides just one of the possibilities for a van der Waals force.

91. B is correct.

92. E is correct.

93. D is correct. Ionic bonds involve electrostatic interactions between oppositely charged atoms, and electrons from a metal atom are transferred to a non-metal atom, giving both atoms a full valence shell. The resulting charged particles are arranged in a highly ordered microscopic structure known as a crystalline network.

94. D is correct.

95. E is correct. A double bond consists of a sigma (single) and a pi bond (π) whereby a single bond has only a sigma bond. Pi bonds are weaker than sigma bonds. Thus a double bond (sigma and pi) is stronger than a single bond (sigma only) but not as strong as two single bonds (sigma and sigma). Therefore, a double bond has less energy per pair of electron than a single bond.

96. D is correct.

97. A is correct.

98. C is correct.

99. C is correct.

100. C is correct.

101. A is correct. Use the provided formula to calculate potential energy for each molecule of NaCl:

$$E = q_1 q_2 / k \cdot r$$

$$E = (1.602 \times 10^{-19}\,C)\,(-1.602 \times 10^{-19}\,C)\,/\,1.11 \times 10^{-10}\,C^2\,J^{-1}\,m^{-1} \times 282 \times 10^{-12}\,m$$

$$E = -8.20 \times 10^{-19}\,J$$

That's for one NaCl molecule. Now calculate the energy released for one mole of NaCl:

$$-8.20 \times 10^{-19}\,J\,\times 6.02 \times 10^{23}\,mol^{-1} = -493{,}640\,J \approx -494\,kJ/mol$$

102. E is correct.

103. D is correct.

104. C is correct. $14\,/\,(14 + [2 \times 16]) = 14\,/\,(14 + 32) = = 14\,/\,(46) = 30.4\%$

105. B is correct.

106. E is correct.

107. D is correct. The water spider can walk on the surface of water because the water molecules are held very close together. This is known as the cohesive property of water (H_2O), which gives the water surface tension, causing it to acquire the least surface area possible.

108. C is correct.

109. D is correct.

110. B is correct.

111. C is correct. Intermolecular forces are between molecules. Dipole-dipole interactions primarily occur between different molecules whereas ionic bonds, covalent and coordinate covalent bonds hold molecules together (i.e. intramolecular forces).

112. B is correct.

113. E is correct.

114. C is correct.

115. D is correct.

116. B is correct. Resonance spreads the double-bond character equally among all three C—S bonds.

117. A is correct.

118. E is correct.

119. B is correct.

120. E is correct.

121. C is correct.

122. A is correct.

123. A is correct.

124. D is correct.

125. A is correct. $C_3H_7NH_2$ ($9 \times 1 + 14 = 23$) has a slightly lower mass compared to C_3H_7OH ($8 \times 1 + 16 = 24$).

126. B is correct.

127. C is correct.

128. B is correct.

129. E is correct. Hydrogen bonds are the strongest intermolecular (between molecules) forces, followed by dipole-dipole and then van der Waals forces (weakest intermolecular).

130. D is correct. Electronegativity is a chemical property υσεδ το describe an atom's tendency to attract electrons towards itself. The most common use of electronegativity pertains to bond polarity. Generally, the greater the difference in electronegativity between two atoms, the more polar of a bond these atoms would form whereby the atom with the higher electronegativity would be the negative end of the dipole.

131. A is correct.

132. D is correct.

133. C is correct.

134. E is correct. OCl_6 is a common industrial chemical.

A: hydrogen forms a negative ion in NaH (sodium hydride) or $LiAlH_4$.

B: lead, although not a transition metal does have two common valences: +2 and +4.

C: fluorine in SF_6 does not have an expanded octet because each F is bonded only to S. The sulfur has an expanded octet but it is in the 3rd row of the periodic table and has empty d orbitals.

135. A is correct.

136. D is correct. Formula to calculate dipole moment:

$$\mu = qr$$

where μ is dipole moment (unit: coulomb per meter or C/m), q is charge (unit: coulomb or C), and r is radius (unit: meter or m)

Convert the unit of dipole moment from Debye to C/m.

The conversion factor is $1\ D = 3.34 \times 10^{-30}$ C/m

$$0.16\ D \times 3.34 \times 10^{-30}\ C/m\ D^{-1} = 5.34 \times 10^{-31}\ C/m$$

Convert the unit of radius to meter:

$$115\ pm \times 1 \times 10^{-12}\ m/pm = 115 \times 10^{-12}\ m$$

Rearrange the dipole moment equation to solve for q:

$$q = \mu / r$$
$$q = 5.34 \times 10^{-31}\ C/m / 115 \times 10^{-12}\ m$$
$$q = 4.65 \times 10^{-21}\ C$$

Express the charge in terms of electron charge (e). Each electron has a charge of 1.602×10^{-19} C.

$$4.65 \times 10^{-21}\ C / 1.602 \times 10^{-19}\ C/e = 0.029\ e$$

In this NO molecule, oxygen is the more electronegative atom. Because of that, the charge experienced by the oxygen atom will be negative: $-0.029\ e$.

137. A is correct.

138. C is correct.

139. D is correct. CCl_4 has an atomic mass of:

$$12g + (4 \times 35.5g) = 154$$
$$Cl = 4 \times (35.5g) = 142$$

The % by mass $= 142/154 \times 100 = 92.2\%$

140. E is correct.

141. B is correct.

142. B is correct.

143. A is correct.

144. C is correct. Ionic crystals are most stable when the arrangement of ions and cations is closest while repulsion forces are minimized.

145. A is correct.

146. E is correct.

147. B is correct.

148. D is correct. Total mass is about 50 with the mass of hydrogen $(2 \times 1) = 2$. 2/50 is about 0.04 or 4% hydrogen.

A: total mass is $35.5 + 2 \times 12 + 5 \times 1 =$ about 65. Five Hs have a % by mass of about 5/65, which is greater than 4%.

B: total mass is $2 \times 35.5 + 12 + 2 \times 1 = 85$. Two Hs have a % by mass of 2/85 for the H which is less than 4%.

C: % by mass of H in $ClCH_3$: $35.5 + 12 + 3 \times 1 =$ about 50. H: $3 \times 1 = 3$. 3/50 = about 0.06.

149. C is correct. Formula to calculate dipole moment:

$$\mu = qr$$

where μ is dipole moment (unit: coulomb per meter or C/m), q is charge (unit: coulomb or C), and r is radius (unit: meter or m)

Convert the unit of radius to meter:

$$154 \text{ pm} \times 1 \times 10^{-12} \text{ m/pm} = 154 \times 10^{-12} \text{ m}$$

Convert the charge to coulomb:

$$0.167 \, e \times 1.602 \times 10^{-19} \text{ C/e}^- = 2.68 \times 10^{-20} \text{ C}$$

Use these values to calculate dipole moment:

$$\mu = qr$$
$$\mu = 2.68 \times 10^{-20} \text{ C} \times 154 \times 10^{-12} \text{ m}$$
$$\mu = 4.13 \times 10^{-30} \text{ C·m}$$

Finally, convert the dipole moment to Debye:

$$4.13 \times 10^{-30} \text{ C·m} \, / \, 3.34 \times 10^{-30} \text{ C·m·D}^{-1} = 1.24 \text{ D}$$

150. E is correct.

151. D is correct.

152. B is correct. The molecular weight is approximately 99. Determine the molecular weight. Note, unlike % by mass, there is no division. $Cl_2C_2H_4$: $2 \times 35.5g + 2 \times 12g + 4 \times 1g = 99g$.

153. E is correct.

154. A is correct.

155. B is correct.

156. C is correct.

CH_3COOH has two C, four H and two O. Reduce by dividing by two.

157. C is correct.

158. B is correct.

159. E is correct.

160. A is correct. HO has a hydrogen fraction $1 / (1 \text{ g} + 16 \text{ g}) = 0.06 = 6\%$.

H_2O has twice the H for greater than 10% for H.

The others are not empirical formulae.

161. D is correct.

162. C is correct. H_2CO molecule has a C=O bond and two C–H bonds. Because the bonds are between different atoms, there will be a difference in dipole moment and this will result in three polar bonds.

163. D is correct.

164. E is correct.

165. B is correct.

166. A is correct.

Chapter 3.   STATES OF MATTER: GASES, LIQUIDS, SOLIDS

1. C is correct. Boyle's law (sometimes called Mariotte's law or the Boyle-Mariotte Law) is an experimental gas law that describes how the volume of a gas tends to increase as the pressure tends to decrease (i.e. they are inversely proportional), as long as the temperature is constant. This law is often expressed using the formula $P_1V_1 = P_2V_2$.

2. B is correct.

3. E is correct. Add 273 to the temperature in °C. 212 °F = boiling water which is equivalent to 100 °C, and 100 °C + 273 = 373.

Or convert °F to °C using the formula:

°C = 5/9 (°F – 32), then add 100 to the °C value.

4. A is correct. Gases do *not* have definite volumes and shapes; rather they take up the volume and shape of the container that they are in. This is different from both liquids (which have a definite volume, but take up the shape of the container that they are in) and solids (which have both a definite volume and a definite shape). Ideal gases are modeled as having perfectly elastic collisions, meaning that they have no intermolecular interactions. Essentially, the molecules in a gas are separate from one another.

5. E is correct. Gases always form homogeneous mixtures, regardless of the identities or relative proportions of the component gases. There is a relatively long distance between gas molecules (as opposed to solids or liquids where the molecules are much closer together). When a pressure is applied to gas, its volume readily decreases, and thus gases are highly compressible. There are no attractive forces between gas molecules, which is why molecules of a gas can move about freely.

6. C is correct.

7. A is correct. Deposition, also known as desublimation, is the name given to the thermodynamic process where gas transitions directly into a solid. An example of deposition occurs in sub-freezing air, when water vapor changes directly to ice without becoming a liquid.

8. C is correct. At –40 °, the temperature is the same in °C and °F.

9. B is correct. Difference of mercury height on both necks indicates the capacity of a manometer. In this problem, the difference is 800mm – 180mm = 620 mm.

Historically, the pressure unit of torr is set to equal 1 mmHg, or the rise/dip of 1 mm of mercury in a manometer. Because this manometer uses mercury, the height difference (620 mm) is equal to its measuring capacity in torr (620 torr).

10. D is correct. Liquids have a definite volume, but take up the shape of the container than they are in. Liquids have moderate intermolecular attractions, compared to the strong intermolecular attractions of solids (that consist of tightly-packed molecules) and weak, almost non-existent, intermolecular attractions of gas molecules (that move freely).

11. C is correct. Scientists realized that the relationships between pressure, temperature and volume of a sample of gas hold true for all gases, and the gas laws were developed. These include Boyle's Law ($P_1V_1 = P_2V_2$), Charles' Law ($V_1/T_1 = V_2/T_2$), and Gay-Lussac's Law ($P_1/T_1 = P_2/T_2$).

12. A is correct. The combined gas law ($PV = k_5T$) states that *the pressure exerted by a gas is inversely proportional to its volume and directly proportional to its temperature in Kelvin.* It is a combination of Boyle's Law ($P_1V_1 = P_2V_2$), Charles' Law ($V_1/T_1 = V_2/T_2$), and Gay-Lussac's Law ($P_1/T_1 = P_2/T_2$).

13. D is correct.

14. E is correct. $PV = nRT$, units of R can be calculated by $R = PV/nT = 1 \cdot atm/mol \cdot K$.

15. E is correct.

16. A is correct.

17. B is correct. Dalton's law, also called Dalton's law of partial pressures, states that *the pressure exerted by a mixture of gases is equal to the sum of the individual gas pressures.* It is an empirical law that was observed by English chemist John Dalton, and is related to the ideal gas laws.

18. A is correct.

19. D is correct. To obtain volume percent of Ar, first set the total and partial volume/mole conditions of Ar equal to each other:

$$(V_T / n_T) = (V_{Ar} / n_{Ar})$$

Solve for the volume of Ar:

$$V_{Ar} = (0.600 \text{ moles Ar}) \times [(6.50 \text{ L total}) / (1.10 \text{ moles total})]$$

$$V_{Ar} = 3.55 \text{ L Ar}$$

Then divide partial volume of Ar by total volume of flask, and multiply by 100%:

$$V_{Ar}\% = [(3.55 \text{ L Ar}) / (6.50 \text{ L total})] \times 100\% = 54.5\%$$

20. E is correct.

21. B is correct.

22. D is correct. For exothermic reactions, the vapor pressure deviates negatively for Raoult's law. Depending upon the ratios of the liquids in solution, the vapor pressure could be lower than either or just lower than *X* because *X* is a higher boiling point thus a lower vapor pressure. The boiling point has increased from *Y* because the vapor pressure decreased.

23. C is correct.

24. D is correct. The pressure of a gas is the force that it exerts on the walls of its container. This is essentially the frequency and energy with which the gas molecules collide with the container's walls.

Partial pressure refers to the individual pressure of a gas that is in a mixture of gases.

Vapor pressure refers to the pressure of a vapor in thermodynamic equilibrium with its solid or liquid phases.

Atmospheric pressure is the pressure exerted by the weight of air in the atmosphere.

25. B is correct.

26. B is correct.

190 torr = 190 mm Hg

760 mm Hg = 1 atm. 190/760 = 0.25 atm

27. C is correct. Solids have a definite shape and volume. For example, a block of granite will not change its shape or its volume regardless of the container in which it is placed. Molecules in a solid are very tightly packed due to the strong intermolecular attractions, which prevents the molecules from moving around.

28. E is correct.

29. A is correct.

30. C is correct.

31. B is correct. The molecules of an ideal gas exert no attractive forces. Therefore, a real gas behaves most nearly like an ideal gas when it is at high temperature and low pressure, because under these conditions the molecules are far apart from each other and exert little or no attractive forces on each other.

32. D is correct.

33. B is correct.

34. E is correct. The ideal gas law is PV = nRT, where P is pressure, V is volume, n is the number of molecules, R is the ideal gas constant, and T is temperature of the gas. Therefore, decreasing the volume, increasing temperature or increasing the number of molecules would all increase the pressure of a gas.

35. A is correct.

36. E is correct. Ideal gases occupy no volume and do not exhibit *inter*molecular forces.

37. B is correct. Start by applying Boyle's Law:

$(P_1V_1) = (P_2V_2)$

Solve for the final volume:

$V_2 = [(0.983 \text{ atm}) \times (4.626 \text{ L})] / (1.388 \text{ atm})]$

$V_2 = 3.28 \text{ L}$

38. D is correct. Gas molecules are further apart than liquid molecules, which is why gases have a smaller density. Because there is such a large amount of space between each molecule in a gas, the extent to which the gas molecules can be pushed together is much larger than the extent to which liquid molecules can be pushed together. Therefore, gases have a greater compressibility than liquids.

39. B is correct. Start by applying Boyle's Law:

$$(P_1V_1) = (P_2V_2)$$

Solve for the final pressure:

$$P_2 = [(280 \text{ torr}) \times (8.00 \text{ L } O_2)] / (14.0 \text{ L } O_2)]$$

$$P_2 = 160 \text{ torr}$$

Notice that pressure units are left in torr.

40. A is correct.

Start by applying Boyle's Law:

$$(P_1V_1) = (P_2V_2)$$

Solve for the final pressure:

$$P_2 = [(75.0 \text{ psi}) \times (0.100 \text{ L Kr})] / (0.450 \text{ L})]$$

$$P_2 = 16.7 \text{ psi}$$

Notice that pressure units are left in psi.

41. E is correct.

42. D is correct. Evaporation is the phase change from a liquid to a gas. This occurs in the Earth's water cycle, when solar energy heats water and causes it to evaporate and become water vapor. Evaporation is an endothermic process (i.e. heat is absorbed).

43. C is correct. The kinetic-molecular theory defines temperature in terms of the *average* speed of the molecules and assumes differences in speed.

44. C is correct.

45. E is correct. Start by applying Charles' Law:

$$(V_1 / T_1) = (V_2 / T_2)$$

Solve for the final temperature:

$$T_2 = (0.050 \text{ L } N_2) \times [(420 \text{ K}) / (0.100 \text{ L } N_2)]$$

$$T_2 = 210 \text{ K}$$

Notice that we keep in mind the correct number of significant figures.

46. A is correct.

47. E is correct. The kinetic theory assumes random motion of molecules, elastic collisions, no significant volume occupied by molecules, and little attraction between molecules. It also assumes, at the same temperature, that the average kinetic energy of molecules of different gases is the same, regardless of differences in mass.

48. C is correct. Start by applying the ideal gas equation:

$$PV = nRT$$

Next, convert the given temperature units from Celsius to Kelvin:

$T_1 = 22.4°C + 273 = 295.4$ K

$T_2 = 184.4°C + 273 = 457.4$ K

Set the initial and final P/V/T conditions equal to each other:

$(P_1 V_1 / T_1) = (P_2 V_2 / T_2)$

Solve for the final pressure:

$P_2 = [(457.4$ K$) \times (772.2$ torr$) \times (16.44$ L$)] / [(16.60$ L$) \times (295.4$ K$)]$

$P_2 = 1{,}184$ torr

49. D is correct. Condensation is the transition from the gas phase to the liquid phase. It is an essential part of the Earth's water cycle. Condensation occurs when atmospheric water vapor in clouds condenses to form droplets of liquid water that become heavy enough to fall due to gravity, which results in rain.

50. D is correct. When the temperature of a gas increases or decreases, the kinetic energy of the gas correspondingly increases or decreases. An increase in kinetic energy results in a more rapid motion of the molecules, and this rapid motion results in the breaking of intermolecular bonds. The breaking of bonds allows molecules to escape from the solution, thus affecting the solubility of gas molecules.

51. A is correct. Start by applying Boyle's Law:

$(P_1 V_1) = (P_2 V_2)$

Solve for the final pressure:

$P_2 = [(0.925$ atm$) \times (2.50$ L He$)] / (0.350$ L He$)$

$P_2 = 6.61$ atm

52. E is correct. Start by applying Gay-Lussac's Law:

$(P_1 / T_1) = (P_2 / T_2)$

Solve for the final pressure:

$P_2 = (449$ K$) \times [(7.50$ atm$) / (220$ K$)]$

$P_2 = 15.3$ atm

53. D is correct.

54. E is correct. Start by applying the ideal gas equation:

$PV = nRT$

Next convert the given temperature units from Celsius to Kelvin:

$T_1 = 22°C + 273 = 295$ K

$T_2 = 60°C + 273 = 333$ K

Then convert the given volume units from mL to L:

$$V_1 = 400 \text{ mL} = 0.400 \text{ L}$$

$$V_2 = 300 \text{ mL} = 0.300 \text{ L}$$

Set the initial and final P/V/T conditions equal to each other:

$$(P_1V_1 / T_1) = (P_2V_2 / T_2)$$

Solve for the final pressure:

$$P_2 = [(1.2 \text{ atm}) \times (0.400 \text{ L}) \times (333 \text{ K})] / [(295 \text{ K}) \times (0.300 \text{ L})]$$

Notice that the question does not ask to solve for the final pressure, but to leave the answer in its formula.

55. B is correct.

56. C is correct.

57. B is correct. The kinetic-molecular theory of gases assumes the volume of each gas molecule equals zero.

58. C is correct. Increasing the pressure of the gas above the liquid puts stress on the equilibrium of the system. Gas molecules start to collide with the liquid surface more often, which increases the rate of gas molecules entering the solution, thus increasing the solubility.

59. E is correct.

60. D is correct. Vapor pressure is the pressure of a vapor in thermodynamic equilibrium with its condensed phases (solid or liquid) in a closed container. Vapor pressure is dependent on temperature only. The relationship between vapor pressure and temperature is exponential, and as temperature increases, vapor pressure increases.

61. B is correct.

62. C is correct. 22.4 liters of gas at STP = 1 mole. Therefore, C_2H_6 = 0.2 mole, CH_4 = 0.5 mole. Total = 0.4 mole of carbon from C_2H_6 (ratio of carbon in C_2H_6 is 2:1 in CH_4). Carbon from CH_4 = 0.4 mole + C_2H_6 = 0.5 mole = 0.90 mole of carbon.

63. A is correct.

64. B is correct.

65. C is correct.

66. E is correct.

67. A is correct. Start by applying the ideal-gas equation:

$$PV = nRT$$

Set the initial and final P/V/T conditions equal to each other:

$$(P_1V_1 / T_1) = (P_2V_2 / T_2)$$

Solve for the volume at STP (remember that STP condition is 0°C/273 K and 1 atm):

$$V_2 = [(273 \text{ K}) \times (583 \text{ torr}) \times (1.425 \text{ L})] / [(760 \text{ torr}) \times (298.4 \text{ K})]$$

$$V_2 = 1.000 \text{ L}$$

68. D is correct.

69. A is correct.

70. E is correct. London dispersion forces are present in all molecules; they are the attractive forces that hold molecules together. They are the weakest of all the intermolecular forces, and their strength increases with increasing size and polarity of the molecules involved.

71. D is correct. Convert the initial temperature from Celsius to Kelvin:

$$27 \text{ °C} = 273 + 27 = 300 \text{ K}$$

Apply Charles' Law:

$$(V_1 / T_1) = (V_2 / T_2)$$

Solve for the final volume:

$$V_2 = (50 \text{ K}) \times [(1.00 \text{ L}) / (300 \text{ K})]$$

$$V_2 = 0.167 \text{ L} = 167 \text{ mL}$$

72. A is correct. Start by applying the ideal-gas equation:

$$PV = nRT$$

Set the initial and final P/V/T conditions equal to each other:

$$(P_1 V_1 / T_1) = (P_2 V_2 / T_2)$$

Remember that STP condition is 0°C/273 K and 1 atm.

Solve for the final temperature:

$$T_2 = [(0.9915 \text{ atm}) \times (0.1642 \text{ L}) \times (273 \text{ K})] / [(1.00 \text{ atm}) \times (0.1224 \text{ L})]$$

$$T_2 = 363.12 \text{ K}$$

Then convert temperature units to degrees Celsius:

$$T_2 = (363.12 \text{ K} - 273 \text{ K})$$

$$T_2 = 90.12\text{°C} \approx 90.2\text{°C}$$

73. B is correct.

74. C is correct. The ideal gas law is $PV = nRT$, where P is pressure, V is volume, n is the number of molecules, R is the ideal gas constant, and T is temperature of the gas. The volume and temperature are directly proportional; if one increases, the other increases as well.

75. C is correct.

76. E is correct.

77. C is correct. The molecules of an ideal gas do not occupy a significant amount of space and exert no intermolecular forces, while the molecules of a real gas do occupy space and do exert (weak) intermolecular forces. However, both an ideal gas and a real gas have pressure, which is created from molecular collisions with the walls of the container.

78. A is correct. Start by applying Boyle's Law:

$$(P_1V_1) = (P_2V_2)$$

Solve for the final pressure:

$$P_2 = [(360 \text{ mmHg}) \times (400 \text{ mL})] / (800 \text{ mL})$$

$$P_2 = 180 \text{ mmHg}$$

79. A is correct. Start by applying Charles' Law:

$$(V_1 / T_1) = (V_2 / T_2)$$

Solve for the final volume:

$$V_2 = (313 \text{ K}) \times [(10.0 \text{ L}) / (296 \text{ K})]$$

$$V_2 = 10.6 \text{ L } O_2$$

80. B is correct. Start by applying Dalton's Law of Partial Pressures:

$$P_T = P_1 + P_2 + P_3 + \ldots$$

Set the total pressure equal to partial vapor pressure of water and partial pressure of hydrogen:

$$P_T = P_{H2O} + P_{H2}$$

Solve for the partial pressure of hydrogen:

$$P_{H2} = P_T - P_{H2O} = (763 \text{ mmHg}) - (17.5 \text{ mmHg})$$

$$P_{H2} = 745.5 \text{ mmHg}$$

81. B is correct. Start by converting the given kg of flour to grams:

$$1.2 \text{ kg} = 1200 \text{ g flour}$$

Next add the mass of all the components to find the total mass of the system:

$$M_T = M_{salt} + M_{flour} + M_{sugar}$$

$$M_T = (150 \text{ g salt}) + (1200 \text{ g flour}) + (650 \text{ g sugar}) = 2000 \text{ g total}$$

Then divide mass of salt by total mass, and multiply by 100%:

$$(150 \text{ g salt}) / (2000 \text{ g total}) = 0.075$$

$$0.075 \times (100) = 7.5\% \text{ salt by mass}$$

82. D is correct. Start by applying Charles' Law:

$$(V_1 / T_1) = (V_2 / T_2)$$

In Charles' Law, and all gas-related laws, T is always expressed in K. Convert the initial temperature to K:

$$44 \text{ °C} + 273 = 317 \text{ K}$$

Solve for the final temperature:

$$T_2 = (3.78 \text{ L}) \times [(317 \text{ K}) / (4.39 \text{ L})]$$

$T_2 = 273$ K

Convert the temperature to Celcius:

273 K − 273 = 0 °C

83. A is correct. Start by applying Dalton's Law of Partial Pressures:

$P_T = P_1 + P_2 + P_3 + \ldots$

Set the total pressure equal to partial vapor pressure of water and partial pressure of oxygen:

$P_T = P_{H2O} + P_{O2}$

Solve for the partial pressure of oxygen:

$P_{O2} = P_T − P_{H2O} = (775 \text{ torr}) − (23.8 \text{ torr})$

$P_{O2} = 751$ torr O_2

84. B is correct. Liquids take the shape of the container that they are in (i.e. they have an indefinite shape). This can be easily visualized by considering of a liter of water poured into a cylindrical bucket or a square box. In both cases, it takes up the shape of the container. However, liquids have definite volume. The volume of water in the given example will always be 1 L regardless of the container it is in.

85. B is correct. The diffusion rate is the inverse root of the molecular weights of the gases. Therefore, the rate of diffusion of $O_2/H_2 = \sqrt{2/32} = 1/4$.

86. C is correct. Start by writing the balanced chemical equation. Combustion of a hydrocarbon (C_xH_y) means that it is reacted with oxygen to create carbon dioxide and water. For methane, the reaction would be:

$CH_4 + 2O_2 \rightarrow CO_2 + 2H_2O$

Next by using the balanced coefficients from the written equation we can apply dimensional analysis to solve for the volume of O_2 needed to react to completion:

$V_{O2} = V_{CH4} \times (\text{mole } O_2 / \text{ mole } CH_4)$

$V_{O2} = (11.2 \text{ L } CH_4) \times (2 \text{ mole } O_2 / 1 \text{ mole } CH_4)$

$V_{O2} = 22.4$ L O_2

(Reminder: in STP condition, 1 mole of gas has a volume of 22.4 L.)

87. B is correct.

88. C is correct. A faster molecule has more momentum and thus exerts more force on the wall of the container. Likewise, more collisions mean greater average force. The volume of a molecule is irrelevant to the average force because volume does not factor into Newton's laws.

89. A is correct.

90. E is correct.

91. D is correct. The kinetic theory of gases describes a gas as a large number of small molecules in constant, random motion. However, it does not say that all molecules have the kinetic energy or the same velocity, and it does not say that all molecular collisions must have the same energy. Therefore, none of the above is true.

92. C is correct.

93. E is correct.

> 32 g of CH_4 = 2 moles of CH_4 (16 g/mole)
>
> NH_3 is 17 g/mole = ½ mole
>
> The partial pressure of NH_3 gas = the mole fraction of NH_3 = ½ mole / 2.5 moles = 0.2
>
> Partial pressure = (0.2)(1.8 atm) = 0.36 atm.

94. C is correct.

95. D is correct.

96. C is correct.

97. E is correct. Start by applying Boyle's Law:

> $(P_1V_1) = (P_2V_2)$

Solve for the final volume:

> V_2 = [(0.900 atm) × (130 mL)] / (0.300 atm)
>
> V_2 = 390 mL

98. A is correct.

99. D is correct.

100. E is correct. Gas molecules have a large amount of space between them, therefore they can be pushed together and gases are thus very compressible. Molecules in solids and liquids are already close together, therefore they cannot be pushed together even further, and are thus nearly incompressible.

101. B is correct. To calculate number of molecules, start by calculating the moles of gas using the ideal gas equation:

> n = PV/RT

Because the gas constant R is in L atm K^{-1} mol^{-1}, the pressure has to be converted into atm:

> 300 mmHg × (1/760 atm/mmHg) = 300/760 atm

(Leave it in this fraction form because the answers all are in this format.)

Convert the temperature to Kelvin:

> 10 °C + 273 = 283 K

Substitute those values into the ideal gas equation:

$n = PV/RT$

$n = (300/760) \times 5 / 0.0821 \times 283$

This expression represents the number of gas moles present in the container. Now calculate the number of atoms:

number of atoms = moles × Avogadro's number

number of atoms = {(300/760) × 5 / 0.0821 × 283} × 6.02 × 10²³

number of atoms = $(300/760)(5)(6 \times 10^{23}) / (0.0821)(283)$

102. C is correct. Start by observing information about gas C: temperature, pressure, and volume of the gas is indicated. Input those data into the ideal gas equation to determine the number of moles:

$PV = nRT$

$n = PV / RT$

Before calculating, notice that the gas constant is 0.0821 L atm K⁻¹ mol⁻¹. Convert all the units to match units indicated in gas constant:

volume = 658.5 mL × (1/1000) L/mL

volume = 0.659 L

pressure = 748.5 torr × (1/760) atm/torr

pressure = 0.985 atm

temperature = 30.4 + 273.15

temperature = 303.6 K

$n = PV / RT$

$n = (0.985 \text{ atm} \times 0.659 \text{ L}) / (0.0821 \text{ L atm K}^{-1} \text{ mol}^{-1} \times 303.6 \text{ K})$

$n = 0.026$ mole

Law of mass conservation states that total mass of products = total mass of reactants. Based on this law, mass of gas C can be determined:

mass product = mass reactant

mass A = mass B + mass C

4.962 g = 3.684 g + mass C

mass C = 1.278 g

Calculate molar mass of C:

molar mass = 1.278 g / 0.026 mole

molar mass = 49.1 g / mole

103. E is correct. Start by applying Gay-Lussac's Law:

$$(P_1 / T_1) = (P_2 / T_2)$$

Solve for the final pressure:

$$P_2 = (60 \text{ K}) \times [(3.00 \text{ atm}) / (30 \text{ K})]$$

$$P_2 = 6.00 \text{ atm}$$

104. D is correct. Gas molecules have a wide range of velocities. In a gas at 200 °C, the *average* speed of a molecule is greater than in a gas at 100 °C but the range of speeds will be large for both temperatures.

105. C is correct.

106. B is correct.

107. A is correct.

108. D is correct. Van der Waals equation describes factors that must be accounted for when the ideal gas law is used to calculate values for nonideal gases. The terms that affect the pressure and volume of the ideal gas law are intermolecular forces and volume of nonideal gas molecules.

109. D is correct.

110. C is correct.

111. B is correct. The ideal gas law is $PV = nRT$, where P is pressure, V is volume, n is the number of molecules, R is the ideal gas constant, and T is temperature of the gas. As can be derived from this equation, if both pressure and temperature are halved, there would be no effect on the volume.

112. A is correct.

113. E is correct.

114. C is correct. Convert the masses of the gases into moles:

0.5 mole O_2 (32 g/mole)

0.5 mole N_2 (28 g/mole)

2 moles CO_2 (44 g/mole)

for a total of 3 moles.

The total pressure of 1 atm (or 760 mm Hg) has a 40 mm Hg contributor as H_2O vapor.

Therefore, only 720 mm Hg of the total pressure is due to the N_2. $O_2 = CO_2$.

The partial pressure of CO_2 = the mole fraction (2 moles CO_2 / 3 moles total gas) × total pressure of the gas mixture less H_2O vapor (720 mm Hg) = 480 mm Hg.

115. D is correct. Start by calculating moles of each gas:

moles H_2 = mass H_2 / molar mass H_2

moles H_2 = 8.00 g / (2 × 1.01 g/mole)

moles H_2 = 3.96 moles

moles Ne = 12.00 g / 20.18 g/mole

moles Ne = 0.595 moles

Next calculate the mole fraction of H:

Mole fraction of H = moles of H / total moles in mixture

Mole fraction of H = 3.96 moles / (3.96 moles + 0.595 moles)

Mole fraction of H = 0.869 moles ≈ 0.870 moles

116. B is correct. The ideal gas law: PV = nRT. Using proportions, if the temperature is increased by a factor of 1.5 and the pressure is increased by a factor of 1.5 (constant number of moles), volume is unchanged.

117. E is correct.

118. D is correct.

119. E is correct.

120. C is correct. The melting point of a substance depends on the pressure that it is at. Generally, melting points are given at standard pressure. If the substance is more dense in the solid than in the liquid state (which is true of most substances), the melting point increases when pressure is increased. This is what happens with CO_2. However, with certain substances including water, the solid is actually less dense than the liquid state (e.g. ice is less dense than water), so the reverse is true and melting point decreases when pressure increases.

121. B is correct. Start by applying Graham's Law of Effusion:

$[Rate_A / Rate_B] = \sqrt{[(M_A) / (M_B)]}$

Set the rate of effusion of krypton over the rate of effusion of methane:

$Rate_{Kr} / Rate_{CH4} = \sqrt{[(M_{Kr}) / (M_{CH4})]}$

Solve for the ratio of effusion rates:

$Rate_{Kr} / Rate_{CH4} = \sqrt{[(83.798 \text{ g/mol}) / (16.04 \text{ g/mol})]} = 2.29$

Next since we know that larger gas molecules must effuse at a slower rate, the effusion rate of Kr gas molecules must be slower than methane molecules:

$Rate_{Kr} = [Rate_{CH4} / (2.29)] = [(631 \text{ m/s}) / (2.29)]$

$Rate_{Kr} = 276 \text{ m/s}$

122. A is correct. Partial pressure of molecules in a mixture are proportional to their molar ratios. Use the coefficients of the reaction to determine molar ratio.

Based on that information, calculate the pressure of O_2:

Pressure O_2 = (coefficient O_2 / sum of coefficients in mixture) × total pressure

Pressure O_2 = {1/(2+1)} × 1340 torr

Pressure O_2 = 446.67 torr ≈ 447 torr

123. E is correct.

124. A is correct. To calculate number of molecules, start by calculating the moles of gas using the ideal gas equation:

$n = PV/RT$

Because the gas constant R is in L atm K^{-1} mol^{-1}, the pressure has to be converted into atm:

800 torr × (1/760 atm/torr) = 1.053 atm

Convert the volume to liters:

500 mL × 0.001 L/mL = 0.5 L

Substitute those values into the ideal gas equation:

$n = PV/RT$

n = 1.053 atm × 0.5 L / 0.08206 L atm K^{-1} mol^{-1} × 300 K

n = 0.0214 ≈ 0.022

125. A is correct.

126. D is correct. The temperature of the helium in the balloon decreases when the balloon is placed in a cold freezer. This is because the surroundings are colder than the balloon, and heat will be transferred from the balloon to the surrounding air until thermal equilibrium is reached.

When temperature of a gas decreases, the molecules move more slowly and become closer together, causing the volume of the balloon to decrease. This can be seen in the ideal gas law, $PV = nRT$. If temperature decreases, volume must also decrease (assuming that pressure remains constant).

127. C is correct.

128. B is correct. Boiling is the rapid vaporization of a liquid where its phase changes from a liquid to a gas. It occurs when the liquid's vapor pressure is equal to or greater than the external pressure. The lower the pressure of a gas above a liquid, the lower the temperature at which the liquid will boil.

129. E is correct.

130. B is correct. As the automobile travels the highway, friction is generated between the road and its tires. The heat energy from friction increases the temperature of the air inside the tires, causing the molecules to move around more quickly. These fast-moving molecules collide with the walls of the tire at a higher rate, and thus pressure is increased. From the ideal gas equation ($PV = nRT$), if temperature is increased, pressure must also increase.

131. A is correct. Hydrogen bond occurs between a very electronegative atom (N, O, F) and a highly positive hydrogen. In this molecule, there are 2 oxygen atoms. Each of them has 2 free electron pairs and those free pairs can function as hydrogen bonding sites, for the total of 4 possible hydrogen bonds. On top of that, there is a hydrogen attached to an oxygen atom. This brings up the total to 5 possible hydrogen bonding sites.

132. D is correct. Solids, liquids and gases all have a vapor pressure which increases from solid to gas. Vapor pressure is a colligative property of a substance and depends only on the quantity of solutes present, not on their identity.

133. A is correct.

134. B is correct. Under STP conditions, 1 mole of gas has a volume of 22.4 L.

Moles of gas = volume / 22.4 L mol^{-1}

Moles of gas = 10 L / 22.4 L mol^{-1}

Moles of gas = 0.446 moles

135. A is correct. Use the ideal gas law, $PV = nRT$. If the volume is reduced by ½ the number of moles is reduced by ½. In addition, the pressure is reduced to 90%, so the number of moles should be reduced by this factor. With constant temperature, the number of moles is 45% of the original. Since mass is proportional to number of moles for a given gas, mass is 45% of 40 grams, or 18 grams.

136. D is correct.

137. A is correct. An ideal gas has no intermolecular forces, indicating that its molecules have no attraction to each other. The molecules of a real gas, however, do have intermolecular forces, although these forces are extremely weak. Therefore, the molecules of a real gas are slightly attracted to one another, although the attraction is nowhere near as strong as the attraction in liquids and solids.

138. E is correct.

139. C is correct.

140. A is correct. At a pressure and temperature corresponding to the triple point of a substance, all three states (gas, liquid and solid) exist in equilibrium.

141. E is correct.

142. D is correct.

143. E is correct.

144. C is correct.

145. D is correct. Dissolving a solute into a solvent alters the solvent's freezing point, melting point, boiling point and vapor pressure.

146. B is correct. Start by applying the Kinetic Molecular Theory of Gas Molecules, which states that the average kinetic energy per molecule in a system is proportional to the temperature of the gas.

Next since we know that both containers X & Y are both at the same temperature and pressure, then both gas molecules must possess the same amount of average kinetic energy per gas molecule.

147. C is correct. Start by understanding that since both samples of He and Ne are at the same temperature, pressure, and volume, they both must possess equal moles of each gas.

Next even though there are equal moles of each gas of He and Ne, if we use the molar masses given in the periodic table, we will notice that the samples contain different masses of each sample.

148. A is correct. Ten grams of O_2 has substantially less moles than ten grams of H_2 because the molecular weight of O_2 is much greater. Since pressure is directly proportional to the number of moles, the pressure of the H_2 is greater than the pressure for the O_2.

149. C is correct.

150. B is correct.

151. A is correct. Vaporization refers to the change of state from a liquid to a gas. There are two types of vaporization: boiling and evaporation, which are differentiated based on the temperature at which they occur (i.e. evaporation occurs at a temperature below the boiling point). However, vaporization is the general term that covers both of these processes.

152. D is correct.

153. C is correct. The vapor pressure of a liquid decreases when a nonvolatile substance is dissolved into a liquid. The lowering of the vapor pressure of a substance is proportional to the number of moles of the solute dissolved in a definite weight of the solvent known as Raoult's law.

154. E is correct. Start by writing the balanced chemical equation:

$N_2 + 3H_2 \rightarrow 2NH_3$

Next, by using the balanced coefficients from the written equation, we can apply dimensional analysis to solve for the volume of H_2 needed to react to completion with 11.2 L N_2:

$V_{H2} = V_{N2} \times$ (mole H_2 / mole N_2)

$V_{H2} = (11.2 \text{ L } N_2) \times (3 \text{ mole } H_2 / 1 \text{ mole } N_2)$

$V_{H2} = 33.6 \text{ L } H_2$

155. C is correct. Start by writing the balanced chemical equation:

$N_2 + 3H_2 \rightarrow 2NH_3$

Next, by using the balanced coefficients from the written equation, we can apply dimensional analysis to solve for the volume of H_2 needed to produce 10.6 L NH_3:

$V_{H2} = V_{NH3} \times$ (mole H_2 / mole NH_3)

$V_{H2} = (10.6 \text{ L } NH_3) \times (3 \text{ mole } H_2 / 2 \text{ mole } NH_3)$

$V_{H2} = 15.9 \text{ L } H_2$

156. A is correct. Sublimation is the direct change of state from a solid to a gas, skipping the intermediate liquid phase. An example of a compound that undergoes sublimation is solid carbon dioxide, also known as dry ice, which goes directly from solid to gas and is often used as a cooling agent.

157. A is correct. Start by dividing the given concentration of Ca^{2+} by 2:

$[Ca^{2+}] = [36 \text{ mEq } Ca^{2+}] / 2 = 18 \text{ mM } Ca^{2+}$

mEq is equivalent to milimolar (mM).

Next by dividing the concentration of Ca^{2+} by 1000, we obtain the concentration of Ca^{2+} in units of molarity:

$[Ca^{2+}] = 18 \text{ mM } Ca^{2+} \times [(1 \text{ M}) / (1000 \text{ mM})] = 0.018 \text{ M } Ca^{2+}$

158. C is correct. Addition of solute to a pure solvent lowers the vapor pressure of the solvent; therefore a higher temperature is required to bring the vapor pressure of the solution in an open container up to the atmospheric pressure. This increases the boiling point. Because adding solute lowers the vapor pressure, the freezing point of the solution decreases (automobile antifreeze is an example).

159. A is correct.

160. C is correct. All of the conditions of the ideal gases are the same so the number of moles (and molecules) is the equal. The mass, however, is different, since the molar mass of oxygen and nitrogen are different. Therefore, their densities are not equal.

161. D is correct.

162. B is correct. Start by writing the balanced chemical equation:

$C_3H_8 + 5O_2 \rightarrow 3CO_2 + 4H_2O$

Next, by using the balanced coefficients from the written equation, we can apply dimensional analysis to solve for the volume of H_2O gas produced from the given volume of 1.8 L C_3H_8 reacted:

$V_{H2O} = V_{C3H8} \times (\text{mole } H_2O / \text{mole } C_3H_8)$

$V_{H2O} = (1.8 \text{ L } C_3H_8) \times (4 \text{ mole } H_2O / 1 \text{ mole } C_3H_8)$

$V_{H2O} = 7.2 \text{ L } H_2O$

163. D is correct. Condensing refers to a change of state from a gas to a liquid. For example, condensation occurs when atmospheric water vapor in clouds condenses to form droplets of liquid water that become heavy enough to fall due to gravity. This results in rain, an essential part of the Earth's water cycle.

164. B is correct. When a solution is diluted, the moles of solute is constant. Use this formula to calculate the new molarity:

$M_1V_1 = M_2V_2$

$125 \text{ mL} \times 2.50 \text{ M} = 575 \text{ mL} \times M_2$

$M_2 = (125 \text{ mL} / 575 \text{ mL}) \times 2.50 \text{ M}$

$M_2 = 0.543 \text{ M}$

165. D is correct. Boiling point elevation = iKm

where I = number of particles produced when molecule dissociates, K = constant (depends on substance), m = molality

molality = (moles) / (kg solvent)

molality = [(90g) / (180g/mole)] / 0.5 kg

molality = 1.0 m

BP elev = (1)(0.52)(1.0)

BP elev = 0.52 K

The BP of H_2O = 373 K

With solute:

BP H_2O = 373 K + 0.52 K = 373.52 K

166. D is correct.

167. E is correct. With consideration to the ideal gas law, there is no difference between He and Ar since pressure, volume, temperature, and number of moles are known quantities. The identity of the gas would only be relevant to convert from moles to mass or vice-versa.

168. B is correct.

169. E is correct. Start by applying the formula for the molar concentration of a solution:

$M_1V_1 = M_2V_2$

Next, by substituting the given volume and molar concentrations of HCl, solve for the final volume of HCl of the resulting dilution:

$V_2 = [M_1V_1] / (M_2)$

V_2 = [(2.00 M HCl) × (0.125 L HCl)] / (0.400 M HCl)

V_2 = 0.625 L HCl

Then solve for the volume of water needed to add to the initial volume of HCl to obtain the final diluted volume of HCl:

$V_{H2O} = V_2 - V_1$

V_{H2O} = (0.625 L HCl) – (0.125 L HCl)

V_{H2O} = 0.500 L H_2O = 500 mL H_2O

170. B is correct. Freezing point depression = –iKm = –10K

Toluene does not dissociate, so i = 1– (1)(5.0)(x) = –10 K

K value of solvent x = 2 molal

2 moles toluene/kg benzene = x moles / 0.1 kg benzene = 0.2 mole toluene

171. E is correct. Start by applying the ideal gas equation:

PV =nRT

Set the total and partial mole/pressure conditions of Ar equal to each other:

$(n_T / P_T) = (n_{Ar} / P_{Ar})$

Solve for the partial-pressure of Ar:

$P_{Ar} = n_{Ar} / (n_T / P_T)$

$P_{Ar} = (0.40$ moles Ar$) / [(1.00$ moles total$) / (1.10$ atm total$)]$

$P_{Ar} = 0.44$ atm Ar

172. A is correct.

173. B is correct.

174. E is correct. The ideal gas law is PV = nRT, where P is pressure, V is volume, n is the number of molecules, R is the ideal gas constant, and T is temperature of the gas. At STP (standard conditions for temperature and pressure), it is known that the pressure and temperature for all three flasks are the same. It is also known that the volume is the same in each case – 2.0 L. Therefore, since R is a constant, the number of molecules "n" must be the same for the ideal gas law to hold true.

175. C is correct. Start by calculating the molecular mass of NaOH using the atomic mass of Na, O, and H:

Molecular mass of NaOH = atomic mass of Na + atomic mass of O + atomic mass of H

Molecular mass of NaOH = (22.99 g/mole) + (15.99 g/mole) + (1.01 g/mole)

Molecular mass of NaOH = 40 g/mole NaOH

Next convert the given mass of 45 g NaOH to moles of NaOH using the molar mass of NaOH:

Moles of NaOH = mass of NaOH × (molar mass of NaOH)

Moles of NaOH = 45 g NaOH × [(1.00 moles NaOH) / 40 g NaOH)]

Moles of NaOH = 1.125 moles NaOH

Then divide moles of NaOH by the total volume of solution:

[NaOH] = [(1.125 moles NaOH) / (0.250 L NaOH)]

[NaOH] = 4.5 M NaOH

176. B is correct.

Freezing point depression = –iKm = –2 K

$-(1)(40)(x) = -2$

$x = 0.05$ molal

Assume that compound x does not dissociate.

0.5 mole compound (x) / kg camphor = 25 g / kg camphor

Therefore, if 0.05 mole = 25 g

1 mole = 500 g

177. A is correct. Hydrogen bonds between water molecules have a duration of about 10^{-10} seconds. The hydrogen bonds quickly form, break, and re-form, and the structure can best be described as flickering clusters.

B: a hydrogen bond is the electrostatic attraction that occurs when a hydrogen atom bound to an electronegative atom (e.g. oxygen, as in water) experiences attraction to another electronegative atom. The oxygen of a water molecule has two lone pairs of electrons, and each lone pair can hydrogen bond with the hydrogen of another molecule. Therefore, each water molecule can form 4 hydrogen bonds: 2 from two lone pairs of electrons and 2 from two hydrogens.

C and D: water molecules form more hydrogen bonds when they are in the solid phase (ice), as opposed to the liquid phase.

178. A is correct. Start by calculating the moles of CO, using the fact that 1 mole of CO has 6.02×10^{23} CO molecules:

moles of CO = 6.21×10^{24} molecules / 6.02×10^{23} molecules/mole

moles of CO = 10.32 moles

In STP condition, 1 mole of gas has a volume of 22.4 L.

Calculate volume of CO:

volume of CO = 10.32 moles × 22.4 L/mole

volume of CO = 231 L

179. E is correct. The kinetic theory of gases describes a gas as a large number of small particles in constant rapid motion. These particles collide with each other and with the walls of the container. Their average kinetic energy depends only on the absolute temperature of the system. At high temperatures, the particles are moving quickly, and at a temperature of 0 K, there is no movement of gas particles. Therefore, as temperature decreases, kinetic energy decreases, and so does the velocity of the gas molecules.

180. D is correct. Start by applying the formula for the molar concentration of a solution:

$M_1V_1 = M_2V_2$

Next by substituting the given volume and molar concentrations of the solution, solve for the final volume of the solution of the resulting dilution:

$V_2 = [M_1V_1] / (M_2)$

$V_2 = [(0.150 \text{ M soln}) \times (1.25 \text{ L soln})] / (2.75 \text{ M soln})$

$V_2 = 0.068 \text{ L soln}$

Then convert the volume of solution to units of mL:

$V_2 = 0.068 \text{ L soln} = 68.2 \text{ mL soln}$

181. C is correct. In STP condition, 1 mole of gas has a volume of 22.4 L.

Calculate moles of O_2:

moles of O_2 = 15.0 L / 22.4 L/mole

moles of O_2 = 0.67 mole

Calculate the moles of O_2, using the fact that 1 mole of O_2 has 6.02×10^{23} O_2 molecules:

molecules of O_2 = 0.67 mole $\times$ 6.02×10^{23} molecules/mole

molecules of O_2 = 4.03×10^{23} molecules

182. B is correct.

183. E is correct.

184. C is correct.

185. D is correct. The boiling point will depend on the intermolecular bonding of those molecules. All of the options are nonpolar halogen molecules. The dominant intermolecular force will be dispersion force (or induced dipole). As the number of electron shells increase, the valence electrons are further from the nucleus and these molecules would be more prone to temporary induced dipole. Therefore, larger molecules will have stronger bonds and higher boiling points. Answer: I_2.

186. C is correct. Start by applying the ideal gas equation:

PV = nRT

Set the initial and final P/V/T conditions equal to each other:

$(P_1 V_1 / T_1) = (P_2 V_2 / T_2)$

Solve for the final volume:

V_2 = [(295 K) $\times$ (760 mmHg) $\times$ (0.180 L N_2)] / [(640 mmHg) $\times$ (273 K)]

V_2 = 0.231 L N_2

187. B is correct. Start by applying the formula for the molar concentration of a solution:

$M_1 V_1 = M_2 V_2$

Next, by substituting the given volume and molar concentrations of the NaOH solution, solve for the initial concentrated volume of NaOH solution needed to prepare the 2.40 L of 0.500 M of dilute NaOH:

V_1 = [$M_2 V_2$] / (M_1)

V_1 = [(0.500 M dilute NaOH) $\times$ (2.40 L dilute NaOH)] / (8.25 M concentrated NaOH)

V_1 = 0.145 L concentrated NaOH

Then convert the volume of solution to units of mL:

V_2 = 0.145 L concentrated NaOH = 145 mL concentrated NaOH

188. E is correct.

189. A is correct. At STP (standard conditions for temperature and pressure), we know that the pressure and temperature are the same regardless of the gas. The ideal gas law is $PV = nRT$, where P is pressure, V is volume, n is the number of molecules, R is the ideal gas constant, and T is temperature of the gas. Therefore, one molecule of each gas will occupy the same amount of volume at STP. Since CO_2 molecules have the largest mass, CO_2 gas will have a greater mass in the same volume, and thus it will have the greatest density.

190. B is correct. At STP, total pressure is 760 torr.

The partial pressure of $N_2 = 760 - 300 - 20 - 8 = 432$ torr.

Start by applying Dalton's Law of Partial Pressures:

$$P_T = P_1 + P_2 + P_3 + \dots$$

Set the total pressure equal to partial pressures of each component of the container:

$$P_T = P_{H2O} + P_{N2} + P_{CO2} + P_{O2} + P_{H2O}$$

Solve for the partial pressure of nitrogen:

$$P_{N2} = P_T - [P_{O2} + P_{CO2} + P_{H2O}]$$

$$P_{N2} = (760 \text{ torr total}) - [300 \text{ torr } O_2 + 20 \text{ torr } CO_2 + 8 \text{ torr } H_2O]$$

$$P_{N2} = 432 \text{ torr } N_2$$

191. D is correct. When dealing with a problem that involves densities of gas, use this modification of the ideal gas law. The default form of ideal gas law is:

$$PV = nRT$$

where n is the number of moles, which is equal to mass/molecular weight (MW). Substitute that expression into the ideal gas equation:

$$PV = (\text{mass/MW}) RT$$

Density (ρ) is equal to mass/volume. Rearrange the equation to get mass/volume on one side and everything else on the other side:

$$\text{mass/volume} = (P \times MW) / RT$$

$$\text{density } (\rho) = (P \times MW) / RT$$

Now rearrange the equation to solve for molecular weight (MW):

$$MW = \rho RT / P$$

The problem indicates that the gas is in STP condition, which has T of $0 \ ^\circ C = 273.15$ K and P of 1 atm. Use those values to calculate MW:

$$MW = 1.34 \text{ g/L} \times 0.0821 \text{ L atm K}^{-1} / 1 \text{ atm}$$

$$MW = 30.05 \text{ g} \approx 30.0 \text{ g}$$

Chapter 4.   SOLUTIONS

1. D is correct.

2. C is correct.

3. E is correct.

4. A is correct.

5. E is correct. Solutions can be gases, liquids, or solids. All three statements are possible types of solutions. An example of gas-in-liquid solution (statement III) is a hydrochloride/HCl. In its pure form, HCl is a gas. It is passed through water to create aqueous solution of HCl.

6. B is correct. Unsaturated solution is the one where a solute dissolves completely, leaving no remaining substances. Saturated solution is the one where solute is unable to dissolve any further, leaving the undissolved substances at the bottom of the container. Supersaturated solution contains more solute than the solvent can normally dissolve. Certain conditions (e.g. temperature) must be met to prepare a supersaturated solution.

7. E is correct.

8. D is correct. By definition, molarity equals moles of solute divided by liters of solution. Since $1 \text{ cm}^3 = 1$ mL, the molarity of this solution is $(0.5 \text{ mol}) / (0.05 \text{ L}) = 10$ M.

9. D is correct. A "solution" is a homogeneous mixture. Therefore, an alloy is a homogeneous structure considered to be a solution, since it is composed of more than one chemical compound, as are options I and II.

10. C is correct.

11. A is correct.

12. A is correct.

13. E is correct.

14. B is correct.

15. C is correct. Ideally dilute solutions are so dilute that solute molecules never interact, whereby the mole fraction of the solvent approaches one.

16. A is correct.

17. C is correct.

18. D is correct.

19. E is correct. When a solution is diluted, the moles of solute (n) is constant. However, the molarity and volume will change. Because $n = MV$:

$$n_1 = n_2$$

$$M_1 V_1 = M_2 V_2$$

Solve for V_2:

$$M_2 = (M_1 V_1) / V_2$$

$$M_2 = (4 \text{ M} \times 1 \text{ mL}) / 15 \text{ mL}$$

$$M_2 = 0.267 \text{ M} \approx 0.270 \text{ M}$$

Usually in molarity calculations, volumes are expressed in liters. However, because this problem involves a volume comparison, they can both be in milliliters because the units will cancel out in the end.

20. B is correct. Ideal solutions obey Raoult's law. The solvent and solute make similar bonds and are similar in size and shape.

21. A is correct.

22. B is correct.

23. C is correct.

24. E is correct.

25. B is correct. Like dissolves like which actually means that polar substances tend to dissolve in polar solvents, and nonpolar substances in nonpolar solvents. Since benzene is nonpolar, look for a nonpolar substance. Silver chloride is ionic, while CH_2Cl_2, H_2S and SO_2 are both polar.

26. D is correct.

27. B is correct. First determine the moles of NaCl:

Moles of NaCl = mass of NaCl / molecular mass of NaCl

Moles of NaCl = 25 g / (23 g/mol + 35.45 g/mol)

Moles of NaCl = 0.427 mole

Then use this information to calculate the molarity:

Molarity = moles/volume

Molarity = 0.427 mole / 0.625 L

Molarity ≈ 0.684 M

28. A is correct.

29. C is correct.

30. D is correct.

31. E is correct.

32. C is correct. The concentration of the solute is $(0.25 \text{ mol}) / (0.05 \text{ kg}) = 5 \text{ m}$. Given that the molecule does not dissociate (i.e. $i = 1$), the freezing point depression is:

$$\Delta T_f = k_f m$$

$$\Delta T_f = (-1.86 \text{ °C/m})(5 \text{ m}) = -9.3 \text{ °C}$$

Thus, $T_f^l = (0 \text{ °C}) - 9.3 \text{ °C} = -9.3 \text{ °C}$

33. E is correct.

34. B is correct. Ammonia forms hydrogen bonds and SO_2 is polar.

35. C is correct.

36. E is correct.

37. C is correct. Since 1 mole of H_2SO_4 produces 2 moles of H^+:

10 M H_2SO_4 = 20 N H_2SO_4

0.5 M = 1.0 N

(V)(normality) = (V)(normality)

$(x)(20 N) = (600 ml)(1 N)$

$x = 30$ ml

38. A is correct.

39. B is correct. Hydrogen bonding in H_2O is stronger than van der Waals forces in benzene.

40. D is correct.

41. E is correct.

42. A is correct.

43. C is correct. *Like dissolves like* whereby van der Waals forces in the hydrocarbons are relatively weak, while hydrogen bonds between H_2O molecules are strong intermolecular bonds.

44. D is correct.

45. B is correct. Molarity = moles/volume.

Rearrange the equation to solve for volume:

Volume = moles/molarity

Volume = 3.12 mole / 6.67 M

Volume = 0.468 L

46. A is correct.

47. B is correct.

48. D is correct. The addition of a solute always elevates the boiling point temperature of a liquid. Since NaCl dissociates into 2 ions in solution, i = 2, so:

$\Delta T_b = k_b mi$

$\Delta T_b = (0.51 \degree C/m)(2 m)(2)$

$\Delta T_b = 2 \degree C$

Thus, $\Delta T_b^1 = (100 \degree C) + 2 \degree C = 102 \degree C$

49. E is correct.

50. A is correct. The intermolecular bonding in all alkanes is similar.

51. D is correct.

52. B is correct.

53. E is correct. To determine the number of equivalents:

$$\frac{4 \text{ moles}}{\text{liter}} \times \frac{3 \text{ equivalents}}{\text{mole}} \times \frac{1}{3} \text{ liter}$$

$$= 4 \text{ equivalents}$$

54. C is correct.

55. D is correct. The mass of a solution is always calculated by taking the total mass of the solution and container and subtracting the mass of the container.

56. A is correct.

57. E is correct.

58. C is correct.

59. A is correct. The solvent is the component with the largest proportion in the mixture.

60. C is correct. A colloid consists of particles larger than those of a solution, but not large enough to settle out due to gravity.

61. C is correct.

62. B is correct.

63. D is correct. Neither bond energy nor vapor pressure changes with a change in pressure. Boiling occurs when the vapor pressure of a liquid equals the atmospheric pressure. Water boils at a lower temperature at high altitudes because the atmospheric pressure decreases as altitude increases.

64. A is correct.

65. E is correct. Colloidal particles are too small to be extracted by simple filtration.

66. D is correct.

67. B is correct.

68. B is correct. Solvent is the component with the highest % volume composition.

69. D is correct. Osmolarity is the number of molecules contributing to osmotic pressure in solutions. Every ion in ionic compounds contribute to osmotic pressure. For example, in a solution, 1 mol of $NaCl$ will dissociate into 1 mol of Na^+ and 1 mol of Cl^-, which means that its osmolarity is $1 + 1 = 2$ moles.

Calculate the osmolarity of all the options by multiplying the molarity with total number of ions in each molecule.

KF: osmolarity $= 0.14 \text{ M} \times 2 = 0.28 \text{ M}$

$CaBr_2$: osmolarity $= 0.2 \text{ M} \times 3 = 0.6 \text{ M}$

$NaCl$: osmolarity $= 0.6 \text{ M} \times 2 = 1.2 \text{ M}$

AlCl₃: osmolarity = 0.35 M × 4 = 1.4 M

KNO₃: osmolarity = 0.10 M × 2 = 0.2 M

AlCl₃ has the highest osmolarity value.

70. E is correct.

71. C is correct.

72. A is correct. Start by calculating the moles of NaCl required:

moles NaCl = molarity × volume

moles NaCl = 4 M × (100 mL × 0.001 L/mL)

moles NaCl = 0.4 mol

Then use this information to calculate the mass:

mass NaCl = moles NaCl × molar mass of NaCl

mass NaCl = 0.4 mol × (23.00 g/mol + 35.45 g/mol)

mass NaCl = 23.4 g

73. B is correct. The Tyndall effect results when a beam of light shone through a colloid is dispersed so that the beam becomes visible to the naked eye from the side. In a true solution, the beam shines right through and is invisible from the side.

74. E is correct.

75. A is correct.

76. C is correct.

77. E is correct. As the name suggests, solubility product constant (K_{sp}) is a product of solubility of each ion in an ionic compound.

Start by writing down the dissociation equation of AgCl in a solution:

AgCl (s) → Ag⁺ (aq) + Cl⁻ (aq)

Solubility of AgCl is provided the problem: 1.3×10^{-4} mol/L. This is the maximum amount of AgCl that can be dissolved in water in standard conditions.

There are 1.3×10^{-4} mol AgCl dissolved in one liter of water, which means that there are 1.3×10^{-4} mol of Ag⁺ ions and 1.3×10^{-4} mol of Cl⁻ ions.

K_{sp} is calculated using the same method as equilibrium constant: concentration of ion to the power of ion coefficient. Only aqueous species are included in the calculation.

For AgCl: K_{sp} = [Ag][Cl]

$K_{sp} = (1.3 \times 10^{-4})(1.3 \times 10^{-4})$

$K_{sp} = 1.69 \times 10^{-8} \approx 1.7 \times 10^{-8}$

78. D is correct.

79. A is correct.

80. C is correct. In coagulation, heating or adding an electrolyte to a colloid causes the particles to bind together, increasing their mass and allowing them to settle due to gravity.

81. B is correct.

82. D is correct.

83. B is correct.

84. C is correct. When the ion product is equal to or greater than K_{sp}, precipitation of the salt occurs. If the ion product value is less than K_{sp}, precipitation does not occur.

85. A is correct. Calculate the number of ions in each option:

A: $Li_3PO_4 \rightarrow 3Li^+ + PO_4^{3-}$ (4 ions)

B: $Ca(NO_3)_2 \rightarrow Ca^{2+} + 2NO_3^-$ (3 ions)

C: $MgSO_4 \rightarrow Mg^{2+} + SO_4^{2-}$ (2 ions)

D: $(NH_4)_2SO_4 \rightarrow 2NH_4^+ + SO_4^{2-}$ (3 ions)

E: $(NH_4)_4Fe(CN)_6 \rightarrow 4NH_4^+ + Fe(CN)_6^{4-}$ (5 ions)

86. D is correct.

87. E is correct. The names of polyatomic anions containing oxygen include the suffixes –ite and –ate. –ate is used for the most common oxyanion while –ite is used for the anion with the same charge but one less oxygen. Hypo– means low, indicating the species with one less oxygen than the –ite species.

88. A is correct.

Mass of KCl = mass % × mass of solution

Mass of KCl = 16% × 26 g

Mass of KCl = 4.16 g

89. D is correct.

90. D is correct.

91. E is correct. The concentrations of the dissolved ions must exceed the value of the K_{sp} for precipitation. Given the dissolution of $PbSO_4$:

$PbSO_4 \leftrightarrow Pb^{2+} (aq) + SO_4^{2-} (aq)$

$K_{sp} = [Pb^{2+}][SO_4^{2-}]$

Therefore, the minimum concentration of SO_4^{2-} for precipitation is:

$[SO_4^{2-}] = K_{sp} / [Pb^{2+}]$

$[SO_4^{2-}] = (1.6 \times 10^{-8}) / (1.25 \times 10^{-3})$

$[SO_4^{2-}] = 1.3 \times 10^{-5}$ M

92. C is correct.

93. B is correct. First determine moles of NaCl:

Moles of NH_3 = mass of NH_3 / molecular weight of NH_3

Moles of NH_3 = 15.0 g / (14.01 g/mol + 3 × 1.01 g/mol)

Moles of NH_3 = 0.88 mol

Then determine the volume of the solution:

Volume of solution = mass / density

Volume of solution = 250 g / 0.974 g/mL

Volume of solution = 256.7 mL

Convert volume to liters

Volume = 256.7 mL × 0.001 L / mL

Volume = 0.2567 L

Divide moles by the volume to calculate molarity:

Molarity = moles / volume

Molarity = 0.88 mol / 0.2567 L

Molarity = 3.42 M

94. C is correct.

95. B is correct.

96. E is correct.

97. A is correct. The bicarbonate ion is the conjugate base of carbonic acid: H_2CO_3.

98. D is correct.

99. E is correct. Ionic product constant of water:

$K_w = [H_3O^+][OH^-]$

Rearrange equation to solve for $[OH^-]$:

$[OH^-] = K_w / [H_3O^+]$

$[OH^-] = 1 × 10^{-14} / 1 × 10^{-5}$

$[OH^-] = 1 × 10^{-9}$

100. A is correct.

101. A is correct.

102. B is correct.

103. E is correct.

104. C is correct.

105. B is correct. The –ate ending indicates the species with more oxygen, but it does not indicate a specific number of oxygen.

106. E is correct. Solubility is proportional to pressure. Use simple proportions to compare solubility in different pressures:

$P_1/S_1 = P_2/S_2$

$S_2 = P_2 / (P_1/S_1)$

$S_2 = 5.55 \text{ atm} / (1.00 \text{ atm} / 1.90 \text{ cc/100 mL})$

$S_2 = 10.55 \text{ cc} / 100 \text{ mL}$

107. D is correct. Ionic product constant of water:

$K_w = [H_3O^+][OH^-]$

Rearrange equation to solve for $[OH^-]$:

$[OH^-] = K_w / [H_3O^+]$

$[OH^-] = 1 \times 10^{-14} / 1 \times 10^{-8}$

$[OH^-] = 1 \times 10^{-6}$

108. C is correct. The glucose content is 8.50 % (m/v). It means that the solute (glucose) is measured in grams but the solution volume is measured in milliliters. Therefore, in this problem the mass and volume of the solution are interchangeable (1 g = 1 mL).

% (m/v) of glucose = mass of glucose / volume of solution

volume of solution = mass of glucose / % (m/v) of glucose

volume of solution = 50 g / 8.50%

volume of solution = 588 mL

109. A is correct. The addition of dissolved F^- (by adding NaF) decreases the solubility of CaF_2. This is the common ion effect (Le Châtelier's Principle).

110. D is correct.

111. E is correct. Given the dissolution of $PbCl_2$:

$PbCl_2 \rightarrow Pb^{2+} + 2Cl^-$
$K_{sp} = [Pb^{2+}][Cl^-]^2$

When X moles of $PbCl_2$ fully dissociate, X moles of Pb and 2X moles of Cl^- are produced:

$K_{sp} = (X)(2X)^2$

$K_{sp} = 4X^3$

112. B is correct.

113. D is correct.

114. E is correct.

115. A is correct.

116. C is correct.

117. B is correct. % (m/m) means that both solute and solvent are measured by their mass.

If the solution contains 12% (m/m), it means that the rest of it is water, or:

$$100\% - 12\% = 88\%$$

Use this percentage to determine the mass:

$$\text{mass of water} = 88\% \times 148 \text{ grams}$$

$$\text{mass of water} = 130.24 \text{ g} \approx 130 \text{ g}$$

118. A is correct.

119. E is correct.

120. D is correct. When AgCl dissociates, equal amounts of Ag^+ and Cl^- are produced. If the concentration of Cl^- is B, this must also be the concentration of Ag^+. The concentration of silver ion can be determined by dividing the K_{sp} by the concentration of chloride ion: $K_{sp} = [Ag^+][Cl^-]$.

Therefore, the concentration of Ag can be A/B moles/liter.

121. C is correct.

122. B is correct.

123. D is correct.

124. A is correct. When an ion is hydrated, it is surrounded and bonded by water molecules. The average number of water molecules bonding to an ion is known as its hydration number. Hydration numbers vary but often are either 4 or 6.

125. C is correct.

$$\text{mass of sucrose} = \text{concentration} \times \text{volume}$$

$$\text{mass of sucrose} = 0.5 \text{ g/L} \times 5.0 \text{ L}$$

$$\text{mass of sucrose} = 2.5 \text{ g}$$

126. E is correct. The NaOH content is 5.0% (m/v). It means that the solute (NaOH) is measured in grams but the solution volume is measured in milliliters. Therefore, in this problem, the mass and volume of the solution are interchangeable (1 g = 1 mL).

$$\text{mass of NaOH} = \% \text{ NaOH} \times \text{volume of solution}$$

$$\text{mass of NaOH} = 5.0\% \times 75.0 \text{ mL}$$

$$\text{mass of NaOH} = 3.75 \text{ g}$$

127. C is correct.

128. D is correct.

129. C is correct.

130. E is correct.

131. B is correct. Strong electrolytes dissociate completely (or almost completely) in water. Strong acids and bases both dissociate nearly completely, but weak acids and bases dissociate only slightly.

132. D is correct.

133. A is correct.

Mass % NaCl = (mass of NaCl / total mass) × 100%

Mass % NaCl = {17.2 g / (17.2 g + 149 g)} × 100%

Mass % NaCl = 10.3 %

134. E is correct.

135. B is correct. Since the empirical formula for magnesium iodide is MgI_2, two moles of dissolved I^- result from each mole of dissolved MgI_2. Therefore, if $[MgI_2] = 0.40$ M, then $[I^-] = 2(0.40$ M$) = 0.80$ M.

136. A is correct. Henry's Law:

$k_H = c/p$

where k_H = Henry's law constant, c = concentration of gas in solution, and p = partial pressure of gas

Rearrange the equation to solve for c:

$c = k_H × p$

$c = 6.8 × 10^{-4}$ mol/L-atm × 0.826 atm

$c = 5.62 × 10^{-4}$ M

137. D is correct. First determine the number of moles:

Moles of $CuSO_4$ = mass of $CuSO_4$ / molecular mass of $CuSO_4$

Moles of $CuSO_4$ = 0.967 g / (63.55 g/mol + 32.06 g/mol + 4 × 16 g/mol)

Moles of $CuSO_4$ = 6.06 × 10^{-3} moles

Convert volume to liters:

20 mL × 0.001 L/mL = 0.02 L

Divide moles by volume to calculate molarity:

Molarity = moles/volume

Molarity = 6.06 × 10^{-3} moles / 0.02 L

Molarity = 0.303 M

138. A is correct. For the dissolution of $PbCl_2$:

$$PbCl_2 \rightarrow Pb^{2+} + 2Cl^-$$

$$K_{sp} = [Pb^{2+}][2Cl^-]^2 = 10^{-5}$$

$$K_{sp} = (x)(2x)^{2+} = 10^{-5}$$

$$4x^3 = 10^{-5}$$

$$x \cong 0.014$$

$$[Cl^-] = 2(0.014)$$

$$[Cl^-] = 0.028$$

For the dissolution of AgCl:

$$AgCl \rightarrow Ag^+ + Cl^-$$

$$K_{sp} = [Ag^+][Cl^-]$$

$$K_{sp} = (x)(x)$$

$$10^{-10} = x^2$$

$$x = 10^{-5}$$

$$[Cl^-] = 10^{-5}$$

139. A is correct. Find concentrations of ions of $Mg(NO_3)_2$ and K_2SO_4 upon complete dissociation.

$Mg(NO_3)_2 \rightarrow$ Mg^{2+} $+$ $2NO_3^-$
0.03 mole   0.03 mole   0.06 mole

$$1 \text{ liter } Mg(NO_3)_2 \times \frac{0.03 \text{ mole}}{\text{liter}} = \frac{0.03 \text{ mole}}{Mg(NO_3)_2}$$

$$2 \text{ liters } K_2SO_4 \times \frac{0.06 \text{ mole}}{\text{liter}} = 0.12 \text{ mole } K_2SO_4$$

Now what is the concentration of Mg^{2+} in the mixture?

$$[Mg^{2+}] = \frac{0.03 \text{ mole}}{3 \text{ liters total volume}} = 0.01 \text{ M}$$

How about SO_4^{2+}?

$$[SO_4^{2-}] = \frac{0.12 \text{ mole}}{3 \text{ liters total volume}} = 0.04 M$$

The ion product is Q:

$$Q = [Mg^{2+}][SO_4^{2-}]$$

$$Q = [0.01][0.04]$$

$$Q = [1 \times 10^{-2}][4 \times 10^{-2}]$$

$$Q = 4 \times 10^{-4}$$

Because $Q > K_{sp}$, more solid must form to decrease the ion product to the K_{sp} value; therefore, precipitation does occur.

140. E is correct. Adding NaCl increases [Cl⁻] in solution (i.e. common ion effect) which increases the precipitation of $PbCl_2$ because the ion product increases. This increase causes lead chloride to precipitate and the concentration of free chloride in solution to decrease.

141. A is correct. AgCl has a stronger tendency to form than $PbCl_2$ because of its smaller K_{sp}. Therefore, as AgCl forms, an equivalent amount of $PbCl_2$ dissolves.

142. E is correct. Solubility is proportional to pressure. Use simple proportions to calculate solubility in a different pressure:

$\text{Solubility}_2 / \text{Solubility}_1) = (\text{Pressure}_2 / \text{Pressure}_1)$

$\text{Solubility}_2 = (\text{Pressure}_2 / \text{Pressure}_1) \times \text{Solubility}_1$

$\text{Solubility}_2 = (10.0 \text{ atm} / 1.0 \text{ atm}) \times 1.45 \text{ g/L}$

$\text{Solubility}_2 = 14.5 \text{ g/L}$

143. D is correct.

144. B is correct. Potassium oxide contains a metal and nonmetal, which makes it a salt. Salts contain ionic bonds and are strong electrolytes.

145. D is correct. Calculation of concentration in ppm (parts per million) is similar to percentage calculation; the only difference is the multiplication factor: 10^6 ppm instead of 100%.

Concentration of contaminant = (mass of contaminant / mass of solution) × 10^6 ppm

Concentration of contaminant = (9.86×10^{-3} g / 4865 g) × 10^6 ppm

Concentration of contaminant = 2.03 ppm

146. E is correct.

147. C is correct. If the attraction between solute molecules is equal or less than the attraction between solvent molecules, a solute has infinite solubility because solvent-solute attraction is stronger than solute-solute attraction.

148. B is correct.

149. C is correct. Molality is the number of solute moles dissolved in 1000 grams of solvent. The total mass of the solution is 1000 g + mass of solute.

Mass of solute (CH_3OH) = moles CH_3OH × molecular mass of CH_3OH

Mass of solute (CH_3OH) = 9.55 moles × (12.01 g/mol + 4 × 1.01 g/mol + 16 g/mol)

Mass of solute (CH_3OH) = 306.1 g

Total mass of solution: 1000 g + 306.1 g = 1306.1 g

Volume of solution = mass / density

Volume of solution = 1306.1 g / 0.937 g/mL

Volume of solution = 1393.92 mL

Divide moles by volume to calculate molarity:

Molarity = number of moles / volume

Molarity = 9.55 moles / 1393.92 mL

Molarity = 6.85 M ≈ 6.86 M

150. C is correct.

151. A is correct.

152. D is correct. Calculate concentration of each option. Because all solutions have the same solute and solvent, concentration expressed in g/mL can be used to compare concentration.

A: 2.4 g / 2 mL = 1.2 g/mL

B: 2.4 g / 5 mL = 0.48 g/mL

C: 20 g / 50 mL = 0.4 g/mL

D: 30 g / 150 mL = 0.2 g/mL

E: 50 g / 175 mL = 0.286 g/mL

Answer: 30 g solute in 150 mL solution.

153. B is correct.

154. C is correct. Hydrochloric acid contains two nonmetals, and is a covalently bonded molecule. Hydrochloric acid is also a strong acid and dissociates into ions when placed in water (i.e. strong electrolyte).

155. C is correct.

156. D is correct.

157. B is correct.

158. E is correct.

Mass % of protein = (mass of protein / mass of blood plasma) × 100%

Mass % of protein = (0.870 g / 10.279 g) × 100%

Mass % of protein = 8.46%

159. D is correct.

The addition of solute to a liquid lowers the vapor pressure of the liquid.

160. C is correct.

161. C is correct.

Mass % of solute = (mass of solute / total urine mass) × 100%

Mass % of solute = (1.929 g / 25.725 g) × 100%

Mass % of solute = 7.499%

162. E is correct.

163. A is correct.

164. D is correct.

Mass % of solute = (mass of solute × mass of seawater) × 100%

Mass % of solute = (1.295 g / 25.895 g) × 100%

Mass % of solute = 5.001%

165. B is correct. The reaction is endothermic because the temperature of the solution drops as the reaction absorbs heat from the environment, and $\Delta H°$ is positive. The solution is unsaturated at 1 molar so dissolving more salt at standard conditions is spontaneous, and $\Delta G°$ is negative.

166. C is correct.

167. A is correct. Start by calculating the moles of H_3PO_4 required:

moles H_3PO_4 = molarity of solution × volume

moles H_3PO_4 = 0.175 M × (175 mL × 0.001 L/mL)

moles H_3PO_4 = 0.031 mole

Then use this information to calculate mass:

Mass of H_3PO_4 = moles × molar mass

Mass of H_3PO_4 = 0.031 moles × (3 × 1.01 g/mol + 30.97 g/mol + 4 × 16 g/mol)

Mass of H_3PO_4 = 3.038 g ≈ 3.00 g

168. E is correct. By definition, a 15.0% aqueous solution of KI contains 15% KI and the remainder (100 % – 15% = 85%) is water. If there are 100 g of KI solution, it will have 15 g of KI and 85 g of water.

Option E (15 g KI and 100 g water) is incorrect because 100 g is the mass of the solution; the actual mass of water should is 85 g.

Answer: 15.0 g KI / 100 g water

169. A is correct. The barium hydroxide dissolved reversibly via the reaction:

$$Ba(OH)_2 (s) \leftrightarrow Ba^{2+} (aq) + 2OH^- (aq)$$

Therefore, the equilibrium expression is $K_{sp} = [Ba^{2+}][OH^-]^2$.

170. E is correct.

171. B is correct. Mass % = mass of solute / mass of solution

Rearrange that equation to solve for mass of solution:

mass of solution = mass of solute / mass %

mass of solution = 2.50 g / 10.0%

mass of solution = 2.50 g / 0.1

mass of solution = 25.0 g

172. A is correct.

173. D is correct. The heat of solution is the enthalpy change (or energy absorbed as heat at constant pressure) when a solution forms. For solution formation, solvent-solvent bonds and solute-solute bonds must be broken while solute-solvent bonds are formed. The breaking of bonds absorbs energy, while the formation of bonds releases energy. If the heat of solution is negative, energy is released.

174. E is correct. Mass % = mass of solute / mass of solution

Rearrange that equation to solve for mass of solution:

mass of solution = mass of solute / mass %

mass of solution = 122 g / 7.50%

mass of solution = 122 g / 0.075

mass of solution = 1626.67 g $\approx$ 1630 g

175. B is correct.

176. A is correct. Let's start by assuming that there is 1 L of seawater. Molarity is defined as number of moles in 1 L of solution, so starting with 1 L will make calculation easier.

Mass of sea water = volume × density

Mass of sea water = (1 L × 1000 L/mL) × 1.06 g/mL

Mass of sea water = 1060 g

Use the mass of the sea water to determine the mass of KCl:

Mass of KCl = mass % of KCl × mass of sea water

Mass of KCl = 12.5% × 1060 g

Mass of KCl = 132.5 g

Next calculate the number of moles:

Moles of KCl = mass of KCl / molar mass of KCl

Moles of KCl = 132.5 g / (39.1 g/mol + 35.45 g/mol)

Moles of KCl = 1.78 moles

Divide moles by volume to calculate molarity:

Molarity of KCl = moles of KCl / volume of KCl

Molarity of KCl = 1.78 moles / 1 L

Molarity of KCl = 1.78 M

177. B is correct. Start by calculating moles of glucose:

Moles of glucose = mass of glucose / molar mass of glucose

Moles of glucose = 10.0 g / 180.18 g/mol

Moles of glucose = 0.0555 mol

Then divide moles by volume to calculate molarity:

Molarity of glucose = moles of glucose / volume of glucose

Molarity of glucose = 0.0555 mol / (100 mL × 0.001 L/mL)

Molarity = 0.555 M

178. E is correct. The reaction is endothermic if the bonds formed have lower energy than the bonds broken. Therefore, from $\Delta G = \Delta H - T\Delta S$, the entropy of the system increases if the reaction is spontaneous.

179. D is correct.

180. A is correct. First calculate the number of moles:

Moles of sucrose = mass of sucrose / molar mass of sucrose

Moles of sucrose = 10 g / 342.34 g/mol

Moles of sucrose = 0.0292 mol

Then divide moles by volume to calculate molarity:

Molarity of sucrose = moles of sucrose / volume of sucrose

Molarity = 0.0292 mol / (100.0 mL × 0.001 L/mL)

Molarity = 0.292 M

181. C is correct. For dilution problems, the concentration (C) times the volume (V) of all the solutions before mixing must equal the concentration times the volume of the final solution:

$(CV)_{\text{Soln 1}} + (CV)_{\text{Soln 2}} = (CV)_{\text{Final soln}}$

(0.02 M)(15 mL) + (0.04 M)(10 mL) = C(25 mL)

C = 0.028 M

182. D is correct.

183. B is correct. When a solution is diluted, the moles of solute (n) is constant. However, the molarity and volume will change. Because n = MV:

$n_1 = n_2$

$M_1V_1 = M_2V_2$

$M_2 = (M_1V_1) / V_2$

$M_2 = \{6.00 \text{ M} \times (250.0 \text{ mL} \times 0.001 \text{ L/mL})\} / 2.50 \text{ L}$

$M_2 = 0.6$ M

184. D is correct.

185. B is correct.

Molarity of NaCl = moles of NaCl / volume of NaCl

Molarity of NaCl = 3.50 moles / 1.50 L

Molarity of NaCl = 2.33 M

186. C is correct. When a solution is diluted, the moles of solute (n) is constant. However, the molarity and volume will change. Because n = MV:

$n_1 = n_2$

$M_1V_1 = M_2V_2$

$M_2 = (M_1V_1) / V_2$

$M_2 = \{0.500\ M \times (200.0\ mL \times 0.001\ L/mL)\} / 1.00\ L$

$M_2 = 0.1\ M$

187. E is correct. Bond formation releases energy: if the heat of solution is negative, then energy is released. Heat of solution is the net of enthalpy changes for making and breaking bonds. During solution formation, solvent-solvent bonds and solute-solute bonds break while solute-solvent bonds form. The breaking of bonds absorbs energy while the formation of bonds releases energy.

188. D is correct.

189. E is correct. When a solution is diluted, the moles of solute (n) is constant. However, the molarity and volume will change. Because n = MV:

$n_1 = n_2$

$M_1V_1 = M_2V_2$

$M_2 = (M_1V_1) / V_2$

$M_2 = \{1.00\ M \times (500.0\ mL \times 0.001\ L/mL)\} / 2.50\ L$

$M_2 = 0.200\ M$

190. C is correct.

191. B is correct. Start by calculating moles of KOH required:

moles of KOH = molarity × volume

moles of KOH = 0.576 M × (22.0 mL × 0.001 L/mL)

moles of KOH = 0.0127 moles

Then use this information to calculate mass:

mass of KOH = moles of KOH × molar mass of KOH

mass of KOH = 0.0127 × (39.1 g/mol + 16 g/mol + 1.01 g/mol)

mass of KOH = 0.713 g ≈ 0.711 g

192. A is correct. When a solution is diluted, the moles of solute (n) is constant. However, the molarity and volume will change. Because n = MV:

$n_1 = n_2$

$M_1V_1 = M_2V_2$

$V_2 = (M_1V_1) / M_2$

$V_2 = (0.10\ M \times 5.0\ L) / 12\ M$

$V_2 = 0.042\ L$

Convert to milliliters:

$$0.042 \text{ L} \times (1000 \text{ mL} / \text{L}) = 42 \text{ mL}$$

193. E is correct.

%v/v of alcohol = (volume of alcohol / volume of wine) × 100%

%v/v of alcohol = (15 mL / 200 mL) × 100%

%v/v of alcohol = 7.5%

194. A is correct. Start by calculating the number of moles:

Moles of LiOH = mass of LiOH / molar mass of LiOH

Moles of LiOH = 29.4 g / (6.97 g + 16.0 g + 1.01 g)

Moles of LiOH = 1.23 moles

Divide moles by volume to calculate molarity:

Molarity = moles / volume

Molarity = 1.23 moles / (985 mL × 0.001 L/mL)

Molarity = 1.25 M

195. C is correct. Start by calculating moles of $NaHCO_3$:

Moles of $NaHCO_3$ = mass $NaHCO_3$ / molar mass $NaHCO_3$

Moles of $NaHCO_3$ = 0.400 g / 84.01 g/mol

Moles of $NaHCO_3$ = 4.76×10^{-3} mol

In this reaction, both $NaHCO_3$ and HCl have coefficients of 1. Therefore moles $NaHCO_3$ = moles HCl = 4.76×10^{-3} mol. Use this to calculate volume of HCl:

volume of HCl = moles / molarity

volume of HCl = 4.76×10^{-3} mol / 0.255 M

volume of HCl = 0.0187 L

Convert volume to milliliters: 0.0187 L × (1000 mL/L) = 18.7 mL

196. E is correct.

197. C is correct.

% v/v solution = (volume of acetone / volume of solution) × 100%

% v/v solution = {25 mL / (25 mL + 75 mL)} × 100%

% v/v solution = 25%

198. A is correct. First calculate the number of moles:

Moles of Na_2CO_3 = mass Na_2CO_3 / moles of Na_2CO_3

Moles of Na_2CO_3 = 0.125 g / 105.99 g/mol

Moles of Na_2CO_3 = 1.18×10^{-3} mol

Check the reaction to obtain coefficients of HCl and Na_2CO_3.

Moles of HCl required = (coefficient of HCl / coefficient of Na_2CO_3) × moles Na_2CO_3

Moles of HCl required = (2/1) × 1.18×10^{-3} mol

Moles of HCl required = 2.36×10^{-3} mol

Then divide moles by molarity to find the volume:

volume of HCl = moles of HCl / molarity of HCl

volume of HCl = 2.36×10^{-3} mol / 0.115 M

volume of HCl = 0.0205 L

Convert to milliliters:

0.0205 L × (1000 mL/L) = 20.5 mL

199. D is correct. Start by calculating the number of moles:

Moles of $CaCl_2$ = molarity of $CaCl_2$ × volume of $CaCl_2$

Moles of $CaCl_2$ = 0.850 M × 3.20 L

Moles of $CaCl_2$ = 2.72 moles

Use this information to find the mass:

Mass of $CaCl_2$ = moles $CaCl_2$ × molar mass $CaCl_2$

Mass of $CaCl_2$ = 2.72 moles × (40.01 g/mol + 2 × 35.45 g/mol)

Mass of $CaCl_2$ = 301.68 g ≈ 302 g

200. B is correct.

201. C is correct.

202. C is correct.

203. A is correct. Start by calculating the number of moles:

Moles of $FeSO_4$ = molarity × volume

Moles of $FeSO_4$ = 0.500 M × (20.0 mL × 0.001 L/mL)

Moles of $FeSO_4$ = 0.01 mol

Use this information to find the mass:

Mass of $FeSO_4$ = moles $FeSO_4$ × molar mass $FeSO_4$

Mass of $FeSO_4$ = 0.01 mol × (55.85 g/mol + 23.06 g/mol + 4 × 16 g/mol)

Mass of $FeSO_4$ = 1.52 g

204. E is correct.

205. D is correct.

206. C is correct.

207. D is correct. Let's start by assuming that there are 1 L of $NaNO_3$ solution. Molarity is defined as number of moles in 1 L of solution; starting with 1 L will make calculation easier. Calculate the mass of the solution:

Mass of solution = volume × density

Mass of solution = (1 L x 1000 mL / L) × 1.24 g/mL

Mass of solution = 1240 g

Determine the mass of $NaNO_3$:

Mass of $NaNO_3$ = mass % of $NaNO_3$ × mass of solution

Mass of $NaNO_3$ = 25% × 1240 g

Mass of $NaNO_3$ = 310 g

Use this information to determine the number of moles:

Moles of $NaNO_3$ = mass of $NaNO_3$ / molar mass of $NaNO_3$

Moles of $NaNO_3$ = 310 g / (22.99 g/mol + 14.01 g/mol + 3 × 16 g/mol)

Moles of $NaNO_3$ = 3.647 moles

Divide moles by volume to calculate molarity:

Molarity of $NaNO_3$ = moles of $NaNO_3$ / volume of $NaNO_3$

Molarity of $NaNO_3$ = 3.647 moles / 1 L

Molarity of $NaNO_3$ = 3.647 M ≈ 3.65 M

208. A is correct.

209. C is correct. Because the % of NaOH is a (w/v) percentage, the solute is measured by weight and solvent is measured by volume. Therefore, the mass of solution can be used interchangeably with volume of solution, with 1 g = 1 mL. Volume is 750 mL, so the mass is 750 g.

Mass of NaOH = % mass NaOH × mass of solution

Mass of NaOH = 2.5% × 750 g

Mass of NaOH = 18.75 g ≈ 19 g

Chapter 5. ACIDS AND BASES

1. E is correct.

2. B is correct. An acid is a chemical substance with a pH less than 7 which produces H^+ ions in water. An acid can be neutralized by a base (i.e. a substance with a pH above 7) to form salt. Acids are known to have a sour taste (e.g. lemon juice). However, acids are not known to have a slippery feel; this is a characteristic of bases.

3. C is correct.

$$Kb = \frac{[NH_4^+][OH^-]}{[NH_3]} = 2 \times 10^{-5}$$

If $pH = 10, pOH = 4, [OH^-] = 1 \times 10^{-4}$

Therefore,

$$Kb = \frac{[NH_4^+][1 \times 10^{-4}]}{[4 \times 10^{-1}]}[2 \times 10^{-5}]$$

$$2 \times 10-5 = \frac{[NH_4^+][1 \times 10^{-4}]}{[4 \times 10^{-1}]}[2 \times 10^{-5}]$$

$$[NH_4^+] = 0.08 \text{ M}$$

4. D is correct.

5. C is correct.

6. B is correct. When the NH_3 molecule accepts a proton to form ammonium, the reaction is: $NH_3 + H^+ \rightarrow NH_4^+$

When NH_3 (charge = 0) combines with the proton (charge = +1), the product molecule must have a charge of $0 + 1 = +1$. Additionally, since NH_3 has eight electrons and H^+ has none, the NH_4^+ molecule must also have 8 electrons.

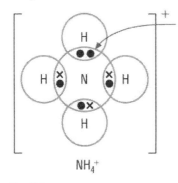

From the Lewis dot structure, when NH_3 donates a lone pair to H^+ to form the coordinate covalent bond, both of the electrons involved in forming the new N-H bond come from the lone pair on the nitrogen atom in the NH_3 molecule (since there are no electrons at all in a bare proton). The nitrogen shares its lone pair of electrons with the proton, resulting in a formal charge of +1 on the nitrogen.

7. C is correct.

8. A is correct.

9. D is correct.

10. B is correct. Brønsted-Lowry acids are defined as proton donors (e.g., HCl, H_2SO_4). Brønsted-Lowry bases are defined as proton acceptors (e.g., HSO_4^-, NO_3^-). Lewis acids are defined as electron pair acceptors, whereas Lewis bases are electron pair donors.

11. D is correct.

12. E is correct.

13. A is correct.

14. E is correct.

15. A is correct.

16. C is correct.

17. A is correct.

18. B is correct. The acid requires two equivalents of base to be fully titrated and therefore is a diprotic acid. At point A, the acid is fully protonated, for example, oxalic acid ($H_2C_2O_4$). At point A, the acid is 50% fully protonated, 50% monoprotonated (50% $H_2C_2O_4$, $HC_2O_4^-$).

At point C, the acid exists in the monoprotonated form only (100% $HC_2O_4^-$).

At point D, the acid exists in the 50% HSO_4^- form and 50% in the SO_4^{2-} form.

Finally, at point E, the acid exists as 100% $C_2O_4^{2-}$.

Point A is known as pK_1, and point C is pK_2.

19. C is correct. See explanation to question **18** above.

20. A is correct.

21. B is correct.

22. B is correct. The buffer region is the flattest region on the curve (the region that resists pH increases with added base). This acid has two buffer regions: around point A and around point C.

23. A is correct. An acid is a substance that ionizes when dissolved in suitable ionizing solvents such as water. If a high proportion of the solute dissociates to form free ions, it is a strong electrolyte. If most of it does not dissociate, it is a weak electrolyte. The more free ions are there, the better the solution will be at conducting electricity.

24. E is correct. The Arrhenius acid-base theory states that acids produce H^+ ions in H_2O solution and bases produce OH^- ions in H_2O solution. This is just one way to classify acids and bases. Other ways include the Bronsted-Lowry acid-base theory, which focuses on the ability to accept and donate protons, and the Lewis acid-base theory, which focuses on the ability to accept and donate electrons. The Arrhenius acid-base theory states that neutralization happens when acid-base reactions produce water and a salt, and that these reactions must take place in aqueous solution.

25. D is correct.

26. C is correct.

27. E is correct.

28. D is correct. The production of H^+ ions in water is characteristic of an acid, not a base. A base is a chemical substance with a pH less than 7 and will produce hydroxide (OH^-) ions in water. A base can be neutralized by an acid (i.e. a substance with a pH below 7) to form salt. Bases are known to have a slippery or soapy feel, because they dissolve the fatty acids and oils from the skin, cutting down the amount of friction. They are also known to have a bitter taste; for example, coffee is bitter because it contains caffeine, which is a base.

29. A is correct. HCl is a strong acid. Strong acids have weak conjugate bases.

30. B is correct.

31. E is correct. When Ka of an acid is considered, the higher the value, the stronger the acid is. Among the choices, HF (hydrofluoric acid) has the highest Ka value, and is therefore the strongest acid. The second strongest acid is HNO_2 (nitrous acid).

H_2CO_3 – carbonic acid; HCN – hydrocyanic acid; HClO – hypochlorous acid.

32. B is correct.

33. D is correct.

34. C is correct.

35. B is correct.

$$pH = -\log [H^+]$$
$$pH = -\log (1.2 \times 10^{-3})$$
$$pH = 2.92$$

36. A is correct. Lewis bases are electron donors. NH_3 has a lone pair of electrons attached to N which can form bonds to other compounds. NH_3 can also act as a proton acceptor: $NH_3 + H_2O \rightleftharpoons NH_4^+ + OH^-$

37. A is correct.

38. E is correct. The ionic product constant for water K_w is equal to 1×10^{-14}:

$$K_w = [H_3O^+] [OH^-]$$
$$1 \times 10^{-14} = [H_3O^+] [OH^-]$$

Rearrange to solve for $[OH^-]$:

$$[OH^-] = 1 \times 10^{-14} \text{ M} / [H_3O^+]$$
$$[OH^-] = 1 \times 10^{-14} \text{ M} / (3.5 \times 10^{-3} \text{ M})$$
$$[OH^-] = 2.86 \times 10^{-12} \text{ M} \approx 2.9 \times 10^{-12} \text{ M}$$

39. D is correct. Strong acids dissociate completely, or almost completely, when in water. They dissociate into a positively-charged hydrogen ion (H^+) and another ion that is negatively charged. An example is hydrochloric acid (HCl), which dissociates into H^+ and Cl^- ions. Polarity refers to the distribution of electrons in a bond, and if a molecule is polar, one side has a partial positive charge and the other side has a partial negative charge. The more polar the bond, the easier it is for a molecule to dissociate into ions, and therefore the acid is more strongly acidic.

40. B is correct.

41. A is correct. The Brønsted-Lowry acid-base theory focuses on the ability to accept and donate protons, while the Arrhenius acid-base theory focuses on the ability to produce H^+ and OH^- ions. A Brønsted-Lowry acid is the term for a substance that donates a proton in an acid-base reaction, while a Brønsted-Lowry base is the term for the substance that accepts the proton.

42. B is correct. The pH is the negative log of the activity of the hydrogen ion in an aqueous solution. The pH scale runs from 1 to 14, with 7 being a neutral pH. Acidic solutions have a pH below 7, while basic solutions have a pH above 7.

43. D is correct. HNO_3 is the only strong acid.

44. C is correct.

45. C is correct.

46. C is correct. Ashes are basic, so they can react with the oils from a person's skin and convert them into fatty acids. This produces solutions of soap that can be used as a cleaning agent, which is why a person might wash their hands with ashes.

47. D is correct.

48. E is correct. An acid is a chemical substance with a pH less than 7 that turns litmus paper red. An acid can neutralized a base (i.e. a substance with a pH above 7) to form salt. Acids are known to have a sour taste (e.g. lemon juice has a pH of about 2).

49. B is correct.

50. D is correct. The strongest acid has the largest K_a value.

51. A is correct. KOH is a strong base, which means all KOH ions will dissociate into K^+ and OH^-. Therefore, $[KOH] = [OH^-] = 0.035$ M.

To determine pH of bases, start by calculating pOH:

$$pOH = -\log[OH^-]$$

$$pOH = -\log 0.035$$

$$pOH = 1.46$$

Using pOH, determine the pH:

$$pH + pOH = 14$$

$$pH = 14 - pOH$$

$$pH = 14 - 1.46$$

$$pH = 12.54 \approx 12.5$$

52. C is correct.

53. B is correct.

54. E is correct.

55. D is correct.

56. A is correct.

57. B is correct.

58. D is correct.

59. E is correct. Boron has an atomic number of five and has a vacant 2p orbital to accept electrons.

60. B is correct. First, determine the reaction product by writing down the full equation. When an acid reacts with a base, it will result in formation of a salt and water. Exchange the cations and anions from acid and base to form the new salt:

$$NaOH + H_2SO_4 \rightarrow Na_2SO_4 + H_2O$$

Always check if a reaction is balanced before starting calculations. That equation was not balanced, so balance it first. Here is the balanced equation:

$$2NaOH + H_2SO_4 \rightarrow Na_2SO_4 + 2H_2O$$

The residue mentioned in the problem must be Na_2SO_4 residue. Calculate moles of Na_2SO_4:

moles Na_2SO_4 = mass Na_2SO_4 / molecular mass Na_2SO_4

moles Na_2SO_4 = (861 mg × 0.001 g/mg) / (2 × 22.99 g/mol + 32.06 g/mol + 4 × 16 g/mol)

moles Na_2SO_4 = 6.06×10^{-3} mole

Because coefficient Na_2SO_4 = coefficient H_2SO_4, moles Na_2SO_4 = moles H_2SO_4 = 6.06×10^{-3} mole. Use this information to determine the molarity:

Molarity of H_2SO_4 = moles of H_2SO_4 / volume of H_2SO_4

Molarity of H_2SO_4 = 6.06×10^{-3} mole / (36 mL × 0.001 L / mL)

Molarity of H_2SO_4 = 0.168 M

61. C is correct. Use this formula for pH:

pH = – log [H^+]

pH = – log [0.000001]

pH = 6

62. B is correct. Only the extent of dissociation of the dissolved acid or base determines its classification as weak or strong. Strong acids and bases completely dissociate into their constituent ions, while weak acids and weak bases only partially dissociate.

63. A is correct. A weak acid will react with a strong base, and it will be converted to its conjugate weak base, creating an overall basic solution.

A strong acid does react with a strong base, creating a neutral solution.

A weak acid only partially dissociates when dissolved in water; unlike a strong acid, it does not readily form ions.

Strong acids are much more corrosive than weak acids.

64. B is correct.

65. C is correct.

66. C is correct.

67. E is correct. The conjugate base of a chemical species is that species after H^+ has dissociated. Therefore, the conjugate base of HSO_4^- is SO_4^{2-} and the conjugate base of H_3O^+ is H_2O.

68. A is correct.

69. A is correct.

70. D is correct.

71. C is correct. The weakest acid has the strongest conjugate base.

72. C is correct.

73. E is correct. The balanced reaction is as follows:

$$2H_3PO_4 + 3Ba(OH)_2 \rightarrow Ba_3(PO_4)_2 + 6H_2O$$

Even though there are 2 moles of H_3PO_4 in a balanced reaction. However, acids are categorized by the number of H^+ per mole of acid.

For example, HCl is monoprotic, H_2SO_4 is diprotic and H_3PO_4 is triprotic acid, regardless of the number of moles in a reaction.

74. D is correct.

75. D is correct.

$$37 \text{ g} \times \frac{1 \text{ mole}}{74 \text{ g}} = 0.05 \text{ mole } Ca(OH)_2$$

$$\frac{2 \text{ moles OH}^-}{1 \text{ mole } Ca(OH)_2} \times 0.5 \text{ mole } Ca(OH)_2 = 1.0 \text{ mole } {}^-OH$$

$$1 \text{ liter} \times \frac{0.55 \text{ mole } H_2SO_4}{\text{liter}} \times \frac{2 \text{ moles } H^+}{1 \text{ mole } H_2SO_4} = 1.1 \text{ moles } H^+$$

Net $H^+ = 1.1$ moles $H^+ - 1$ mole $OH^- = 0.1$ mole H^+

$pH = -\log(0.1) = 1$

$pOH = 14 - (1) = 13$

76. C is correct.

77. D is correct.

78. C is correct. Perchloric acid ($HClO_4$) is the strongest acid thus is the weakest conjugate base. Hypochlorite (ClO^-) is the strongest base (i.e. least stable anion). In oxy acids, the more oxygen, the greater is the acid strength (i.e. for the weakest conjugate bases).

79. E is correct.

80. B is correct.

81. A is correct.

82. C is correct. Acetic acid (CH_3COOH) is a proton (H^+) donor and a weak acid.

83. E is correct. Acidic solutions contain hydronium ions (H_3O^+). These ions are in the aqueous form because they are dissolved in water. Although chemists often write H^+ (*aq*), referring to a single hydrogen nucleus (a proton), it actually exists as the hydrogen atom.

84. D is correct. pH greater than 7, turns litmus paper blue, and feels slippery are all qualities of bases, not acids. However, a sour taste is a general property of an acidic solution (e.g. lemon juice, pH 2).

85. C is correct.

86. A is correct.

87. A is correct.

88. B is correct.

89. B is correct. An Arrhenius acid increases the concentration of H^+ ions in an aqueous solution. Since pH is the negative log of the activity of H^+ ions in an aqueous solution, this is why acids have a low pH. It is true that an acid can act as a proton donor, but this is the Brønsted-Lowry definition of an acid, not Arrhenius.

90. A is correct. $Ka = \dfrac{[H^+][F^-]}{[HF]} \dfrac{(5 \times 10^{-2})(5 \times 10^{-5})}{(2.5 \times 10^{-1})} = 1 \times 10^{-5}$ or 0.00001

91. D is correct. The ratio of the conjugate base to the acid must be determined from the pH of the solution and the pKa of the acidic component in the reaction. In the reaction, $H_2PO_4^-$ is acting as the acid and HPO_4^{2-} is acting as the base, so the pK_a of $H_2PO_4^-$ should be used in the equation. Plugging in the values, the Henderson-Hasselbalch equation should read:

pH = pK_a + log (salt/acid)

7.2 = 6.86 + log(salt/acid).

Since $H_2PO_4^-$ is acting as the acid, subtract 6.86 from both sides to get:

0.34 = log(salt/acid).

The log base is 10, so the inverse log will give:

$10^{0.34}$ = (salt/acid)

(salt/acid) = 2.18 ≈ 2.2

This means that the ratio between the conjugate base or salt and the acid is 2.2/1.

92. E is correct. The balanced equation is:

$BaCO_3$ (*aq*) + $2HNO_3$ (*aq*) → $Ba(NO_3)_2$ (*aq*) + CO_2 (*g*) + H_2O (*l*)

Therefore, the sum of the coefficients is: 1 + 2 + 1 + 1 + 1 = 6

93. C is correct.

94. B is correct.

95. D is correct.

96. E is correct.

97. D is correct. Start by calculating moles of Na_2CO_3:

moles Na_2CO_3 = mass Na_2CO_3 / molar mass Na_2CO_3

moles Na_2CO_3 = 0.424 g / 105.99 g/mol

moles Na_2CO_3 = 0.004 mole

Then use the coefficients in the equation to determine the moles of HCl:

Moles of HCl = (coefficient HCl / coefficient Na_2CO_3) × moles Na_2CO_3

Moles of HCl = (2/1) × 0.004 mole

Moles of HCl = 0.008 mole

Divide moles by volume to calculate molarity:

Molarity of HCl = moles of HCl / volume of HCl

Molarity of HCl = 0.008 mole / (20 mL × 0.001 L/mL)

Molarity of HCl = 0.4 M

98. C is correct. The formula for pH is:

pH = $-\log[H_3O^+]$

Rearrange to solve for $[H_3O^+]$:

$[H_3O^+] = 10^{-pH}$

$[H_3O^+] = 10^{-2.34}$

$[H_3O^+] = 4.57 \times 10^{-3} \approx 4.6 \times 10^{-3}$ M

99. E is correct. Amophoteric compounds act as Brønsted-Lowry acids and bases. HSO_4^- acts as both a proton donor and a proton acceptor.

100. A is correct. Because both HCl and NaOH have coefficients of 1, moles HCl = moles NaOH:

$n_{HCl} = n_{NaOH}$

Because n = MV:

$M_{HCl} \times V_{HCl} = M_{NaOH} \times V_{NaOH}$

$V_{NaOH} = M_{HCl} \times V_{HCl} / M_{NaOH}$

$V_{NaOH} = 0.1$ M × 10 mL / 0.2 M

$V_{NaOH} = 5.00$ mL

101. B is correct. Although the Lewis dot structure is used more frequently when discussing Lewis acids and bases, it is also applicable to Brønsted-Lowry acid base theory. A Brønsted-Lowry base must carry a lone pair of electrons, which is later transferred to its conjugate acid over the course of the reaction.

102. E is correct. When a strong acid reacts with a weak base, the resulting product will be an acid salt, and the resulting solution will have a pH lower than 7. An example of this is the reaction NH_3 (weak base) + HCl (strong acid) → NH_4Cl. The product is the acid ammonium chloride, which dissociates into NH_4^+ and Cl^-. The ammonium dissociates further into ammonia and a proton, and since it donates a proton, it makes the solution acidic.

103. A is correct.

104. C is correct. According to Brønsted-Lowry acid theory, an acid is the species which contributes proton/hydrogen. H_2CO_3 gave one hydrogen to Na_2HPO_4, which makes H_2CO_3 the acid in this reaction.

105. D is correct.

106. E is correct. Acids and bases react to form H_2O and salts: $NaOH + HCl \rightleftharpoons Na^+Cl^-$ (a salt) $+ H_2O$ (water)

107. D is correct.

108. C is correct.

109. E is correct.

I: water is always produced in neutralization reaction.

II: is only one example of neutralization, but it is not always the case.

III: neutralization occurs when acid donates a proton to the base.

110. C is correct.

111. B is correct.

112. B is correct.

113. D is correct. Weak acids or bases and their salts are the best buffer systems.

114. E is correct. For this question, it is important to identify the acid that is active in the reaction. The parent acid is defined as the most protonated form of the buffer. The number of dissociating protons an acid can donate will depend on the charge of its conjugate base.

$Ba_2P_2O_7$ is given as one of the products in the reaction. Because barium is a group 2B metal, it has a stable oxidation state of +2. Because two barium cations are present in the product, the charge of P_2O_7 ion (the conjugate base in the reaction) must be –4. Therefore, the fully protonated form of this conjugate must be $H_4P_2O_7$, which is a tetraprotic acid because it has 4 protons that can dissociate.

115. B is correct.

116. A is correct.

117. D is correct. By the Brønsted-Lowry definition, a base accepts H^+ (hydrogen) ions.

By the Arrhenius definition, a base donates ^-OH (hydroxide) ions in water.

By the Lewis definition, a base donates electrons.

118. C is correct.

119. A is correct.

120. E is correct.

121. C is correct. A buffer is an aqueous solution that consists of a weak acid and its conjugate base, or vice versa. It resists changes in pH, and is often used to keep pH at a nearly constant value in many chemical applications.

122. A is correct. H_2SO_4 is a strong acid. Weak acids and their salts are good buffers.

123. C is correct.

124. B is correct.

125. A is correct. pI is the symbol for isoeletric point: pH where a protein ion has zero net charge.

To calculate pI of amino acids, take the average of the pK_a's:

$$pI = (pK_a1 + pK_a2) / 2$$

$$pI = (2.2 + 4.2) / 2$$

$$pI = 3.2$$

126. D is correct.

127. C is correct.

128. A is correct. HNO_3 is a strong acid, which means that $[HNO_3] = [H_3O^+] = 0.00756$.

$$pH = - \log [H_3O^+]$$

$$pH = - \log (0.00756)$$

$$pH = 2.1$$

129. A is correct. Salts of strong acids or bases are neutral. For example:

$HCl +$ $NaOH \rightleftharpoons NaCl + H_2O$
Strong   strong   neutral
  acid   base

130. E is correct.

131. C is correct. K_w is water ionization constant (also called water autoprotolysis constant). It can be determined by experiment and has the value 1.011×10^{-14} at 25 °C (1.00×10^{-14} is used in general).

132. B is correct.

133. D is correct.

134. E is correct. The properties listed above (turning litmus paper blue, bitter taste, slippery feel and neutralizing acids) are all true of bases. An acidic solution has opposite qualities. It has a pH lower than 7 and therefore turns litmus paper red. It neutralizes bases, it tastes sour and does not feel slippery.

135. B is correct.

136. E is correct. All reactions either increase the production of H^+ or OH^-, or decrease the production of H^+ or OH^- and therefore resist changes in pH (feature of a buffer system).

137. A is correct. A standard solution contains a precisely known concentration of an element or substance, usually determined to 3-4 significant digits. Standard solutions are often used to determine the concentration of other substances, such as solutions in titrations.

138. B is correct.

139. D is correct.

140. B is correct.

141. E is correct.

142. C is correct. H_2O lost a proton/a hydrogen to form OH^-. The proton is taken by CO_3^{2-} and it becomes HCO_3^-. In other words, H_2O acts as the donor and gives a proton to CO_3^{2-}, which acts as the acceptor.

143. D is correct. HCl completely dissociates in solution:

$$0.001\ M = \frac{0.001\ \text{mole H}^+}{\text{liter}} \quad pH = -\log[H^+] = -\log(10^{-3}) = 3$$

144. E is correct. In a neutralization reaction, cations and anions from acid and base will trade partners, which will result in salt and water.

Complete reaction: $H_2SO_4\ (aq) + 2NaOH\ (aq) \rightarrow Na_2SO_4\ (aq) + 2H_2O\ (l)$

145. A is correct.

146. C is correct.

147. A is correct.

148. D is correct. According to Bronsted-Lowry acid theory, an acid is a molecule which contributes proton/hydrogen. HCN lost a hydrogen/proton and this proton pairs up with HS to form H_2S.

149. C is correct.

Condition 1: pH = 4

$[H_3O^+] = 10^{-pH} = 10^{-4}$

Condition 2: pH = 7

$[H_3O^+] = 10^{-pH} = 10^{-7}$

Ratio of $[H_3O^+]$ in condition 1 and condition 2:

$10^{-4} : 10^{-7} = 1000 : 1$

Solution with pH = 4 has 1000 times greater $[H^+]$ than solution with pH = 7.

(Note: $[H_3O^+]$ is equivalent to $[H^+]$.)

150. B is correct. Use the following relationship between pH and pK_a:

$$pH = pKa + \log\left(\frac{\text{salt}}{\text{acid}}\right)$$

Convert the given K_a into pK_a:

$Ka = 1 \times 10^{-4}$

$$pKa = -\log(10^{-4}) = 4$$

$$pH = 4 + \log\left(\frac{1}{10}\right)$$

$$pH = 4 + \log 10^{-1}$$

$$pH = 4 + -1 = 3$$

151. C is correct.

152. A is correct. The formula for pH is:

$$pH = -\log[H^+]$$

Rearrange to solve for $[H^+]$:

$$[H^+] = 10^{-pH}$$

$$[H^+] = 10^{-6.35}$$

$$[H^+] = 4.47 \times 10^{-7} \approx 4.5 \times 10^{-7} \text{ M}$$

153. E is correct.

154. B is correct.

155. D is correct. Start by calculating the moles of HCl:

Moles HCl = molarity HCl × volume HCl

Moles HCl = 0.1 M × (25 mL × 0.001 L / mL)

Moles HCl = 0.0025 mole

Use the coefficients in the reaction equation to determine the moles of $Ba(OH)_2$:

Moles of $Ba(OH)_2$ = (coefficient $Ba(OH)_2$ / coefficient HCl) × moles HCl

Moles of $Ba(OH)_2$ = (1/2) × 0.0025 mole

Moles of $Ba(OH)_2$ = 0.00125 mole

Divide moles by molarity to calculate volume:

Volume of $Ba(OH)_2$ = moles of $Ba(OH)_2$ / molarity of $Ba(OH)_2$

Volume of $Ba(OH)_2$ = 0.00125 mole / 0.15 M

Volume of $Ba(OH)_2$ = 0.00833 L

Convert volume to milliliters:

0.00833 L × 1000 mL / L = 8.33 mL

156. C is correct.

157. E is correct.

158. A is correct. The dissociation of HF is:

$$HF \ (aq) \leftrightarrow H^+ \ (aq) + F^- \ (aq)$$

Let $[H^+] = [F^-] = x$. Although the actual equilibrium concentration of HF is $(2 - x)$ M due to dissociation, assume that x is very small (compared to 2) and ignore the difference.

[HF] = 2 M at equilibrium

The equilibrium expression for this reaction is:

$K_a = [H^+][F^-] / [HF]$

$K_a = x^2/2$

$x^2 = 2K_a$

$x^2 = 2(6.5 \times 10^{-4})$

$x^2 = 13.0 \times 10^{-4}$

$x = 3.6 \times 10^{-2}$

The assumption x is small compared to 2 is very reasonable; x is less than 2% of 2.

159. D is correct.

160. B is correct. Use the Henderson-Hasselbalch equation:

$pH = pK_a + \log(A^-/HA)$

$pH = -\log(1.8 \times 10^{-5}) + \log(1/10)$

$pH = 4.7 - 1 = 3.7$

161. C is correct. An acid is known to donate hydrogen ions (H^+) in water. It is important to differentiate the hydrogen ion from a hydrogen atom (H), because a hydrogen ion refers to a hydrogen atom that has donated its one electron and thus consists of only a nucleus. A hydrogen ion H^+ is thus equivalent to a proton.

162. E is correct.

163. C is correct.

$pH = -\log [H^+]$

$pH = -\log 0.001$

$pH = 3$

164. D is correct.

165. A is correct.

$$\underset{\text{no. of moles } H^+}{C_1 V_1} = \underset{\text{no. of moles } OH^-}{C_2 V_2}$$

$$(x \text{ ml})(0.15 \text{ M})\left(\frac{2 \text{ moles } H^+}{1 \text{ mole } H_2SO_4}\right) = (40 \text{ ml})(0.2 \text{ M})\left(\frac{1 \text{ mole } OH^-}{1 \text{ mole } NaOH}\right)$$

$x = 27$ ml

166. E is correct.

167. A is correct.

168. D is correct. The ionic product constant of water:

$$K_w = [H_3O^+]\,[OH^-]$$

$$[OH^-] = K_w / [H_3O^+]$$

$$[OH^-] = 1 \times 10^{-14} / 7.5 \times 10^{-9}$$

$$[OH^-] = 1.33 \times 10^{-6} \approx 1.5 \times 10^{-6}$$

169. A is correct.

170. B is correct.

171. D is correct.

172. B is correct. The pH of a buffer is calculated using the Henderson-Hasselbalch equation:

$$pH = pK_a + \log([\text{conjugate base}] / [\text{conjugate acid}])$$

When [acid] = [base], the fraction is 1. Since log 1 = 0, $pH = pK_a$. If the K_a of the acid is 4.5×10^{-4}, which is between 10^{-4} and 10^{-3}, the pK_a (and, therefore, the pH) is between 3 and 4.

173. C is correct.

174. B is correct.

175. E is correct.

176. C is correct.

177. E is correct.

178. C is correct.

179. A is correct.

180. C is correct. Use equation $C_1V_1 = C_2V_2$

where C_1 = original concentration of the solution (before it gets diluted)

C_2 = final concentration of the solution, after dilution,

V_1 = volume about to be diluted,

V_2 = final volume after dilution

Phosphoric acid is triprotic, but 0.1 N indicates that there are 0.1 moles of acidic protons.

$$(0.03\ \text{M})(V_1) = (0.1\ \text{M})(40\ \text{ml})$$

$$V_1 = 133\ \text{ml}$$

When working with acids and bases, normality is sometimes used in place of molarity. Normality indicates the concentration of H^+ ions in acids and OH^- ions in bases.

Some acids and bases have multiple H^+ or OH^- ions per molecule. For example, H_2SO_4 has 2 hydrogen ions, which means that a 1 M solution of H_2SO_4 will have 2 M of hydrogen ions. When expressed in normality, the concentration of this solution will be 2 N.

The problem states that there are 40 ml of 0.1 N H_3PO_4, which means that $[H^+] = 0.1$ M.

Moles of H^+ = volume of acid × normality

Moles of H$^+$ = (40 ml x 0.001 L / mL) × 0.1 N

Moles of H$^+$ = 0.004 mole

A titration is complete when all H$^+$ ions completely reacted with OH$^-$ ions. Therefore, the amount of OH$^-$ required to titrate the acid is also 0.004 mole.

Because NaOH is a strong base,

[NaOH] = [OH$^-$] = 0.03 M

Calculate volume of NaOH required:

volume of NaOH = moles of NaOH / molarity of NaOH

volume of NaOH = 0.004 mole / 0.03 M

volume of NaOH = 0.133 L

Convert to milliliters:

0.133 L × 1000 mL / L = 133 mL

181. A is correct. The pH scale runs from 1 to 14, with acids being less than 7 and bases being above 7. A neutral solution has a pH of 7. If the solution is slightly lower than pH 7, it is weakly acidic, and if the solution is slightly higher than pH 7, it is weakly basic. However, stomach digestive juice has a pH of 2 which is *much* lower than 7 and therefore is *strongly* acidic. Conversely, a substance with a very high pH (close to 14) is said to be *strongly* basic.

182. E is correct. The formula for pH is:

pH = –log[H$_3$O$^+$]

Rearrange to solve for [H$_3$O$^+$]:

[H$_3$O$^+$] = 10^{-pH}

[H$_3$O$^+$] = 10$^{-11.61}$

[H$_3$O$^+$] = 2.45 × 10^{-12}

183. D is correct.

184. A is correct.

185. B is correct.

186. B is correct. A solution is considered acidic if the concentration of [H$_3$O$^+$] is larger than 1×10^{-7}.

If [H$_3$O$^+$] is smaller than 1×10^{-7}, it is a basic solution.

If [H$_3$O$^+$] = 1×10^{-7}, it is neutral.

187. E is correct.

188. C is correct. Start by calculating moles of NaHCO$_3$:

moles of NaHCO$_3$ = mass of NaHCO$_3$ / molecular mass of NaHCO$_3$

moles of NaHCO$_3$ = 0.84 g / 84.01 g/mol

moles of $NaHCO_3$ = 0.01 mol

Using the coefficients in the reaction equation, calculate moles of H_2SO_4:

moles H_2SO_4 = (coefficient H_2SO_4 / coefficient $NaHCO_3$) × moles $NaHCO_3$

moles H_2SO_4 = (1/2) × 0.01 mol

moles H_2SO_4 = 0.005 mol

Divide moles by volume to determine molarity:

Molarity of H_2SO_4 = moles of H_2SO_4 / volume of H_2SO_4

Molarity of H_2SO_4 = 0.005 mol / (30 mL × 0.001 L/mL)

Molarity of H_2SO_4 = 0.167 M

189. A is correct.

190. D is correct. When all the hydrogens are removed, carbonic acid will become carbonate ion (CO_3^{2-}) and sulfuric acid will become sulphate ion (SO_4^{2-}). Both ions have 2 extra electrons that would reside with oxygen atoms. All oxygen atoms are equally capable of housing the extra electrons and the electrons are constantly moving between them.

Sulphate ion (SO_4^{2-}) has 2 extra electrons and 4 oxygen atoms. Using the combination theory, it means that there are 4C2 or (4!/2! × 2!)* = 6 possible resonance structures for sulphate ion.

Carbonate ion (CO_3^{2-}) has 3 oxygen atoms and 2 negative charge. Using the combination theory, it means that there are 3C2 or (3!/2! × 1!)** = 3 possible resonance structures for carbonate ion.

Because sulphate ion is more stable than carbonate ion, sulfuric acid is more likely to release its hydrogens than carbonic acid, which means sulfuric acid is a stronger acid.

* (4 × 3 × 2 × 1) / (2 × 1)·(2 × 1)

** (3 × 2 × 1) / (2 × 1)·(1)

191. E is correct. The hydronium ion is H_3O^+.

pH = – log [H_3O^+]

pH = – log 3.98 × 10^{-9}

pH = 8.400

192. B is correct.

193. D is correct.

194. E is correct. Formula to calculate pH of an acidic buffer:

[H^+] = ([acid]/[salt]) × K_a

Calculate H^+ from pH:

[H^+] = 10^{-pH}

[H^+] = 10^{-4}

Calculate Ka from pK$_a$:

$K_a = 10^{-pKa}$

$K_a = 10^{-3}$

Now substitute those values into the buffer equation:

$[H^+] = ([acid] / [salt]) \times K_a$

$10^{-4} = ([acid] / [salt]) \times 10^{-3}$

$10^{-1} = [acid] / [salt]$

$[salt] / [acid] = 10$

Therefore the ratio of salt to acid would be 10:1.

195. B is correct. A buffer is an aqueous solution that consists of a weak acid and its conjugate base, or vice versa. It resists changes in pH, and is often used to keep pH at a nearly constant value in many chemical applications. It does this by readily absorbing or releasing protons (H^+) and OH$^-$. When an acid is added, the buffer will release OH$^-$ and accept H^+ ions from the acid. When a base is added, the buffer will accept OH$^-$ ions from the base and release protons (H^+).

196. D is correct.

197. A is correct.

198. C is correct.

199. B is correct.

200. D is correct. Start by calculating the moles of KOH (remember to convert the volume to liters):

moles KOH = molarity × volume

moles KOH = 0.500 M × 20.0 mL × 0.001 L/mL

moles KOH = 0.01 mol

Because the coefficients of KOH and HNO$_3$ are equal, moles KOH = moles HNO$_3$.

Calculate the volume of HNO$_3$ required:

volume HNO$_3$ = moles HNO$_3$ / molarity HNO$_3$

volume HNO$_3$ = 0.01 mol / 0.250 M

volume HNO$_3$ = 0.04 L

Convert to liters:

0.04 L × 1000 mL/L = 40 mL

201. E is correct.

202. D is correct. Formic acid is a weak acid which would form a buffer solution in the bloodstream.

For buffer solutions:

$$[H^+] = ([acid]/[conjugate\ base]) \times K_a$$

Calculate H^+ from pH:

$$[H^+] = 10^{-7.4}$$

$$[H^+] = 3.98 \times 10^{-8}$$

Calculate Ka from pK_a:

$$K_a = 10^{-pK_a}$$

$$K_a = 10^{-3.9}$$

$$K_a = 1.26 \times 10^{-4}$$

Solve the buffer equation for the ratio asked by the question:

$$[H^+] = ([acid]/[conjugate\ base]) \times K_a$$

$$[conjugate\ base] / [acid] = K_a / [H^+]$$

Substitute the calculated values:

$$[conjugate\ base] / [acid] = 1.26 \times 10^{-4} / 3.98 \times 10^{-8}$$

$$[conjugate\ base] / [acid] = 3165\ or\ 3.165 \times 10^3$$

203. C is correct.

204. A is correct.

205. D is correct.

206. E is correct.

$$pH = -\log[H_3O^+]$$

$$pH = -\log 8.3 \times 10^{-9}$$

$$pH = 8.08$$

207. B is correct.

208. A is correct. Because HNO_3 is a strong acid, $[HNO_3] = [H_3O^+] = 0.021$ M.

$$pH = -\log[H_3O^+]$$

$$pH = -\log 0.021$$

$$pH = 1.68$$

209. D is correct. The addition of hydroxide (from NaOH) would decrease the solubility of magnesium hydroxide due to the common ion effect. Therefore, the amount of undissociated $Mg(OH)_2$ increases.

210. C is correct. Start by calculating the moles of $CaCO_3$:

Moles of $CaCO_3$ = mass of $CaCO_3$ / molecular mass of $CaCO_3$

Moles of $CaCO_3$ = 0.5 g / 100.09 g/mol

Moles of $CaCO_3$ = 0.005 mol

Use the coefficients in the reaction equation to find moles of HNO_3:

Moles of HNO_3 = (coefficient of HNO_3 / coefficient of $CaCO_3$) × moles of $CaCO_3$

Moles of HNO_3 = (2/1) × 0.005 mol

Moles of HNO_3 = 0.01 mol

Divide moles by volume to calculate molarity:

Molarity of HNO_3 = moles of HNO_3 / volume of HNO_3

Molarity of HNO_3 = 0.01 mol / (25 mL × 0.001 L/mL)

Molarity of HNO_3 = 0.4 M

211. E is correct.

212. D is correct.

213. B is correct.

214. E is correct.

215. A is correct.

216. A is correct.

217. C is correct.

218. B is correct.

219. A is correct.

220. C is correct.

221. B is correct.

222. D is correct.

223. E is correct. For a conjugate pair (e.g. formic acid and the formate ion), the product of K_a of the acid and the K_b of the base is equal to 10^{-14}:

$K_a K_b = 10^{-14}$

Therefore:

$pK_a + pK_b = 14$

Rearrange to solve for pK_b:

$pK_b = 14 - pK_a$

$pK_b = 14 - [-\log(1.8 \times 10^{-4})]$

$pK_b == 14 + \log(1.8 \times 10^{-4})$

224. C is correct.

225. B is correct.

226. D is correct.

227. A is correct.

228. D is correct. The formula for pH is:

$$pH = -\log[H^+]$$

Rearrange to solve for $[H^+]$:

$$[H^+] = 10^{-pH}$$

$$[H^+] = 10^{-2} \text{ M} = 0.01 \text{ M}$$

229. B is correct. Sodium acetate is a basic compound because acetate is the conjugate base of acetic acid, a weak acid ("the conjugate base of a weak acid acts as a base in water"). The addition of a base to any solution, even a buffered solution, increases the pH.

230. E is correct.

231. A is correct. Start by calculating the moles of $Ca(OH)_2$:

$$\text{Moles of } Ca(OH)_2 = \text{molarity } Ca(OH)_2 \times \text{volume of } Ca(OH)_2$$

$$\text{Moles of } Ca(OH)_2 = 0.1 \text{ M} \times (25 \text{ mL} \times 0.001 \text{ L/mL})$$

$$\text{Moles of } Ca(OH)_2 = 0.0025 \text{ mol}$$

Use the coefficients from the reaction equation to determine moles of HNO_3:

$$\text{Moles of } HNO_3 = (\text{coefficient of } HNO_3 / \text{coefficient } Ca(OH)_2) \times \text{moles of } Ca(OH)_2$$

$$\text{Moles of } HNO_3 = (2/1) \times 0.0025 \text{ mol}$$

$$\text{Moles of } HNO_3 = 0.005 \text{ mol}$$

Divide moles by molarity to calculate volume:

$$\text{Volume of } HNO_3 = \text{moles of } HNO_3 / \text{molarity of } HNO_3$$

$$\text{Volume of } HNO_3 = 0.005 \text{ mol} / 0.2 \text{ M}$$

$$\text{Volume of } HNO_3 = 0.025 \text{ L}$$

Convert volume to milliliters:

$$0.025 \text{ L} \times 1000 \text{ mL} / \text{L} = 25 \text{ mL}$$

232. C is correct. The problem is asking for K_a of an acid, which indicates that the acid in question is a weak acid. In aqueous solutions, a hypothetical weak acid HX will partly dissociate and create this equilibrium:

$$HX \leftrightarrow H^+ + X^-$$

with acid equilibrium constant or $K_a = [H^+][X^-] / [HX]$

To calculate K_a, the concentration of all species are needed.

From the given pH, the concentration of H^+ ions can be calculated:

$$[H^+] = 10^{-pH}$$

$$[H^+] = 10^{-7} \text{ M}$$

The number of H^+ and X^- ions are equal, which means that concentration of X^- ions will also be 10^{-7} M.

Those ions came from the dissociated acid molecules. According to the problem, only 24% of the acid is dissociated. Therefore, the rest of acid molecules (100% – 24% = 76%) did not dissociate. Use the simple proportion of percentages to calculate concentration of HX:

$$[HX] = (76\%/24\%) \times 1 \times 10^{-7}\,M$$

$$[HX] = 3.17 \times 10^{-7}\,M$$

Use the concentration values to calculate K_a:

$$K_a = [H^+]\,[X^-]\,/\,[HX]$$

$$K_a = (1 \times 10^{-7}) \times (1 \times 10^{-7})\,/\,3.17 \times 10^{-7})$$

$$K_a = 3.16 \times 10^{-8}$$

Finally, calculate pK_a:

$$pK_a = -\log K_a$$

$$pK_a = -\log (3.16 \times 10^{-8})$$

$$pK_a = 7.5$$

233. C is correct.

234. D is correct.

235. B is correct.

236. E is correct. Boiling point elevation = ikm where i = the number of particles produced the solute dissociates, k = boiling elevation constant, and m = molality. In this problem, acid molality is not known.

237. B is correct. The reduction potential: $2H^+ + 2e^- \rightarrow H_2$ $E = 0$. When this is added to the oxidation of solid zinc, the potential is positive, which means spontaneous.

238. A is correct.

239. C is correct.

240. E is correct.

241. B is correct.

242. B is correct.

243. D is correct. The buffer solution in blood maintains blood pH in the 7.3 – 7.4 range. pH in other parts of the body should be pretty close in value. If pH is too acidic, it will cause acidosis (and very basic pH will cause alkalosis) – both of which are dangerous to human health.

Choose the option with the smallest range around pH = 7, which is option D (6.5 – 8.0).

244. E is correct.

245. A is correct.

246. D is correct.

247. B is correct.

248. A is correct.

249. C is correct.

250. C is correct. Acidic salt is a salt that still contains H^+ in its anion. It is formed when a polyprotic acid is partially neutralized, leaving at least 1 H^+.

For example:

$H_3PO_4 + 2KOH \rightarrow K_2HPO_4 + 2H_2O$ (partial neutralization, K_2HPO_4 is acidic salt)

While:

$H_3PO_4 + 3KOH \rightarrow K_3PO_4 + 3H_2O$ (complete neutralization, K_3PO_4 is not acidic salt)

251. D is correct. Given:

$[OH^-] = 1 \times 10^{-9}$ M

The ion product constant:

$K_w = [H_3O^+] [OH^-]$

$1 \times 10^{-14} = [H_3O^+] [OH^-]$

Rearrange to solve for $[H_3O^+]$:

$[H_3O^+] = 1 \times 10^{-14}$ M / $[OH^-]$

$[H_3O^+] = 1 \times 10^{-14}$ M / 1×10^{-9} M

$[H_3O^+] = 1 \times 10^{-5}$ M

Calculate pH:

$pH = - \log [H_3O^+]$

$pH = - \log 1 \times 10^{-5}$ M

$pH = 5$

252. A is correct. Protons (H^+) travel between amino acid and solvent, depending on the pH of solvent and pK_a of functional groups on the amino acid.

Carboxylic acid groups can donate protons, while amine groups can receive protons.

For carboxylic acid group:

If pH of solution < pK_a	=	group is protonated and neutral
If pH of solution > pK_a	=	group is deprotonated and negative

For amine group:

If pH of solution < pK_a	=	group is protonated and positive
If pH of solution > pK_a	=	group is deprotonated and neutral

253. E is correct.

Chapter 6. STOICHIOMETRY AND GENERAL CONCEPTS

1. D is correct.

2. A is correct.

3. C is correct. Calculations: 0.4 mole $CaCO_3$ × 100 g / 1 mole = 40 g

4. E is correct. Remember that 1 amu (atomic mass unit) = 1 g/mole.

Moles of C = mass of C / atomic mass of C

Moles of C = 3.50 g / 12.01 g/mole

Moles of C = 0.291 mole

5. A is correct.

6. B is correct. Start by calculating the mass of each component:

C: 40.00% × 90 g = 36 g

H: 6.71% × 90 g = 6.04 g

O: 53.29% × 90 g = 47.96 g

To obtain the moles of each element that are present, divide each mass with each elements' atomic mass:

C: 36 g / 12 g/mol = 3 mol

H: 6.04 g / 1 g/mol = 6 mol

O: 47.96 g / 16 g/mol = 3 mol

Therefore, the molecular formula is $C_3H_6O_3$.

7. D is correct.

8. B is correct. At equilibrium, there is no potential and therefore neither direction of the reaction is favored.

9. E is correct. Start by balancing the number of nitrogen by adding 2 to NH_3:

___N_2 + ___H_2 → $2NH_3$

Now balance the hydrogen by adding 3 to H_2:

___N_2 + $3H_2$ → $2NH_3$

The equation is now fully balanced:

N_2 + $3H_2$ → $2NH_3$

Answer: 1, 3, 2

10. A is correct. A single-replacement reaction is a chemical reaction in which one element is substituted for another element in a compound, making a new compound and an element.

B and C: are correctly classified as single-replacement reactions because they each produce a compound (2NaF and $FeSO_4$, respectively) and an element (Cl_2 and Cu).

A double-replacement reaction occurs when parts of two ionic compounds are exchanged to make two new compounds.

A: is incorrectly classified because its products are two new compounds ($BaSO_4$ and 2HCl), so it is a double-replacement reaction.

D: is correctly classified as a synthesis reaction, because two species are combining to form a more complex chemical compound as the product.

11. E is correct.

12. C is correct. To determine the number of moles, divide the number of molecules with Avogadro's constant:

$$\text{number of moles} = 4.0 \times 10^{21} \text{ molecules} / 6.02 \times 10^{23} \text{ molecules/mol}$$

$$\text{number of moles} = 6.6 \times 10^{-3} \text{ mol}$$

13. D is correct. Avogadro's number is equivalent to approximately 6.02×10^{23}: the number of atoms present in 1 g atomic weight of any element.

14. E is correct. Start by assuming that hydrogen and oxygen have their most common oxidation states, which is +1 and –2, respectively. Because the sum of oxidation numbers in a neutral molecule is zero:

$$0 = \text{oxidation state of H} + \text{oxidation state of Cl} + 4(\text{oxidation state of O})$$

$$0 = 1 + \text{oxidation state of Cl} + 4(-2)$$

$$\text{oxidation state of Cl} = +7$$

15. C is correct.

16. B is correct.

17. A is correct.

18. C is correct. Elements are defined by the number of protons (i.e. atomic number). The isotopes are neutral atoms: # electrons = # protons.

19. E is correct. The number of oxygens on both sides of the reaction equation must be equal. On the right side, there are 8 CO_2 molecules; since each CO_2 molecule contains 2 oxygens, multiply $8 \times 2 = 16$. Also on the right side are 10 H_2O molecules; $10 \times 1 = 10$. Add 16 and 10 to get the total number of oxygens on the right side: $16 + 10 = 26$.

Since there are 26 oxygens on the right side, there should be 26 oxygens on the left side. Each O_2 molecule contains 2 oxygens; $26 / 2 = 13$. Therefore, the coefficient 13 is needed to balance the equation.

20. A is correct.

21. D is correct.

22. B is correct.

23. C is correct. Calculations:

wt O / wt of compound → 3(16) / 108 + 14 + 3(16) = 0.28 × 100 = 28%

24. B is correct. Remember that 1 amu (atomic mass unit) = 1 g/mole.

Moles of Mg = mass of Mg / atomic mass of Mg

Moles of Mg = 3.50 g / 24.305 g/mole

Moles of Mg = 0.144 mole

25. D is correct. A decomposition reaction occurs when one chemical compound is split apart into two or more compounds. The compound $2KClO_3$ is split apart into $2KCl$ and $3O_2$.

A and B: are synthesis reactions (also called composition reactions) because they are forming more complex chemical compounds from individual elements.

C: is a combustion reaction because the hydrocarbon is reacting with oxygen. It cannot be a decomposition reaction because it involves two reactants rather than a single substance.

26. C is correct.

27. B is correct. Since atoms cannot be created or destroyed in chemical reactions, there must be equal numbers of atoms on each side of the reaction arrow. The number of atoms present in a reaction can never vary, even if conditions change the reaction. However, the number of products and reactants does not have to be the same. For example, two reactants (on the left side of a reaction arrow) can combine to form one product (on the right side of a reaction arrow). Similarly, the number of molecules on each side of the reaction arrow does not have to be equal.

28. A is correct. This calculation involves multiplication and division. After performing those calculations, the answer should have the least significant figures from the values involved.

The starting values are P = 2.0 atm, V = 10.5 L and T = 298 K. The value with least significant figures is P (2 significant figures). Therefore, the answer should also have 2 significant figures.

29. C is correct.

30. B is correct.

31. A is correct.

32. E is correct. The reactants in a chemical reaction are always on the left side of the reaction arrow, while the products are on the right side. In this reaction, the reactants are $C_6H_{12}O_6$, H_2O and O_2.

33. A is correct. To determine the empirical formula, assume 100 g of a compound.

$$15.8 \text{ g C} \times \frac{1 \text{ mole}}{12 \text{ g}} = 1.3 \text{ moles C}$$

$$36.8 \text{ g N} \times \frac{1 \text{ mole}}{14 \text{ g}} = 2.6 \text{ moles N}$$

$$42.1 \text{ g S} \times \frac{1 \text{ mole}}{32 \text{ g}} = 1.3 \text{ moles S}$$

$$5.3 \text{ g H} \times \frac{1 \text{ mole}}{1 \text{ g}} = 5.3 \text{ moles H}$$

Therefore, the ratio of atoms in the compound: $C_{1.3}S_{1.3}N_{2.6}H_{5.3}$

Divide each by 1.3 = $C_1S_1N_2H_4$, reordering the atoms: N_2H_4CS

34. D is correct. Obtain the atomic masses from the periodic table and calculate the molar mass:

$58.93 + 6(14.01 + 3 \times 1.01) + 3(35.45 + 4 \times 16.00) = 459.47$ amu

35. B is correct. B is incorrectly classified. A single-replacement reaction must result in the production of a compound and an element, but this reaction results in the production of two elements. This reaction is actually a combustion reaction where methane (CH_4) reacts with oxygen.

A: correctly classified as a double-replacement reaction, where parts of two ionic compounds (AgNO3 and KCl) are exchanged to make two new compounds (KNO3 and AgCl).

C: correctly classified as a single-replacement reaction, where one element is substituted for another element in a compound, making a new compound ($ZnSO_4$) and an element (H_2).

D: correctly classified as a decomposition reaction, where one chemical compound ($2KClO_3$) is split apart into two or more pieces (2KCl and $3O_2$).

36. A is correct.

37. D is correct. In one mole of CH_3COOH, mass of O atoms = 2×16 g = 32 g; mass of H atoms = 4×1 g = 4 g. Therefore, the mass % of O is 8 times greater than for H.

Start by calculating the molecular mass (MW) of acetic acid:

MW of CH_3COOH = (2 × atomic mass of C) + (4 × atomic mass of H) + (2 × atomic mass of O)

MW of CH_3COOH = (2 × 12.01 g/mole) + (4 × 1.01 g/mole) + (2 × 16.00 g/mole)

MW of CH_3COOH = 60.05 g/mole

To obtain percent mass composition of each element, calculate the total mass of each element, divide it by the molecular mass, and multiply with 100%.

% mass composition of carbon = [(2 × 12.01 g/mole) / 60.05 g/mole] × 100%

% mass composition of carbon = 40.00%

% mass composition of hydrogen = [(4 × 1.01 g/mole) / 60.05 g/mole] × 100%

% mass composition of hydrogen = 6.71%

% mass composition of oxygen = [(2 × 16.00 g/mole) / 60.05 g/mole] ×100%

% mass composition of oxygen = 53.29%

38. E is correct. The mass of an electron is less than $1/10^{th}$ of one percent the mass of a proton (or neutron). Neutrons and protons have approximately the same mass.

39. C is correct.

40. C is correct. A double-replacement reaction occurs when parts of two ionic compounds (in this example, HBr and KOH) are exchanged to make two new compounds (H_2O and KBr).

A: a decomposition reaction where a compound is broken down into its constituent elements.

B: a synthesis or composition reaction where two species are combining to form a more complex chemical product.

D: a single-replacement reaction, which occurs when one element trades places with another element in a compound (the oxygen atom leaves the Cu and joins H_2).

41. E is correct.

42. E is correct.

43. B is correct. First, calculate the molecular mass (MW) of $MgSO_4$:

MW of $MgSO_4$ = atomic mass of Mg + atomic mass of S + (4 × atomic mass of O)

MW of $MgSO_4$ = 24.3 g/mole + 32.1 g/mole + (4 × 16.00 g/mole)

MW of $MgSO_4$ = 120.4 g/mole

Then use the molecular mass to determine the number of moles:

Moles of $MgSO_4$ = mass of $MgSO_4$ / MW of $MgSO_4$

Moles of $MgSO_4$ = 40.1 g / 120.4 g/mole

Moles of $MgSO_4$ = 0.33 mole

44. B is correct.

45. D is correct.

46. C is correct.

47. A is correct.

48. E is correct. The mass number is an approximation of the atomic weight of the element as amu (or g/mole); 13 grams = 1 mole; 26 grams = 2 mole.

49. D is correct. $2Na\ (l) + Cl_2\ (g) \rightarrow 2NaCl\ (s)$

50. D is correct.

51. C is correct.

52. A is correct.

53. E is correct. Assume 100 g of a compound.

$$49.3\text{ g C} \times \frac{1\text{ mole}}{12\text{ g}} = 4.1\text{ moles C}$$

$$43.8\text{ g O} \times \frac{1\text{ mole}}{16\text{ g}} = 2.7\text{ moles O}$$

$$6.9\text{ g H} \times \frac{1\text{ mole}}{1\text{ g}} - 6.9\text{ moles H}$$

Therefore, the compound is $C_{4.1}O_{2.7}H_{6.9}$

Divide each by 2.7 = $C_{1.5}O_1H_{2.5}$

Multiply by 2 = $C_3O_2H_5$

The compound weighs 73 g/mole which is 3 × less than the molecular weight of the unknown: 219. Therefore, multiply by 3 to get the molecular formula: $C_9O_6H_{15}$

54. D is correct. Formula mass is a synonym of molecular mass/molecular weight (MW).

MW = (16 × atomic mass of C) + (30 × atomic mass of H) + (4 × atomic mass of O)

MW = (16 × 12.01 g/mole) + (30 × 1.01 g/mole) + (4 × 16.00 g/mole)

MW = 286.41 g/mole

Remember that 1 amu = 1 g/mole.

55. B is correct.

56. C is correct.

57. E is correct.

58. B is correct. The "(II)" in copper (II) chloride. Cu has a +2 charge; Cl is a halogen and has a charge of –1: copper (II) chloride is $CuCl_2$. Likewise, carbonate has a charge of –2, so iron (II) carbonate is $FeCO_3$.

59. A is correct.

60. D is correct.

61. C is correct.

62. E is correct.

63. A is correct. The balanced equation is:

$2RuS + 9/2\ O_2 + 2H_2O \rightarrow Ru_2O_3 + 2H_2SO_4$

To avoid fractional coefficients, multiply all the coefficients by 2:

$4RuS + 9O_2 + 4H_2O \rightarrow 2Ru_2O_3 + 4H_2SO_4$

Add all the coefficients:

$4 + 9 + 4 + 2 + 4 = 23$

The sum of the coefficients is 23.

64. C is correct. First, calculate the moles of NaCl:

moles NaCl = mass NaCl / molar mass NaCl

moles NaCl = 146 g / (23 g + 35.45 g)

moles NaCl = 2.50 mol

Now calculate the number of NaCl molecules:

2.5 mol × 6.02 × 10^{23} molecules/mol = 1.50 × 10^{24} molecules

Formula unit is equivalent to empirical formula, or the simplest ratio of elements in a molecule. Because NaCl is already the simplest ratio and can't be simplified further, the number of molecules is equal to the formula units: 1.50 × 10^{24}.

65. D is correct.

66. E is correct.

67. B is correct. One mole of H_2SO_4 contains 32.1 g of S and 4 × 16 g = 64 g of O. Therefore, the % mass of O is twice the % mass of S.

Start by calculating the molecular mass of H_2SO_4:

(2 × atomic mass of H) + atomic mass of S + (4 × atomic mass of O)

Molecular mass of H_2SO_4 = (2 × 1.01 g/mole) + 32.07 g/mole + (4 x 16.00 g/mole)

Molecular mass of H_2SO_4 = 98.09 g/mole

To obtain percent mass composition of each element, calculate the total mass of each element, divide it by the molecular mass, and multiply with 100%.

Mass % of hydrogen = [(2 × 1.01 g/mole) / 98.09 g/mole] × 100%

Mass % of hydrogen = 2.06%

Mass % of sulfur = (32.07 g/mole / 98.09 g/mole) × 100%

Mass % of sulfur = 32.69%

Mass % of oxygen = [(4 × 16.00 g/mole) / 98.09 g/mole] × 100%

Mass % of oxygen = 65.25%

68. A is correct.

69. D is correct. 2Na (*l*) + Cl_2 (*g*) → 2NaCl (*s*)

70. B is correct.

71. C is correct.

72. D is correct.

73. E is correct. Calculation:

$$49 \text{ g} \times \frac{1 \text{ mole}}{98 \text{ g}} = 0.5 \text{ mole } H_2SO_4$$

If 0.5 mole H_2SO_4 is produced, set up a ratio for O_2 consumed.

$$\frac{9O_2}{4H_2SO_4} = \frac{x \text{ moles } O_2}{0.5 \text{ mole } H_2SO_4} \qquad x = 1.25 \text{ moles } O_2 \cdot \frac{22.4 \text{ liters}}{1 \text{ mole}} = 25.2 \text{ liters}$$

74. B is correct. Calculate the moles of each gas in the mixture:

moles CH_4 = mass of CH_4 / molecular mass of CH_4

moles CH_4 = 16.0 g / (12 g + 4 × 1 g)

moles CH_4 = 1 mol

moles O_2 = mass of O_2 / molecular mass of O_2

moles O_2 = 16.0 g / (2 × 16 g)

moles O_2 = 0.5 mol

moles SO_2 = mass of SO_2 / molecular mass of SO_2

moles SO_2 = 16.0 g / (32 g + 2 × 16 g)

moles SO_2 = 0.33 mol

moles CO_2 = mass of CO_2 / molecular mass of CO_2

moles CO_2 = 16.0 g / (12 g + 2 × 16 g)

moles CO_2 = 0.36 mol

Total = 1 mol + 0.5 mol + 0.33 mol + 0.36 mol = 2.49 mol ≈ 2.50 mol

75. A is correct.

76. D is correct.

77. B is correct.

78. E is correct. The ideal gas law works for partial pressures and for total pressure. At 1 atmosphere and 0 °C, 22.4 L = 1 mole. Compared to STP, the volume and pressure are half, and the temperature is slightly higher, so the number of moles is ~1/2 × 1/2 = 1/4. ¼ mole of N_2 gas = ~7 g.

79. C is correct.

80. B is correct.

81. A is correct. To obtain percent mass composition of oxygen, calculate the total mass of oxygen in the molecule, divide it by the molecular mass, and multiply with 100%.

% mass of oxygen = (mass of oxygen in molecule/molecular mass) × 100%

% mass of oxygen = [(4 moles × 16.00 g/mole)/303.39 g/mole] × 100%

% mass of oxygen = 21.09%

82. E is correct.

83. C is correct. Note the following calculation:

22.4 liters O_2 at STP = 1 mole O_2

67 g RuS × 1 mole/133 g = 0.5 mole RuS

Since 4 RuS molecules combine with 9 O_2 molecules, given 1 mole of O_2 and 0.5 mole RuS, O_2 is the limiting reagent.

Set up ratio for the limiting agent: molar ratio:

$$\frac{9O_2}{4RuS} = \frac{1 \text{ mole } O_2}{x \text{ mole RuS}} \quad x = \frac{4}{9} \text{ mole RuS}$$

Since RuS and H_2SO_4 have the same ratio, $\frac{4}{9}H_2SO_4$ is produced.

$$\frac{4}{9} \text{ mole } H_2SO_4 \times 98\frac{g}{mole} = 44g$$

84. B is correct. In order to calculate the number of atoms, start by calculating the molecular mass (MW) of fructose:

MW of fructose = (6 × atomic mass of C) + (12 × atomic mass of H) + (6 × atomic mass of O)

MW of fructose = (6 × 12.01 g/mole) + (12 × 1.01 g/mole) + (6 × 16.00 g/mole)

MW of fructose = 180.18 g/mole

Using the molecular mass, calculate the number of moles in fructose sample:

Moles of fructose = mass of fructose / MW of fructose

Moles of fructose = 3.62 g / 180.18 g/mole

Moles of fructose = 0.02 mole

Because there are 6 oxygen atoms for each molecule of fructose:

Moles of oxygen = 6 × moles of fructose

Moles of oxygen = 6 × 0.02 mole

Moles of oxygen = 0.12 mole

One mole of atoms has 6.02×10^{23} atoms (this is known as Avogadro's Number/N_A).

Number of oxygen atoms = moles of oxygen × Avogadro's number

Number of oxygen atoms = 0.12 mole × (6.02×10^{23} atoms/mole)

Number of oxygen atoms = 7.22×10^{22} atoms

85. B is correct.

86. C is correct.

87. A is correct. For an equation to be balanced, the number of each type of atom must be equal on the left side and the right sides. This is true of all the choices except $SO_2 + O_2 \rightarrow SO_3$. There are 4 oxygen atoms on the left side, but only 3 oxygen atoms on the right side.

88. B is correct. Determine the number of moles of He which has a molar mass of 4.0 g/mol; 2 grams = ½ mole. Each mole of He has 2 electrons since He has atomic number 2 (# electrons = # protons for neutral atoms). Therefore, ½ a mole of He × 2 electrons / mole = 1 mole of electrons.

89. D is correct. Formula mass is a synonym of molecular mass/molecular weight (MW).

MW of SO_2 = atomic mass of S + (2 × atomic mass of O)

MW of SO_2 = 32.07 g/mole + (2 × 16.00 g/mole)

MW of SO_2 = 64.02 g/mole

Remember that 1 amu = 1 g/mole.

90. C is correct.

91. E is correct.

92. D is correct.

93. A is correct. Set up a ratio and solve:

$$\frac{4RuS}{2Ru_2O_3} = \frac{7 \text{ moles RuS}}{x \text{ moles } Ru_2O_3}$$

$x = 3.5$ moles

94. D is correct. Start by calculating the molecular mass (MW) of glucose:

MW of glucose = (6 × atomic mass of C) + (12 × atomic mass of H) + (6 × atomic mass of O)

MW of glucose = (6 × 12.01 g/mole) + (12 × 1.01 g/mole) + (6 × 16.00 g/mole)

MW of glucose = 180.18 g/mole

Then multiply the number of moles by the molecular mass:

Mass of glucose = moles of glucose × MW of glucose

Mass of glucose = 5.20 moles × 180.18 g/mole

Mass of glucose = 936.94 g

95. C is correct.

96. A is correct. The law of constant composition states that *all samples of a given chemical compound have the same chemical composition by mass*. This is true for all compounds, including ethyl alcohol. This law is also sometimes called the law of definite proportions or Proust's Law because this observation was first made by the French chemist Joseph Proust.

97. E is correct. From the balanced equation, 4 moles of Ag are produced for each mole of O_2. Therefore, if 1 mole of Ag is produced, ¼ mole of O_2 is produced. The mass of ¼ mole of O_2 is (1/4)(2)(16 g) = 8 g.

98. A is correct. The atomic mass of a natural sample of Si is 28.1 which is much less than the mass of ^{29}Si or ^{30}Si.

99. E is correct.

100. D is correct.

101. B is correct.

102. D is correct.

>Mass of Ca = moles of Ca × atomic mass of Ca

>Mass of Ca = 3.61 moles × 40.08 g/mole

>Mass of Ca = 144.69 g ≈ 145 g

103. E is correct. The balanced equation: $2Al + Fe_2O_3 \rightarrow 2Fe + Al_2O_3$

The sum of the coefficients of the products is 3.

104. B is correct. Start by calculating molecular mass of CO_2:

>Molecular mass of CO_2 = atomic mass of C + (2 × atomic mass of O)

>Molecular mass of CO_2 = 12.01 g/mole + (2 × 16.00 g/mole)

>Molecular mass of CO_2 = 44.01 g/mole

Calculate the moles of CO_2:

>Moles of CO_2 = mass of CO_2 / molecular mass of CO_2

>Moles of CO_2 = 154 g / 44.01 g/mole

>Moles of CO_2 = 3.5 moles

One mole of atoms has 6.02×10^{23} atoms (this is known as Avogadro's Number or N_A).

>Number of CO_2 atoms = moles of CO_2 × Avogadro's number

>Number of CO_2 atoms = 3.5 moles × (6.02×10^{23} atoms/mole)

>Number of CO_2 atoms = 2.107×10^{24} atoms

105. A is correct.

106. C is correct.

107. B is correct. The subscripts are the small numbers to the right of a chemical symbol that denote how many atoms of a certain element are there (e.g. for carbon dioxide CO_2, the subscript 2 is showing that there are 2 oxygen atoms). If the subscripts in a chemical formula are changed, the substance itself is being changed. For example, if subscript is removed from CO_2, the resulting CO stands for carbon monoxide, which is very different from carbon dioxide.

Subscripts may never be changed to make an equation simpler to balance, because it would alter the meaning of the equation. Instead, place coefficients in front of formulas are used to balance the equation, since it is only changing the amount of each substance, not the identity of the substance itself.

108. E is correct. H_2 is the limiting reagent. 22 moles of H_2 should produce 22 × 2/3 = 14.6 moles of NH_3. If only 12 moles are produced, the yield = 12/14.6 = 82%.

109. A is correct. Since one mole of nitrogen is 14 grams, 7 grams of nitrogen contains 0.5 moles.

110. B is correct.

111. C is correct.

112. D is correct. To find what the reaction yields, look at the right side of the equation. There are 6 CO_2 atoms: $6 \times 2 = 12$. There are 12 H_2O atoms: $12 \times 1 = 12$.

$12 + 12 = 24$, so the reaction yields 24 atoms of oxygen.

113. C is correct. Identify the limiting reagent: Al is the limiting reagent because 2 atoms of Al combine with 1 molecule of ferric oxide to produce the products. If the reaction starts with equal numbers of moles of each reagent, Al is depleted.

Use moles of Al and coefficients to calculate moles of other products/reagents. Because coefficient of Al = coefficient of Fe, the moles of iron produced will also be 0.1 mole.

114. E is correct. Methane is CH_4, combustion is combination with oxygen.

115. D is correct.

116. E is correct.

117. A is correct.

118. D is correct. Start by calculating molecular mass of NO:

Molecular mass of NO = atomic mass of N + atomic mass of O

Molecular mass of NO = 14.01 g/mole + 16.00 g/mole

Molecular mass of NO = 30.01 g/mole

Then use this information to calculate moles of NO:

Moles of NO = mass of NO / molecular mass of NO

Moles of NO = 10.0 g / 30.01 g/mole

Moles of NO = 0.333 mole

Remember that in STP conditions, 1 mole of gas has a volume of 22.4 L:

Volume of NO = moles of NO × 22.4 L/mole

Volume of NO = 0.333 mole × 22.4 L

Volume of NO = 7.46 L

119. E is correct. For calculations, assume 100 g of the compound; 64 g of Ag, 8 g of N and 28 g of O.

Therefore, the number of moles of each of these elements is:

Ag: (64 g) / (108 g/mol) = 0.6 mol

N: (8 g) / (14 g/ mol) = 0.6 mol

O: (28 g) / (16 g/mol) = 1.8 mol

120. B is correct. Ethanol is C_2H_5OH, combustion is combination with oxygen.

121. A is correct. Formula mass is a synonym of molecular mass/molecular weight (MW).

Molecular mass = atomic mass of C + (2 × atomic mass of O)

Molecular mass = 12.01 g/mole + (2 × 16.00 g/mole)

Molecular mass = 44.01 g/mole

Remember that 1 amu = 1 g/mole.

122. C is correct.

123. C is correct.

124. A is correct.

125. D is correct.

Using half reactions, the balanced reaction is:

$$\text{To balance hydrogen} \qquad \text{To balance oxygen}$$

$$\downarrow \qquad\qquad\qquad \downarrow$$

$$4(5e^- + 8H^+ + MnO_4 \rightarrow Mn^{2+} + 4(H_2O))$$

$$5(H_2O) + C_3H_7OH \rightarrow C_2H_5CO_2H + 4H^+ + 4e^-$$

$$\overline{\qquad\qquad\qquad\qquad\qquad\qquad\qquad\qquad}$$

$$12H^+ + 4MnO_4^- + 5C_3H_7OH \rightarrow$$

$$11H_2O + 4Mn^{2+} + 5C_2H_5CO_2H$$

Multiply by a common multiple of 4 and 5:

the sum of the product's coefficients = 11 + 4 + 5 = 20.

126. A is correct. First calculate the molecular mass (MW) of K_2CrO_4:

MW of K_2CrO_4 = (2 × atomic mass of K) + atomic mass of Cr + (4 × atomic mass of O)

MW of K_2CrO_4 = (2 × 39.10 g/mole) + 52.00 g/mole + (4 × 16.00 g/mole)

MW of K_2CrO_4 = 194.20 g/mole

To obtain percent by mass composition of chromium, divide the mass of a Cr atom by the molecular mass, and multiply with 100%.

% mass of Cr = (mass of Cr in molecule / molecular mass of K_2CrO_4) × 100%

% mass of Cr = (52.00g / 194.20 g/mole) × 100%

% mass of Cr = 26.776%

127. D is correct.

128. E is correct. First calculate the molecular mass (MW) of CH_4:

Molecular mass of CH_4 = atomic mass of C + (4 × atomic mass of H)

Molecular mass of CH_4 = 12.01 g/mole + (4 × 1.01 g/mole)

Molecular mass of CH_4 = 16.05 g/mole

Use this information to determine the number of moles:

Moles of CH_4 = mass of CH_4 / molecular mass of CH_4

Moles of CH_4 = 3.20 g / 16.05 g/mole

Moles of CH_4 = 0.2 mole

Then multiply by Avogadro's Number to obtain the number of molecules:

Number of CH_4 molecules = moles of CH_4 × Avogadro's Number

Number of CH_4 molecules = 0.2 moles × 6.02 × 10^{23} molecules/mole

Number of CH_4 molecules = 1.20 × 10^{23} molecules

129. B is correct. When thinking about electrons, the mnemonic "OIL RIG" may be helpful: Oxidation Is Loss and Reduction Is Gain). If the substance loses electrons (being oxidized), another substance must be gaining electrons (being reduced). So, the original substance is referred to as a reducing agent, even though it is being oxidized.

130. D is correct. At lower temperatures, the potential energy due to the intermolecular forces is more noticeable compared to the kinetic energy which causes the pressure to be reduced because the gas molecules are attracted to each other.

131. C is correct.

132. B is correct.

133. E is correct.

134. C is correct.

135. E is correct. Al is the limiting reagent because 2 atoms of Al combine with 1 molecule of ferric oxide to produce the products. If the reaction starts with equal numbers of moles of each reagent, Al is depleted.

136. A is correct.

Moles of Al = mass of Al / atomic mass of Al

Moles of Al = 4.56 g / 26.982 g

Moles of Al = 0.169 moles

137. E is correct.

138. A is correct.

139. D is correct.

140. C is correct. Balance the reaction: $C_6H_{12}O_6 (s) + 6O_2 (g) \rightarrow 6CO_2 (g) + 6H_2O (g)$

141. B is correct.

142. A is correct. The ClO^- and Cl^- combine to form Cl_2. The oxidation state of chlorine in Cl_2 is defined as 0. The oxidation state of chlorine in ClO^- is +1 and as Cl^- –1. Because chlorine is being oxidized and reduced in the same reaction, this reaction is an example of disproportionation. All other choices do not show the same atom undergoing both oxidation and reduction.

143. C is correct.

144. D is correct.

145. E is correct. The most common definition of oxidation is loss of electrons. In terms of oxygen transfer, it can also be defined as a gain of oxygen. Oxidation can also be defined as a loss of hydrogen, but it is not a common definition and may be encountered in organic chemistry.

146. B is correct. If the quantity of carbon atoms is known, the quantity of potassium atoms can be calculated directly using the ratio of coefficients.

Number of potassium atoms = number of carbon atoms × (coefficient of potassium / coefficient of carbon)

Number of potassium atoms = 1.084×10^{24} atoms × (3/6)

Number of potassium atoms = 5.42×10^{23} atoms

147. D is correct.

148. B is correct.

149. A is correct. Salts of group 1A metals and all nitrate salts are known to completely dissociate in water and will have no equilibrium constant. The salts can be identified by the (*aq*) notation, which means that it will dissociate. Ag_2SO_4 is a salt that precipitates out of solution because of the (*s*) notation.

150. C is correct. The mole fraction is 60/760 = 0.08; set equal to 100 moles of gas present; 8 moles of C, with a mass of 8 × 44 = 352 g =20% of the total mass. The other species must = 4.5 times that mass = 1584 grams. Since the other species has 92 moles, its molar mass would be ~1600/92, or 17.4 g/mol = methane (CH_4) is close.

151. C is correct. Hydrogen is being oxidized (or ignited) to produce water. The balanced equation that describes the ignition of hydrogen gas in air to produce water is:

$$\tfrac{1}{2}\,O_2 + H_2 \rightarrow H_2O$$

This equation suggests that for every mole of water that is produced in the reaction, 1 mole of hydrogen and ½ mole of oxygen gas is needed. The maximum amount of water that can be produced in the reaction is determined by the amount of limited reagent available. This will require identifying which reactant is the limited reagent, this can be done by comparing the number of moles of oxygen and hydrogen.

From the question, there are 10 grams of oxygen gas and 1 gram of hydrogen gas. This is equivalent to 0.3125 moles of oxygen and 0.5 moles of hydrogen. Because the reaction requires twice as much hydrogen as oxygen gas, the limited reagent is hydrogen gas (0.3215 moles of O_2 will require 0.625 moles of hydrogen, but only 0.5 moles of H_2 are available). Since one equivalent of water is produced for every equivalent of hydrogen that is burned, the amount of water produced is 18 gram/mol H_2O × 0.5 mol H_2O = 9 grams of H_2O.

152. D is correct.

153. E is correct.

154. B is correct.

155. E is correct. In the balanced equation, the molar ratio of Sn^{4+} and Sn^{2+} are equal because the number of moles of Sn^{2+} (reactant) = number of moles of Sn^{4+} (product).

156. B is correct. In order to compare quantities of carbon and oxygen in a molecule, the moles of each type of atom has to be determined.

> Moles of oxygen = mass of oxygen / atomic mass of oxygen

> Moles of oxygen = 1.99 g / 16.00 g/mole

> Moles of oxygen = 0.124 mole

In C_2H_5OH, there are 2 carbon atoms for each oxygen atom.

> Moles of carbon = 2 × 0.124 mole

> Moles of carbon = 0.248 mole

Using the moles and the atomic mass, the mass of carbon in the molecule can be calculated:

> Mass of carbon = moles of carbon × atomic mass of carbon

> Mass of carbon = 0.248 mole × 12.01 g/mole

> Mass of carbon = 2.98 g

157. A is correct. Remember the acronym OIL RIG: Oxidation Is Loss, Reduction is Gain (of electrons). Therefore, the substance that is reduced always gains. It does not have to contain an element that increases in oxidation number. It is not the reducing agent; the substance that is reduced is called the oxidizing agent.

158. D is correct. I: total ionic charge of reactants must equal total ionic charge of products, which means that no electrons can "disappear" from the reaction, they can only be transferred from one atom to another. Therefore, the total charge will always be the same.

II: atoms of each reactant must equal atoms of product, which is true for all chemical reactions, because atoms in chemical reactions cannot be created or destroyed.

III: any electrons that are gained by one atom must be lost by another atom.

159. A is correct.

160. E is correct. Balance the reaction: $2C_6H_{14}(g) + 19O_2(g) \rightarrow 12CO_2(g) + 14H_2O(g)$.

161. B is correct. Start by writing down the equation of reaction:

> $H_2 + O_2 \rightarrow H_2O$

Balance the equation by adding coefficients to each molecule. There are two hydrogens on each side so hydrogen is already balanced. Meanwhile, there are 2 oxygen atoms on the left and one on the right. Assign 1/2 as the coefficient of oxygen:

> $H_2 + 1/2\, O_2 \rightarrow H_2O$

Multiply all the equations by 2 to remove the fraction:

> $2H_2 + O_2 \rightarrow 2H_2O$

The next step is to find the limiting reactant, or the reactant that runs out first. Before performing this calculation, first calculate the moles of each reactant:

Moles of hydrogen = mass of hydrogen / (2 × atomic mass of hydrogen)

Moles of hydrogen = 25 g / (2 × 1.01 g/mole)

Moles of hydrogen = 12.38 moles

Moles of oxygen = mass of oxygen / (2 × atomic mass of oxygen)

Moles of oxygen = 225 g / (2 × 16.00 g/mole)

Moles of oxygen = 7.03 moles

To find the limiting reactant, divide the moles of each reactant with its coefficient. After this division, the reactant with the smaller number of moles will be the limiting reactant.

Hydrogen = 12.38 moles / 2

Hydrogen = 6.19 moles

Oxygen = 7.03 moles / 1

Oxygen = 7.03 moles

Because hydrogen has a smaller number of moles after the division, hydrogen is the limiting reactant and all hydrogen will be used up in the reaction. Look at the reaction again:

$2H_2 + O_2 \rightarrow 2H_2O$

Both hydrogen and water have 2 as their coefficients; therefore those two molecules would have the same number of moles. There are 12.38 moles of hydrogen, which means there will be 12.38 moles of water produced by this reaction.

Molecular mass of H_2O = (2 × molecular mass of hydrogen) + atomic mass of oxygen

Molecular mass of H_2O = (2 × 1.01 g/mole) + 16.00 g/mole

Molecular mass of H_2O = 18.02 g/mole

Mass of H_2O = moles of H_2O × molecular mass of H_2O

Mass of H_2O = 12.38 moles × 18.02 g/mole

Mass of H_2O = 223.09 g

162. D is correct.

163. A is correct. A molecular formula expresses the actual number of atoms of each element in a molecule.

An empirical formula is the simplest formula for a compound. For example, if the molecular formula of a compound is C_6H_{16}, the empirical formula is C_3H_8.

Elemental formula and atomic formula are not chemistry terms.

164. B is correct.

165. E is correct. A reducing agent reduces a compound and itself becomes oxidized in the process.

166. A is correct.

167. B is correct.

168. C is correct.

169. D is correct.

170. C is correct. 10 moles of N_2O_4 (l) could produce 24 moles of H_2O. The other reactant must be depleted first.

171. A is correct.

172. D is correct. According to the problem, there are 0.850 moles of nitrate ion in a $Fe(NO_3)_3$ solution. Because there are three nitrate (NO_3) ions for each $Fe(NO_3)_3$ molecule, the moles of $Fe(NO_3)_3$ can be calculated:

$(1/3) \times 0.850$ moles $= 0.283$ moles

Calculate the volume of solution:

Volume of solution = moles of solute / molarity

Volume of solution = 0.283 moles / 0.4 mol/L

Volume of solution = 0.708 L

Convert the volume into milliliters:

0.708 L $\times$ 1000 mL/L = 708 mL

173. C is correct. As the volume of the container is decreased, the molecules approach each other more closely which leads to an increase in the number and strength of intermolecular attractions among the molecules. As these attractions increase, the number and intensity of collisions between the molecules and the wall decrease leading to a decrease in the pressure exerted on the walls of the container by the gas.

174. E is correct.

175. C is correct. Note the following calculation:

$$\frac{2Al}{1Al_2O_3} = \frac{0.1 \text{ mole Al}}{x \text{ moles Al}_2O_3}$$

$x = 0.05$ mole

Therefore (0.5 mole)(102 g/mole) = 5.1 g

176. A is correct.

Number of molecules = moles $\times$ Avogadro's constant

Number of molecules = 1.4 mol $\times$ 6.02 $\times$ 10^{23} molecules/mol

Number of molecules = 8.428 $\times$ 10^{23} molecules

There are 4 atoms in each PF_3 molecule, which means that there are:

$$4 \times 8.428 \times 10^{23} = 3.372 \times 10^{24} \text{ atoms}$$

177. C is correct. Start by assuming that hydrogen and oxygen have their most common oxidation states, which is +1 and –2, respectively. Because the sum of oxidation numbers in a neutral molecule is zero:

0 = oxidation state of H + oxidation state of Br + 4(oxidation state of O)

0 = 1 + oxidation state of Br + 4(–2)

oxidation state of Br = +7

178. E is correct.

179. B is correct.

180. C is correct. Balance the reaction: $C_{12}H_{22}O_{11}\ (l) + 12O_2\ (g) \rightarrow 12CO_2\ (g) + 11H_2O\ (g)$.

181. D is correct. Formula mass is a synonym of molecular mass/molecular weight (MW).

MW of $C_6H_{12}O_6$ = (6 × atomic mass of C) + (12 × atomic mass of H) + (6 × atomic mass of O)

MW of $C_6H_{12}O_6$ = (6 × 12.01 g/mole) + (12 × 1.01 g/mole) + (6 × 16.00 g/mole)

MW of $C_6H_{12}O_6$ = 180.18 g/mole

182. B is correct.

183. D is correct.

184. E is correct.

185. B is correct. Cu^{+2} gains electrons (i.e. oxidizing agent) and is neutralized.

186. C is correct. According to the law of mass conservation, there should be equal amounts of carbon in the product (CO_2) and reactant (the hydrocarbon sample).

Start by calculating the amount of carbon in the product (CO_2). In order to do so, first calculate the mass % of carbon in CO_2:

Molecular mass of CO_2 = atomic mass of carbon + (2 × atomic mass of oxygen)

Molecular mass of CO_2 = 12.01 g/mole + (2 × 16.00 g/mole)

Molecular mass of CO_2 = 44.01 g/mole

Mass % of carbon in CO_2 = (mass of carbon / molecular mass of CO_2) × 100%

Mass % of carbon in CO_2 = (12.01 g/mole / 44.01 g/mole) × 100%

Mass % of carbon in CO_2 = 27.3%

Now calculate the mass of carbon in the CO_2:

Mass of carbon = mass of CO_2 × mass % of carbon in CO_2

Mass of carbon = 8.398 g × 27.3%

Mass of carbon = 2.29 g

The mass of carbon in the starting reactant (the hydrocarbon sample) should also be 2.29 g.

Mass % of carbon in hydrocarbon sample = (mass of carbon in sample / total mass sample) × 100%

Mass % of carbon in hydrocarbon sample = (2.29 g / 6.987 g) × 100%

Mass % of carbon in hydrocarbon sample = 32.8%

187. D is correct. D: incorrectly classified which makes it the correct answer. The decomposition part is correct, because one complex compound is being broken down into two or more parts. However, the redox part is wrong. It is actually a non-redox reaction because the reactants and products are all compounds (no single elements) and there is no change in oxidation state (i.e. no gain or loss of electrons).

A: correctly classified as a double-replacement reaction (sometimes referred to as double-displacement) because parts of two ionic compounds are exchanged to make two new compounds. It is also a non-redox reaction because the reactants and products are all compounds (no single elements) and there is no change in oxidation state (i.e. no gain or loss of electrons).

B: correctly classified as a synthesis reaction because two species are combining to form a more complex chemical compound as the product. It is also a redox reaction because the F atoms in F_2 are oxidized (they lose electrons) and the Cl atoms in Cl_2 are reduced (they gain electrons), leading to Cl^- and F^+ which interact to form an ionic compound.

C: correctly classified as a synthesis reaction because two species are combining to form a more complex chemical compound as the product. It is also a non-redox reaction because the reactants and products are all compounds (no single elements) and there is no change in oxidation state (i.e. no gain or loss of electrons).

188. A is correct.

189. A is correct.

190. C is correct. 33 moles of H_2 (*g*) should react with 33/3 = 11 moles of N_2 (*g*). Since 13.5 moles of N_2 (*g*) were the reactant, the product should be 27.0 moles. The reaction did not go to completion. From the moles of NH_3, 18 moles of NH_3 require 9 moles of N_2, and the reaction started with 13.5 with 4.5 moles remaining.

191. D is correct.

192. E is correct.

193. B is correct. A mole is a unit of measurement used to express amounts of a chemical substance. The number of molecules in a mole is 6.02×10^{23}, which is Avogadro's number. However, Avogadro's number relates to the number of molecules, not the amount of substance.

Molar mass refers to the mass per mole of a substance.

Formula mass is a term that is sometimes used to mean molecular mass or molecular weight, and it refers to the mass of a certain molecule.

194. D is correct.

195. E is correct. H = +1; O = –2; Cl = –1. Cr must have an oxidation number of +4.

H	Cr$_2$	O$_4$	Cl
(1 × 1)	(2x)	(4 × –2)	(1 × –1)

$$1 + -8 + -1 + 2x = 0 \qquad\qquad x = 4$$

196. C is correct.

197. B is correct. B: incorrectly classified. The decomposition part of the classification is correct, because one more complex compound (H_2O_2) is being broken down into two or more parts (H_2O and O_2). However, it is a redox reaction because oxygen is being lost from H_2O_2, which is one of the three indicators of a redox reaction (i.e. electron loss/gain, hydrogen loss/gain, oxygen loss/gain). Additionally, one of the products is a single element (O_2), which is also a clue that it is a redox reaction.

A: correctly classified as a non-redox reaction because the reactants and products are all compounds (no single elements) and there is no change in oxidation state (i.e. no gain or loss of electrons). It is also a precipitation reaction, because the chemical reaction occurs in aqueous solution and one of the products formed (AgOH) is insoluble, which makes it a precipitate.

C: correctly classified as a redox reaction because the nitrate (NO_3^-), which dissociates, is oxidized (loses electrons) and the Na^+ is reduced (gains electrons), and the two combine to form the ionic compound $NaNO_3$. It is a single-replacement reaction because one element is substituted for another element in a compound, making a new compound (2NaNO3) and an element (Pb).

D: correctly classified as a non-redox reaction because the reactants and products are all compounds (no single elements) and there is no change in oxidation state (i.e. no gain or loss of electrons). It is also a double-replacement reaction because parts of two ionic compounds are exchanged to make two new compounds.

198. A is correct.

199. E is correct. In this molecule, Br has the oxidation number of –1. Because the sum of charges in a neutral molecule is zero:

0 = oxidation state of Fe + 3 × oxidation state of Br

0 = oxidation state of Fe + 3 × (–1)

oxidation state of Fe = +3

200. A is correct. The coefficients in balanced reactions refer to moles (or molecules) but not grams. 1 mole of N_2 gas reacts with 3 moles of H_2 gas to produce 2 moles of NH_3 gas.

201. C is correct.

202. A is correct. Start by balancing the overall reaction:

$$6HCl\ (aq) + 2Fe\ (s) \rightarrow 2FeCl_3\ (aq) + 3H_2\ (g)$$

Now identify the component that undergoes oxidation (increasing oxidation number). For this problem, it would be Fe because it went from 0 in elemental iron to Fe^{3+} in $FeCl_3$.

Write them in a half-reaction with their coefficients:

$$2Fe \rightarrow 2Fe^{3+}$$

Add electrons to balance the charges:

$$2Fe \rightarrow 2Fe^{3+} + 6e^-$$

203. D is correct. Start by calculating moles of cobalt:

Moles of cobalt = mass of cobalt sample / atomic mass of cobalt

Moles of cobalt = 58.93 g / 58.93 g

Moles of cobalt = 1.000 mole

Then use this information and Avogadro's number to calculate the number of atoms:

Number of atoms = number of moles × Avogadro's number

Number of atoms = 1.000 mole × 6.02×10^{23} atoms/mole

Number of atoms = 6.02×10^{23} atoms

204. B is correct.

205. D is correct. Using ½ reactions, the balanced reaction is:

$$6\ (\underline{Fe}^{2+} \rightarrow \underline{Fe}^{3} + 1e^-)$$

$$\underline{6e^- + 14H^+ + \underline{Cr_2O_7}^{2-} \rightarrow 2\underline{Cr}^{3+} + 7H_2O}$$

$$Cr_2O_7^{2-} + 14H^+ + 6Fe^{2+} \rightarrow 2Cr^{3+} + 6Fe^{3+} + 7H_2O$$

The sum of coefficients in the balanced reaction is 36.

206. B is correct. The sum of all the oxidation numbers in any neutral molecule must be zero. In this reaction, the oxidation number of each H is +1 and the oxidation number of each O is –2. If x denotes the oxidation number of S in H_2SO_4, then $2(+1) + x + 4(-2) = 0$, which means $x = +6$.

207. C is correct.

208. A is correct. See explanation to question **163**.

209. E is correct.

210. A is correct. First, calculate the molar mass of phosphorous trichloride:

Molar mass of PCl_3 = atomic mass of P + (3 × atomic mass of Cl)

Molar mass of PCl_3 = 30.97 g/mole + (3 × 35.45 g/mole)

Molar mass of PCl_3 = 137.32 g/mole

Then use this information to calculate the number of moles:

Moles of PCl_3 produced = mass of PCl_3 / molar mass of PCl_3

Moles of PCl_3 = 275 g / 137.32 g/mole

Moles of PCl_3 = 2.00 moles

The reaction equation is:

$P_4 + 6Cl_2 \rightarrow PCl_3$

Always confirm that a reaction equation is balanced before doing mole comparisons. Presence of coefficient(s) doesn't always indicate a fully-balanced equation; this reaction is one of those.

To balance the equation, assign 4 as coefficient of PCl_3:

$P_4 + 6Cl_2 \rightarrow 4PCl_3$

With a balanced equation, moles of P_4 can be determined by comparison of coefficients:

Moles P_4 = (coefficient P_4 / coefficient PCl_3) × moles PCl_3

Moles P_4 = (1/4) × 2.00

Moles P_4 = 0.5 moles

From the balanced reaction, ½ mole of $P_4(s)$ is needed.

Mass of P_4 = moles of P_4 × molar mass of P_4

Mass of P_4 = 0.5 moles × (4 × 30.97 g/mole)

Mass of P_4 = 61.94 g

211. B is correct.

212. A is correct.

213. E is correct.

214. D is correct.

215. B is correct. The net charge of H_2SO_4 = 0. Hydrogen has a common oxidation number of +1 whereas each oxygen atom has an oxidation number of –2.

$$\begin{array}{ccc} H_2 & S & O_4 \\ (2 \times 1) & x & (4 \times -2) \end{array}$$

$2 + x + -8 = 0$

$x = 6$

216. C is correct.

217. B is correct.

218. C is correct.

219. E is correct. The mole fraction of the CO_2 = 30/760 = about 0.04. But since CO_2 has a somewhat higher molar mass than N_2, it has a slightly higher % by mass than mole fraction.

To calculate, assume 100 moles of gas because the % does not depend on the number of moles. There are 8 moles of CO_2 and 92 moles of N_2. The total mass = (8 × 44) + (92 × 28), and the fraction of CO_2 by mass $= 8 \times 44/ ([8 \times 44] + [92 \times 28]) = 352/ (352 + 2576) = 352/ 2928 = 0.12 \times 100 = 12\%$.

220. C is correct.

221. D is correct.

222. E is correct. Assume acidic conditions and use the formation of water as one of two half reactions:

$$Sn^{2+} \rightarrow Sn^{4+} \qquad 2(Sn^{2+} \rightarrow Sn^{4+} + 2e^-)$$

$$O_2 \rightarrow 2H_2O \qquad \underline{4\ e^- + 4H^+ + O_2 \rightarrow 2H_2O}$$

$$2Sn^2 + 4H^+ + O_2 \rightarrow 2Sn^{4+} + 2H_2O$$

Balance oxygen by adding water.

223. D is correct. HCl has a molar mass of 36.5 g/mol: 365 grams = 10 moles. 10 moles is 75% of total yield, so enough PCl_3 produces 13.5 moles of HCl. Apply the mole ratios: 13.5 moles of HCl is produced by 4.5 moles of PCl_3.

224. A is correct. Start by balancing the overall reaction:

$$2Fe\ (s) + 3CuSO_4\ (aq) \rightarrow Fe_2(SO_4)_3(aq) + 3Cu\ (s)$$

Now identify the component that undergoes reduction (decreasing oxidation number). For this problem, it would be Cu because it went from +2 in $CuSO_4$ to 0 in elemental Cu.

Write them in a half-reaction with their coefficients:

$$3Cu^{2+} \rightarrow 3Cu$$

Add electrons to balance the charges:

$$3Cu^{2+} + 6e^- \rightarrow 3Cu$$

225. A is correct. Standard temperature and pressure are conditions that were set for experimental measurements to allow comparisons to be made between different sets of data. IUPAC established this standard temperature as 0 °C (273.15 K) and the standard pressure as 1 atm (100,000 Pa).

226. A is correct.

227. A is correct.

228. D is correct.

229. A is correct.

230. C is correct. Remember that in STP conditions, 1 mole of gas has a volume of 22.4 L.

First, determine the moles of N_2:

Moles of N_2 = mass of N_2 / molecular mass of N_2

Moles of N_2 = 0.750 g / (2 × 14.01 g/mole)

Moles of N_2 = 0.027 mole

Then use this information to find the volume:

Volume of N_2 = moles of N_2 × 22.4 L/mole

Volume of N_2 = 0.027 mole × 22.4 L/mole

Volume of N_2 = 0.605 L

231. E is correct.

232. D is correct. Start by calculating the moles of Cl^- ion:

Moles of Cl^- ion = number of Cl^- atoms / Avogadro's number

Moles of Cl^- ion = $6.8 × 10^{22}$ atoms / $6.02 × 10^{23}$ atoms/mole

Moles of Cl^- ion = 0.113 moles

In a solution, $BaCl_2$ will dissociate according to this equation:

$BaCl_2 \rightarrow Ba^{2+} + 2Cl^-$

The moles of from Cl^- previous calculation can be used to calculate the moles of Ba^{2+}:

Moles of Ba^{2+} = (coefficient of Ba^{2+} / coefficient Cl^-) × moles of Cl^-

Moles of Ba^{2+} = (1/2) × 0.113 moles

Moles of Ba^{2+} = 0.0565 moles

Finally, calculate the mass of Ba^{2+}:

Mass of Ba^{2+} = moles of Ba^{2+} × atomic mass of Ba

Mass of Ba^{2+} = 0.0565 moles × 137.33 g/mole

Mass of Ba^{2+} = 7.76 g

233. B is correct.

Mass % of chlorine = (mass of chlorine in molecule / molecular mass) × 100%

Mass % of chlorine = (2 × 35.45 g/mol / 159.09 g/mol) × 100%

Mass % of chlorine = 44.57%

234. D is correct. All of the choices for experiments depend on the mass of the gas molecules.

235. C is correct.

236. E is correct.

237. B is correct. The most likely reason for non ideal behavior of a gas is strong intermolecular forces.

238. E is correct. For most substances, the solid form is denser than the liquid phase. Therefore, a block of most solids sinks in the liquid. With regards to pure water though, a block of ice (solid phase) floats in liquid water because ice is less dense.

Like other substances, when liquid water is cooled from room temperature, it becomes increasingly dense. However, at approximately 4 °C (39 °F), water reaches its maximum density, and as it's cooled further, it expands and becomes less dense. This phenomenon is knows as negative thermal expansion and is attributed to strong intermolecular interactions that are orientation-dependent.

The density of water is about 1 g/cm^3 and depends on the temperature. When frozen, the density of water is decreased by about 9%. This is due to the decrease in intermolecular vibrations, which allows water molecules to form stable hydrogen bonds with other water molecules around. As these hydrogen bonds form, molecules are locking into positions similar to the hexagonal structure. Even though hydrogen bonds are shorter in the crystal than in the liquid, this position locking decreases the average coordination number of water molecules as the liquid reaches the solid phase.

Chapter 7.   CHEMICAL EQUILIBRIA AND CHEMICAL KINETICS

1. E is correct.

2. C is correct.

3. A is correct. Initiation reactions are defined as reactions that produce free radicals. Propagation reactions involve no net loss of free radicals. A free radial reaction for Cl_2 follows.

Initiation:

$$Cl_2 \xrightarrow{\text{UV light}} 2Cl\cdot$$

Propagation: $Cl\cdot + CH_3R \rightarrow CH_3R\cdot + HCl$

Termination: $CH_3R\cdot + Cl\cdot \rightarrow CH_3RCl$

4. C is correct. Rate of formation/consumption of all species in a reaction are proportional to their coefficients. If the rate of a species is known, the rate of other species can be calculated using simple proportions.

coefficient of NOBr/coefficient of Br_2 = Rate of formation of NOBr / Rate of consumption of Br_2

Rate of consumption of Br_2 = Rate of formation of NOBr / (Coefficient NOBr/Coefficient Br_2)

Rate of consumption of Br_2 = 4.50×10^{-4} mol L^{-1} s^{-1} / (2/1)

Rate of consumption of Br_2 = 2.25×10^{-4} mol L^{-1} s^{-1}

5. B is correct.

6. E is correct.

7. B is correct.

8. C is correct. The balanced equation is:

$$C_2H_6O + 3O_2 \rightarrow 2CO_2 + 3H_2O.$$

Rate of reaction/consumption is proportional to the coefficients, which means that the rate of carbon dioxide production will be twice the rate of ethanol consumption:

$$2 \times 3.0 \text{ M s}^{-1} = 6.0 \text{ M s}^{-1}$$

9. A is correct.

10. B is correct.

11. D is correct.

12. E is correct.

13. A is correct.

14. B is correct. This is a propagation reaction because the free radical electron has been transferred.

15. B is correct. Rate of formation/consumption of all species in a reaction are proportional to their coefficients. If the rate of a species is known, the rate of other species can be calculated using simple proportions.

Rate of consumption of CH_4O / Rate of consumption of O_2 = coefficient of CH_4O / coefficient of O_2

Rate of consumption of CH_4O = (coefficient of CH_4O / coefficient of O_2) × Rate of consumption of O_2

Rate of consumption of CH_4O = $(2/3) × 0.400$ mol L^{-1} s^{-1}

Rate of consumption of CH_4O = 0.267 mol L^{-1} s^{-1}

16. C is correct.

17. D is correct.

18. A is correct.

19. D is correct. Add the exponents to determine the rate of the reaction.

20. E is correct. Calculation of solubility constant (K_{sp}) is similar to equilibrium constant. The concentration of each species is raised to the power of their coefficients and multiplied with each other. For K_{sp}, only aqueous species are included in the calculation. Therefore the K_{sp} or this reaction is: $K_{sp} = [Ag^+]^2 [SO_4^{2-}]$.

21. B is correct.

22. D is correct.

23. C is correct.

24. E is correct. When changing the conditions of a reaction, Le Châtelier's principle states that the position of equilibrium will shift to counteract the change. If the reaction temperature, pressure or volume is changed, the position of equilibrium will change. However, adding a catalyst does not affect the position of equilibrium because a catalyst speeds up the forward and backward reaction to the same extent.

25. A is correct.

Activated complexes decompose rapidly, have specific geometries, are extremely reactive but may not be chemically isolated (compare to intermediates which can be isolated).

26. D is correct. Rate of formation/consumption of all species in a reaction are proportional to their coefficients. If the rate of a species is known, the rate of other species can be calculated using simple proportions.

Because the rate of formation of a species is already known, there's no need to calculate the rate. (The extra information on the problem are just there to deceive test takers).

Rate of consumption of H_2 / Rate of formation of NO_2 = coefficient of H_2 / coefficient of NO_2

Rate of consumption of H_2 = (coefficient of H_2 / coefficient of NO_2) × Rate of formation of NO_2

Rate of consumption of H_2 = $(4 / 2) × 2.6 × 10^{-4}$ M/min

Rate of consumption of H_2 = $5.2 × 10^{-4}$ M/min

27. A is correct.

28. E is correct.

29. D is correct. The reaction rate is the speed at which a chemical reaction proceeds. The factors that affect reaction rates include the solvent, concentrations of reactants, the physical state of the reactants and their dispersion, temperature and the presence of a catalyst.

30. A is correct. Any single step reaction has a rate law in which the powers are the numbers of molecules of a given type which collide. Half a molecule cannot collide.

31. E is correct.

32. A is correct. General formula for the equilibrium constant of a reaction:

$aA + bB \leftrightarrow cC + dD$

$K_{eq} = ([C]^c \times [D]^d) / ([A]^a \times [B]^b)$

For equilibrium constant calculation, only include species in aqueous or gas phases.

For this problem:

$K_{eq} = [NO]^4[H_2O]^6 / [NH_3]^4[O_2]^5$

33. C is correct.

34. D is correct.

35. E is correct. The rate-determining step has the highest activation energy.

36. B is correct.

37. B is correct. Enzymes (biological catalysts) bind to substrates to form an enzyme-substrate complex. While in this complex, they often align reactive chemical groups and hold them close together. Enzymes can induce structural changes that strain substrate bonds. Therefore, catalysts can actively participate in reactions.

38. C is correct.

39. B is correct. This is a tricky question because all of the events described by the options occur in a chemical reaction. You must choose one that doesn't have to happen for a reaction to occur.

The number of collisions doesn't have to be large for a reaction to occur. However, there is a minimum threshold of collisions that need to be reached before a reaction can happen. Reactions tend to happen more readily at higher temperatures because higher temperatures = larger number of collisions.

Argument for option B (a large enough number of collisions must occur): the number of collisions doesn't have to be large for a reaction to occur. On the other hand, there is a minimum threshold of collisions that need to be reached before a reaction can happen. Reactions tend to happen more at higher temperatures because higher temperatures = larger number of collisions.

Arguments can also be made for option E (chemical bonds in the product must form): some reactions (such as radical cleavage of chlorine in ozone decomposition process) only break bonds and don't form new bonds. For option C (chemical bonds in the reactants must break), not all bonds in the reactants will be broken for a reaction to occur.

But for the purposes of this problem, Option B seems to be the best answer.

40. E is correct. The forward and reverse rates are equal at equilibrium. Setting the rates equal and solving for products over reactants gives $K = k_1/k_{-1}$.

41. A is correct. $CaF_2 (s) \rightarrow Ca^{2+} (aq) + 2F^- (aq)$

Concentration of fluorine ions can be determined using concentration of calcium ions:

$$[F^-] = 2 \times [Ca^{2+}]$$

$$[F^-] = 2 \times 0.00021 \text{ M}$$

$$[F^-] = 4.2 \times 10^{-4} \text{ M}$$

Then K_{sp} can be determined:

$$K_{sp} = [Ca^{2+}][F^-]^2$$

$$K_{sp} = 2.1 \times 10^{-4} \text{ M} \times (4.2 \times 10^{-4} \text{ M})^2$$

$$K_{sp} = 3.7 \times 10^{-11}$$

42. A is correct.

43. C is correct.

44. E is correct.

45. D is correct. Removing NH_3 (I) and adding N_2 (IV) would shift equilibrium to right, while removing N_2 (III) or adding NH_3 (II) would shift equilibrium to the left.

46. D is correct. All are important conditions for chemical reactions to occur.

47. C is correct.

48. A is correct.

49. C is correct.

50. B is correct.

51. E is correct.

52. C is correct. Order of reaction is the sum of individual reactant orders, which is expressed as the power on each reactant's concentration. In this problem, the order for $[A]$ is 1 and $[B]^3$ is 3. Overall order $= 1 + 3 = 4$.

53. D is correct. General formula for the equilibrium constant of a reaction:

$$aA + bB \rightarrow cC + dD$$

$$K_{eq} = ([C]^c \times [D]^d) / ([A]^a \times [B]^b)$$

For equilibrium constant calculation, only include species in aqueous or gas phases (which, in this case, is all of them):

$$K_i = [H^+][H_2PO_4^-] / [H_3PO_4]$$

54. C is correct. Endothermic reactions consume energy, which means that there should be heat in the reactants' side. There is only one option that fulfills this criterion. This reaction is the Degussa process for the production of hydrogen cyanide, ΔH is +251 KJ/mol.

55. A is correct.

56. C is correct.

57. B is correct.

58. C is correct. Because there are 2 moles of molecules on each side, change in pressure (or volume) will not affect equilibrium.

59. E is correct. Two peaks in this reaction indicate two energy-requiring steps with each peak as an activated complex (high-energy intermediate).

60. B is correct. The activation energy for the reverse reaction is from the lowest energy point to the highest energy-activated complex.

The net energy for the forward reaction is the difference between A and E.

61. B is correct. Activation energies for forward exothermic reactions are the distance from the original, ground-state energy of the starting material to the energy content of the activated complex.

62. B is correct. The change in energy for this reaction (or ΔH) is the difference between energy contents of the reactants and the products.

63. B is correct.

64. E is correct.

65. A is correct.

66. A is correct. Lowering the temperature decreases the rate of a reaction because the molecules involved in the reaction will move around and collide more slowly, so the reaction will occur at a slower speed. Increasing the concentration of reactants or adding a catalyst will increase the rate of a reaction.

67. B is correct. Relationship between constant units and reaction order:

zero order = mol $L^{-1}s^{-1}$

first order = s^{-1}

second order = L $mol^{-1}s^{-1}$

Because the constant (k) unit is s^{-1}, this is a first order reaction.

Integrated rate equation for a first order reaction:

$\ln [A_t] - \ln [A_o] = -\,kt$

where A_t = concentration at t, A_o = initial concentration, k = rate constant, t = time

Partial pressure can be substituted for concentration.

$\ln [A_t] = -kt + \ln [A_o]$

$\ln [A_t] = -1 \times 10^{-4} \text{ s}^{-1} \times 23{,}000 \text{ s} + \ln [100]$

$\ln [A_t] = -2.3 + 4.6$

$\ln [A_t] = 2.3$

$[A_t] = e^{2.3} = 9.97 \approx 10 \text{ torr}$

Alternatively, use the equation:

$\log[A]_t = -kt/2.303 + \log[A]_0.\ \log[A]_0 = \log[100] = 2$

$-kt/2.303 = -1 \times 10^{-4} \times 23{,}000/2.3 = -1.$

Thus $\log[A]_t = 1$ or $[A]_t = 10$.

68. B is correct. In equilibrium, only gaseous and aqueous species will affect equilibrium; solids and liquids won't have any effect. Addition of solid PbI_2 would not affect the equilibrium.

69. C is correct.

70. E is correct.

71. A is correct.

72. D is correct.

73. C is correct. In exothermic reactions, heat released is a product of the forward reaction. If the temperature of the system is raised, heat and the other product of the forward reaction (e.g. methanol) combine to make the reaction go in the reverse direction. The perturbation of adding heat to this reaction causes the system, originally at equilibrium, to adjust to the perturbation, by consuming heat and shifting the equilibrium to the left.

74. C is correct. To shift equilibrium to the right (towards reactants), either concentration of reactants has to be reduced or concentration of products has to be decreased. In equilibrium, only gaseous and aqueous species will affect equilibrium. Solids and liquids won't have any effect, so PbI_2 has no affect on equilibrium. Therefore, the only correct option is decrease $[I^-]$.

75. E is correct.

76. B is correct. Rate of formation/consumption of all species in a reaction are proportional to their coefficients. If the rate of a species is known, the rate of other species can be calculated using simple proportions.

Rate of formation of C_2H_4 / Rate of consumption of C_4H_8 = coefficient of C_2H_4 / coefficient of C_4H_8

Rate of formation of C_2H_4 = (coefficient of C_2H_4 / coefficient of C_4H_8) × Rate of consumption of C_4H_8

Rate of formation of C_2H_4 = (2 / 1) × 4.25×10^{-4} mol L^{-1} s^{-1}

Rate of formation of C_2H_4 = 8.5×10^{-4} mol L^{-1} s^{-1}

77. C is correct.

78. D is correct.

79. E is correct.

80. A is correct. Reagents that do not affect the rate are order 0.

81. D is correct. Add the molar coefficients in the balanced reaction. Note that this sum is three for the reactants and two for the products. Decreasing the pressure tends to favor the side of the reaction that has a higher molar coefficient sum (left). Decreasing the volume favors the side of the reaction that has a smaller molar coefficient sum. Decreasing the temperature of the system favors the production of more heat, and favors a shift of equilibrium to the right.

82. E is correct. A catalyst increases the rate of a reaction through lowering the activation energy (i.e. the energy of the reaction's transition state) by providing an alternative chemical pathway for the reaction. There are many different mechanisms that the catalyst can use to provide this alternative pathway, including changing the proximity and orientation of the reactants, forming ionic bonds with the intermediates and creating bond strain.

83. A is correct.

84. C is correct.

85. B is correct.

86. E is correct.

87. C is correct. The rate constant is related to the activation energy by the following equation:

$$k = Ae^{-Ea/RT}$$

k = rate constant Ea = activation energy

A = constant R = 1.99 cal/mol·K

88. A is correct. To determine order of reactant A, find 2 experiments where the concentrations of B are identical and concentrations of A are different. In this problem, that would be experiments 2 and 3. Use data from those experiments to calculate order of A:

$$Rate_3 / Rate_2 = ([A]_3 / [A]_2)^{order\ of\ A}$$

$$0.500 / 0.500 = (0.060 / 0.030)^{order\ of\ A}$$

$$1 = (2)^{order\ of\ A}$$

Order of A = 0

89. B is correct.

90. D is correct.

91. A is correct. General formula for the equilibrium constant of a reaction:

$$aA + bB \leftrightarrow cC + dD$$

$$K_{eq} = ([C]^c \times [D]^d) / ([A]^a \times [B]^b)$$

For equilibrium constant calculation, only include species in aqueous or gas phases.

$$K_{eq} = 1 / [CO][H_2]^2$$

92. C is correct.

93. B is correct. Consider the exponents.

94. D is correct.

95. E is correct.

96. D is correct.

97. B is correct.

98. D is correct.

99. A is correct.

100. E is correct.

101. D is correct. By Le Châtelier's principle, if the concentration of H_2 increases then the equilibrium shifts to the right which leads to a greater production of HF and increased consumption of F_2.

102. A is correct. Catalysts increase the rates of reactions by lowering the activation energy. Catalysts increase both forward and backward reaction rates equally but do not shift the equilibrium or change equilibrium concentrations.

103. B is correct.

104. E is correct.

105. C is correct. General formula for the equilibrium constant of a reaction:

$$aA + bB \leftrightarrow cC + dD$$

$$K_{eq} = ([C]^c \times [D]^d) / ([A]^a \times [B]^b)$$

For equilibrium constant calculation, only include species in aqueous or gas phases (which, in this case, is all of them).

$$K_i = [H^+] [HS^-] / [H_2S]$$

106. C is correct.

107. D is correct.

108. A is correct. General formula for the equilibrium constant of a reaction:

$$aA + bB \leftrightarrow cC + dD$$

$$K_{eq} = ([C]^c \times [D]^d) / ([A]^a \times [B]^b)$$

For equilibrium constant calculation, only include species in aqueous or gas phases.

$$K_{eq} = [CO_2]$$

109. B is correct.

110. B is correct.

111. A is correct. General formula for the equilibrium constant of a reaction:

$aA + bB \leftrightarrow cC + dD$

$K_{eq} = ([C]^c \times [D]^d) / ([A]^a \times [B]^b)$

For the reaction above:

$K_{eq} = [C]^2 / [A] [B]^3$

112. E is correct.

113. C is correct. Catalysts lower activation energy by creating a new path towards the transition state.

114. C is correct. General formula for the equilibrium constant of a reaction:

$aA + bB \leftrightarrow cC + dD$

$K_i = ([C]^c \times [D]^d) / ([A]^a \times [B]^b)$

For equilibrium constant calculation, only include species in aqueous or gas phases (which, in this case, is all of them).

$K_i = [H^+] [HCO_3^-] / [H_2CO_3]$

115. A is correct. General formula for the equilibrium constant of a reaction:

$aA + bB \leftrightarrow cC + dD$

$K_{eq} = ([C]^c \times [D]^d) / ([A]^a \times [B]^b)$

Analyze the given K expression to determine the reaction:

$K = [H_2]^2 [O_2] / [H_2O]$

Reaction $= 2H_2O \leftrightarrow 2H_2 + O_2$

116. C is correct.

117. E is correct.

118. B is correct. General formula for the equilibrium constant of a reaction:

$aA + bB \leftrightarrow cC + dD$

$K_{eq} = ([C]^c \times [D]^d) / ([A]^a \times [B]^b)$

For equilibrium constant calculation, only include species in aqueous or gas phases.

$K_c = 1 / [CO_2]$

119. B is correct.

120. C is correct. A catalyst is never consumed in a reaction. A catalyst lowers the energy of the high-energy transition state (i.e. the activation energy), but it does not change the energy of the reactants of the reactants or the products. Catalysts alter the rate of chemical reactions causing the reactions to occur faster.

121. A is correct.

122. D is correct. General formula for the equilibrium constant of a reaction:

$aA + bB \leftrightarrow cC + dD$

$K_{eq} = ([C]^c \times [D]^d) / ([A]^a \times [B]^b)$

For equilibrium constant calculation, only include species in aqueous or gas phases.

$K_{eq} = [O_2]^3$

123. E is correct.

124. C is correct. In order to write a complete rate law, the order of each reactant is required. The order of each reactant has been provided by the problem (first order in each).

The total order is a sum of the individual orders, which would be $1 + 1 = 2$. Total order is usually not expressed in the rate law.

$\text{Rate} = k[NO][O_2]$

125. B is correct.

126. D is correct.

127. B is correct.

128. C is correct. Use the equilibrium concentrations to calculate K_c:

$K_c = [N_2] [H_2]^3 / [NH_3]^2$

$K_c = 0.04 \times (0.12)^3 / (0.4)^2$

$K_c = 4.3 \times 10^{-4}$

129. A is correct.

130. E is correct. General formula for the equilibrium constant of a reaction:

$aA + bB \leftrightarrow cC + dD$

$K_{eq} = ([C]^c \times [D]^d) / ([A]^a \times [B]^b)$

For equilibrium constant calculation, only include species in aqueous or gas phases.

$K_c = [CO_2] [H_2O]^2 / [CH_4]$

131. B is correct. The rate law is determined by comparing trials and determining how changes in the initial concentrations of the reactants affect the initial rate of the reaction. Comparing Trials 1 and 3, [A] increased by a factor of 3 as did the reaction rate; thus, the reaction is first order with respect to A. Comparing Trials 1 and 2, [B] increased by a factor of 4 and the reaction rate increased by a factor of $16 = 4^2$. Thus, the reaction is second order with respect to B. Therefore, the rate $= k[A][B]^2$.

132. A is correct. General formula for the equilibrium constant of a reaction:

$aA + bB \leftrightarrow cC + dD$

$K_{eq} = ([C]^c \times [D]^d) / ([A]^a \times [B]^b)$

For the reaction above:

$K_{eq} = [C] / [A]^2 [B]^3$

133. D is correct.

134. E is correct. To find the order with respect to W, look at trials 2 and 4. The concentrations of X and Y do not change when comparing trials 2 and 4, but the concentration of W changes from 0.015 to 0.03 which corresponds to an increase by a factor of two. However this increase in concentration corresponds to no increase rate (0.08 to 0.08). Therefore, the order with respect to W is zero.

The order for X can be found by looking at trials 1 and 3. The concentrations for W and Z are constant, and the concentration for X increases by a factor of 3 (from 0.5 to 0.15). This corresponds to a rate increase of 9 x (0.04 to 0.36). The order with respect to X is two. The order with respect to Y is found by looking at trials 1 to 5. [W] and [X] do not change but [Y] goes up by a factor of four. The rate from trial 1 to five goes up by a factor of 2. This corresponds to an order that is a square root function or ½ power for Y. The overall order is found by taking the sum of the orders for X, Y, and Z: $0 + 2 + ½ = 2½$.

135. B is correct. Since the order with respect to W is zero, the rate of formation of Z does not depend on the concentration of W.

136. D is correct. Use the partial orders determined in #134 to write the rate law:

rate = $k[W]^0[X]^2[Z]^{1/2}$

Plug in the values from one of the trials. In this case, Trial #1 was chosen:

$0.04 = k\,[0.01]^0[0.05]^2[0.04]^{1/2}$
$0.04 = (k)(1)(2.5 \times 10^{-3})(2 \times 10^{-1})$

$k = 80$

137. C is correct.

138. E is correct. The final amount of NOBr is known (0.47 mol) which means the amount of NO and Br_2 used can be calculated by comparing coefficients:

NO = (2/2) × 0.47 mol = 0.47 mol

Br_2 = (1/2) × 0.47 mol = 0.235 mol

Calculate final concentration of the reactants:

NO = 0.56 mol – 0.47 mol = 0.09 mol

Br_2 = 0.380 mol – 0.235 mol = 0.145 mol ≈ 0.15 mol

Final composition: 0.09 mol NO and 0.15 mol Br_2

139. D is correct. General formula for the equilibrium constant of a reaction:

aA + bB ↔ cC + dD

$K_{eq} = ([C]^c \times [D]^d) / ([A]^a \times [B]^b)$

For equilibrium constant calculation, only include species in aqueous or gas phases (which, in this case, is all of them).

$K_i = [H^+]\,[HSO_3^-] / [H_2SO_3]$

140. A is correct.

141. D is correct.

142. C is correct. General formula for the equilibrium constant of a reaction:

$$aA + bB \leftrightarrow cC + dD$$

$$K_{eq} = ([C]^c \times [D]^d) / ([A]^a \times [B]^b)$$

For equilibrium constant calculation, only include species in aqueous or gas phases (which, in this case, is all of them).

$$K_{eq} = [CH_4][H_2S]^2 / [CS_2][H_2]^4$$

143. B is correct. General formula for the equilibrium constant of a reaction:

$$aA + bB \leftrightarrow cC + dD$$

$$K_{eq} = ([C]^c \times [D]^d) / ([A]^a \times [B]^b)$$

For equilibrium constant calculation, only include species in aqueous or gas phases.

$$K_{eq} = [CH_4] / [H_2]^2$$

144. A is correct.

145. C is correct. All chemical reactions eventually reach equilibrium, the state at which the reactants and products are present in concentrations that have no further tendency to change with time. Catalysts speed up reactions, and therefore increase the rate at which equilibrium is reached, but they never alter the thermodynamics of a reaction and therefore do not change free energy ΔG.

146. B is correct. Note the following calculation:

$$Cl_2 \rightleftharpoons 2Cl$$

Before equilibrium: 1M   0

At equilibrium: 1M − x   2x

$$K = \frac{[Cl]^2}{[Cl_2]}$$

$$= \frac{(2x)^2}{(1-x)} = \frac{4x^2}{1} = 4 \times 10^{-4}$$

(ignore x in denominator because it is small).

$$x = 0.01$$
$$2x = 0.02$$

147. D is correct. In order to write a complete rate law, the order of each reactant is required. To determine order of reactant B, find 2 experiments where the concentrations of C are identical and concentrations of B are different. In this problem, that would be experiments 1 and 2. Use data from those experiments to calculate order of B:

$$Rate_2 / Rate_1 = ([B]_2/[B]_1)^{order\ of\ B}$$

$$0.000500 / 0.000250 = (0.200/0.100)^{order\ of\ B}$$

$2 = (2)^{\text{order of B}}$

Order of B $= 1$

Use the same procedure to calculate order of C. Based on data from experiments 1 and 3:

$\text{Rate}_3 \, / \, \text{Rate}_1 = ([C]_3/[C]_1)^{\text{order of C}}$

$0.001000 \, / \, 0.000250 = (0.500/0.250)^{\text{order of C}}$

$4 = (2)^{\text{order of C}}$

Order of C $= 2$

$\text{Rate} = k[B][C]^2$

148. E is correct. $3A + 2B \rightarrow 4C$

Moles of A used in the reaction $= 1.4$ moles $- 0.9$ moles $= 0.5$ moles

Moles of C formed $=$ (coefficient C / coefficient A) $\times$ moles of A used

Moles of C formed $= (4 / 3) \times 0.5$ moles $= 0.67$ moles

149. A is correct. General formula for the equilibrium constant of a reaction:

$aA + bB \leftrightarrow cC + dD$

$K_{eq} = ([C]^c \times [D]^d) \, / \, ([A]^a \times [B]^b)$

For the reaction above:

$K_{eq} = [B] \, [C]^3 \, / \, [A]^2$

150. C is correct. General formula for the equilibrium constant of a reaction:

$aA + bB \leftrightarrow cC + dD$

$K_{eq} = ([C]^c \times [D]^d) \, / \, ([A]^a \times [B]^b)$

For equilibrium constant calculation, only include species in aqueous or gas phases (which, in this case, is all of them):

$K_{eq} = [CO_2]^2 \, / \, [CO]^2[O_2]$

151. C is correct. Do not confuse kinetics with equilibrium. Rate laws cannot be determined from the balanced equation unless the reaction occurs in a single step. From the data, when the concentration is doubled, the rate quadruples. Since four is two squared, the rate law is second order.

152. A is correct.

153. C is correct.

154. A is correct. To find the K_{sp} take the molarities or concentrations of the products (cC and dD) and multiply them. If any of the products have coefficients in front of them, raise the product to that coefficient power and multiply the concentration by that coefficient:

$K_{sp} = [C]^c[D]^d$

$K_{sp} = [Cu^{2+}]^3 \, [PO_4{}^{3-}]^2$

The reactant (aA) is not included in the K_{sp} equation. Solids are not included when calculating equilibrium constant expressions, because their concentrations do not change the expression. Any change in their concentrations are insignificant, and thus omitted.

155. B is correct.

156. A is correct. Note the following balanced reaction and calculation:

$$2NH_3 \rightarrow N_2 + 3H_2$$

$$K = \frac{[H_2]^3 [N_2]}{[NH_3]^2}$$

$$K = \frac{(0.3)^3 (02)}{(0.1)^2}$$

157. C is correct.

158. E is correct.

159. C is correct. General formula for the equilibrium constant of a reaction:

$$aA + bB \leftrightarrow cC + dD$$

$$K_{eq} = ([C]^c \times [D]^d) / ([A]^a \times [B]^b)$$

For equilibrium constant calculation, only include species in aqueous or gas phases (which, in this case, is all of them):

$$K_{eq} = [NO_2]^2 / [N_2O_4]$$

Plug in the values for each concentration:

$$K_{eq} = (0.400)^2 / 0.800$$

$$K_{eq} = 0.200$$

160. D is correct.

161. B is correct. The rate depends upon the specific reaction, not the order of the reaction.

162. D is correct. General formula for the equilibrium constant of a reaction:

$$aA + bB \leftrightarrow cC + dD$$

$$K_{eq} = ([C]^c \times [D]^d) / ([A]^a \times [B]^b)$$

For equilibrium constant calculation, only include species in aqueous or gas phases.

$$K_{eq} = 1 / [Cl]^2$$

163. E is correct. Catalysts lower the activation energy of a reaction, which is the minimum amount of energy that must be input to cause a chemical reaction. By doing this, they cause a reaction to occur faster and thus increase the rate of the reaction.

164. B is correct.

165. D is correct. Rate expressions are determined experimentally from rate data for a reaction. The calculation is not similar to that for the equilibrium constant. Since rate data are not given for this reaction, the rate expression cannot be determined.

166. C is correct.

167. D is correct.

168. E is correct.

169. B is correct.

170. A is correct. For a reaction to occur, the molecules must have enough energy during a collision and strike each other with the proper spatial orientation.

171. E is correct.

172. A is correct.

173. D is correct.

174. E is correct.

175. B is correct. An increase in the rate constant equals a faster reaction rate. Increasing the temperature of a reaction always increases the reaction rate.

176. C is correct. Mass action expression is identical to equilibrium constant expression. General formula for the equilibrium constant of a reaction:

$aA + bB \leftrightarrow cC + dD$

$K_{eq} = ([C]^c \times [D]^d) / ([A]^a \times [B]^b)$

To determine the mass action expression, only include species in aqueous or gas phases.

$K_c = [CrCl_3]^4 / [CCl_4]^3$

177. A is correct. Start by calculating the concentrations of each species:

$O_2 = 0.343$ mol $/ 3.25$ L $= 0.106$ M

$SO_2 = 0.00419$ mol $/ 3.25$ L $= 1.289 \times 10^{-3}$ M

$SO_3 = 0.0212$ mol $/ 3.25$ L $= 0.00652$ M

Use the concentrations to calculate K_c:

$K_c = [SO_2]^2 [O_2] / [SO_3]^2$

$K_c = (1.29 \times 10^{-3})^2 \times 0.106 / (0.0065)^2$

$K_c = 4.14 \times 10^{-3}$

178. D is correct.

179. E is correct.

180. D is correct. All the coefficients of the reaction have been doubled therefore the powers in the equilibrium expression have doubled.

When coefficients in equations are multiplied by a number, the equilibrium constant (K) will be raised to the power of the multiplier. When coefficients in equations are divided by a number, take the root of K with the divisor as the root factor.

In this problem, the equation is multiplied by 2, so the new K will be $125^2 = 1.5 \times 10^4$.

181. B is correct. Amount of PCl_5 used = 0.84 moles – 0.72 moles = 0.12 moles.

All of the species have the same coefficient, so amount of PCl_3 and Cl_2 created = 0.12 moles each.

Because the volume of container is 1.0 L, number of moles = concentration.

$$K_{eq} = [PCl_3]\,[Cl_2]\,/\,[PCl_5]$$

$$K_{eq} = 0.12 \times 0.12 / 0.72$$

$$K_{eq} = 0.02$$

182. E is correct.

183. D is correct.

184. B is correct. The rate-determining step of a reaction is the slowest step (i.e. takes the most time).

185. C is correct.

186. A is correct.

187. D is correct. General formula for the equilibrium constant of a reaction:

$$aA + bB \rightarrow cC + dD$$

$$K_{eq} = ([C]^c \times [D]^d) / ([A]^a \times [B]^b)$$

The given $K_{sp} = [Fe^{3+}]^2[CrO_4^{2-}]^3$

The powers in the given solubility product expression indicate the number of ions present (2 for Fe, 3 for CrO_4). Ion charges are already indicated by the problem.

Answer: $Fe_2(CrO4)_3 \leftrightarrow 2Fe^{3+} + 3CrO_4^{2-}$

188. E is correct. The main function of catalysts is lowering the activation energy of a reaction, thus increasing its rate. Although they do decrease the amount of energy required to reach the rate-limiting transition state, they do *not* decrease the amount of energy consumed by the reaction (ΔG).

189. B is correct. This is usual for reaction at equilibrium. Catalysts, by definition, are regenerated during the course of a reaction and are not consumed by the reaction.

190. C is correct.

191. E is correct. Comparing the first two lines, doubling the hydrogen concentration doubles the rate. Since $2^1 = 2$, the reaction is first order for H_2. Comparing line 2 to line 4, tripling the NO concentration increases the rate by about nine times. Since $3^2 = 9$, the reaction is second order for NO.

192. E is correct.

193. B is correct. The rate law is determined by comparing trials and determining how changes in the initial concentrations of the reactants affect the initial rate of the reaction. Comparing Trials 1 and 2, [A] increased by a factor of 2 and so did the reaction rate; thus, the reaction is first order with respect to A. Comparing Trials 2 and 3, [B] increased by a factor of 2 as did the reaction rate; thus, the reaction is also first order with respect to B.

194. C is correct.

195. A is correct. Expression for equilibrium constant:

$$K = [H_2O]^2 [Cl_2]^2 / [HCl]^4 [O_2]$$

Solve for $[Cl_2]$:

$$[Cl_2]^2 = (K \times [HCl]^4[O_2]) / [H_2O]^2$$

$$[Cl_2]^2 = \{46 \times (0.150)^4 \times 0.395\} / (0.625)^2$$

$$[Cl_2]^2 = 0.0235$$

$$[Cl_2] = 0.153$$

196. E is correct.

197. A is correct. General formula for the equilibrium constant of a reaction:

$$aA + bB \leftrightarrow cC + dD$$

$$K_{eq} = ([C]^c \times [D]^d) / ([A]^a \times [B]^b)$$

For the reaction above:

$$K_{eq} = [C]^2[D] / [A][B]^2$$

198. D is correct. Calculate the value of the equilibrium expression under these conditions (the reaction quotient): hydrogen iodide concentration decreases for equilibrium to be reached.

To determine the state of a reaction, calculate its reaction quotient (Q). Q has the same method of calculation as equilibrium constant (K); the difference is K has to be calculated at point of equilibrium, whereas Q can be calculated at any time.

If $Q > K$ reaction will shift towards reactants (more reactants, less products)

If $Q = K$ reaction is at equilibrium

If $Q < K$ reaction will shift towards products (more products, less reactants)

$$Q = [HI]^2 / [H_2][I_2]$$

$$Q = (3)^2 / 0.4 \times 0.6$$

$$Q = 37.5$$

Because $Q > K$, the reaction will shift towards reactant and the amount of product (HI) will decrease. Answer: [hydrogen iodide] decreases.

199. A is correct.

200. C is correct.

201. B is correct.

202. E is correct. The rate law is determined by comparing trials and determining how changes in the initial concentrations of the reactants affect the initial rate of the reaction. Comparing Trials 1 and 4, we see that [A] increased by a factor of 2 and the reaction rate increased by a factor of 4 = 2^2; thus, the reaction is second order with respect to A. Comparing Trials 1 and 3, [B] increased by a factor of 2 and the reaction rate increased by a factor of 4 = 2^2; thus, the reaction rate is also second order with respect to B. Comparing Trials 1 and 2, [C] increased by a factor of 2 as does the reaction rate; thus, the reaction is first order with respect to C.

203. A is correct. When two or more reactions are combined to create a new reaction, the K of the resulting reaction is a product of Ks of individual reactions.

When a reaction is reversed, new K = 1 / old K.

Start by analyzing all the reactions provided the problem:

    (1) $2NO + Cl_2 \leftrightarrow 2NOCl$ $K_c = 3.2 \times 10^3$

    (2) $2NO_2 \leftrightarrow 2NO + O_2$ $K_c = 15.5$

    (3) $NOCl + \frac{1}{2}O_2 \leftrightarrow NO_2 + \frac{1}{2}Cl_2$ $K_c = ???$

Reaction 3 can be created by combining reactions 1 and 2.

Let's start with reaction 1. Notice that on reaction 3, NOCl is located on the left. To match reaction 3, reverse reaction 1. The K of this reversed reaction will be 1 / (3.2×10^{-3}) = 312.5

    $2NOCl \leftrightarrow 2NO + Cl_2$ $K_c = 312.5$

Reaction 2 also needs to be reversed to match the position of NO in reaction 3. The new K will be 1/15.5 = 0.0645

    $2NO + O_2 \leftrightarrow 2NO_2$ $K_c = 0.065$

Now add those reactions together. K of the resulting reaction is the product of K from both reactions:

    $312.5 \times 0.064 = 20.16$

    $2NOCl \leftrightarrow 2NO + Cl_2$

    $2NO + O_2 \leftrightarrow 2NO_2$

    ─────────────────── +

    $2NOCl + O_2 \leftrightarrow 2NO_2 + Cl_2$ $K_c = 20.16$

All that's left is to divide the equation by 2. The new K will be the square root of initial K:

    $\sqrt{20.16} = 4.49$

    $NOCl + \frac{1}{2}O_2 \leftrightarrow NO_2 + \frac{1}{2}Cl_2$ $K_c = 4.49$

204. D is correct.

205. A is correct.

206. C is correct.

207. A is correct. Whenever the fast step proceeds the slow step, the fast step is assumed to reach equilibrium and the equilibrium concentrations are used for the rate law of the slow step.

208. B is correct.

209. C is correct.

210. E is correct. None of the stated changes tend to decrease the *magnitude* of the equilibrium constant K. For exothermic reactions, decreasing the temperature increases the magnitude of K. Changes in volume, pressure or concentration do not affect the magnitude of K.

211. D is correct. When two or more reactions are combined to create a new reaction, the K of the resulting reaction is a product of Ks of individual reactions.

When a reaction is reversed, new K = 1 / old K.

$$PCl_3 + Cl_2 \leftrightarrow PCl_5 \qquad K = K_1$$
$$2NO + Cl_2 \leftrightarrow 2NOCl \qquad K = K_2$$

Reverse the 1st equation:

$$PCl_5 \leftrightarrow PCl_3 + Cl_2 \qquad K = 1/K_1$$

Add those two reactions to create a third reaction:

$$PCl_5 \leftrightarrow PCl_3 + Cl_2 \qquad K = 1/K_1$$
$$2NO + Cl_2 \leftrightarrow 2NOCl \qquad K = K_2$$
$$\overline{} \; +$$
$$PCl_5 + 2NO \leftrightarrow PCl_3 + 2NOCl$$
$$K = (1/K_1) \times K_2 = K_2/K_1$$

212. E is correct.

213. B is correct.

$$K_{sp} = [C]^c[D]^d$$
$$K_{sp} = [Au^{3+}] \, [Cl^-]^3$$

See explanation for question **154** for more information.

214. A is correct. General formula for the equilibrium constant of a reaction:

$$aA + bB \leftrightarrow cC + dD$$
$$K_{eq} = ([C]^c \times [D]^d) / ([A]^a \times [B]^b)$$

For equilibrium constant calculation, only include species in aqueous or gas phases (which, in this case, is all of them):

$$K_{eq} = [H_2O]^6[NO]^4 / [NH_3]^4[O_2]^5$$

215. D is correct.

216. B is correct.

217. D is correct.

218. A is correct.

Chapter 8.   THERMODYNAMICS AND THERMOCHEMISTRY

1. B is correct.

2. A is correct.

3. D is correct.

4. E is correct.

5. A is correct. The overall reaction is the sum of the two individual reactions. The overall ΔH_{rxn} is (–802 kJ/mlol) + (–88 kJ/mol) = –890 kJ/mol.

6. C is correct.

7. A is correct.

8. E is correct.

9. D is correct.

10. B is correct. It is not an isolated system because work is being done on the system but it is a closed system because no matter moves in or out.

11. C is correct.

12. C is correct.

13. A is correct. Since $\Delta G = \Delta H + T\Delta S$ and T is always positive, a – ΔH and a +ΔS always = –ΔG.

14. B is correct.

15. E is correct. Bell jars are designed to not let air or other materials in or out. Insulated means that heat cannot get in or out. The fact that the contents do not begin in equilibrium is of no consequence.

16. B is correct.

17. A is correct.

18. C is correct.

19. D is correct. Changes in entropy, enthalpy, and free energy are state functions, because they depend only on the initial and final states of the system, and are independent of the paths taken to reach the final state.

20. E is correct. No matter or energy leaks out of the system. The presence of non-equilibrium processes inside the bunker is irrelevant.

21. B is correct.

22. A is correct.

23. C is correct.

ΔH_{rxn} = total ΔH_f of the products – total ΔH_f of the reactants.

ΔH_{rxn} = ($\Delta H_{f, products}$) – ($\Delta H_{f, reactants}$)

ΔH_{rxn} = (–635.5 kJ/mol + –395.5 kJ/mol) – (–1206.5 kJ/mol)

ΔH_{rxn} = (–1,031 kJ/mol) – (–1206.5 kJ/mol)

ΔH_{rxn} = 177.5 kJ/mol.

24. E is correct.

25. D is correct.

26. A is correct.

27. D is correct.

28. E is correct.

29. C is correct. H_2O removes heat from the body at a greater rate than air through direct contact as conduction. Conduction is different than the heat removed by water (i.e. evaporation) which is related to the latent heat of vaporization of water.

30. A is correct. Heat = mass × specific heat × change in temperature

In symbolic form:

$q = m \times c \times \Delta t$

$q = 36.5g \times 0.908 \text{ J/g } ^\circ C \times (84.1^\circ C - 56.8^\circ C)$

$q = 904.77 \text{ J} \approx 905 \text{ J}$

31. B is correct.

32. E is correct.

33. C is correct. Air and vacuum are the excellent insulators. For example, storm windows which have air wedged between two glass panes also work by utilizing this principle of conduction.

34. B is correct.

35. E is correct. The ΔG for an element in its standard state is zero by convention.

36. E is correct. More stable product means that the molecules lost energy = $-\Delta H$.

A more orderly arrangement for products than the reactants means entropy decreased = $-\Delta S$.

37. D is correct. The change in enthalpy (ΔH) is defined as the quantity of heat absorbed (energy change) when a reaction occurs constant pressure.

A: refers to the energy change independent of pressure.

B: refers to the change in free energy.

D: refers to the change in entropy or randomness of a system.

38. C is correct. Conduction (i.e. transfer of thermal energy through matter) can be reduced by introducing an insulator, the air or vacuum between the two walls is a highly effective insulator.

39. D is correct.

40. E is correct. Heat = mass × specific heat × change in temperature

In symbolic form:

$$q = m \times c \times \Delta t$$
$$q = 16.0 \text{ g} \times 0.382 \text{ J/g} \,^{\circ}\text{C} \times (66.1 \,^{\circ}\text{C} - 23.0 \,^{\circ}\text{C})$$
$$q = 263.4 \text{ J} \approx 263 \text{ J}$$

41. B is correct.

42. A is correct.

43. C is correct. Convection is defined as the movement of heat through liquids and gases. The lid prevents fluid (including air) from leaking out.

44. D is correct. Heat = mass × specific heat × change in temperature

In symbolic form:

$$q = m \times c \times \Delta t$$

Rearrange to solve for mass:

$$m = q / (c \times \Delta t)$$
$$m = 9.86 \text{ J} / \{0.90 \text{ J/g} \,^{\circ}\text{C} \times (30.5 \,^{\circ}\text{C} - 23.2 \,^{\circ}\text{C})\}$$
$$m = 1.5 \text{ g}$$

45. B is correct.

46. B is correct.

A catalyst lowers the energy of activation which increases the rate of the reaction.

47. D is correct. Thermal radiation is the emission of electromagnetic waves (i.e. energy carried via photons) from all matter that has a temperature (i.e. kinetic energy) greater than absolute zero. A mirror-like surface reflects radiation, keeping heat inside the thermos.

48. A is correct.

49. E is correct. Heat = mass × specific heat × change in temperature

In symbolic form:

$$q = m \times c \times \Delta t$$

Rearrange the equation to solve for Δt:

$$\Delta t = q / (m \times c)$$
$$\Delta t = 336 \text{ J} / (25 \text{ g} \times 4.184 \text{ J/g} \,^{\circ}\text{C})$$
$$\Delta t = 3.2 \,^{\circ}\text{C}$$

The problem indicates that heat is removed from H_2O, which means that its temperature will decrease.

$$\text{Final t} = \text{initial t} - \Delta t$$

Final t = 19.6 °C – 3.2 °C

Final t = 16.4 °C

50. A is correct.

51. A is correct.

52. D is correct. Heat carried by gases (i.e. hot air) is prevented from leaving the system through the lid.

53. E is correct. *Heat capacity* is amount of heat required to increase temperature of *the whole sample* by 1 °C while *specific heat capacity* is heat required to increase temperature of *1 gram* of sample by 1 °C.

Heat capacity = mass × specific heat capacity

Heat capacity = 84.0 g × 4.184 J/g °C

Heat capacity = 351.5 J/°C ≈ 351 J/°C

54. B is correct.

55. D is correct. Gas molecules transfer kinetic energy between each other.

56. B is correct.

57. D is correct.

58. C is correct.

59. A is correct. In this problem, heat flows from Au to Ag.

q released by Au = q captured by Ag

For this example, let Au be sample 1 and Ag be sample 2.

$m_1 \times c_1 \times \Delta t_1 = m_2 \times c_2 \times \Delta t_2$

Solving for the unknown (mass of Ag or m_2):

$m_2 = (m_1 \times c_1 \times \Delta t_1) / (c_2 \times \Delta t_2)$

$m_2 = [22 \text{ g} \times 0.130 \text{ J/g °C} \times (95.5°C – 26.4°C)] / [0.240 \text{ J/g °C} \times (36 °C – 23 °C)]$

$m_2 = 63.34 \text{ g} \approx 63 \text{ g}$

60. C is correct.

61. B is correct. Exothermic reactions are spontaneous and more stable than endothermic reactions.

62. A is correct. Work and heat relate to the change in energy of a system when it moves from one state to another which depends on how a system changes between states.

63. E is correct. Heat = mass × specific heat × change in temperature

In symbolic form:

$q = m \times c \times \Delta t$

Rearrange the equation to solve for mass:

$$m = q / (c \times \Delta t)$$

$$m = 468 \text{ J} / \{0.130 \text{ J/g °C} \times (33.2 \text{ °C} - 21.6 \text{ °C})\}$$

$$m = 310 \text{ g}$$

64. D is correct.

65. A is correct.

66. E is correct. The zero law of thermodynamics states that no object can reach absolute zero. At absolute zero, all motion ceases and the material could not radiate heat.

67. D is correct. Heat = mass × specific heat × change in temperature

In symbolic form:

$$q = m \times c \times \Delta t$$

Rearrange the equation to solve for Δt:

$$\Delta t = q / (m \times c)$$

Check the units of specific heat in the problem – in this case, it's 4.18 J/g °C. It means that the energy has to be converted to joules.

$$6.90 \times 10^2 \text{ calories} \times 4180 \text{ J/calorie} = 2{,}884{,}200 \text{ J}$$

Most of the time, heat will be expressed in kilojoules (kJ). Because the specific heat is in joules, remember to convert kilojoules into joules.

$$59.1 \text{ kg} \times 1000 \text{ g/kg} = 59{,}100 \text{ g}$$

Use those values in the rearranged heat equation to obtain Δt:

$$\Delta t = q / (m \times c)$$

$$\Delta t = 2{,}884{,}200 \text{ J} / (59{,}100 \text{ g} \times 4.18 \text{ J/g °C})$$

$$\Delta t = 11.68 \text{ °C} \approx 11.7 \text{ °C}$$

68. B is correct.

69. C is correct. One mole of an ideal gas occupies 22.4 L at STP. Therefore, three moles of a gas = 67.4 L.

70. B is correct. The first law is a statement of conservation of energy.

71. D is correct.

72. A is correct. Relationship between enthalpy (ΔH) and internal energy (ΔE):

Enthalpy = Internal energy + work (for gases, work = PV)

$$\Delta H = \Delta E + \Delta (PV)$$

Solving for ΔE:

$$\Delta E = \Delta H - \Delta (PV)$$

According to ideal gas law:

$$PV = nRT$$

Substitute ideal gas law to the previous equation:

$$\Delta E = \Delta H - \Delta(nRT)$$

R and T are constant, which leaves Δn as the variable.

The reaction is C_2H_2 (g) + $2H_2$ (g) $\rightarrow$ C_2H_6 (g). There are three gas molecules on the left and one on the right, which means $\Delta n = 1 - 3 = -2$.

In this problem, the temperature is not provided. However, the presence of degree symbols (ΔG^o, ΔH^o, ΔS^o) indicates that those are standard values, which are measured at 25°C or 298.15 K.

Always double check the units before performing calculations; ΔH is in kilojoules while the gas constant (R) is 8.314 J/mol K. Convert ΔH to joules before calculating.

Use the Δn and T values to calculate ΔE:

$$\Delta E = \Delta H - \Delta nRT$$

$$\Delta E = -311,500 \text{ J/mol} - (-2 \times 8.314 \text{ J/mol K} \times 298.15 \text{ K})$$

$$\Delta E = -306,542 \text{ J} \approx -306.5 \text{ kJ}$$

73. C is correct.

74. B is correct. Convert calories to joules using this conversion factor:

$$1 \text{ calorie} = 4.18 \text{ J}$$

Convert joules to kilojoules using this conversion factor:

$$1000 \text{ J} = 1 \text{ kilojoule (kJ)}$$

Converting from calories to kilojoules:

$$212 \text{ calories} \times 4.18 \text{ J/calorie} \times 0.001 \text{ kJ/J} = 0.887 \text{ kJ}$$

75. E is correct.

76. A is correct. Diffusion rate is proportional to the speed of the gas. Since lighter gases travel faster than heavier gases, H_2 diffuses faster than O_2.

At the same temperature, two gases have the same average molecular kinetic energy: $(\frac{1}{2})m_H v_N^2 = (\frac{1}{2})m_o v_o^2$, which implies $(v_H/v_o)^2 = m_o/m_H$. Since $m_o/m_H = 16$, $(v_H/v_o)^2 = 16 = v_H/v_o = 4:1$ ratio.

77. C is correct. Intensive properties do not depend on the amount of the material present. Density is an intensive property because if a container of liquid is reduced by a percentage, the density is the same as the density of the original liquid sample.

78. D is correct.

79. B is correct.

80. E is correct.

81. B is correct. Determine the moles of N_2:

moles N_2 = mass N_2 / molecular mass N_2

moles N_2 = 50.0g / (2 × 14.01 g/mol)

moles N_2 = 1.78 moles

ΔH is positive, which means energy is consumed by the reaction. ΔH value indicated in the reaction is for one mole of N_2 (or one mole of O_2 / 2 moles of NO).

Calculate the heat consumed by 1.78 moles of N_2:

1.78 × 43.2 kcal = 76.9 kcal ≈ 77.1 kcal consumed

82. C is correct. An extensive property is a property that varies with amount of matter. An intensive property is a property that doesn't vary with amount of matter. Because the problem indicates that change of heat is an extensive property, it should be proportional to the amount of matter involved in the reaction. Therefore, three times more mass results in three times the chance in the property.

(330 grams/110 grams) × – 45 kJ

3 × – 45 kJ = – 135 kJ

83. A is correct.

84. A is correct.

85. C is correct. $\Delta G = \Delta H - T\Delta S$. ΔG is most negative (most spontaneous) when ΔH is lowest and ΔS is greatest.

86. E is correct. Intensive properties do not depend on the amount of material.

87. D is correct.

88. C is correct.

89. B is correct. The mixture is 40% CO_2. The partial pressure of CO_2 = (0.4)(700 torr) = 280 torr.

90. E is correct. Relationship between enthalpy (ΔH) and internal energy (ΔE):

Enthalpy = Internal energy + work (for gases, work = PV)

$\Delta H = \Delta E + \Delta(PV)$

Solving for ΔE:

$\Delta E = \Delta H - \Delta(PV)$

According to ideal gas law:

PV = nRT

Substitute ideal gas law to the previous equation:

$\Delta E = \Delta H - \Delta nRT$

The reaction is NH_3 (g) + HCl (g) → NH_4Cl (s). There are two gas molecules on the left and none on the right, which means $\Delta n = 0 - 2 = -2$.

In this problem, the temperature is not provided. However, the presence of degree symbols (ΔG°, ΔH°, ΔS°) indicates that those are standard values, which are measured at 25°C or 298.15 K.

Always double check the units before performing calculations; ΔH is in kilojoules while the gas constant (R) is 8.314 J/mol K. Convert ΔH to joules before calculating.

Use the Δn and T values to calculate ΔE:

$$\Delta E = \Delta H - \Delta nRT$$

$$\Delta E = -175,900 \text{ J/mol} - (-2 \times 8.314 \text{ J/mol K} \times 298.15 \text{ K})$$

$$\Delta E = -170942 \text{ J} \approx -170.9 \text{ kJ}$$

91. B is correct. Bond energy is internal potential energy (PE) while thermal energy is internal kinetic energy (KE).

92. A is correct.

93. D is correct.

94. D is correct. The pressure due to N_2 and $CO_2 = 320 + 240 = 560$ torr. The total pressure is 740 torr, so the partial pressure of O_2 is: 740 – 560 = 180 torr. 180/740 = ~ 24%.

The % pressure of $O_2 = 24\%$.

95. B is correct. For an ideal gas, internal energy is a function of temperature only. Since there are no intermolecular forces in an ideal gas, changing the distance between the molecules of an ideal gas, while holding temperature constant, does not affect the internal energy. The kinetic energy of the molecules is a function of temperature: K.E. = 3/2 *RT*. Molecular rotational and vibration energies are also a function of temperature.

96. E is correct.

97. C is correct.

98. A is correct. In a chemical reaction, bonds within reactants are broken down and new bonds will be formed to create products. Therefore, in bond dissociation problems, $\Delta H_{reaction}$ = sum of bond energy in reactants – sum of bond energy in products. Remember that this is the opposite of ΔH_f problems, where $\Delta H_{reaction}$ = sum of ΔH_f product – sum of ΔH_f reactant.

For $N_2 + O_2$ → 2NO

$\Delta H_{reaction}$ = sum of bond energy in reactants – sum of bond energy in products

$\Delta H_{reaction}$ = [(N≡N) + (O=O)] – 2(N–O)

$\Delta H_{reaction}$ = (226 kcal + 199 kcal) – (2 × 145 kcal)

$\Delta H_{reaction}$ = 135 kcal

99. C is correct. Internal energy can changes forms from potential (i.e. chemical) to kinetic (i.e. thermal) energy or some of the chemical energy is used to do work which decreases the internal energy of the system.

100. D is correct.

101. A is correct.

102. A is correct.

103. C is correct. In an exothermic reaction, the bonds formed are stronger than the bonds broken.

104. D is correct.

105. C is correct.

106. B is correct. The equation should show the reactant of methane and the products of diatomic gases:

$$CH_4 + 2O_2 \rightarrow CO_2 + 2H_2O \quad (-191.8)$$
$$CO_2 \rightarrow C + O_2 \quad\quad\quad (94.0)$$
$$\underline{2(H_2O) \rightarrow H_2 + \tfrac{1}{2}O_2 \quad\quad 2(57.8)}$$
$$CH_4 \rightarrow C + 2H_2 \quad\quad \Delta H = +17.8 \text{ kJ}$$

107. C is correct.

Any formula with ΔT can be expressed in either Celsius or Kelvin temperature.

108. E is correct.

$$\Delta H_{fusion} = mass \times heat\ of\ fusion$$

$$\Delta H_{fusion} = 12.9 \text{ g} \times 205 \text{ J/g}$$

$$\Delta H_{fusion} = 2644.5 \text{ J} \approx 2640 \text{ J}$$

109. B is correct.

110. C is correct. P, n, and R are constants. The ideal gas law, $PV = nRT$ means V is proportional to T. Since the absolute temperature decreased by a factor of 3 (from 300 K to 100 K), the volume decreases by a factor of 3. The new volume: $(300 \text{ cm}^3)/3 = 100 \text{ cm}^3$.

111. B is correct. Change in temperature is equivalent when measured in either Celsius or Kelvin.

112. D is correct.

113. E is correct.

114. D is correct.

115. C is correct. Kinetic energy is proportional to temperature.

In most thermodynamic equations, temperatures are expressed in Kelvin, so convert the Celsius temperatures to Kelvin:

$$25 + 273.15 = 298.15 \text{ K}$$

$$50 + 273.15 = 323.15 \text{ K}$$

Now calculate the kinetic energy using simple proportions:

$(323.15 / 298.15) \times 500 \text{ J} = 541.9 \text{ J} \approx 540 \text{ J}$

116. D is correct.

$q = \text{mass} \times \text{heat of condensation}$

$q = 14 \text{ g} \times 1,380 \text{ J/g}$

$q = 19,320 \text{ J} \approx 19,000 \text{ J}$

117. D is correct.

118. E is correct. If V, R, and T are constants, then the ideal gas law, $PV = nRT$, implies that P is proportional to n. Therefore, increasing n causes an increase in P.

119. B is correct.

$\Delta L/L = \alpha \Delta T$

where α is the coefficient of linear expansion

$(1.00022 \text{ cm} - 1 \text{ cm})/(1 \text{ cm}) = \alpha [0 \text{ °C} - (-10 \text{ °C})]$

$0.00022 = \alpha(10 \text{ °C})$

$\alpha = (2.2 \times 10^{-4}) / 10 \text{ °C}$

It is not necessary to convert to meters because $\Delta L/L$ cancels units as any conversion factor applies to both the numerator and the denominator.

120. A is correct.

121. E is correct.

122. A is correct.

123. E is correct. Enthalpy: $U + PV$.

124. B is correct.

125. A is correct. There are two different methods available to solve this problem. Both methods are based on the definition of ΔH formation as energy required/released when one mole of molecule is produced from its elemental atoms.

Method 1: rearrange and add all the equations together to create the formation reaction of C_2H_5OH.

Information provided by the problem:

$C_2H_5OH + 3O_2 \rightarrow 2CO_2 + 3H_2O$ $\Delta H = 327 \text{ kcal}$

$H_2O \rightarrow H_2 + \frac{1}{2}O_2$ $\Delta H = 68.3 \text{ kcal}$

$C + O_2 \rightarrow CO_2$ $\Delta H = -94.1 \text{ kcal}$

Place C_2H_5OH on the product side. For the other two reactions, arrange them so the elements are on the left and the molecules are on the right (remember that the goal is to create a formation reaction: elements forming a molecule). When reversing the direction of a reaction, change the positive/negative sign of ΔH. Multiplying the whole reaction with a coefficient would also multiply ΔH by the same ratio.

$$2CO_2 + 3H_2O \rightarrow C_2H_5OH + 3O_2 \qquad \Delta H = -327 \text{ kcal}$$

$$3H_2 + 3/2 \; O_2 \rightarrow 3H_2O \qquad \Delta H = -204.9 \text{ kcal}$$

$$2C + 2O_2 \rightarrow 2CO_2 \qquad \Delta H = -188.2 \text{ kcal}$$

$$\overline{2C + 3H_2 + 1/2 \; O_2 \rightarrow C_2H_5OH \qquad \Delta H = -720.1 \text{ kcal}} \; +$$

ΔH formation of C_2H_5OH is −720.1 kcal.

Method 2: Heat of formation (ΔH$_f$) data can be used to calculate ΔH of a reaction:

ΔH$_{reaction}$ = sum of ΔH$_f$ product – sum of ΔH$_f$ reactant

Apply the formula on the first equation: $C_2H_5OH + 3O_2 \rightarrow 2CO_2 + 3H_2O$ ΔH = 327 kcal

ΔH$_{reaction}$ = sum of ΔH$_f$ product – sum of ΔH$_f$ reactant

327 kcal = (ΔH$_f$ CO_2 + 3 × ΔH$_f$ H_2O) – (ΔH$_f$ C_2H_5OH + 3 × ΔH$_f$ O_2)

Oxygen (O_2) is an element, which means its ΔH$_f$ is zero. As for CO_2 and H_2O, ΔH$_f$ information can be obtained from the other 2 reactions:

$$H_2O \rightarrow H_2 + 1/2 \; O_2 \qquad \Delta H = 68.3 \text{ kcal}$$

$$C + O_2 \rightarrow CO_2 \qquad \Delta H = -94.1 \text{ kcal}$$

The CO_2 reaction is already a formation reaction – creation of one mole of a molecule from its elements. Therefore, ΔH$_f$ of CO_2 is −94.1 kcal.

If the H_2O reaction is reversed, it will also be a formation reaction.

$$H_2 + 1/2 \; O_2 \rightarrow H_2O \qquad \Delta H = -68.3 \text{ kcal}$$

Using those values, calculate ΔH$_f$ of C_2H_5OH:

327 kcal = (2 × ΔH$_f$ CO_2 + 3 × ΔH$_f$ H_2O) – (ΔH$_f$ C_2H_5OH + 3 × ΔH$_f$ O_2)

327 kcal = (2 × –94.1 kcal + 3 × – 68.3 kcal) – (ΔH$_f$ C_2H_5OH + 3 × 0 kcal)

ΔH$_f$ C_2H_5OH = −720.1 kcal

126. B is correct. For an ideal gas, enthalpy (ΔH) depends only on temperature because internal energy (U) depends only upon temperature and $PV = nRT$. Thus enthalpy (U + PV) can be expressed as $U + nRT$ for an ideal gas which is a function that depends upon temperature only.

127. D is correct.

q = mass × heat of vaporization

Solving for heat of vaporization:

heat of vaporization = q/mass

heat of vaporization = 6,823 J / 58.0 g

heat of vaporization = 117.64 J/g ≈ 118 J/g

128. C is correct.

129. E is correct. Boiling occurs when the vapor pressure of a liquid equals atmospheric pressure. Vapor pressure always increases as the temperature increases, Liquid A boils at a lower temperature than B because the vapor pressure of Liquid A is closer to the atmospheric pressure.

130. C is correct. Enthalpy is different than work because it assumes no work was done by gases. The answer includes a change in the number of moles of gas.

131. D is correct.

132. A is correct.

133. B is correct. $S + O_2 \rightarrow SO_2 + 69.8$ kcal

The reaction indicates that 69.8 kcal of energy is released by the reaction (because it's located on the product side).

All species in this reaction have the coefficient of 1, which means that the ΔH value is calculated by reacting 1 mole of each reagent to create 1 mole of product. The atomic mass of sulfur is 32.1 g, which means that this reaction uses 32.1 g of sulfur.

Conclusion: 69.8 kcal are produced when 32.1 of sulfur reacts.

134. C is correct. Negative enthalpy indicates an exothermic reaction. Since the entropy change is negative, it cannot be determined from the information given if the reaction is spontaneous under standard conditions.

135. D is correct.

$q = \text{mass} \times \text{heat of vaporization}$

$q = 17.6 \text{ g} \times 1380 \text{ J/g}$

$q = 24{,}288 \text{ J} \approx 24{,}300 \text{ J}$

136. E is correct.

137. B is correct. Substitute the given K_c value into the ΔG equation:

$\Delta G = -RT \ln K_c$

$\Delta G = -8.314 \text{ J/mol K} \times (427 + 273.15)\text{K} \times \ln (9.4 \times 10^{-5})$

$\Delta G = -53974 \text{ J/mol} \approx -56 \text{ kJ}$

138. E is correct. Enthalpy is an extensive property: it varies with quantity of the matter.

Reaction 1 : $P_4 + 6Cl_2 \rightarrow 4PCl_3$ $\qquad \Delta H = -1289$ kJ/mol

Reaction 2 : $3P_4 + 18Cl_2 \rightarrow 12PCl_3$ $\qquad \Delta H = ??$

The only difference between reactions 1 & 2 are the coefficients; in reaction 2, all coefficients are three times bigger than reaction 1. It means that reaction 2 consumes three times as much reactant as reaction 1 and in turn reaction 2 will also release three times as much energy as reaction 1.

$\Delta H = 3 \times -1289 \text{ kJ/mol} = -3837 \text{ kJ/mol}$

139. A is correct.

140. C is correct.

141. A is correct. A gas can be liquefied by bringing the molecules closer together by 1) increasing the external pressure on the gas or 2) by decreasing its temperature. Neither occurs here so a gas remains.

142. D is correct. In this problem, both reactions presented in the problem are identical, except for the direction of reaction. Therefore, the enthalpy of both reactions would have equal values with opposing signs. Because the reaction with given enthalpy value has a negative sign (–1274 kJ/mol), the opposite reaction's enthalpy is +1274 kJ/mol.

143. B is correct. Because the sample in this problem absorbs heat and undergoes a phase change, calculation of the heat has to be done in steps:

a) Ice temperature increases from –10 °C to 0 °C

$$q = m \times c \times \Delta t$$

$$q = 10.0 \text{ g} \times 2.09 \text{ J/g°C} \times 10°C$$

$$q = 209 \text{ J}$$

b) Ice reaches melting point and starts melting to form water at 0 °C

$$q = m \times \text{heat of fusion}$$

$$q = 10.0 \text{ g} \times 334 \text{ J/g}$$

$$q = 3340 \text{ J}$$

c) Water temperature increases from 0°C to 10 °C

$$q = m \times c \times \Delta t$$

$$q = 10.0 \text{ g} \times 4.18 \text{ J/g°C} \times 10 °C$$

$$q = 418 \text{ J}$$

Add all the results to obtain total required heat = 209 J + 3340 J + 418 J = 3967 J ≈ 3970 J

144. C is correct.

145. B is correct.

146. E is correct. Heat of formation is defined as the heat required or released upon creation of one mole of the substance from its elements. If the given reaction is reversed and divided by two, it would be the formation reaction of NH_3:

$$\frac{1}{2} N_2 + \frac{3}{2} H_2 \rightarrow NH_3$$

ΔH of this reaction would also be reversed (plus to minus sign) and divided by two:

$$-(92.4 \text{ kJ/mol}) / 2 = -46.2 \text{ kJ/mol}$$

147. D is correct.

148. E is correct.

149. B is correct. The reaction is spontaneous if ΔG is negative; reaction is exothermic if ΔH is negative.

150. C is correct. The heat of formation of water vapor is essentially the same as the very exothermic process for the heat of combustion of hydrogen. Heat is required to convert H_2O (l) into vapor, therefore the heat of formation of water vapor must be less exothermic than of H_2O (l).

151. B is correct.

152. E is correct.

153. C is correct.

154. A is correct. Gases have much higher entropy than the other phases.

155. C is correct.

156. E is correct.

157. D is correct. The heat of reaction (ΔH) is not a function of temperature. Since the reaction is exothermic, Le Châtelier's Principle states that increasing the temperature decreases the forward reaction.

158. E is correct.

159. A is correct. Gases have the highest entropy. Solutions have higher entropy than pure phases since the species are more scattered. The liquid phase has less entropy than the aqueous phase.

160. D is correct.

161. E is correct.

162. D is correct. Decreasing external pressure increases the distance between gas molecules. Therefore, the phase change is likely from liquid $\rightarrow$ gas.

163. C is correct.

164. E is correct. Entropy has no absolute zero value and a substance at zero Kelvin has zero entropy. This value of zero is arbitrary, not absolute.

165. C is correct.

166. D is correct.

167. B is correct.

168. A is correct. The compound exists as a liquid if the external pressure > compound's vapor pressure. A substance boils when vapor pressure = external pressure.

169. A is correct. Find the heat of combustion of 60 g (2 moles) of ethane.

$\Delta H = \Delta H_f$ products $- \Delta H_f$

$\Delta H = [4(-94.1) + 6(-57.8)] - [2(-20.2) + 0]$

$\Delta H = -682.8$ kcal

Heat for 2 moles $C_2H_6 = -682.9$ kcal; do *not* multiply by 2.

170. D is correct. The Second Law implies but irreversible reactions. If a statement describes a process as in only one direction, it could be a consequence of the Second Law.

171. C is correct.

172. B is correct.

173. B is correct. Two gases having the same temperature have the same average molecular kinetic energy. Therefore, $(1/2)m_I v_I^2 = (1/2)m_{II} v_{II}^2$; yields $m_{II}/m_I = (v_I/v_{II})^2$. Since $v_I/v_{II} = 2$, $m_{II}/m_I = 2^2 = 4$. The only gases listed with a mass ratio of about 4 to 1 are titanium (47.8 g/mol) and carbon (12 g/mol).

174. E is correct. The disorder of the system appears to be decreasing, as more complex and ordered molecules are forming from the reaction of H_2 and O_2 gases. 3 mole of gas are combining to form 2 mole of gas.

175. C is correct.

176. D is correct. According to the second law of thermodynamics, the entropy gain of the universe must always be positive. The entropy of a system, however, can be negative if the surroundings experience an increase in entropy greater than the negative entropy change experienced by the system.

177. A is correct. In a chemical reaction, bonds within reactants are broken down and new bonds will be formed to create products. Therefore, in bond dissociation problems, $\Delta H_{reaction}$ = sum of bond energy in reactants – sum of bond energy in products.

Remember that this is the opposite of ΔH_f problems, where $\Delta H_{reaction}$ = sum of ΔH_f product – sum of ΔH_f reactant.

For $N_2 + 3H_2 \rightarrow 2NH_3$

$\Delta H_{reaction}$ = sum of bond energy in reactants – sum of bond energy in products

$\Delta H_{reaction} = [(N\equiv N) + 3(H–H)] – [2 \times 3(N–H)]$

$\Delta H_{reaction} = (946\ kJ + 3 \times 436\ kJ) – (2 \times 3 \times 389\ kJ)$

$\Delta H_{reaction} = –80\ kJ$

178. C is correct. The problem provides temperature required by each substance to reach the same vapor pressure (400 mmHg). The substance that needs the highest temperature to reach 400 mmHg has the slowest rate of change in vapor pressure. If all of those substances are heated to the same temperature, the substance with lowest rate of change will have the lowest vapor pressure. Answer: SnI_4.

179. C is correct. ΔG is always negative for spontaneous reactions.

180. B is correct.

181. D is correct. Entropy is based on probability. The greater the sample space, the greater the entropy. Increased volume provides more possible positions for molecules. Greater moles offer more objects to fill the positions. Greater temperature means greater movement, so more possible combinations.

182. E is correct.

183. A is correct. Since both sides of the reaction have 2 gas molecules, a change in pressure has no effect on equilibrium. According Le Châtelier's principle, endothermic reactions shift to the right at higher temperatures.

184. D is correct. Entropy is the unavailable energy which cannot be converted into mechanical work. Gases contain more energy than liquids of the same element and they have a higher degree of randomness.

185. A is correct.

$$\Delta G = -\,RT \ln K_c$$

$$-69.7 \text{ kJ} = -8.314 \text{ J/mol K} \times 298.15 \text{ K} \times \ln K_c$$

$$28.12 = \ln K_c$$

$$K_c = e^{28.12}$$

$$K_c = 1.63 \times 10^{12}$$

186. E is correct. The equation relates the change in entropy (ΔS) at different temperatures. Entropy increases with increasing temperature.

187. B is correct.

188. E is correct.

189. B is correct.

190. A is correct. According to Le Châtelier's principle, increasing the pressure shifts the reaction to the side with the fewer gas molecules. Reactants: $1 + 3 = 4$ gas molecules while the product side has just 2. The forward reaction is favored and fewer gas molecules mean a smaller volume.

191. E is correct. Spontaneity of a reaction is determined by evaluating the Gibbs free energy, or ΔG.

The formula is $\Delta G = \Delta H - T\Delta S$

A reaction is spontaneous if $\Delta G < 0$ (or ΔG is negative). For ΔG to be negative, ΔH has to be less than $T\Delta S$. A reaction is nonspontaneous if $\Delta G > 0$ (or ΔG is positive). Therefore, the answer is $\Delta H > T\Delta S$.

192. C is correct. In a chemical reaction, bonds within reactants are broken down and new bonds will be formed to create products. Therefore, in bond dissociation problems, $\Delta H_{reaction} =$ sum of bond energy in reactants – sum of bond energy in products.

Remember that this is the opposite of ΔH_f problems, where $\Delta H_{reaction} =$ sum of ΔH_f product – sum of ΔH_f reactant.

$$O=C=O + 3H_2 \rightarrow CH3-O-H + H-O-H$$

$\Delta H_{reaction}$ = sum of bond energy in reactants − sum of bond energy in products

$\Delta H_{reaction}$ = [2(C=O) + 3(H–H)] − [3(C–H) + (C–O) + (O–H) + 2(O–H)]

$\Delta H_{reaction}$ = [2 × 743 kJ + 3 × 436 kJ] − [3 × 412 kJ + 360 kJ + 463 kJ + 2 × 463 kJ]

$\Delta H_{reaction}$ = −191 kJ

193. B is correct.

194. C is correct. ΔG is only spontaneous if pressure and temperature remain constant.

195. C is correct.

196. D is correct.

197. B is correct. ΔG tends to be positive, so the reaction is nonspontaneous.

198. D is correct.

199. A is correct.

200. B is correct. $\Delta G = \Delta H - T\Delta S$ requires that only temperature remain constant. If pressure changes, a negative ΔG does not necessarily indicate a spontaneous reaction.

201. C is correct.

202. C is correct.

203. E is correct.

204. D is correct. ΔG indicates the energy made available to do non P–V work. This is a useful quantity for processes like batteries and living cells which lack expanding gases.

205. E is correct. This answer cannot be determined because when the given $\Delta G = \Delta H - T\Delta S$ both terms cancel. The system is at equilibrium when $\Delta G = 0$, but in this question both sides of the equation cancel:

$$\underbrace{X - RY}_{\Delta G \text{ term}} = \underbrace{X - RY}_{\substack{\Delta H - T\Delta S \\ \text{terms}}}, \quad \text{so} \quad 0 = 0$$

206. A is correct. Calculation of standard free-energy (ΔG) uses the same method with heat of formation (ΔH_f) problems: sum of ΔG products − sum of ΔG reactants.

For $NO_2 + SO_2 \rightarrow NO + SO_3$

$\Delta G_{reaction}$ = sum of ΔG products − sum of ΔG reactants

$\Delta G_{reaction}$ = (86.69 kJ − 370.0 kJ) − (51.84 kJ − 300.0 kJ)

$\Delta G_{reaction}$ = −35.15 kJ

207. B is correct.

208. C is correct. ΔG of the universe decreases with each reaction so it does not follow the conservation of energy law.

209. A is correct.

210. D is correct. In a chemical reaction, bonds within reactants are broken down and new bonds will be formed to create products. Therefore, in bond dissociation problems, ΔH reaction = sum of bond energy in reactants – sum of bond energy in products.

Remember that this is the opposite of ΔH_f problems, where $\Delta H_{reaction}$ = sum of ΔH_f products – sum of ΔH_f reactants.

For $H_2C=CH_2 + H_2 \rightarrow CH_3–CH_3$

$\Delta H_{reaction}$ = sum of bond energy in reactants – sum of bond energy in products

$\Delta H_{reaction}$ = [(C=C) + 4(C–H) + (H–H)] – [(C–C) + 6(C–H)

$\Delta H_{reaction}$ = [612 kJ + 4 × 412 kJ + 436 kJ] – [348 kJ + 6 × 412 kJ]

$\Delta H_{reaction}$ = –124 kJ

211. B is correct.

212. D is correct. Bond dissociation energy is the energy required to break a bond between two gaseous items and is useful in estimating the enthalpy change in a reaction.

213. E is correct. The magnitude of a negative Gibbs energy (ΔG) is the amount of work that can be done on the surroundings by the reaction. The spontaneity of a reaction is independent of its rate.

214. D is correct. A catalyst lowers the activation energy (E_a) of a reaction.

215. A is correct.

216. C is correct.

217. B is correct. All thermodynamic functions in $\Delta G = \Delta H - T\Delta S$ refer to the system.

218. E is correct.

219. D is correct.

220. B is correct. Nonspontaneous reactions can occur by coupling them to a more spontaneous reaction so that the total ΔG is negative.

221. A is correct.

222. C is correct. Bond dissociation energy:

ΔH_{rxn} = Σ bond energy broken – Σ bond energy formed bonds

ΔH_{rxn} = [2(495) + 4(410)] – [2(720) + 4(460)] = [990 + 1640] – [1440 + 1840]

ΔH_{rxn} = –650 kJ/mole.

The reaction is exothermic.

223. B is correct. Calculation of standard free-energy (ΔG) uses the same method with heat of formation (ΔH_f) problems: sum of ΔG products – sum of ΔG reactants.

Start by calculating ΔG using this formula: $\Delta G° = \Delta H° - T\Delta S°$. In this problem, the temperature is not provided. However, the presence of degree symbols ($\Delta G°$, $\Delta H°$, $\Delta S°$) indicates that those are standard values, which are measured at 25°C or 298.15 K.

Always check the units of ΔH° and ΔS° before calculating; sometimes one of them will be in kilojoules and the other one will be in joules.

$H_2 + I_2 \rightarrow 2HI$

H_2: $\quad \Delta G^\circ = \Delta H^\circ - T\,\Delta S^\circ$

$\quad\quad \Delta G^\circ = 0 - 298.15\ K \times 130.6\ J/mol\ K$

$\quad\quad \Delta G^\circ = -38.9\ kJ/mol$

I_2: $\quad \Delta G^\circ = \Delta H^\circ - T\,\Delta S^\circ$

$\quad\quad \Delta G^\circ = 0 - 298.15\ K \times 116.12\ J/mol\ K$

$\quad\quad \Delta G^\circ = -34.6\ kJ/mol$

HI: $\quad \Delta G^\circ = \Delta H^\circ - T\,\Delta S^\circ$

$\quad\quad \Delta G^\circ = 26{,}000\ J/mol - 298.15\ K \times 206\ J/mol\ K$

$\quad\quad \Delta G^\circ = -35.4\ kJ$

ΔG° for total reaction:

$\quad\quad \Delta G^\circ_{reaction} = \Delta G^\circ\ products - \Delta G^\circ\ reactants$

$\quad\quad \Delta G^\circ_{reaction} = (2 \times \Delta G^\circ\ HI) - (\Delta G^\circ\ H_2 + \Delta G^\circ\ I_2)$

$\quad\quad \Delta G^\circ_{reaction} = (2 \times -35.4\ kJ) - (-34.6\ kJ - 38.9\ kJ)$

$\quad\quad \Delta G^\circ_{reaction} = 2.7\ kJ$

224. A is correct. Calculation of standard free-energy (ΔG) uses the same method with heat of formation (ΔH_f) problems: sum of ΔG products – sum of ΔG reactants.

Start by calculating ΔG using this formula: $\Delta G^\circ = \Delta H^\circ - T\,\Delta S^\circ$. In this problem, the temperature is not provided.

Convert the temperature to Kelvin: $815 + 273.15 = 1088.15\ K$

Always check the units of ΔH° and ΔS° before calculating; sometimes one of them will be in kilojoules and the other one will be in joules.

$CaCO_3 \rightarrow CaO + CO_2$

$CaCO_3$: $\Delta G^\circ = \Delta H^\circ - T\,\Delta S^\circ$

$\quad\quad \Delta G^\circ = -1{,}207{,}000\ J/mol - 1088.15\ K \times 92.9\ J/mol\ K$

$\quad\quad \Delta G^\circ = -1308\ kJ/mol$

CaO: $\quad \Delta G^\circ = \Delta H^\circ - T\,\Delta S^\circ$

$\quad\quad \Delta G^\circ = -635{,}500\ J/mol - 1088.15\ K \times 40\ J/mol\ K$

$\quad\quad \Delta G^\circ = -679\ kJ/mol$

CO$_2$: $\Delta G° = \Delta H° - T\,\Delta S°$

$\Delta G° = -394{,}000$ J/mol $- 1088.15$ K $\times 213.6$ J/mol K

$\Delta G° = -626.4$ kJ/mol

$\Delta G°$ for total reaction:

$\Delta G°_{\text{reaction}} = \Delta G°$ products $- \Delta G°$ reactants

$\Delta G°_{\text{reaction}} = (\Delta G°\,CaO + \Delta G°\,CO_2) - (\Delta G°\,CaCO_3)$

$\Delta G°_{\text{reaction}} = (-679$ kJ/mol $- 626.4$ kJ/mol$) - (-1308$ kJ/mol$)$

$\Delta G°_{\text{reaction}} = 2.6$ kJ/mol

Chapter 9.   ELECTROCHEMISTRY

1. C is correct.

2. A is correct. Since the reduction potentials for Li^+ (*aq*) and Na^+ (*aq*) are both negative, neither process is spontaneous. Reversing each of the reactions listed in the table supports that Li (*s*) is more easily oxidized than Na (*s*), because 3.05 V > 2.71 V.

3. B is correct.

4. E is correct.

5. E is correct. One faraday is equivalent to 1 mole of electrons. To electrolyze 5 moles of H_2O_2, 10 moles of electrons are required. 10 moles of electrons = 10 faradays.

6. D is correct. One mole of e^- has a charge of 96,500 coulombs.

Conversion factor: 1 mole e^- / 96,500 coulombs

10 moles of H_2O need 10 moles of e^-.

To calculate charge:

10 moles of e^- × 96,500 coulombs / 1 mole e^- = 965,000 coulombs

7. C is correct. 1 amp = 1 coulomb/sec.

2 moles of H_2O need 2 moles of e^-.

To calculate moles of H_2O:

$$2 \text{ moles } e^- \times \frac{96,500 \text{ coul}}{1 \text{ mole } e^-} \times \frac{1 \text{ sec}}{2 \text{ coul}} = 9.65 \times 10^4 \text{ sec}$$

8. A is correct. Half reaction:

$NO_3^- \rightarrow NH_4^+$

Balancing half-reaction in acidic conditions:

Step 1: Balance all atoms except for H and O

$NO_3^- \rightarrow NH_4^+$ (N is already balanced)

Step 2: To balance oxygen, add H_2O to the side with less oxygen atoms

$NO_3^- \rightarrow NH_4^+ + 3H_2O$

Step 3: To balance hydrogen, add H^+ to the opposing side of H_2O added in the previous step

$NO_3^- + 10 H^+ \rightarrow NH_4^+ + 3H_2O$

Step 4: Balance charges by adding electrons to the side with higher/more positive total charge

Total charge on left side: $10(+1) - 1 = +9$

Total charge on right side: +1

Add 8 electrons to left side:

$$NO_3^- + 10\,H^+ + 8e^- \rightarrow NH_4^+ + 3H_2O$$

Total electrons required: $8e^-$ on the left side

9. D is correct.

10. B is correct.

11. A is correct. The oxidizing and reducing agents are always reactants, not products, in a redox reaction. The oxidizing agent is the species that gets reduced that is, the one that gains electrons; this is Cu^{2+}.

12. E is correct.

13. B is correct.

14. B is correct. In all cells, reduction occurs at the cathode while oxidation occurs at the anode (The following mnemonic can be used: RED CAT / AN OX).

15. E is correct. Calculating mass of metal deposited in cathode.

Step 1: Calculate total charge using current and time

Q = current × time

Q = 5.2 A × (45.0 minutes × 60 s/minute)

Q = 14040 A·s = 14040 C

Step 2: Calculate moles of electron which has that same amount of charge

moles e^- = Q / 96500 C/mol

moles e^- = 14040 C / 96500 C/mol

moles e^- = 0.146 mol

Step 3: Calculate moles of metal deposit

The solution contains chromium (III) sulfate. Half-reaction of chromium (III) ion reduction:

$$Cr^{3+}\,(aq) + 3e^- \rightarrow Cr\,(s)$$

Use the moles of electron from the previous calculation to calculate moles of Cr:

moles Cr = (coefficient Cr / coefficient electron) × moles electron

moles Cr = (1/3) × 0.146 mol

moles Cr = 0.0487 mol

Step 4: Calculate mass of metal deposit

mass Cr = moles Cr × molecular mass of Cr

mass Cr = 0.0487 mol × 52.00 g/mol

mass Cr = 2.5 g

16. C is correct.

---

17. A is correct.

18. D is correct. Oxidation always occurs at the anode while reduction always occurs at the cathode. Mg^{2+} does not lose any more electrons and Cl^- does not gain any more electrons.

19. C is correct.

20. A is correct.

21. E is correct. E° tends to be negative and G positive because electrolytic cells are nonspontaneous. Electrons must be forced into the system for the reaction to proceed.

22. D is correct. Balancing half-reaction in basic conditions:

The first few steps are identical to balancing reactions in acidic conditions.

Step 1: Balance all atoms except for H and O

$C_8H_{10} \rightarrow C_8H_4O_4^{2-}$ C is already balanced

Step 2: To balance oxygen, add H₂O to the side with less oxygen atoms

$C_8H_{10} + 4H_2O \rightarrow C_8H_4O_4^{2-}$

Step 3: To balance hydrogen, add H⁺ to the opposing side of H₂O added in the previous step

$C_8H_{10} + 4H_2O \rightarrow C_8H_4O_4^{2-} + 14H^+$

This next step is the unique additional step for basic conditions.

Step 4: Add equal amounts of OH⁻ on both sides. The number of OH⁻ should match the number of H⁺ ions. Combine H⁺ and OH⁻ on the same side to form H₂O. If there are H₂O molecules on both sides, subtract accordingly to end up with H₂O on one side only.

There are 14 H^+ ions on the right, so add $14OH^-$ ions on both sides:

$C_8H_{10} + 4H_2O + 14OH^- \rightarrow C_8H_4O_4^{2-} + 14H^+ + 14OH^-$

Combine H^+ and OH^- ions to form H_2O:

$C_8H_{10} + 4H_2O + 10OH^- \rightarrow C_8H_4O_4^{2-} + 14H_2O$

There are H₂O molecules on both sides. Those will cancel out and some H₂O will remain on one side:

$C_8H_{10} + 14OH^- \rightarrow C_8H_4O_4^{2-} + 10H_2O$

Step 5: Balance charges by adding electrons to the side with higher/more positive total charge

Total charge on left side: $14(-1) = -14$

Total charge on right side: -2

Add 12 electrons to right side:

$C_8H_{10} + 14OH^- \rightarrow C_8H_4O_4^{2-} + 10H_2O + 12e^-$

Total electrons required: $12e^-$ on the right side

23. E is correct.

24. C is correct.

25. B is correct. Oxidation always occurs at the anode while reduction always occurs at the cathode. In reaction 2, each I⁻ anion must lose one electron to produce neutral I_2 in the process of oxidation.

26. A is correct.

27. D is correct.

28. E is correct.

Oxidation of Mg (s): $Mg\ (s) \rightleftarrows Mg^{2+} + 2e^-$ E° = 2.37 V

       Reduction of Pb (s): $Pb^{2+} + 2e^- \rightleftarrows Pb\ (s)$ E° = –1.26 V

       Net Reaction: $Mg\ (s) + Pb^{2+} \rightleftarrows Pb\ (s) + Mg^{2+}$ E° = 2.244 V

       Note: when a reaction reverses, the sign of E° changes.

29. B is correct.

30. D is correct.

31. B is correct.

32. E is correct. Oxidation is defined as an increase in oxidation number and is the loss of electrons.

33. C is correct.

34. D is correct.

35. C is correct. The anode in galvanic cells attracts anions. Anions in solution flow toward the anode while cations flow toward the cathode. Oxidation (i.e. loss of electrons) occurs at the anode. Positive ions are formed while negative ions are consumed at the anode. Therefore, negative ions flow toward the anode to equalize the charge.

36. A is correct. Half reaction:

    $Cl_2O_7 \rightarrow HClO$

Balancing half-reaction in acidic conditions:

Step 1: Balance all atoms except for H and O

    $Cl_2O_7 \rightarrow 2HClO$

Step 2: To balance oxygen, add H_2O to the side with less oxygen atoms

    $Cl_2O_7 \rightarrow 2HClO + 5H_2O$

Step 3: To balance hydrogen, add H^+ to the opposing side of H_2O added in the previous step

    $Cl_2O_7 + 12\ H \rightarrow 2HClO + 5H_2O$

Step 4: Balance charges by adding electrons to the side with higher/more positive total charge

    Total charge on left side: $12(+1) = +12$

Total charge on right side: 0

Add 12 electrons to left side:

$Cl_2O_7 + 12 H^+ + 12e^- \rightarrow 2HClO + 5H_2O$

Total electrons required: $12e^-$ on the left side

37. C is correct. $2Na \rightarrow 2Na^+$

Balance the charges by adding electrons:

$2Na \rightarrow 2Na^+ + 2e^-$

According to the balanced reaction, Na lost electrons to form Na^+ ions.

Answer: $2e^-$ are lost.

38. E is correct.

39. B is correct. Electrolytic cells are nonspontaneous chemical reactions. The oxidation occurs at the anode while reduction occurs at the cathode in all electrochemical cells.

40. A is correct.

41. C is correct.

42. B is correct.

The problem has already specified the net reaction:

$Cu + Li^+ \rightarrow Cu^{2+} + Li$

Rearrange the provided equations to end up with the net reaction upon addition:

$Cu \rightarrow Cu^{2+} + 2e^-$ $E^o = -0.337$ V

$Li^+ + e^- \rightarrow Li$ $E^o = -3.03$ V

Multiply the second equation by 2 to match the number of electrons from 1st reaction:

$2Li^+ + 2e^- \rightarrow 2Li$ $E^o = -3.03$ V

(E^o values are constant and not affected by change in coefficients)

Now add those equations together to obtain the net reaction:

$Cu \rightarrow Cu^{2+} + 2e^-$ $E^o = -0.337$ V

$\underline{2Li^+ + 2e^- \rightarrow 2Li}$ $\underline{E^o = -3.03 \text{ V}}$

$Cu + 2Li^+ \rightarrow Cu^{2+} + 2Li$ $E^o = -3.367$ V

Answer: -3.367 V

43. C is correct. Since $E^°$ is negative and G is positive, the reaction is not spontaneous as written and proceeds in the opposite direction.

44. E is correct.

45. D is correct. $Na \rightarrow Na^+$

Balance the charges by adding an electron:

$$Na \rightarrow Na^+ + e^-$$

According to the balanced reaction, Na lost an electron to form Na^+ ion.

Answer: 1 e^- is lost.

46. A is correct.

47. E is correct.

48. B is correct.

49. D is correct.

50. A is correct. Oxidation occurs at the anode in all types of electrochemical cells.

51. E is correct.

52. A is correct. $Cl_2 \rightarrow 2Cl^-$

Balance the charges by adding electrons:

$$Cl_2 + 2e^- \rightarrow 2Cl^-$$

According to the balanced reaction, Cl_2 gained 2 electrons to form Cl^- ions.

Answer: 2 e^- are gained.

53. B is correct.

54. A is correct. A reducing agent is the reactant that is oxidized. Therefore, the best reducing agent is most easily oxidized. Reversing each of the half-reactions shows that the oxidation of Cr (*s*) has a potential of +0.74 V, which is greater than the potential (+0.14 V) for the oxidation of Sn^{2+} (*aq*). Thus, Cr (*s*) is stronger reducing agent.

55. B is correct.

56. E is correct.

57. B is correct. Since $G° = -nFE$, when E° is positive, G is negative.

58. D is correct.

59. E is correct.

60. A is correct.

61. B is correct. Calculate its E°:

$$2Br^- (aq) \rightarrow Br_2 (l) + 2e^- \qquad E° = -1.07 \text{ V}$$

$$F_2 (g) + 2e^- \rightarrow 2F^- (aq) \qquad E° = +2.87 \text{ V}$$

$$\overline{F_2 (g) + 2Br^- (aq) \rightarrow Br_2 (l) + 2F^- (aq)} \; E° = +1.80 \text{ V}$$

Answer: E° = +1.80 V and spontaneous

62. A is correct. Ionization energy (IE) is the energy required to release one electron from an element. Higher IE means the element is more stable.

Elements with high IE are usually elements that only need one or two more electrons to achieve stable configuration. It's more likely for those elements to gain electron and reach stability than lose electron. When an atom gains electron(s), its oxidation number goes down and it is reduced. Therefore, elements with high IE are easily reduced.

In reduction-oxidation reactions, species that undergo reduction are called oxidator/oxidizing agent, because their presence allows the other reactant to be oxidized. Because elements with high IE are easily reduced, they are strong oxidizing agents.

On the other hand, reducing agents are species that undergo oxidation. Elements with high IE do not undergo oxidation readily, which means that they are weak reducing agents.

63. D is correct.

64. E is correct. Electrochemical and galvanic cells are identical. Concentration cells have no chemical reactions occurring.

65. C is correct.

66. A is correct.

67. D is correct.

68. C is correct.

69. D is correct.

70. E is correct. A redox reaction, or oxidation-reduction reaction, involves the transfer of electrons between two reacting substances. An oxidation reaction specifically refers to the substance that is losing electrons and a reduction reaction specifically refers to the substance that is gaining reactions. The oxidation and reduction reactions alone are called half-reactions, because they always occur together to form a whole reaction.

The key to this question is that it is about the *transfer* of electrons between *two* species, so it is talking about the whole redox reaction in its entirety, not just one half reaction.

An electrochemical reaction takes place during the passage of electric current, and does involve redox reactions. However, it is not the correct answer to the question posed.

71. C is correct. Calculating mass of metal deposited in cathode:

Step 1: Calculate total charge using current and time

Q = current × time

Q = 8 A × (2 minutes × 60 s/minute)

Q = 960 A·s = 960 C

Step 2: Calculate moles of electron which has that same amount of charge

moles e^- = Q / 96500 C/mol

moles e⁻ = 960 C / 96500 C/mol

moles e⁻ = 0.01 mol

Step 3: Calculate moles of metal deposit

Half-reaction of silver ion reduction:

$Ag^+ (aq) + e^- \rightarrow Ag (s)$

Because all coefficients in that reaction are 1, moles e⁻ = moles Ag = 0.00995 mol

Step 4: Calculate mass of metal deposit

mass Ag = moles Ag × molecular mass of Ag

mass Ag = 0.00995 mol × 108 g/mol

mass Ag = 1.07 g

72. D is correct. Start by calculating moles of chromium:

moles Cr = mass Cr / molecular mass of Cr

moles Cr = 35.0 g / 52.0 g/mol

moles Cr = 0.673 mol

The solution is aqueous $CrCl_3$, which dissociates into the following ions:

$CrCl_3 \rightarrow Cr^{3+} + 3Cl^-$

Half reaction of chromium reduction:

$Cr^{3+}(aq) + 3e^- \rightarrow Cr (s)$

In order to calculate charge required to deposit metal, calculate the moles of electron:

moles of electron = (coefficient e⁻ / coefficient Cr) × moles Cr

moles of electron = (3/1) × 0.673 mol

moles of electron = 2.02 mol

Calculate total charge:

charge = moles of electron × Coulomb's constant

charge = 2.02 mol × 96500 C/mol

charge = 194930 C ≈ 1.95×10^5 C

73. B is correct.

74. A is correct.

75. C is correct.

76. C is correct. It is true that more than one electron can be transferred in an oxidation and reduction reaction.

A: either neutral or charged atoms can be formed in oxidation and reduction reactions.

B: a half-reaction is a term used for either oxidation reactions or reduction reactions.

D: it is impossible for half an electron to be transferred because electrons cannot be broken into parts in chemical reactions.

77. D is correct. Electrolysis is a method of using a direct electric current to provide electricity to a nonspontaneous redox process to drive the reaction. The direct electric current must be passed through an ionic substance or solution that contains electrolytes. Electrolysis is often used to separate elements.

78. E is correct. Calculating mass of metal deposited in cathode:

Step 1: Calculate total charge using current and time

Q = current × time

Q = 1 A × (10 minutes × 60 s/minute)

Q = 600 A·s = 600 C

Step 2: Calculate moles of electron which has that same amount of charge

moles e^- = Q / 96500 C/mol

moles e^- = 600 C / 96500 C/mol

moles e^- = 6.22×10^{-3} mol

Step 3: Calculate moles of metal deposit

Half-reaction of zinc ion reduction:

$Zn^{2+}(aq) + 2e^- \rightarrow Zn\ (s)$

moles of Zn = (coefficient Zn / coefficient e^-) × moles e^-

moles of Zn = (1 /2) × 6.22×10^{-3} mol

moles of Zn = 3.11×10^{-3} mol

Step 4: Calculate mass of metal deposit

mass Zn = moles Zn × molecular mass of Zn

mass Zn = 3.11×10^{-3} mol × 65 g/mol

mass Zn = 0.20 g

79. B is correct.

80. B is correct. Half reaction: $C_2H_6O \rightarrow HC_2H_3O_2$

Balancing half-reaction in acidic conditions:

Step 1: Balance all atoms except for H and O

$C_2H_6O \rightarrow HC_2H_3O_2$ (C is already balanced)

Step 2: To balance oxygen, add H_2O to the side with less oxygen atoms

$C_2H_6O + H_2O \rightarrow HC_2H_3O_2$

Step 3: To balance hydrogen, add H⁺ to the opposing side of H₂O added in the previous step

$$C_2H_6O + H_2O \rightarrow HC_2H_3O_2 + 4\ H^+$$

Step 4: Balance charges by adding electrons to the side with higher/more positive total charge

Total charge on left side: 0

Total charge on right side: $4(+1) = +4$

Add 4 electrons to right side:

$$C_2H_6O + H_2O \rightarrow HC_2H_3O_2 + 4\ H^+ + 4e^-$$

Total electrons required: 4 electrons on the right side.

81. D is correct.

82. A is correct.

83. E is correct.

84. A is correct.

85. B is correct. Electrochemistry is the branch of physical chemistry that studies chemical reactions that take place at the interface of an ionic conductor (i.e. the electrolyte) and an electrode. Electric charges move between the electrolyte and the electrode through a series of redox reactions, and chemical energy is converted to electrical energy.

86. A is correct. The cell reaction is:

$$Co\ (s) + Cu^{2+}\ (aq) \rightarrow Co^{2+}(aq) + Cu\ (s)$$

Separate it into half reactions:

$$Cu^{2+}(aq) \rightarrow Cu\ (s)$$
$$Co\ (s) \rightarrow Co^{2+}\ (aq)$$

The potentials provided by the problem are written in this format:

$$Cu^{2+}\ (aq)\ |\ Cu\ (s)$$

+0.34 V

It means that for the reduction reaction $Cu^{2+}\ (aq) \rightarrow Cu\ (s)$, the potential is +0.34 V.

The reverse reaction, or oxidation reaction $Cu\ (s) \rightarrow Cu^{2+}\ (aq)$ will have opposing potential value: –0.34 V.

Obtain the potential values for both half-reactions. Remember to reverse sign for potential values of oxidation reactions:

$$Cu^{2+}\ (aq) \rightarrow Cu\ (s) \quad = +0.34\ V \quad (reduction)$$
$$Co\ (s) \rightarrow Co^{2+}\ (aq) \quad = +0.28\ V \quad (oxidation)$$

Determine the standard cell potential:

Standard cell potential = sum of half-reaction potential

Standard cell potential = 0.34 V + 0.28 V

Standard cell potential = 0.62 V

87. E is correct.

88. D is correct.

89. C is correct.

90. C is correct.

91. B is correct.

92. E is correct. Half reaction:

$$H_2S \rightarrow S_8$$

Balancing half-reaction in acidic conditions:

Step 1: Balance all atoms except for H and O

$$8H_2S \rightarrow S_8$$

Step 2: To balance oxygen, add H_2O to the side with less oxygen atoms

There is no oxygen at all, so skip this step.

Step 3: To balance hydrogen, add H^+ to the opposing side of H_2O added in the previous step

$$8H_2S \rightarrow S_8 + 16H^+$$

Balance charges by adding electrons to the side with higher/more positive total charge

Total charge on left side: 0

Total charge on right side: $16(+1) = +16$

Add 16 electrons to right side:

$$8H_2S \rightarrow S_8 + 16H^+ + 16e^-$$

Total electrons required: 16 electrons on the right side.

93. A is correct.

94. B is correct.

95. D is correct.

96. C is correct.

97. D is correct. A redox reaction, or oxidation-reduction reaction, involves the transfer of electrons between two reacting substances. An oxidation reaction specifically refers to the substance that is losing electrons and a reduction reaction specifically refers to the substance that is gaining reactions. The oxidation and reduction reactions alone are called half-reactions, because they always occur together to form a whole reaction. Therefore, half-reaction is the answer because it can represent either a separate oxidation process or a separate reduction process.

98. A is correct.

99. E is correct.

100. C is correct.

101. D is correct.

102. B is correct.

103. A is correct.

104. C is correct.

105. A is correct.

106. D is correct.

107. B is correct. Oxidation number, also known as oxidation state, indicates the degree of oxidation (i.e. loss of electrons) in an atom. If an atom is electron-poor, that means that it has lost electrons, and would therefore have a positive oxidation number. If an atom is electron-rich, that means that it has gained electrons, and would therefore have a negative oxidation number.

108. C is correct.

109. E is correct.

110. D is correct.

111. B is correct. Reduction potential is the measure of a substance's ability to acquire electrons (i.e. undergo reduction). The more positive the reduction potential, the more likely it is that the substance will be reduced. Reduction potential is generally measured in volts.

112. D is correct.

113. C is correct.

114. E is correct.

115. A is correct.

116. B is correct.

117. E is correct.

118. C is correct.

119. B is correct.

120. A is correct.

121. E is correct.

122. D is correct.

123. C is correct.

124. C is correct.   *Balancing Redox Equations*

From the balanced equation, the coefficient for the proton can be determined. Balancing a redox equation not only requires balancing the atoms that are in the equation, but the charges must be balanced as well. To do this, the equations must be separated into two different half reactions. One of the half-reactions will address the oxidizing component and the other will address the reducing component.

In this reaction, the magnesium is being oxidized, therefore the unbalanced oxidation half-reaction will be:

$$Mg \ (s) \rightarrow Mg^{2+} \ (aq)$$

Furthermore, the nitrogen is being reduced, therefore the unbalanced reduction half-reaction will be:

$$NO_3^- \ (aq) \rightarrow NO_2 \ (aq)$$

At this stage, each half reaction needs to be balanced for each atom, and the net electric charge on each side of the equations must be balanced as well.

Order of operations for balancing half-reactions:

1) Balance atoms except for oxygen and hydrogen

2) Balance the oxygen atom count by adding water

3) Balance the hydrogen atom count by adding protons

   a. If in basic solution, add equal amounts of hydroxide to each side to cancel the protons

4) Balance the electric charge by adding electrons

5) If necessary, multiply the coefficients of one half reaction equation by a factor that will cancel the electron count when both equations are combined.

6) Cancel any ions or molecules that appear on both sides of the overall equation

After determining the balanced overall redox reaction, the stoichiometry will reveal the moles of the protons that are involved.

For magnesium:

$$Mg \ (s) \rightarrow Mg^{2+} \ (aq)$$

The magnesium is already balanced with a coefficient of 1. There are no hydrogen or oxygen atoms present in the equation. The magnesium cation has a +2 charge, so to balance the charge, 2 moles of electrons should be added to the right side. The balanced half reaction for oxidation will be:

$$Mg \ (s) \rightarrow Mg^{2+} \ (aq) + 2e^-$$

For nitrogen:

$$NO_3^- \ (aq) \rightarrow NO_2 \ (aq)$$

The equation is already balanced for nitrogen because one nitrogen atom appears on both sides of the reaction. The nitrate reactant has three oxygen atoms, while the nitrite product has two oxygen atoms. To balance the oxygen, one mole of water should be added to the right side to give:

$$NO_3^- \ (aq) \rightarrow NO_2 \ (aq) + H_2O$$

Adding water to the right side of the equation introduces hydrogen atoms to that side. Therefore, the hydrogen atom count needs to be balanced. Water possesses two hydrogen atoms, therefore, two protons need to be added to the left side of the reaction. This will give:

$$NO_3^- (aq) + 2H^+ \rightarrow NO_2 (aq) + H_2O$$

The reaction is occurring in acidic conditions. If the reaction was basic, then OH^- would need to be added to both sides to cancel the protons.

Next, the net charge will need to be balanced. The left side has a net charge of $+1$ ($+2$ from the protons and -1 from the electron), while the right side is neutral. Therefore, one electron should be added to the left side. This will give:

$$NO_3^- (aq) + 2H^+ + e^- \rightarrow NO_2(aq) + H_2O$$

When half reactions are recombined, the electrons in the overall reaction must cancel out. The reduction half reaction will contribute one electron to the left side of the overall equation, while the oxidation half reaction will contribute two electrons to the product side. Therefore, the coefficients of the reduction half reaction should be doubled. This will give:

$$2 \times [NO_3^- (aq) + 2H^+ + e^- \rightarrow NO_2 (aq) + H_2O] = 2NO_3^- (aq) + \mathbf{4H^+} + 2e^- \rightarrow 2NO_2 (aq) + 2H_2O$$

You can tell the answer will be 4 at this step.

Combining both half reactions will give:

$$Mg (s) + 2NO_3^- (aq) + \mathbf{4H^+} + 2e^- \rightarrow Mg^{2+} (aq) + 2e^- + 2NO_2 (aq) + 2H_2O$$

The electrons that appear on both sides of the reaction will cancel to give the following balanced net equation:

$$Mg (s) + 2NO_3^- (aq) + \mathbf{4H^+} \rightarrow Mg^{2+} (aq) + 2NO_2 (aq) + 2H_2O$$

This equation is now fully balanced for mass, oxygen, hydrogen, and electric charge.

The coefficient of the proton is 4.

Share your opinion

Your feedback is important because we strive to provide the highest quality prep materials. If you are satisfied with the content of this book, post your review on Amazon, so others can benefit from your experience.

If you have any questions or comments about the material, email us at info@sterling-prep.com and we will resolve any issues to your satisfaction.

Made in the USA
San Bernardino, CA
18 February 2016